American Legislative Leaders in the South, 1911–1994

American Legislative Leaders in the South, 1911–1994

James Roger Sharp and
Nancy Weatherly Sharp, *Editors*

Kevin G. Atwater and Gina Petonito, *Assistant Editors*
Charles F. Ritter and Jon L. Wakelyn, *Advisory Editors*

GREENWOOD PRESS
Westport, Connecticut • London

Library of Congress Cataloging-in-Publication Data

American legislative leaders in the South, 1911–1994 / James Roger
  Sharp and Nancy Weatherly Sharp, editors ; Kevin G. Atwater and
  Gina Petonito, assistant editors ; Charles F. Ritter and Jon L.
  Wakelyn, advisory editors.
      p.   cm.
    Includes bibliographical references and index.
    ISBN 0–313–30213–8 (alk. paper)
    1. Legislators—Southern States—Biography—Dictionaries.
  2. Legislators—United States—States—Biography—Dictionaries.
  3. Legislative bodies—Southern States—Leadership.   4. Southern
  States—Biography—Dictionaries.   I. Sharp, James Roger, 1936–   .
  II. Sharp, Nancy Weatherly.
  F208.A44   1999
  328.73'092'275—dc21
  [B]   98–23549

British Library Cataloguing in Publication Data is available.

Library of Congress Catalog Card Number: 98–23549
ISBN: 0–313–30213–8

First published in 1999

Greenwood Press, 88 Post Road West, Westport, CT 06881
An imprint of Greenwood Publishing Group, Inc.
www.greenwood.com

Printed in the United States of America

The paper used in this book complies with the
Permanent Paper Standard issued by the National
Information Standards Organization (Z39.48–1984).

10 9 8 7 6 5 4 3 2 1

CONTENTS

TABLES

PREFACE

This book is part of a four-volume project to provide a biographical dictionary of state house speakers in each region of the United States from 1911 to 1994. In process for more than a decade, the project turned out to be much larger and more difficult than we had anticipated when asked to undertake it by the editors at Greenwood Press. It represented the talents and hard work of a large number of researchers, librarians, and archivists throughout the country as well as assistants and student workers at Syracuse University. Most of the latter subsequently left the university for various professional fields, but some showed their commitment to the project by continuing to be involved.

The challenge that the project presented became obvious early on when we encountered difficulty in getting the names of all the speakers in all the states. For about half of the states, this was perfunctory. We wrote to whom we saw as the appropriate official, and a list was forthcoming. Elsewhere, simply putting together correctly spelled names and speakership dates constituted a major achievement. An even more difficult challenge was determining political party affiliations. In the end we identified a total of 1,472 speakers.

Once we had the names, dates, and parties of the speakers, our goal was to recruit outstanding scholars of state history and politics to write biographies and fill out questionnaires for each individual. There were many disappointments along the way, but in the end we enlisted a dedicated group of contributors from every state in the Union. The extent to which they went to track down information about the speakers often amazed us. For instance, one contributor wrote of finding crucial information in an old graveyard.

The introductions to these volumes were based on literature about state legislative politics as well as the information we collected. They were drafted by James Roger Sharp, professor of history at Syracuse University, and based on suggestions and revisions offered by co-editor Nancy Weatherly Sharp, professor of newspaper journalism and assistant dean for graduate professional studies at the S. I. Newhouse School of Public Communications at Syracuse. Other revisions were supplied by the volumes' assistant editors, Gina Petonito and Kevin

G. Atwater. Ms. Petonito, who earned a Ph.D. in sociology from Syracuse in 1992 and is now on the faculty at Western Illinois University, Macomb, Illinois, joined the project in 1985 and was invaluable in helping to coordinate it. The same is true of Mr. Atwater, who became associated with the project in 1986 while completing an M.A. in geography from Syracuse and who now works in the Bibliographic Services Department of the university's E. S. Bird Library.

After our contributors sent us the individual biographies, we had to transcribe them onto computer disks. This painstaking work was performed by several people including Nada Al-Mudawwar, Tara Watson, Joyce Bell, Wendy Herron Angell, and Prof. Petonito. The biographies were then meticulously edited by Prof. Nancy Sharp as well as by Prof. Petonito and Mr. Atwater. Information was verified against a variety of sources, and the writing was polished with the objectives of making the style and organization as consistent and the text as readable as possible.

Tremendous effort went into compiling a database from the questionnaire responses. Patrick Scully, then a doctoral student in social science at Syracuse University and now vice president of the Topsfield Foundation, Pomfret, Connecticut, took the leading role in developing the questionnaire. We also relied on Dr. Scully's knowledge and excellent research skills to help launch the project in other ways. Prof. Petonito designed a form for coding the data, and she, Mr. Atwater, David List, Nancy Jones, and Sugita Katyal did the coding. The recipient of a Ph.D. in social science from Syracuse in 1988, Mr. List is now an adjunct professor on the community faculty of Metropolitan State University in St. Paul, Minnesota. Mr. Atwater and Prof. Petonito input and cleaned the data online, carefully checking it for accuracy and supplementing it through other sources. They then ran analyses using the SAS System. Regrettably, only a portion of our database could be listed in the appendices.

Meanwhile we continued to keep track of the speakers. More than 500 were still alive when we received their biographies and questionnaires, which thus remained open to revision. As the end of the project approached we contacted our contributors once more to gather as much current information and clear up as many loose ends as possible. Credit for this mighty effort must be given to Mr. Atwater, Prof. Petonito, Bonnie Datt, Beth Rosenstein, and Teresa Starr Fugit. Mark D. Scott and Ms. Fugit were essential in the final organization of the biographies and in adding and editing the bibliographical references. In addition, James McQuivey helped with the bibliographies, and Tim Barger, Mr. McQuivey, and Mr. Atwater prepared the tables and appendices. Other project tasks were performed by Jane Reeves, Jenny Robb, and J. Brian O'Laughlin. Kay Banning did an admirable job in preparing the index for this volume.

Readers should be aware of several decisions we made concerning the parameters of these volumes. The 1,472 individuals covered in the biographies served as speakers of *state lower legislative chambers between 1911 and 1994*, with the three following exceptions. For Alaska and Hawaii we included the speakers of the territorial houses prior to statehood in 1959. Nebraska shifted to a one-chamber legislature (the Unicameral) in 1937, after which we covered the speakers of that body. We also included William Bruce Anthony of Oklahoma, who presided over a special session in late 1910, since he was not listed in an earlier book in the Greenwood series, *American Legislative Leaders, 1850–1910* by Charles F. Ritter and Jon L. Wakelyn.

In contrast, the database contained 1,410 observations, as we omitted two separate groups among the 1,472 speakers. One group consisted of the 16 individuals first presiding before 1911 who had already been covered in the Ritter and Wakelyn book. The other comprised the 46 speakers who attained the post after 1990, the previous cutoff date for our project, because it was decided to include biographies for them only after we had completed our data analyses.

It would be useful for readers to understand four basic differences in legislative practices and politics among states during our period of coverage. First, in most cases the lower chamber was known as the House of Representatives. However, it was called the Assembly in California, Nevada, New York, and Wisconsin, and the General Assembly in New Jersey. In Maryland, Virginia, and West Virginia it was the House of Delegates. As previously mentioned, the Nebraska legislature was called the Unicameral after 1937. While applying the appropriate nomenclature in individual biographies, we used the term *house* when referring in general to a lower chamber.

Second, there was a variation among states concerning the length and starting dates of speakership terms. In most cases speakers served two-year terms that began in odd years. However, Alabama, Louisiana, and Mississippi had four-year terms. Terms in Alabama started in odd years, whereas those in the other two states began in even years. Maryland had two-year terms starting in even years until 1924, and four-year terms beginning in odd years since 1927. Four states originally had one-year terms: Rhode Island until 1912, Massachusetts until 1920, New York until 1938, and New Jersey until 1971. All of them then switched to two-year terms, starting in odd years in the first three states and even years in New Jersey. Virginia's two-year terms began in even years. In Vermont terms started in even years until 1912 and odd years since 1915, whereas in Kentucky they began in even years until 1992 and odd years since 1993. Both Arizona and New Mexico had terms in odd years except for 1911 and 1913, replacing those with ones held upon statehood in 1912.

Although terms often officially began in December or ended in January, we sought consistency by labeling them by their first *calendar* year in the biographies and appendices. Thus someone who was speaker between December 1984 and December 1986 was listed as presiding during the 1985 session. In Appendix 2 we also gave the last calendar year for terms. It should be noted that in many states, especially early in our period of coverage, the house convened only for a few months every other year. However, all speakers were listed as serving full terms unless it was known that they left office or died. When such instances did occur, the particulars were discussed in the biographies.

   A third difference among states involved political party affiliations. The only prominent parties in most states throughout our period of coverage were the Democrats and Republicans. However, two others controlled speakerships during the 1930s: the Progressive Party in Wisconsin and the Farmer-Labor Party in Minnesota. The latter merged with the Democrats in 1944 to form the Democratic-Farmer-Labor Party, and their opponents later became known as the Independent Republicans. In North Dakota the primary political division from 1915 to 1956 was between liberal and conservative Republicans, and these factions were given in the biographies. After the Democrats incorporated the populist Nonpartisan League, they were known as the Democratic-NPL Party. The Nebraska Unicameral was always officially non-partisan, whereas the Minnesota House was non-partisan from 1913 to 1973. For those cases, we provided the speaker's affiliation "outside" of the house. If an individual switched parties at some point, we noted this in his or her biography. We gave the individual's party affiliation *while speaker* in Appendix 1.

   The fourth disparity among states concerned the prominent unit of local government, which determined our definition of house districts. For most bibliographies we provided the counties (parishes in Louisiana) represented by the speaker. However, we listed the towns represented by speakers from New England states and the communities represented by Alaska speakers. The speaker's home unit was always given first, followed by all other units wholly or partially within the district. In Appendix 1 we listed the home county or its equivalent for speakers from *all* states. When a district's boundaries changed over time, we noted this in the biography and gave the home county *while speaker* in the appendix.

   There were other variables that we fully described in the biographies, but simplified to fit in the appendices. If we did not know a speaker's birth date but had both a death date and an age at death, the more probable year of birth was input in Appendix 4. For an individual's occupations (Appendix 7) or public offices outside of the house (Appendices 9 and 10), we separated those held prior to the individual's becoming speaker from those begun during or after the speakership. The religious affiliation, military rank, and marital status given in Appendix 6 were those at the point of becoming speaker, whereas educational background (Appendix 5) and membership in voluntary organizations (Appendix 8) covered an individual's entire life.

   In our complete database we provided room for more than one response to several variables, including occupations and public offices. If a particular response was deemed noteworthy, it was always listed first and thus became the entry given in the appendices. For example, attorney was highlighted among occupations held before becoming speaker, whereas lobbying was emphasized among post-speakership occupations. When a speaker held multiple public offices, we gave leadership positions priority.

   We also developed procedures for coding variables in cases where nothing was known. No information about reasons for leaving the speakership and house

(Appendix 3), education, religion, military rank, marital status, and pre-speakership occupations was coded as blank. As a result, any speaker for whom we did not know one of the above variables was excluded from the appropriate frequency tables in the introduction. However, we treated a lack of information on post-speakership occupations, voluntary organizations, and public offices as evidence of no activity and coded the variables as zero. The affected speakers were therefore included in those frequency distributions.

Variables concerned with dates and length of house service (Appendix 2) covered all such bodies within the given state. Thus in several cases territorial and state house tenures were added together, and in Nebraska House and Uni-cameral tenures were combined. However, service in another state's house was *not* included. Data for each of these variables were kept as current as possible through the end of 1994.

James Roger Sharp
Nancy Weatherly Sharp
Kevin G. Atwater
Gina Petonito
Syracuse, New York

ACKNOWLEDGMENTS

A number of our colleagues at Syracuse University were generous in their backing of this project. Dr. Bennie R. Ware, Vice President of Research and Computing, Dean John Palmer of the Maxwell School of Citizenship and Public Affairs, Dean David Rubin of the Newhouse School of Public Communications, and the Newhouse School's Development and Leaves Committee were marvelously supportive. Their aid at several crucial points was essential in allowing us to hire students to help us perform a variety of tasks, including collecting, coding, and manipulating our enormous data set. The Maxwell School provided us with an office and computer facilities, and the Office of Computing and Media Services supplied both equipment and expertise in setting up our database. We would also like to thank Professor Jeffrey Stonecash of the Maxwell School for his time and expertise.

In addition, we received encouragement from the other editors of the *American Legislative Leaders* series. It was James H. Broussard of Lebanon Valley College who originally saw the value of such a project. Jon L. Wakelyn of Kent State University advanced the series with Greenwood Press and also was one of our contributors. Cynthia Harris of Greenwood Press was with the project from the beginning and proved very patient.

We would like to thank our two children, Sandy and Matt. They were not driectly involved in the production of this book, and they even may have been responsible for some of the delays. Nonetheless, they have been a continuing source of joy and pride during the years we have been engaged in this project.

Finally, we would like to dedicate this volume to Nancy's parents, the late Edward and Anne Ferring Weatherly.

INTRODUCTION

In 1911 William Howard Taft was serving in the third year of his only term as president of the United States. He led a country that over the previous 100 years had undergone major and dislocating change. The rural, agricultural, inward-looking, relatively homogeneous society of the early nineteenth century had been transformed into the urban, industrial, imperialist, multiethnic, multiracial society of the early twentieth century. Federal, state, and local governments faced a host of severe economic and social problems accompanying urbanization and industrialization. The population of the United States in 1911 stood at slightly more than 92 million, which was more than six times greater than it had been 80 years earlier. During that time the population density had jumped from 7.4 to 31 inhabitants per square mile.[1]

Presidential politics, with the exception of Democrat Grover Cleveland's two terms, had been dominated by the Republican Party since the election of Abraham Lincoln in 1860. The Civil War and Reconstruction had consolidated the hold of the GOP on national power as the party that had saved the Union and the Republic. Even more persuasively, the Republicans were seen as the protectors and embodiment of those middle-class and Protestant values that were celebrated by the rags-to-riches stories of Horatio Alger and elevated to doctrinal canon by the *McGuffey Readers*. The Democrats, in sharp contrast, were portrayed by the Republicans as the party of rum, Romanism, and rebellion—a party that stood for alien, hostile, and dangerous values.

Whereas the nineteenth century had been a period of tremendous development, the political, economic, social, and demographic geography of the United States would be even more dramatically recast in the 80 years from 1911 to 1990. Indeed, the ways Americans lived, worked, and played were revolutionized in the twentieth century. Transportation was just one area affected. In 1905 there were only about 78,000 registered automobiles in the country, but by 1990 there were more than 188 million registered motor vehicles. The first automobile trip across the United States (from San Francisco to New York) was made in 1903 in 52 days. By the last decade of this century the country was crisscrossed by 45,000 miles of interstate highways, making long-distance road travel commonplace for many Americans. The country's public health also showed marked improvement. For example, life expectancy between 1900 and the late twentieth century increased from 48 to 75 years for males and from 52 to 79 years for females.[2]

In 1990, during the middle of George Bush's only presidential term, the population of the United States stood at close to 250 million people, a 172 percent increase from 1911. The population density had increased to more than 70 persons per square mile. As important as the overall increase was, the most significant demographic developments were the internal migrations that had taken place during the 80-year period. Among these were the large number of African Americans who had left the South for northern cities and the later exodus of waves of Americans from the Northeast and Midwest to what were perceived as the greener pastures of the South and West. Consequently Miami, Atlanta, Dallas, Houston, Phoenix, Los Angeles, and other cities experienced major population booms from the 1940s on. The Great Depression and World Wars I and II were the primary catalysts in prompting this movement, although the numerous recessions, loss of manufacturing jobs, lure of good weather, and development of air conditioning also had an impact.

Among the country's regions,[3] the South experienced relative growth during this period. Whereas the South had 31.6 percent of the total national population in 1910, that figure had fallen to 30.4 percent in 1960 but then risen to 34.1 percent in 1990. The two most populous states in the South, Texas and Florida, were respectively ranked as numbers 5 and 33 in the country in 1910. In 1990 they were numbers 3 and 4.[4]

Meanwhile the West increased its share of the population from 7.7 percent in 1910 to 21.2 percent in 1990. The Midwest and Northeast showed relative declines, respectively falling from 32.4 to 24 percent and from 28.3 to 20.7 percent. These demographic shifts were, of course, reflected in the transfer of electoral votes. In 1948 the South had a total of 128 electors, but by 1988 that figure had reached 176.[5]

The partisan landscape of the United States also experienced critical changes between the Taft and Bush presidencies. These changes, which are reflected in the database of the *American Legislative Leaders* project,[6] can best be understood by looking at three eras that made up the period (see Table 1). The first, 1911–1932, was a time of Republican hegemony on both the state level and the national level, except for Woodrow Wilson's two presidential terms. The second, 1933–1964, was shaped by the Great Depression and the New Deal and dominated nationally by the Democratic Party. The third and last era, 1965–1990, was heavily influenced by historic U.S. Supreme Court decisions ordering the states to redistrict according to population. It was characterized by continued Democratic dominion, at least in the U.S. Congress and state legislatures.

In the period 1911–1932 the control of state houses—as reflected through the selection of speakers—demonstrated the Republican strength of the time, with

Table 1
Party Affiliation of Speakers

A. By Year

Frequency Percent	Democrat	Republican	Other	Total
1911–1932	179	278	0	**457**
	39.17	60.83	0.00	
1933–1964	323	271	4	**598**
	54.01	45.32	0.67	
1965–1990	211	144	0	**355**
	59.44	40.56	0.00	
Total	**713**	**693**	**4**	**1,410**
	50.57	**49.15**	**0.28**	**100**

B. By Region

Frequency Percent	Democrat	Republican	Other	Total
MIDWEST	91	253	4	**348**
	26.15	72.70	1.15	
NORTHEAST	85	230	0	**315**
	26.98	73.02	0.00	
SOUTH	348	8	0	**356**
	97.75	2.25	0.00	
WEST	189	202	0	**391**
	48.34	51.66	0.00	
Total	**713**	**693**	**4**	**1,410**
	50.57	**49.15**	**0.28**	**100**

C. By Region (1911–1932)

Frequency Percent	Democrat	Republican	Other	Total
MIDWEST	19	94	0	**113**
	16.81	83.19	0.00	
NORTHEAST	14	93	0	**107**
	13.08	86.92	0.00	
SOUTH	117	7	0	**124**
	94.35	5.65	0.00	
WEST	29	84	0	**113**
	25.66	74.34	0.00	
Total	**179**	**278**	**0**	**457**
	39.17	**60.83**	**0.00**	**100**

Table 1 (continued)

D. By Region (1933–1964)

Frequency *Percent*	Democrat	Republican	Other	Total
MIDWEST	38	101	4	143
	26.57	70.63	2.80	
NORTHEAST	27	107	0	134
	20.15	79.85	0.00	
SOUTH	148	0	0	148
	100.00	0.00	0.00	
WEST	110	63	0	173
	63.58	36.42	0.00	
Total	323	271	4	598
	54.01	45.32	0.67	100

60.8 percent[7] of all speakers belonging to the GOP. A respective 86.9, 83.2, and 74.3 percent of speakers in the Northeast, Midwest, and West were Republicans, whereas 94.4 percent of speakers in the South were Democrats.[8]

Of the southern states, Alabama, Arkansas, Florida, Georgia, Louisiana, Maryland, Mississippi, North Carolina, South Carolina, Tennessee, Texas, and Virginia were unanimous in their support of Democratic speakers from 1911 to 1932. West Virginia was the only state with significant Republican strength, choosing that party's members as speakers 55.6 percent of the time.[9]

There was a sharp reversal in the partisan balance in the next period, 1933–1964. The Great Depression and the New Deal had the effect of discrediting the Republicans and forcing a national realignment of party strength. As a consequence the Democrats held the presidency for 28 of the next 36 years. On the state level realignment was not as clear-cut, although 54 percent of all speakers were Democrats. That party's members composed 100 percent of the speakers in the South and 63.6 percent of those in the West. The Northeast and the Midwest continued to be bastions of Republican strength, with a respective 79.9 and 70.6 percent of speakers in those regions being affiliated with the GOP.[10]

Looking at the South in the 1933–1964 period, we see that the region became an even stronger bastion of Democratic support. Every speaker in every southern state during those years was a Democrat.[11]

During the 1965–1990 period there was another shift in the political pattern. This resulted in part from a series of U.S. Supreme Court decisions that revolutionized the nature of legislative representation in the states. Until these decisions, representation in many, if not most, states reflected a historic rural dominance. The redistricting of state legislatures was rare: Vermont had not done so since 1793, Connecticut since 1818, Mississippi since 1890, Delaware since 1897, and Alabama since 1901. Urban voters had thus been grievously underrepresented. The five largest counties in New Jersey and Florida, which

Table 1 (continued)

E. By Region (1965–1990)

Frequency Percent	Democrat	Republican	Other	Total
MIDWEST	34	58	0	92
	36.96	63.04	0.00	
NORTHEAST	44	30	0	74
	59.46	40.54	0.00	
SOUTH	83	1	0	84
	98.81	1.19	0.00	
WEST	50	55	0	105
	47.62	52.38	0.00	
Total	**211**	**144**	**0**	**355**
	59.44	**40.56**	**0.00**	**100**

contained about half of the population of each state, had respectively only 5 of 21 and 5 of 38 state senate seats. In Connecticut the four largest cities (with 23 percent of the population) had only 8 of the 279 members in the state house.

However, in the early 1960s the Supreme Court ruled—in *Baker v. Carr* (1962) followed by *Reynolds v. Sims* (1964), among others—that legislators "represent people, not trees or acres," and that "as a basic constitutional standard, the Equal Protection Clause requires that the seats in both houses of a bicameral state legislature must be apportioned on a population basis." This meant that state legislative elections could no longer be based upon political boundaries, as had always been the case in the U.S. Senate. Instead, they had to be established on the basis of population and the principle of "one person, one vote."[12]

Although the Republicans controlled the presidency for 18 of the 26 years from 1965 to 1990, the Democrats dominated the U.S. Congress. They also increased their hold on the state houses, with 59.4 percent of all speakers being Democrats. For the first time the Democrats gained the upper hand in the Northeast, at 59.5 percent. The Midwest continued to favor the Republicans with 63 percent, whereas the South, despite gains made by GOP presidential candidates, remained a Democratic stronghold with that party controlling 98.8 percent of the speakerships. The West was the most closely contested region, with Republican speakers accounting for 52.4 percent of the total.[13]

In the South during the period 1965–1990, Democratic speakers continued their complete domination. The speakerships were held by Democrats 100 percent of the time in every state except Tennessee, where the figure was 80 percent.[14]

At the end of the 80-year span, the 1990 election continued the Democratic dominance of state legislatures. The Democrats controlled both legislative chambers in 30 states, whereas the Republicans slipped to a mere five. Only in the

Table 1 (continued)

F. By Southern State (1911–1932)

Frequency Percent	Democrat	Republican	Total
ALABAMA	5 100.00	0 0.00	5
ARKANSAS	11 100.00	0 0.00	11
FLORIDA	9 100.00	0 0.00	9
GEORGIA	4 100.00	0 0.00	4
KENTUCKY	8 88.89	1 11.11	9
LOUISIANA	7 100.00	0 0.00	7
MARYLAND	9 100.00	0 0.00	9
MISSISSIPPI	3 100.00	0 0.00	3
NORTH CAROLINA	11 100.00	0 0.00	11
OKLAHOMA	13 92.86	1 7.14	14
SOUTH CAROLINA	6 100.00	0 0.00	6
TENNESSEE	11 100.00	0 0.00	11
TEXAS	11 100.00	0 0.00	11
VIRGINIA	5 100.00	0 0.00	5
WEST VIRGINIA	4 44.44	5 55.56	9
Total	117 94.35	7 5.65	124 100

South did the Republicans show a major improvement. Although they could not contest the Democrats' command of the speakerships, they so increased their numbers that by 1990 they held ''more seats in southern legislatures than at any time in this century.''[15]

The above statistics undoubtedly portray too stark a partisan division and perhaps exaggerate the strength of party loyalty of state legislators. Just looking at the results of speakership choices might lead a casual observer to faulty

Table 1 (continued)

G. By Southern State (1933–1964)

Frequency Percent	Democrat	Republican	Total
ALABAMA	9	0	9
	100.00	0.00	
ARKANSAS	15	0	15
	100.00	0.00	
FLORIDA	15	0	15
	100.00	0.00	
GEORGIA	7	0	7
	100.00	0.00	
KENTUCKY	14	0	14
	100.00	0.00	
LOUISIANA	6	0	6
	100.00	0.00	
MARYLAND	9	0	9
	100.00	0.00	
MISSISSIPPI	4	0	4
	100.00	0.00	
NORTH CAROLINA	16	0	16
	100.00	0.00	
OKLAHOMA	15	0	15
	100.00	0.00	
SOUTH CAROLINA	5	0	5
	100.00	0.00	
TENNESSEE	8	0	8
	100.00	0.00	
TEXAS	13	0	13
	100.00	0.00	
VIRGINIA	4	0	4
	100.00	0.00	
WEST VIRGINIA	8	0	8
	100.00	0.00	
Total	**148**	**0**	**148**
	100.00	**0.00**	**100**

conclusions. There is a danger, as has been pointed out by political scientist Jeffrey M. Stonecash, of oversimplifying complex political phenomena.[16] In some states the minority party was sometimes open to intriguing with a dissident faction of the majority party in order to overthrow a sitting speaker or otherwise defy the will of the majority.

For example, in 1983 conservative Democrat Gibson D. Lewis won the speakership of the Texas House by convincing Republican members to vote for him

Table 1 (continued)

H. By Southern State (1965–1990)

Frequency *Percent*	Democrat	Republican	Total
ALABAMA	4	0	4
	100.00	0.00	
ARKANSAS	13	0	13
	100.00	0.00	
FLORIDA	12	0	12
	100.00	0.00	
GEORGIA	1	0	1
	100.00	0.00	
KENTUCKY	5	0	5
	100.00	0.00	
LOUISIANA	5	0	5
	100.00	0.00	
MARYLAND	4	0	4
	100.00	0.00	
MISSISSIPPI	3	0	3
	100.00	0.00	
NORTH CAROLINA	9	0	9
	100.00	0.00	
OKLAHOMA	5	0	5
	100.00	0.00	
SOUTH CAROLINA	3	0	3
	100.00	0.00	
TENNESSEE	4	1	5
	80.00	20.00	
TEXAS	6	0	6
	100.00	0.00	
VIRGINIA	2	0	2
	100.00	0.00	
WEST VIRGINIA	7	0	7
	100.00	0.00	
Total	**83**	**1**	**84**
	98.81	**1.19**	**100**

in order to prevent a liberal Democrat from being named. Not surprisingly, Lewis announced that he was "not a big fan of partisan politics." Thus Lewis won not just because he was a Democrat but because he was able to patch together a bipartisan conservative coalition.[17]

The same dynamic was present in the 1989 Oklahoma and Connecticut houses. In Oklahoma, a group of dissident Democrats allied themselves with the Republicans to oust the "heavy handed" Democratic speaker, Jim L. Barker.[18]

Liberal Democratic Speaker Irving Jules Stolberg of Connecticut was foiled in his attempt to win a third term by a coalition of conservative Democrats and Republicans. The successful challenger, Democrat Richard J. Balducci, was an auto salvage executive and former high school football coach who was described as "the quintessential blue-collar legislator, likeable and competent."[19]

A similar situation in Florida had a different outcome. During the 1989 session the liberal Democratic speaker-designee, Tom Gustafson, faced opposition from conservative Democrats and Republicans. Gustafson preserved his position by allying himself with Dade County Hispanic Republicans, promising more money for Dade County and more attention to Hispanic affairs.[20]

Thus one cannot necessarily assume that selections to the speakership exactly reflect the partisan division of a house. In the aforementioned cases the majority Democratic Party was split between liberal and conservative wings and the eventual winner, while Democratic, was named only after appealing to Republicans.

The 1989 "legislative coup d'etat" in North Carolina, in which 20 Democrats banded with 45 Republicans to deny a fifth term to Democratic Speaker Liston Bryan Ramsey, illustrates some of the same issues. It also sheds some light on the political changes that took place in the South in recent decades. During most of the twentieth century the Democratic Party dominated North Carolina politics. Every four years a new Democratic governor would be elected, and every two years a new Democrat would occupy the speakership. However, by the time of Republican Dwight D. Eisenhower's presidential campaign in 1952, the political scene in the state was beginning to shift, with the popular World War II general winning an unprecedented 46.1 percent of North Carolina's vote. By 1970 the state had four Republican congressmen, and two years later voters elected the first GOP governor in the twentieth century. During the 1980s both of North Carolina's U.S. senators were Republicans. The political transformation was also occurring in the state legislature, where the Republicans had increased their numbers in the 120-member North Carolina House from 26 in 1966 to 46 in 1988.

The increase in Republican strength in North Carolina was only a part of the dynamic that defeated Ramsey in 1989. In the late 1970s the Democratic-controlled house had changed its rules to allow the speaker to serve more than one term, and Ramsey became only the second person to do so. The election of 1988, while returning a comfortable majority of Democrats to the North Carolina House, had still resulted in "the loss of ten House seats to the Republicans, the largest Democratic legislative losses of any state in the country" that year. Some Democratic legislators—who became known as the "kamikaze" group—blamed their loss upon negative public perception of the house leadership and the increasingly "arbitrary and dictatorial fashion" with which "power was [being] wielded" there. As a result, they decided to meet with the Republicans, hammering out an agreement to reorganize the house committee structure and give the GOP proportional representation on the subcommittees. With that agreement the Republicans were virtually unanimous in supporting dissident Democrat Josephus L. Mavretic in his victorious bid for speaker.[21]

These internecine battles were not limited to recent times. Over the years conflicts concerning such issues as road construction, prohibition, and even placement of the state capital have rocked houses, splintered parties, and resulted in bitter battles for the speakership.

In Iowa, for example, the Republican-dominated house sessions of 1917 and 1919 divided over the "hard roads" versus "mud roads" issue. The "hard roads" faction—who favored state control over highway improvements—fought for the passage of the 1913 Highway Commission Act, which created a state commission. "Mud roads" adherents, hoping to retain county control, were led by Republican Governor William L. Harding. In a rare move, Harding named Milton Bird Pitt as his candidate for speaker in 1917. Pitt was chosen, and he pushed the "mud roads" agenda. However, the next term "hard roads" nominee Arch W. McFarlane captured the speakership and blocked the repeal of the Highway Commission Act. McFarlane then presided for a second term, becoming only the third speaker in Iowa history to do so. The "hard roads" victory over legislative policy was secured with Joseph H. Anderson's speakership in 1923, a reward for his defying of Harding several years earlier.[22]

Although Harding's meddling in the legislative process was rare in Iowa, in other states the governor's dominance over the house was the norm and often resulted in divisive intraparty battles. In Louisiana, flamboyant Democratic Governor Huey P. Long dominated state politics. The 1929 session's business was overshadowed by a movement to impeach the governor led by Democrat Ralph Norman Bauer and his "Dynamite Squad." This attempt was foiled by Long's supporters, including Speaker John Baptiste Fournet, Allen Joseph Ellender, and Lorris M. Wimberly. For several years in the 1930s loyalty to the governor was rewarded with political prizes. Fournet became a Louisiana Supreme Court justice; Ellender and Wimberly became speakers. Bauer had to wait until after Long's assassination in 1935 to capture the speakership, presiding in 1940 and 1944.[23]

The momentous demographic shifts and the changes in the partisan alignment were only two indicators of the vast political transformation that occurred in the United States between 1911 and 1990. The role of state government, or perhaps more accurately the relationship between state government and federal government, had undergone what can be described as a sea change since the founding of the country. According to one 1985 study, in the period from 1789 to the New Deal, the states were the "paramount actors and innovators in the political and public policy areas, the exclusive legal architects of local government that at the time actually provided most of the public services available, effective restrainers of national government activities, and strong partners in the federal system." In the early part of the twentieth century the states had the "primary responsibility for domestic government in the United States." They were, in the main, "direct service providers in their own right, particularly in the fields of criminal justice, health and hospitals, transportation, higher education and business relations through commercial codes,'' as well as the ''prime regulators in guarding the public health, safety, welfare, good order and convenience of their citizens through the use of their police power.''[24]

From the New Deal in the 1930s down to 1960, however, ''the scope of the states' police powers lessened somewhat, their performance as policy innovators eroded significantly and their involvement with national program goals through federal grants expanded.''[25]

It was in the period from the 1960s to the mid-1980s that the states' role went through even more significant change, with the states acquiring ''new responsibilities, though not to the point of totally losing their traditional ones.'' The study claims that ''in contrast to their earlier basic functions, the role of the modern states essentially is to assume two main responsibilities: planning and controlling big and frequently intergovernmental programs and using their position as the major intermediate level of government and of politics to mobilize political consent for these programs.''[26]

These new responsibilities given to the states and their institutions have not brought a corresponding increase in serious scholarly attention. Part of the problem has been a long-held belief that state legislatures are unprogressive, anachronistic institutions mired in corruption, with votes commonly being auctioned off to the highest bidder. Consequently, of all the institutions of state government, the legislatures have been the most maligned. Daniel Webster was supposed to have remarked: ''Now is the time when men work quietly in the fields and women weep softly in the kitchen. The legislature is in session and no man's property is safe.''[27]

As late as 1966 a similar complaint was made by Alexander Heard, a former chancellor of Vanderbilt University. ''State legislatures may be our most extreme example of institutional lag,'' he lamented. ''In their formal qualities they are largely 19th-century organizations and they must, or should address themselves to 20th-century problems.'' Condemnations of state legislatures, he continued, ranged

from allegations of personal bribery to the doleful conclusion that much of the time these institutions of representative government so conduct themselves that the popular will is thwarted. Even if all legislators were models of efficiency and rectitude, as indeed some of them are, most state legislatures would remain poorly organized and technically ill-equipped to do what is expected of them. They do not meet often enough nor long enough; they lack space, clerical staffing, professional assistance; they are poorly paid and overworked; they are prey to special interests, sometimes their own; their procedures and committee systems are outmoded; they devote inordinate time to local interests that distract them from general public policy; they sometimes cannot even get copies of bills on which they must vote. They work, in short, under a host of conditions that dampen their incentive and limit their ability to function effectively.[28]

If state legislatures themselves have been institutionally unresponsive to the problems of twentieth-century America, most scholars have also been remiss in not recognizing the potential value in analyzing and charting the evolution and development of these critically important governmental organizations. In particular the changing roles of the state houses and their leadership have been neglected.

Almost 25 years ago historian Ballard Campbell complained that "American state legislatures are an underdeveloped historical resource." He reminded his readers that there had been too much of a concentration of scholarly attention on the national political institutions despite the fact that the states "were the primary structural components of American government in the nineteenth and early twentieth centuries." Among other things, Campbell urged scholars to examine "long run structural changes in state legislatures, including membership patterns."[29]

There is no doubt that state legislatures and their membership patterns have been slighted by scholars. However, this is especially true of the leadership of those legislatures. Almost three decades ago political scientists Douglas Camp Chaffey and Malcolm E. Jewell complained that "political scientists have devoted relatively little attention to the study of legislative party leaders—how they are selected, the roles that they play, or the sources of their power—particularly at the state legislative level. Our understanding of the recruitment process for legislative party leaders comes primarily from a relatively few studies of the United States House of Representatives."[30] As recently as 1981, the editor of *Legislative Studies Quarterly* lamented that "among the most neglected topics in state legislative studies is leadership," for we "know almost nothing about leadership selection and turnover . . . the tactics of leadership, or the styles and roles of leaders."[31]

One scholar has written recently that "the skills, attitudes, and goals of legislators are the product of their total life experience. Thus, knowledge about who legislators are and how they got to be there should contribute to a better understanding of legislative behavior and institutions."[32] This challenge has not been met by students of politics, for even though the "Speaker of the House is generally considered to be one of the most important and powerful figures in his [or her] state," it has been argued as late as 1990 that "relatively little research . . . has been done on either the social origins, career patterns or stability in office of speakers."[33]

The four volumes of the *American Legislative Leaders* project address many of the concerns of these scholars. Among the several questions about state house speakers they attempt to answer are these: Who and what kind of persons occupied positions of leadership in the various houses? What was the nature of legislative leadership and how did it evolve in the twentieth century? Why were some speakers apparently more successful in their leadership roles than others? Finally, what was the extent of professionalization in state houses?

It should come as no surprise that the overwhelming number of speakers were white, male, and middle-aged (see Table 2). In fact, as the century unfolded, the average age of speakers increased, for they tended to have longer house

Table 2
Characteristics of Speakers by Year

A. Age

Frequency Percent	21–39	40–49	50+	Total
1911–1932	151	169	124	**444**
	34.01	38.06	27.93	
1933–1964	165	227	195	**587**
	28.11	38.67	33.22	
1965–1990	86	155	114	**355**
	24.23	43.66	32.11	
Total	**402**	**551**	**433**	**1,386**
	29.00	**39.75**	**31.24**	**100**

Frequency Missing = 24

tenures before assuming their posts. During the 1911–1932 period 34 percent of the speakers were named before their fortieth birthdays, as contrasted to 28.1 percent in 1933–1964 and 24.2 percent in 1965–1990.[34]

Of the 1,410 speakers in the database, 1,401 (99.4 percent) were male and only 9 (0.6 percent) were female. The small number of women who became speakers reflects the overall appalling lack of a female presence in U.S. politics. For example, women comprised only 2 percent of all members of the U.S. Congress from 1917 to 1965.[35] Even as late as 1986, women made up only 15.5 percent of the membership in all state legislatures.[36] The first woman speaker was Republican Minnie Craig of North Dakota, who was named in 1933. There was not another woman chosen as speaker until Consuelo Northrop Bailey won the nod in Vermont in 1953. A total of three women speakers were named in the 1960s, none in the 1970s, and four in the 1980s.[37] The nine women consisted of four from the West (two in Wyoming, and one each in Arizona and Oregon), three from the Midwest (two in North Dakota and one in South Dakota), and two from the Northeast (New Jersey and Vermont). None were from the South.[38]

One of the most successful of the women speakers was Oregon's Vera Katz, who was named on the 101st ballot of the 1985 Democratic caucus. Initially some of her colleagues "just couldn't believe that a woman was tough enough to be speaker," but the liberal Katz confounded her skeptics by becoming the first speaker in Oregon history to serve three terms.[39] A longtime observer of Oregon politics opined that Katz could be "as tough as whang leather or as soft and cajoling as a cooing dove."[40]

Our database indicates that 1,389 of the 1,410 speakers (98.5 percent) were white. The minority speakers consisted of 3 African Americans (0.2 percent), 6 Hispanics (0.4 percent), 2 Native Americans (0.1 percent), and 10 Asians or Pacific Islanders (0.7 percent).[41]

Table 2 (continued)

B. Gender

Frequency Percent	Male	Female	Total
1911–1932	457 100.00	0 0.00	**457**
1933–1964	596 99.67	2 0.33	**598**
1965–1990	348 98.03	7 1.97	**355**
Total	**1,401** **99.36**	**9** **0.64**	**1,410** **100**

All three African-American speakers were Democrats.[42] S. Howard Woodson, Jr., of New Jersey was named in 1974, followed by K. Leroy Irvis of Pennsylvania in 1977, 1983, 1985, and 1987. The third, Willie Lewis Brown, Jr., of California, was the most prominent and successful of all the nonwhite speakers. Taking advantage of a gridlock between two candidates in his own party, Brown was chosen in 1980 with Republican support and became the longest-serving speaker in California's history as well as "one of the most influential blacks in American politics."[43]

Of the six Hispanic speakers, five were from New Mexico and one from Colorado. Hispanic participation in New Mexico politics spanned the political spectrum from landed gentry Republicans in the early part of the century to "Young Turk" Democrats in recent years. Secundino Romero and Antonio A. Sedillo, named speaker in 1915 and 1919 respectively, were both from prominent local families. After that, Hispanics dropped from the state political leadership (with the exception of George Washington Armijo in 1939) until the emergence in 1971 of the "Mama Lucy" faction led by speakers Walter K. Martinez and Raymond G. Sanchez. This group consisted of largely Hispanic liberal and moderate Democrats who wrested New Mexico House control from the "Old Guard," mostly white conservative Democrats. Other than the 1979, 1981, and 1985 terms, the "Mama Lucy" faction remained in power through 1990.[44]

Both Native American speakers were from Oklahoma. The first was William Alexander Durant, a Choctaw chief who was chosen in 1911. In 1973 the second, William Pascal Willis, was named.

All ten Asian or Pacific Islander speakers were from Hawaii.[45] Asians of both parties have occupied Hawaii's speakership throughout the twentieth century, with perhaps the most prominent being Republican Hiram Leong Fong in 1949, 1951, and 1953. In 1959 Fong became the first Asian member of the U.S. Senate. The Hawaii House was controlled by Asian Democratic speakers from 1968 through 1990.

Table 2 (continued)

C. Racial Background

Frequency Percent	White	African American	Hispanic	Native American	Asian/ Pacific Islander	Total
1911–1932	453 99.12	0 0.00	2 0.44	1 0.22	1 0.22	457
1933–1964	593 99.16	0 0.00	1 0.17	0 0.00	4 0.67	598
1965–1990	343 96.62	3 0.85	3 0.85	1 0.28	5 1.41	355
Total	**1,389** **98.51**	**3** **0.21**	**6** **0.43**	**2** **0.14**	**10** **0.71**	**1,410** **100**

A total of 81.9 percent of the speakers were Protestants (see Table 3). The Methodists (19.7 percent), Presbyterians (12.6 percent), Episcopalians (9.7 percent), Baptists (8.7 percent), Congregationalists (8.4 percent), and Lutherans (6.4 percent) represented the bulk of the Protestant affiliations. Of the nation's 50 Mormon speakers, 49 were from the West. Catholics accounted for 16 percent of the speakers, and 1.9 percent were Jewish.[46]

For the most part Catholic speakers were rare until Irish and Italian Americans began to flex their political muscles well into the twentieth century. Only 9 percent of the speakers in the period 1911–1932 were Catholics, but that figure jumped to 25.3 percent in the years 1965–1990. Thomas P. O'Neill, Jr., was the first Democrat and the first Catholic to hold the speakership in the Massachusetts House when he assumed the post in 1949.[47] There were relatively fewer Catholic speakers in the South, where during the entire 1911–1990 period the figure was only 8 percent.

A similar increase in political participation by Jews was seen. During the 1911–1932 period there were five Jewish speakers, but by 1965–1990 the figure had doubled to ten. Despite their small overall numbers at least one Jewish speaker presided during each decade between 1911 and 1990, beginning with Benjamin Selling of Oregon in 1915. Jewish speakers could be found in all areas of the United States, from Alaska's Richard Carl Rothenburg in 1929 to Nebraska's Harry Leon Pizer in 1959. Perhaps the most remarkable of them was Solomon Blatt of South Carolina, who presided for 33 years—longer than anybody else in state history. Furthermore, when Blatt died in 1986 at age 91, he had held his South Carolina House seat for 54 consecutive years—the longest tenure of any state legislator in the country.[48]

Speakers in this century have, by and large, been well educated (see Table 4). A total of 81.8 percent attended college and/or had some professional training during their lifetimes.[49] The colleges from which speakers earned their highest degree were scattered throughout the country. Harvard educated the most speakers (48), followed by Yale (27). The large state universities in the Midwest and South also trained a significant number of speakers, with Nebraska, Michigan, Wisconsin, and Florida each graduating at least 20. Clearly this reflected the strong public education systems that were in place in midwestern and southern states from the beginning of this century. These systems offered young men— and later young women—relatively inexpensive educations close to home as well as a chance to develop important state and regional networks of acquaintance and friendship with other ambitious young people.

A recent study of state house speakers from 1960 to 1989 concludes that the proportion for whom law was the primary occupation declined from 50 percent of the total in the 1960s to 38 percent in the 1980s.[50] Among all state legislators, the proportion of attorneys dropped from 22 percent in 1976 to 16 percent in 1986. One scholar speculates about this decline. She writes that in the past it was considered unethical for lawyers to advertise, and thus the "best way for an attorney . . . to establish himself [or herself] in the community, was to run

Table 3
Religious Affiliation of Speakers

A. By Year

Frequency Percent	Methodist	Mormon	Other Protestant	Catholic	Greek Orthodox	Jewish	Total
1911–1932	68	13	217	30	0	5	333
	20.42	3.90	65.17	9.01	0.00	1.50	
1933–1964	113	20	303	76	0	7	519
	21.77	3.85	58.38	14.64	0.00	1.35	
1965–1990	52	17	164	83	2	10	328
	15.85	5.18	50.00	25.30	0.61	3.05	
Total	**233**	**50**	**684**	**189**	**2**	**22**	**1,180**
	19.75	**4.24**	**57.97**	**16.02**	**0.17**	**1.86**	**100**

Frequency Missing = 230

B. By Region

Frequency Percent	Methodist	Mormon	Other Protestant	Catholic	Greek Orthodox	Jewish	Total
MIDWEST	65	0	195	35	0	2	297
	21.89	0.00	65.66	11.78	0.00	0.67	
NORTHEAST	26	0	151	68	2	10	257
	10.12	0.00	58.75	26.46	0.78	3.89	
SOUTH	102	1	192	26	0	6	327
	31.19	0.31	58.72	7.95	0.00	1.83	
WEST	40	49	146	60	0	4	299
	13.38	16.39	48.83	20.07	0.00	1.34	
Total	**233**	**50**	**684**	**189**	**2**	**22**	**1,180**
	19.75	**4.24**	**57.97**	**16.02**	**0.17**	**1.86**	**100**

Frequency Missing = 230

Table 4
Highest Level of Education of Speakers by Region

Frequency Percent	High School or Less	College	Professional	Total
MIDWEST	61	120	164	345
	17.68	34.78	47.54	
NORTHEAST	76	72	160	308
	24.68	23.38	51.95	
SOUTH	38	93	215	346
	10.98	26.88	62.14	
WEST	74	152	140	366
	20.22	41.53	38.25	
Total	**249**	**437**	**679**	**1,365**
	18.24	**32.01**	**49.74**	**100**

Frequency Missing = 45

for the state legislature and put posters up on all the telephone poles.'' Now that the American Bar Association no longer disapproves of advertising, attorneys who once would have served "their one or two terms in the legislature for personal and private, career-oriented gain" do not have to run for public office.[51]

In general, the *American Legislative Leaders* database corroborates these findings (see Table 5). During the 1911–1932 period 55.6 percent of the speakers were lawyers, compared to 44 percent in 1933–1964 and 40.3 percent in 1965–1990. Over the entire period from 1911 to 1990, 46.8 percent were attorneys. There were, however, some major regional distinctions. Speakers in the South were more than twice as likely to be lawyers (63.9 percent) as those in the West (30.9 percent).

The proportion of speakers involved in agriculture held relatively steady over the years at 11.4 percent in 1911–1932, 15.7 percent in 1933–1964, and 12.5 percent in 1965–1990. During the entire period 13.5 percent were farmers. Speakers with agriculture-related occupations were more common in the Midwest and West, at 22.1 percent and 19 percent respectively. For the South and Northeast, only a respective 6.6 percent and 4.9 percent held such occupations.[52] It is worth noting that agricultural interests continued to be influential despite the decline of farming as an occupation from 10.9 million workers in 1900 to 6.9 million in 1950.[53]

Focusing upon the South, Alabama, Georgia, Maryland, Mississippi, North Carolina, South Carolina, Tennessee, and Texas each named lawyers to the speakership at least two thirds of the time. However, less than half of speakers in Arkansas, Kentucky, and Virginia were attorneys. At least 10 percent of the speakers in Florida, Kentucky, and Mississippi came from agricultural backgrounds.[54]

In the past it was assumed that citizen-legislators were citizens who primarily

Table 5
Primary Occupation of Speakers before Speakership

A. By Year

Frequency Percent	Lawyer	Other Professional	Business	Agriculture	Other	Total
1911–1932	248 55.61	21 4.71	118 26.46	51 11.43	8 1.79	446
1933–1964	258 44.03	43 7.34	172 29.35	92 15.70	21 3.58	586
1965–1990	139 40.29	33 9.57	115 33.33	43 12.46	15 4.35	345
Total	**645** **46.84**	**97** **7.04**	**405** **29.41**	**186** **13.51**	**44** **3.20**	**1,377** **100**

Frequency Missing = 33

B. By Region

Frequency Percent	Lawyer	Other Professional	Business	Agriculture	Other	Total
MIDWEST	150 44.25	19 5.60	87 25.66	75 22.12	8 2.36	339
NORTHEAST	155 50.49	28 9.12	92 29.97	15 4.89	17 5.54	307
SOUTH	221 63.87	19 5.49	78 22.54	23 6.65	5 1.45	346
WEST	119 30.91	31 8.05	148 38.44	73 18.96	14 3.64	385
Total	**645** **46.84**	**97** **7.04**	**405** **29.41**	**186** **13.51**	**44** **3.20**	**1,377** **100**

Frequency Missing = 33

Table 5 (continued)

C. By Southern State

Frequency / Percent	Lawyer	Other Professional	Business	Agriculture	Other	Total
ALABAMA	12 / 66.67	0 / 0.00	6 / 33.33	0 / 0.00	0 / 0.00	18
ARKANSAS	18 / 46.15	4 / 10.26	15 / 38.46	2 / 5.13	0 / 0.00	39
FLORIDA	22 / 61.11	1 / 2.78	8 / 22.22	4 / 11.11	1 / 2.78	36
GEORGIA	11 / 91.67	0 / 0.00	0 / 0.00	1 / 8.33	0 / 0.00	12
KENTUCKY	13 / 46.43	3 / 10.71	5 / 17.86	5 / 17.86	2 / 7.14	28
LOUISIANA	10 / 58.82	1 / 5.88	5 / 29.41	1 / 5.88	0 / 0.00	17
MARYLAND	15 / 75.00	1 / 5.00	3 / 15.00	1 / 5.00	0 / 0.00	20
MISSISSIPPI	7 / 70.00	1 / 10.00	1 / 10.00	1 / 10.00	0 / 0.00	10
NORTH CAROLINA	27 / 75.00	1 / 2.78	6 / 16.67	2 / 5.56	0 / 0.00	36
OKLAHOMA	19 / 59.38	2 / 6.25	9 / 28.13	2 / 6.25	0 / 0.00	32
SOUTH CAROLINA	13 / 92.86	0 / 0.00	1 / 7.14	0 / 0.00	0 / 0.00	14
TENNESSEE	17 / 77.27	0 / 0.00	4 / 18.18	1 / 4.55	0 / 0.00	22
TEXAS	18 / 66.67	2 / 7.41	6 / 22.22	1 / 3.70	0 / 0.00	27
VIRGINIA	4 / 36.36	0 / 0.00	5 / 45.45	1 / 9.09	1 / 9.09	11
WEST VIRGINIA	15 / 62.50	3 / 12.50	4 / 16.67	1 / 4.17	1 / 4.17	24
Total	**221 / 63.87**	**19 / 5.49**	**78 / 22.54**	**23 / 6.65**	**5 / 1.45**	**346 / 100**

Frequency Missing = 10

Table 6
Highest U.S. Military Rank of Speakers

A. By Year

Frequency Percent	None	Enlisted	Officer	Total
1911–1932	251	41	41	**333**
	75.38	12.31	12.31	
1933–1964	244	141	106	**491**
	49.69	28.72	21.59	
1965–1990	131	134	83	**348**
	37.64	38.51	23.85	
Total	**626**	**316**	**230**	**1,172**
	53.41	**26.96**	**19.62**	**100**

Frequency Missing = 238

engaged in their regular occupations and only secondarily devoted time to their legislative duties. This, however, appears increasingly unlikely in the future. By the mid-1980s one study questioned whether the "Citizen Legislator [was] Becoming Extinct." It was pointed out that 11 percent "of all state legislators now consider themselves full-time legislators" and that "legislatures in nine states are generally considered full time: California, Illinois, Massachusetts, Michigan, New Jersey, New York, Ohio, Pennsylvania and Wisconsin." This process has been brought on by "the diversity and complexity of state legislating as an activity, as well as the need for legislators to legislate." Some celebrate such a trend: "If I'm sick, I want professional help. . . . I feel the same way about public affairs. I want legislators who are knowledgeable and professional." Others do not: "When Legislators spend all their time in the capitol, there's a tendency to feel that the whole world revolves around the capitol," according to one observer. When this happens, says another, "you're more influenced by the lobbyists than by your constituents." Another analysis rejects the notion that the trend toward full-time legislators will engulf all the states, claiming that "in smaller or more sparsely populated states, legislatures can afford to limit—and will continue to limit—their focus," whereas in "larger or more densely populated states . . . the business of being a state legislator has become much more complicated."[55]

Although the United States fought in four major wars between 1911 and 1990, only 46.6 percent of the speakers had military service prior to assuming their posts (see Table 6). Of the total, 27 percent were enlisted men and 19.6 percent were officers. The South had the highest proportion of speakers who had been in the armed forces at 53.6 percent.[56] Speakers were also apparently the marrying kind, for only 4.7 percent were never espoused before attaining their posts (see Table 7).[57]

Table 6 (continued)

B. By Region

Frequency Percent	None	Enlisted	Officer	Total
MIDWEST	158	77	53	288
	54.86	26.74	18.40	
NORTHEAST	154	53	52	259
	59.46	20.46	20.08	
SOUTH	136	89	68	293
	46.42	30.38	23.21	
WEST	178	97	57	332
	53.61	29.22	17.17	
Total	**626**	**316**	**230**	**1,172**
	53.41	**26.96**	**19.62**	**100**

Frequency Missing = 238

A total of 63.6 percent of the speakers were affiliated with at least one fraternal organization. The Masons claimed the largest membership at 40.8 percent;[58] the Elks were second at 25.6 percent. Other fraternal groups to which significant numbers of speakers belonged included the Odd Fellows, Knights of Pythias, Grange, Eagles, Moose, and Woodmen.

In addition, speakers were members of a wide variety of non-fraternal voluntary organizations. The most common were the American Legion (20.4 percent), Chamber of Commerce (18.9 percent), American Bar Association (13.9 percent), and Rotary (13.5 percent). Five speakers belonged to the National Rifle Association, five to the National Association for the Advancement of Colored People, three to the American Civil Liberties Union, and two to the Ku Klux Klan.

Our database also shows that there were eight pairs of fathers and sons who were each speaker. A total of 31 speakers were charged with crimes, 11 died in accidents, 4 apparently committed suicide, and 1 was murdered. Two ran on U.S. presidential tickets—Alfred Emanuel Smith of New York, the Democratic candidate for president in 1928, and Fielding Lewis Wright of Mississippi, the Dixiecrat vice-presidential nominee in 1948.

A classic study of state legislators written more than 30 years ago by Heinz Eulau and others contends that a "political career, like other careers, is a more or less typical sequence of events, a pattern in the life histories of men moving into positions made available by the framework of institutions. Political careers, therefore, can tell us a great deal about governmental institutions, which in turn are formalized and regularized patterns of action that shape and are shaped by political behavior." In their research Eulau and his colleagues found that "the more competitive [i.e., closely balanced] the state's party system, the more likely

Table 7
Marital Status of Speakers by Region

Frequency Percent	Never Married	Married	Total
MIDWEST	12 3.70	312 96.30	324
NORTHEAST	22 8.27	244 91.73	266
SOUTH	15 4.55	315 95.45	330
WEST	12 3.25	357 96.75	369
Total	**61** **4.73**	**1,228** **95.27**	**1,289** **100**

Frequency Missing = 121

it is for legislators to have had some prior governmental service.'' Whereas only a third of the legislators in New Jersey, a highly competitive state, had not held any office beforehand, half the legislators in the less competitive states of California and Tennessee were political beginners.[59]

Our *American Legislative Leaders* study, which is based upon a significantly larger database, finds that 59.9 percent of individuals had occupied public offices outside their state house prior to becoming speaker (see Table 8). A total of 49.4 percent of the speakers had been local office holders, whereas 18 percent had held state posts. Of the 6.7 percent who had been federal officials, all had been bureaucrats aside from U.S. House members Samuel Lafort Collins of California and James Alfred Taylor of West Virginia. It should be noted that it was more likely for a speaker to have held a prior public office in 1911–1932 (65.2 percent) than in 1965–1990 (54.9 percent).[60]

For the South as a whole, 55.9 percent of the speakers had previously been in a public position. The figures in Alabama, Georgia, and North Carolina were a respective 88.9, 91.7, and 75 percent. However, in Kentucky, Louisiana, South Carolina, and Texas less than 40 percent of the speakers had held any public office.[61]

Once legislators are in the state house, what factors determine their length of service and shape the contours of their individual careers? Has the length of service changed over time? What impact has this had on the state house?

Some scholars have argued that ''turnover in state legislatures is excessive and that rapid turnover detracts from the performance of both the lawmaking and watchdog functions and weakens the institution.''[62] One study based on an examination of 49 state houses (excluding Nebraska's Unicameral) for the 1963, 1965, 1967, 1969, and 1971 sessions predicts that ''state legislative turnover

Table 8
Number of Public Offices Held by Speakers before Speakership

A. By Year

Frequency Percent	0	1–2	3+	Total
1911–1932	159	213	85	457
	34.79	46.61	18.60	
1933–1964	246	265	87	598
	41.14	44.31	14.55	
1965–1990	160	145	50	355
	45.07	40.85	14.08	
Total	565	623	222	1,410
	40.07	44.18	15.74	100

rates will decline, at least gradually, in the years ahead.'' Making comparisons with earlier studies, the author points out that while he found 35.4 percent of the members to be new to legislative service during the period 1963–1971, the proportion of newcomers in sessions from 1925 to 1935 was larger (39.6 percent).[63]

A more comprehensive study of state legislatures from 1931 to 1976 also concludes that overall turnover rates have been declining. "In general," the authors report, "turnover has been notably higher over time" in southern states such as Alabama, Louisiana, Maryland, Mississippi, and North Carolina and in the northeastern state of Maine. However, turnover "has been consistently lower in some urban, industrial states such as New York, California, Illinois, and Massachusetts." Many other states exhibited no pattern, and "turnover varied substantially from one decade to another."[64]

One political scientist, David Ray, maintains that the causes of turnover need to be examined, suggesting that legislators who leave due to voluntary retirement should be analyzed separately from legislators who are defeated at the polls. In a study of eight legislatures—those of Illinois, Iowa, Michigan, Minnesota, Missouri, New Jersey, West Virginia, and Wisconsin—from 1897 to 1967, he discovers that the "most obvious trend is a gradual but very substantial decline in the number of legislators who voluntarily retire." Early in the period (1897–1917), "the percentage of legislators who voluntarily retired was always substantially larger than the percentage who were defeated at the polls." After 1917 voluntary retirement continued to be the major factor in turnover in Iowa, New Jersey, and West Virginia, whereas in the other five states "the percentage of legislators who were defeated at the polls has exceeded the percentage who voluntarily retired in slightly more than half the cases since 1927."[65]

High turnover, of course, implies legislative instability as a result of newcomers to the process coming into service each new term. However, in another study Ray questions some of the scholarly conventional wisdom about the instability

Table 8 (continued)

B. By Region

Frequency *Percent*	0	1–2	3+	Total
MIDWEST	131	164	53	**348**
	37.64	47.13	15.23	
NORTHEAST	90	141	84	**315**
	28.57	44.76	26.67	
SOUTH	157	161	38	**356**
	44.10	45.22	10.67	
WEST	187	157	47	**391**
	47.83	40.15	12.02	
Total	**565**	**623**	**222**	**1,410**
	40.07	**44.18**	**15.74**	**100**

of membership in the state legislatures. He points out that it is often asserted that more than half of the approximately 7,800 state legislators in the country "must be replaced every other year." After studying the legislatures in Connecticut, Michigan, and Wisconsin for the period 1893–1969, he concludes that all "had a substantial decline in the number of first-term legislators" as "exemplified by the Michigan House of Representatives, which contained 80 per cent freshmen in 1893 and only 14 per cent in 1969." Ray is not interested in *just* the proportion of freshman legislators, wanting to know how many legislators *sought* reelection. In other words, how many were interested in legislative careers? All three states, he finds, have shown "a substantial increase in the percentage of legislators who have sought re-election." "In 1893," he continues, "only 9 per cent of the members of the Connecticut House of Representatives sought reelection, a figure which rose to 30 per cent in 1917, 61 per cent in 1937, and 80 per cent in 1969."[66]

The decline in turnover and the trend toward legislators becoming careerists has at least in some states led to a professionalization of legislatures over the course of the twentieth century—especially in recent years. In the late 1960s political scientist Nelson Polsby published a path-breaking article on the institutionalization of the U.S. House of Representatives. Finding that there was a dramatic decline in turnover among House members from 1789 down to the mid-1960s, Polsby equates this decline with an increasing institutionalization of the House as exemplified by more clearly defined boundaries, a more complex organization with "interdependent" parts, and "automatic rather than discretionary methods for conducting . . . internal business."

The speakership of the U.S. House, Polsby argues, holds special significance as an index of this institutionalization. "Before 1899," he points out, "the mean years of service of members selected for the Speakership was six; after 1899, the mean rises steeply to twenty-six." Polsby concludes that the speakers' ca-

Table 8 (continued)

C. By Southern State

Frequency Percent	0	1–2	3+	Total
ALABAMA	2 11.11	13 72.22	3 16.67	18
ARKANSAS	18 46.15	16 41.03	5 12.82	39
FLORIDA	16 44.44	18 50.00	2 5.56	36
GEORGIA	1 8.33	8 66.67	3 25.00	12
KENTUCKY	17 60.71	8 28.57	3 10.71	28
LOUISIANA	11 61.11	7 38.89	0 0.00	18
MARYLAND	13 59.09	9 40.91	0 0.00	22
MISSISSIPPI	4 40.00	6 60.00	0 0.00	10
NORTH CAROLINA	9 25.00	20 55.56	7 19.44	36
OKLAHOMA	13 38.24	15 44.12	6 17.65	34
SOUTH CAROLINA	9 64.29	4 28.57	1 7.14	14
TENNESSEE	10 41.67	9 37.50	5 20.83	24
TEXAS	19 63.33	11 36.67	0 0.00	30
VIRGINIA	3 27.27	8 72.73	0 0.00	11
WEST VIRGINIA	12 50.00	9 37.50	3 12.50	24
Total	**157** **44.10**	**161** **45.22**	**38** **10.67**	**356** **100**

reers in the U.S. House are "a strong indication of the development of the speakership as a singular occupational specialty," with speakers specializing in House leadership and prizing and valuing their career as a fulfillment of their political ambitions. This "development of a specifically House leadership, the increase in the overall seniority of members, and the decrease in the influx of newcomers" have had "the effect not only of separating the house from other organizations in the political system, but also of facilitating the growth of stable ways of doing business within the institution."[67]

Table 9
Number of Years Speakers Served in House before Speakership

A. By Year

Frequency Percent	0	1–4	5–8	9+	Total
1911–1932	55	259	111	29	**454**
	12.11	57.05	24.45	6.39	
1933–1964	18	202	231	147	**598**
	3.01	33.78	38.63	24.58	
1965–1990	2	45	118	190	**355**
	0.56	12.68	33.24	53.52	
Total	**75**	**506**	**460**	**366**	**1,407**
	5.33	**35.96**	**32.69**	**26.01**	**100**

Frequency Missing = 3

In an effort to test in the state legislatures Polsby's conclusions about the U.S. Congress, Douglas Camp Chaffey and Malcolm Jewell examine the "selection and turnover for the speaker and party floor leaders in the lower houses" of New York, Pennsylvania, Illinois, Wisconsin, Connecticut, Rhode Island, Iowa, and Montana from 1945 to 1970. In the more professionalized legislatures of New York and Pennsylvania, as measured by compensation, scope of legislative staff support, number of bills, and number of days in a legislative session, they find "few leadership elections in the . . . lower houses" that were "the result of openly-contested elections." However, in the least professional legislature, that of Montana, "an automatic or predictable pattern of selection of legislative party leaders" had not been established. Agreeing with Polsby's national findings, they conclude that in the more professional legislatures the tenure of the leaders is longer, leaders serve longer periods of apprenticeship, incumbents are less likely to be challenged, there is a "pattern of succession to top leadership positions," and there are "fewer contests for leadership positions."[68]

Our *American Legislative Leaders* database reaffirms many of these conclusions (see Table 9). The length of time necessary to attain the speakership dramatically increased in the years from 1911 to 1990. During the 1911–1932 period 69.2 percent of the speakers were in the state house for four or less years before attaining their positions; only 6.4 percent needed nine or more years. In the next period, 1933–1964, 36.8 percent took four or less years, but 24.6 percent needed at least nine years. By the 1965–1990 period the proportion of speakers needing four or less years had declined to 13.2 percent, whereas those requiring nine or more years had increased to 53.5 percent.[69]

There were notable regional variations during the 1911–1932 era. A total of 37.4 percent of southern and 36.4 percent of northeastern speakers needed at least five years in the state house before attaining their posts, whereas only 25.9

Table 9 (continued)

B. By Region

Frequency *Percent*	0	1–4	5–8	9+	Total
MIDWEST	10 2.88	115 33.14	116 33.43	106 30.55	347
NORTHEAST	15 4.76	124 39.37	99 31.43	77 24.44	315
SOUTH	25 7.04	110 30.99	116 32.68	104 29.30	355
WEST	25 6.41	157 40.26	129 33.08	79 20.26	390
Total	**75** **5.33**	**506** **35.96**	**460** **32.69**	**366** **26.01**	**1,407** **100**

Frequency Missing = 3

percent of midwestern and 23.2 percent of western speakers required that much time. Those regional distinctions had all but disappeared by the period 1965–1990, with more than 80 percent of speakers in each region serving at least five years in the house beforehand.[70]

In the South, during the entire 1911–1990 period 46.2 percent of the speakers in Arkansas, 44.4 percent of those in Louisiana, 50 percent of those in Maryland, and 72.7 percent of those in Virginia served nine or more years prior to gaining their posts. However, over half of the speakers in Tennessee and West Virginia required four or less years.[71]

Not only did speakers serve increasingly longer house apprenticeships in the years after 1911, they also tended to have increasingly long tenures in the speakership (see Table 10). In the period 1911–1932, 81.6 percent held the office two or less years and only 4.4 percent for five or more years. By the period 1965–1990, 54.6 percent were speakers for two or less years, whereas 23.7 percent remained in their posts for five or more years.[72]

The South tended to have the longest-serving speakers, with 6.5 percent holding office for at least five years in 1911–1932, in contrast to 3.7, 3.5, and 3.5 percent in the Northeast, Midwest, and West respectively. The same pattern continued in 1933–1964 with 12.2, 6.7, 9.8, and 6.9 percent holding office for five or more years in the respective regions. By the most recent period, 1965–1990, 35.7 percent of southern speakers were in office at least five years as compared to 23 percent in the Northeast, 21.7 percent in the Midwest, and 16.2 percent in the West.[73] As a rule, speakers in the West took less time to attain their positions and served for shorter periods of time—which perhaps indicates that western houses were less institutionalized than those in the other regions.[74]

Within the South, patterns of holding office varied considerably from state to

Table 9 (continued)

C. By Region (1911–1932)

Frequency / Percent	0	1–4	5–8	9+	Total
MIDWEST	10	73	22	7	112
	8.93	65.18	19.64	6.25	
NORTHEAST	7	61	29	10	107
	6.54	57.01	27.10	9.35	
SOUTH	17	60	37	9	123
	13.82	48.78	30.08	7.32	
WEST	21	65	23	3	112
	18.75	58.04	20.54	2.68	
Total	**55**	**259**	**111**	**29**	**454**
	12.11	**57.05**	**24.45**	**6.39**	**100**

Frequency Missing = 3

D. By Region (1933–1964)

Frequency / Percent	0	1–4	5–8	9+	Total
MIDWEST	0	32	68	43	143
	0.00	22.38	47.55	30.07	
NORTHEAST	6	55	42	31	134
	4.48	41.04	31.34	23.13	
SOUTH	8	41	57	42	148
	5.41	27.70	38.51	28.38	
WEST	4	74	64	31	173
	2.31	42.77	36.99	17.92	
Total	**18**	**202**	**231**	**147**	**598**
	3.01	**33.78**	**38.63**	**24.58**	**100**

E. By Region (1965–1990)

Frequency / Percent	0	1–4	5–8	9+	Total
MIDWEST	0	10	26	56	92
	0.00	10.87	28.26	60.87	
NORTHEAST	2	8	28	36	74
	2.70	10.81	37.84	48.65	
SOUTH	0	9	22	53	84
	0.00	10.71	26.19	63.10	
WEST	0	18	42	45	105
	0.00	17.14	40.00	42.86	
Total	**2**	**45**	**118**	**190**	**355**
	0.56	**12.68**	**33.24**	**53.52**	**100**

Table 9 (continued)

F. By Southern State

Frequency Percent	0	1–4	5–8	9+	Total
ALABAMA	2 11.11	6 33.33	4 22.22	6 33.33	18
ARKANSAS	1 2.56	10 25.64	10 25.64	18 46.15	39
FLORIDA	3 8.33	7 19.44	21 58.33	5 13.89	36
GEORGIA	0 0.00	2 16.67	6 50.00	4 33.33	12
KENTUCKY	2 7.14	10 35.71	10 35.71	6 21.43	28
LOUISIANA	2 11.11	3 16.67	5 27.78	8 44.44	18
MARYLAND	3 13.64	6 27.27	2 9.09	11 50.00	22
MISSISSIPPI	1 10.00	1 10.00	4 40.00	4 40.00	10
NORTH CAROLINA	0 0.00	7 19.44	18 50.00	11 30.56	36
OKLAHOMA	1 3.03	15 45.45	12 36.36	5 15.15	33
SOUTH CAROLINA	1 7.14	5 35.71	3 21.43	5 35.71	14
TENNESSEE	5 20.83	13 54.17	4 16.67	2 8.33	24
TEXAS	0 0.00	14 46.67	9 30.00	7 23.33	30
VIRGINIA	0 0.00	0 0.00	3 27.27	8 72.73	11
WEST VIRGINIA	4 16.67	11 45.83	5 20.83	4 16.67	24
Total	25 7.04	110 30.99	116 32.68	104 29.30	355 100

Frequency Missing = 1

state. Whereas Georgia, Maryland, Mississippi, South Carolina, and Virginia had a respective 41.7, 31.8, 60, 35.7, and 63.4 percent of their speakers serve for five or more years, no speakers in Arkansas and Florida were in office that long.[75]

National or even regional statistics often obscure practices that are unique to one or a few states. The authors of one study on the tenure of state legislative

Table 10
Number of Years Speakers Served as Speaker

A. By Year

Frequency Percent	0–1	2	3–4	5+	Total
1911–1932	68	305	64	20	**457**
	14.88	66.74	14.00	4.38	
1933–1964	80	375	90	53	**598**
	13.38	62.71	15.05	8.86	
1965–1990	24	170	77	84	**355**
	6.76	47.89	21.69	23.66	
Total	**172**	**850**	**231**	**157**	**1,410**
	12.20	**60.28**	**16.38**	**11.13**	**100**

B. By Region

Frequency Percent	0–1	2	3–4	5+	Total
MIDWEST	19	242	49	38	**348**
	5.46	69.54	14.08	10.92	
NORTHEAST	91	145	49	30	**315**
	28.89	46.03	15.56	9.52	
SOUTH	27	197	76	56	**356**
	7.58	55.34	21.35	15.73	
WEST	35	266	57	33	**391**
	8.95	68.03	14.58	8.44	
Total	**172**	**850**	**231**	**157**	**1,410**
	12.20	**60.28**	**16.38**	**11.13**	**100**

C. By Region (1911–1932)

Frequency Percent	0–1	2	3–4	5+	Total
MIDWEST	10	86	13	4	**113**
	8.85	76.11	11.50	3.54	
NORTHEAST	41	47	15	4	**107**
	38.32	43.93	14.02	3.74	
SOUTH	12	79	25	8	**124**
	9.68	63.71	20.16	6.45	
WEST	5	93	11	4	**113**
	4.42	82.30	9.73	3.54	
Total	**68**	**305**	**64**	**20**	**457**
	14.88	**66.74**	**14.00**	**4.38**	**100**

Table 10 (continued)

D. By Region (1933–1964)

Frequency Percent	0–1	2	3–4	5+	Total
MIDWEST	5 3.50	106 74.13	18 12.59	14 9.79	143
NORTHEAST	36 26.87	77 57.46	12 8.96	9 6.72	134
SOUTH	12 8.11	82 55.41	36 24.32	18 12.16	148
WEST	27 15.61	110 63.58	24 13.87	12 6.94	173
Total	**80** **13.38**	**375** **62.71**	**90** **15.05**	**53** **8.86**	**598** **100**

leaders from 1947 to 1980 found that Arkansas, North Dakota, Utah, and Wyoming routinely named a new speaker every term, whereas in Alaska, Connecticut, Iowa, Kansas, Montana, Nevada, Oregon, South Dakota, and Wisconsin speakers never held office for longer than one or two terms. At the other extreme, individual speakers retained their positions for 18 or more years in Georgia, Mississippi, South Carolina, and Virginia.[76]

What are the factors, other than tradition or house rules, that influence the selection and length of tenure of speakers? Party competitiveness is an obvious issue. When there is a competitive balance within a state and thus a periodic shift in power from one party to another in the house, the speakership will also frequently change hands. In Indiana, for instance, "the more frequent turnover . . . has often been due to changes in partisan control of the House, which shifted eight times between 1947 and 1979."[77]

There are other considerations as well. Southern states such as Alabama, Georgia, Louisiana, Kentucky, and Maryland have had a long history of the governor playing a major role in choosing the speaker. The Louisiana speaker has traditionally held office concomitantly with the governor, each remaining in office for four years. Furthermore, in some states the term of the speaker has lengthened to match that of the governor. The removal of constitutional restraints restricting a governor to a single term "has reduced the opportunities for upward mobility of leaders, and forced them to serve longer; it has also reduced the likelihood of a new governor seeking to change leaders after four years." However, in most states the governor's influence in naming the speaker has been on the decline.[78]

Rivalries within state parties have also influenced the selection process. For example, the Republican-dominated Vermont legislature established a pattern of succession to the top state jobs—speaker first, then lieutenant governor and governor. Set by the precedent of Franklin Swift Billings, Sr., in the 1920s, this pattern

Table 10 (continued)

E. By Region (1965–1990)

Frequency Percent	0–1	2	3–4	5+	Total
MIDWEST	4 4.35	50 54.35	18 19.57	20 21.74	92
NORTHEAST	14 18.92	21 28.38	22 29.73	17 22.97	74
SOUTH	3 3.57	36 42.86	15 17.86	30 35.71	84
WEST	3 2.86	63 60.00	22 20.95	17 16.19	105
Total	**24** **6.76**	**170** **47.89**	**77** **21.69**	**84** **23.66**	**355** **100**

became regular during the next two decades. In order to avoid fierce intraparty battles for the offices, a "mountain rule" was followed whereby governors were limited to single two-year terms and the office traditionally alternated between eastern and western Vermonters. Moreover, western governors had eastern lieutenant governors and vice versa. The pattern was broken in 1975 when Democrat Timothy J. O'Connor, Jr., won the speakership.[79] O'Connor was not only the first Democratic speaker in Vermont in this century but also the state's first Catholic speaker and first three-term speaker since the 1700s.[80]

When general elections resulted in a house being evenly divided between parties, representatives devised unique solutions for choosing a speaker. In the past some compromise was reached such as soliciting votes to break the deadlock or dividing committee chairs. A remarkable example occurred in New Jersey in 1919, when Republican Arthur N. Pierson's name was drawn from a hat. These methods may have been fine for states where speakers were mere titular heads or wielded limited power. However, in modern times more is at stake in choosing a speaker. Our database shows a new trend, that of the dual speakership. First tried in Washington in 1979,[81] dual speakerships have also been utilized in the Indiana House in 1989 and the Michigan House in 1993.[82]

The Indiana example is illuminating. After the 1988 election resulted in a 50–50 deadlock between parties, the Indiana House named Democrat Michael Keith Phillips and Republican Paul Steven Mannweiler as co-speakers. Phillips and Mannweiler alternated days in presiding over the chamber. In a legislature that had made the speaker arguably the most powerful individual in state government, the new arrangement was nothing less than revolutionary. It forced not only a sharing of the speakership but a sharing of the chairmanships of each committee, the naming of two clerks, and so on.[83]

The Texas system for choosing speakers, at least in the 1970s and 1980s, was unusual in that it did not ordinarily follow party lines. Instead the minority

Table 10 (continued)

F. By Southern State

Frequency Percent	0–1	2	3–4	5+	Total
ALABAMA	1	5	8	4	18
	5.56	27.78	44.44	22.22	
ARKANSAS	1	37	1	0	39
	2.56	94.87	2.56	0.00	
FLORIDA	3	28	5	0	36
	8.33	77.78	13.89	0.00	
GEORGIA	0	2	5	5	12
	0.00	16.67	41.67	41.67	
KENTUCKY	4	12	10	2	28
	14.29	42.86	35.71	7.14	
LOUISIANA	1	1	12	4	18
	5.56	5.56	66.67	22.22	
MARYLAND	3	5	7	7	22
	13.64	22.73	31.82	31.82	
MISSISSIPPI	1	1	2	6	10
	10.00	10.00	20.00	60.00	
NORTH CAROLINA	3	29	3	1	36
	8.33	80.56	8.33	2.78	
OKLAHOMA	8	19	2	5	34
	23.53	55.88	5.88	14.71	
SOUTH CAROLINA	1	5	3	5	14
	7.14	35.71	21.43	35.71	
TENNESSEE	0	17	4	3	24
	0.00	70.83	16.67	12.50	
TEXAS	1	22	5	2	30
	3.33	73.33	16.67	6.67	
VIRGINIA	0	1	3	7	11
	0.00	9.09	27.27	63.64	
WEST VIRGINIA	0	13	6	5	24
	0.00	54.17	25.00	20.83	
Total	**27**	**197**	**76**	**56**	**356**
	7.58	**55.34**	**21.35**	**15.73**	**100**

Republicans were courted by Democratic rivals, so that speakers were named by Democratic factions along with sympathetic Republicans. From 1947 until the 1970s Texas speakers served only one or two terms, but in the 1970s Billy Wayne Clayton became the first speaker in state history to hold the office for three consecutive terms. Clayton's successor, Gibson D. Lewis, outdid him by retaining the speakership for five terms. In recent years aspiring speakers in Texas have made their intentions known several years in advance. Furthermore, the speakership contests have not been limited to the halls of the Texas House but have become statewide races, with contenders frequently traveling to raise money and to recruit friendly legislative candidates.[84]

Despite the individual variations in the states regarding the tenure and selection of speakers, by 1990 speakers generally held onto their offices longer and also put in lengthier apprenticeships than their counterparts in the first part of the century. This tends to substantiate the work of those scholars who have argued that there has been a strong trend toward more professional, or institutionalized, state legislatures this century.

There are, of course, indices in addition to those involving leadership that suggest that state legislatures are becoming more professionalized, albeit slowly and unevenly. In 1970 the Citizens Conference on State Legislatures, after a major study, made a number of recommendations for streamlining and improving the efficiency and representativeness of those bodies. These recommendations were the basis for at least some changes. Among other things, the conference recommended reducing the size of state houses to no more than 100 members. However, in the early 1980s a total of 22 states still exceeded this number, with New Hampshire having 400 representatives. A recommendation to reduce the number of state House committees, in order to make them more efficient and reduce unnecessary complexity, had more success with a decline from 1,356 committees in 1955 to 914 committees in 1981. The need to improve compensation for legislators was also suggested. Although there was some improvement by the early 1980s, there was still wide variation among states. For instance, New Hampshire paid legislators annual salaries of $100 at the same time Michigan paid them $31,000. In order to make legislators independent from information given by lobbyists and/or the governor, it has long been recommended that professional legislative staffs be retained. By the end of the 1970s, 32 states provided professional staffs for all committees, 41 states did so for most, and only 4 western states—Idaho, Montana, Nevada, and Wyoming—did not provide committees with professional staffs.[85]

Why do speakers leave office? One recent study argues: "Most leaders leave voluntarily either to seek higher office, pursue other career paths or retire. They are motivated by political ambition and circumstances, a need to make more money than legislative salaries provide, a sense of accomplishment about their legislative goals or, in some instances, by fatigue or burnout. A few leave involuntarily because of electoral defeat, ouster by a leadership challenge or changes in party control." Stanley Fink, a four-term New York speaker, revealed that his decision to retire resulted from the lack of suitable political opportunities and the demand for fresh, more dynamic leadership. Personally and professionally, he said, he needed "to go out and climb new mountains." The problem that Fink and other legislative leaders have faced is that "there are very few other jobs that are attractive and politically possible."[86]

Scholars who have studied the U.S. Congress and the state legislatures have argued that as legislative branches have become more institutionalized, fewer

Table 11
Speakers' Reasons for Leaving House

A. By Year

Frequency Percent	Other Office	Retired	Defeated	Died	Total
1911–1932	162	155	20	16	**353**
	45.89	43.91	5.67	4.53	
1933–1964	254	190	29	36	**509**
	49.90	37.33	5.70	7.07	
1965–1990	121	81	27	11	**240**
	50.42	33.75	11.25	4.58	
Total	**537**	**426**	**76**	**63**	**1,102**
	48.73	**38.66**	**6.90**	**5.72**	**100**

Frequency Missing = 308

of their members have voluntarily retired and the speakership has increasingly been seen as a significant career goal in itself rather than as a stepping stone to a higher office. For example, Polsby, in his study of Congress, concludes that the speakers' legislative careers strongly indicate that the speakership has become "a singular occupational specialty."[87] In a similar vein, Andrew McNitt and Edward Brazil find that from 1960 to 1989 the speakership became "a more exclusively legislative career" and state legislatures became "increasingly independent organizations." They also show that speakers from that period were less likely to be elected to higher office than those in the past.[88]

Our *American Legislative Leaders* database indicates that 48.7 percent of the speakers from 1911 to 1990 left the state house for another elective or appointive post, 38.7 percent retired from the house, 6.9 percent lost reelection, and 5.7 percent died in office (see Table 11). Those seeking another position rose from 45.9 percent in the 1911–1932 period to 50.4 percent in the years 1965–1990, whereas those who retired decreased from 43.9 percent in the first period to 33.8 percent in the most recent era.[89]

In the South, 39.6 percent of the speakers left the state house for another office. The figure was more than 50 percent in Georgia, Maryland, and South Carolina. A different situation was apparent in Virginia, where only 9.1 percent sought another position.[90]

Among all speakers, 49 percent held a state office after leaving the state house (see Table 12). The highest office reached by 4.6 percent was governor; 7.5 percent attained a lower executive position, 11.9 percent state senator, 5.8 percent state judge, and 19.2 percent a bureaucratic office. A total of 15.7 percent of the speakers later held a federal position.[91] Two of those were Samuel Taliaferro Rayburn of Texas and Thomas P. O'Neill, Jr., of Massachusetts, each of whom became speaker of the U.S. House of Representatives.

Table 11 (continued)

B. By Region

Frequency Percent	Other Office	Retired	Defeated	Died	Total
MIDWEST	133	105	13	16	**267**
	49.81	39.33	4.87	5.99	
NORTHEAST	149	79	11	12	**251**
	59.36	31.47	4.38	4.78	
SOUTH	110	126	20	22	**278**
	39.57	45.32	7.19	7.91	
WEST	145	116	32	13	**306**
	47.39	37.91	10.46	4.25	
Total	**537**	**426**	**76**	**63**	**1,102**
	48.73	**38.66**	**6.90**	**5.72**	**100**

Frequency Missing = 308

Although extremely valuable for setting the general contours of who the speakers have been, how long they have served, and what they have done afterward, the overall statistics say nothing about why some speakers were more successful than others. Why were some able to win the support of their colleagues session after session? As might be expected, some speakers spent a large portion of their adult lives in the state house. A total of 13.3 percent served 20 years or more, with 3.1 percent serving 30 years or more.

The champion of longevity was South Carolina Democrat Solomon Blatt, who as previously mentioned was speaker for 33 years—from 1937 to 1973 with the exception of the 1947 and 1949 sessions. Known as a political "arm twister," Blatt was supported and sustained as leader by the Democratic "Barnwell Ring." That faction was often at odds with another politically powerful South Carolinian, Strom Thurmond. In New York, Republican Oswald D. Heck held the longest tenure in state history, presiding from 1937 to 1959. Enjoying bipartisan support throughout his career, Heck was the last speaker from upstate New York.

Whereas Blatt and Heck were political novices when first elected to their houses, Democrat Walter Sillers of Mississippi belonged to a legislative dynasty, with his father having been a state representative and his father-in-law a state senator. Sillers was a member of the Mississippi House for 51 years and speaker from 1944 to 1966. He ascended to the speakership with the support of other committee chairs and then consolidated his position, becoming known as the "most powerful figure in Mississippi." A rabid segregationist and fiscal conservative, Sillers did not support his party's presidential nominees from Harry S. Truman through Lyndon B. Johnson and attempted to thwart desegregation by abolishing the state public school system.

Table 11 (continued)

C. By Southern State

Frequency Percent	Other Office	Retired	Defeated	Died	Total
ALABAMA	6	7	1	2	16
	37.50	43.75	6.25	12.50	
ARKANSAS	10	10	1	3	24
	41.67	41.67	4.17	12.50	
FLORIDA	9	13	0	2	24
	37.50	54.17	0.00	8.33	
GEORGIA	4	2	1	1	8
	50.00	25.00	12.50	12.50	
KENTUCKY	6	10	3	2	21
	28.57	47.62	14.29	9.52	
LOUISIANA	6	4	0	3	13
	46.15	30.77	0.00	23.08	
MARYLAND	11	7	2	0	20
	55.00	35.00	10.00	0.00	
MISSISSIPPI	3	2	0	3	8
	37.50	25.00	0.00	37.50	
NORTH CAROLINA	14	13	2	2	31
	45.16	41.94	6.45	6.45	
OKLAHOMA	9	13	4	0	26
	34.62	50.00	15.38	0.00	
SOUTH CAROLINA	6	5	0	1	12
	50.00	41.67	0.00	8.33	
TENNESSEE	6	13	1	0	20
	30.00	65.00	5.00	0.00	
TEXAS	12	14	2	0	28
	42.86	50.00	7.14	0.00	
VIRGINIA	1	8	1	1	11
	9.09	72.73	9.09	9.09	
WEST VIRGINIA	7	5	2	2	16
	43.75	31.25	12.50	12.50	
Total	**110**	**126**	**20**	**22**	**278**
	39.57	**45.32**	**7.19**	**7.91**	**100**

Frequency Missing = 78

What does it take to build a long career as speaker? In the aforementioned cases, the speakers had created virtual local political baronies, making party affiliation of secondary importance to the maintaining or wielding of power. State or local issues and alliances were the stuff that made for long-term political survival. However, the careers of three recently prominent speakers indicate that there is no one leadership style that guarantees success.

Table 12
Speakers' Offices after Speakership by Region

A. Highest State Office

Frequency Percent	None	Governor	Lower Executive	Senate	Judge	Bureaucrat	Total
MIDWEST	182 54.17	16 4.76	35 10.42	24 7.14	13 3.87	66 19.64	336
NORTHEAST	129 42.02	19 6.19	24 7.82	45 14.66	21 6.84	69 22.48	307
SOUTH	195 56.03	17 4.89	25 7.18	29 8.33	28 8.05	54 15.52	348
WEST	197 50.90	11 2.84	20 5.17	66 17.05	18 4.65	75 19.38	387
Total	**703** **51.02**	**63** **4.57**	**104** **7.55**	**164** **11.90**	**80** **5.81**	**264** **19.16**	**1,378** **100**

Frequency Missing = 32

B. Highest Federal Office

Frequency Percent	None	Congress	Cabinet	Judge	Bureaucrat	Total
MIDWEST	271 80.65	18 5.36	2 0.60	3 0.89	42 12.50	336
NORTHEAST	256 83.39	21 6.84	1 0.33	4 1.30	25 8.14	307
SOUTH	306 87.93	15 4.31	0 0.00	0 0.00	27 7.76	348
WEST	329 85.01	12 3.10	0 0.00	1 0.26	45 11.63	387
Total	**1,162** **84.33**	**66** **4.79**	**3** **0.22**	**8** **0.58**	**139** **10.09**	**1,378** **100**

Frequency Missing = 32

By all accounts Democrat Willie Lewis Brown, Jr., of California (named in 1980, 1981, 1983, 1985, 1987, 1989, 1991, and 1993) was one of the most successful recent speakers. Not aspiring to higher office, Brown said that his "goal in life [was] really to be speaker as long as the house will have me." This focus upon the speakership paid big dividends and won him unprecedented longevity in the post. Despite the decline of the institutional power of the speakership over the years, Brown, "because of his intelligence, his parliamentary skill and his vast knowledge," maintained the image of the "all powerful speaker." He was elected to the California Assembly as a radical ideologue in 1964 but later won the reputation of being the consummate pragmatist—a "members' speaker" who rarely strayed from the consensus of the Democratic caucus and worked behind the scenes to give credit to individual members for passage of legislation. Using his unmatched fund-raising skill to benefit his supporters, Brown cemented an already strong bond of allegiance among his friends.[92]

The career of Vera Katz of Oregon (chosen in 1985, 1987, and 1989) showed a similar trajectory to that of Brown. Katz also entered the legislature as a liberal Democrat, working to expand health care and protect the rights of consumers and tenants. Faced with a declining economy in the Northwest and an expanding state responsibility for providing essential services under Ronald Reagan's New Federalism, Katz said that in the 1980s she was forced "to move toward new policies and weigh a great many old claims." Therefore, when she became speaker she focused upon "managing the institution . . . not in engaging in ideological battles over divisive issues." As with Brown, she was a consensus builder striving to satisfy "individual members' needs" in order "to retain the loyalty of senior members who [had] not moved up in leadership." This attention to her relationships with individual members was an important factor in her success. She also claimed that being a woman was an advantage. The "female perspective on politics is different" and "conveys trust and fairness to a process that is basically dog eat dog," she concluded.[93]

Vernal G. Riffe, Jr., of Ohio (named in 1975, 1977, 1979, 1981, 1983, 1985, 1987, 1989, 1991, and 1993) worked to build solid relationships with his colleagues and to act, first and foremost, as a facilitator for the efficient operation of the legislature. In contrast to Brown and Katz, Riffe was a conservative Democrat who adopted more of the operating style of the old-time political boss. He was called "the most powerful speaker in Ohio's history." Riffe astonished friends and foes alike with his political power by overriding a decision of the Ohio Board of Regents and successfully pushing the Ohio House into creating a state university in his district. Ruling with an iron fist, he rewarded his friends by supporting their bills and getting contributions for their campaign coffers. He even created more committees in order to assure every senior House Democrat a chair with its additional stipend. When legislators opposed a Riffe-endorsed bill or criticized his methods, they often were stripped of committee chairs and found it impossible to get bills on the house calendar.

Part of Riffe's power and the key to his effectiveness was his unmatched knowledge of the details of the legislative process and the problems and needs of the various communities around the state. He resembled a banker, constantly engaged in granting or calling in political loans or favors. Critics condemned Riffe for the lack of deliberation in the Ohio House, the emphasis upon businesslike legislative efficiency rather than democratic consensus building, and the allegedly cozy working relationship between lobbyists and the leadership. Notwithstanding his critics, Riffe transformed the Ohio House from a body that was consistently meeting in all-night sessions and failing to meet budget deadlines to a more streamlined chamber that rarely failed to deliver a balanced budget on time.[94]

Brown, Katz, and Riffe each offer somewhat different perspectives on what it takes to make it as a speaker. Their examples show that successful speakers are successful politicians who effectively cultivate networks of friendly working relationships with their colleagues in order to expedite and facilitate the activities of the house.

There are, however, a number of important differences between legislative leaders in 1911 and 1990. Speakers in 1990 served longer apprenticeships in the state house than their counterparts early in the century, thereby bringing to their positions a greater expertise and professionalism. In addition, there was a little more ethnic, racial, and gender diversity among speakers by 1990. At least in general, the later speakers led house colleagues who were better paid and more professional in their conduct of legislative business. Notwithstanding these advances, however, state houses across the United States have a long way to go in order to meet the challenges of the twenty-first century and to preserve representative democracy.

NOTES

1. U.S. Bureau of the Census, *Statistical Abstract of the United States*, 111th ed. (Washington, DC: U.S. Government Printing Office, 1991), 7.

2. Ibid., 73, 605–610; and Laurence Urdang, ed., *The Timetables of American History* (New York: Simon & Schuster, 1981), 264–281.

3. This project divides the United States into four regions, with a volume devoted to each: the Midwest (Illinois, Indiana, Iowa, Kansas, Michigan, Minnesota, Missouri, Nebraska, North Dakota, Ohio, South Dakota, and Wisconsin); the Northeast (Connecticut, Delaware, Maine, Massachusetts, New Hampshire, New Jersey, New York, Pennsylvania, Rhode Island, and Vermont); the South (Alabama, Arkansas, Florida, Georgia, Kentucky, Louisiana, Maryland, Mississippi, North Carolina, Oklahoma, South Carolina, Tennessee, Texas, Virginia, and West Virginia); and the West (Alaska, Arizona, California, Colorado, Hawaii, Idaho, Montana, Nevada, New Mexico, Oregon, Utah, Washington, and Wyoming).

4. U.S. Bureau of the Census, *Statistical Abstract of the United States*, 19; and U.S. Bureau of the Census, *Historical Statistics of the United States, Colonial Times to 1957* (Washington, DC: U.S. Government Printing Office, 1960), 12–13.

5. U.S. Bureau of the Census, *Statistical Abstract of the United States*, 19, 251.

6. A thorough discussion of the database is given in the Preface.

7. We have rounded off all percentages to the nearest tenth.

8. See Tables 1A–1C.

9. See Table 1F.

10. See Tables 1A–1B, 1D.

11. See Table 1G.

12. Russell W. Maddox and Robert F. Fuquay, *State and Local Government*, 4th ed. (New York: D. Van Nostrand, 1981), 87–89; and Advisory Commission on Intergovernmental Relations, *The Question of State Government Capability* (Washington, DC: Advisory Commission on Intergovernmental Relations, 1985), 66, 68.

13. See Tables 1A–1B, 1E.

14. See Table 1H.

15. Karen Hansen, "To the Democrats Go the Spoils," *State Legislatures* 16 (November/December 1990), 15–20.

16. Stonecash warns: "Efforts to create indexes for all states may be inherently flawed in that they seek to use simple means to capture complex phenomena. Developing such indexes may be attractive because it is easier than doing intensive work on each political system. Having such indexes is also attractive because it is easier than doing intensive work on each political system. . . . But the whole process may lead to fundamental misrepresentation of the political reality." It is his contention based upon his work on New York legislative politics that indicators constructed for studying all the states "may not come even remotely close to capturing the political situation in New York." See Jeffrey M. Stonecash, "Observations from New York: The Limits of 50-State Studies and the Case for Case Studies," *Comparative State Politics* 12 (August 1991), 1–9.

17. Dave McNeely, "Last of the Good Old Boys," *State Legislatures* 15 (November/December 1989), 27–29.

18. "Oklahoma Ousts Speaker," *State Legislatures* 15 (July 1989), 9.

19. Michele Jacklin, "Conservative Democrats Are Victorious in Connecticut House," *State Legislatures* 15 (April 1989), 13–15.

20. Lucy Morgan, "In Florida a Coalition Saves Speaker-Designee," *State Legislatures* 15 (April 1989), 22–23.

21. Thad L. Beyle, "Political Change in North Carolina: A Legislative Coup D'Etat," *Comparative State Politics Newsletter* 10 (April 1989), 3–15; Rob Christensen, "Growing Republican Ranks Help Topple Speaker in North Carolina," *State Legislatures* 15 (April 1989), 16–19; and Joel A. Thompson, "The 1989 North Carolina General Assembly: Beirut on a Bad Day," *Comparative State Politics* 10 (December 1989), 13–17.

22. See the biographies of the Iowa speakers.

23. See the biographies of the Louisiana speakers.

24. Advisory Commission on Intergovernmental Relations, *The Question of State Government Capability*, 5–6, 385.

25. Ibid., 385.

26. Ibid., 386.

27. Ibid., 65.

28. Ibid., 65–66.

29. Ballard Campbell, "The State Legislature in American History: A Review Essay," *Historical Methods Newsletter* 9 (September 1976), 185.

30. Douglas Camp Chaffey and Malcolm E. Jewell, "Selection and Tenure of State

Legislative Party Leaders: A Comparative Analysis,'' *The Journal of Politics* 34 (November 1972), 1278.

31. Malcolm E. Jewell, ''Editor's Introduction: The State of U.S. State Legislative Research,'' *Legislative Studies Quarterly* 6 (February 1981), 8.

32. Donald R. Matthews, ''Legislative Recruitment and Legislative Careers,'' in Gerhard Loewenberg, Samuel C. Patterson, and Malcolm E. Jewell, eds., *Handbook of Legislative Research* (Cambridge, MA: Harvard University Press, 1985), 17.

33. Edward Brazil and Andrew McNitt, ''Speakers of the State Houses in an Era of Legislative Change,'' paper presented at the April 1990 meeting of the Midwest Political Science Association, Chicago.

34. See Table 2A.

35. Matthews, ''Legislative Recruitment and Legislative Careers,'' 21.

36. Brazil and McNitt, ''Speakers of the State Houses in an Era of Legislative Change,'' 2.

37. See Table 2B.

38. Two more women (in Alaska and Minnesota) were speakers between 1991 and 1994.

39. Larry Morandi, ''She's Got Clout,'' *State Legislatures* 15 (November/December 1989), 16–17. This article mistakenly contends that Katz was only the second woman speaker in U.S. history. In fact, she was the seventh.

40. Cecil Edwards's communication with the editors. Whang leather is normally made of deerskin and used for thongs and laces.

41. See Table 2C.

42. Another African American, Daniel T. Blue, Jr., was speaker in North Carolina in 1991 and 1993.

43. Richard C. Paddock, ''A Speaker of Prominence,'' *State Legislatures* 15 (November/December, 1989), 22–24.

44. See the biographies of the New Mexico speakers.

45. Another Asian was named speaker in Hawaii in 1993.

46. See Tables 3A–3B.

47. See the biography of Thomas P. O'Neill, Jr.

48. See the biography of Solomon Blatt.

49. See Table 4.

50. Andrew McNitt and Edward Brazil, ''Speakers of the State Houses: 1960–1989,'' *Comparative State Politics* 14 (February 1993), 31–42.

51. Andrea Paterson, ''Is the Citizen Legislator Becoming Extinct?'' *State Legislatures* 12 (July 1986), 22.

52. See Tables 5A–5B.

53. U.S. Bureau of the Census, *Historical Statistics of the United States, Colonial Times to 1957*, 74.

54. See Table 5C.

55. Paterson, ''Is the Citizen Legislator Becoming Extinct?'' 22–25.

56. See Tables 6A–6B.

57. See Table 7.

58. Members of any of the various Masonic orders were included here.

59. Heinz Eulau et al., ''Career Perspectives of American State Legislators,'' in Dwaine Marvick, ed., *Political Decision-Makers* (New York: Free Press of Glencoe, 1961), 218, 224.

60. See Tables 8A–8B.

61. See Table 8C.

62. Alan Rosenthal, "Turnover in State Legislatures," *American Journal of Political Science* 18 (August 1974), 609.

63. Ibid., 616.

64. Kwang S. Shin and John S. Jackson, III, "Membership Turnover in U.S. State Legislatures: 1931–1976," *Legislative Studies Quarterly* 4 (February 1979), 95–104.

65. David Ray, "Voluntary Retirement and Electoral Defeat in Eight State Legislatures," *The Journal of Politics* 38 (May 1976), 426–433.

66. David Ray, "Membership Stability in Three State Legislatures: 1893–1969," *The American Political Science Review* 68 (March 1974), 106–112.

67. Nelson W. Polsby, "The Institutionalization of the U.S. House of Representatives," *The American Political Science Review* 62 (March 1968), 144–168. See also H. Douglas Price, "The Congressional Career: Then and Now," in Nelson W. Polsby, ed., *Congressional Behavior* (New York: Random House, 1971), 14–27; and H. Douglas Price, "Congress and the Evolution of Legislative 'Professionalism,' " in Norman J. Ornstein, ed., *Congress in Change: Evolution and Reform* (New York: Praeger, 1975), 2–23.

68. Chaffey and Jewell, "Selection and Tenure of State Legislative Party Leaders: A Comparative Analysis," 1278–1286.

69. See Table 9A. In their study of speakers from 1960 to 1988, Brazil and McNitt conclude: "Individuals who wish to become speaker must be willing to devote a decade or more to obtaining that post" ("Speakers of the State Houses in an Era of Legislative Change," 9).

70. See Tables 9B–9E.

71. See Table 9F.

72. See Table 10A. Speakers still serving as of 1994 are credited with their number of years in office through 1994.

73. This does not take into account differences in the lengths of speakership terms among states. See the Preface for details.

74. See Tables 10B–10E. Brazil and McNitt comment: "Sixty percent of speakers serve only one term as speakers" ("Speakers of the State Houses in an Era of Legislative Change," 11). However, as can be seen by our data, there is considerable variation in length of service by period and region.

75. See Table 10F.

76. "Survey on Selection of State Legislative Leaders," *Comparative State Politics Newsletter* 1 (May 1980), 7–21.

77. Ibid., 11.

78. Ibid.

79. Ibid., 12.

80. See the biographies of the Vermont speakers.

81. See the biographies of John A. Bagnariol and Duane L. Berentson.

82. In Michigan Curtis Hertel and Paul Hillegonds were labeled "stereo speakers." See George Weeks and Don Weeks, "Taking Turns," *State Legislatures* 19 (July 1993), 19–25.

83. Robert X. Browning, "Indiana Elects Democratic Governor and Equally Divided House," *Comparative State Politics Newsletter* 10 (April 1989), 1–2; and Patrick J. Traub, "Speakers du Jour in Indiana," *State Legislatures* 15 (July 1989), 17–22.

84. McNeely, "Last of the Good Old Boys," 27–29; and "Survey on Selection of State Legislative Leaders," 10, 12, 17–18.

85. Advisory Commission on Intergovernmental Relations, *The Question of State Government Capability*, 65–109.

86. Lucinda Simon, "When Leaders Leave," *State Legislatures* 13 (February 1987), 16–18.

87. Polsby, "Institutionalization of the U.S. House of Representatives," 144–168.

88. McNitt and Brazil, "Speakers of the State Houses: 1960–1989," 40; and Brazil and McNitt, "Speakers of the State Houses in an Era of Legislative Change," 9.

89. See Tables 11A–11B.

90. See Table 11C.

91. See Tables 12A–12B.

92. Paddock, "A Speaker of Prominence," 22–24.

93. Morandi, "She's Got Clout," 16–17.

94. Lee Leonard, "Pro among Pros," *State Legislatures* 15 (November/December 1989), 13–15.

A

ABINGTON, WILLIAM H. (Arkansas, 1929) was born in Des Arc, Arkansas, on January 2, 1871. Earning an M.D. from Arkansas Medical College in 1892, he became a physician, pharmacist, and hospital owner in Beebe, Arkansas. Abington served in the U.S. Army's Medical Corps during World War I, rising to the rank of major. In addition, he belonged to the Masons, Elks, Knights of Pythias, Woodmen of the World, and Christian Church (Disciples of Christ). He was married.

A Democrat, Abington served Beebe as mayor, town councilman, and school board president. He won election to the Arkansas House of Representatives from White County in 1926 and 1928, and he was named speaker for the 1929 session. The following year Abington successfully ran for the Arkansas Senate. Elected to additional terms in each legislative chamber, he left the House in 1946. Abington was a member of the Senate when he died on March 19, 1951, at age 81.

Diane D. Blair, *Arkansas Politics and Government* (Lincoln: University of Nebraska Press, 1988), 160–184; Jerry E. Hinshaw, *Call the Roll* (Little Rock: Rose Publishing, 1986); *Historical Report of the Secretary of State, Arkansas* (Little Rock: Secretary of State, 1958–   ); Walter Nunn, *Readings in Arkansas Government* (Little Rock: Rose Publishing, 1973), 59–133.

CAL LEDBETTER, JR.

ADAMS, CHARLES CRAYTON, III (Alabama, 1959) was born December 7, 1912, in Alexander City, Alabama, to Charles Crayton and Lessie Valera (Nolen) Adams. His grandfather and his great-grandfather were mayors of Alexander City. Educated in local public schools, he received a B.S. from the Alabama Polytechnic Institute (now Auburn University) in Auburn in 1936. Adams then entered the real estate and insurance business in Alexander City. During World War II he served with the U.S. Army field artillery in the North African and European theaters, rising to the rank of lieutenant colonel. He was awarded the Bronze Star and the French Croix de Guerre.

In 1950 Adams successfully ran for the Alabama House of Representatives as a Democrat from Tallapoosa County. He served three consecutive four-year terms. Supporting the successful 1958 gubernatorial campaign of John Patterson, Adams was chosen as speaker for the 1959 session with Patterson's backing. While in office he worked to pass legislation to improve Alabama's educational system, highways, and mental institutions.

Adams resigned from the House in 1960, when he was appointed to the Tallapoosa County Probate Court. He was the regional director of the U.S. Department of Housing and Urban Development in Atlanta, Georgia, from 1965 to 1974. Named "Man of the Year" by the Alexander City Chamber of Commerce in 1959, Adams was a steward of the Methodist Church. In addition he belonged to the Masons, Elks, Lions, Chamber of Commerce, and Sons of the American Revolution. Adams died on March 8, 1982, at the age of 70.

Alabama Official and Statistical Register (Montgomery: State of Alabama, Department of Archives and History, 1903–); Frank L. Grove, ed., *Library of Alabama Lives* (Hopkinsville, KY: Historical Records Association, 1961); Murray C. Havens, *City versus Farm: Urban-Rural Conflict in the Alabama Legislature* (University, AL: Bureau of Public Administration, University of Alabama, 1957); Henry S. Marks, *Alabama Past Leaders* (Huntsville: Strode Publishers, 1982); *Who's Who in Alabama* (Birmingham: Sayers Enterprises, 1965–).

REID BADGER

ADAMS, SAMUEL W. (Kentucky, 1924) was born in Boone County, Kentucky, on June 23, 1873, to William and Frances Adams. Educated in local public schools, he earned a degree from the Kent College of Law in Chicago, Illinois, in 1896. Adams then began a private practice in Covington, Kentucky. He also belonged to the Masons, Elks, Knights of Pythias, Moose, and Eagles. A Baptist, he married Ida Patton in 1916.

In 1901 and 1903 Adams successfully ran for the Kentucky House of Representatives as a Democrat from Kenton County. Again elected to the House in 1921 and 1923, he was chosen as speaker for the 1924 session. He won election to the Kentucky Senate in 1925 and 1929. Afterward he returned to his law practice. Adams died on September 19, 1954, at the age of 81.

George T. Blakey, *Hard Times and the New Deal in Kentucky, 1929–1939* (Lexington: University Press of Kentucky, 1986); Malcolm E. Jewell and Everett W. Cunningham, *Kentucky Politics* (Lexington: University Press of Kentucky, 1968); Malcolm E. Jewell and Penny Miller, *The Kentucky Legislature: Two Decades of Change* (Lexington: University Press of Kentucky, 1988); Robert F. Sexton, "Kentucky Politics and Society, 1919–1932" (Ph.D. dissertation, University of Washington, 1970).

CAROL CROWE-CARRACO

ALARIO, JOHN A., Jr. (Louisiana, 1984, 1992) was born in New Orleans, Louisiana, on September 15, 1943. Educated in local public schools, he received a B.A. from Southeastern Louisiana University in Hammond in 1965. Alario then became an accountant. Eventually he established the John A. Alario, Jr., Income Tax Service.

A Democrat, Alario sat on the executive committee of the New Orleans Democratic Committee from 1965 to 1973. He also attended the 1972 Democratic National Convention and 1973 Louisiana Constitutional Convention. In 1971 he won election to the Louisiana House of Representatives from Jefferson Parish. Chosen as speaker by Governor Edwin W. Edwards in 1984, Alario was again named to the post for the 1992 session. While in office he emphasized economic development, education, health care, and social services.

Alario was named Southeastern Louisiana's "Outstanding Alumnus" in 1981. In addition, he belonged to the National Society of Public Accountants and Catholic Church. He married Alba Williamson in 1965, and the couple had four children. As of this writing Alario remains in the speakership.

GINA PETONITO

ALBRIGHT, JOSEPH PAUL (West Virginia, 1985) was born on November 8, 1938, in Parkersburg, West Virginia, to Melvin P. and Catherine (Rathbone) Albright. Educated in local public schools, he worked for his family's furniture business in Belpre, Ohio. He was named secretary and director of the company in 1959. Albright earned a B.B.A. *cum laude* (1961) and a J.D. (1962) from the University of Notre Dame in Indiana. Afterward he began a law practice in Parkersburg, becoming a partner in the firm of Albright, Bradley & Ellison in 1984.

A Democrat, Albright was Wood County assistant prosecutor in 1965–68 and Parkersburg city attorney in 1968. He successfully ran for the West Virginia House of Delegates from Wood and Wirt counties in 1970 and for the West Virginia Senate two years later. Albright was again elected to the House in 1974, serving six consecutive terms. Chair of the Education Committee and the Judiciary Committee, he was chosen as speaker for the 1985 session.

In 1986 Albright was defeated for reelection to the House. Returning to his private practice, he also belonged to the Elks, American, West Virginia, and Wood County bar associations, and Catholic Church. He married Patricia Ann Deem in 1958, and the couple had four children. Albright continues to live in Parkersburg at this writing.

LISLE G. BROWN

ALEXANDER, CECIL LEWIS (Arkansas, 1975) was born in Heber Springs, Arkansas, on August 2, 1935. Educated in local public schools, he received a B.A. in business from Hendrix College in Conway, Arkansas. Alexander worked as a teacher for two years before operating his family's restaurant and service station in Heber Springs from 1960 to 1971. He then began a real estate firm.

In 1962 Alexander was elected to the Arkansas House of Representatives as a Democrat from Cleburne and Van Buren counties. Serving eight consecutive terms, he was named speaker for the 1975 session. Alexander lost the 1978 Democratic primary for the U.S. House of Representatives from the 2nd District of Arkansas, despite attracting support from the business community due to his fight to maintain the state's ban against union shops and his pledge to reduce government regulations. He was narrowly defeated for the nomination for lieutenant governor of Arkansas in 1980.

Later that year Alexander became director of state governmental affairs for the Arkansas Power and Light Company. He was also president of the Chamber of Commerce, Young Business Men, and Cleburne County Board of Realtors. A Methodist, Alexander married Patricia Ann Leming in 1957.

SUZANNE MABERRY

ALMON, EDWARD BERTON (Alabama, 1911) was born on April 18, 1860, in Moulton, Alabama. Educated in local public schools, he earned a B.S. from the State Normal College (now the University of North Alabama) in Florence in 1882 and an LL.B from the University of Alabama in 1883. Almon practiced law in Belle Green (now Belgreen), Alabama, until 1885, when he moved to Tuscumbia, Alabama. In addition, he belonged to the Masons, Elks, Knights of Pythias, Good Roads Association, and Methodist Church. He married Luie Clopper in 1887.

A Democrat, Almon chaired the Colbert County Democratic Committee. He successfully ran for the Alabama Senate in 1891 and sat on the state's 11th Circuit Court from 1898 to 1906. Elected to the Alabama House of Representatives from Colbert County in 1910, Almon was named speaker for his only term in 1911. In 1914 he won election to the U.S. House of Representatives from the 8th District of Alabama. Almon was still serving in that body when he died in Washington, D.C., on June 22, 1933, at age 73.

BENJAMIN B. WILLIAMS AND DONALD B. DODD

AMOS, JOHN ELLISON (West Virginia, 1943, 1945, 1947) was born in Charleston, West Virginia, on July 16, 1905, to John Ellison and Louise Hampton (Delaney) Amos. Attending public schools and Augusta Military Academy in Fort Defiance, Virginia, he earned an LL.B. from West Virginia University in 1929. Amos then began practicing law in Charleston. He married Edith Johnston in 1935, and the couple had two children.

In 1934 Amos won election to one term in the West Virginia House of Delegates as a Democrat from Kanawha County. Again elected to the House in 1938, he served five consecutive terms. Amos was chosen as speaker for the 1943, 1945, and 1947 sessions. While in the speakership he introduced a bill on unemployment compensation. He successfully ran for the West Virginia Senate in 1948 and 1952, becoming that body's majority leader in 1953.

Returning to his Charleston practice, Amos was also a director of transportation, manufacturing, and utility companies. He was president of the West Virginia Board of Regents and the American Trucking Association and a member of the Elks and the Methodist Church. From 1959 to 1968 Amos sat on the Democratic National Committee.

WILLIAM T. DOHERTY

ANGELLE, ROBERT (Louisiana, 1957) was born in 1896 in Cecilia, Louisiana, and moved to Breaux Bridge, Louisiana, at age 15. Educated in local schools, he took a commercial course at the Southwestern Louisiana Institute (now the University of Southwestern Louisiana) in Lafayette. Angelle became chief clerk of the lumber and hardware firm of J. W. Begnaud in Breaux Bridge in 1917. Later he worked for the Standard Oil Company and the Louisiana Oil Company. He became a general contractor in 1936, and he also operated a dairy farm.

A Democrat, Angelle was elected mayor of Breaux Bridge in 1923. The following year he joined Huey P. Long's successful gubernatorial campaign. Angelle won election to the Louisiana House of Representatives from St. Martin Parish in 1935 and served seven consecutive four-year terms. He was named speaker in 1957 after the resignation of incumbent Lorris M. Wimberly. While in office Angelle supported programs providing old age pensions, school lunches, free textbooks, and the homestead exemption from the state real estate tax. In addition, he secured funding for Evangeline State Park and introduced a bill declaring Breaux Bridge "the crayfish capital of the world."

In 1963 Angelle retired from the House. Noted for never having lost an election, he outlined his political philosophy by stating, "I don't belong to that reform crowd. . . . I am a spoils politician." He was married, and he became president of the Breaux Bridge Bank and Trust Company in 1961. Angelle died on September 22, 1979.

Castille, Jeanne, "Robert Angelle," *A Dictionary of Louisiana Biography* (New Orleans: Louisiana Historical Association, 1988), I: 15–16; *Membership in the Legislature of Louisiana, 1880–1980* (Baton Rouge, 1979).

RAYMOND O. NUSSBAUM

ANGLIN, WILLIAM THOMAS (Oklahoma, 1933) was born in Osage, Virginia, on June 13, 1883, of Irish ancestry. Attending public schools and a military academy in Martinsville, Virginia, he earned a B.S. from Milligan College in Tennessee (1902) and an LL.B. from the University of Virginia (1905). Anglin then practiced law in Allen, Indian Territory (now Oklahoma), and in Calvin, Oklahoma. In 1914 he moved to Holdensville, Oklahoma, where he established the law firm of Anglin and Stevenson. He also engaged in farming and banking.

Originally a Republican, Anglin joined the Democrats after losing a race for Hughes County attorney. He served as county chair of each party and was a delegate to the 1920 and 1932 Democratic national conventions. Anglin won election to the Oklahoma House of Representatives from Hughes County in 1918 and to the Oklahoma Senate in 1920. While in the Senate he chaired the Appropriations Committee, sponsored an unsuccessful anti–Ku Klux Klan bill, and was president *pro tem* in 1923. Again elected to the House in 1932, Anglin was chosen as speaker for the 1933 session. He became the first person to lead both chambers of the Oklahoma legislature.

Losing the 1934 Democratic nomination for governor of Oklahoma to E. W. Marland, Anglin was returned to the Senate in 1938 and was again named president *pro tem* in 1943. He remained there until 1950, helping to write state laws concerning public schools and ad *valorem* taxes. In addition, he was chair of the Oklahoma Interstate Oil Compact Commission and the Hughes County Liberty Loan drive and a member of the Elks, Rotary, Chamber of Commerce, and Christian Church (Disciples of Christ). Anglin died on July 15, 1953, at the age of 70.

TIMOTHY A. ZWINK

ANTHONY, WILLIAM BRUCE (Oklahoma, 1910) was born in Bedford County, Tennessee, on January 9, 1871, to Jacob L. and Martha (Bruce) Anthony. After earning a degree in education from Terrill College in Decherd, Tennessee, in 1892, he worked as a teacher in Tennessee. In 1895 Anthony moved to Marlow, Indian Territory (now Oklahoma), where he published the *Marlow Review* and sold real estate. He married Sarah S. Shaw in 1893, and the couple had seven children.

A Democrat, Anthony successfully ran for mayor of Marlow in 1900. He was elected to the Oklahoma House of Representatives from Stephens County upon statehood in 1907, and he served three consecutive terms. Anthony chaired the Tax and Revenue Committee. Concurrently private secretary to Governor Charles N. Haskell, he was instrumental in the move of the Oklahoma capital from Guthrie to Oklahoma City in 1910. The shift had been approved in a referendum, but it was then halted by a court injunction. One night Anthony hid the state seal in a bundle of laundry and slipped it past a retinue of deputy sheriffs. He was named speaker for the special session in December 1910 that confirmed the relocation.

Leaving the House in 1912, Anthony was appointed to the State Capitol Commission. He was city manager of Walters, Oklahoma, from 1919 to 1923. Afterward Anthony settled in Norman, Oklahoma, and worked for the Oklahoma Gas and Electric Company. In addition, he was a director of the City National Bank of Oklahoma City and the First National Bank of Norman and a member of the Masons, Odd Fellows, Knights of Pythias, and Methodist Church. Anthony died in Norman on August 11, 1933, at the age of 62.

GORDON MOORE

ARNOLD, MALCOLM R. (West Virginia, 1941) was born on April 7, 1909, in Racine, West Virginia, to John and Evaline (McCutcheon) Arnold. Earning a B.S. from West Virginia University (1932) and an M.A. from Columbia University (1939), he also attended the University of Chicago. He became a principal and an athletic coach in Bloomingrose, West Virginia.

A Democrat, Arnold served Boone County as assistant superintendent of schools. In 1940 and 1942 he was elected to the West Virginia House of Delegates from Boone County. Arnold was chosen as speaker for the 1941 session. Forced to resign from the House in 1943 due to a scandal, he was convicted and spent eighteen months in prison.

Afterward Arnold returned to his career in education. In addition, he belonged to the Masons, Red Men, United Mine Workers, and Presbyterian Church. He was married in 1935 to Reba Thompson, with whom he had two children, and he later remarried and had two more children. Arnold died in Charleston, West Virginia, on October 31, 1979, at the age of 70.

Jim Comstock, ed., *The West Virginia Heritage Encyclopedia*, 25 vols. (Richwood, WV, 1976); Phil Conley, ed., *The West Virginia Encyclopedia* (Charleston: West Virginia Publishing, 1929).

PATRICK J. CHASE

ASHWORTH, VIRGIS MARION (Alabama, 1961) was born in Herrin, Illinois, on November 25, 1911, to Amos Asbury and Mary (Jones) Ashworth. As a child he moved with his family to West Blockton, Alabama. He attended local public schools and the University of Alabama. Ashworth was forced to leave college during the Depression, working as a miner in West Blockton. Eventually earning a B.A. from Alabama and an LL.B. from the Birmingham School of Law, he began a private practice in Centreville, Alabama, in 1937. For a year he was a special agent for the Federal Bureau of Investigation.

A Democrat, Ashworth served as solicitor of Bibb County and city attorney of Brent, Alabama. In addition, he sat on the Bibb County Democratic Executive Committee. He won election to the Alabama House of Representatives from Bibb County in 1954 and 1958, and he was chosen as speaker *pro tem* for the 1959 session. Ashworth was named speaker in 1961 following the resignation of incumbent Charles C. Adams. Admired for his personality and his fairness, he presided over a debate on legislative redistricting.

In 1962 Ashworth was rumored to be a candidate for lieutenant governor of Alabama, but he instead decided to return to his Centreville practice. He was president of the Kiwanis and a member of the Baptist Church. Appointed district attorney for Alabama's 4th Judicial Circuit Court in 1969, he later became a judge on that body. Ashworth still sat on the bench when he died of an apparent suicide on June 18, 1975, at age 63.

Alabama Official and Statistical Register (Montgomery: State of Alabama, Department of Archives and History, 1903–); Frank L. Grove, ed., *Library of Alabama Lives* (Hopkinsville, KY: Historical Records Association, 1961); Murray C. Havens, *City versus Farm: Urban-Rural Conflict in the Alabama Legislature* (University, AL: Bureau of Public Administration, University of Alabama, 1957); Henry S. Marks, *Alabama Past Leaders* (Huntsville: Strode Publishers, 1982); *Who's Who in Alabama* (Birmingham: Sayers Enterprises, 1965–).

REID BADGER

ATKINSON, JAMES BUFORD (South Carolina, 1921) was born on January 13, 1872, in Chester, South Carolina, to E. T. and Eliza McClure (Alexander) Atkinson. He attended local schools and received a B.A. from Furman University as class valedictorian. Atkinson then became a teacher and a school principal in Anderson, South Carolina. Earning an LL.B. from the University of South Carolina in 1897, he worked for the state attorney general for several years. Later he briefly practiced law in Blackville, South Carolina, before moving to Spartanburg, South Carolina.

Atkinson was elected to the South Carolina House of Representatives as a Democrat from Spartanburg County in 1916. Serving four consecutive terms, he was a leading proponent of compulsory education and a statewide system of highways. In 1921 Atkinson became speaker *pro tem*. He was chosen as speaker following incumbent Thomas P. Cothran's resignation in January 1921.

Retiring from the House in 1924, Atkinson returned to his Spartanburg practice. In addition, he was an attorney for the Southern Railroad. He married Corrine Searson, and the couple had three daughters. Atkinson died on September 25, 1942, at the age of 70.

WALTER B. EDGAR

AYCOCK, CLARENCE C. "Taddy" (Louisiana, 1952) was born in Franklin, Louisiana, on January 13, 1915. His father, grandfather, aunt, and uncle were local officials. Educated in local public schools, Aycock earned a degree from Spring Hill College in Mobile, Alabama, and an LL.B. from Loyola University in New Orleans, Louisiana. He then began a law practice, and he belonged to the Louisiana Bar Association. During World War II Aycock served as an officer in the U.S. Army's Judge Advocate General's Corps, earning a Bronze Star. A Catholic, he was married and had six children.

Aycock successfully ran for the Louisiana House of Representatives as a Democrat from St. Mary Parish in 1951 and 1955. He was chosen as speaker for the 1952 session, working closely with Governor Robert F. Kennon. However, his conservative orientation later brought him into conflict with Governor Earl K. Long.

In 1959 Aycock was elected lieutenant governor of Louisiana on a ticket with Jimmie H. Davis. While in office he opposed the civil rights movement and allied himself with segregationist leader Leander H. Perez. Although he remained a Democrat, Aycock supported Republican Barry Goldwater in the 1964 presidential campaign. He returned to his law practice after losing a bid for governor in 1971. Aycock died in Franklin on January 6, 1987, at the age of 71.

Chaillot, Jane B., "C. C. 'Taddy' Aycock," *A Dictionary of Louisiana Biography* (New Orleans: Louisiana Historical Association, 1988), I: 27; *Membership in the Legislature of Louisiana, 1880–1980* (Baton Rouge, 1979).

RAYMOND O. NUSSBAUM

B

BAILEY, THOMAS LOWRY (Mississippi, 1924, 1928, 1932) was born in Maben, Mississippi, on January 6, 1888. Educated in local public schools, he earned an A.B. (1909) and an LL.B. (1912) from Millsaps College in Jackson, Mississippi. After that Bailey began a law practice in Meridian, Mississippi. He was married, and he belonged to the Kiwanis and the Methodist Church.

Bailey was elected to the Mississippi House of Representatives as a Democrat from Lauderdale County in 1915 and served six consecutive four-year terms. He joined Joseph W. George, Lawrence T. Kennedy, and Walter Sillers in a group known as the "Big Four," which dominated the fiscally conservative "low pressure" faction of the Democratic Party. Named speaker for the 1924, 1928, and 1932 sessions, Bailey was a proponent of industrial development. In 1936 he withdrew from renomination to the speakership in favor of Horace S. Stansel.

Defeated for governor of Mississippi in 1939, Bailey successfully ran for the post in 1943. While in office he broke with the "low pressure" faction and implored the legislature to look to the future. He recommended an ambitious state budget that included a $55 million highway construction program, but this was eventually scaled down. Bailey was still governor when he died on November 2, 1946, at age 58.

Albert Kirwan, *The Revolt of the Rednecks: Mississippi Politics 1876–1925* (Lexington: University of Kentucky Press, 1951); Dale Krane and Stephen D. Shaffer, eds., *Mississippi Government & Politics: Modernizers versus Traditionalists* (Lincoln: University of Nebraska Press, 1992); Richard A. McLemore, *A History of Mississippi*, 2 vols. (Jackson: University and College Press of Mississippi, 1973); *Mississippi Official and Statistical Register* (Jackson: Secretary of State).

DAVID G. SANSING

BARKER, JIM L. (Oklahoma, 1983, 1985, 1987, 1989) was born on June 20, 1935, in Muskogee, Oklahoma, to Fred and Pearl Gullett (Hill) Barker. After earning an A.A. from the Oklahoma Military Academy in 1955 and a B.S. from

Northeastern State College (now University) in Tahlequah, Oklahoma, in 1957, he served in the U.S. Army and rose to the rank of first lieutenant. Barker became president of Muskogee Restaurant Supply, Inc., in Muskogee in 1959. He belonged to the Chamber of Commerce and the Aircraft Owners and Pilots Association. A Methodist, he married Kay Frances Tucker; the couple had two children.

Barker was elected to the Oklahoma House of Representatives as a Democrat from Muskogee County in 1976. He remained there for seven consecutive terms, and he sat on the board of the State Legislative Leaders Foundation. Chosen as speaker in 1983 after the expulsion of incumbent Daniel D. Draper, Jr., Barker was renamed to the post in 1985, 1987, and 1989. In May 1989, he was ousted from the speakership by a coalition of Republicans and dissident Democrats. He left the House in 1990. At this writing Barker continues to live in Muskogee.

"Oklahoma Ousts Speaker," *State Legislatures* 15 (July 1989), 9.

GINA PETONITO

BARNES, BEN FRANK (Texas, 1965, 1967) was born on April 17, 1938, in Gorman, Texas, to B. F. and Ina B. (Carrigan) Barnes. Earning a B.B.A. from the University of Texas in 1960, he settled in De Leon, Texas. Barnes belonged to the Elks, Jaycees, Chamber of Commerce, Southwestern Cattle Growers Association, and Methodist Church. He was married in 1957 to Martha Jane Morgan, with whom he had two children, and in 1971 to Nancy Sayres.

In 1960 Barnes won election to the Texas House of Representatives as a Democrat. Serving four consecutive terms, he represented Comanche, Brown, Coleman, Erath, Hood, Parker, Runnels, and Wise counties until 1966 and Comanche, Brown, Coleman, and Runnels counties thereafter. Barnes was chosen as speaker in 1965 after collecting pledges in a well-publicized all-night telephone marathon, becoming the youngest person to hold the post in Texas history at age 26. He was unanimously renamed for the 1967 session. While in the speakership he helped enact measures to create the Consumer Credit Code, improve air and water quality, and provide programs for the elderly, mentally ill, and handicapped.

Elected lieutenant governor of Texas in 1968 and 1970, Barnes lost the 1972 gubernatorial race. In addition, he sat on the U.S. Commission on Intergovernmental Relations, attended the 1968 Democratic National Convention, and was active in the Council of State Governments and the National Conference of State Legislative Leaders. He later moved to Brownwood, Texas, where he was the president of several real estate and financial firms and a rancher. Barnes was named one of "Five Outstanding Young Texans" by the state Jaycees in 1965 and one of "Ten Outstanding Young Men in America" by the U.S. Chamber of Commerce in 1970.

LUTHER G. HAGARD, JR.

BARRON, WINGATE STUART (Texas, 1929) was born in Brazos County, Texas, on February 6, 1889, and moved with his family to Grimes County,

Texas, in 1899. Attending Allen Academy in Bryan, Texas, he earned a degree from Sam Houston Normal Institute (now State University) in Huntsville, Texas, and a law degree from the University of Texas. Barron began a private practice in Anderson County, Texas, in 1914. Three years later he settled in Bryan.

A Democrat, Barron was school superintendent of Grimes County in 1910–14. He was elected to the Texas House of Representatives from Brazos and Grimes counties in 1924 and served three consecutive terms. Barron was chosen as speaker for the 1929 session, although ill health limited his power. While in the speakership he emphasized education issues, particularly those involving Texas A&M College.

Returning to his Bryan law practice, Barron was secretary-treasurer of a federal land bank during the 1930s. From 1940 to 1955 he sat on the 85th District Court of Texas. In addition, Barron was a director of the Texas Bar Association and a member of the Masons and Baptist Church. He never married. Barron died on February 12, 1984, six days after his ninety-fifth birthday.

Norman D. Brown, *Hood, Bonnet, and Little Brown Jug: Texas Politics, 1921–1928* (College Station: Texas A&M University Press, 1984); Dallas *Morning News*, January 10, 1929; *Presiding Officers of the Texas Legislature, 1846–1982* (Austin: Texas Legislative Council, 1982), 166–167.

ALWYN BARR

BARRY, WILLIAM FRANCIS, Jr. (Tennessee, 1925) was born in Union City, Tennessee, on February 2, 1900, to William Francis and Etta Lee (Moore) Barry. His father was speaker of the Tennessee Senate in 1927. Barry moved with his family to Jackson, Tennessee, in 1906, and he was educated in local public schools. During World War I he served in the U.S. armed forces. Attending Union University in Jackson, Barry earned a degree from George Washington University in Washington, D.C., and an LL.B. from Cumberland University in Lebanon, Tennessee, in 1921. He then began to practice law in Jackson.

Elected to the Tennessee House of Representatives as a Democrat from Madison County in 1922 and 1924, Barry was chosen as speaker for the 1925 session. He was assistant attorney general of Tennessee (1926–28) and Tennessee solicitor general (1939–51). Barry won election to the National Democratic Executive Committee in 1935 and 1937. In 1947 he was appointed to the Tennessee Tax Pension Committee.

Settling in Nashville, Tennessee, in 1935, Barry continued his private practice. He became vice-president and general counsel of the National Life and Accident Insurance Company in 1944 and an attorney for the WSM Broadcasting Company in 1953. In addition, Barry belonged to the Elks, Chamber of Commerce, American and Tennessee bar associations, American Legion, and Sons of the American Revolution. A Baptist, he married Eleanor Tyne in 1935; the couple had no children. Barry died in Nashville on June 4, 1967, at age 67, and he was buried in Union City.

JAMES H. EDMONSON

BARRY, WILLIAM LOGAN (Tennessee, 1963, 1965) was born in Lexington, Tennessee, on February 9, 1926, to Henry Daniel and Mary (Logan) Barry. Educated in local public schools, he received a B.A. (1948) and an LL.B. (1950) from Vanderbilt University in Nashville, Tennessee. Barry then began practicing law in Lexington. During the Korean conflict he served in the U.S. Army, rising to the rank of first lieutenant.

A Democrat, Barry was an alderman in Lexington in 1953–55. He was elected to the Tennessee House of Representatives from Henderson and Madison counties in 1954, remaining there for six consecutive terms. While in office he worked with the Democratic faction headed by Governor Frank G. Clement, but he maintained his independence. Barry was named majority floor leader in 1959 and 1961 and speaker for the 1963 and 1965 sessions. After his home district was divided by legislative reapportionment, he decided not to seek reelection to the House in 1966.

Barry was executive assistant to Governor E. Buford Ellington in 1967–70 and an assistant attorney general of Tennessee. Following that he returned to his private practice. President of the Lions in 1957–58, Barry also belonged to the Elks, Knights of Pythias, Farm Bureau, Tennessee Bar Association, American Legion, VFW, and Baptist Church. He married Elizabeth Coffman in 1966. At this writing Barry continues to live in Lexington.

Biographical Directory, Tennessee General Assembly, 1796–1969 (Nashville: State Library and Archives).

LEE S. GREENE

BAUER, RALPH NORMAN (Louisiana, 1940, 1944) was born in Patterson, Louisiana, on June 12, 1899, of French and English ancestry. He attended local schools and Louisiana State University. During World War I Bauer served in the U.S. Army. Earning an LL.B. from Louisiana State in 1920, he helped form the law firm of Brumby and Bauer in 1925.

Bauer won election to the Louisiana House of Representatives as a Democrat from St. Mary Parish in 1927, 1931, 1939, and 1943. While in office he was a leader of the faction known as the "Dynamite Squad," which unsuccessfully attempted to impeach Governor Huey P. Long in 1929. Named speaker for the 1940 and 1944 terms, Bauer worked with Governor Sam H. Jones to reform state government. He was also city attorney of both Berwick and Patterson, Louisiana, and a member of the Louisiana Democratic Committee.

In 1949 Bauer and his brother began a law partnership that became one of the most prominent in southern Louisiana. President of the Patterson State Bank, he was vice-president of the Teche Savings and Loan Association. He was married, and he belonged to the Masons, Elks, Rotary, and American and Louisiana bar associations. Bauer died in Franklin, Louisiana, on March 13, 1963, at the age of 63.

Edwin Adams Davis, *The Story of Louisiana* (New Orleans: J. F. Hyer, 1960).

BEATRICE R. OWSLEY

BEASLEY, THOMAS DeKALB (Florida, 1947, 1959) was born in a log cabin in Barbour County, Alabama, on August 16, 1904. One of eleven children, he was educated at home before attending high school. Beasley earned a B.A. from the University of Alabama and an LL.B. from Cumberland University in Lebanon, Tennessee. Afterward he moved to Florida, where he was an editor of the *Gulf Coast News* in Panama City and the *News* in Jasper. He later began practicing law in De Funiak Springs, Florida.

Beasley was elected to the Florida House of Representatives as a Democrat from Walton County in 1938, 1942, 1944, 1946, 1948, 1950, 1954, 1956, 1958, and 1960. He was named speaker for the 1947 session. During his speakership the legislature failed to approve any new tax laws, believing that the post–World War II economic boom would provide the necessary revenues for increased appropriations. Among the bills passed were those converting the University of Florida and Florida State College for Women (now Florida State University) into coeducational institutions, giving broader powers to the state highway patrol, and reopening the St. Johns River and Lake Okeechobee to commercial fishing.

Chosen as speaker again in 1959, Beasley became the first person to preside over two terms since 1917. In 1962 he left the House, returning to his private practice. He was married, and he belonged to the Lions and the Methodist Church. Beasley died on January 14, 1988, at the age of 83.

Paul S. George, *A Guide to the History of Florida* (Westport, CT: Greenwood Press, 1989); *Miami Daily News; Miami Herald; Tallahassee Democrat; Tampa Tribune.*

PAUL S. GEORGE

BECK, WILLIAM MORRIS (Alabama, 1947) was born on October 11, 1903, in Oxford, Alabama, to David Reese and Emma Josephine Beck. Educated in local public schools, he served in the U.S. Army. Beck attended Newberry College in South Carolina and earned an A.B. from Jacksonville State Teachers College (now University) in Alabama in 1926. He then worked as a teacher in Calhoun and De Kalb counties in Alabama while studying law. In 1932 he began a private practice in Fort Payne, Alabama.

Beck successfully ran for the Alabama House of Representatives as a Democrat from De Kalb County in 1938, but the next year he was appointed to the De Kalb County Court. He enlisted in the U.S. Marines during World War II, rising to the rank of master sergeant. Again elected to the House in 1946, Beck was named speaker for the 1947 session with the backing of Governor James E. Folsom. While in the post he advocated increased public support for education and state tourism, sponsored legislation aimed at restricting liquor advertising and Communist Party activity, and opposed the "Dixiecrat" movement to split from the national Democratic Party. He also sat on the Alabama Board of Education.

Losing a bid for governor of Alabama in 1950, Beck returned to his Fort Payne practice. He was acting president of Judson College in Marion, Alabama, in 1965. In addition, Beck was chair of the Boy Scouts, vice-president of the Alabama Bar Association, a trustee of Birmingham Baptist Hospitals, and a member of the Odd Fellows, Rotary, and De Kalb County Bar Association. A Baptist, he married Vera Isbell. His son, William M. Beck, Jr., was elected to the Alabama House in 1966. The elder Beck died on February 26, 1990, at the age of 86.

Alabama Official and Statistical Register (Montgomery: State of Alabama, Department of Archives and History, 1903–); Frank L. Grove, ed., *Library of Alabama Lives* (Hopkinsville, KY: Historical Records Association, 1961); Murray C. Havens, *City versus Farm: Urban-Rural Conflict in the Alabama Legislature* (University, AL: Bureau of Public Administration, University of Alabama, 1957); *A Manual for Alabama Legislators* (Montgomery: Legislative Reference Service, State of Alabama, 1942–); Henry S. Marks, *Alabama Past Leaders* (Huntsville: Strode Publishers, 1982); *Who's Who in Alabama* (Birmingham: Sayers Enterprises, 1965–).

                                                                          REID BADGER

BETHELL, JOHN PINCKNEY, Sr. (Arkansas, 1961) was born on July 4, 1907, in Columbia, Tennessee. Attending the University of Arkansas, he was a teacher and coach in Des Arc and Hazen, Arkansas, from 1942 to 1952. Bethell was also a founder of the Des Arc Museum. He married Eloise Willis Dailey in 1932, and the couple had four children.

A Democrat, Bethell was chair of the local Ration Board during World War II and mayor of Des Arc in 1942–43. In 1948 he was elected to the Arkansas House of Representatives from Prairie County. Bethell served twelve consecutive terms, chairing the Education Committee and the Public Welfare Committee. He was chosen as speaker for the 1961 session.

Leaving the House in 1972, Bethell returned to Des Arc. He acquired extensive land holdings in Prairie County. From 1957 to 1960 Bethell chaired the advisory council of the Arkansas Vocational School Board. In addition, he belonged to the Masons, Lions, and Presbyterian Church. Bethell died on January 2, 1981, at age 73, and he was buried in Des Arc.

                                                                          LEON C. MILLER

BILLINGSLEY, WALTER ASBURY (Oklahoma, 1949) was born in Salem, Arkansas, on August 12, 1890, to Luther A. and Mintie (Estes) Billingsley. He moved with his family to Stuart, Indian Territory (now Oklahoma) in 1905. Educated in public schools, he worked as a teacher for ten years. Billingsley attended East Central State Teachers College (now University) in Ada, Oklahoma, and he read law. He began a private practice in Wewoka, Oklahoma, in 1921.

A Democrat, Billingsley served Seminole County as school superintendent (1917–21), assistant county attorney, county attorney (1924–26), voting registrar, and election board member. In 1938 he was appointed special judge of the Oklahoma Supreme Court. Billingsley also sat on the Seminole County Democratic Central Committee. Elected to the Oklahoma House of Representatives from Seminole County in 1940, he remained there for five consecutive terms. He was caucus chair before being named speaker for the 1949 session.

Returning to his law practice, Billingsley served as an Oklahoma special district judge from 1969 to 1975. In addition, he was chair of the American Red Cross and a member of the Masons, Lions, Oklahoma and Seminole County bar associations, and Church of Christ. He married Alice O'Neal in 1916, and the couple had one son. Billingsley died on December 5, 1985, at the age of 95.

"Ex-Official Billingsley Dies at 95," *Saturday Oklahoman & Times*, December 7, 1985: 8; Gaston Litton, *History of Oklahoma at the Golden Anniversary of Statehood*, 4 vols. (New York: Lewis Historical Publishing, 1957).

DONOVAN L. REICHENBERGER

BISHOP, WILLIAM BURTON (Florida, 1935) was born in Jefferson County, Florida, on November 3, 1890. Receiving a B.A. from the Florida Normal Institute in Madison in 1908, he taught school in northern Florida for eight years. Afterward Bishop began to manage a farm in Nash, Florida, which grew to 2,700 acres. He also operated lumber mills.

Bishop was elected to the Florida House of Representatives as a Democrat from Jefferson County in 1920, 1922, 1924, 1932, and 1934. He was named speaker for the 1935 session. During Bishop's speakership Governor David Sholtz sought to convince the legislature of the need to obtain federal monies and strengthen the state government. A sales tax bill narrowly failed, but the legislature passed a workmen's compensation act, social welfare act, and moratorium on all public indebtedness for two years. In addition, it approved a state liquor law and created the Florida Employment, Forestry, Planning, and Tuberculosis boards, Citrus and Everglades Park commissions, and Park Service.

Returning to his Nash farm, Bishop later lost a race for Florida commissioner of agriculture. Outside of politics he was president of the Monticello Production Credit Association and a member of the Masons, Elks, and Methodist Church. He was married. Bishop died in 1954.

GARY R. MORMINO

BLANDFORD, DONALD JOSEPH (Kentucky, 1986, 1988, 1990, 1992) was born on April 4, 1938, to Joseph Ellis and Maude (Merrimee) Blandford. After attending Catholic schools in Owensboro, Kentucky, he began raising purebred cattle in Philpot, Kentucky. Blandford was a member of the Farm Bureau, National Farmers Association, and American Polled Hereford Association. He married Mary Jane O'Bryan in 1961.

In 1967 Blandford was elected to the Kentucky House of Representatives as a Democrat from Daviess County. He served thirteen consecutive terms and was named speaker for the 1986, 1988, 1990, and 1992 sessions, the longest tenure in the post in Kentucky history. After an FBI investigation, he was indicted for allegedly accepting money to kill a bill disliked by harness racing interests in 1992 and resigned from the speakership. Blandford was ousted from the House when he was convicted along with five former state legislators in April 1993. As a result, the Kentucky legislature passed reforms regulating lobbyists. At this writing Blandford continues to live in Philpot.

Tom Loftus and Al Cross, "Lies, Bribes and Videotapes," *State Legislatures* 19 (July 1993), 42–47.

                                                                GINA PETONITO

BLATT, SOLOMON (South Carolina, 1937, 1939, 1941, 1943, 1945, 1951, 1953, 1955, 1957, 1959, 1961, 1963, 1965, 1967, 1969, 1971, 1973) was the longest-serving state house speaker in U.S. history. He was born on February 27, 1896, in Blackville, South Carolina, to Russian Jewish immigrants Nathan and Mollie Blatt. Educated in local schools, he earned an LL.B. from the University of South Carolina in 1917. Blatt then joined a law practice in Barnwell, South Carolina. During World War I he served as a sergeant with the U.S. Army in France.

A Democrat, Blatt lost the 1930 primary for the South Carolina House of Representatives from Barnwell County. He was elected to the House in 1932 and remained there for twenty-seven consecutive terms. Blatt was chosen as speaker *pro tem* in 1935 and as speaker for the 1937, 1939, 1941, 1943, and 1945 sessions with the support of the local faction known as the "Barnwell Ring." Declining to seek the speakership in 1947 or 1949 due in part to Governor Strom Thurmond's opposition to the "Barnwell Ring," he was again named to the post in 1951, 1953, 1955, 1957, 1959, 1961, 1963, 1965, 1967, 1971, and 1973.

While in office Blatt gained a reputation as a political "arm-twister" who demanded a balanced budget. In July 1973 he resigned from the speakership. Outside of politics he was a trustee of the University of South Carolina and the Barnwell School as well as a member of the Masons and the American Legion. He married Ethel Green in 1920, and the couple had one son. Blatt was still a member of the House when he died on May 14, 1986, at age 90.

John K. Cauthen, *Speaker Blatt: His Challenges Were Greater* (Columbia: University of South Carolina Press, 1978); *South Carolina Legislative Manual* (Columbia: General Assembly of South Carolina, 1916–   ); *The State* (Columbia).

                                                    MARIAN ELIZABETH STROBEL

BLUE, DANIEL TERRY, Jr. (North Carolina, 1991, 1993) was born on April 18, 1949, in Lumberton, North Carolina, to Daniel Terry and Allene (Morris) Blue. Educated in public schools, he earned a B.S. in mathematics from North Carolina Central University in Durham (1970) and a J.D. from Duke University in Durham (1973). Blue began a law practice in Raleigh, North Carolina, becoming a partner in the firm of Thigpen, Blue, Stephens, and Fellers. Later he joined the firm of Sanford, Adams, McCullough and Beard. He also taught at the National Institute for Trial Law Advocacy.

In 1980 Blue was elected to the North Carolina House of Representatives as a Democrat from Wake County. He chaired the Judiciary Committee and the Appropriations Committee. Chair of the Legislative Black Caucus in 1984–89, he was chosen as speaker for the 1991 and 1993 sessions.

Blue was a member of the Kiwanis, American, North Carolina, and Wake County bar associations, American Trial Lawyers Association, and North Carolina Association of Black Lawyers. He received the Humanities Award from the NAACP and the Friend of the Working People Award from the North Carolina AFL-CIO. A Presbyterian, he married Edna Earle Smith; the couple had three children. At this writing Blue remains in the House.

North Carolina Manual (Raleigh: North Carolina Historical Commission, 1917–).

JON L. WAKELYN

BLUE, HERBERT CLIFTON (North Carolina, 1963) was born in Cumberland County (now Hoke County), North Carolina, on August 29, 1910. Graduating from high school in Vass, North Carolina, he settled in Aberdeen, North Carolina. Blue began working for the *Sandhill Citizen*, and he later published the *Robbins Record* and the *Montgomery Herald*. He was married.

A Democrat, Blue was a commissioner of Aberdeen (1945) and president of the Moore County Young Democrats. He won election to the North Carolina House of Representatives from Moore County in 1946 and served nine consecutive terms. During the 1950s he became associated with a small band of ''backbenchers'' who supported increases in spending, particularly for education. Blue was named speaker for the 1963 session. While in the post he oversaw several issues affecting education, the most controversial being the Speaker Ban Law that prohibited Communists and persons who had pleaded the Fifth Amendment in relation to subversive activities from speaking at state-supported colleges.

Losing the 1964 Democratic primary for lieutenant governor of North Carolina to Robert Scott, Blue returned to his newspapers. In 1949–52 he was secretary of the North Carolina Democratic Executive Committee. He was also president of the Lions and the North Carolina Press Association and a member of the Masons, Woodmen of the World, and Presbyterian Church. Blue died in Pinehurst, North Carolina, on March 10, 1990, at the age of 79.

Hugh Talmage Lefler and Albert Ray Newsome, *The History of a Southern State: North Carolina* (Chapel Hill: University of North Carolina Press, 1973); *The News and Observer* (Raleigh, North Carolina); William S. Powell, *North Carolina through Four Centuries* (Chapel Hill: University of North Carolina Press, 1989).

FRED D. RAGAN

BLUME, NORBERT (Kentucky, 1972, 1974) was born on August 30, 1922, in Louisville, Kentucky. He attended the University of Louisville and the University of Kentucky. During World War II Blume served as a chief petty officer in the U.S. Navy. Becoming a labor union official in Louisville, he was secretary-treasurer of Local 783 of the International Brotherhood of Teamsters for thirty-one years.

In 1963 Blume was elected to the Kentucky House of Representatives as a Democrat from Jefferson County. Remaining there for seven consecutive terms, he lost a 1970 bid for the speakership but was named to the post for the 1972 and 1974 sessions. Blume became the first speaker from Louisville in Kentucky history. While in office he cosponsored a bill that brought the University of Louisville into the state education system. He also introduced civil rights legislation, worked to increase the House's independence from the governor, and raised the salaries of the legislative staff.

Blume withdrew from the 1976 race for speaker as a result of splits within the Democratic Party concerning civil rights, and he was defeated for reelection to the House in 1977. He then worked as a lobbyist. In addition, Blume was a founder of the Kentucky Civil Liberties Union and a member of the Americans for Democratic Action and the VFW. A Catholic, he was married. At this writing Blume continues to live in Louisville.

Gary S. Cox, "The Kentucky Legislative Interim Committee System, 1968–1974" (Ph.D. dissertation, University of Kentucky, 1975); Malcolm E. Jewell, *Representation in State Legislatures* (Lexington: University Press of Kentucky, 1982); Malcolm E. Jewell and Everett W. Cunningham, *Kentucky Politics* (Lexington: University Press of Kentucky, 1968); Malcolm E. Jewell and Penny Miller, *The Kentucky Legislature: Two Decades of Change* (Lexington: University Press of Kentucky, 1988); Malcolm E. Jewell and Samuel C. Patterson, *The Legislative Process in the United States*, 4th ed. (New York: Random House, 1986); John Ed Pearce, *Divide and Dissent: Kentucky Politics, 1930–1963* (Lexington: University Press of Kentucky, 1987).

H. LEW WALLACE

BLUMHAGEN, E. (Oklahoma, 1941) was born in Drake, North Dakota, on November 1, 1907, of German ancestry. Educated in local public schools, he earned an LL.B. from Howard College (now Samford University) in Birmingham, Alabama, in 1928. Blumhagen then worked for West Publications in St. Paul, Minnesota. In 1932 he began a law practice in Watonga, Oklahoma. He was married.

A Democrat, Blumhagen was elected to the Oklahoma House of Representatives from Blaine County in 1936. He served three consecutive terms and was chosen as speaker for the 1941 session. In addition he was city attorney of Watonga. Blumhagen belonged to the Kiwanis and the American and Oklahoma bar associations.

TIMOTHY A. ZWINK

BOARD, CHARLES RAYMOND (Oklahoma, 1947) was born in Butler, Missouri, on November 9, 1901, to Charles Walter and Gertrude (Raybourn) Board. In 1903 he moved with his family to Okfuskee County, Indian Territory (now

Oklahoma). Educated in local public schools, he attended the University of Oklahoma. Board earned an LL.B. from Cumberland University in Lebanon, Tennessee, in 1925. He practiced law in Okemah, Oklahoma, before settling in Boise City, Oklahoma, around 1930.

A Democrat, Board was secretary of the Okfuskee County election board. In addition, he served Cimarron County as attorney (1932–36) and judge (1936–40). Board won election to the Oklahoma House of Representatives from Cimarron County in 1940 and served four consecutive terms. He was chosen as speaker for the 1947 session.

Judge of the 1st District Court of Oklahoma from 1950 to 1966, Board also sat on the Oklahoma Tax Court. He was president of the Oklahoma Judicial Conference, Rotary, and Chamber of Commerce and a member of the Masons, American and Oklahoma bar associations, and Baptist Church. Board was married.

Gaston Litton, *History of Oklahoma at the Golden Anniversary of Statehood*, 4 vols. (New York: Lewis Historical Publishing, 1957).

DONOVAN L. REICHENBERGER

BOBBITT, ROBERT LEE (Texas, 1927) was born in Hill County, Texas, on January 24, 1888, of Scotch-Irish descent. Attending local schools and Carlisle Military Academy in Arlington, Texas, he earned a degree from North Texas State Normal College (now the University of North Texas) in Denton and an LL.B. from the University of Texas. Bobbitt settled in Laredo, Texas, in 1916, and the next year he joined the law firm of Hicks, Hicks, Dickson and Bobbitt. During World War I he served in the U.S. Army, rising to the rank of captain. He was married.

A Democrat, Bobbitt sat on the Texas Democratic Executive Committee for two years. In 1922 he was elected to the Texas House of Representatives from Webb and Zapata counties. Bobbitt remained there for three consecutive terms. Becoming closely associated with Governor Daniel Moody, he was named speaker for the 1927 session. He was Webb County district attorney (1928–29) and attorney general of Texas (1929–31).

Moving to San Antonio, Texas, around 1935, Bobbitt sat on the 4th Court of Civil Appeals of Texas and the Texas Highway Commission. He chaired the board of Texas A&I College in Kingsville. In addition, he was district governor of the Rotary, president of the Chamber of Commerce, commander of the American Legion, and a member of the Elks, American and Texas bar associations, and Presbyterian Church. Bobbitt died on September 14, 1972, at the age of 84.

Austin *American*, September 18, 1972; Emory E. Bailey, ed., *Who's Who in Texas: A Biographical Directory Being a History of Texas* (Dallas: Who's Who Publishing, 1931), 98; Norman D. Brown, *Hood, Bonnet, and Little Brown Jug: Texas Politics, 1921–1928* (College Station: Texas A&M University Press, 1984); Dallas *Morning News*, January 9, 1927; *Presiding Officers of the Texas Legislature, 1846–1982* (Austin: Texas Legislative Council, 1982), 164–165.

ALWYN BARR

BOIARSKY, IVOR F. (West Virginia, 1969, 1971) was born in Charleston, West Virginia, on April 7, 1920, to Mose and Rae D. Boiarsky. Educated in local public schools and the Blair Academy in Blairstown, New Jersey, he studied at Middlebury College in Vermont. He received a B.A. from Brown University in 1941. Boiarsky served in the U.S. Coast Guard during World War II, and he later became a lieutenant commander in the Coast Guard Reserve. Earning an LL.B. from the University of Virginia in 1947, he began a law practice in Charleston.

From 1952 to 1958 Boiarsky directed the drafting service for the West Virginia House. He was elected to the West Virginia House of Delegates as a Democrat from Kanawha County in 1958 and remained there for seven consecutive terms. Boiarsky chaired the Committee on Finance before being named to the speakership for the 1969 and 1971 sessions. While in the post he introduced tax legislation and cosponsored bills creating the West Virginia Labor Management Relations Board, Department of Program Development and Management, and Board of Regents.

In other affairs Boiarsky was president of the Charleston Federal Savings and Loan Association. A Jew, he married Barbara Faith Polan in 1948; the couple had two sons. Boiarsky was still speaker when he died of a heart attack on March 12, 1971. He was 50.

WILLIAM T. DOHERTY

BOMAR, JAMES LA FAYETTE, Jr. (Tennessee, 1953, 1955, 1957, 1959, 1961) was born in Raus, Tennessee, on July 1, 1914, to James La Fayette and Aetna (Hix) Bomar. Educated in local public schools, he earned an A.B. (1935) and an LL.B. (1936) from Cumberland University in Lebanon, Tennessee. After that Bomar began practicing law in Shelbyville, Tennessee. He served in the U.S. Navy during World War II, rising to the rank of lieutenant (j.g.).

Bomar won election to the Tennessee House of Representatives as a Democrat from Bedford and Moore counties in 1942 and 1948. In 1946 he successfully ran for the Tennessee Senate. Again elected to the House in 1952, Bomar remained there for five consecutive terms. He was named speaker for the 1953, 1955, 1957, 1959, and 1961 sessions with the support of Governors Frank G. Clement and E. Buford Ellington. While in the post he oversaw the creation of the Legislative Council Committee to aid in research and bill drafting.

Returned to the Senate in 1962, Bomar was that body's speaker for the 1963 session. He then resumed his Shelbyville practice. Bomar was state president of the American Cancer Society (1960–61) and president of the Rotary. In addition, he belonged to the Elks, Moose, Farm Bureau, American Legion, VFW, and American and Tennessee bar associations. A Presbyterian, Bomar married Edith Dees in 1940; the couple had two sons.

Lee Seifert Greene, David H. Grubbs, and Victor C. Hobday, *Government in Tennes-*

see, 4th ed. (Knoxville: University of Tennessee Press, 1982); *Tennessee Blue Book* (Nashville: Tennessee Secretary of State).

LEE S. GREENE

BOONE, A. GORDON (Maryland, 1963) was born in Baltimore County, Maryland, on December 2, 1910. Educated in local schools, he earned an A.B. from Johns Hopkins University in Baltimore, Maryland (1934) and an LL.B. from the University of Baltimore (1937). Boone then practiced law in Towson, Maryland. During World War II he served in the U.S. Navy, participating in the invasion of Normandy and rising to the rank of lieutenant commander. He was married in 1932 but divorced in 1946.

A Democrat, Boone was counsel to the Baltimore County Welfare Board in 1940–42. He was elected to the Maryland House of Delegates from Baltimore County in 1946 and remained there for five consecutive four-year terms. Boone was named majority leader and chair of the Ways and Means Committee in 1951, but he was defeated for the speakership in 1959 by Perry O. Wilkinson. In addition, he lost a 1952 bid for the U.S. House of Representatives from Maryland's 2nd District.

Chosen as speaker for the 1963 session, Boone was forced to resign in February 1963 after being indicted for mail fraud involving his association with the Security Financial Insurance Corporation. He was convicted in 1964, leaving the House and spending thirteen months in federal prison. Governor Marvin Mandel granted Boone a partial pardon in 1971. In 1973 he moved to Swans Island, Maine. Boone died there on October 14, 1988, at the age of 77.

Baltimore *Evening Sun*; Baltimore *Sun*, October 15, 1988; Robert J. Brugger, *Maryland: A Middle Temperament, 1634–1980* (Baltimore: Johns Hopkins University Press, 1988); George H. Callcott, *Maryland and America, 1940–1980* (Baltimore: Johns Hopkins University Press, 1985); *Maryland Manual: Annual Publication of State Officers* (Annapolis: Hall of Records Commission).

WHITMAN H. RIDGWAY

BOST, EUGENE THOMPSON, Jr. (North Carolina, 1953) was born in Cabarrus County, North Carolina, on July 11, 1907, to Eugene Thompson and Zula (Hinshaw) Bost. Educated in local public and private schools, he attended the Mount Pleasant Collegiate Institute and earned an LL.B. from Duke University in Durham, North Carolina, in 1933. Bost then began practicing law in Concord, North Carolina. He married Bernice Hahn in 1937, and the couple had three children.

In 1936 Bost successfully ran for the North Carolina House of Representatives as a Democrat from Cabarrus County. He served nine consecutive terms, chairing the Finance Committee and the 1951 Democratic caucus. While in office he proposed the first prison work-release program in state history. Bost was named speaker without opposition for the 1953 session, gaining a reputation as an efficient, no-nonsense leader. Again elected to the House in 1956, he was defeated for reelection two years later.

Afterward Bost became corporate counsel for the powerful Cannon family. President of Cannon of the West Coast, Inc., he was also vice-president of the Charles A. Cannon Charitable Trust and the Cannon Foundation. He belonged to the American and North Carolina bar associations and the Methodist Church. Bost died of a heart attack in April 1977 at the age of 69.

OTIENO OKELO

BOSWORTH, JOE F. (Kentucky, 1920) was born in Fayette County, Kentucky, on October 3, 1867, to Benjamin and Mary (Cloud) Bosworth. Educated in public schools in Kentucky, he attended the University of Kentucky and University of Virginia. In 1889 he began a law practice in Middlesboro, Kentucky.

A Republican, Bosworth served Middlesboro as a councilman (1891), judge (1894–02), and city attorney (1902–05). He successfully ran for the Kentucky House of Representatives from Bell County in 1905 and for the Kentucky Senate two years later. Again elected to the House in 1919, 1921, 1923, and 1931, Bosworth was named speaker for the 1920 session. While in office he worked for better roads and improved courts in Eastern Kentucky, becoming known as the "Father of Good Roads."

Outside of politics Bosworth was president of the state Elks and the Kentucky Good Roads Association and a member of the Baptist Church. He was married in 1890 to Elizabeth Veal, with whom he had two children, and in 1912 to Bessie L. Sherlock. Bosworth died on October 8, 1939, at the age of 72.

Malcolm E. Jewell and Everett W. Cunningham, *Kentucky Politics* (Lexington: University Press of Kentucky, 1968); Malcolm E. Jewell and Penny Miller, *The Kentucky Legislature: Two Decades of Change* (Lexington: University Press of Kentucky, 1988); Robert F. Sexton, "Kentucky Politics and Society, 1919–1932" (Ph.D. dissertation, University of Washington, 1970).

CAROL CROWE-CARRACO

BOUANCHAUD, HEWITT LEONIDAS (Louisiana, 1916) was born in Poydras Plantation, Louisiana, on August 19, 1877. Attending Louisiana State University, he received a law degree from Tulane University in New Orleans, Louisiana. Later Bouanchaud practiced law in Pointe Coupee Parish, Louisiana. He belonged to the Catholic Church.

A Democrat, Bouanchaud won election to the Louisiana House of Representatives from Pointe Coupee Parish in 1907 and served three consecutive four-year terms. He was named speaker for the 1916 session. Bouanchaud was elected lieutenant governor of Louisiana on a reform ticket with John M. Parker in 1919. In addition, he presided over the 1921 Louisiana Constitutional Convention. Running for governor in 1923 against Henry L. Fuqua and Huey P. Long, Bouanchaud claimed that his opponents actively sought Ku Klan Klan support.

The charge was probably true about Fuqua, the eventual winner, but almost certainly false about Long.

In 1929 Bouanchaud was elected district attorney of the 16th Judicial District of Louisiana, but he took office only after defeating a challenge by one of Long's allies. Remaining in the post until 1936, he then returned to his law practice and began raising cattle in New Roads, Louisiana. Bouanchaud died there on October 17, 1950, at the age of 73.

Bergeron, Arthur W., "Hewitt Leonidas Bouanchaud," *A Dictionary of Louisiana Biography* (New Orleans: Louisiana Historical Association, 1988), I: 93; Dave H. Brown, comp., *A History of Who's Who in Louisiana Politics in 1916* (New Orleans: Coste and Frichter, 1916); *Membership in the Legislature of Louisiana, 1880–1980* (Baton Rouge, 1979).

RAYMOND O. NUSSBAUM

BRANSFORD, JOHN McKINNIS (Arkansas, 1937, 1939) was born in Lonoke, Arkansas, on November 29, 1901, to William Y. and Mattie (McKinnis) Bransford. Educated in local public schools, he earned a degree from the University of Arkansas. Bransford then became a cotton broker and a farmer. He belonged to the Masons and the Christian Church (Disciples of Christ).

In 1930 Bransford was elected to the Arkansas House of Representatives as a Democrat from Lonoke County, succeeding his father. Serving five consecutive terms, he was chair of the Legislative Joint Budget Committee in 1933. Bransford was named speaker for the 1937 and 1939 sessions, becoming the first person in state history to hold the post for two consecutive terms. He lost the 1940 race for lieutenant governor of Arkansas, but he chaired the Arkansas Agricultural and Industrial Commission during World War II.

Moving to Little Rock, Arkansas, Bransford was an office manager for the brokerage of Clayton Anderson and Company. Concurrently he was president of the Little Rock Cotton Exchange. He became a director of the Arkansas Industrial Pipeline Corporation in 1959. Bransford died in Little Rock on September 10, 1967, at age 65, and he was buried in Lonoke.

Arkansas Democrat; Arkansas Gazette; The Arkansas Handbook (Little Rock: Arkansas History Commission, 1936–   ).

RUSSELL PIERCE BAKER

BREWER, ALBERT PRESTON (Alabama, 1963) was born on a farm near Bethel Springs, Tennessee, on October 26, 1928, to Daniel Austin and Clara (Yarber) Brewer. In 1935 he moved with his family to Decatur, Alabama, where he attended public schools. Brewer earned an A.B. and an LL.B. from the University of Alabama, and he began a law practice in Decatur. A Baptist, he married Martha Helen Farmer; the couple had two daughters.

Brewer successfully ran for the Alabama House of Representatives as a Democrat from Morgan County in 1954 and served three consecutive four-year terms. While in office he was a strong supporter of Governor George C. Wallace.

With Wallace's backing, Brewer was chosen as speaker for the 1963 session when he was only 34. He was named "Outstanding Member of the House" by the Capital Press Corps and one of four "Outstanding Young Men of Alabama" by the state Jaycees.

Elected lieutenant governor of Alabama in 1966, Brewer rose to the governorship upon the death of incumbent Lurleen Wallace in May 1968. As governor he restructured the executive branch to increase its efficiency, sponsored legislation to strengthen Alabama's public school system, and began a series of programs designed to promote economic development. In addition, he was forced to address several controversial civil rights suits against various state agencies. Brewer was vice-chair of the Southern Governors' Conference (1969) and a member of the executive committee of the National Governors' Conference (1970). He lost the 1970 gubernatorial primary to his former ally George Wallace.

Afterward Brewer practiced law in Montgomery, Alabama, until 1978, when he was again an unsuccessful gubernatorial candidate. Outside of politics he was inducted into the Alabama Academy of Honor in 1969, and he belonged to the Masons, Jaycees, American Legion, and American, Alabama, and Morgan County bar associations. Returning to Decatur, he became a partner in the firm of Brewer, Lentz, Nelson and Whitmore. He also taught law at Samford University in Birmirgham, Alabama, and headed the Public Affairs Research Council of Alabama. Brewer continues to live in Decatur at this writing.

Alabama Official and Statistical Register (Montgomery: State of Alabama, Department of Archives and History, 1903–); Frank L. Grove, ed., *Library of Alabama Lives* (Hopkinsville, KY: Historical Records Association, 1961); Murray C. Havens, *City Versus Farm: Urban-Rural Conflict in the Alabama Legislature* (University, AL: Bureau of Public Administration, University of Alabama, 1957); Henry S. Marks, *Alabama Past Leaders* (Huntsville: Strode Publishers, 1982); John C. Stewart, *The Governors of Alabama* (Gretna, LA: Pelican Publishing Company, 1975); *Who's Who in Alabama* (Birmingham: Sayers Enterprises, 1965–).

                                                                                      REID BADGER

BREWER, RICHARD LEWIS, Jr. (Virginia, 1920, 1922, 1924) was born in Prince George County, Virginia, on May 27, 1864. His father was the first mayor of Suffolk, Virginia. After attending Suffolk Military Academy, Brewer operated his family's Brewer Jewelry Company until 1923. He was also an investment and insurance broker and vice-president of the American Bank and Trust Company in Suffolk.

A Democrat, Brewer was mayor of Suffolk from 1891 to 1903. He was elected to the Virginia House of Delegates from the city of Suffolk and Nansemond County (now part of Suffolk) in 1911 and served eleven consecutive terms. Brewer became the first chair of the Appropriations Committee in 1914, and he was named speaker for the 1920, 1922, and 1924 sessions. Part of a delegation of Virginians that presented the British government with a statue of

George Washington in 1921, he sat on the Virginia Board of Public Welfare for almost thirty years.

In 1933 Brewer retired from the House. Active in the Methodist Church, he was president of the Virginia Methodist Conference Orphanage Board. He belonged to the Masons, Elks, and Knights of Pythias. Brewer died in Suffolk on April 5, 1947, at the age of 82.

E. Griffith Dodson, ed., *Speakers and Clerks of the Virginia House of Delegates, 1776–1976*, rev. under the direction of Joseph H. Holleman, Jr. (Richmond, 1976), 120–143; *History of Virginia* (Chicago: American Historical Society, 1924): IV–VI; *Suffolk News-Herald*, April 5, 1947.

JAMES R. SWEENEY

BRISCOE, JOHN HANSON (Maryland, 1973, 1975) was born in Leonard-town, Maryland, on April 10, 1934, to John Henry Thomas and Hilda (Maddox) Briscoe. Educated in local private schools, he earned an A.B. from Mount Saint Mary's College in Emmitsburg, Maryland (1956) and an LL.B. from the University of Baltimore (1960). Afterward Briscoe began practicing law in Leonardtown. He was president of the St. Mary's County Bar Association and a member of the Elks, Lions, Rotary, Knights of Columbus, and Maryland Bar Association. A Catholic, he married Sylvia Weiss in 1956; the couple had four children.

Briscoe was appointed to the Maryland House of Delegates as a Democrat from St. Mary's County in 1962 and elected to the post later that year. He served four consecutive four-year terms. Chair of the Ways and Means Committee in 1971, Briscoe refused an offer to become majority leader because he disagreed with the efforts of Speaker Thomas H. Lowe to concentrate power. In addition, he chaired the Southern Legislative Conference in 1971–72 and was a delegate to the 1976 Democratic National Convention.

Chosen as speaker in November 1973 following Lowe's resignation, Briscoe was renamed to the post for the 1975 session. While in office he was known for his moderation and his willingness to negotiate, but he asserted the need for legislative independence from the governor. He declined to seek reelection to the House in 1978, returning to his private practice and becoming a state lobbyist. In 1986 Briscoe was appointed to the 7th Circuit Court of Maryland, a position he continues to hold at this writing.

Baltimore *Evening Sun*; Baltimore *News American*; Baltimore *Sun*; Robert J. Brugger, *Maryland: A Middle Temperament, 1634–1980* (Baltimore: Johns Hopkins University Press, 1988); George H. Callcott, *Maryland and America, 1940–1980* (Baltimore: Johns Hopkins University Press, 1985); *Maryland Manual: Annual Publication of State Officers* (Annapolis: Hall of Records Commission).

WHITMAN H. RIDGWAY

BRITT, DAVID MAXWELL (North Carolina, 1967) was born in McDonald, North Carolina, on January 3, 1917, to Dudley H. and Martha Mae (Hall) Britt.

His family had lived in the area since the early eighteenth century. Educated in local public schools, he earned a law degree from Wake Forest College (now University) in North Carolina. Britt began a private practice in Fairmont, North Carolina, after waiting six months to reach the minimum age of 21. During World War II he served in the U.S. Army. He married Louise Teague, and the couple had four children.

A Democrat, Britt served Fairmont as solicitor of the Recorder's Court (1940–44), city attorney (1946–67), and chair of the school board (1954–58). In 1958 he was elected to the North Carolina House of Representatives from Robeson, Hoke, and Scotland counties. Remaining there for five consecutive terms, he became chair of the Appropriations Committee in 1963. Britt chaired a state commission that recommended revisions to the controversial Speaker Ban Law, which the legislature adopted in the 1965 special session. He also belonged to the North Carolina Courts Commission and the North Carolina and Robeson County Democratic executive committees.

Britt was named speaker in 1967, but near the end of that year he was appointed to the North Carolina Court of Appeals. Sitting on the North Carolina Supreme Court from 1978 to 1982, he then returned to his law practice. He was district governor of the Rotary, president of the Wake Forest Alumni Association, and a member of the American, North Carolina, and Robeson County bar associations and the Baptist Church. At this writing Britt continues to live in Fairmount.

Hugh Talmage Lefler and Albert Ray Newsome, *The History of a Southern State: North Carolina* (Chapel Hill: University of North Carolina Press, 1973); *The News and Observer* (Raleigh, North Carolina); William S. Powell, *North Carolina through Four Centuries* (Chapel Hill: University of North Carolina Press, 1989).

FRED D. RAGAN

BROOME, JAMES JESSE (Tennessee, 1943) was born March 10, 1884, in Palmyra, Tennessee. Educated in elementary schools, he became a farmer and a real estate dealer. Broome belonged to the Masons, Odd Fellows, United American Mechanics, and Presbyterian Church. He married Beulah Davis in 1918.

A Democrat, Broome served Montgomery County as justice of the peace and a member of the Quarterly County Court (1912–52). Eventually he successfully ran for the Tennessee Senate. He was elected to the Tennessee House of Representatives from Montgomery County in 1942, 1944, and 1948, and he was named speaker for the 1943 session. Broome died on May 25, 1952, at the age of 67.

Biographical Directory, Tennessee General Assembly, 1796–1969 (Nashville: State Library and Archives); *Tennessee Blue Book* (Nashville: Tennessee Secretary of State).

LEE S. GREENE

BROWN, EDGAR ALLAN (South Carolina, 1925) was born in Aiken County, South Carolina, on July 11, 1888, to Augustus Abraham and Elizabeth Barker

(Howard) Brown. As a youth he was afflicted with tuberculosis. Brown attended local public schools, Graniteville Academy in South Carolina, and Osborne's Business College in Augusta, Georgia. After serving in the U.S. National Guard in 1906–07, he moved to Barnwell, South Carolina. He married Annie Love Sitgreaves in 1913, and the couple had one daughter.

A Democrat, Brown was stenographer for South Carolina's 2nd Circuit Court (1908–18) and a military aide to Governor Robert A. Cooper. He chaired the South Carolina Democratic Executive Committee. In 1920 Brown successfully ran for the South Carolina House of Representatives from Barnwell County. Remaining there for three consecutive terms, he was named speaker for the 1925 session. Brown was elected to the South Carolina Senate in 1928, becoming that body's president *pro tem* and chair of the Finance Committee for thirty years. While in office he helped lead the influential "Barnwell Ring," championing fiscal responsibility, tax law revision, and educational television. He retired from the Senate in 1972.

In the national political arena Brown lost races for the U.S. Senate from South Carolina in 1926, 1938, and 1954, and he was a delegate to several Democratic national conventions.

Outside of politics Brown sat on the board of trustees of Clemson College (now University), becoming its president in 1966. A member of the Masons, Knights of Pythias, Woodmen of the World, and Methodist Church, he was awarded honorary degrees by the Medical College of South Carolina and Clemson. His biography, *The Bishop from Barnwell: The Political Life and Times of Edgar Brown* by W. D. Workman, Jr., was published in 1963. Brown died on June 26, 1975, two weeks after the dedication of a state House office complex named for him. He was 86.

N. Louise Bailey, Mary L. Morgan, and Carolyn R. Taylor, eds., *Biographical Dictionary of the South Carolina Senate, 1776–1985*, 3 vols. (Columbia: University of South Carolina Press, 1986); *Biographical Directory of the South Carolina House of Representatives* (Columbia: University of South Carolina Press, 1974–); *South Carolina Legislative Manual* (Columbia: General Assembly of South Carolina, 1916–).

NANCY VANCE ASHMORE COOPER

BROWN, J. SINCLAIR (Virginia, 1930, 1932, 1934) was born in Warm Springs, Virginia, on September 30, 1880. He attended public schools in Virginia, Burnsville Academy in West Virginia, and the University of Virginia. Joining the Farmers National Bank in Salem, Virginia, in 1914, Brown became the bank's president in 1922 and chair of its board in 1954. In addition, he was president of the Virginia Bankers Association and vice-president of the American Bankers Association.

Brown was elected to the Virginia House of Delegates as a conservative Democrat from Roanoke County in 1915, and he served ten consecutive terms. While in office he sat on commissions that planned the state highway system and codified banking laws. Named chair of the Appropriations Committee in

1920, Brown played a major role in establishing the executive budget. He was chosen as speaker for the 1930, 1932, and 1934 sessions. The Richmond *News Leader* described him as "steadfastly the voice of courage, of moderation and of sound judgment."

After sitting on the Virginia Commission of Game and Inland Fisheries in 1937–39, Brown was appointed to the Virginia Board of Education. In 1945 he presided over the Virginia Constitutional Convention that exempted servicemen on active duty from paying poll taxes. He was president of the Kiwanis and a member of the Masons, Odd Fellows, Knights of Pythias, Chamber of Commerce, and Presbyterian Church. Brown died in Roanoke on January 15, 1965, at the age of 84.

E. Griffith Dodson, ed., *Speakers and Clerks of the Virginia House of Delegates, 1776–1976*, rev. under the direction of Joseph H. Holleman, Jr. (Richmond, 1976), 120–143; *History of Virginia* (Chicago: American Historical Society, 1924): IV–VI; *Richmond Times-Dispatch*, January 16, 1965; *Roanoke Times*, January 16, 1965.

                                                                    JAMES R. SWEENEY

BROWN, JAMES HYATT (Florida, 1979) was born in Orlando, Florida, on July 12, 1937, to James Adrian and Elizabeth (Worley) Brown. Educated in public schools, he received a B.S. from the University of Florida in 1959. He then settled in Daytona Beach, Florida, where he became president of an insurance company.

Brown entered politics in 1972 when he was elected to the Florida House of Representatives as a Democrat from Volusia County. He served four consecutive terms. Chair of the Growth and Energy Committee in 1975 and Government Operations Committee in 1978, he was named speaker for the 1979 session. While in the speakership Brown successfully sought tax reform and increased funding for education. The House also approved bills regulating hazardous waste, deregulating the trucking industry, increasing penalties for drug abuse, and requiring electric companies to institute energy conservation programs.

Afterward Brown returned to his insurance business. In addition, he belonged to the Masons, Kiwanis, Chamber of Commerce, YMCA, United Way, Salvation Army, and Baptist Church. He married Cynthia Rodriguez in 1965, and the couple had three children. Brown lives in Ormond Beach, Florida, at this writing.

                                                                    J. LARRY DURRENCE

BROWN, JOHN YOUNG (Kentucky, 1932) was born in Union County, Kentucky, on February 1, 1900, to Jessie C. and Lucy (Keefer) Brown. He was named for the governor of Kentucky in 1891–95. Brown attended local schools and received a degree from Centre College in Danville, Kentucky, in 1921. After working as a high school coach and principal in Marion County, Kentucky, for two years, he earned an LL.B. from the University of Kentucky in 1926. He then began a law practice in Lexington, Kentucky.

A Democrat, Brown won election to the Kentucky House of Representatives from Fayette County in 1929 and 1931. He was chosen as speaker for the 1932 session. Later that year Brown successfully ran for the U.S. House of Representatives from Kentucky. However, he later failed in several attempts to regain his seat. Brown was defeated in the 1935 Democratic primary for governor of Kentucky. Again elected to the Kentucky House in 1945, 1953, 1961, and 1965, he lost a 1959 bid for lieutenant governor.

Outside of politics Brown was president of the Kiwanis and a member of the Masons and the Methodist Church. In 1970 he published *The Legend of the Praying Colonels*, a history of the famed Centre College football team of the 1920s. He married Dorothy Inman in 1929, and the couple had five children. His son, John Young Brown, Jr., was elected governor of Kentucky in 1979. The elder Brown died of pneumonia on June 16, 1985, at the age of 85.

George T. Blakey, *Hard Times and the New Deal in Kentucky, 1929–1939* (Lexington: University Press of Kentucky, 1986); Malcolm E. Jewell and Everett W. Cunningham, *Kentucky Politics* (Lexington: University Press of Kentucky, 1968); Malcolm E. Jewell and Penny Miller, *The Kentucky Legislature: Two Decades of Change* (Lexington: University Press of Kentucky, 1988); Robert F. Sexton, "Kentucky Politics and Society, 1919–1932" (Ph.D. dissertation, University of Washington, 1970).

NANCY DISHER BAIRD

BROWN, ROBERTS HENRY (Alabama, 1951) was born on October 3, 1907, in Dothan, Alabama, to James Vandiver and Laura Augusta Brown. He attended local public schools, San Marcos Academy in Texas, and the Culver Military Academy in Indiana. After studying at Mercer University in Macon, Georgia, Brown earned a B.S. from the Alabama Polytechnic Institute (now Auburn University) in Auburn in 1930 and an LL.B. from the University of Georgia. In 1936 he settled in Auburn and began a law practice, which he later moved to Opelika, Alabama.

A Democrat, Brown was recorder for the Auburn Police Court in 1936–41. He successfully ran for the Alabama House of Representatives from Lee County in 1938 and 1942. Brown resigned in 1943 to serve with the U.S. Army Air Forces in the European theater during World War II, seeing action in the D-Day invasion. Again elected to the House in 1946, he remained there for three consecutive four-year terms. While in office Brown advocated public support for education and opposed Governor James E. Folsom's tax program in 1949. He was chosen as speaker in 1951 with the support of Governor Gordon Person, but he was not renamed to the post for the 1955 session.

Retiring from the House in 1958, Brown returned to his Opelika practice. In addition, he was a trustee of Auburn University and a member of the Kiwanis, American Legion, VFW, and Presbyterian Church. Brown died on November 18, 1971, at the age of 64.

Alabama Official and Statistical Register (Montgomery: State of Alabama, Department of Archives and History, 1903–); Frank L. Grove, ed., *Library of Alabama Lives*

(Hopkinsville, KY: Historical Records Association, 1961); Murray C. Havens, *City versus Farm: Urban-Rural Conflict in the Alabama Legislature* (University, AL: Bureau of Public Administration, University of Alabama, 1957); *A Manual for Alabama Legislators* (Montgomery: Legislative Reference Service, State of Alabama, 1942–   ); Henry S. Marks, *Alabama Past Leaders* (Huntsville: Strode Publishers, 1982); *Who's Who in Alabama* (Birmingham: Sayers Enterprises, 1965–   ).

REID BADGER

BROWN, WALLACE (Kentucky, 1935) was born on October 11, 1874, on a farm near Bloomfield, Kentucky, to George Washington and Ann (Greer) Brown. His parents were natives of the state. Educated in local schools, he attended Kentucky Wesleyan College in Winchester (now Owensboro) and earned a B.A. with honors from Centre College in Danville, Kentucky, in 1896. Brown worked in the insurance business, and he founded the Kentucky *Standard* in 1901. Later he read law and briefly operated a private practice.

A Democrat, Brown was Nelson County Circuit Court clerk for twelve years. He won election to one term in the Kentucky House of Representatives from Nelson County in 1911, and he was floor leader in 1912. Brown sat on the Nelson County Court in 1913–25. In 1925 he successfully ran for the Kentucky Senate. Returning to the House in 1933 and 1935, he was named speaker for the February 1935 special session.

From 1937 to 1948 Brown was again a county judge. While in office he sought to safeguard public funds, even using his own amateur carpentry skills to repair the courthouse. In addition, Brown chaired the Nelson County Democratic Campaign and belonged to the Masons and the Methodist Church. He married Nancy Jackson Williams in 1904, and the couple had two sons. Brown died on November 4, 1964, at the age of 90.

George T. Blakey, *Hard Times and the New Deal in Kentucky, 1929–1939* (Lexington: University Press of Kentucky, 1986); Malcolm E. Jewell and Everett W. Cunningham, *Kentucky Politics* (Lexington: University Press of Kentucky, 1968); Malcolm E. Jewell and Penny Miller, *The Kentucky Legislature: Two Decades of Change* (Lexington: University Press of Kentucky, 1988); Robert F. Sexton, "Kentucky Politics and Society, 1919–1932" (Ph.D. dissertation, University of Washington, 1970).

NANCY DISHER BAIRD

BRUMMITT, DENNIS GARFIELD (North Carolina, 1919) was born in Granville County, North Carolina, on February 7, 1881. After earning an A.B. and an LL.B. from Wake Forest College (now University) in North Carolina, he worked as a teacher for a year. Brummitt then began a law practice in Oxford, North Carolina. He was married.

A liberal Democrat, Brummitt was mayor of Oxford in 1909–13. In addition, he sat on the Democratic executive committees of Granville County (1908–14) and North Carolina (1913–24). Brummitt successfully ran for the North Carolina House of Representatives from Granville County in 1914. Serving three consecutive terms, he was named speaker for the regular session of 1919 and the 1920 special session. He was a presidential elector in 1920.

Elected attorney general of North Carolina in 1924, Brummitt retained that position until 1934. He was a trustee of North Carolina State College and Wake Forest College and a member of the Masons, Odd Fellows, and North Carolina Bar Association. Brummitt died on April 12, 1935, at the age of 54.

John L. Cheney, Jr., *North Carolina Government, 1585–1974: A Narrative and Statistical History* (Raleigh: North Carolina Department of the Secretary of State, 1975); Hugh Talmadge Lefler and Albert Ray Newsome, *The History of a Southern State: North Carolina* (Chapel Hill: University of North Carolina Press, 1973); William S. Powell, *North Carolina through Four Centuries* (Chapel Hill: University of North Carolina Press, 1989).

CLAUDE HARGROVE

BRYAN, L. L. "Doc" (Arkansas, 1993) was born in Coal Hill, Arkansas, on January 31, 1920. After attending Arkansas Polytechnic College (now Arkansas Tech University) in Russellville, he served in the U.S. Navy during World War II. Bryan became director of industrial relations for the Arkansas Poultry Federation in Russellville. In addition, he belonged to the Lions, Arkansas Broadcasters Association, American Legion, VFW, and Christian Church (Disciples of Christ). He married Evelyn Chronister, and the couple had two daughters.

Bryan was elected to the Arkansas House of Representatives as a Democrat from Pope County in 1966. Vice-chair of the Joint Committee on Energy, he was chosen as speaker for the 1993 session. He then became majority leader. As of this writing Bryan remains in the House.

JON L. WAKELYN

BRYANT, CECIL FARRIS (Florida, 1953) was born on July 26, 1914, near Ocala, Florida, to Charles Cecil and Lela Margaret (Farris) Bryant. His uncle, Ion L. Farris, was speaker of the Florida House in 1909 and 1913. Earning a B.S. from the University of Florida in 1935 and an LL.B. from Harvard University in 1938, Bryant began a law practice in Ocala. He was president of the Rotary and a member of the Masons, Elks, Chamber of Commerce, American Legion, VFW, and American and Florida bar associations. A Methodist, he married Julia Burnett in 1940; the couple had three daughters.

Bryant won election to the Florida House of Representatives as a Democrat from Marion County in 1942, but he resigned to serve in the U.S. Navy during World War II. In 1946 he was again elected to the House. Remaining there for five consecutive terms, he was named the ''Most Promising First Term Legislator'' and chosen as speaker for the 1953 session. While in the post Bryant worked with Governor Daniel T. McCarty to create a state turnpike authority, increase funding for economic development, and raise salaries for teachers. He chaired the state delegations to the 1952 and 1960 Democratic national conventions.

Losing the 1956 Democratic primary for governor of Florida to Leroy Collins, Bryant won the post in 1960 on a platform of fiscal conservatism and racial segregation. He supported increased funding for public schools, expansion of the state university system, reorganization of the scandal-ridden Road Department, and improvements in mental health facilities and prisons. Bryant then moved to Jacksonville, Florida, where he became chair of the board of the Voyager Life Insurance Company. In addition, he was director of the U.S. Office of Emergency Planning in 1966–67. At this writing Bryant continues to live in Jacksonville.

J. LARRY DURRENCE

BULLARD, JAMES MARVIN (Oklahoma, 1951) was born on April 13, 1901, near Elmore City, Indian Territory (now Oklahoma), to Sidney A. and Minnie E. (Burns) Bullard. Soon thereafter he moved with his family to Lawton, Oklahoma. Educated in public schools in Jefferson County, Oklahoma, he earned a degree from Chickasha Business College in Oklahoma in 1919. Bullard moved to Duncan, Oklahoma, where he worked in a bank and for the Duncan Abstract Company. He then became a drilling contractor, helping organize the Independent Petroleum Association of America in 1929. The next year he began operating a ranch.

A Democrat, Bullard served Stephens County as assistant treasurer (1924–26) and treasurer (1934–38). In 1938 he won election to one term in the Oklahoma House of Representatives from Stephens County. Bullard was again elected to the House in 1942 and remained there for ten consecutive terms. Chosen as speaker in 1951, he was majority floor leader for the 1955 and 1957 sessions. He lost the Democratic primary for the U.S. House of Representatives from Oklahoma's 6th District in 1962, but later that year he successfully ran for Oklahoma secretary of state.

Afterward Bullard was an assistant director of the Oklahoma Corporation Commission and a deputy insurance commissioner of Oklahoma. President of the Kiwanis and the Beaver Cow Creek Watershed Development Association, he belonged to the Masons, Elks, Chamber of Commerce, YMCA, and Baptist Church. He married Edith Marion Furst, and the couple had one daughter. Bullard died on July 21, 1978, at the age of 77.

"Former State Official James M. Bullard Dies," *The Daily Oklahoman*, July 22, 1978: 22; Gaston Litton, *History of Oklahoma at the Golden Anniversary of Statehood*, 4 vols. (New York: Lewis Historical Publishing, 1957).

DONOVAN L. REICHENBERGER

BURNLEY, CHARLES W. (Kentucky, 1952, 1954) was born on July 9, 1904, in McCracken County, Kentucky. Graduating from high school, he was a fireman and later an engineer for the Illinois Central Railroad. In addition, he worked as a prison guard and a used car salesman. Burnley belonged to the Brotherhood of Locomotive Engineers and the Christian Church (Disciples of Christ). He was married.

A Democrat, Burnley was postmaster of Kuttawa, Kentucky. He won election to the Kentucky House of Representatives from McCracken County in 1943 and remained there for seven consecutive terms. While in office he was known as the "Casey Jones of the House" as a result of his railroad background. Named speaker for the 1952 and 1954 sessions, Burnley worked with progressive Governor Lawrence W. Wetherby. Afterward he was Kentucky deputy commissioner of rural highways. Burnley died on October 5, 1962, following an automobile accident. He was 58.

Louisville *Courier-Journal; Kentucky Directory for the Use of the Courts, State and County Officials, and General Assembly of the State of Kentucky* (Frankfort, KY: 1914–); John E. Kleber, ed., *The Kentucky Encyclopedia* (Lexington: University Press of Kentucky, 1992); Penny M. Miller, *Kentucky Politics and Government* (Lincoln: University of Nebraska Press, 1994); Robert F. Sexton, ed., *The Public Papers of the Governors of Kentucky* (Lexington: University Press of Kentucky, 1975).

ROGER TATE

BURWELL, WILLIAM HIX (Georgia, 1913, 1915) was born in Baltimore, Maryland, on April 21, 1869, and moved with his family to Sparta, Georgia, in 1872. Attending local public schools, he read law and began a private practice in Sparta. In addition, Burwell belonged to the Masons, Odd Fellows, and Presbyterian Church. He was married.

Burwell won election to the Georgia House of Representatives as a Democrat from Hancock County in 1894, 1896, and 1906. From 1898 to 1900 he was mayor of Sparta. Defeated in a 1902 bid for the Georgia Senate, he successfully ran for the post in 1908. Two years later Burwell was again elected to the House, where he served four consecutive terms. While in office he led the fight to abolish the convict leasing system and backed an amendment to the Georgia Constitution to impede black suffrage by creating a literacy test and poll tax.

Named speaker for the 1913 and 1915 sessions, Burwell cast the deciding vote in the passage of Governor John M. Slanton's bill to establish a low inheritance tax. He also supported strengthening the Georgia Railroad Commission and instituting a tax reform law. Burwell lost renomination to the speakership in 1917. Afterward he returned to his Sparta law practice. Settling in Miami, Florida, in 1924, Burwell died there on February 22, 1953. He was 83.

James F. Cook, *Governors of Georgia* (Huntsville, AL: Strode, 1979); *The Georgia Annual: A Compendium of Useful Information about Georgia* (Atlanta: A. B. Caldwell, 1911–); Lucian L. Knight, ed., *Encyclopedia of Georgia Biography* (Atlanta: A. H. Cawston, 1931); *Leaders of the Georgia General Assembly, 1913–1914* (Atlanta: J. C. Reese and H. Branch, 1914).

CHARLES J. WEEKS

BYRD, RICHARD EVELYN (Virginia, 1912; also 1908, 1910) was a Democrat from the city of Winchester and Frederick County. He served as speaker of the Virginia House of Delegates for the 1912 session, having previously presided in 1908 and 1910.

Charles F. Ritter and Jon L. Wakelyn, *American Legislative Leaders, 1850–1910* (New York: Greenwood Press, 1989), 95–96.

KEVIN G. ATWATER

BYRNE, WILLIAM ESTON RANDOLPH (West Virginia, 1923) was born October 26, 1862, in Fort Defiance, Virginia, to Benjamin Wilson and Mary L. (Holt) Byrne. After attending public schools in West Virginia, he worked as a civil engineer for five years. Byrne studied law under his uncle in 1884. The following year he moved to Braxton County, West Virginia, where he began a private practice. He married Amanda Austin in 1889, and the couple had five children.

A Democrat, Byrne was prosecuting attorney of Braxton County. In addition, he was clerk of both the West Virginia Senate (1893–97) and House (1899). Byrne successfully ran for the West Virginia House of Delegates from Kanawha County in 1922. He was chosen as speaker for the 1923 term, his only one in the House.

Outside of politics Byrne belonged to the Presbyterian Church. He wrote *Tale of the Elk*, a book of facts and stories about the Elk River Valley. Appointed clerk of the West Virginia Court of Appeals in 1937, Byrne still held that post when he died on December 11, 1937, at age 75.

His cousin, Homer A. Holt, was governor of West Virginia in 1937–41.

ROBERT L. HUNT

C

CALVERT, ROBERT WILBURN (Texas, 1937) was born near Pulaski, Tennessee, on February 22, 1905, to Porter and Maud (Richardson) Calvert. Family problems following his father's death in 1913 led to his being sent to an orphan's home near Corsicana, Texas. There Calvert graduated from high school. Earning a B.A. and an LL.B. (1931) from the University of Texas, he began a law practice in Hillsboro, Texas. He was married in 1931 to Frances Freeland, with whom he had two children, and in 1962 to Corinne Lundgren.

Calvert successfully ran for the Texas House of Representatives as a Democrat from Hill and Navarro counties in 1932 and served three consecutive terms. Losing a 1935 bid for speaker to Coke R. Stevenson, he was named to the post for the 1937 session as a supporter of Governor James V. Allred. The next year he was defeated for attorney general of Texas. In addition, Calvert was president of the Hillsboro school board, Hill County attorney (1943–46), and chair of the Texas Democratic Executive Committee (1946–48). He won election to the Texas Supreme Court in 1950, becoming its chief justice from 1960 to 1972.

Chairing the National Conference of State Chief Justices in 1970, Calvert was president of the Texas Constitutional Revision Commission in 1973. In 1983–85 he sat on the Texas Ethics Advisory Commission. Calvert was also a consulting counsel for the firm of McGinnis, Lockridge and Kilgore in Austin, Texas. He was chair of the Red Cross, a founder of the Texas Rural Roads Association, and a member of the Rotary, Chamber of Commerce, and Baptist Church. At this writing Calvert continues to live in Austin.

Calvert, Robert W., *Here Comes the Judge: From State Home to State House* (Waco: Texian Press, 1977); George Norris Green, *The Establishment in Texas Politics: The Primitive Years, 1938–1957* (Westport, CT: Greenwood Press, 1979); *Presiding Officers of the Texas Legislature, 1846–1982* (Austin: Texas Legislative Council, 1982), 172–173.

ALWYN BARR

CAMPBELL, JAMES R., Jr. (Arkansas, 1951) was born in Tuskegee, Alabama, on December 4, 1893, to James R. and Mamie (Jackson) Campbell. Educated in local public schools, he earned a B.S. and an M.S. from Alabama Polytechnic Institute (now Auburn University) in Auburn and an LL.B. from Cumberland University in Lebanon, Tennessee. Campbell was an English teacher in Jasper, Alabama, before moving to Sevier County, Arkansas. He served as a captain in the U.S. Army during World War I, receiving the Purple Heart.

A Democrat, Campbell was superintendent of schools of Horatio, Arkansas, city attorney of DeQueen, Arkansas, and prosecuting attorney of the 9th Judicial District of Arkansas. In 1928 he won election to one term the Arkansas House of Representatives from Sevier County. Later Campbell settled in Hot Springs, Arkansas. Elected to the House from Garland County in 1934, he remained there for ten consecutive terms and was named speaker for the 1951 session. While in the House he sponsored a bill creating the Arkansas Legislative Council and became its first chair. He was given the "Statesman Award" in 1945.

Leaving the House in 1954, Campbell returned to Hot Springs. In addition, he was president of the Garland County Bar Association, commander of the American Legion, and a member of the Elks, Arkansas Bar Association, and Methodist Church. He was married. Campbell died on November 3, 1981, at the age of 87.

Arkansas Gazette, November 3, 1981; *The Arkansas Handbook* (Little Rock: Arkansas History Commission, 1936–   ).

JANE McBRIDE GATES

CAPPS, JOHN PAUL (Arkansas, 1983) was born in Steprock, Arkansas, on April 17, 1934, to Edwin H. and Vivian (Pinegar) Capps. Graduating from local public schools as valedictorian and senior class president, he attended Beebe Junior College (now part of Arkansas State University). Capps served in the U.S. Army Reserve. He became a radio broadcaster in 1955, working for stations in Searcy and Little Rock, Arkansas, before establishing KAPZ in Searcy in 1980.

In 1962 Capps successfully ran for the Arkansas House of Representatives as a Democrat from White County. Vice-chair of the Revenue and Taxation Committee, he was chosen as speaker for the 1983 session. While in the speakership Capps emphasized education, highways, and economic development. He was majority leader in 1985.

Capps presided over the boards of North Arkansas Human Services and the Community Action Program of Central Arkansas. In addition he was president of the Jaycees, Chamber of Commerce, Arkansas Broadcasters Association, PTA, and 4-H Club and a member of the Lions and the Church of Christ. He married Elizabeth Ann Vaughan in 1955, and the couple had three children. At this writing Capps remains in the House and continues to operate his Searcy radio station.

SUZANNE MABERRY

CARDIN, BENJAMIN LOUIS (Maryland, 1979, 1983) was born on October 5, 1943, in Baltimore, Maryland, to Meyer M. and Dora (Green) Cardin. His father and his uncle, Maurice Cardin, were state legislators. Educated in local public schools, the younger Cardin earned a B.A. *cum laude* from the University of Pittsburgh (1964) and a law degree with honors from the University of Maryland (1967). He then began a law practice in Baltimore.

In 1966 Cardin was elected to the Maryland House of Delegates as a Democrat from the city of Baltimore. He served five consecutive four-year terms and became chair of the Ways and Means Committee in 1974. Cardin was named speaker for the 1979 and 1983 sessions, working to increase House efficiency and decentralize power to achieve a greater policy consensus. With the support of Governor Harry Hughes, he also successfully sought to expand the legislature's independence from executive domination. While in the speakership he chaired several committees of the National Conference of State Legislators.

Cardin won election to the U.S. House of Representatives from the 3rd District of Maryland in 1986, and he was assistant majority whip in 1993. He was a trustee of St. Mary's College and the Baltimore Museum of Art. In addition, Cardin belonged to the Masons, United Nations Association, Council on Foreign Affairs, and American, Maryland, and Baltimore bar associations. A Jew, he married Myrna Edelman in 1964; the couple had two children. At this writing Cardin remains in the U.S. House.

Baltimore *Evening Sun*; Baltimore *News American*; Baltimore *Sun*; Robert J. Brugger, *Maryland: A Middle Temperament, 1634–1980* (Baltimore: Johns Hopkins University Press, 1988); George H. Callcott, *Maryland and America, 1940–1980* (Baltimore: Johns Hopkins University Press, 1985); Robert Douglas, "Ben Cardin and the Family Dilemma," *Baltimore Magazine* 74 (February 1981), 56–61; John Feinstein, "Annapolis Ringmaster: Benjamin Cardin Rules Md. Power Politics," *Washington Post*, April 18, 1982; *Maryland Manual: Annual Publication of State Officers* (Annapolis: Hall of Records Commission); "Questions and Answer: Cardin & Sachs," Baltimore *Jewish Times*, May 4, 1984.

WHITMAN H. RIDGWAY

CARMICHAEL, ARCHIBALD HILL (Alabama, 1915; also 1907) was born on June 17, 1864, in Sylvan Grove, Alabama, to Jesse M. and Amanda J. (Smith) Carmichael. His father was a state legislator. Educated in local public schools, he earned both an A.B. and an LL.B from the University of Alabama in 1886. The following year Carmichael began a law practice in Tuscumbia, Alabama. In addition, he was a trustee of the University of Alabama and a member of the Masons, Knights of Pythias, and Methodist Church. He married Annie Sugg in 1890.

A Democrat, Carmichael was assistant clerk of the Alabama House of Representatives in 1888 and 1890. He was solicitor of the District Court of Colbert and Lauderdale counties (1891–94) and of the state's 11th Judicial Circuit Court (1894–98). Carmichael attended the 1901 Alabama Constitutional Convention. Elected to the Alabama House from Colbert County in 1906, he served three consecutive four-year terms. In March 1907 he was unanimously chosen as speaker following the death of incumbent William L. Martin. While in the post

Carmichael helped pass a prohibition amendment to the Alabama Constitution, but it was rejected in a state referendum. He was again named to the speakership for the 1915 session.

Carmichael successfully ran for the Alabama Senate in 1918, but he lost the 1926 Democratic primary for governor of Alabama to D. Bibb Graves. He was also a delegate to the 1916, 1928, and 1932 Democratic national conventions. Winning a special election to the U.S. House of Representatives from Alabama's 8th District in 1933, he remained there for two terms. Carmichael died in Tuscumbia on July 15, 1947, at the age of 83.

BENJAMIN B. WILLIAMS AND DONALD B. DODD

CARR, WAGGONER (Texas, 1957, 1959) was born in Fairlie, Texas, on October 1, 1918, to Vincent and Ruth (Warlick) Carr. He moved with his family to Lubbock, Texas. Attending local schools, he earned a B.A. from Texas Technological College (now Texas Tech University) in Lubbock in 1940. Carr served as a specialist in military intelligence in the U.S. Army Air Forces during World War II. In 1947 he received an LL.B. from the University of Texas. He married Ernestine Story in 1941, and the couple had one son.

A Democrat, Carr was assistant district attorney of the 72nd Judicial District of Texas and Lubbock County attorney (1949–51). He won election to the Texas House of Representatives from Lubbock County in 1950 and remained there for five consecutive terms. Carr was named speaker for the 1957 and 1959 sessions. While in the speakership he helped pass constitutional amendments to create the Texas Water Development Board and to authorize tourism promotion and industrial development. Other bills established a code of legislative ethics, created the Texas Youth Council, modernized workers' compensation statutes, reorganized the Texas Insurance Board, and financed a new state library and archives building.

Carr unsuccessfully ran for attorney general of Texas in 1960, but he was elected to the post in 1962. He was chosen as the outstanding attorney general in the country by his peers in 1966. That same year Carr lost a race for the U.S. Senate from Texas to incumbent John Tower. Defeated in the 1968 Democratic primary for governor of Texas, he was a regent of Texas Tech University in 1969–72. In addition, Carr belonged to the Masons, Knights of Pythias, Lions, Farm Bureau, American Legion, Texas and Lubbock County bar associations, and Methodist Church.

LUTHER G. HAGARD, JR.

CARROLL, JULIAN MORTON (Kentucky, 1968, 1970) was born on April 16, 1931, in Paducah, Kentucky, to Elvie Beeler and Eva (Heady) Carroll. He earned an A.A. (1952) from Paducah Junior College and an A.B. (1954) and an LL.B. (1956) from the University of Kentucky. After that he served as a lieutenant in the U.S. Air Force. Carroll began a law practice in Paducah in 1959.

A Presbyterian, he married Charlann Harting in 1951; the couple had four children.

In 1961 Carroll was elected to the Kentucky House of Representatives as a Democrat from McCracken County. Serving five consecutive terms, he was named speaker for the 1968 and 1970 sessions. While in office he was known as a deliberate and efficient leader who enjoyed bipartisan support. Many observers credited Carroll with increasing the power and prestige of the House and speakership, particularly through his creation of a functional committee system. He also helped pass bills regulating the bail bond industry, raising the state sales tax, and increasing funds for education.

Carroll successfully ran for lieutenant governor of Kentucky in 1971 and for governor in 1975. Moving his law practice to Frankfort, Kentucky, he lost the 1987 Democratic gubernatorial primary to Wallace Wilkinson. He belonged to the Masons, Kiwanis, Jaycees, and American, Kentucky, and Franklin County bar associations. As of this writing Carroll continues to live near Frankfort.

Gary S. Cox, "The Kentucky Legislative Interim Committee System, 1968–1974" (Ph.D. dissertation, University of Kentucky, 1975); Malcolm E. Jewell, *Representation in State Legislatures* (Lexington: University Press of Kentucky, 1982); Malcolm E. Jewell and Everett W. Cunningham, *Kentucky Politics* (Lexington: University Press of Kentucky, 1968); Malcolm E. Jewell and Penny Miller, *The Kentucky Legislature: Two Decades of Change* (Lexington: University Press of Kentucky, 1988); Malcolm E. Jewell and Samuel C. Patterson, *The Legislative Process in the United States*, 4th ed. (New York: Random House, 1986); John Ed Pearce, *Divide and Dissent: Kentucky Politics, 1930–1963* (Lexington: University Press of Kentucky, 1987).

H. LEW WALLACE

CARTER, REX LYLE (South Carolina, 1973, 1975, 1977, 1979) was born on June 20, 1925, in Honea Path, South Carolina, to D. B. and Eunice Carter. After attending schools in Greenville, South Carolina, he served with the U.S. Coast Guard in the Atlantic and Pacific theaters during World War II. Carter earned an A.B. from Erskine College in Due West, South Carolina (1950) and an LL.B. from the University of South Carolina (1952). While at the latter he was president of the law school student body. He then began practicing law in Greenville, eventually becoming a partner in the firm of Carter, Philpot, Johnson & Smith.

In 1952 Carter was elected to the South Carolina House of Representatives as a Democrat from Greenville County. Remaining there for fourteen consecutive terms, he developed friendly relations with the "Barnwell Ring" faction and was speaker *pro tem* from 1957 to 1973. Carter was chosen as speaker following the resignation of incumbent Solomon Blatt in July 1973. He was renamed to the speakership for the 1975, 1977, and 1979 sessions. Retiring from the House in September 1980, he returned to his law practice and later became a political lobbyist. At this writing Carter continues to live in Greenville.

South Carolina Legislative Manual (Columbia: General Assembly of South Carolina, 1916–); *The State* (Columbia).

MARIAN ELIZABETH STROBEL

CAUDLE, REECE ARTHUR (Arkansas, 1927) was born on June 16, 1888, in Scottsville, Arkansas. After earning a degree from the University of Arkansas, he worked as a teacher in Pope County, Arkansas, until 1918. Caudle began practicing law in Russellville, Arkansas, in 1922. He was married.

A Democrat, Caudle was Pope County circuit clerk from 1918 to 1922. In the latter year he was elected to the Arkansas House of Representatives from Pope County. Caudle served three consecutive terms and was chosen as speaker for the 1927 session. He sat on the Arkansas Railroad Commission in 1929–33, and he was appointed to the Arkansas Flood Control Commission in 1941.

President of the Arkansas Soil Conservation District Supervisors Association for nine years, Caudle was later the executive secretary of the Arkansas Flood Control Association. In addition, he was an elder of the Christian Church (Disciples of Christ) and a member of the Masons. Caudle died on June 21, 1955, at the age of 67.

Diane D. Blair, *Arkansas Politics and Government* (Lincoln: University of Nebraska Press, 1988), 160–184; Jerry E. Hinshaw, *Call the Roll* (Little Rock: Rose Publishing, 1986); *Historical Report of the Secretary of State, Arkansas* (Little Rock: Secretary of State, 1958–   ); Walter Nunn, *Readings in Arkansas Government* (Little Rock: Rose Publishing, 1973), 59–133.

CAL LEDBETTER, JR.

CAZORT, WILLIAM LEE, Sr. (Arkansas, 1917) was born in Lamar, Arkansas, in 1887. Graduating from high school in Fort Smith, Arkansas, he attended Hendrix College in Conway, Arkansas, and the University of Arkansas. Cazort received a law degree from Washington and Lee University in Lexington, Virginia, in 1910. He then began a private practice in Johnson County, Arkansas. In addition, Cazort was president of the Arkansas Horticultural Society and the Arkansas Livestock Association and a member of the Masons. A Methodist, he was married.

Cazort won election to the Arkansas House of Representatives as a Democrat from Johnson County in 1914 and 1916. He was chosen as speaker for the 1917 session. Elected to the Arkansas Senate in 1918 and 1920, Cazort was that body's president in 1921. While in the legislature he authored bills on tick eradication and the creation of the Arkansas Livestock Board and Apiary Board.

Defeated in the 1924 race for governor of Arkansas, Cazort successfully ran for the lieutenant governorship in 1928 and moved to Little Rock, Arkansas. In 1932 and 1934 he was again elected lieutenant governor. While in office he sponsored state constitutional amendments to provide free textbooks for public elementary schools and to create a homestead tax exemption. In 1936 Cazort lost another gubernatorial race. He was a U.S. bankruptcy referee from 1937 to 1964. Cazort died in Little Rock on October 6, 1969.

Arkansas Democrat; Arkansas Gazette.

CARL H. MONEYHON

CHAMBERS, ROBERT CHARLES "Chuck" (West Virginia, 1987, 1989, 1991, 1993) was born in Mingo County, West Virginia, on August 27, 1952, to James Edgar and Geraldine (Kiser) Chambers. Educated in public schools in Barboursville, West Virginia, he earned an A.B. in political science from Marshall University in Huntington, West Virginia (1974) and a J.D. from West Virginia University (1978). He then practiced law with his father in the firm of Chambers, Chambers & Heilmann in Huntington.

A Democrat, Chambers was legal counsel to the West Virginia Elections Committee in 1978. That same year he was elected to the West Virginia House of Delegates from Cabell County after winning the Democratic primary when a tabulation error was discovered. He chaired the Judiciary Committee in 1985, overcoming critics of his pro-labor reputation. Chambers was named to the speakership for the 1987, 1989, 1991, and 1993 sessions. While in the post he focused upon the issues of education, economic development, and legislative ethics.

In other affairs Chambers belonged to the executive committee of the National Conference of State Legislators. He joined the Bucci Law Offices in 1991. Chambers was a member of the West Virginia and Cabell County bar associations, American Trial Lawyers Association, West Virginia Wildlife Federation, and Methodist Church. Married three times, he had three children. At this writing Chambers remains speaker.

LISLE G. BROWN

CHAPPELL, WILLIAM VENROE, Jr. (Florida, 1961) was born in Kendrick, Florida, on February 3, 1922, to William Venroe and Laura C. (Kemp) Chappell. Educated in local public schools, he served as an aviator in the U.S. Navy during World War II. Later he rose to the rank of captain in the Naval Reserve. Chappell earned a B.A. (1947) and an LL.B. (1949) from the University of Florida, and he began a law practice in Ocala, Florida, in 1950. In addition, he belonged to the Masons and the Methodist Church. He was married and had four children.

A Democrat, Chappell was Marion County prosecuting attorney in 1950–54. He was elected to the Florida House of Representatives from Marion County in 1954, remaining there until 1968 with the exception of the 1965 term. Chappell joined fellow Florida conservative Mallory E. Horne in campaigning for a constitutional amendment to limit the U.S. Supreme Court's powers after its 1954 decision in *Brown v. Board of Education*. Named speaker for the 1961 session, he helped pass organizational changes aimed at improving the efficiency of the legislative process.

In 1968 Chappell successfully ran for the U.S. House of Representatives from Florida's 4th District. Serving ten consecutive terms, he sat on the Appropriations Committee and the Banking and Currency Committee. While in office Chappell supported balancing the national budget and maintaining a strong national defense; he also sponsored legislation relating to conservation and clean air. He lost reelection to the U.S. House to Craig T. James in 1988. Chappell died on March 30, 1989, at the age of 67.

JERRELL H. SHOFNER

CHERRY, ROBERT GREGG (North Carolina, 1936, 1937) was born in Catawba Junction, South Carolina, on October 17, 1891, to Chancellor Lafayette and Hattie (Davis) Cherry. Orphaned as a child, he was raised in Gastonia, North Carolina. He received an A.B. (1912) and a law degree (1914) from Trinity College (now Duke University) in Durham, North Carolina. While in college he was captain of the basketball team, earning the nickname "Cherry the Terrible." Cherry then began practicing law in Gastonia. Serving with the U.S. Army in Europe during World War I, he later became a major in the North Carolina National Guard. He married Mildred Stafford in 1921; the couple had no children.

A Democrat, Cherry was mayor of Gastonia in 1919–23. In 1930 he won election to the North Carolina House of Representatives from Gaston County. Cherry remained there for five consecutive terms, promoting social welfare programs. He was named speaker for the December 1936 special session, 1937 regular session, and extra session of 1938, and his military background led to his becoming known as the "Iron Major." Concurrently Cherry chaired the North Carolina Democratic Executive Committee. He successfully ran for the North Carolina Senate in 1940 and 1942.

Elected governor of North Carolina in 1944, Cherry refused to join the "Dixiecrat" opposition to the national Democratic Party and led the state's delegation to the 1948 party convention. He served North Carolina by sitting on the School Commission, Textbook Commission, and Board of Charities and Public Welfare. In addition Cherry was a trustee of Duke University and the University of North Carolina. State chancellor of the Knights of Pythias and commander of the American Legion, he belonged to the Masons, Odd Fellows, Kiwanis, American, North Carolina, and Gaston County bar associations, and Methodist Church. Cherry died on June 25, 1957, at age 65.

William S. Powell, ed., *Dictionary of North Carolina Biography*, 6 vols. (Chapel Hill: University of North Carolina Press, 1979–1996).

CHARLES H. BOWMAN, JR.

CHRISTIE, WILLIAM McLEAN (Florida, 1937) was born in Jacksonville, Florida, on August 8, 1892. Attending local schools and the University of North Carolina, he earned a B.A. and an LL.B. (1913) from the University of Florida. During World War I Christie served as a captain in the U.S. Army's 70th Division in Europe. He later began a private law practice.

A Democrat, Christie was assistant U.S. attorney of Duval County in 1921–24. He was elected to the Florida House of Representatives from Duval County in 1932 and remained there for four consecutive terms. Christie lost a 1935 bid for speaker to William B. Bishop of Jefferson County, but he was unopposed for the post in 1937. Described by the *Miami Herald* as a "brilliant presiding officer," Christie oversaw a legislature that passed Social Security and unemployment insurance programs and provided nearly $12 million for education. The legislature also abolished the state poll tax, banned slot machines, increased the alcohol tax, and submitted a proposed constitutional amendment to extend homestead tax exemptions.

Afterward Christie was mentioned as a candidate for governor of Florida. Married with one child, he belonged to the Elks, American Legion, and Episcopal Church. Christie was still a member of the House when he drowned in a car accident near Kissimmee, Florida, on July 9, 1939. He was 46.

Paul S. George, *A Guide to the History of Florida* (Westport, CT: Greenwood Press, 1989); *Miami Daily News; Miami Herald; Tallahassee Democrat; Tampa Tribune.*

PAUL S. GEORGE

CLARK, JAMES STERLING (Alabama, 1987, 1991) was born on October 7, 1921, in Eufaula, Alabama, to Edward Ephriam and Stella Lee (Floyd) Clark. Educated in local public schools, he attended college in Alabama. During World War II Clark served as a sergeant in the U.S. Army Air Forces. He became a partner in the Johnston-Clark Company in 1960 and chair of the Citizens' Bank of Eufaula in 1965.

A Democrat, Clark was mayor and a member of the Planning and Industry Development Board in Eufaula. In 1958 he successfully ran for the Alabama Senate, where he remained until 1974. He was elected to the Alabama House of Representatives from Barbour and Russell counties in 1984. Clark chaired the Rules Committee before being named speaker for the 1987 and 1991 sessions. While in office, he emphasized the restructuring of state government and the development of highways.

President of the Kiwanis, Clark was a member of the Association of Independent Insurance Agents and the Methodist Church. In addition, he worked to help develop programs for the mentally disabled. He married Marie Turner Kendall in 1949, and the couple had three children. Clark continues to hold the speakership at this writing.

GINA PETONITO

CLARKE, P. JOSEPH (Kentucky, 1993) was born in Danville, Kentucky, on March 12, 1933, to Phillip Joseph and Marie (Newton) Clarke. He earned a B.S. in chemical engineering from the University of Notre Dame in Indiana in 1955 and a J.D. from Georgetown University in Washington, D.C., in 1960. Clarke then began a private practice in Danville. A Catholic, he married Anne Dooling; the couple had four sons.

In 1969 Clarke was elected to the Kentucky House of Representatives as a Democrat from Boyle and Lincoln counties. Chair of the Appropriations and Revenue Committee, he was chosen as speaker for the 1993 session. He was also active in the Council of State Governments and the National Conference of State Legislators. Clarke remains in the House at this writing.

JON L. WAKELYN

CLAYTON, BILLY WAYNE (Texas, 1975, 1977, 1979, 1981) was born in Olney, Texas, on September 11, 1928, to William Thomas and Myrtle F. (Chitwood) Clayton. At age 3 he moved with his family to Springlake, Texas. Attending local public schools and Allen Academy in Bryan, Texas, he earned a B.S. in agricultural economics from Texas A&M University in 1950. Clayton then operated his family's farm in Springlake. He also acquired interests in a bank, insurance business, radio station, and several retail firms.

A conservative Democrat, Clayton attended the 1960 Democratic National Convention. He was elected to the Texas House of Representatives from Lamb and Deaf Smith counties in 1962 and served ten consecutive terms. While in office he sponsored legislation enacting the Texas Water Code in 1971. Clayton was named speaker for the 1975, 1977, 1979, and 1981 sessions, the longest tenure in the post in state history at that time. Interested in modernizing the House, he successfully pushed bills to create standing committees and to encourage professional committee staffs and the prefiling of legislation. In 1977 he oversaw passage of the Texas Sunset Law, designed to improve services by state agencies.

Indicted in 1980 for allegedly taking a bribe as part of the FBI's Brilab sting operation, Clayton was acquitted but declined to run for reelection to the House in 1982. Afterward he became a lobbyist for state utilities, osteopathic physicians, and acupuncturists. Clayton switched to the Republican Party during the mid-1980s. In addition, he sat on the board of Texas A&M University and belonged to the Masons, Lions, and Baptist Church. He married Delma Jean Dennis in 1950, and the couple had two children. At this writing Clayton continues to live in Springlake.

LUTHER G. HAGARD, JR.

COCKRILL, STERLING ROBERTSON, Jr. (Arkansas, 1967) was born in Little Rock, Arkansas, on April 7, 1925, to Sterling Robertson and Helen (Bracy) Cockrill. During World War II he served in the U.S. Navy, rising to the rank of lieutenant. Attending Arkansas A&M College in Monticello and Northwestern University in Evanston, Illinois, Cockrill earned a B.S. in business administration from the University of Arkansas in 1948. He then joined his father's Little Rock insurance company.

Cockrill was elected to the Arkansas House of Representatives as a Democrat in 1956. Remaining there for seven consecutive terms, he represented Pulaski County until 1966 and Pulaski and Perry counties thereafter. While in office Cockrill opposed the "Old Guard" faction loyal to conservative Governor Orval E. Faubus. He was vice-chair of the Insurance Committee before being named speaker for the 1967 session. In 1969 Cockrill was majority leader and chair of the Insurance Committee.

Claiming that the "Old Guard" had stymied his attempts to reform the House, Cockrill joined the Republican Party but lost a 1970 bid for lieutenant governor of Arkansas. He was appointed a deputy director of the U.S. Department of Housing and Urban Development in 1971 and a director four years later. Cockrill became executive director of Metrocentre Improvement District No.1 in Little Rock in 1978. In addition, he was president of the Arkansas Association of Insurance Agents and a member of the Jaycees and the Chamber of Commerce. An Episcopalian, Cockrill married Adrienne Storey in 1945; the couple had two daughters.

LEON C. MILLER

CONLON, THOMAS EDWARD (Maryland, 1939, 1943) was born in Toledo, Ohio, on June 27, 1883. He attended local public and private schools. Joining the Baltimore and Ohio Railroad in 1901, he began working as a stenographer and clerk in Pittsburgh, Pennsylvania, in 1903. Conlon became a traveling freight agent for the railroad in 1914, and four years later he was transferred to its home office in Baltimore, Maryland, as supervisor of freight suits. Eventually he was promoted to assistant claim agent. A Catholic, he married Marcella Elizabeth Quigley; the couple had six children.

Conlon enrolled in the charter law school class of the University of Baltimore in Maryland, earning an LL.B. in 1928. He delayed taking the bar examination until his son, Thomas E. Conlon, Jr., had completed his law studies. When they passed the Maryland bar in 1933, they became the first father and son to do so at the same time. The elder Conlon also belonged to the Optimists and the Knights of Columbus.

In 1934 Conlon was elected to the Maryland House of Delegates as a Democrat from the city of Baltimore. He served three consecutive four-year terms and was named speaker for the 1939 and 1943 sessions. Resigning from the House in 1943, he successfully ran for president of the Baltimore City Council. Conlon collapsed and died on October 28, 1943, while attending a city government meeting. He was 60.

MORGAN H. PRITCHETT

CONNER, DOYLE E. (Florida, 1957) was born near Starke, Florida, on December 17, 1928, to James Leon and Ruby Mae (Clemons) Conner. He earned a B.S. in agriculture from the University of Florida in 1952. Afterward he became a farmer and rancher in Starke. A Baptist, he was married and had three children.

In 1950 Conner was elected to the Florida House of Representatives as a Democrat from Bradford County. He served five consecutive terms. Conner was named speaker for the 1957 regular session and the special session later that year. At age 28, he was the youngest person to hold the post in state history.

During Conner's speakership the legislature approved programs for screwworm and cattle fever tick eradication and the authorization of agricultural assessments. However, the House spent much of its time trying to find legal ways to block desegregation.

Conner successfully ran for Florida commissioner of agriculture in 1960. He remained in that post until retiring in 1990, setting a record for tenure in the state cabinet. Outside of politics he was national president of the Future Farmers of America and a member of the Masons, Elks, Rotary, Kiwanis, Chamber of Commerce, and Farm Bureau. As of this writing Conner lives in Tallahassee, Florida.

J. LARRY DURRENCE

CONNER, MARTIN SENNETT (Mississippi, 1916, 1920) was born on August 31, 1891, in Hattiesburg, Mississippi, and raised in Seminary, Mississippi. Earning a B.S. from the University of Mississippi in 1910, he received an LL.B *cum laude* from Yale University in 1913. Conner then began a law practice in Seminary. He was married, and he belonged to the Masons and the Methodist Church.

In 1915 and 1919 Conner was elected to the Mississippi House of Representatives as a Democrat from Covington County. Supported by Governor Theodore G. Bilbo and the party's populist "redneck" faction, he was chosen as speaker in 1916 when he was only 24. He later joined the fiscally conservative "low pressure" faction, and with their backing he was again named to the speakership for the 1920 session.

Conner unsuccessfully ran for governor of Mississippi in 1923 and 1927, but he won election to the post in 1931. While in the governorship he championed industrial development, helped pass a state sales tax, slashed government services, and reduced the number of state employees. Losing a bid for the U.S. Senate from Mississippi in 1936, Conner was defeated in the 1939 and 1943 gubernatorial races. From 1940 to 1948 he was the first commissioner of athletics for the Southeastern Conference. Conner died in Jackson, Mississippi, on September 18, 1950, at the age of 59.

Albert Kirwan, *The Revolt of the Rednecks: Mississippi Politics 1876–1925* (Lexington: University of Kentucky Press, 1951); Dale Krane and Stephen D. Shaffer, eds., *Mississippi Government & Politics: Modernizers versus Traditionalists* (Lincoln: University of Nebraska Press, 1992); Richard A. McLemore, *A History of Mississippi*, 2 vols. (Jackson: University and College Press of Mississippi, 1973); *Mississippi Official and Statistical Register* (Jackson: Secretary of State).

DAVID G. SANSING

CONNOR, GEORGE WHITFIELD (North Carolina, 1913) was born on October 24, 1872, in Wilson, North Carolina, to Henry Groves and Kate (Whitfield) Connor. His father was speaker of the North Carolina House in 1899 and a state Supreme Court justice. Educated in local public schools, he earned an A.B. *cum* *laude* from the University of North Carolina in 1892. Connor worked as a school principal in Goldsboro, North Carolina, before returning to Wilson. He studied law and began a private practice in 1899.

A conservative Democrat, Connor served Wilson as school superintendent (1894–97) and school board chair (1897–99). In 1900, 1910, and 1912 he won election to the North Carolina House of Representatives from Wilson County. While in office Connor unsuccessfully opposed ratification of the 16th Amendment to the U.S. Constitution creating a federal income tax. He was chosen as speaker for the 1913 session.

Appointed to the North Carolina Superior Court in 1913, Connor remained there until being named to the North Carolina Supreme Court in 1924. In addition, he was a trustee of the University of North Carolina and a member of the Masons and the Episcopal Church. He married Bessie Hadley in 1894, and the couple had four children. Connor still sat on the Supreme Court when he died of a heart attack on April 23, 1938, at age 65.

John L. Cheney, Jr., *North Carolina Government, 1585–1974: A Narrative and Statistical History* (Raleigh: North Carolina Department of the Secretary of State, 1975); Hugh Talmadge Lefler and Albert Ray Newsome, *The History of a Southern State: North Carolina* (Chapel Hill: University of North Carolina Press, 1973); William S. Powell, *North Carolina through Four Centuries* (Chapel Hill: University of North Carolina Press, 1989).

CLAUDE HARGROVE

COOKE, JOHN WARREN (Virginia, 1968, 1970, 1972, 1974, 1976, 1978) was born in Mathews, Virginia, on February 28, 1915. His father, Giles B. Cooke, served as an aide to Confederate General Robert E. Lee. Educated in local public and private schools, the younger Cooke attended the Virginia Military Institute in Lexington. Eventually he became publisher of the *Gloucester-Mathews Gazette-Journal*. He married Anne Brown Rawn.

A conservative Democrat, Cooke was deputy clerk of the Mathews County Court from 1936 to 1942. In 1941 he was elected to the Virginia House of Delegates. Cooke served nineteen consecutive terms, originally representing Mathews, Gloucester, and Middlesex counties and later Mathews, Charles City, Gloucester, Middlesex, and New Kent counties. Named majority leader in 1958, he opposed the enactment of a state sales tax until 1966. He remained close to the dominant Democratic faction led by U.S. Senator Harry F. Byrd, Sr., despite rejecting their policy of "massive resistance" to the U.S. Supreme Court decision against school segregation in *Brown v. Board of Education*.

Cooke was chosen as speaker for the 1968, 1970, 1972, 1974, 1976, and 1978 sessions. He gained a reputation for being innovative and fair-minded, appointing Republicans and Democrats outside the Byrd faction to influential committees. When the Citizens Conference on State Legislatures (CCSL) published a national study giving Virginia a very low rating, Cooke chaired a commission that successfully proposed installing modern computer systems and providing individual legislators with offices and staffs. The CCSL responded by awarding Cooke its national legislative leadership award in 1975.

Afterward Cooke returned to his newspaper. In addition, he was president of Tidewater Newspapers, Inc. Chair of the House of Delegates Ethics Advisory Panel, Cooke sat on the Commission on Virginia's Future (1982–84) and the Commision for the Preservation of the Capitol. He belonged to the Rotary and the Episcopal Church. Cooke continues to live in Mathews at this writing.

E. Griffith Dodson, ed., *Speakers and Clerks of the Virginia House of Delegates, 1776–1976*, rev. under the direction of Joseph H. Holleman, Jr. (Richmond, 1976), 120–143; Guy Friddell, "Cooke's Style: Fairness, Innovation," *Norfolk Virginian-Pilot*, March 8, 1979; Guy Friddell, "Cooke of Pud'n' Creek," *Norfolk Virginian-Pilot*, April 6, 1980; James Latimer, "Byrd Organization Man Became Legislative Innovator," *Richmond Times-Dispatch*, February 25, 1979.

JAMES R. SWEENEY

COOPER, WILLIAM PRENTICE (Tennessee, 1915) was born on September 27, 1870, in Henderson County, Kentucky, to James W. and Elizabeth A. (Royster) Cooper. Attending the Webb School in Bell Buckle, Tennessee, he received a law degree from Vanderbilt University in Nashville, Tennessee, in 1891. Cooper practiced law in Henderson County until 1902, when he moved to Shelbyville, Tennessee. He was president of the People's National Bank in Shelbyville and vice-president of both the Bank of Bell Buckle and the Huntsville Bank and Trust Company in Alabama. A Methodist, he married Argentine Shofner in 1894.

In 1914 Cooper was elected to the Tennessee House of Representatives as a Democrat from Bedford, Lincoln, and Moore counties. He was chosen as speaker for the 1915 term, his only one in the House. Returning to his business interests in Shelbyville, he was district governor of the Rotary in 1934–35. His son, William Prentice Cooper, Jr., was governor of Tennessee from 1939 to 1945. The elder Cooper died on July 4, 1961, at the age of 90.

Biographical file of Tennessee legislators, Tennessee State Library and Archives, Nashville; Philip M. Hamer, ed., *Tennessee: A History* (New York, 1933), IV: 488; *Lawmakers and Public Men of Tennessee* (Nashville, 1915), 67; Nashville *Banner*, January 4, 5, 1915, July 4, 1961.

FRED A. BAILEY

COTHRAN, THOMAS PERRIN (South Carolina, 1918, 1919, 1921) was born in Abbeville, South Carolina, on October 24, 1857, to James Sproull and Emma Chiles (Perrin) Cothran. Educated in local schools, he attended the University of Virginia. Cothran studied law and began a private practice in Abbeville in 1878. He later moved to Greenville, South Carolina, where he became a partner in the law firm of Cothran, Dean and Cothran. In addition, he was assistant division counsel for the Southern Railroad.

Cothran successfully ran for the South Carolina House of Representatives as a Democrat from Greenville County in 1904, 1906, 1908, 1914, 1916, 1918, and 1920. While in office he coauthored the Carey-Cothran Local Option Bill, which effectively abolished the much-abused state liquor monopoly established by Governor Benjamin R. Tillman. Following the resignation of incumbent James A. Hoyt, Cothran was chosen as speaker in January 1918. He was renamed to the speakership for the 1919 and 1921 sessions.

However, Cothran resigned from the House in January 1921 when he was appointed to the South Carolina Supreme Court. He was a member of the Masons, Odd Fellows, United American Mechanics, Kiwanis, and Presbyterian Church. In 1886 he married Ione Smith, who died a year later. Cothran died on April 11, 1934, at the age of 76.

WALTER B. EDGAR

COTTRELL, JOHN HALL, Jr. (Arkansas, 1965) was born in Shirley, Arkansas, on November 15, 1917, and moved with his family to Little Rock, Arkansas, in 1925. Attending Abilene Christian College in Texas, he earned an LL.B. from the University of Arkansas in 1941. During World War II Cottrell served with the U.S. Army in the Panama Canal Zone as head of the Criminal Investigation Division and as assistant provost marshal, rising to the rank of major. He then entered the insurance business in Little Rock. In 1950 Cottrell bought the United Loan Investment Company, a business founded by his father. A member of the Church of Christ, he married Mary Ann Burr; the couple had two sons.

Cottrell was elected to the Arkansas House of Representatives as a Democrat from Pulaski County in 1954. He served six consecutive terms, becoming vice-chair of the Rules Committee and chair of the Committee on Banks and Banking. After opposing a purge of Little Rock school employees by segregationists, Cottrell was appointed to that city's school board in 1959. His stance brought him into conflict with conservative Governor Orval E. Faubus.

Despite this, Cottrell maintained close ties to the governor's "Old Guard" faction and was Pulaski County campaign manager for Faubus in 1964. With the backing of the "Old Guard," he was named speaker for the 1965 session by defeating Ray S. Smith, Jr., in the first open floor fight in Arkansas since 1917. Cottrell lost reelection to the House to Paul Meers in 1966, and he was again defeated for the post two years later. Following that Cottrell returned to his Little Rock investment firm.

LEON C. MILLER

COX, EDWIN PIPER (Virginia, 1914) was born in Bland County, Virginia, on May 2, 1870. After attending private schools in Richmond, Virginia, and Prince Edward Academy in Worsham, Virginia, he earned a B.A. from Hampden-Sydney College in Virginia and an LL.B. from the University of Virginia. He then began practicing law in Richmond.

Cox was elected to the Virginia House of Delegates as a Democrat from the city of Richmond in 1903. Remaining there for six consecutive terms, he chaired the General Laws Committee and sat on a commission that examined public schools. In addition, Cox helped write major changes in the state tax code. He was chosen as speaker for the 1914 session.

Returning to his private practice, Cox served on the U.S. Selective Service Appeals Board during World War I. In 1924 he was appointed judge of Virginia's 4th Judicial Circuit Court. He was also grand commander of the Sons of Confederate Veterans, master of the Masons, and a member of the Episcopal Church. Cox still sat on the bench when he died in Richmond on March 11, 1938, at age 67.

E. Griffith Dodson, ed., *Speakers and Clerks of the Virginia House of Delegates, 1776–1976*, rev. under the direction of Joseph H. Holleman, Jr. (Richmond, 1976), 120–143; *History of Virginia* (Chicago: American Historical Society, 1924): IV–VI; *Richmond Times-Dispatch*, March 12, 1938.

JAMES R. SWEENEY

CRANK, MARION HARLAN (Arkansas, 1963) was born in Bearden, Arkansas, on February 18, 1915, to Julius Walrath and Mary (Hughes) Crank. As a child he moved with his family to Oklahoma. Earning a B.S. in agriculture from Oklahoma A&M University (now Oklahoma State University), he attended the University of Arkansas. Crank worked for the U.S. Farmers Home Administration in Dallas, Texas, and for the United Nations Relief and Rehabilitation Administration as chief agricultural officer in Hankow, China, following World War II. He then moved to Foreman, Arkansas, where he became a teacher and a farmer. In addition, he owned the Foreman Feed and Supply Company.

Crank was elected to the Arkansas House of Representatives as a Democrat from Little River County in 1950. Serving nine consecutive terms, he was named co-chair of the Joint Budget Committee in 1961 and speaker for the 1963 session. While in office Crank became identified as part of the "Old Guard" faction that supported conservative Governor Orval E. Faubus, although he denied the association. He chaired the Legislative Council in 1968, the same year he was defeated for governor of Arkansas by incumbent Republican Winthrop Rockefeller.

Afterward Crank returned to Foreman. An officer in several local development agencies, he was president of the Foreman Industrial Development Corporation and vice-president of the Arkansas Cement Corporation. He was also president of the Rotary and the Farm Bureau and a member of the Episcopal Church. Crank married Mary Pauline Yauger, and the couple had four children.

LEON C. MILLER

CRARY, EVANS, Sr. (Florida, 1945) was born in Tampa, Florida, on June 25, 1905. Educated in local public schools, he received a B.A. and an LL.B. (1927) from the University of Florida. Crary then moved to Stuart, Florida, where he began to practice law. He was married and had two sons.

A Democrat, Crary was a municipal judge in 1928–36, county attorney in

1931–37, and attorney to the county board of commissioners for twenty-three years. He won election to the Florida House of Representatives from Martin County in 1936 and served five consecutive terms. Crary was named speaker for the 1945 regular session and for an extra session later that year, the first in state history. During his speakership the legislature increased taxes on several items, created a small network of vocational schools, and approved a reapportionment bill.

Successfully running for the Florida Senate in 1946, Crary remained there until 1954. Afterward he returned to his Stuart law practice. He was president of the Rotary and Chamber of Commerce and a member of the Elks, Martin County Bar Association, and Methodist Church. Crary died on April 16, 1968, at the age of 62.

Paul S. George, *A Guide to the History of Florida* (Westport, CT: Greenwood Press, 1989); *Miami Daily News; Miami Herald; Tallahassee Democrat; Tampa Tribune.*

PAUL S. GEORGE

CROWE, ROBERT T. (Kentucky, 1918) was born in Ontario, Canada, on May 27, 1875, to William J. and Mary F. Crowe. He worked as a lumberjack in order to attend St. Lawrence Academy in New York and the State University of New York. Moving to La Grange, Kentucky, in 1897, Crowe was a member of a railroad gang while reading law. Afterward he began a private practice.

A Democrat, Crowe was Oldham County attorney from 1908 to 1914. He was elected to the Kentucky House of Representatives from Oldham and Trimble counties in 1915 and 1917, chairing the Court of Appeals Committee in his first term. Crowe was named speaker for the 1918 session. While in the post he prosecuted the impeachment of a county judge before the Kentucky Senate. In addition, he served as a special state counsel in an action to take control of land claimed by the Shakers.

Returning to his law practice, Crowe also sat on the La Grange school board. He was a presidential elector in 1920 and the state chair of his friend William G. McAdoo's unsuccessful 1924 campaign for president. In 1927 Crowe lost the Democratic nomination for governor of Kentucky to J. C. W. Beckham, despite having the support of Governor William J. Fields and the racing and coal industries. Outside of politics he was a master of the Masons and a member of the Methodist Church. He married Fannye Eastes in 1909, and the couple had two children. Crowe died on October 19, 1937, at the age of 62.

Malcolm E. Jewell and Everett W. Cunningham, *Kentucky Politics* (Lexington: University Press of Kentucky, 1968); Malcolm E. Jewell and Penny Miller, *The Kentucky Legislature: Two Decades of Change* (Lexington: University Press of Kentucky, 1988); Robert F. Sexton, "Kentucky Politics and Society, 1919–1932" (Ph.D. dissertation, University of Washington, 1970).

CAROL CROWE-CARRACO

CUMMINGS, JAMES HARVEY, II (Tennessee, 1967) was born in Woodbury, Tennessee, on November 8, 1890, to John Morgan and Lula (Land) Cummings. His grandfather, James Harvey Cummings, and his older brother were state legislators. Educated in local public and private schools, the younger Cummings earned an LL.B. from both the YMCA Law School in Nashville, Tennessee (1922) and Cumberland University in Lebanon, Tennessee (1923). Afterward he practiced law in Woodbury. In addition, Cummings belonged to the Elks, Knights of Pythias, Lions, and Farm Bureau. He married Hesta Harding McBroom in 1925; the couple had no children.

A Democrat, Cummings was clerk of the Cannon County Circuit Court from 1914 to 1922. He first won election to the Tennessee House of Representatives from Cannon County in 1930. Cummings then served additional terms in the House as well as the Tennessee Senate. From 1949 to 1952 he was Tennessee secretary of state. Again elected to the House in 1958, he remained there for seven consecutive terms and was named speaker for the 1967 session.

While in office Cummings gained a reputation for intelligence, shifting his alliances between factions of the state Democratic Party. He joined with Walter Haynes of Winchester and I. D. Beasley of Carthage to form a group often dubbed the ''unholy trinity'' by their opponents. Strongly supporting rural interests, Cummings fought against legislative reapportionment and backed educational improvement. In 1972 he retired from the House with the longest legislative tenure in Tennessee history. Cummings died on November 1, 1979, a week short of eighty-ninth birthday.

Biographical Directory, Tennessee General Assembly, 1796–1969 (Nashville: State Library and Archives); Lee Seifert Greene, David H. Grubbs, and Victor C. Hobday, *Government in Tennessee*, 4th ed. (Knoxville: University of Tennessee Press, 1982).

LEE S. GREENE

CUMMINS, JOHN WILLIAM (West Virginia, 1929) was born in Wheeling, West Virginia, on July 24, 1881, to John and Annie (Campbell) Cummins. Educated in local public schools, he received a B.A. from West Virginia University (1905) and an LL.B. from Georgetown University in Washington, D.C. (1907). Afterward Cummins began a law practice in Wheeling. He served as a first lieutenant in the U.S. Army Air Service during World War I.

Cummins won election to the West Virginia House of Delegates as a Republican from Ohio County in 1926 and remained there for three consecutive terms. In 1929 he was chosen as speaker. When the Democrats gained control of the House in 1931, Cummins was forced to step down from the speakership and to become minority leader. He was elected to one additional House term in 1938, and he again held the minority leadership for the 1939 session.

In other affairs Cummins was exalted leader of the Elks, commander of the American Legion, and a member of the Kiwanis and United Workmen. He sat on the board of the American Legislature Association. A Catholic, he was married to Jean Welty in 1912 and later to Bess Hybart. Cummins died on December 27, 1965, at the age of 84.

ROBERT L. HUNT

CUNNINGHAM, ERNEST G. (Arkansas, 1987) was born on July 4, 1936, in Helena, Arkansas. Educated in local public schools, he earned a degree in accounting and business administration from the University of Arkansas in 1958. Cunningham then served in the U.S. Army's Finance Corps for two years. He became co-owner of the Cunningham Gas Company, and he belonged to the Chamber of Commerce. An Episcopalian, he married Cathy Martin; the couple had two children.

In 1968 Cunningham was elected to the Arkansas House of Representatives as a Democrat from Helena and Phillips counties. Chosen as speaker for the 1987 session, he focused on promoting agriculture, economic development, and educational reform. He was majority leader in 1989. Cunningham continues to serve in the House at this writing.

GINA PETONITO

CURTIS, FRANCIS P. (Maryland, 1924) was born in Baltimore, Maryland, on July 18, 1866. He studied law while working for his father's produce business. Curtis then began a private practice in Baltimore. A Catholic, he was married and belonged to the Knights of Columbus.

In 1899 Curtis won election to one term in the Maryland House of Delegates as a Democrat from the city of Baltimore. He was affiliated with the party machines of Isaac F. Rasin, John J. Mahon, and John S. Kelly, becoming an assessor for the Appeal Tax Court and a member of the Baltimore City Council (1911–15). Again elected to the House in 1915, Curtis served five consecutive terms and was named speaker for the 1924 session. Afterward he sat on the Baltimore Board of Commissioners for Opening Streets. Curtis died on February 7, 1933, at the age of 66.

GARY L. BROWNE

D

DANIEL, J. T. (Oklahoma, 1937) was born on December 21, 1893, in Poetry, Texas, and moved with his family to Ryan, Oklahoma. He earned degrees from East Texas Normal College (now Texas A&M University at Commerce), North Texas State Teachers College (now the University of North Texas) in Denton, and the University of Oklahoma. For eleven years Daniel was a teacher and a school superintendent in Stoneburg, Texas, and Terral and Ringling, Oklahoma. A Baptist, he was married.

Daniel was elected to the Oklahoma House of Representatives as a Democrat from Jefferson County in 1926, 1928, 1930, 1932, 1936, and 1940. Named majority floor leader in 1931, he was chosen as speaker for the 1937 session with the support of Governor E. W. Marland. He later sat on the Jefferson County Court.

In 1939 Daniel became publisher and editor of the Ryan *Leader*. Convicted of income tax evasion, he spent eight months in federal prison. He was reinstated to the state bar by the Oklahoma Supreme Court over the protest of the Oklahoma Bar Association. Daniel died on January 1, 1965, at the age of 71.

TIMOTHY A. ZWINK

DANIEL, MARION PRICE, Jr. (Texas, 1973) was born in Austin, Texas, on June 8, 1941, to Marion Price and Jean Houston (Baldwin) Daniel. His father was Texas speaker in 1943 as well as state attorney general, U.S. senator, governor, and Supreme Court justice. Daniel moved with his family to Liberty, Texas, and Washington, D.C. Graduating from high school in Austin, he earned a B.B.A. (1964) and an LL.B. (1966) from Baylor University in Waco, Texas. While in college Daniel operated a rare book business by mail. He then began a law practice in Liberty.

A Democrat, Daniel was Liberty County justice of the peace in 1966–67. He was elected to the Texas House of Representatives from Liberty, Polk, San Jacinto, Trinity, and Tyler counties in 1968 and served three consecutive terms.

Daniel was chosen as speaker for the 1973 session, when over half of the 150 House members were new to their seats as a result of the Sharpstown financial scandal and redistricting. This turnover led to the passage of ethics and financial disclosure laws, more stringent regulations on lobbyists, a revision of open meetings laws, and a new open records act. In 1974 the legislature reconvened as the first state constitutional convention in almost a century, and Daniel was named its president.

Returning to his Liberty practice, Daniel lost the Democratic nomination for attorney general of Texas in 1978. He was a professor of government and law at the University of Houston, Texas Southern University, and South Texas College of Law. In addition, Daniel belonged to the Rotary, Jaycees, Liberty County and Chambers County bar associations, and Texas Trial Lawyers Association. A Methodist, he married Diane Wommack in 1966; the couple had one son. Daniel died in Liberty on January 19, 1981, after being shot by his second wife, Vicki Moore Daniel. He was 39.

LUTHER G. HAGARD, JR.

DANIEL, MARION PRICE, Sr. (Texas, 1943) was one of the most famous politicians in Texas history. He was born in Dayton, Texas, on October 10, 1910, to Marion Price and Nannie (Partlow) Daniel. Educated in public schools, he earned a B.A. in journalism (1931) and an LL.B. (1932) from Baylor University in Waco, Texas. After that Daniel began a law practice in Liberty, Texas. In addition, he was publisher of the *Liberty Vindicator* and the *Anahuac Progress*.

Daniel won election to the Texas House of Representatives as a Democrat from Liberty and Hardin counties in 1938 and served three consecutive terms. He was unanimously named speaker for the 1943 session when he was only 32. During World War II he served in the U.S. Army's Judge Advocate General's Corps, rising to the rank of captain. Attorney general of Texas in 1947–52, Daniel argued to uphold a law excluding black applicants from state educational institutions on the grounds that conflict would result "if the races got too close together." The U.S. Supreme Court declared the law unconstitutional in the case of *Sweatt v. Painter* in 1950.

Elected to the U.S. Senate from Texas in 1952, Daniel gained a reputation for speaking his mind and occasionally breaking party ranks. In 1956 he successfully ran for governor of Texas. While in the governorship Daniel led campaigns against pornography, drug trafficking, and legalized gambling, and he attempted to improve public education and water conservation. He was defeated for reelection in the 1962 Democratic primary by John Connally.

Daniel then returned to his private practice in Liberty. He was a delegate to the 1968 Democratic National Convention, the director of the U.S. Office of Emergency Planning, and a member of the Texas Supreme Court from 1970 to 1979. In addition, Daniel belonged to the Masons and the American and Texas bar associations. A Baptist, he married Jean Houston Baldwin; the couple had four children. His son, Marion Price Daniel, Jr., was speaker of the Texas House in 1973. The elder Daniel died on August 25, 1988, at the age of 77.

RICHARD B. RILEY

DAVID, THOMAS E. "Ted" (Florida, 1955) was born in Comer, Georgia, on April 2, 1920, and moved with his family to Hollywood, Florida, at age 3. Attending local public schools and the Riverside Military Academy in Hollywood, he earned a degree in business administration from the University of Georgia. During World War II David served as a captain in the U.S. Army. He then received a law degree with honors from the University of Miami in Florida and began a private practice in Hollywood.

While still in law school, David was elected to the Florida House of Representatives as a Democrat from Broward County in 1948. He served four consecutive terms. David was named speaker for the 1955 regular session and the special sessions of 1955 and 1956. During those sessions the House unsuccessfully sought to reapportion itself in favor of underrepresented southern Florida and failed to resolve the matter of school desegregation following the U.S. Supreme Court's decision in *Brown v. Board of Education*.

Losing races for governor of Florida in 1960 and 1964, David returned to his law practice and business concerns. He was attorney for the Broward County school board for ten years and a trustee of Florida Presbyterian (now Eckerd) College. In addition, David sat on the commission that revised the Florida Constitution in 1968.

JERRELL H. SHOFNER

DAVIS, FRED HENRY (Florida, 1927) was born in Greenville, South Carolina, on May 18, 1894, and moved with his family to Tallahassee, Florida, in 1907. Educated in public schools, he read law in the Florida Supreme Court Library and began a private practice in Tallahassee. During World War I Davis served in the U.S. armed forces. He belonged to the Masons, Elks, Odd Fellows, and Sons of the Confederacy.

A Democrat, Davis was Wakulla County attorney and Leon County prosecutor from 1919 to 1925. He won election to the Florida House of Representatives from Leon County in 1920 and remained there for four consecutive terms. Davis was chosen as speaker for the 1927 session, but he resigned from the House later that year to become state attorney general. In 1931 he successfully ran for the Florida Supreme Court. Appointed chief justice in 1933, Davis still held that post when he died on June 26, 1937, at age 43.

Robert J. Huckshorn, ed., *Government and Politics in Florida* (Gainesville: University of Florida Press, 1991); Allen Morris, *The Florida Handbook* (Tallahassee: Peninsular Publishing, 1947–).

GEORGE E. POZZETTA

DAWSON, JOHN GILMER (North Carolina, 1923) was born in Lenoir County, North Carolina, on April 19, 1882. Educated in local public schools, he earned an A.B. and an LL.B. from the University of North Carolina. Dawson then began a law practice in Kinston, North Carolina. He was married.

A Democrat, Dawson was city attorney of Kinston from 1914 to 1924. He successfully ran for the North Carolina House of Representatives from Lenoir County in 1918 and served three consecutive terms. Dawson was named speaker for the regular session of 1923 and the 1924 special session. Chair of the state Democratic Party, he was a presidential elector in 1948 and won election to the North Carolina Senate in 1956.

In the 1930s Dawson helped organized seven radio stations in southeastern North Carolina. He was also president of the Society of Cincinnati, a trustee of the University of North Carolina, and a member of the Masons, Odd Fellows, American Bar Association, and Episcopal Church. Dawson died on January 18, 1966, at the age of 83.

John L. Cheney, Jr., *North Carolina Government, 1585–1974: A Narrative and Statistical History* (Raleigh: North Carolina Department of the Secretary of State, 1975); Hugh Talmadge Lefler and Albert Ray Newsome, *The History of a Southern State: North Carolina* (Chapel Hill: University of North Carolina Press, 1973); William S. Powell, *North Carolina through Four Centuries* (Chapel Hill: University of North Carolina Press, 1989).

CLAUDE HARGROVE

DELONY, VAIL MONTGOMERY (Louisiana, 1964) was born in East Carroll Parish, Louisiana, in 1901. Educated in public schools, he earned a degree from a local business college. Delony then became a farmer and contractor in Lake Providence, Louisiana. In addition, he was president of the Lake Providence Savings and Loan Association. He was married, and he belonged to the Episcopal Church.

A Democrat, Delony was mayor of Lake Providence. In 1939 he won election to the Louisiana House of Representatives from East Carroll Parish. He served seven consecutive four-year terms and was named speaker for the 1964 session. While in office Delony worked closely with Governors John J. McKeithen and Jimmie H. Davis. As a result of his strong support of road improvement legislation, he became known as "Mr. Highway." Delony still held the speakership when he died on November 18, 1967.

Edwin Adams Davis, *The Story of Louisiana* (New Orleans: J. F. Hyer, 1960).

BEATRICE R. OWSLEY

DICKSON, STANLEY S. (Kentucky, 1942) was born in Bourbon County, Kentucky, on July 30, 1897. Attending Centre College in Danville, Kentucky, and Princeton University, he served in the U.S. Army during World War I. Afterward he became a tobacco farmer in Paris, Kentucky. Dickson belonged to the American Legion and the Christian Church (Disciples of Christ), a denomination that had originated in Bourbon County during the nineteenth century. He married Mildred Collins in 1921, and the couple had two children.

A Democrat, Dickson won election to the Kentucky House of Representatives from Bourbon County in 1933, 1935, 1939, and 1941. He was named speaker for the 1942 regular session and the special session later that year. During Dickson's speakership the legislature enacted two landmark bills requested by Governor Keen Johnson. One bill authorized the first legislative redistricting in Kentucky since 1893; the other permitted cities to purchase low cost electricity from the Tennessee Valley Authority. Dickson died in Paris on November 16, 1973, at the age of 76.

Louisville *Courier-Journal; Kentucky Directory for the Use of the Courts, State and County Officials and General Assembly of the State of Kentucky* (Frankfort, KY: 1914–); John E. Kleber, ed., *The Kentucky Encyclopedia* (Lexington: University Press of Kentucky, 1992); Penny M. Miller, *Kentucky Politics and Government* (Lincoln: University of Nebraska Press, 1994); Robert F. Sexton, ed., *The Public Papers of the Governors of Kentucky* (Lexington: University Press of Kentucky, 1975).

ROGER TATE

DIMOS, JIMMY N. (Louisiana, 1988) was born on October 18, 1938. Educated in public schools, he earned a B.A. from Northeast Louisiana State University in Monroe in 1960 and a J.D. from Tulane University in New Orleans, Louisiana, in 1963. Dimos then began a law practice in Monroe, and he served in the U.S. Army Reserve. He was president of Northeast Louisiana's Alumni Association, vice-president of the Optimists, and a member of the Jaycees. An Episcopalian, he married Gale Guilkey; the couple had four children.

In 1975 Dimos was elected to the Louisiana House of Representatives as a Democrat from Ouachita Parish. While in office he emphasized issues involving the budget and appropriations, economic development, and education. He was chosen as speaker for the 1988 session. Dimos then stepped down from the speakership, but he remains in the House at this writing.

GINA PETONITO

DORAN, ADRON (Kentucky, 1950) was born on September 1, 1909, in Weakley County, Tennessee. Attending Tennessee public schools and Freed-Hardeman College in Jackson, Tennessee, he received a B.S. from Murray State Teachers College (now University) in Kentucky in 1932. Doran was then a teacher, school principal, and minister of the Church of Christ in Wingo, Kentucky. He married Magnon McClain in 1941.

In 1943 Doran won election to the Kentucky House of Representatives as a Democrat from Calloway County. He remained there for four consecutive terms and was chosen as speaker for the 1950 session. During his speakership the legislature successfully defied Democratic Governor Earle C. Clements on several occasions.

Earning an Ed.D. from the University of Kentucky in 1950, Doran was president of Morehead State College (now University) in Kentucky from 1954 to

1977. Afterward he became an evangelist for his church. He also belonged to the Kiwanis. Doran lives in Lexington, Kentucky, at this writing.

Louisville *Courier-Journal; Kentucky Directory for the Use of the Courts, State and County Officials and General Assembly of the State of Kentucky* (Frankfort, KY: 1914–   ); John E. Kleber, ed., *The Kentucky Encyclopedia* (Lexington: University Press of Kentucky, 1992); Penny M. Miller, *Kentucky Politics and Government* (Lincoln: University of Nebraska Press, 1994); Robert F. Sexton, ed., *The Public Papers of the Governors of Kentucky* (Lexington: University Press of Kentucky, 1975).

ROGER TATE

DOUGHTON, JAMES KEMP (North Carolina, 1957) was born in Sparta, North Carolina, on May 18, 1884, to Rufus Alexander and Sue (Parks) Doughton. His father was North Carolina speaker in 1891 as well as lieutenant governor. The younger Doughton attended local public schools, the Oak Ridge Military Academy in North Carolina, and the University of North Carolina. Briefly working as a teacher at Oak Ridge, he moved to Raleigh, North Carolina, around 1906. Doughton was later a banker in Winston-Salem, Salisbury, and Washington, North Carolina. He belonged to the Methodist Church.

A Democrat, Doughton served in the North Carolina treasurer's office and was state bank examiner. Afterward he was chief bank examiner for the U.S. Federal Reserve in Atlanta, Georgia, and Richmond, Virginia. Doughton moved to Baltimore, Maryland, in 1933 to chair the board of the Federal Land Bank and the Federal Intermediate Credit Bank. Returning to Sparta in 1946, he bought farm land. He also became a trust officer of the Northwestern Bank in North Wilkesboro, North Carolina.

In 1948 Doughton was elected to the North Carolina House of Representatives from Alleghany County. Remaining there for five consecutive terms, he was named chair of the Appropriations Committee in 1953 and speaker for the 1957 session. He was married in 1910 to Josephine Brown, with whom he had three children, and in 1950 to Ivey Doughton, a distant cousin. Doughton died in 1972 at the age of 88.

OTIENO OKELO

DOUGLAS, JAMES STUART (Louisiana, 1924) was born in Mansfield, Louisiana, on July 29, 1876. His father was a state legislator. Educated in local schools, the younger Douglas moved to Caddo Parish, Louisiana, in 1897. He worked in a plantation store before heading the mercantile firm of J. S. Douglas and Company. In addition, he was the owner of a cotton plantation, a partner in a contracting firm in Shreveport, Louisiana, and president of the First State Bank in Belcher, Louisiana. He was married, and he belonged to the Ku Klux Klan and the Presbyterian Church.

Douglas was elected to the Louisiana House of Representatives as a Democrat from Caddo Parish in 1915 and served three consecutive four-year terms. Despite strong legislative opposition as a result of his Klan affiliation, he was named speaker for the 1924 session with the backing of Governor Henry L. Fuqua. While in office Douglas worked to curb Klan power and supported bills concerning labor, charitable institutions, and child welfare. His reputation for hard work earned him respect as well as the nickname "Old Taskmaster." Douglas still held the speakership when he died on September 20, 1924, at age 48.

Henry E. Chambers, *A History of Louisiana: Wilderness—Colony—Province—Territory—State—People* (Chicago: American Historical Society, 1925); Edwin Adams Davis, *The Story of Louisiana* (New Orleans: J. F. Hyer, 1960).

BEATRICE R. OWSLEY

DOVELL, GROVER ASHTON (Virginia, 1936, 1938, 1940) was born on June 8, 1885, in Madison County, Virginia. Educated in local schools, he received a B.A. from the College of William and Mary in Williamsburg, Virginia (1908) and an LL.B. from the University of Virginia (1912). Dovell briefly practiced law in Tacoma, Washington, before settling in Williamsburg. He trained to be a U.S. Army officer during World War I.

A Democrat, Dovell successfully ran for commonwealth's attorney of James City County and Williamsburg in 1920. In 1923 he was elected to the Virginia House of Delegates from the city of Williamsburg and Charles City, James City, New Kent, and York counties. Dovell served nine consecutive terms and was named speaker from the 1936, 1938, and 1940 sessions. Highly regarded as an orator and parliamentarian, he took a particular interest in public education. He also spent twelve years as chair of a committee that monitored state welfare institutions.

Afterward Dovell's progressive views led to a break with the conservative Democratic faction led by Harry F. Byrd, Sr. Losing the Democratic nomination to the U.S. House of Representatives from Virginia in 1945, Dovell supported Byrd's opponent in the 1946 U.S. Senate primary. Outside of politics he was president of the Rotary and the Virginia Bar Association, a trustee of Colonial Williamsburg, and a member of the Masons, American Legion, American Bar Association, and Episcopal Church. Dovell died on October 28, 1949, at the age of 64.

E. Griffith Dodson, ed., *Speakers and Clerks of the Virginia House of Delegates, 1776–1976*, rev. under the direction of Joseph H. Holleman, Jr. (Richmond, 1976), 120–143; *Norfolk Virginian-Pilot*, October 29, 1949; *Richmond Times-Dispatch*, October 29, 1949; *Virginia Gazette*, November 4, 1949.

JAMES R. SWEENEY

DOWD, WILLIAM CAREY (North Carolina, 1911) was born on March 21, 1865, in Moore County, North Carolina. Educated at the Carolina Military Institute, he earned an A.B. from Wake Forest College (now University) in North Carolina in 1889. Dowd then moved to Charlotte, North Carolina, where he became publisher of *The Charlotte News*. He was married.

A Democrat, Dowd successfully ran for the North Carolina Senate in 1894. In addition, he was a delegate to the 1896 and 1900 Democratic national conventions and a presidential elector in 1900 and 1908. Dowd was elected to the North Carolina House of Representatives from Mecklenburg County in 1906 and served four consecutive terms. He was chosen as speaker for the 1911 session.

In 1914 Dowd left the House, returning to his Charlotte newpaper. President of the North Carolina Press Association, he belonged to the Masons, Odd Fellows, Rotary, Chamber of Commerce, and Baptist Church. He was also a trustee of the University of North Carolina. Dowd died on September 23, 1927, at the age of 62.

John L. Cheney, Jr., *North Carolina Government, 1585–1974: A Narrative and Statistical History* (Raleigh: North Carolina Department of the Secretary of State, 1975); Hugh Talmadge Lefler and Albert Ray Newsome, *The History of a Southern State: North Carolina* (Chapel Hill: University of North Carolina Press, 1973); William S. Powell, *North Carolina through Four Centuries* (Chapel Hill: University of North Carolina Press, 1989).

CLAUDE HARGROVE

DRAKE, THOMAS E. (Alabama, 1983) was born on December 5, 1930, in Falkville, Alabama, and later moved with his family to Cullman, Alabama. Educated in local public schools, he earned a B.S. from the University of Chattanooga (now the University of Tennessee at Chattanooga) in 1953. Drake received an M.Ed. (1960) and an LL.B. (1963) from the University of Alabama, and he then began a law practice in Cullman. He served in the U.S. Army.

In 1962 Drake successfully ran for the Alabama House of Representatives as a Democrat from Cullman and Morgan counties. He remained there for four consecutive four-year terms. Again elected to the House in 1982, Drake was named speaker for the 1983 session. After that he stepped down from the speakership.

Drake sat on the Alabama Space and Rocket Exhibit Commission and the advisory boards of Snead State Junior College in Boaz, Alabama, and George C. Wallace State Community College in Hanceville, Alabama. He was a member of the Masons, Elks, Moose, American Legion, American Bar Association, American Trial Lawyers Association, and American Judicature Society. A Baptist, he married Christine McCoy; the couple had four children. As of this writing Drake remains in the House.

GINA PETONITO

DRAPER, DANIEL DAVID, Jr. (Oklahoma, 1979, 1981, 1983) was born near Tahlequah, Oklahoma, on April 12, 1940. His father was a state representative. Earning a B.S. in accounting from Oklahoma State University in 1961, the younger Draper studied law at the University of Oklahoma and received an LL.B. from George Washington University in Washington, D.C., in 1964. While at George Washington he was a clerk for the secretary of the U.S. Senate. Draper then began a law practice in Stillwater, Oklahoma. He was married.

In 1970 Draper was elected to the Oklahoma House of Representatives as a Democrat from Payne County. He served seven consecutive terms. Chosen as speaker for the 1979, 1981, and 1983 sessions, he presided during years of economic growth due to the revival of the oil and gas industry. While in the speakership Draper helped dramatically increase state funding for education, mental health, and capital improvements in various governmental institutions. Political analysts often gave him more credit than the governor for setting the legislative agenda.

Convicted of conspiracy and mail fraud in 1983, Draper was expelled from the House. A federal judge overturned the ruling due to perjury, and Draper was reinstated to his House seat in 1984. Later that year he declined to seek reelection.

Outside of politics Draper was state vice-president of the Jaycees, president of the Chamber of Commerce and the Stillwater Bar Association, and chair of the March of Dimes. Draper also belonged to the Oklahoma Bar Association and the Christian Church (Disciples of Christ).

KENNY L. BROWN

DRURY, GEORGE LUCIAN (Kentucky, 1926) was born on December 12, 1875, in Union County, Kentucky, to George H. and Ellen (Harris) Drury. Educated in local public schools, he briefly worked as a teacher before earning a law degree from the University of Louisville in Kentucky in 1899. Drury then began a private law practice with his brother in Morganfield, Kentucky. He was also a farmer and a businessman. A Catholic, he married Margaret Hite in 1906.

Drury won election to the Kentucky House of Representatives as a Democrat from Union County in 1911, 1921, 1923, and 1925, and he was chosen as speaker for the 1926 session. Afterward he returned to practicing law. In addition, he belonged to the Kiwanis and the Knights of Columbus. Recognized as a historian, philosopher, poet, and humorist, Drury died on February 21, 1940. He was 64.

Malcolm E. Jewell and Everett W. Cunningham, *Kentucky Politics* (Lexington: University Press of Kentucky, 1968); Malcolm E. Jewell and Penny Miller, *The Kentucky Legislature: Two Decades of Change* (Lexington: University Press of Kentucky, 1988); Robert F. Sexton, "Kentucky Politics and Society, 1919–1932" (Ph.D. dissertation, University of Washington, 1970).

NANCY DISHER BAIRD

DUFFY, HUGH CORNELIUS (Kentucky, 1916) was born in 1854 in Gallatin, Tennessee, to Michael and Cornelia (Read) Duffy. Educated in private schools, he earned a degree from the University of Virginia. Duffy then moved to Cynthiana, Kentucky, where he practiced law and bred horses and livestock. In addition, he belonged to the Harrison County Bar Association. He married Fannie Desha, the daughter of a Confederate general, and the couple had six children.

A Democrat, Duffy was elected to the Kentucky House of Representatives from Harrison County in 1909, 1913, 1915, 1919, 1921, and 1923. He was named speaker by acclamation for the 1916 session. In 1922 he withdrew his name from consideration for the speakership. Duffy died of a cerebral hemorrhage on July 22, 1941.

Malcolm E. Jewell and Everett W. Cunningham, *Kentucky Politics* (Lexington: University Press of Kentucky, 1968); Malcolm E. Jewell and Penny Miller, *The Kentucky Legislature: Two Decades of Change* (Lexington: University Press of Kentucky, 1988); Robert F. Sexton, "Kentucky Politics and Society, 1919–1932" (Ph.D. dissertation, University of Washington, 1970).

CAROL CROWE-CARRACO

DURANT, WILLIAM ALEXANDER (Oklahoma, 1911) was born on March 18, 1866, in Bennington, Indian Territory (now Oklahoma). His parents, Sylvester and Martha Durant, were each half Choctaw Indian. From 1881 to 1919 he lived in Durant, Indian Territory (now Oklahoma), a town named for his family. Educated in Choctaw Nation schools, Durant earned an M.A. from Presbyterian College in Batesville, Arkansas, in 1886. For seven years he was an attorney for the Missouri, Kansas and Texas Railroad. Durant belonged to the Masons, Elks, Knights of Pythias, and Presbyterian Church. He married Ida May Corber in 1892, and the couple had three children.

A Democrat, Durant was superintendent of Jones Academy in Hartshorne, Indian Territory (now Oklahoma). In addition, he served the Choctaw Nation as inspector of academies, special judge, and speaker of the National Council (1891). Durant attended the 1896 and 1904 Democratic national conventions. He sat on the Durant City Council in 1902 and was a delegate and an assistant sergeant-at-arms at the 1906–07 Oklahoma Constitutional Convention.

Oklahoma achieved statehood in 1907, and Durant was elected to the Oklahoma House of Representatives from Bryan County. He remained there for five consecutive terms and was named speaker for the 1911 session with the support of Governor Lee Cruce. Leaving the House in 1916, Durant was an oil and gas agent for the Oklahoma School Land Office for five years and secretary of the Oklahoma School Land Commission for six years. In 1934 he was appointed principal chief of the Choctaw Nation. Durant died in Tuskahoma, Oklahoma, on August 1, 1948, at the age of 82.

GORDON MOORE

E

EDGE, L. DAY (Florida, 1923) was born in Glennville, Georgia, on November 21, 1891, and moved with his family to Groveland, Florida, in 1900. Attending local public schools and Stetson University in De Land, Florida, he earned a degree from Southern College in Sutherland, Florida, in 1913. Edge studied law at the University of Florida for a year. He then began operating mercantile and turpentine businesses in Groveland.

A Democrat, Edge successfully ran for the Florida House of Representatives from Lake County in 1914 when he was only 22. He remained there for five consecutive terms. While in the House he was noted for an interest in issues concerning forestry, naval stores, and road improvement. Edge was named speaker *pro tem* in 1921 and speaker for the 1923 session. In 1924 he won election to one term in the Florida Senate.

Returning to his Groveland business interests, Edge also became a rancher. He was one of the first individuals in Florida to raise large numbers of Brahman cattle. In addition, he served Groveland as mayor and as a member of the city council. Edge died on December 6, 1971, at the age of 80.

Robert J. Huckshorn, ed., *Government and Politics in Florida* (Gainesville: University of Florida Press, 1991); Allen Morris, *The Florida Handbook* (Tallahassee: Peninsular Publishing, 1947–).

GEORGE E. POZZETTA

ELLENDER, ALLEN JOSEPH (Louisiana, 1932) was born in Montegut, Louisiana, on September 24, 1890. Earning a B.A. from St. Aloysius College in New Orleans, Louisiana, he received an M.A. (1909) and an LL.B. (1913) from Tulane University in New Orleans. Ellender then began a law practice in Houma, Louisiana. During World War I he served in the U.S. Army's artillery corps.

A Democrat, Ellender was Houma city attorney in 1913–15 and district attorney of Terrebonne Parish in 1915–16. He was a delegate to the 1921 Louisiana Constitutional Convention. Ellender won election to the Louisiana House of Representatives from Terrebonne Parish in 1923 and remained there for four consecutive four-year terms. While in office he supported Governor Huey P. Long. Majority floor leader in 1928, Ellender was named speaker for the 1932 session. He survived a 1934 attempt to oust him from the speakership. In addition, he managed successful U.S. Senate bids by Long in 1930 and John H. Overton in 1932.

Elected to the U.S. Senate from Louisiana in 1936, Ellender served six consecutive terms and became that body's president *pro tem* in 1971. Outside of politics he belonged to the Catholic Church. He married Helen Calhoun Donnelly, and the couple had one son. Ellender was still a U.S. senator when he died on July 27, 1972, at age 81.

Membership in the Legislature of Louisiana, 1880–1980 (Baton Rouge, 1979).

RAYMOND O. NUSSBAUM

ELLIOTT, ELMER B. (Florida, 1951) was born in Texas in 1903, and he moved to Palm Beach County, Florida, in 1922. A vegetable farmer, he also began operating an automobile dealership in Pahokee, Florida, during the 1930s. Elliott obtained several contracts to plant Australian pines along the Palm Beach Canal. He was exalted ruler of the Elks and a member of the Masons and the Methodist Church.

In 1944 Elliott was elected to the Florida House of Representatives as a Democrat from Palm Beach County. Serving four consecutive terms, he was chosen as speaker for the 1951 session. He then returned to his business interests. Elliott died of cancer around 1960.

JERRELL H. SHOFNER

EVANS, RANDALL, Jr. (Georgia, 1941) was born on May 3, 1906, in Thomson, Georgia, where he attended public schools. He received a degree from Maynard's Law School in 1925 and began a private law practice in Macon, Georgia. Later Evans returned to Thomson. A Baptist, he was married.

Evans won election to the Georgia House of Representatives as a Democrat from McDuffie County in 1930 and 1932 and the Georgia Senate in 1934. Concurrently he was mayor, city attorney of Thomson, and attorney of McDuffie County. Again elected to the House in 1936, Evans served three consecutive terms. He was named speaker for the 1941 session. In 1969 he was appointed to the Georgia Court of Appeals. Evans retired from the bench in 1976.

AMOS ST. GERMAIN

F

FARRIS, ION L. (Florida, 1913; also 1909) was a Democrat from Marion County. He served as speaker of the Florida House of Representatives for the 1913 session, having previously presided in 1909.

Charles F. Ritter and Jon L. Wakelyn, *American Legislative Leaders, 1850–1910* (New York: Greenwood Press, 1989), 223.

KEVIN G. ATWATER

FITE, ERNEST RANKIN (Alabama, 1955, 1967) was born in Montgomery, Alabama, on September 1, 1916, to Ernest Baxter and Minnie (Pierce) Fite. His father, uncle, and cousin sat in the state House. Raised in Hamilton, Alabama, he attended local public schools and the Starke University School in Montgomery. Fite earned an LL.B. from the University of Alabama in 1939 and began a law practice in Hamilton. During World War II he served with the U.S. Army Air Forces in the European theater, rising to the rank of first lieutenant.

A Democrat, Fite successfully ran for the Alabama Senate in 1946. He was elected to the Alabama House of Representatives in 1950, 1954, 1962, 1966, and 1970, representing Marion County until 1966 and Marion and Winston counties thereafter. Fite was chosen as speaker for the 1955 session with the support of Governor James E. Folsom. Speaker *pro tem* in 1963, he was again named to the speakership in 1967 under Governor Lurleen Wallace. While in the post he used his parliamentary skills and his fiery oratory to become one of the legislature's most powerful and controversial leaders.

Declining to seek reelection to the House in 1974 as a result of ill health, Fite returned to his Hamilton practice. He also sat on the Alabama Oil and Gas Board, Alabama Board of Education, and Tennessee-Tombigbee Waterway Development Authority. In 1955 Fite became president of the Marion County Banking Company. A Methodist, he married Ruby Morris in 1941; the couple had one son. Fite died of an apparent heart attack on November 6, 1980, at age 64.

Alabama Official and Statistical Register (Montgomery: State of Alabama, Department of Archives and History, 1903–   ); Frank L. Grove, ed., *Library of Alabama Lives* (Hopkinsville, KY: Historical Records Association, 1961); Murray C. Havens, *City versus Farm: Urban-Rural Conflict in the Alabama Legislature* (University, AL: Bureau of Public Administration, University of Alabama, 1957); Henry S. Marks, *Alabama Past Leaders* (Huntsville: Strode Publishers, 1982); John C. Stewart, *The Governors of Alabama* (Gretna, LA: Pelican Publishing Company, 1975); *Who's Who in Alabama* (Birmingham: Sayers Enterprises, 1965–   ).

REID BADGER

FITZPATRICK, THOMAS P. (Kentucky, 1956) was born in Covington, Kentucky, on March 2, 1894. Graduating from local Catholic schools, he worked as an insurance agent in Covington. Fitzpatrick served in the U.S. Army during World War I. He was married, and he belonged to the Eagles and the Knights of Columbus.

As a youth Fitzpatrick was a featherweight prize fighter who won his first eighteen bouts. However, a loss in his last fight convinced him to enter what he labeled the more benign field of politics. Fitzpatrick became a precinct leader of the Democratic Party in 1916. Winning election to the Kentucky House of Representatives from Kenton County in 1933, he served five consecutive terms. He successfully ran for mayor of Covington in 1942 and for sheriff of Campbell County three years later.

In 1953 Fitzpatrick was again elected to the House. Remaining there for another five consecutive terms, he was named speaker for the 1956 session under progressive Governor A. B. Chandler. His help in passing legislation initiated by Chandler gained Fitzpatrick the governor's support for his own projects. Among these were bills giving more power to local governments and allowing cities to set hours for beer and whiskey sales. Fitzpatrick was still a member of the House when he died on June 22, 1962, at age 68.

Malcolm E. Jewell, *Representation in State Legislatures* (Lexington: University Press of Kentucky, 1982); Malcolm E. Jewell and Everett W. Cunningham, *Kentucky Politics* (Lexington: University Press of Kentucky, 1968); Malcolm E. Jewell and Penny Miller, *The Kentucky Legislature: Two Decades of Change* (Lexington: University Press of Kentucky, 1988); Malcolm E. Jewell and Samuel C. Patterson, *The Legislative Process in the United States*, 4th ed. (New York: Random House, 1986); John Ed Pearce, *Divide and Dissent: Kentucky Politics, 1930–1963* (Lexington: University Press of Kentucky, 1987); Seymour Sher, "Conditions for Legislative Control," *Journal of Politics* 25 (1963), 526–551.

H. LEW WALLACE

FLANNERY, W. E. "Bill" (West Virginia, 1949, 1951, 1953, 1955, 1957) was born on August 6, 1904, in Jacobs, Kentucky, and raised on a farm in Elliott County, Kentucky. He attended local elementary schools, and he claimed never to have seen a paved road or a train while growing up. Afterward Flannery moved to West Virginia, where he worked on a railroad. A Methodist, he married Mildred Burton Davis in 1922.

Flannery eventually saved enough money to attend Morehead State Teachers College (now University) in Kentucky. Earning an A.B. and an M.A. from the University of Kentucky, he became a teacher and a principal in Man, West Virginia. Later Flannery received a law degree from West Virginia University. He settled in Logan, West Virginia, around 1956.

Backed by labor interests, Flannery was elected to the West Virginia House of Delegates as a Democrat from Logan County in 1944. He served seven consecutive terms and was named speaker for the 1949, 1951, 1953, 1955, and 1957 sessions. While in the post Flannery helped pass legislation creating the West Virginia Board of Health, civil defense system, West Virginia Business Development Authority, and Office of the Commissioner of Public Institution. In 1958 he announced his intention to run for the U.S. House of Representatives from West Virginia. However, Flannery died on March 7, 1958, at the age of 54.

WILLIAM T. DOHERTY

FLEEMAN, EUGENE CECIL (Arkansas, 1959) was born in Harrisburg, Arkansas, on April 13, 1907, to Mack and Eliza (Burton) Fleeman. Graduating from public schools in Mississippi County, Arkansas, he became president of the Merchants and Planters Bank in Manila, Arkansas. In addition, Fleeman owned a service station, theater, and insurance agency. He was president of the Lions and a member of the Kiwanis. A Methodist, he was married.

Fleeman was elected to the Arkansas House of Representatives as a Democrat from Mississippi County in 1944. Serving nine consecutive terms, he was chosen as speaker for the 1959 session. In 1949 he was Arkansas's emissary to the inauguration of President Harry S. Truman. Fleeman was still a member of the House when he died of a heart attack in Palm Beach, Florida, on February 4, 1962. He was 54.

Arkansas Gazette, February 4, 1961.

JANE McBRIDE GATES

FORD, TIMOTHY ALAN (Mississippi, 1988, 1992) was born in Winter Haven, Florida, on October 22, 1951. Educated in public schools in Baldwyn, Mississippi, he earned a B.A. (1973) and a J.D. (1977) from the University of Mississippi. He later became a partner in the law firm of Carnathan, Malski and Ford in Tupelo, Mississippi.

Ford was elected to the Mississippi House of Representatives as a Democrat from Lee and Prentiss counties in 1983. He was chosen as speaker for the 1988 and 1992 sessions. A Presbyterian, he married Mary Cox Foose; the couple had two children. As of this writing Ford remains in the speakership.

GINA PETONITO

FOUNTAIN, RICHARD TILLMAN (North Carolina, 1927) was born on February 15, 1885, in Edgecombe County, North Carolina. Educated in local public and private schools, he earned a law degree from the University of North Carolina in 1907. Fountain began a private practice in Rocky Mount, North Carolina, where he also owned farm land. He was married.

A Democrat, Fountain served Rocky Mount as a member of the Municipal Court (1911–18) and as school board chair. In 1918 he successfully ran for the North Carolina House of Representatives from Edgecombe County. He remained there for five consecutive terms and was named speaker for the 1927 session, gaining a reputation as a parliamentarian. Fountain was elected lieutenant governor of North Carolina in 1928 and 1930. Known as a liberal for his backing of President Franklin D. Roosevelt, he lost bids for governor in 1932 and 1940 and for the U.S. Senate from North Carolina in 1936 and 1942.

In other affairs Fountain chaired the North Carolina Board of Equalization and sat on the state Park Commission and the Great Smoky Mountains National Park Commission. Chair of the board of the Eastern North Carolina Industrial Training School for Boys, he was a trustee of the University of North Carolina and a director of three banks. He was also president of the Civitan Club and the Rocky Mount Bar Association and a member of the Knights of Pythias, American and North Carolina bar associations, and Presbyterian Church. Fountain died on February 21, 1945, at the age of 60.

William S. Powell, ed., *Dictionary of North Carolina Biography*, 6 vols. (Chapel Hill: University of North Carolina Press, 1979–1996).

CHARLES H. BOWMAN, JR.

FOURNET, JOHN BAPTISTE (Louisiana, 1928) was born on July 27, 1895, in St. Martinville, Louisiana. Educated in local public schools, he earned a degree from Louisiana State Normal College (now Northwestern State University) in Natchitoches in 1915. Fournet was then a teacher and principal. During World War I he served in the U.S. armed forces. He received an LL.B. from Louisiana State University in 1920 and began a law practice in Jefferson Davis Parish, Louisiana.

Fournet won election to the Louisiana House of Representatives as a Democrat from Jefferson Davis Parish in 1927. He was named speaker for his only term in 1928 with the support of newly elected Governor Huey P. Long. Closely tying his career to Long's, Fournet often used dubious tactics to get recalcitrant House members to follow the governor. In 1931 he successfully ran for lieutenant governor of Louisiana.

Elected to the Louisiana Supreme Court in 1934, Fournet was with Long when the latter was assassinated in the state capitol in September 1935. He remained on the Supreme Court until 1970, becoming its chief justice in 1949. Outside of politics he belonged to the Masons, Elks, and American Bar Association. Fournet died in Jackson, Mississippi, on June 3, 1984, at the age of 88.

Membership in the Legislature of Louisiana, 1880–1980 (Baton Rouge, 1979); Frank W. Wurzlow, Jr., "John Baptiste Fournet," *A Dictionary of Louisiana Biography* (New Orleans: Louisiana Historical Association, 1988), I: 384.

RAYMOND O. NUSSBAUM

FOUTCH, McALLEN (Tennessee, 1949, 1951) was born on June 14, 1909, in Alexandria, Tennessee. Educated in local schools, he received an LL.B. from Andrew Jackson University in Nashville, Tennessee, in 1938. Afterward he began practicing law in Smithville, Tennessee. Foutch was a member of the Elks, Lions, Civitan Club, Exchange Club, and Baptist Church. He was married twice, the second time to Sallie Parker in 1948.

A Democrat, Foutch was city attorney of Smithville. He won election to the Tennessee House of Representatives from De Kalb County in 1942 and served six consecutive terms. While in office he was allied with the party faction led by Governor Gordon W. Browning. Foutch was named speaker for the 1949 and 1951 sessions, but he was forced to step down following the 1952 victory of anti-Browning forces led by Governor Frank G. Clement. He became a leading opponent of Clement's policies.

In 1954 Foutch successfully ran for the Tennessee Senate. Elected to one additional term in the House in 1956, Foutch then returned to his Smithville practice. He later died.

Biographical Directory, Tennessee General Assembly, 1796–1969 (Nashville: State Library and Archives); Lee Seifert Greene, David H. Grubbs, and Victor C. Hobday, *Government in Tennessee*, 4th ed. (Knoxville: University of Tennessee Press, 1982).

LEE S. GREENE

FREEMAN, HAROLD (Oklahoma, 1943) was born in Pauls Valley, Indian Territory (now Oklahoma), on October 4, 1902. Educated in local public schools and at a military school in Lyndon, Kentucky, he attended the University of Oklahoma. Freeman received an LL.B. from Cumberland University in Lebanon, Tennessee, in 1927. He was married.

A Democrat, Freeman helped organized the Garvin County Young Democrats and was assistant county attorney. He was elected to the Oklahoma House of Representatives from Garvin County in 1934 and remained there for five consecutive terms. Freeman was chosen as speaker for the 1943 session. Resigning from the House later that year, he served in the U.S. Army during World War II and was awarded the Bronze Star.

After that Freeman entered law practice and operated a ranch. He was named chair of the Oklahoma State Board of Public Affairs in 1955, the same year he was appointed to the Oklahoma Corporation Commission. In 1962 he chaired the Oklahoma Heart Fund Association. Freeman also belonged to the Masons, Kiwanis, Chamber of Commerce, American Legion, VFW, and Presbyterian Church.

TIMOTHY A. ZWINK

FULLER, FRANKLIN OLIVER (Texas, 1917) was born on November 2, 1873, in Melrose, Texas, to Benjamin Franklin and Josephine (Green) Fuller. Educated in local public schools, he became a teacher. Fuller attended Sam Houston Normal Institute (now State University) in Huntsville, Texas, and he earned an LL.B. from Southern Normal University in Huntington, Tennessee, in 1901. He then began a law practice in Coldspring, Texas.

A Democrat, Fuller was San Jacinto County attorney in 1904–06. He won election to the Texas House of Representatives from San Jacinto County in 1906, 1908, 1912, 1914, and 1916. Fuller supported prohibition, but he managed to gain respect from colleagues on both sides of the issue and was unanimously named speaker for the 1917 session. After populist Governor James E. Ferguson vetoed the appropriation for the University of Texas, Fuller called a special session to investigate charges that the governor had mishandled public funds. That action was a flagrant violation of the Texas Constitution, but it eventually led to Ferguson's impeachment.

During World War I Fuller chaired the San Jacinto Council of Defense and was a captain in the U.S. Army's Judge Advocate General's Corps. Moving to Houston, Texas, in 1920, he established the law firm of Fuller and Fuller. He was married. Fuller died on August 7, 1934, at the age of 60.

Austin Statesman, January 8, 1917; Eldon Stephen Branda, ed., *The Handbook of Texas: A Supplement* (Austin: Texas State Historical Association, 1976); "Ex-Speaker of the House at Austin Dies," *Houston Chronicle*, August 9, 1934; *Presiding Officers of the Texas Legislature, 1846–1982* (Austin: Texas Legislative Council, 1982).

EDWARD WELLER

G

GARRETT, JOHN SIDNEY (Louisiana, 1968) was born in Haynesville, Louisiana, in 1922. Educated in local public schools, he earned a B.A. from Louisiana Tech University in Ruston. Garrett served in the U.S. Army during World War II. He then became involved in banking, ranching, and retailing in Haynesville.

In 1947 Garrett was elected to the Louisiana House of Representatives as a Democrat from Claiborne and Webster parishes. Remaining there for six consecutive four-year terms, he chaired the Joint Committee on Segregation. Garrett was named speaker for the 1968 session. He also sat on the Louisiana Democratic Central Committee.

Afterward Garrett became chair of the board of the Planters Bank and Trust Company. He belonged to the Masons, Lions, Farm Bureau, Louisiana Cattlemen's Association, American Legion, and Methodist Church. Garrett continues to live in Haynesville at this writing.

Edwin Adams Davis, *The Story of Louisiana* (New Orleans: J. F. Hyer, 1960).

BEATRICE R. OWSLEY

GEORGE, WILLIAM TAYLOR (West Virginia, 1913) was born in Barbour County, West Virginia, in 1870, to John R. and Gaytura (Taylor) George. He attended local public schools, the Burnsville Academy in Volga, West Virginia, and the United Brethren Academy in Buckhannon, West Virginia. George earned a law degree from the Stockton Normal School in California, where he also worked as a teacher. Settling in Philippi, West Virginia, in 1896, he began practicing law.

George was elected to the West Virginia House of Delegates as a Republican from Barbour County in 1912. He was chosen as speaker for the 1913 term, his only one in the House, after the GOP gained a majority. In 1920 he was a delegate to the Republican National Convention. Returning to his private practice, George was also a member of the Elks and the Methodist Church. He married Dora May Howell in 1892, and before her death in 1918 the couple had five children. George died in Philippi on March 9, 1957, at the age of 87.

ROBERT L. HUNT

GETZEN, SAMUEL WYCHE (Florida, 1929) was born in Lake City, Florida, on February 13, 1898. Attending local public schools and Baptist College in Jacksonville, Florida, he earned a law degree from the University of Florida. Afterward Getzen moved to Webster, Florida, where he practiced law and operated a naval store business. He served in the U.S. Army Officer's Training Corps during World War I.

Getzen successfully ran for the Florida House of Representatives as a Democrat from Sumter County in 1922 and remained there for four consecutive terms. While in office he introduced the state Workman's Compensation Law and consistently supported school appropriations. Chair of the Corporations Committee, Getzen was named speaker *pro tem* in 1927 and speaker for the 1929 session. He won election to the Florida Senate in 1930 and to one additional House term in 1934.

In other affairs Getzen was both solicitor and attorney of Sumter County in 1929–32. He was president of the Webster State Bank and a member of the Masons, Odd Fellows, and Knights of Pythias. A Methodist, he was married. Getzen died on April 11, 1960, at the age of 62.

Robert J. Huckshorn, ed., *Government and Politics in Florida* (Gainesville: University of Florida Press, 1991); Allen Morris, *The Florida Handbook* (Tallahassee: Peninsular Publishing, 1947–).

GEORGE E. POZZETTA

GIBBONS, MURRAY F. (Oklahoma, 1923) was born in Purcell, Indian Territory (now Oklahoma), on February 28, 1891. Attending Wentworth Military Academy in Berkeley, California, he earned an A.B. from the University of Oklahoma. Gibbons later began practicing law in Purcell, Oklahoma. He served in the U.S. Navy for four years and as a captain in the U.S. Army's 87th Division for three years.

In 1920 and 1922 Gibbons was elected to the Oklahoma House of Representatives as a Democrat from McClain County. He was named speaker for the 1923 session with the support of Governor John C. Walton. Caught in a growing legislative rebellion against Walton's reform policies, Gibbons exerted less and less influence. A special session was called in October 1923 to consider impeaching the governor, and Gibbons was forced to resign from the House.

Afterward Gibbons was appointed head of the U.S. Veterans Bureau in Oklahoma City, Oklahoma. Indicted on eight counts of bribery in 1929, he was later acquitted. He returned to his practice in Purcell, where he also belonged to the American Legion. Gibbons married Francis Leiper, and the couple had two children.

GORDON MOORE

GIBSON, JAMES BREEDEN (South Carolina, 1933) was born on December 30, 1879, in Marlboro County, South Carolina, to Simeon and Elizabeth (Breeden) Gibson. Educated in public schools in Gibson, North Carolina, he earned a B.A. from Wofford College in Spartanburg, South Carolina, and an LL.B. from the University of North Carolina in 1903. Afterward Gibson began a law practice in Dillon, South Carolina.

In 1930 and 1932 Gibson was elected to the South Carolina House of Representatives as a Democrat from Marlboro County. He was chosen as speaker for the 1933 session. Declining to run for governor of South Carolina in 1934, he was president of the 1934 South Carolina Democratic Convention.

Outside of politics Gibson belonged to the Masons, Elks, Woodmen of the World, and United American Mechanics. A Methodist, he married Argent Bethea in 1909; the couple had two children. Gibson died on June 22, 1934, at the age of 54.

WALTER B. EDGAR

GILMER, CLAUD H. (Texas, 1945) was born on March 12, 1901, in Rocksprings, Texas. After attending local public schools and Meridian Junior College, he worked as a teacher, football coach, and principal in Rocksprings in 1921–24. Gilmer later studied law and began a private practice. He married Georgia Carson in 1923, and he belonged to the Masons and the Baptist Church.

A Democrat, Gilmer was elected Edwards County judge in 1924. He successfully ran for the Texas House of Representatives from Edwards, Bandera, Crockett, Kerr, Kimble, Mason, Menard, Real, Schleicher, and Sutton counties in 1938 and served five consecutive terms. Gilmer was named speaker for the 1945 session. However, he was best remembered for joining state Senator A. M. Aiken, Jr., in calling for a review of the public school system. The two men were appointed to a committee, many of whose recommendations were later passed in legislation popularly known as the "Gilmer-Aiken Bill." Among these were higher pay for teachers, increased and more equitable state funding, and reorganization of the Texas Board of Education.

Returning to his law practice, Gilmer also owned a ranch and operated his family's telephone company. He chaired the Texas Board of State Hospitals and Special Schools from 1949 to 1955. In 1952 Gilmer helped Governor R. Allan Shivers retain control of the state Democratic Party and rallied support for Republican presidential candidate Dwight D. Eisenhower. President of the Texas Telephone Association, he was that organization's legislative lobbyist. Gilmer died in San Antonio, Texas, on February 26, 1983, at age 81.

Eugene W. Jones, Joe E. Ericson, Lyle C. Brown, and Robert S. Trotter, Jr., *Practicing Texas Politics*, 8th ed. (Boston: Houghton Mifflin, 1992); *Presiding Officers of the Texas Legislature, 1846–1982* (Austin: Texas Legislative Council, 1982), 180–181.

LYLE C. BROWN

GODWIN, PHILIP PITTMAN (North Carolina, 1969, 1971) was born in 1925 in Gatesville, North Carolina, to Adolphus Pilston and Mabel Claire (Hayes) Godwin. He attended local public schools and the Fishburne Military School in Waynesboro, Virginia. During World War II Godwin served with the U.S. Army Air Forces in the Pacific theater. Earning a B.S. (1953) and an LL.B. (1956) from Wake Forest College (now University) in North Carolina, he began practicing law in Gatesville.

Godwin was elected without opposition to the North Carolina House of Representatives as a Democrat from Gates, Camden, Chowan, Currituck, Pasquotank, and Perquimans counties in 1960. He remained there for six consecutive terms. In 1963 Godwin successfully introduced what he initially labeled a "harmless bill." Popularly known as the Speaker Ban Law, it prohibited Communists and persons who had pleaded the 5th Amendment in relation to subversive activities from speaking at state-supported colleges. The law was modified in the 1965 special session but declared unconstitutional by a federal district court in 1968.

Chosen as speaker in late 1969 following the resignation of incumbent Earl W. Vaughn, Godwin was renamed to the post for the 1971 session. He won election to one term in the North Carolina Senate in 1972 and then returned to his law practice. Godwin was president of the First District Bar Association, a trustee of Wake Forest College and Chowan College, and a member of the Masons and the North Carolina Bar Association. A Baptist, he married Anita Thomas Freeman in 1950; the couple had one son. At this writing Godwin continues to live in Gatesville.

Hugh Talmage Lefler and Albert Ray Newsome, *The History of a Southern State: North Carolina* (Chapel Hill: University of North Carolina Press, 1973); *The News and Observer* (Raleigh, North Carolina); William S. Powell, *North Carolina through Four Centuries* (Chapel Hill: University of North Carolina Press, 1989).

FRED D. RAGAN

GORFINE, EMANUEL "Mannie" (Maryland, 1935) was born in Baltimore, Maryland, on November 28, 1895, into a Jewish family. His mother had emigrated from Latvia. Educated in local public schools, Gorfine received an LL.B. from the University of Maryland in 1917. Afterward he began practicing law in Baltimore with the firm of Silberstein and Gorfine. He served in the U.S. Navy during World War I.

Gorfine was elected to the Maryland House of Delegates as a Democrat from the city of Baltimore in 1930 and 1934. Named speaker for the 1935 session, he stated that he believed in "less laws for Maryland and more innovations in the way of social legislation." In 1938 Gorfine successfully ran for the Maryland Senate, where he chaired the Judicial Proceedings Committee. He narrowly lost reelection in 1942.

Sitting on the Maryland Accident Commission from 1942 to 1950, Gorfine became its chair in 1943. In addition, he was president of the Mount Washington

Improvement Association and a member of the Masons, Odd Fellows, Knights of Pythias, American Legion, and American, Maryland, and Baltimore bar associations. He married his childhood sweetheart, Lillian Miller, in 1920, and the couple had two children. Gorfine died on September 28, 1984, at the age of 88.

MORGAN H. PRITCHETT

GRAHAM, ALEXANDER HAWKINS "Sandy" (North Carolina, 1929) was born in Hillsborough, North Carolina, on August 9, 1890. His grandfather, William Alexander Graham, was governor of North Carolina in 1845–48. Educated in private schools, the younger Graham earned an A.B. (1912) and a law degree (1913) from the University of North Carolina. He studied law at Harvard University before beginning a private practice in Hillsborough in 1914. During World War I he served with the U.S. Army in France, rising to the rank of captain.

A Democrat, Graham was Orange County attorney, Hillsborough city attorney, and chair of the Orange County Democratic Executive Committee (1919–47). In 1920 he won election to the North Carolina House of Representatives from Orange County. Graham remained there for five consecutive terms and was named speaker for the 1929 session. While in office he sought to reorganize the highway and public works systems, create a new budget system, and improve public schools and prison administration. He was elected lieutenant governor of North Carolina in 1932 and 1934, but he lost a 1936 bid for governor.

Returning to his Hillsborough practice, Graham chaired the North Carolina Board of Education and the state Highway and Public Works Commission. He sat on the North Carolina Board of Equalization and attended the 1936, 1940, and 1944 Democratic national conventions. In addition Graham was a trustee of the University of North Carolina and a director of the Rocky Mount Cotton Mills. Commander of the state 81st Veterans Association and the American Legion, he belonged to the North Carolina Bar Association and the Episcopal Church. He was married. Graham died on April 3, 1977, at age 86.

William S. Powell, ed., *Dictionary of North Carolina Biography*, 6 vols. (Chapel Hill: University of North Carolina Press, 1979–1996).

CHARLES H. BOWMAN, JR.

GREEN, JAMES COLLINS (North Carolina, 1975) was born in Halifax County, Virginia, on February 24, 1921, to John Collins and Frances Sue (Oliver) Green. He attended local public schools and Washington and Lee University in Lexington, Virginia. Serving as a corporal in the U.S. Marine Corps during World War II, he participated in the invasion of Iwo Jima. Green then began farming in Clarkton, North Carolina, and owned tobacco warehouses in North Carolina, Virginia, and Tennessee. In addition, he was president of the Rotary and active in the Masons, American Legion, VFW, and Presbyterian Church.

A Democrat, Green sat on the Bladen County school board (1955–61) and the Bladen County Democratic Executive Committee. He won election to the North Carolina House of Representatives from Bladen, Columbus, and Sampson counties in 1960, 1962, and 1964, and to the North Carolina Senate in 1966. Again elected to the House in 1968, he remained there for four consecutive terms. Green was named speaker for the 1975 session, gaining notoriety for calling committee chairs before him to read their "charge." He surprised observers by appointing an African American to chair the Human Resources Committee, the highest assignment a black had received since Reconstruction.

Winning 1976 and 1980 races for lieutenant governor of North Carolina, Green was defeated in the 1984 Democratic gubernatorial primary. From 1985 to 1991 he was Republican Governor James G. Martin's special assistant for legislative affairs. Green also served North Carolina as chair of the Advisory Council on Government, co-chair of the Board on Economic Development, and a member of the Board of Education, Board of Community Colleges, Commission on Indian Affairs, Capital Planning Commission, and Board of Transportation. He married Alice McAulay Clark in 1943, and the couple had three children. At this writing Green continues to live in Clarkton.

William S. Powell, ed., *Dictionary of North Carolina Biography*, 6 vols. (Chapel Hill: University of North Carolina Press, 1979–1996).

CHARLES H. BOWMAN, JR.

GRIER, HARRY PERCY (North Carolina, 1921) was born in Yorkville, South Carolina, on March 20, 1871. Orphaned as a child, he moved to his uncle's home in Statesville, North Carolina. Grier attended local public and private schools before reading law. In 1894 he began a private practice in Statesville. He was married, and he belonged to the Congregational Church.

A conservative Democrat, Grier was mayor of Statesville in 1907–11. He successfully ran for the North Carolina House of Representatives from Iredell County in 1912 and served five consecutive terms. Grier was named speaker for the 1921 session. In addition, he was a trustee of the University of North Carolina. Elected to the North Carolina Senate in 1922, Grier still held that post when he died on October 10, 1932. He was 61.

John L. Cheney, Jr., *North Carolina Government, 1585–1974: A Narrative and Statistical History* (Raleigh: North Carolina Department of the Secretary of State, 1975); Hugh Talmadge Lefler and Albert Ray Newsome, *The History of a Southern State: North Carolina* (Chapel Hill: University of North Carolina Press, 1973); William S. Powell, *North Carolina through Four Centuries* (Chapel Hill: University of North Carolina Press, 1989).

CLAUDE HARGROVE

GRIFFITH, ROBERT WILLIAM (Arkansas, 1943) was born in North Little Rock, Arkansas, on October 7, 1906, to Robert W. and Flora (Farley) Griffith. Educated in local public schools, he earned a degree from the University of the South in Sewanee, Tennessee, and an LL.B. from the Arkansas Law School in Little Rock. Griffith began a private practice in Pulaski County, Arkansas, around 1931. He was secretary of the Central Arkansas Board of Bar Examiners (1933–35), a member of the Masons, and a stamp collector.

Defeated for the Arkansas House of Representatives as a Democrat from Pulaski County in 1936, Griffith was elected to the position two years later. He served three consecutive terms and was chosen as speaker for the 1943 session. In 1956 Griffith lost a bid for attorney general of Arkansas. An Episcopalian, he was married. Griffith died on October 21, 1960, at age 54; he was buried in Little Rock.

Arkansas Democrat; *Arkansas Gazette*; *The Arkansas Handbook* (Little Rock: Arkansas History Commission, 1936–   ).

RUSSELL PIERCE BAKER

GUSTAFSON, TOM (Florida, 1989) was born in Ocean City, New Jersey, on October 9, 1949. Earning a B.A. from the University of Notre Dame (1971) and a J.D. from the University of Florida (1974), he began practicing law in Fort Lauderdale, Florida. He married Lynne Soowal in 1984, and the couple had two children.

A Democrat, Gustafson won election to the Florida House of Representatives from Broward County in 1976. He remained there for seven consecutive terms, chairing the Insurance Committee and the Committee on Criminal Justice. In 1988 he was acknowledged as the leading candidate to become the next speaker until being challenged by a coalition of Republicans and conservative Democrats led by Carl Carpenter. Gustafson responded by helping raise $1.5 million to reelect liberal Democrats and garnering the support of Hispanic GOP members. As a result, he was named to the speakership for the 1989 session.

Afterward Gustafson returned to his law practice. In addition, he belonged to the Jaycees, Chamber of Commerce, Urban League, and American, Florida, and Broward County bar associations. He received awards for his legislative service from the Florida Association of Domestic Insurance Companies and the Florida Trial Lawyers Association. Gufstafson continues to live in Fort Lauderdale at this writing.

Morgan, Lucy, "In Florida a Coalition Saves Speaker-Designee," *State Legislatures* 15 (April 1989), 22–23.

GINA PETONITO

H

HABEN, RALPH H., Jr. (Florida, 1981) was born in Atlanta, Georgia, on November 25, 1941, and moved with his family to Florida in 1946. Earning a B.A. from the University of Florida in 1964, he received a J.D. from Cumberland University in Lebanon, Tennessee, in 1967. Afterward Haben began a law practice in Palmetto, Florida. He served in the Florida National Guard.

A Democrat, Haben was an aide in the Florida Senate in 1967 and became assistant state attorney for Florida's 12th Judicial District in 1969. He was also city prosecutor of Palmetto and a judge in Palmetto and Anna Maria, Florida. In 1972 he was elected to the Florida House of Representatives from Manatee County. Remaining there for five consecutive terms, Haben was named speaker for the 1981 session. While in the speakership he helped pass bills creating single-member legislative districts and increasing the sales tax. Haben then returned to Palmetto, where he continues to live at this writing.

JERRELL H. SHOFNER

HAINKEL, JOHN JOSEPH, Jr. (Louisiana, 1980) was born in New Orleans, Louisiana, on March 24, 1938, to John Joseph and Alida (Bonnette) Hainkel. Educated in local schools, he received a B.A. (1958) and an LL.B. (1961) from Tulane University in New Orleans. Hainkel then began a law practice in New Orleans. A Catholic, he married Kathleen Roth in 1961; the couple had three children.

In 1967 Hainkel was elected to the Louisiana House of Representatives as a Democrat from Orleans Parish. He served five consecutive four-year terms. Hainkel was named speaker for the 1980 session with the backing of Governor David C. Treen, the first Republican to hold that post since Reconstruction. While in office he supported Treen's pro-business and good government agenda. In addition, Hainkel emphasized the professionalization of the House by expecting legislators to develop specialized expertise. Self-consciously conservative at times, he admitted that groups such as the AFL-CIO and the Black Legislative Caucus would have preferred a more liberal speaker.

Hainkel was replaced as speaker in 1984 following the election of Governor Edwin W. Edwards. He successfully ran for the Louisiana Senate in 1987 and later joined the Republican Party. Outside of politics he belonged to the Chamber of Commerce, Farm Bureau, Knights of Columbus, and American, Louisiana, and New Orleans bar associations. As of this writing Hainkel remains in the Senate.

Membership in the Legislature of Louisiana, 1880–1980 (Baton Rouge, 1979).

RAYMOND O. NUSSBAUM

HALL, FRANK SAMPSON (Tennessee, 1923) was born in Dyersburg, Tennessee, on September 26, 1890. Attending the Mooney School in Murfreesboro, Tennessee, and local public schools, he earned an LL.B. from Cumberland University in Lebanon, Tennessee. Hall then began practicing law in Dickson, Tennessee. During World War I he served in the U.S. Army. He married Pauline Clark in 1913, and the couple had one daughter.

A Democrat, Hall entered politics when he successfully ran for the Tennessee House of Representatives from Dickson County in 1918 and 1922. He was chosen as speaker for the 1923 session. The next year he lost the Democratic primary for the U.S. House of Representatives from Tennessee's 7th District to incumbent Edward E. Eslick. Hall was Tennessee's commissioner of finance and taxation (1925–27) and a member of the Reelfoot Lake Commission (1925–31). In 1928 he won election to one term in the Tennessee Senate.

Returning to his private practice, Hall was again elected to the state House in 1940 and 1942. He was a presidential elector in 1952 and a delegate to the 1953 Tennessee Constitutional Convention. In addition, he belonged to the Masons, American Legion, Tennessee and Dickson County bar associations, and Presbyterian and Methodist churches. Hall died in Dickson on February 21, 1958, at the age of 67.

JAMES H. EDMONSON

HAMBLIN, JOHN KNAPP (South Carolina, 1927, 1929, 1931) was born on March 22, 1881, in Magnolia, North Carolina, to J. C. and Rebecca (Carroll) Hamblin. After earning a B.A. and a law degree from the University of North Carolina, he was a teacher in Pelham, Georgia. Hamblin began a law practice in Union, South Carolina, in 1903. In addition, he taught Sunday school at the Baptist Church. He was married to Eva Croon, and after her death to Mary Atkins, with whom he had two children.

A Democrat, Hamblin was city attorney of Union and attorney of Union County. In 1916 he won election to the South Carolina House of Representatives from Union County. Serving eight consecutive terms, Hamblin authored legislation requiring compulsory education in South Carolina, prohibiting the sale of alcoholic patent medicines, and requiring the dental and medical inspection of all school children in the state. He was named speaker for the 1927, 1929, and 1931 sessions. Hamblin died on August 7, 1933, at the age of 52.

WALTER B. EDGAR

HAND, FREDRICK BARROW (Georgia, 1947, 1949, 1951, 1953) was born in Pelham, Georgia, on October 26, 1904. After attending Georgia Military College in Milledgeville and earning a B.A. from the University of Georgia, he became a farmer and a businessman in Pelham. Hand was president of the Rotary and a member of the Methodist Church. He was married.

A Democrat, Hand successfully ran for the Georgia Senate in 1930. Two years later he was elected to the Georgia House of Representatives from Mitchell County, serving until 1954 with the exception of the 1939 term. Hand was speaker *pro tem* before being named speaker for the 1947, 1949, 1951, and 1953 sessions. In 1954 he lost the race for governor of Georgia to S. Marvin Griffin and returned to his Pelham business interests. Hand died in 1978.

Georgia Department of History and Archives, *Georgia's Official Register* (Atlanta: Longino and Porter, 1923–1967/68).

JANE W. HERNDON

HARDAGE, JOSIAH "Joe" (Arkansas, 1913) was born in 1868 on a farm in Clark County, Arkansas. He earned a degree from Ouachita College in Arkadelphia, Arkansas (1891), and a law degree from Cumberland University in Lebanon, Tennessee (1893). Hardage practiced law for one year in Oklahoma City, Oklahoma Territory, before settling in Arkadelphia. In addition, he belonged to the Baptist Church.

A Democrat, Hardage sat on the Clark County Court from 1902 to 1908. He won election to the Arkansas House of Representatives from Clark County in 1910, 1912, and 1916. Hardage was chosen as speaker for the 1913 session with the support of Governor James T. Robinson. In 1921–23 he was a member of the Arkansas Railroad Commission. Again appointed to the county court in 1927, Hardage still held that post when he died in Arkadelphia on December 30, 1928. He was 60.

Arkansas Democrat; Arkansas Gazette.

CARL H. MONEYHON

HARDEE, CARY AUGUSTUS (Florida, 1915, 1917) was born on November 13, 1876, on a farm near Perry, Florida, to Georgia natives James B. and Amanda (Johnson) Hardee. Educated in public schools, he became a teacher. Hardee then read law and began a private practice. In addition, he helped establish the First National Bank in Live Oak, Florida.

A Democrat, Hardee was state's attorney for the 3rd Judicial Circuit of Florida from 1905 to 1913. He won election to the Florida House of Representatives from Suwannee County in 1914 and 1916, and he was named speaker for the 1915 and 1917 sessions. During Hardee's speakership the legislature created the Florida Road Department, increased public education funding, approved state prohibition, and allowed counties to require cattle dipping. However, it failed to abolish the controversial convict lease system due to fear that doing so might lead to higher taxes.

In 1920 Hardee won election to one term as governor of Florida. While he was in office, cattle dipping was made compulsory and convict leasing was eliminated with his reluctant support. The newly created Hardee County was named for him. Hardee was married, and he belonged to the Masons, Elks, and Baptist Church. He died in Live Oak on November 22, 1957, at the age of 81.

J. LARRY DURRENCE

HARKEY, BYRON E. "Bill" (Oklahoma, 1955, 1957) was born near De Kalb, Texas, on July 6, 1911, and moved with his family to a farm near Idabel, Oklahoma, in 1915. Graduating from high school in Edmond, Oklahoma, he attended Oklahoma State University and earned a law degree from Oklahoma City University in 1939. During World War II Harkey served with the U.S. Navy in the Pacific theater. He then began practicing law in Oklahoma City.

A Democrat, Harkey was secretary of the Oklahoma Insurance Board (1939–40) and a judge on the state Industrial Commission (1941–42). He won election to the Oklahoma House of Representatives from Oklahoma County in 1950 and remained there for four consecutive terms. Harkey was named speaker for the 1955 and 1957 sessions, supporting the agenda of Governor Raymond D. Gary. While in the speakership he helped ratify a constitutional amendment that made Oklahoma the first segregated state to comply with the the U.S. Supreme Court's decision in *Brown v. Board of Education.*

Losing the Democratic nomination for governor of Oklahoma in 1958, Harkey returned to his private practice. Later he sat on the Oklahoma Ethics Commission. He was married. Harkey belonged to the Masons, Kiwanis, Chamber of Commerce, American Legion, VFW, and Episcopal Church.

KENNY L. BROWN

HARPER, JESSE B. (Oklahoma, 1925) was born in Greenwood, Arkansas, and moved to Talihina, Oklahoma, in 1911. Receiving an LL.B. from Columbia University, he began practicing law in Talihina. Harper belonged to the Masons, Lions, and Baptist Church. He married Effie Norris; the couple had no children.

In 1916 Harper was elected to the Oklahoma House of Representatives as a Democrat from Le Flore County. Serving five consecutive terms, he was named speaker for the 1925 session with the support of Governor Martin E. Trapp. He successfully ran for the Oklahoma Senate in 1926. Harper was director of the Oklahoma Public Welfare Commission from 1930 to 1947.

GORDON MOORE

HARRINGTON, T. BARTON (Maryland, 1933) was born in Baltimore, Maryland, on July 6, 1897, into a prominent Catholic family. Educated in local public and parochial schools, he earned a B.A. from Loyola College in Baltimore (1921) and an LL.B. from the University of Maryland (1924). Harrington then began practicing law in Baltimore. He belonged to the Knights of Columbus and the American, Maryland, and Baltimore bar associations. In addition, he collected books and antique weapons.

A Democrat, Harrington won election to one four-year term in the Maryland House of Delegates from the city of Baltimore in 1930. He was named speaker in 1933 following the resignation of incumbent Francis A. Michel. Harrington was appointed an assistant U.S. attorney in July 1934. In 1944 he became assistant state attorney of Maryland.

Returning to his private practice in 1946, Harrington later lost the Democratic nomination for Maryland attorney general. He chaired the Maryland Democratic Central Committee for four years before unsuccessfully running for mayor of Baltimore in 1955. After that he served Baltimore as police magistrate-at-large and as chief judge of the Municipal Court in 1961–66. Harrington died on April 10, 1974, at the age of 76.

MORGAN H. PRITCHETT

HARRIS, REGINALD LEE (North Carolina, 1933) was born in Roxboro, North Carolina, on September 9, 1890. He attended local public schools and the Virginia Military Institute in Lexington, Virginia. Harris began to work for the Roxboro Cotton Mills in 1910. A Methodist, he was married.

In 1926 Harris won election to the North Carolina House of Representatives as a Democrat from Person County. Remaining there for five consecutive terms, he was named speaker for the 1933 session. Harris also served North Carolina by sitting on the Educational Commission (1929–31), Textbook Commission (1935–43), and Board of Education (1943–45). He was a delegate to the 1936, 1940, and 1944 Democratic national conventions.

Leaving the House in 1936, Harris successfully ran for lieutenant governor of North Carolina in 1940 and 1942. He was again elected to the House in 1946 and 1948. Chair of the board of Person Memorial Hospital, Harris was a trustee of the University of North Carolina and a director of the North Carolina State College Foundation and the state tuberculosis sanatorium. In addition, he was president of the North Carolina Cotton Manufacturers Association and a member of the Rotary. Harris died on October 27, 1959, at the age of 69.

William S. Powell, ed., *Dictionary of North Carolina Biography*, 6 vols. (Chapel Hill: University of North Carolina Press, 1979–1996).

CHARLES H. BOWMAN, JR.

HARRIS, ROY VINCENT (Georgia, 1937, 1939, 1943, 1945) was born in Mitchell, Georgia, on October 2, 1895. He received an A.B. from the University of Georgia. During World War I Harris served in the U.S. Army, rising to the rank of second lieutenant. Earning an LL.B. from Georgia in 1919, he began a law practice in Louisville, Georgia. Later he moved to Augusta, Georgia.

Harris won election to the Georgia House of Representatives as a Democrat from Jefferson County in 1920 and remained there for four consecutive terms.

In 1930 he successfully ran for the Georgia Senate. Elected to the House from Richmond County in 1932, Harris served another seven consecutive terms. He was chosen as speaker for the 1937, 1939, 1943, and 1945 sessions.

Losing reelection to the House in 1946, Harris returned to his Augusta practice. He was city attorney of Augusta, and he sat on the Georgia Board of Regents. In addition, Harris was president of the Kiwanis, commander of the American Legion, and a member of the Masons and the Knights of Pythias. A Methodist, he was married. Harris died on January 15, 1985, at the age of 89.

Georgia Department of History and Archives, *Georgia's Official Register* (Atlanta: Longino and Porter, 1923–1967/68).

JANE W. HERNDON

HAYNES, WALTER MILLER "Pete" (Tennessee, 1931, 1935, 1937) was born in Decherd, Tennessee, on October 2, 1897. Educated in local public schools, he received an LL.B. from Cumberland University in Lebanon, Tennessee, in 1918. The following year Haynes began a law practice in Winchester, Tennessee. He was a referee in bankruptcy proceedings in 1925.

Haynes successfully ran for the Tennessee House of Representatives as a Democrat from Franklin County in 1922 and served eight consecutive terms. He was named speaker for the 1931, 1935, and 1937 sessions. In 1930 he was also an assistant attorney general of Tennessee. Elected to the Tennessee Senate in 1948, 1950, and 1958, Haynes was that body's speaker in 1949 and 1951 and Tennessee's first lieutenant governor in 1951. He was elected to one additional House term in 1960.

In other affairs Haynes was chair of the 1952 Tennessee Democratic Convention and a delegate to the 1953 Tennessee Constitutional Convention. He belonged to the Masons, Elks, and American, Tennessee, and Franklin County bar associations. An Episcopalian, he married Virginia Wilson in 1929; the couple had no children. Haynes died on May 29, 1967, at the age of 69.

Tennessee Blue Book (Nashville: Tennessee Secretary of State).

WILLIE H. PIGG

HENDRIX, B. G. (Arkansas, 1989) was born in Jenny Lind, Arkansas, on December 16, 1922, to Bert Garrett and Thelma H. (Dodson) Hendrix. Educated in local public schools, he attended the University of Tulsa in Oklahoma and Central College of Arkansas. Hendrix served in the U.S. Coast Guard during World War II. Eventually he became a consultant to the Western Arkansas Planning and Development District in Fort Smith, Arkansas.

A Democrat, Hendrix served as a justice of the peace for Fort Smith for four years and as Sebastian County coroner for four years. He was elected to the Arkansas House of Representatives from Sebastian County in 1962. Hendrix was chosen as speaker for the 1989 session. While in the speakership he focused on budget and taxation issues, the criminal justice system, and economic development.

Outside of politics Hendrix was commander of the Amvets and a member of the Masons, Chamber of Commerce, VFW, and Methodist Church. He married Janis Evans Williams in 1945, and the couple had two children. Hendrix remains in the House at this writing.

GINA PETONITO

HENDRIX, CARL EDWARD (Arkansas, 1949) was born on August 8, 1906, in Sevier County, Arkansas, to Benjamin E. and Edith W. (Youtsey) Hendrix. His father was from Georgia, and his mother from Missouri. Educated in local public schools, he earned degrees from Magnolia A&M College in Arkansas and the University of Arkansas. Hendrix then settled in Horatio, Arkansas, becoming president of the Horatio State Bank. He was married.

A Democrat, Hendrix chaired the Sevier County Democratic Committee. In 1944 he was elected to the Arkansas House of Representatives from Sevier County. He served three consecutive terms and was chosen as speaker for the 1949 session. Outside of politics Hendrix was chairman of the board of Magnolia A&M College and a member of the Masons and the Baptist Church.

The Arkansas Handbook (Little Rock: Arkansas History Commission, 1936–).

JANE McBRIDE GATES

HENRY, EDGERTON L. "Bubba" (Louisiana, 1972, 1976) was born on February 10, 1936, in Jonesboro, Louisiana, to Dallas E. and Ruby (Lewis) Henry. He attended local public schools, and he earned a B.A. from Baylor University in Waco, Texas (1958) and a J.D. from Louisiana State University (1961). Afterward Henry began a law practice in Jonesboro. A Baptist, he married Frances Turner in 1958; the couple had two children.

Henry was elected to the Louisiana House of Representatives as a Democrat from Jackson Parish in 1967 and served three consecutive four-year terms. He was chosen as speaker for the 1972 and 1976 sessions. While in the post Henry sought to increase the professionalization of the House. In addition, he chaired the 1973 Louisiana Constitutional Convention, which replaced a fifty-year-old Constitution so burdened by voter-added amendments that it had become the second longest public document in the world.

Losing the 1979 primary for governor of Louisiana, Henry was state commissioner of administration under Republican Governor David C. Treen from 1980 to 1984. He joined the GOP in 1982. Outside of politics Henry was regional vice-president of the Jaycees and a member of the Kiwanis and the Lions. In 1972 he was named "Young Man of the Year" by the Louisiana Jaycees. Henry lives in Baton Rouge, Louisiana, at this writing.

Louisiana Legislature, 1992–1996: Grass Roots Guide (Lafayette, LA, 1992); *Membership in the Legislature of Louisiana, 1880–1980* (Baton Rouge, 1979).

RAYMOND O. NUSSBAUM

HEWLETT, ADDISON, Jr. (North Carolina, 1959) was born in Masonboro Sound, North Carolina, on May 4, 1912, to Addison and Ethel (Herring) Hewlett. His father chaired the New Hanover County Board of Commissioners. Educated in local public schools, Hewlett earned a B.S. (1933) and an LL.B. (1934) from Wake Forest College (now University) in North Carolina. While in college he was student body president. Hewlett then began practicing law in Wilmington, North Carolina. He served with the U.S. Army Air Forces in the Pacific theater during World War II, rising to the rank of captain.

In 1950 Hewlett was elected to the North Carolina House of Representatives as a Democrat from New Hanover County. Remaining there for five consecutive terms, he gained a reputation for hard work. While in office he helped pass the controversial Financial Responsibility Act as well as bills raising workman's compensation, improving the state's ports, and creating an educational program for mentally retarded children. Hewlett was chair of the Judiciary II Committee as well as vice-chair of the Finance Committee and the Appropriations Committee. He was named speaker for the 1959 session.

After losing the 1960 Democratic nomination for the U.S. Senate from North Carolina to B. Everett Jordan, Hewlett returned to his private practice. He was president of the Civitan Club and the New Hanover County Bar Association, commander of the American Legion, and a trustee of Wake Forest College. In addition, Hewlitt belonged to the Red Men and the North Carolina Bar Association. A Baptist, he married Annie Crockett Williams in 1939; the couple had one son. Hewlett continues to live in Masonboro Sound at this writing.

OTIENO OKELO

HILL, JOHNSON DAVIS (Oklahoma, 1945) was born on December 12, 1887, in El Dorado Springs, Missouri. Earning a B.A. and an LL.B. from the University of Missouri, he was vice-president and general counsel of the Waite Phillips Oil Company in Okmulgee, Oklahoma, in 1923–26. Hill then moved to Tulsa, Oklahoma, where he founded the Tulsa Trust Company. In 1932 he became president of the Atlas Life Insurance Company. He was married.

A Democrat, Hill entered politics in 1942 when he failed to gain the nomination for lieutenant governor of Oklahoma. However, that same year he was elected to the Oklahoma House of Representatives from Tulsa County. While successfully campaigning for reelection in 1944, he promised to quit if the state school superintendent was not impeached within thirty days. Hill was named speaker for the 1945 session, but he resigned from the House when the impeachment bill was narrowly defeated. In 1946 he lost the Democratic primary for governor of Oklahoma despite declaring himself ''The Man Who Keeps His Word.''

Returning to his insurance business, Hill became chair of its board in 1952. He chaired the Carver Memorial Trust, an organization dedicated to improving impoverished northern Tulsa, and he initiated Tulsa's Carver Youth Center for African Americans. In addition, he was a member of the Masons and the Episcopal Church. Hill died on April 27, 1977, at the age of 89.

''Former House Speaker Dies,'' *Tulsa World*, April 28, 1977; Joseph E. Howell,

"Johnson Hill Sr., State Figure Dies," *Tulsa Tribune*, April 28, 1977; Gaston Litton, *History of Oklahoma at the Golden Anniversary of Statehood*, 4 vols. (New York: Lewis Historical Publishing, 1957).

DONOVAN L. REICHENBERGER

HILL, THOMAS AUSTIN (Arkansas, 1925) was born in Pine Bluff, Arkansas, on July 24, 1889. Graduating from local public schools, he became a professional baseball player in the Cotton States League. Hill managed theaters in Pine Bluff and Little Rock, Arkansas, before entering the advertising business in Pine Bluff. He belonged to the Elks, Eagles, and United Workmen. A Methodist, he was married.

In 1918 Hill successfully ran for the Arkansas House of Representatives as a Democrat from Jefferson County. He served four consecutive terms and was chosen as speaker for the 1925 session. Secretary-treasurer of the National Council of State Legislatures in 1925–29, Hill lost bids for lieutenant governor of Arkansas in 1928 and 1930. Afterward he returned to his advertising firm. Hill died on June 25, 1937, at the age of 47.

Diane D. Blair, *Arkansas Politics and Government* (Lincoln: University of Nebraska Press, 1988), 160–184; Jerry E. Hinshaw, *Call the Roll* (Little Rock: Rose Publishing, 1986); *Historical Report of the Secretary of State, Arkansas* (Little Rock: Secretary of State, 1958–   ); Walter Nunn, *Readings in Arkansas Government* (Little Rock: Rose Publishing, 1973), 59–133.

CAL LEDBETTER, JR.

HINDS, H. IREDELLE (Oklahoma, 1945) was born in Siloam Springs, Arkansas, on April 14, 1895, and moved with his family to Pryor, Oklahoma, in 1900. He served in the U.S. Army Air Service during World War I. After attending Northeastern State Teachers College (now University) in Tahlequah, Oklahoma, he became a teacher. Hinds organized the Hulbert Mercantile Company in Hulbert, Oklahoma, in 1920. In 1939 he settled in Tahlequah, where he established the Hinds Mercantile and Department Store.

A Democrat, Hinds was a member of the the Delaware County election board. He won election to the Oklahoma House of Representatives from Cherokee County in 1930, 1932, 1942, and 1944. Hinds was named speaker following the resignation of incumbent Johnson D. Hill in February 1945. Chair of the state Democratic Party, he was also U.S. marshal for the Eastern District of Oklahoma. Later he was Oklahoma collector of internal revenue, administrative assistant to Governor J. Howard Edmondson, and chair of the Tahlequah Utilities Board.

Outside of politics Hinds continued to operate his store until 1963. In addition, he was a director of the Tahlequah Savings and Loan Association and a member of the Masons, American Legion, and Methodist Church. He was married. Hinds died on July 11, 1972, at the age of 77.

"H. I. Hinds, Ex-Demo Chief, Dies," *Tulsa Tribune*, July 12, 1972; "Hinds Rites Set Friday," *The Daily Oklahoman*, July 13, 1972: 17; Gaston Litton, *History of Oklahoma at the Golden Anniversary of Statehood*, 4 vols. (New York: Lewis Historical Publishing, 1957); "Rites Held for Former Speaker of the House," *Tahlequah Pictorial Press*, July 20, 1972.

DONOVAN L. REICHENBERGER

HINER, RALPH McCLUNG (West Virginia, 1933) was born in Pendleton County, West Virginia, on December 25, 1896, to Ben H. and Maude (McClung) Hiner. After attending Randolph-Macon College in Ashland, Virginia, he served in the U.S. Army's 14th Infantry Division during World War I. Hiner earned an LL.B. from West Virginia University, and he began practicing law in Pendleton County. He was a member of the Masons, Elks, and American Legion.

In 1928 Hiner was elected to the West Virginia House of Delegates as a Democrat from Pendleton County. Remaining there for four consecutive terms, he was named speaker for the 1933 session. While in the speakership he introduced bills related to banking, indebtedness, workmen's compensation, and the distribution of general school funds. Hiner left the House in 1936.

WILLIAM T. DOHERTY

HOLDER, JOHN NATHANIEL (Georgia, 1911, 1917, 1919; also 1909) was a Democrat from Jackson County. He served as speaker of the Georgia House of Representatives for the 1911, 1917, and 1919 sessions, having previously presided in 1909.

Charles F. Ritter and Jon L. Wakelyn, *American Legislative Leaders, 1850–1910* (New York: Greenwood Press, 1989), 310–11.

KEVIN G. ATWATER

HOLLENSWORTH, CARROLL C. (Arkansas, 1953) was born in Columbia County, Arkansas, to Eli Asa and Mary Elizabeth (Lee) Hollensworth. Attending public schools in Warren, Arkansas, Hendrix College in Conway, Arkansas, and Tyler Commercial College in Little Rock, Arkansas, he earned a degree from the Chicago School of Law in Illinois. Hollensworth was also a graduate student at Loyola University in New Orleans, Louisiana, Cumberland University in Lebanon, Tennessee, and the Institute of Applied Science in Chicago. He began practicing law in Warren.

In 1934 Hollensworth was elected to the Arkansas House of Representatives as a Democrat from Bradley County. Serving thirteen consecutive terms, he was parliamentarian in 1935–38 and 1943–46. Hollensworth wrote a book entitled *Rules of Representatives of the State of Arkansas* and established the Institute of Legislative Procedure. He was named speaker for the 1953 session.

Outside of politics Hollensworth belonged to the Masons, Elks, Lions, American Legion, Arkansas and Bradley County bar associations, and American Judicature Society. A Presbyterian, he was married. Hollensworth was still a member of the House when he died of a heart attack on May 19, 1959.

The Arkansas Handbook (Little Rock: Arkansas History Commission, 1936–   ).

JANE McBRIDE GATES

HORNE, MALLORY ELI (Florida, 1962, 1963) was born on April 17, 1925, in Tavares, Florida, of Scotch-Irish ancestry. During World War II he served as a pilot in the U.S. Army Air Forces. Attending the University of Tennessee and Florida State University, he earned a law degree from the University of Florida. Horne joined the law firm of Caldwell, Parker, Foster, and Wigginton while its senior member, Millard Caldwell, was governor of Florida. He became a partner in the firm of Horne and Rhodes in Tallahassee, Florida, during the 1950s.

A Democrat, Horne won election to the Florida House of Representatives from Leon County in 1954 and remained there for five consecutive terms. He and fellow conservative legislator William V. Chappell, Jr., campaigned to limit the powers of the U.S. Supreme Court after the latter's 1954 decision in *Brown v. Board of Education*. Horne was chosen as speaker for the extra session of 1962 and for the 1963 regular session. In addition, he co-chaired the state campaign of 1964 Republican presidential nominee Barry Goldwater.

Elected to the Florida Senate in 1966 and named that body's president in 1972, Horne became the only person to preside over both branches of the state legislature in this century. Afterward he returned to his law practice and worked as a lobbyist. Home also amassed a sizable personal fortune as a partner in the real estate company of Killearn Properties, Inc. He was president of the Exchange Club. At this writing Horne continues to live in Tallahassee.

JERRELL H. SHOFNER

HOUSTON, HARRY RUTHERFORD (Virginia, 1916, 1918) was born on May 20, 1878, in Fincastle, Virginia. Receiving a B.A. from Hampden-Sydney College in Virginia in 1899, he established a printing business in Hampton, Virginia, the following year. Houston later became editor and publisher of the Hampton *Monitor*. He was a trustee of Hampden-Sydney College and a member of the Masons, Elks, Rotary, and Presbyterian Church.

A conservative Democrat, Houston was elected to the Virginia House of Delegates in 1905, 1907, 1911, 1913, 1915, 1917, and 1923. He represented the city of Hampton and Accomack and Elizabeth City counties until 1909 and the city of Hampton and Elizabeth City County (now part of Hampton) thereafter. While in office he supported legislation creating the Virginia School for the Deaf and Blind in Newport News, Virginia, serving as president of its board of visitors from 1906 to 1940. Houston was named speaker for the 1916 and 1918 sessions. In addition, he chaired the Virginia Democratic Convention three times.

Virginia commissioner of fisheries from 1926 to 1930, Houston was associate director of the Federal Housing Administration in Virginia in 1934–35. During World War II he sat on the U.S. Office of Price Administration rationing board for Hampton and Elizabeth City County and the Hampton Roads Regional Defense Council. He also played a prominent role in developing Langley Field, a U.S. Army Air Forces Base in Hampton. Houston died on November 13, 1960, at the age of 82.

E. Griffith Dodson, ed., *Speakers and Clerks of the Virginia House of Delegates, 1776–1976*, rev. under the direction of Joseph H. Holleman, Jr. (Richmond, 1976), 120–143; *History of Virginia* (Chicago: American Historical Society, 1924): IV–VI; *Newport News Daily Press*, November 14–15, 1960.

JAMES R. SWEENEY

HOYT, JAMES ALFRED (South Carolina, 1915, 1917) was born on October 11, 1837, in Waynesboro, Virginia, to J. Perkins and Jane (Johnson) Hoyt. He moved with his family to Laurens, South Carolina, in the 1840s. Entering the newspaper business when he was 14, he worked for the Laurensville *Herald*. Hoyt then settled in Anderson, South Carolina, where he edited the *Gazette* before starting to publish the *Intelligencer* in 1860. During the Civil War he served in the Confederate Army, rising to the rank of colonel for "gallant and meritorious conduct on the field" and being severely wounded.

Hoyt resumed his career in journalism in 1877 with the Columbia, South Carolina, *Reporter*. Purchasing the *Working Christian*, he moved the paper to Greenville, South Carolina, and renamed it the *Baptist Courier*. In 1892 Hoyt bought the Greenville *Mountaineer*. He was president of the State Baptist Convention and a trustee of Furman University.

A Democrat, Hoyt chaired the state party committee and became chair of the National Democratic Committee in 1890. He unsuccessfully ran for governor of South Carolina as a prohibition candidate in 1900. From 1909 to 1914 Hoyt was clerk of the South Carolina House of Representatives. Elected to the House from Greenville County in 1914 and 1916, he was chosen as speaker for the 1915 and 1917 sessions. Hoyt resigned from the House in January 1918 to enter private business in Detroit, Michigan.

WALTER B. EDGAR

HUGHES, WILLIAM CLARK (Louisiana, 1926) was born in Bossier Parish, Louisiana, on January 31, 1868. Educated in local public schools, he attended Louisiana State University and Tulane University in New Orleans, Louisiana. Hughes moved to Hughes Spur, Louisiana, in 1888. He operated a farm and later became a merchant.

A Democrat, Hughes won election to the Louisiana House of Representatives from Bossier Parish in 1903. He served seven consecutive four-year terms and was named speaker in 1926 after the death of incumbent James S. Douglas. In 1929 Hughes was one of a group of conservative leaders who attempted to impeach Governor Huey P. Long. As a result, Long unsuccessfully tried to have him recalled. Hughes was still serving in the House when he died in 1930.

Dave H. Brown, comp., *A History of Who's Who in Louisiana Politics in 1916* (New Orleans: Coste and Frichter, 1916); *Membership in the Legislature of Louisiana, 1880–1980* (Baton Rouge, 1979).

RAYMOND O. NUSSBAUM

HUNT, JOSEPH MARVIN (North Carolina, 1961) was born in Greensboro, North Carolina, on October 19, 1906. After attending the Riverside Military Academy in Gainesville, Georgia, and Duke University in Durham, North Carolina, he became vice-president of the Wimbish Insurance Agency in Greensboro. Hunt was president of the Association of Insurance Agents, a trustee of North Carolina A&T State University, and a member of the Kiwanis, Chamber of Commerce, and Methodist Church. He was married.

A Democrat, Hunt served Greensboro by sitting on the special school board and chairing the Municipal Study Commission. He was elected to the North Carolina House of Representatives from Guilford County in 1952. Hunt remained there for five consecutive terms, supporting efforts to expand programs for people with learning disabilities and to increase teacher salaries. Gaining a widespread reputation as a humorist, he was chosen as speaker for the 1961 session.

In 1962 Hunt lost a bid for the North Carolina Senate, publicly blaming the result on Governor J. Terry Sanford's expansion of the sales tax. Returning to his insurance business, he later chaired the North Carolina Highway Commission. He was an advisor to his cousin, James B. Hunt, when the latter successfully ran for governor in 1976. Hunt died in Greensboro on May 2, 1978, at the age of 71.

Hugh Talmage Lefler and Albert Ray Newsome, *The History of a Southern State: North Carolina* (Chapel Hill: University of North Carolina Press, 1973); *The News and Observer* (Raleigh, North Carolina); William S. Powell, *North Carolina through Four Centuries* (Chapel Hill: University of North Carolina Press, 1989).

FRED D. RAGAN

J

JENKINS, WILLIAM LEWIS (Tennessee, 1969) was born on November 29, 1936, in Detroit, Michigan, to Lewis C. and Maud (Wilson) Jenkins. As a child he moved with his family to Rogersville, Tennessee. Educated in local public schools, he earned a B.S. from Tennessee Technological University in Cookeville in 1958. Jenkins then served in the U.S. Army and the Army Reserve, rising to the rank of captain. He earned a J.D. from the University of Tennessee in 1961. The following year he became a partner in the Rogersville law firm of Hyder, Jenkins & Boyd.

Jenkins was elected to the Tennessee House of Representatives as a Republican from Hawkins and Hancock counties in 1962. He served four consecutive terms and was minority leader. When the GOP gained control of the House in 1969 for the first time in eighty-eight years, Jenkins was chosen as speaker. In 1971 he was appointed commissioner of the Tennessee Department of Conservation.

After sitting on the board of the Tennessee Valley Authority from 1972 to 1978, Jenkins resumed practicing law in Rogersville. In addition, he owned a farm. He was a member of the Masons, Kiwanis, Jaycees, Farm Bureau, Tennessee and Hawkins County bar associations, and Baptist Church. Jenkins married Mary Kathryn Myers in 1959, and the couple had four children.

Tennessee Blue Book (Nashville: Tennessee Secretary of State).

LEE S. GREENE

JENNINGS, FRANK E. (Florida, 1921) was born in Centralia, Kansas, on June 9, 1877. Educated in local public schools, he earned an LL.B. from the University of Missouri in 1901. Jennings then helped compile a law encyclopedia in New York, New York. In 1904 he moved to Jacksonville, Florida, where he began practicing law. He served in the U.S. Army during World War I.

A Democrat, Jennings was elected port commissioner of Jacksonville in 1912. The following year he was appointed to the Florida Board of Control. Jennings was elected to the Florida House of Representatives from Duval County in 1920 and named speaker for his only term in 1921. During his speakership the legislature defeated a proposal to move the state capital from Tallahassee, but it approved the creation of Charlotte, Dixie, Glades, Hardee, Highlands, Sarasota, and Union counties.

Unsuccessfully running for governor of Florida in 1924, Jennings returned to his law practice. In addition, he was a member of the Masons, Odd Fellows, Chamber of Commerce, American Legion, and Christian Church (Disciples of Christ). He was married. Jennings died in Jacksonville in 1966.

GARY R. MORMINO

JENNINGS, THOMAS ALBERT (Florida, 1911) was born in Jennings, Florida, on January 8, 1865. After attending Florida public schools and Emory College (now University) in Atlanta, Georgia, he became president of the Bank of Jennings. He later moved to Pensacola, Florida, where he operated the Jennings Naval Stores Company.

A Democrat, Jennings was a delegate to the Democratic national conventions in 1888, 1892, 1908, and 1912 and a presidential elector in 1904. In 1909 he chaired the Pensacola Board of Public Works. Jennings won election to the Florida House of Representatives from Escambia County in 1910, and he was named speaker for his only term in 1911. During his speakership the legislature defeated attempts to legalize horse racing, launch a $10 million road system, and move the state capital from Tallahassee to a more central location. However, it did adopt a union school test bill and approve the creation of Pinellas County.

Returning to Pensacola, Jennings organized the Globe Naval Stores Company in 1913. In addition, he was a director of the Gulf, Florida, and Alabama Railway Company. He was married, and he belonged to the Masons, Elks, Knights of Pythias, and Methodist Church. Jennings died in 1917.

GARY R. MORMINO

JEWELL, J. THOMAS (Louisiana, 1960) was born on March 6, 1909, in Mix, Louisiana, a town named for his grandfather, Thomas Mix. His family had been active in state politics since 1847. Educated in local public schools, he received an LL.B. from Louisiana State University in 1931. Jewell then began a law practice in New Roads, Louisiana. He was married.

A Democrat, Jewell joined the Louisiana Democratic Committee in 1932. He was elected to the Louisiana House of Representatives from Pointe Coupee Parish in 1935 and served eight consecutive four-year terms. While in office he helped pass bills to improve rural roads, drainage, and education. Jewell was unanimously chosen as speaker for the 1960 session. That same year he attended the Democratic National Convention.

Outside of politics Jewell was active in the Louisiana State Law Institute and the World Peace through Law Center in Washington, D.C. He was also president of the Lions, a governor of the Louisiana Bar Association, and a member of the American Bar Association, American Judicature Society, Farm Bureau, Pointe

Coupee Parish Historical Society, and Catholic Church. Jewell died in New Roads in December 1993 at the age of 84.

Edwin Adams Davis, *The Story of Louisiana* (New Orleans: J. F. Hyer, 1960).

BEATRICE R. OWSLEY

JOHNSON, BOLLEY L. "Bo" (Florida, 1993) was born in Milton, Florida, on November 15, 1951, to Leroy and Madie (Cooper) Johnson. His father was a Santa Rosa County commissioner. Earning an A.A. from Pensacola Junior College in Florida in 1971 and a B.S. from Florida State University in 1973, Johnson entered the real estate business in Milton. He eventually became the owner of Bo Johnson Associates and vice-president of the Halford Company.

A conservative Democrat, Johnson was an aide to state Senator E. Mallory Horne (1973–74) and to U.S. Senator Lawton Chiles of Florida (1974–78). He was elected to the Florida House of Representatives from Santa Rosa, Escambia, and Okaloosa counties in 1978 and served eight consecutive terms. While in office Johnson opposed organized crime and supported legislative term limits. Chair of the Tourism and Economic Development Committee and the Community Affairs Committee, he was named speaker for the 1993 session.

Johnson then returned to his business interests. In addition he belonged to the Masons, Rotary, Kiwanis, Chamber of Commerce, Board of Real Estate Brokers, National Rifle Association, and Methodist Church. He married Judi Ellen Maness, and the couple had two children. At this writing Johnson continues to live in Milton.

Guidebook to Florida Legislators (Baltimore: Legislative Guidebooks, 1993/94–); *The Miami Herald Almanac of Florida Politics* (Miami: Miami Herald Publishing, 1994–).

JON L. WAKELYN

JOHNSON, GLEN D., Jr. (Oklahoma, 1991, 1993) was born in Oklahoma City, Oklahoma, on April 20, 1954, to Glen D. and Imogene (Storms) Johnson. Educated in local schools, he earned a B.A. (1976) and a J.D. (1979) from the University of Oklahoma. Johnson then began a law practice in Okemah, Oklahoma. In addition, he was president of the Lions and the Okfuskee County Bar Association and a member of the Chamber of Commerce, Oklahoma Bar Association, Okfuskee County Historical Society, and Catholic Church. He married Melinda Pierce.

A Democrat, Johnson was chair of the Okfuskee County Democratic Committee in 1981–85. In 1982 he won election to the Oklahoma House of Representatives from Okfuskee, Hughes, and Okmulgee counties. He was chosen as speaker for the 1991 and 1993 sessions. Johnson remains in the speakership at this writing.

Directory of Oklahoma: State Almanac (Oklahoma City: Oklahoma Department of Libraries).

JON L. WAKELYN

JOHNSON, ROBERT GRADY (North Carolina, 1935) was born in Pender County, North Carolina, on May 5, 1895. After attending local public schools and the University of North Carolina, he served as a medical records clerk in the U.S. Army during World War I. In 1919–25 he was an assistant cashier of the Bank of Pender. Johnson studied law at Wake Forest College (now University) in North Carolina before beginning to practice in Burgaw and Raleigh, North Carolina. He was a trustee of the University of North Carolina, and he belonged to the Masons, American Legion, and North Carolina and Pender County bar associations.

A Democrat, Johnson was Pender County register of deeds, a Burgaw alderman (1922–28), and chair of the Pender County Board of Elections (1923–25). He also sat on the North Carolina Democratic Executive Committee. Johnson successfully ran for the North Carolina Senate in 1928. Elected to the North Carolina House of Representatives from Pender County in 1930, he remained there for three consecutive terms and was named speaker for the 1935 session.

Following that Johnson was secretary of the North Carolina Petroleum Industries Committee and sat on the State Highway and Public Works Commission. Director of the North Carolina Division of Prisons in 1937–41, he introduced reforms emphasizing modernization, recreation, and rehabilitation. In addition, Johnson served North Carolina as coordinator for national defense, chair of the Board of Alcoholic Control, and a member of the Utilities Commission. He was married after leaving the House. Johnson died on June 22, 1951, at age 56.

William S. Powell, ed., *Dictionary of North Carolina Biography*, 6 vols. (Chapel Hill: University of North Carolina Press, 1979–1996).

CHARLES H. BOWMAN, JR.

JOHNSON, VERNON EMIL (West Virginia, 1915, 1927) was born in Berkeley Springs, West Virginia, in 1880. He attended public schools and Eastman Business College in Poughkeepsie, New York. After working in his father's general merchandise store, Johnson established an insurance business. In 1908 he became president of the Bank of Berkeley Springs.

A Republican, Johnson was a trustee and a councilman in Berkeley Springs as well as chair of the Morgan County draft board. In addition, he was a military aide to Governors William E. Glasscock and Henry D. Hatfield. Johnson successfully ran for the West Virginia House of Delegates from Morgan County in 1910 and served three consecutive terms. Chosen as speaker in 1915, he introduced a bill changing the terms and schedules of the state's circuit courts. He was later again elected to the House, and he was returned to the speakership for the 1927 session.

Declining to run for governor of West Virginia, Johnson was appointed a collector for the U.S. Bureau of Internal Revenue in 1928. That same year he sat on the West Virginia Game, Fish and Forestry Commission. Outside of politics Johnson belonged to the Masons and the Chamber of Commerce. He was married to Willie Rice in 1901, and later to Ethel Harmison. Johnson was a candidate for auditor of West Virginia when he died in April 1944.

WILLIAM T. DOHERTY

JOINER, JOSEPH WILLIAM (Arkansas, 1920, 1921) was born in Magnolia, Arkansas, on August 1, 1888. His father was treasurer of Columbia County. Earning a bachelor's degree (1912) and a law degree (1913) from the University of Arkansas, Joiner briefly worked as a teacher before beginning a private practice in Magnolia. In addition, he owned farm land. He belonged to the Odd Fellows, Woodmen of the World, and Baptist Church.

Joiner won election to one term in the Arkansas House of Representatives as a Democrat from Columbia County in 1914. During World War I he served in the U.S. Army. Again elected to the House in 1918 and 1920, Joiner was chosen as speaker for the special session of 1920 and the 1921 regular session. He was Columbia County treasurer in 1923–26. In 1929 he was appointed prosecuting attorney for the 13th Judicial District of Arkansas. Joiner still held that post when he died in El Dorado, Arkansas, on June 2, 1932, at age 44.

Arkansas Democrat; Arkansas Gazette.

CARL H. MONEYHON

JUNKIN, JOHN RICHARD (Mississippi, 1966, 1968, 1972) was born in Natchez, Mississippi, on December 16, 1896. Graduating from local schools, he became a gravel contractor and farmer in Natchez. Junkin belonged to the American Legion and Catholic Church. He was married.

A Democrat, Junkin sat on the Adams County Board of Supervisors in 1928–36. In 1943 he was elected to the Mississippi House of Representatives from Adams County. He served eight consecutive four-year terms and chaired the Appropriations Committee. While in office Junkin supported fiscally conservative policies, once describing the sales tax as ''the most equitable tax that could be placed on people.'' Chosen as speaker following the death of incumbent Walter Sillers in September 1966, he was renamed to the post for the 1968 and 1972 sessions. Junkin still held the speakership when he died on October 12, 1975, at age 78.

Dale Krane and Stephen D. Shaffer, eds., *Mississippi Government & Politics: Modernizers versus Traditionalists* (Lincoln: University of Nebraska Press, 1992); Richard A. McLemore, *A History of Mississippi*, 2 vols. (Jackson: University and College Press of Mississippi, 1973); *Mississippi Official and Statistical Register* (Jackson: Secretary of State).

DAVID G. SANSING

K

KEATLEY, EDWIN MINER (West Virginia, 1921, 1925) was born on May 12, 1868, in Barton, New York, to William and Elizabeth (Swallow) Keatley. His father was from Ireland, and his mother from Pennsylvania. Educated in public schools in Luzerne County, Pennsylvania, he earned a degree from the Wyoming Seminary in Kingston, Pennsylvania. In 1891 Keatley moved to West Virginia, where he worked as an engineer at coal mines owned by J. P. Morgan. He began practicing law in Charleston, West Virginia, in 1897.

A Republican, Keatley became an assistant attorney general of West Virginia in 1897. From 1901 to 1918 he was clerk of the U.S. District Court. Keatley was elected to the West Virginia House of Delegates from Kanawha County in 1920, 1924, 1926, and 1928, and he was chosen as speaker for the 1921 and 1925 sessions. He lost a 1930 bid for reelection to the House.

Outside of politics Keatley was president of the Virginia Electric and Machine Works. In addition, he presided over the Charleston Chamber of Commerce and belonged to the Masons, Rotary, and Episcopal Church. He was married to Alethia McCreery, with whom he had four children, and later to Lenore Gosling, with whom he had three more. Keatley died on May 31, 1933, at the age of 65.

ROBERT L. HUNT

KENTON, WILLIAM G. (Kentucky, 1976, 1978, 1980) was born in Maysville, Kentucky, on August 28, 1941. He was a descendant of the pioneer Simon Kenton. Attending the University of Virginia, Kenton received an A.B. and an LL.B. from the University of Kentucky. Afterward he began a law practice in Lexington, Kentucky.

As an attorney Kenton gained a reputation for taking controversial stands, including his successful defense of the cast of the musical "Oh, Calcutta!" against obscenity charges in 1977. He belonged to the Rotary, Jaycees, American and Kentucky bar associations, and American Trial Lawyers Association. A Baptist, he was married.

Kenton was elected to the Kentucky House of Representatives as a Democrat from Fayette County in 1969 and served six consecutive terms. Named speaker for the 1976, 1978, and 1980 sessions, he increased the post's power and independence from the governor. While in office Kenton became known for his booming voice and a style that mixed stern stewardship with wit and humor. He was also chair of the Kentucky Cancer Commission. Kenton still held the speakership when he died on November 5, 1981, at age 40.

Malcolm E. Jewell, *Representation in State Legislatures* (Lexington: University Press of Kentucky, 1982); Malcolm E. Jewell and Penny Miller, *The Kentucky Legislature: Two Decades of Change* (Lexington: University Press of Kentucky, 1988); Malcolm E. Jewell and Samuel C. Patterson, *The Legislative Process in the United States*, 4th ed. (New York: Random House, 1986); John Ed Pearce, *Divide and Dissent: Kentucky Politics, 1930–1963* (Lexington: University Press of Kentucky, 1987).

H. LEW WALLACE

KERR, JOHN HOSEA, Jr. (North Carolina, 1943) was born in Warrenton, North Carolina, on May 19, 1900, to John Hosea and Lillian (Foote) Kerr. His family descended from the plantation aristocracy of eastern North Carolina. Educated in local public schools, he received an A.B. from the University of North Carolina in 1921. During World War I he served in the U.S. armed forces. Kerr studied law at George Washington University in Washington, D.C., and earned an LL.B. from Wake Forest College (now University) in North Carolina in 1923. He practiced law in Edgecombe County, North Carolina, before returning to Warrenton.

In 1928 Kerr won election to one term in the North Carolina House of Representatives as a Democrat from Edgecombe County. Elected to the House from Warren County in 1938, he remained there for six consecutive terms and was named speaker for the 1943 session. While in office he delivered a memorable speech on behalf of legislation appropriating $1 million to set up the nation's first state-supported art museum. Kerr successfully ran for the North Carolina Senate in 1954 and again for the House in 1956, 1958, 1960, and 1962. He was also chair of the Warren County Democratic Executive Committee.

Resuming his Warrenton practice, Kerr was chair of the board of Warren General Hospital and a director of the People's Bank and Trust Company in Norlina, North Carolina. In addition, he belonged to the North Carolina Bar Association and the Baptist Church. He married Mary Hinton Duke, and the couple had one son. Kerr died of a cerebral hemorrhage on May 30, 1968, at the age of 68.

OTIENO OKELO

KIRTLEY, JOHN D. (Kentucky, 1936, 1938) was born in Island, Kentucky, on January 19, 1900. He attended local public schools and became a farmer and a sawmill operator. In addition, Kirtley belonged to the Masons and the Elks. A Methodist, he married Viola Tally in 1921.

Kirtley was elected to the Kentucky House of Representatives as a Democrat from McLean County in 1933 and served three consecutive terms. He was chosen as speaker for the 1936 and 1938 sessions. In 1938 Kirtley supported Governor A. B. Chandler's campaign for the U.S. Senate from Kentucky. Chandler lost the primary, but he appointed Kirtley to the Kentucky Public Service Commission.

Becoming chair of the commission in 1940, Kirtley was fired by Governor Keen Johnson two years later for opposing efforts to expand the state's participation in the Tennessee Valley Authority. Afterward he became a director of the Kentucky Utilities Company and worked in the insurance industry. Kirtley died in Owensboro, Kentucky, on June 19, 1978, at the age of 78.

Louisville *Courier-Journal; Kentucky Directory for the Use of the Courts, State and County Officials, and General Assembly of the State of Kentucky* (Frankfort, KY: 1914–); John E. Kleber, ed., *The Kentucky Encyclopedia* (Lexington: University Press of Kentucky, 1992); Penny M. Miller, *Kentucky Politics and Government* (Lincoln: University of Nebraska Press, 1994); Robert F. Sexton, ed., *The Public Papers of the Governors of Kentucky* (Lexington: University Press of Kentucky, 1975).

ROGER TATE

KOPP, DONALD LEE (West Virginia, 1977) was born on May 23, 1935, in Clarksburg, West Virginia, to Francis and Jenny (Wilkinson) Kopp. After graduating from local public schools, he began working at the Fourco Glass Company in Clarksburg. Kopp was vice-president of Rolland Local Number 6 of the United Glass and Ceramics Workers, a delegate to the Harrison County Federation of Labor, and a member of the Elks, Moose, and Methodist Church. He married Beverly Ann Wycoff in 1955, and the couple had three children.

In 1964 Kopp successfully ran for the West Virginia House of Delegates as a Democrat from Harrison County. Serving seven consecutive terms, he chaired the Industry and Labor Committee and the Judiciary Redistricting Committee. Kopp was chosen as speaker for the 1977 session. He also attended the 1972 and 1976 Democratic national conventions.

Defeated for reelection to the House in 1978, Kopp became first vice-president of the West Virginia Democratic Executive Committee. He was again elected to the House in 1980 and 1982. However, he resigned his seat in December 1982 when he was appointed clerk of the House. Kopp continues to hold that post at this writing.

LISLE G. BROWN

L

LAIRD, PHILIP DANDRIDGE (Maryland, 1916) was born in Montgomery County, Maryland, on November 15, 1847. After graduating from high school and reading law, he practiced law in Rockville, Maryland. Laird was also president of the Farmer's Banking and Trust Company. He was married.

First elected to the Maryland House of Delegates as a Democrat from Montgomery County in 1885, Laird served a total of eleven terms. In addition, he was Maryland land commissioner and a presidential elector in 1912. He was appointed to the Maryland Public Service Commission in 1910, becoming its chair in 1916. Chosen as speaker for the 1916 session, Laird was forced to retire from the House in April 1917 due to illness. Following that he returned to his Rockville practice. Laird died on April 27, 1920, at the age of 72.

GARY L. BROWNE

LANDERS, H. LACY (Arkansas, 1985) was born in Benton, Arkansas, on June 28, 1927. He attended local public schools and Little Rock Junior College in Arkansas. During the Korean conflict he served in the U.S. armed forces. Landers worked for the Aluminum Company of America until 1982. A Baptist, he married Lea Bell; the couple had two children.

In 1962 Landers was elected to the Arkansas House of Representatives as a Democrat from Saline County. He was vice-chair of the Insurance and Commerce Committee, the House Management Committee, and the Joint Budget Committee. Chosen as speaker for the 1985 session, he emphasized issues concerning human services and industry. Landers continues to serve in the House at this writing.

GINA PETONITO

LANEY, JAMES E. "Pete" (Texas, 1993) was born in Plainview, Texas, on March 20, 1943, to Wilbur G. and Frances (Wilson) Laney. After earning a B.S. in engineering from Texas Tech University in Lubbock in 1965, he began farming in Hale Center, Texas. Laney belonged to the Masons, Hale County Soil and Water Conservation Board, and Christian Church (Disciples of Christ). He married Nelda Kay McQuien in 1963, and the couple had three children.

A Democrat, Laney chaired the Hale County Democratic Committee in 1970. In 1972 he was elected to the Texas House of Representatives from Hale, Bailey, Briscoe, Castro, Cochran, Crosby, Dickens, Floyd, Lamb, Motley, Parmer, and Swisher counties. He became chair of the State Affairs Committee in 1983, and he was named speaker for the 1993 session. Laney remains in the speakership at this writing.

JON L. WAKELYN

LANSDEN, JOSEPH MERLE (Oklahoma, 1944) was born on a farm near Forgan, Oklahoma, on July 8, 1907. He received an LL.B. from the University of Oklahoma in 1939 and began a law practice in Beaver, Oklahoma. In addition, Lansden was a member of the American and Oklahoma bar associations. A Catholic, he was married.

Lansden successfully ran for the Oklahoma House of Representatives as a Democrat from Beaver County in 1940 and remained there for three consecutive terms. He was named speaker for the extra session of April 1944, following the resignation of incumbent Harold Freeman. During World War II Lansden served as a legal officer in the U.S. Marine Corps. Elected to one additional House term in 1962, he was judge of Oklahoma's 1st District from 1967 to 1977. Lansden died on October 31, 1989, at the age of 82.

"Former State House Speaker Joseph Lansden Dies at 82," *The Daily Oklahoman*, November 2, 1989: 24; Gaston Litton, *History of Oklahoma at the Golden Anniversary of Statehood*, 4 vols. (New York: Lewis Historical Publishing, 1957).

DONOVAN L. REICHENBERGER

LEACH, ALBERT MARTIN (Tennessee, 1911) was born on June 29, 1859, in Murfreesboro, Tennessee, to James T. and Lucy J. (Winston) Leach. In 1897 he moved to Clarksville, Tennessee, where he and his brother founded the firm of Leach and Leach Buggy Manufacturers. A Methodist, Leach became active in temperance reform. He was married to Fannie Texie Shannon in 1882, and following her death to her sister Frusie Shannon.

Leach was elected to the Tennessee House of Representatives as a Democrat from Montgomery County in 1908 and 1910. Joining the "Fusionist" coalition of prohibitionist Democrats and East Tennessee Republicans, he was named speaker for the 1911 session. Afterward Leach returned to his business interests. He also sat on the Montgomery County Election Commission. Leach died on September 5, 1926, at the age of 67.

Biographical file of Tennessee legislators, Tennessee State Library and Archives, Nashville; Clarksville *Leaf Chronicle*, September 7, 1926; Robert M. McBride, *Preliminary Biographical Directory of Tennessee General Assembly* (Nashville, 1967–), XVII: 34; Nashville *Tennessean and American*, January 3, 1911.

FRED A. BAILEY

LEBUS, FRANK (Kentucky, 1933) was born in Harrison County, Kentucky, on January 22, 1882, to J. F. and Nanie K. Lebus. Educated in local schools, he was involved in tobacco farming and banking in Cynthiana, Kentucky. He married Bettie Belle Goodwin in 1909.

A Democrat, Lebus was a local court magistrate for several years. He won election to the Kentucky House of Representatives from Harrison County in 1933, and he was chosen as speaker for the special session that year. Afterward he returned to Cynthiana. Lebus died on August 28, 1962, at the age of 80.

George T. Blakey, *Hard Times and the New Deal in Kentucky, 1929–1939* (Lexington: University Press of Kentucky, 1986); Malcolm E. Jewell and Everett W. Cunningham, *Kentucky Politics* (Lexington: University Press of Kentucky, 1968); Malcolm E. Jewell and Penny Miller, *The Kentucky Legislature: Two Decades of Change* (Lexington: University Press of Kentucky, 1988); Robert F. Sexton, "Kentucky Politics and Society, 1919–1932" (Ph.D. dissertation, University of Washington, 1970).

NANCY DISHER BAIRD

LEE, EDWARD BROOKE (Maryland, 1927) was born on October 23, 1892, in Washington, D.C., to Blair and Anne (Clymer) Lee. His great-grandfather, Richard Henry Lee, signed the Declaration of Independence, and his father was a U.S. senator from Maryland in 1914–17. Raised in Montgomery County, Maryland, the younger Lee attended Princeton University and earned a law degree from George Washington University in 1917. During World War I he served with the U.S. Army in Europe, rising to the rank of major and receiving the Distinguished Service Cross. Lee later became a colonel in the Maryland National Guard. He founded the North Washington Realty Company in the 1920s.

A Democrat, Lee was elected comptroller of Maryland in 1919 and appointed Maryland secretary of state in 1923. Concurrently he chaired the Maryland Democratic Central Committee. Lee won election to one four-year term in the Maryland House of Delegates from Montgomery County in 1926 and was named speaker for the 1927 session. While in the speakership he supported legislation to develop Montgomery County's public school and park systems.

Returning to his realty firm, Lee also began breeding Hereford cattle in Damascus, Maryland. From 1942 to 1948 he sat on the Maryland Park and Planning Commission. In addition, Lee was a regent of the University of Maryland and a member of the Chamber of Commerce and the Episcopal Church. He was married three times and had three sons. His son, Blair Lee III, was lieutenant governor of Maryland. The elder Lee died of pneumonia in Damascus on September 21, 1984, at age 91.

GARY L. BROWNE

LEE, JOHN L. G. (Maryland, 1922) was born in Harford County, Maryland. A Lutheran, he married Caroline Hunter. In 1917 Lee was elected to the Maryland House of Delegates as a Democrat from Harford County. He served three consecutive terms and was chosen as speaker for the 1922 session. Lee died in Bel Air, Maryland, on May 29, 1952.

GARY L. BROWNE

LEONARD, HOMER L. (Texas, 1941) was born in Licking, Missouri, on January 14, 1899. After working as a telegraph operator, he graduated from high school in Rolla, Missouri. Leonard earned a B.S. in mining engineering from the University of Missouri at Rolla in 1922. For five years he was a teacher and a geologist in Oklahoma and Kansas. Moving to Hidalgo County, Texas, Leonard became co-owner of the *Mission Enterprise* and the *McAllen Monitor*. He later studied law.

In 1930 Leonard successfully ran for the Texas House of Representatives as a Democrat from Hidalgo County. He was elected as a write-in candidate in 1932 after being kept off the ballot by a court ruling. Leonard served eight consecutive terms and was named speaker for the 1941 session. Settling in Austin, Texas, in 1945, he lost a 1946 race for the House from Travis County.

Following that, Leonard became general counsel for the Texas Brewers' Institute, a position he held until 1971. He was also active in the Masons, Rotary, American Legion, and Austin Civic Theatre. A Baptist, he was married. Leonard died in Austin on February 13, 1979, at the age of 80.

Eugene W. Jones, Joe E. Ericson, Lyle C. Brown, and Robert S. Trotter, Jr., *Practicing Texas Politics*, 8th ed. (Boston: Houghton Mifflin, 1992); *Presiding Officers of the Texas Legislature, 1846–1982* (Austin: Texas Legislative Council, 1982), 176–177.

L. GERALD FIELDER

LEWALLEN, W. BUFORD (Tennessee, 1947) was born on September 20, 1920, in Clinton, Tennessee, to William Everette and Annette (Stansberry) Lewallen. His father was mayor of Clinton. Lewallen attended local public schools and Carson-Newman College in Jefferson City, Tennessee. While serving as a cadet in the U.S. Army Air Forces, he was severely injured in a plane crash and spent two years in hospitals. He married Celdon Medaris in 1939.

In 1946 Lewallen was elected to the Tennessee House of Representatives as a Democrat from Anderson and Morgan counties. He was chosen as speaker for the 1947 session, his only one in the House, when he was only 26. Afterward he earned an LL.B. from the University of Tennessee and began practicing law in Clinton.

Lewallen and his father successfully helped end the violence that arose from the racial integration of the Clinton schools in 1956. From 1958 to 1977 he sat on the Anderson County Trial Justice Court. Joining the law firm of Daniel, Claiborne & Lewallen, he later established the Main Bank and Trust Company. He was a member of the Elks, American Legion, and Baptist Church. At this writing Lewallen continues to live in Clinton.

Tennessee Blue Book (Nashville: Tennessee Secretary of State).

LEE S. GREENE

LEWIS, E. CLAY, Jr. (Florida, 1931) was born on September 18, 1901, in Marianna, Florida. Earning a degree from the University of Florida, he began working in lumber mills in Port St. Joe, Florida, in 1923. Lewis then returned to the University of Florida, becoming student body president and receiving an LL.B. in 1929. He was married, and he belonged to the Elks and the Rotary.

A Democrat, Lewis was a clerk in the Florida comptroller's office, assistant reading clerk to the state House (1925), and the first judge of Gulf County (1925–26). In 1926 he won election to the Florida House of Representatives from Gulf County. Lewis served three consecutive terms and was named speaker for the 1931 regular session and the special session later that year. During his speakership the House was bitterly divided between urban and rural counties over allocation of gas tax revenues. It killed bills to create sales, cigarette, and income taxes, but it mandated state control of public education funding and overturned Governor Doyle Carlton's veto of parimutuel race track wagering.

From 1937 to 1948 Lewis was attorney to the Gulf County Board of Commissioners and county prosecuting attorney. He was again elected to the House in 1938 and remained there for three more consecutive terms. Appointed assistant attorney of the 14th Judicial Circuit Court of Florida in 1944, he became that body's judge in 1948. Lewis died on April 27, 1961, at the age of 59.

GARY R. MORMINO

LEWIS, GIBSON D. "Gib" (Texas, 1983, 1985, 1987, 1989, 1991) was born in a log cabin in Oletha, Texas, on October 22, 1936, to Jack and Marie Gibson (Croft) Lewis. Graduating from high school in Cleveland, Texas, he attended Sam Houston State University in Huntsville, Texas, and Texas Christian University in Fort Worth. From 1957 to 1961 he served in the U.S. Air Force. Lewis then worked as a salesman for the Olmsted-Kirk Paper Company. He founded Lewis Label Productions, Inc., in Fort Worth in 1964, and he was also part-owner of a gun store called the Shooter's Palace.

A conservative Democrat, Lewis was a River Oaks, Texas, city councilman in 1968–70. He won election to the Texas House of Representatives from Tarrant County in 1970 and remained there for eleven consecutive terms. While in office Lewis supported the Surface Mining and Reclamation Act as well as bills creating the Fort Worth State School and the Texas College of Osteopathic Medicine. Chosen as speaker with bipartisan support in 1983 and renamed for the 1985, 1987, 1989, and 1991 sessions, he held the longest tenure in the post in state history. Lewis won praise for making committee appointments that were balanced ideologically and racially. In addition, he helped pass legislation to strengthen the authority of the speakership.

Afterward Lewis returned to his printing business. President of the Jaycees and the Printing Craftsmen, he belonged to the Rotary, Lions, YMCA, Cancer

Society, United Fund, and Church of Christ. He married Sandra Majors, and the couple had two daughters. Lewis continues to live in Fort Worth at this writing.

McNeely, Dave, "Last of the Good Old Boys," *State Legislatures* 15 (November/December 1989), 27–29.

LUTHER G. HAGARD, JR.

LEWIS, STEPHEN C. (Oklahoma, 1989) was born in Oklahoma City, Oklahoma, on January 6, 1943, to Dudley T. and Charlene Berger (Roberts) Lewis. Graduating from high school in Shawnee, Oklahoma, he earned a B.A. from Oklahoma Baptist University in Shawnee (1964) and a J.D. from the University of Oklahoma (1967). Lewis served in the U.S. Navy for four years before beginning a law practice in Shawnee. In addition, he belonged to the Kiwanis. He married Carolyn J. Woodward, and the couple had two children.

A Democrat, Lewis was assistant district attorney and district attorney of Shawnee. He won election to the Oklahoma House of Representatives from Pottawatomie County in 1980 and remained there for five consecutive terms. In May 1989 Lewis was chosen as speaker by a coalition of dissident Democrats and Republicans who had ousted incumbent Jim L. Barker. Leaving the House in 1990, Lewis continues to live in Shawnee at this writing.

"Oklahoma Ousts Speaker," *State Legislatures* 15 (July 1989), 9.

GINA PETONITO

LINDSEY, JIM THURSTON (Texas, 1955) was born near Texarkana, Texas, on February 1, 1927, to James Luke and Bertie Lee Lindsey. After attending local public schools, he worked part time to fund his education at North Texas Agriculture College (now the University of Texas at Arlington). During World War II Lindsey served in the U.S. Army Air Forces. He earned a B.A. and a law degree with honors (1950) from Baylor University in Waco, Texas. A Baptist, he married Moya Yvonne Birdwell.

Lindsey was elected to the Texas House of Representatives as a conservative Democrat from Bowie County in 1948. He remained there for four consecutive terms and chaired several committees. In addition, Lindsey was involved in creating the Texas Legislative Council and the Legislative Budget Board, which provided trained staff assistance. Named speaker by acclamation for the 1955 session, he was best known for helping pass legislation to revise state corporation law and the Texas Probate Code.

In 1956 Lindsey briefly became executive vice-president of the Texas Good Roads Association. Chair of the state Democratic Party in 1956–59, he backed the efforts of Governor M. Price Daniel, Sr., to maintain the control of the conservative faction. Lindsey practiced law and operated a real estate and investment firm in Austin, Texas, from 1959 to 1991. He was a member of the Masons and the Jaycees. Later Lindsay moved to Red Wood Valley, California, where he continues to live at this writing.

THOMAS R. MYERS

LIPTON, JOHN M. (Arkansas, 1991) was born in Warren, Arkansas, on February 26, 1936. Educated in local public schools, he received a degree from the University of Arkansas. Afterward Lipton became a wholesale oil and gas consultant in Warren. He was a member of the Chamber of Commerce and the Bradley County Industrial Development Corporation. A Baptist, he married Jenelle Neal; the couple had three children.

In 1968 Lipton was elected to the Arkansas House of Representatives as a Democrat from Bradley, Calhoun, and Union counties. He served twelve consecutive terms. Chair of the Joint Performance Review Committee, he was chosen as speaker for the 1991 session. Lipton then returned to Warren, where he continues to live at this writing.

JON L. WAKELYN

LITTLEJOHN, CAMERON BRUCE (South Carolina, 1947, 1949) was born on July 22, 1913, in Pacolet, South Carolina, to Cameron and Lady Sara (Warmoth) Littlejohn. He grew up near Spartanburg, South Carolina. Littlejohn received an A.B. from Wofford College in Spartanburg in 1935 and an LL.B. from the University of South Carolina in 1936. A Baptist, he was widowed and had two children.

In 1936 Littlejohn successfully ran for the South Carolina House of Representatives as a Democrat from Spartanburg County. Remaining there for four consecutive terms, he resigned from the House in October 1943. Littlejohn served in the U.S. Army during World War II, rising to the rank of first lieutenant after helping prosecute Japanese war criminals in the Philippines. He again won election to the House in 1946 and 1948 and was named speaker for the 1947 and 1949 sessions with the support of Governor Strom Thurmond.

Littlejohn stepped down from the speakership in May 1949 and was appointed to the state's 7th Circuit Court later that year. Elected to the South Carolina Supreme Court in 1966, he was its chief justice in 1984–85 before retiring. He belonged to the American Legion, VFW, and American Bar Association. His memoirs, *Littlejohn's Half Century at the Bench and Bar*, were published in 1987. At this writing Littlejohn continues to live in Spartanburg.

Bruce Littlejohn, *Littlejohn's Half Century at the Bench and Bar* (Columbia: South Carolina Bar Foundation, 1987); *South Carolina Legislative Manual* (Columbia: General Assembly of South Carolina, 1916–   ); *The State* (Columbia).

MARIAN ELIZABETH STROBEL

LIVINGSTON, CLINT GRAHAM (Oklahoma, 1959) was born on May 1, 1918, in Burneyville, Oklahoma. After graduating from high school at Stringtown, Oklahoma, he worked with the U.S. Civilian Conservation Corps in California for six months. Livingston attended the University of Oklahoma before becoming the superintendent of a temporary air base in Denton, Texas, in 1941.

During World War II he served in the U.S. Army Air Forces. Earning a law degree from Oklahoma in 1948, he began a private practice in Marietta, Oklahoma. He was married.

A Democrat, Livingston entered politics as Love County attorney in 1949–50. In 1950 and 1952 he successfully ran for the Oklahoma House of Representatives from Love County. Livingston lost a 1954 bid for the Oklahoma Senate. Again elected to the House in 1956 and 1958, he was chosen as speaker for the 1959 session. He was commissioner of the Oklahoma Insurance Fund (1959–60) as well as a member of the state Industrial Court (1961–62) and the Cleveland County Superior Court (1962).

After practicing law in Norman, Oklahoma, Livingston was a referee for the Oklahoma Supreme Court in 1964–66. He was then an administrative judge for the U.S. Social Security Administration in Fort Worth, Texas, and for the U.S. Coast Guard in Houston, Texas. Returning to Marietta in 1971, Livingston sat on Oklahoma's 20th District Court in 1974–78 and was appointed to the state Worker's Compensation Court in 1982. From 1978 to 1982 he was a lay minister in the Methodist Church. Livingston also belonged to the Masons and the Lions.

KENNY L. BROWN

LONG, JOHN LEE (Alabama, 1927) was born on January 12, 1867, in Greenville, Alabama. After attending local private schools, he began working as a cotton buyer in Greenville. Long served as an officer in the Alabama Militia. He belonged to the Episcopal Church, and he married Sallie Josephine Dickerson in 1900.

A Democrat, Long served Greenville as a city councilman, treasurer, and clerk. He was president of the Butler County Board of Revenue and chair of the county Democratic Executive Committee. In 1901 he was a delegate to the Alabama Constitutional Convention.

Long was elected to the Alabama House of Representatives from Butler County in 1906, 1910, 1918, 1922, and 1926. Chosen as speaker for the 1927 session, he sponsored legislation to build fifteen toll bridges throughout the state. He still held the speakership when he died in Montgomery, Alabama, on February 20, 1929, at age 62. The next year a highway bridge in Miller's Ferry, Alabama, was named for Long.

BENJAMIN B. WILLIAMS AND DONALD B. DODD

LOVE, CHARLES HOWARD (Tennessee, 1929) was born in South Carrollton, Kentucky, on August 10, 1874. After working for the Murfreesboro, Tennessee, *Free Press*, he became a foreman for the Madisonville, Kentucky, *Hustler*. Love spent eleven years with the *Robertson County Times* in Springfield, Tennessee. He was also an assistant investigator for the U.S. Bureau of Internal Revenue and a special agent for the U.S. Department of the Interior for three years.

Love won election to one term in the Tennessee House of Representatives as a Democrat from Robertson County in 1904. In 1918–22 he was clerk of the Robertson County Circuit Court. Again elected to the House in 1926 and 1928, Love was named speaker for the 1929 session. He was Tennessee commissioner of labor (1931–33) and head of the Sales Tax Division of the Tennessee Department of Finance and Taxation.

A member of the Robertson County Democratic Executive Committee, Love was county campaign manager for the gubernatorial campaigns of Austin Peay and Henry Horton and state coordinator of the 1930 Democratic campaign. In addition, he was president of the Chamber of Commerce and a member of the Knights of Pythias and the Methodist Church. He married Nannie Smith in 1898; the couple had no children. Love died on May 16, 1950, at the age of 75.

Tennessee Blue Book (Nashville: Tennessee Secretary of State).

WILLIE H. PIGG

LOWE, THOMAS HUNTER (Maryland, 1969, 1971) was born in McDaniel, Maryland, on January 8, 1928, to Denton Scott and Louise (Price) Lowe. Educated in local public schools, he served in the U.S. Marine Corps during World War II. Lowe attended Baltimore City College in Maryland and earned an A.A. from Towson State Teachers College (now University) in Maryland (1950), an A.B. from Washington College in Chestertown, Maryland (1952), and an LL.B. from the University of Maryland (1956). He then began a law practice in Easton, Maryland.

In 1958 Lowe won election to the Maryland House of Delegates as a Democrat from Talbot County. Remaining there for four consecutive four-year terms, he became chair of the Judiciary Committee in 1963 and majority leader in 1967. Lowe was chosen as speaker in January 1969 after incumbent Marvin Mandel became governor, and he was renamed to the post for the 1971 session. While in the speakership he cultivated a loud and confrontational image that sometimes obscured his political innovations. He helped pass Mandel's programs and attempted to concentrate legislative power in the speakership.

Appointed to the Maryland Court of Special Appeals in October 1973, Lowe was elected to the position the following year. He was president of the Jaycees and the Talbot County Bar Association and a member of the Elks, Lions, Chamber of Commerce, American Legion, and VFW. An Episcopalian, he married Jane Bradley in 1953; the couple had two sons. Lowe died of an apparent heart attack on June 13, 1984, at age 56.

Baltimore *Evening Sun*; Baltimore *News American*; Baltimore *Sun*; Robert J. Brugger, *Maryland: A Middle Temperament, 1634–1980* (Baltimore: Johns Hopkins University Press, 1988); George H. Callcott, *Maryland and America, 1940–1980* (Baltimore: Johns Hopkins University Press, 1985); Easton *Star-Democrat*, June 18, 1984; *Maryland Manual: Annual Publication of State Officers* (Annapolis: Hall of Records Commission).

WHITMAN H. RIDGWAY

LOWMAN, HARRY KING (Kentucky, 1960, 1962) was born in Louisville, Kentucky, on August 8, 1913, and moved with his family to Ashland, Kentucky, as a child. Earning a B.S. from Morehead State College (now University) and an M.Ed. from the University of Kentucky, he worked as a teacher and a real estate developer in Ashland. Lowman also owned the T and L Construction Company. He was married, and he belonged to the Christian Church (Disciples of Christ).

A Democrat, Lowman was a member of the Young Democrats and the state Central-Executive Committee. He won election to one term in the Kentucky House of Representatives from Boyd County in 1941. During World War II Lowman served in the U.S. Army. Again elected to the House in 1945, he remained there for nine consecutive terms. Lowman was named majority leader in 1952 and 1954 and speaker for the 1960 and 1962 sessions. However, his power was limited by the strong legislative influence of the governor.

Withdrawing from the 1962 Democratic primary for the U.S. Senate from Kentucky, Lowman lost reelection to the House in 1963. In addition, he was defeated in the 1967 primary for lieutenant governor of Kentucky. After that he returned to his Ashland real estate and construction businesses. Lowman died on February 23, 1977, at the age of 63.

Malcolm E. Jewell, *Representation in State Legislatures* (Lexington: University Press of Kentucky, 1982); Malcolm E. Jewell and Everett W. Cunningham, *Kentucky Politics* (Lexington: University Press of Kentucky, 1968); Malcolm E. Jewell and Penny Miller, *The Kentucky Legislature: Two Decades of Change* (Lexington: University Press of Kentucky, 1988); Malcolm E. Jewell and Samuel C. Patterson, *The Legislative Process in the United States*, 4th ed. (New York: Random House, 1986); John Ed Pearce, *Divide and Dissent: Kentucky Politics, 1930–1963* (Lexington: University Press of Kentucky, 1987); Seymour Sher, "Conditions for Legislative Control," *Journal of Politics* 25 (1963), 526–551.

H. LEW WALLACE

LUBER, JOHN CHRISTOPHER (Maryland, 1951, 1955) was born on November 22, 1903, in Baltimore, Maryland. His father was a state legislator in 1922. Educated in local Catholic schools until he was 15, Luber began working as an accountant for the Baltimore and Ohio Railroad. He was married, and he belonged to the Moose.

A Democrat, Luber became an active ward politician. In 1938 he was elected to the Maryland House of Delegates from the city of Baltimore with the backing of party boss William Curran. Luber served five consecutive four-year terms, becoming chair of the Baltimore delegation in 1941 and majority leader and chair of the Ways and Means Committee two years later. He was stripped of those positions in 1946 when he supported a losing candidate for governor.

Playing an instrumental role in the passage of a sales tax bill in 1947, Luber was named speaker for the 1951 and 1955 sessions. His tenure coincided with the governorship of Republican Theodore R. McKeldin. While in the speakership Luber enjoyed more independence and power than most of his predecessors, in part because he was able to build support from regional coalitions within his party. He lost reelection to the House in the 1958 Democratic primary, and he then became a state lobbyist for the Baltimore and Ohio Railroad. Luber died on July 9, 1962, at the age of 58.

Baltimore *Evening Sun*; Baltimore *News-Post*, July 10, 1962; Baltimore *Sun*; Robert J. Brugger, *Maryland: A Middle Temperament, 1634–1980* (Baltimore: Johns Hopkins University Press, 1988); George H. Callcott, *Maryland and America, 1940–1980* (Baltimore: Johns Hopkins University Press, 1985); *Maryland Manual: Annual Publication of State Officers* (Annapolis: Hall of Records Commission); Morris L. Radoff, *The Old Line State: A History of Maryland* (Hopkinsville, KY: Historical Records Association, 1956), II: 477–480.

WHITMAN H. RIDGWAY

LUMPKIN, SAMUEL E. (Mississippi, 1940) was born on April 21, 1908, in Hudsonville, Mississippi, and as a child moved with his family to Tupelo, Mississippi. Educated in local schools, he earned an LL.B. from Cumberland University in Lebanon, Tennessee, in 1931. Afterward he began a law practice in Tupelo. Lumpkin was district governor of the Lions, commander of the American Legion, and a member of the Masons, Knights of Pythias, VFW, and Methodist Church. He was married.

A Democrat, Lumpkin was Tupelo city attorney for eight years and a school trustee. He won election to the Mississippi House of Representatives from Lee County in 1931 when he was only 23. Lumpkin remained there for three consecutive four-year terms, and he was unanimously chosen as speaker for the 1940 session. While in office he coauthored homestead and old age pension legislation and helped pass bills to offer free public school textbooks and to purchase the right-of-way for the Natchez Trace Parkway. Resigning from the House in March 1942, he served as an intelligence officer with the U.S. Army Air Forces in the Pacific theater during World War II.

In 1947 Lumpkin successfully ran for lieutenant governor of Mississippi. He narrowly lost to Hugh L. White in the 1951 gubernatorial race. Again elected to the House in 1955, Lumpkin was defeated for the post in 1963. During that time he increasingly distanced himself from the national Democratic Party, helping to organize the 1948 "Dixiecrat" movement and publicly backing Republican presidential candidates in 1952, 1956, and 1960. Lumpkin died of a heart attack in Tupelo on July 9, 1964, at age 56.

Dale Krane and Stephen D. Shaffer, eds., *Mississippi Government & Politics: Modernizers Versus Traditionalists* (Lincoln: University of Nebraska Press, 1992); Richard A. McLemore, *A History of Mississippi*, 2 vols. (Jackson: University and College Press of Mississippi, 1973); *Mississippi Official and Statistical Register* (Jackson: Secretary of State).

DAVID G. SANSING

LYNNE, SEABOURN ARTHUR (Alabama, 1920) was born in Apple Grove, Alabama, on July 5, 1877. Attending public schools and Somerville Academy in Alabama, he earned a B.S. (1895) and a B.A. (1896) from Morgan County College in Alabama. For one year he worked as a principal and teacher in

Lacey's Spring, Alabama. Lynne received an LL.B. from the University of Alabama, where he also worked as a law librarian. He practiced law in New Decatur, Alabama, from 1898 to 1901, when he moved to Decatur, Alabama.

A Democrat, Lynne was Decatur city attorney in 1901. He was elected to one term in the Alabama Senate in 1902 and to the Alabama House of Representatives from Morgan County in 1918. Lynne was majority floor leader for the 1919 session. In 1920 he was chosen as speaker following the resignation of incumbent Henry P. Merritt.

After that Lynne returned to his Decatur practice. Appointed to Alabama's 8th Circuit Court in 1951, he won election to the post the next year but was defeated in 1958. Lynne belonged to the Odd Fellows, Knights of Pythias, and Baptist Church. He married Anne Leigh Harris in 1906, and the couple had three children. His son, Seabourn Harris Lynne, was a federal judge. The elder Lynne died on July 12, 1960, at the age of 83.

BENJAMIN B. WILLIAMS AND DONALD B. DODD

LYONS, GEORGE SAGE (Alabama, 1971) was born on October 1, 1936, in Mobile, Alabama, to Mark and Ruth (Kelly) Lyons. After attending the University Military School in Mobile, he earned a B.A. in economics from Washington and Lee University in Lexington, Virginia (1958) and an LL.B. from the University of Alabama (1960). Lyons then served in the U.S. Army Reserve with the Judge Advocate General's Corps, rising to the rank of captain. In 1962 he began a law practice in Mobile, where he eventually became a partner in the firm of Lyons, Pipes and Cook. He married Elsie Crain, and the couple had two children.

A Democrat, Lyons was Mobile County coordinator of Lurleen Wallace's successful gubernatorial campaign in 1966. In addition, he worked on the 1968 presidential bid of George C. Wallace. Lyons was appointed to the Alabama House of Representatives from Mobile County in 1969 and elected to the post the next year. With Governor George Wallace's support, he was named speaker for the 1971 session. While in the speakership Lyons led the House through a difficult period of reapportionment ordered by a federal court. He was able to achieve an unusual degree of independence for the House, and he implemented several recommendations of Alabama's 1970 Legislative Reform Study to improve efficiency.

Afterward Lyons returned to his Mobile law practice. President of the Mobile Chamber of Commerce in 1980, he was chair of the Crain Oil Company in Guntersville, Alabama, and a director of First National Bank in Mobile. Lyons sat on the finance committees of the 1988 and 1992 presidential campaigns of George Bush. He was also active in the Tennessee-Tombigbee Waterway Development Authority, American, Alabama, and Mobile County bar associations, and Episcopal Church. As of this writing Lyons continues to live in Mobile.

Alabama Official and Statistical Register (Montgomery: State of Alabama, Department of Archives and History, 1903–   ); Henry S. Marks, *Alabama Past Leaders* (Huntsville:

Strode Publishers, 1982); Harold W. Stanley, *Senate vs. Governor, Alabama, 1971* (University, AL: University of Alabama Press, 1975); *Who's Who in Alabama* (Birmingham: Sayers Enterprises, 1965–   ).

                                                                                    REID BADGER

M

MAIDEN, SELDEN LONGLEY (Tennessee, 1927) was born in Humphreys County, Tennessee, on August 8, 1883, to George and Rosamond (Hawley) Maiden. His brother, Robert E. Maiden, was solicitor general of Tennessee and a state legislator in 1895. Educated in public and private schools in Weakley County, Tennessee, he earned a degree from Dickson College in Tennessee and a law degree from the University of Memphis in Tennessee. For three years Maiden practiced law in Memphis. He moved to Dresden, Tennessee, in 1913 and later to Greenfield, Tennessee.

Maiden won election to the Tennessee House of Representatives as a Democrat from Weakley County in 1914 and 1916. In 1922 and 1924 he successfully ran for the Tennessee Senate. Again elected to the House in 1926, he was chosen as speaker for the 1927 session.

After that Maiden returned to his law practice. He became president of the Greenfield Banking Company in 1937, and he belonged to the Masons. A Methodist, he married Mamie Brasfield in 1916; the couple had one son. Maiden died in Memphis on May 24, 1949, at age 65, and he was buried in Greenfield.

JAMES H. EDMONSON

MANDEL, MARVIN (Maryland, 1964, 1967) was born on April 19, 1920, in Baltimore, Maryland, into a Jewish family. Educated in local public schools, he earned an LL.B. from the University of Maryland in 1942. During World War II he served in the U.S. Army. Mandel then began to practice law in Baltimore. In addition, he was state commander of the Jewish War Veterans and a member of the American Legion and the American, Maryland, and Baltimore bar associations. He was married twice.

A Democrat, Mandel was a justice of the peace in Baltimore and a member of the Maryland Democratic Central Committee. In January 1952 he was appointed to the Maryland House of Delegates from the city of Baltimore. Mandel remained there for five consecutive four-year terms, and he was majority leader and chair of the Ways and Means Committee in 1963. Becoming acting speaker following the resignation of incumbent A. Gordon Boone in February 1963, Mandel was chosen as speaker the next year. He was renamed to the speakership for the 1967 session. While in office he helped reorganize the House, gaining a reputation for being forceful but nonconfrontational.

Appointed governor of Maryland in January 1969 to replace U.S. Vice President-elect Spiro T. Agnew, Mandel won election to the post in 1970 and 1974. He chaired the National Governors Conference in 1972–73 and attended the 1968 and 1972 Democratic national conventions. Mandel resigned the governorship upon being convicted on federal charges of racketeering and mail fraud in 1977. After spending nineteen months in prison, he became a lobbyist and a radio talk show host in Annapolis, Maryland. His mail fraud conviction was overturned in 1987 as a result of a U.S. Supreme Court decision. At this writing Mandel continues to live in Annapolis.

Baltimore *Daily Record*; Baltimore *Evening Sun*; Baltimore *Sun*; Robert J. Brugger, *Maryland: A Middle Temperament, 1634–1980* (Baltimore: Johns Hopkins University Press, 1988); George H. Callcott, *Maryland and America, 1940–1980* (Baltimore: Johns Hopkins University Press, 1985); *Maryland Manual: Annual Publication of State Officers* (Annapolis: Hall of Records Commission); Morris L. Radoff, *The Old Line State: A History of Maryland* (Hopkinsville, KY: Historical Records Association, 1956), III: 1272–1274.

                                                                    WHITMAN H. RIDGWAY

MANFORD, THOMAS DURWOOD, Jr. (Texas, 1949) was born on March 13, 1917, in Smiley, Texas. Educated in local public schools, he attended Southwestern University in Georgetown, Texas, and earned a B.A. from the University of Texas in 1938. Manford studied law and began a private practice around 1945. He was married, and he belonged to the Masons, Texas Bar Association, and Methodist Church.

In 1940 Manford was elected to the Texas House of Representatives as a conservative Democrat from Gonzales County. Serving five consecutive terms, he gained notoriety as the author of the controversial Manford Act of 1943, which placed labor unions under state regulation. Manford also helped establish the Legislative Budget Board, Legislative Council, and Farm-to-Market Road Program. He was named speaker for the 1949 session.

Afterward Manford helped operate his family's retail business and ranch near Smiley. In addition, he sat on the Texas Board of State Hospitals and Special Schools, Industrial Accident Board, and Board of Water Engineers from 1955 to 1961. Appointed to the Texas Insurance Board in 1961, Manford moved to Austin, Texas. He remained on the Insurance Board until 1982. Manford died on March 24, 1988, at the age of 71.

Eugene W. Jones, Joe E. Ericson, Lyle C. Brown, and Robert S. Trotter, Jr., *Practicing Texas Politics*, 8th ed. (Boston: Houghton Mifflin, 1992); *Presiding Officers of the Texas Legislature, 1846–1982* (Austin: Texas Legislative Council, 1982), 184–185.

                                                                    LYLE C. BROWN

MASSENBURG, GEORGE ALVIN (Virginia, 1947, 1948) was born on September 19, 1894, in Hampton, Virginia. Educated in local public schools, he became a harbor pilot in Hampton in 1912. From 1943 to 1968 Massenburg was president of the Virginia Pilot Association. He served in the U.S. Coast Guard Reserve during World War II, rising to the rank of captain.

Massenburg was elected to the Virginia House of Delegates as a Democrat from the city of Hampton and Elizabeth City County (now part of Hampton) in 1925, and he remained there for twelve consecutive terms. While in office he backed several bills for port development and promoted the construction of bridges and tunnels in the Hampton Roads and Chesapeake Bay regions. Chosen as speaker in 1947 after the resignation of incumbent Thomas B. Stanley, Massenburg was renamed to the post for the 1948 session. He was a staunch supporter of the conservative Democratic faction headed by U.S. Senator Harry F. Byrd, Sr., chairing the state party in 1948–52.

In 1949 Massenburg was defeated for renomination to the House by a liberal candidate. He sat on the Virginia Port Authority (1942–51), the Virginia Conservation and Development Commission (1949–53), and the board of visitors of the Virginia Military Institute (1949–58). President of the Rotary and the Hampton Roads Maritime Association, he also belonged to the Masons, Elks, Eagles, and Methodist Church. Massenburg died on November 25, 1968, at the age of 74.

E. Griffith Dodson, ed., *Speakers and Clerks of the Virginia House of Delegates, 1776–1976*, rev. under the direction of Joseph H. Holleman, Jr. (Richmond, 1976), 120–143; *Newport News Daily Press*, November 26, 1968; *Norfolk Virginian-Pilot*, November 27, 1968.

JAMES R. SWEENEY

MAVRETIC, JOSEPHUS L. (North Carolina, 1989) was born on July 29, 1934, in Powells Point, North Carolina, to Joseph and Virginia (Bateman) Mavretic. He earned an A.B. from the University of North Carolina (1956) and an M.S. from George Washington University in Washington, D.C. (1972). Mavretic served in the U.S. Marine Corps during the Vietnam conflict, flying more than 300 combat missions. Afterward he began farming in Tarboro, North Carolina.

A Democrat, Mavretic was school board chair and director of the North Carolina Council on Alcoholism. He won election to the North Carolina House of Representatives from Edgecombe County in 1980 and remained there for seven consecutive terms. Mavretic was named speaker for the 1989 session following the ouster of incumbent four-term Liston B. Ramsey by a coalition of conservative Democrats and Republicans. In return he agreed (among other things) to grant the GOP proportionality in committee assignments.

Mavretic left the House in 1994. Outside of politics he was a director of the

First Carolina Bank and a member of the Moose, Rotary, American Legion, American Cancer Society, and Methodist Church. He was married and had one son. At this writing Mavretic continues to live in Tarboro.

Christensen, Rob, ''Growing Republican Ranks Help Topple Speaker in North Carolina,'' *State Legislatures* 15 (April 1989), 16–19.

GINA PETONITO

MAXEY, JAMES HARVEY (Oklahoma, 1913) was born around 1889. His father, James Harvey Maxey, was a U.S. commissioner and a state legislator. Raised in Cleveland and Pottawatomie counties, Oklahoma Territory, the younger Maxey settled in Muskogee, Oklahoma, in 1907. He won election to the Oklahoma House of Representatives as a Democrat from Muskogee County. Maxey was chosen as speaker for the 1913 session.

GORDON MOORE

McBEE, WILLIAM DALTON (Oklahoma, 1923) was born on June 10, 1876, in Austin, Texas. He read law and operated a private practice in Comanche, Oklahoma Territory, from 1896 to 1908. McBee then moved to Clovis, New Mexico, where he began publishing the Clovis *Journal* in 1913. Relocating to Nowata, Oklahoma, in 1916, he later returned to Comanche. He was a regent of the University of New Mexico and active in the Masons, Rotary, Izaak Walton League, and Methodist Church.

A Democrat, McBee served Comanche as city assessor and tax collector in 1898. In 1908 he successfully ran for the New Mexico territorial Senate. He was also a member of the school boards of Clovis and Melrose, New Mexico, assistant city district attorney for Clovis (1912), and district judge for Curry County, New Mexico (1912–13). McBee was appointed to the Nowata County Council of Defense during World War I. Elected to one term in the Oklahoma House of Representatives from Stephens County in 1922, he joined three other Democrats to form the ''Four Horsemen,'' who opposed the reforms of Governor John C. Walton.

The governor declared martial law, but he was eventually forced to call the legislature into a special session in October 1923. McBee was named speaker following the expulsion of incumbent Murray F. Gibbons. While in the post he was chief prosecutor in the proceedings that impeached Walton and removed him from office. After briefly practicing law and operating a real estate office in Duncan, Oklahoma, McBee entered the oil business in Oklahoma City, Oklahoma, in 1926. He married Myrtle Montgomery, and the couple had five children. McBee died in Oklahoma City on January 15, 1965, at age 88.

GORDON MOORE

McCALLUM, SHELBY (Kentucky, 1964, 1966) was born in Marshall County, Kentucky, on February 23, 1918. Graduating from local public schools, he served in the U.S. Army during World War II. McCallum eventually became the owner of three radio stations, a drive-in theater, and a newspaper in Benton, Kentucky. He was married.

A Democrat, McCallum was elected to the Kentucky House of Representatives from Marshall County in 1951. He remained there until 1969 with the exception of the 1960 term. McCallum was named speaker for the 1964 and 1966 sessions. While in the speakership he had little power due to the House's limited professional staff and unwieldy committee system.

After leaving the House, McCallum returned to his businesses in Benton. He belonged to the Masons, Rotary, and Methodist Church. In 1981 he was appointed coordinator of a campaign to pass an amendment to the Kentucky Constitution concerning succession. McCallum died on June 14, 1987, at the age of 69.

Malcolm E. Jewell, *Representation in State Legislatures* (Lexington: University Press of Kentucky, 1982); Malcolm E. Jewell and Everett W. Cunningham, *Kentucky Politics* (Lexington: University Press of Kentucky, 1968); Malcolm E. Jewell and Penny Miller, *The Kentucky Legislature: Two Decades of Change* (Lexington: University Press of Kentucky, 1988); Malcolm E. Jewell and Samuel C. Patterson, *The Legislative Process in the United States*, 4th ed. (New York: Random House, 1986); John Ed Pearce, *Divide and Dissent: Kentucky Politics, 1930–1963* (Lexington: University Press of Kentucky, 1987).

H. LEW WALLACE

McCARTY, DANIEL THOMAS (Florida, 1941) was born in Fort Pierce, Florida, on January 18, 1912, to Daniel T. and Frances (Moore) McCarty. He earned a B.S. in agriculture from the University of Florida in 1934. Afterward he operated his family's citrus groves and managed the Indian River Citrus Association, Inc. In addition, McCarty was president of the Chamber of Commerce and a member of the Masons, Elks, Odd Fellows, Rotary, American Legion, and VFW. An Episcopalian, he was married.

McCarty won election to the Florida House of Representatives as a Democrat from St. Lucie County in 1936. Remaining there for three consecutive terms, he was named speaker for the 1941 session when he was only 29. While in office McCarty promoted economy in government, but he also consistently advocated increased funding for public education. He supported increasing taxes on non-essentials such as alcohol and levying new taxes on local governments despite their already heavy debts.

Resigning from the House in late 1941, McCarty served with the U.S. Army's field artillery during World War II. He rose to the rank of colonel and received several medals. In 1948 he lost the Florida Democratic gubernatorial primary to Fuller Warren. Scandals in Warren's administration helped McCarty be elected to the governorship in 1952. Although he suffered a heart attack following his inauguration, he successfully worked to raise teachers' salaries and to create a state turnpike authority. McCarty was still governor when he died on September 28, 1953, at age 41.

J. LARRY DURRENCE

McCARTY, J. D. (Oklahoma, 1961, 1963, 1965) was born in Waurika, Oklahoma, on August 28, 1916, and moved to Oklahoma City, Oklahoma, in 1927. Earning a degree from Capitol Hill Junior College in 1936, he received a B.A. in government and economics from the University of Oklahoma. During World War II McCarty served with the U.S. Navy in the Pacific theater. Afterward he entered the construction and insurance businesses in Oklahoma City. A Methodist, he was married.

In 1940 McCarty was elected to the Oklahoma House of Representatives as a Democrat from Oklahoma County. Remaining there for thirteen consecutive terms, he became known as one of the outspoken "Knothole Gang." McCarty lost a 1959 bid for speaker to Clint G. Livingston, but he was chosen as speaker for the 1961 session with the support of Governor J. Howard Edmondson. While in the speakership he helped protect Edmonson's newly passed reforms concerning central purchasing and the merit system. Renamed to the post in 1963 and 1965, McCarty clashed with Republican Governor Henry L. Bellmon over mental health and educational programs. He also chaired the board of the Council of State Governments.

McCarty lost a bid for reelection to the House in 1966. The following year he was convicted of federal income tax evasion and perjury. After spending several months in prison, McCarty became a lobbyist. He eventually gained a reputation as the "dean of lobbyists" in the Oklahoma legislature. In addition, he was president of the Kiwanis and United Cerebral Palsy of Oklahoma and a member of the Chamber of Commerce and the American Legion. McCarty died of a heart ailment on January 1, 1981, at the age of 69.

KENNY L. BROWN

McCLERKIN, HAYES CANDOR (Arkansas, 1969) was born in Texarkana, Arkansas, on December 16, 1931, to Hayes Candor and Orlean (Maloney) McClerkin. After earning a B.S. from Washington and Lee University in Lexington, Virginia, in 1953, he served in the U.S. Navy for three years and rose to the rank of lieutenant. McClerkin received an LL.B. from the University of Arkansas in 1959. He then began practicing law in Texarkana.

In 1960 McClerkin was elected to the Arkansas House of Representatives as a Democrat from Miller County. Remaining there for five consecutive terms, he became identified with the "Young Turk" faction opposed to conservative Governor Orval E. Faubus and his supporters in the "Old Guard." McClerkin chaired the Public Health Committee and the Efficiency Committee before being named speaker for the 1969 session. While in the speakership he attempted to improve the image of the House by banning all lobbyists from the floor. He also sponsored bills creating a code of ethics for state employees and a Printing Review Committee.

Despite his reputation as a reform candidate, McClerkin lost the 1970 Democratic primary for governor of Arkansas to Dale L. Bumpers. Afterward he returned to his Texarkana practice. McClerkin sat on the Arkansas Oil and Gas Commission in 1980–83. He was also president of the Lions and a member of the American Legion, VFW, and American and Miller County bar associations. A Presbyterian, McClerkin married Lillian Riggs; the couple had three daughters.

LEON C. MILLER

McCORQUODALE, JOSEPH CHARLES, Jr. (Alabama, 1975, 1979) was born on December 2, 1920, in Salitpa, Alabama, to Joseph Charles and Winnie Lee (Griffin) McCorquodale. He attended local public schools, the Marion Institute in Alabama, and the University of Alabama. During World War II McCorquodale served with the U.S. Army Air Forces in the Pacific theater, rising to the rank of first lieutenant. An automobile dealer until 1961, he later became owner of the McCorquodale Insurance Agency and president of Overstreet & McCorquodale Forest Products in Jackson, Alabama. In addition, he was a bank director.

McCorquodale was elected to the Alabama House of Representatives as a Democrat in 1958 and remained there for six consecutive four-year terms. He represented Clarke County until 1966, Clarke, Choctaw, and Washington counties until 1974, and Clarke and Monroe counties thereafter. Becoming vice-chair of the Ways and Means Committee in 1968 and speaker *pro tem* in 1972, McCorquodale was named to the speakership in 1975. His selection process broke Alabama tradition, as he gathered support among House colleagues before gaining the approval of Governor George C. Wallace. He was again chosen as speaker for the 1979 session.

In 1982 McCorquodale unsuccessfully sought the Democratic nomination for governor of Alabama. Returning to his business interests, he was a consultant to the Business Council of Alabama and a legislative adviser to Republican Governor Guy Hunt. McCorquodale belonged to the Chamber of Commerce, American Legion, VFW, and Methodist Church. He married Mary Elizabeth McCrary in 1942, and the couple had two children. As of this writing McCorquodale continues to live in Jackson.

WILLIAM H. STEWART

McCRORY, ALONZO (Oklahoma, 1915) was born in Fayette, Texas, on September 10, 1878, to A. S. and Clara (Wier) McCrory. After attending Baylor University in Waco, Texas, he worked for a bank in Durant, Indian Territory (now Oklahoma), for two years. McCrory moved to Comanche, Oklahoma Territory, and then to Ringling, Oklahoma Territory, in 1905. He became vice-president of the First State Bank of Ringling.

A Democrat, McCrory was deputy clerk of the Jefferson County Court and a member of the Ringling school board. In 1912 and 1914 he was elected to the Oklahoma House of Representatives from Jefferson County. McCrory was chosen as speaker for the 1915 session, working with Governor Robert L. Williams. He sat on the Oklahoma Council of Defense during World War I.

Afterward McCrory returned to his Ringling bank. In addition, he was director of the Cornish Orphans Home and active in the Masons, Woodmen, Rotary, and Baptist Church. He married Una B. Cochran in 1902, and the couple had five children. Convicted of embezzlement in 1932 in connection with the bank's failure, McCrory spent ten years in jail.

GORDON MOORE

McCUISTON, LLOYD CARLISLE, Jr. (Arkansas, 1981) was born on March 26, 1918, in Lucy, Tennessee, to Lloyd Carlisle and Myrtle Ola (Potts) McCuiston. In 1933 he moved with his family to West Memphis, Arkansas, where he graduated from high school. Earning a B.S. in civil engineering from the University of Arkansas in 1940, he briefly worked for the U.S. Corps of Engineers. McCuiston served with the U.S. Navy's Construction Battalion in the Pacific theater during World War II, rising to the rank of lieutenant (s.g.). He then engaged in farming and farm equipment sales in West Memphis, becoming president of the Russell Tractor Company from 1963 to 1983.

A Democrat, McCuiston served Crittenden County as clerk of the Circuit Court (1949–58) and justice of the peace (1958–60). He was elected without opposition to the Arkansas House of Representatives from Crittenden and St. Francis counties in 1960. McCuiston was chosen as speaker for the 1981 session. In addition, he sat on the Arkansas Democratic Committee.

Outside of politics McCuiston was president of the Rotary and the Chamber of Commerce and a member of the American Legion, VFW, and Baptist Church. He married Olivia Lucretia Graham in 1947, and the couple had two children. As of this writing McCuiston remains in the House and continues to operate his farm.

SUZANNE MABERRY

McINTOSH, DAVID GREGG, Jr. (Maryland, 1917) was born in Baltimore County, Maryland, on July 1, 1877. His father was from South Carolina, and his mother from Virginia. He earned a B.A. from Johns Hopkins University in Baltimore, Maryland (1898) and an LL.B. from the University of Maryland (1900). McIntosh then began a law practice in Towson, Maryland. In addition, he was an avid huntsman and a member of the Elks and the Maryland and Baltimore County bar associations. An Episcopalian, he was married.

In 1913 McIntosh successfully ran for the Maryland House of Delegates as a Democrat from Baltimore County. He served three consecutive terms and was named speaker for the special session of June 1917 after the resignation of incumbent Philip D. Laird. Elected to the Maryland Senate in 1923, McIntosh remained there until 1934 and was that body's president in 1924–30. While in office he became well known for his opposition both to Governor Albert Ritchie and to smoking in the Senate chamber. McIntosh died on May 9, 1940, at the age of 62.

GARY L. BROWNE

McKINNEY, JAMES ROBIN (Tennessee, 1971) was born on March 10, 1931, in Smith County, Tennessee, to Theodore R. and Pearl (Bellar) McKinney. During the Korean conflict he served in the U.S. Navy, receiving several medals. McKinney earned a B.S. from Tennessee Technological University in Cookeville (1956) and an LL.B. from the YMCA Law School in Nashville, Tennessee (1964). He then began a private practice in Madison, Tennessee (now part of Nashville).

McKinney was elected to the Tennessee House of Representatives as a Democrat from Davidson County in 1968 and remained there for eight consecutive terms. Minority whip in 1969, he was chosen as speaker when the Democrats gained control of the House for the 1971 session. In 1973 McKinney was defeated for the speakership by Ned R. McWherter. He was also a delegate to the 1972 Democratic National Convention.

After losing the 1984 Democratic primary for the House, McKinney returned to Nashville. He was named "Distinguished Young Man of the Year" by the Madison Jaycees in 1966. In addition he belonged to the Masons, Elks, Lions, American Legion, VFW, and Baptist Church. McKinney married Dorothy Scudder in 1955, and the couple had two sons.

Lee Seifert Greene, David H. Grubbs, and Victor C. Hobday, *Government in Tennessee*, 4th ed. (Knoxville: University of Tennessee Press, 1982); *Tennessee Blue Book* (Nashville: Tennessee Secretary of State).

LEE S. GREENE

McMANUS, LEWIS NICHOLS (West Virginia, 1971, 1973, 1975) was born on September 8, 1929, in Beckley, West Virginia, to Joab L. and Mattie (Ferguson) McManus. Attending local public schools and Beckley College in West Virginia, he earned a B.A. *magna cum laude* from Morris Harvey College (now the University of Charleston) in West Virginia in 1956. McManus then entered the real estate and insurance business in Beckley. He never married.

In 1964 McManus was elected to the West Virginia House of Delegates as a Democrat from Raleigh County. Serving six consecutive terms, he became chair of the Committee on Finance in 1969. McManus was chosen as speaker in March 1971 following the death of incumbent Ivor F. Boiarsky. He was renamed to the speakership for the 1973 and 1975 sessions.

Appointed executive secretary of the West Virginia Public Employees Retirement Board in 1977, McManus resigned from the post in 1983. The following year he began working for West Virginia University President Gordon Gee as a legislative liaison, despite protests from some legislators that colleges were not supposed to hire lobbyists. In other affairs he belonged to the Masons, Elks,

Moose, West Virginia Association of Realtors, and Presbyterian Church. McManus continues to live in Beckley at this writing.

LISLE G. BROWN

McMILLAN, THOMAS SANDERS (South Carolina, 1923) was born on November 22, 1888, in Ulmers, South Carolina, to James Carrol and Mary (Carre) McMillan. Earning a B.A. (1912) and an LL.B. (1913) from the University of South Carolina, he began a law practice in Charleston, South Carolina. McMillan sat on the board of visitors of Clemson College and belonged to the Masons, Lions, and Baptist Church. He married Clara Eloise Gooding in 1916, and the couple had five sons.

In 1916 McMillan successfully ran for the South Carolina House of Representatives as a Democrat from Charleston County. He served four consecutive terms and was named speaker *pro tem* in 1921 and speaker for the 1923 session. Elected to the U.S. House of Representatives from South Carolina's 1st District in 1924 and 1926, McMillan sat on the Appropriations Committee. Afterward he returned to Charleston. McMillan died on September 29, 1939, at the age of 51.

WALTER B. EDGAR

McWHERTER, NED RAY (Tennessee, 1973, 1975, 1977, 1979, 1981, 1983, 1985) was born on October 15, 1930, in Palmersville, Tennessee, to Harmon Ray and Lucille Golden (Smith) McWherter. Graduating from local public schools, he became a beer distributor and a farmer in Dresden, Tennessee. McWherter served in the U.S. Army National Guard, rising to the rank of major. He belonged to the Masons, Elks, Eagles, Lions, Jaycees, Chamber of Commerce, and American Cancer Society. A Methodist, he married Betty Jean Beck; the couple had two children before her death.

In 1968 McWherter successfully ran for the Tennessee House of Representatives as a Democrat from Weakley County. He remained there for nine consecutive terms, chairing the party caucus and the Committee on Calendar and Rules. McWherter was chosen as speaker in 1973 after defeating incumbent James R. McKinney. Renamed speaker for the 1975, 1977, 1979, 1981, 1983, and 1985 sessions, McWherter held the post longer than any person in Tennessee history. While in the speakership he was criticized for appointing committee members in a more partisan manner than his predecessors had done.

McWherter was elected governor of Tennessee in 1986 and 1990. He also attended the 1976 and 1980 Democratic national conventions and sat on the board of the Council of State Governments (CSG). During the 1975 CSG Southern Legislative Conference, he and Georgia Speaker Thomas B. Murphy developed the idea of a ''Super Tuesday'' presidential primary to increase the influence of Southern voters. Leaving the governorship in 1994, McWherter continues to live in Dresden at this writing.

Lee Seifert Greene, David H. Grubbs, and Victor C. Hobday, *Government in Tennes-*

see, 4th ed. (Knoxville: University of Tennessee Press, 1982); *Tennessee Blue Book* (Nashville: Tennessee Secretary of State).

LEE S. GREENE

MERRILL, HUGH DAVIS (Alabama, 1923, 1939) was born on December 20, 1877, in Franklin, Georgia. Educated in public schools in Franklin and in Edwardsville, Alabama, he earned an A.B. from Oxford College in Alabama (1896) and an LL.B. from the University of Alabama. Merrill practiced law with his father in Edwardsville until 1902, when he moved to Anniston, Alabama. He formed a partnership with his brother in Heflin, Alabama, in 1908, but he later returned to Anniston.

A Democrat, Merrill won election to one term in the Alabama House of Representatives from Calhoun County in 1899. He was Anniston city attorney (1906–08) and a member of Alabama's 7th Judicial Circuit Court (1911–20). Merrill was again elected to the House in 1922 and 1926, and he was named to the speakership for the 1923 session. In 1930 he successfully ran for lieutenant governor of Alabama. Returned to the House in 1938, Merrill was once more chosen as speaker in 1939. For twenty years he sat on the Alabama Democratic Executive Committee.

Outside of politics Merrill was a trustee of the Alabama Polytechnic Institute. In addition, he belonged to the Masons, Elks, Knights of Pythias, Kiwanis, and Baptist Church. He was married to Frances Abercrombie in 1899, and after her death to Martha Chitwood in 1906. Merrill died in Anniston on January 6, 1954, at the age of 76.

BENJAMIN B. WILLIAMS AND DONALD B. DODD

MERRITT, HENRY PAUL (Alabama, 1919) was born on June 7, 1873, near Old Spring Hill, Alabama. Educated in schools in Barbour and Bullock counties in Alabama, he attended Southern University in Greensboro, Alabama (now Birmingham-Southern College), and earned a law degree from the University of Virginia. In 1896 Merritt began a private practice in Tuskegee, Alabama. He married Annie Seay King in 1894.

A Democrat, Merritt was elected to the Alabama Senate in 1906. He successfully ran for the Alabama House of Representatives from Macon County in 1910 and served three consecutive four-year terms. Merritt was named speaker for the 1919 session. In addition, he was chair of the Macon County Democratic Executive Committee.

Appointed to the Alabama Court of Appeals in October 1919, Merritt won election to the post the following year. Outside of politics he was a trustee of the Alabama School for the Deaf and Blind and a member of the Masons, Knights of Pythias, and Methodist Church. Merritt still sat on the bench when he died in Birmingham, Alabama, on March 26, 1923, at age 49. He was buried in Midway, Alabama.

BENJAMIN B. WILLIAMS AND DONALD B. DODD

MICHEL, FRANCIS A. (Maryland, 1931) was born on February 19, 1892, in Baltimore, Maryland. He attended Strayer's Business College in Baltimore and earned a law degree from the University of Maryland in 1917. After that he began a private practice in Baltimore. Michel was a member of the Elks, Kiwanis, and American, Maryland, and Baltimore bar associations. A Catholic, he was married.

In 1923 Michel won election to one term in the Maryland House of Delegates as a Democrat from the city of Baltimore. After the House shifted to four-year terms, he was reelected in 1926 and 1930. He was chosen as speaker for the 1931 session, but he left the House the following year.

Returning to his law practice, Michel was a hearing attorney for gasoline violations in the U.S. Office of Price Administration during World War II. He was appointed chair of the Baltimore City Board of Liquor License Commissioners in 1947, and he was a committee chair for George P. Mahoney's unsuccessful 1954 gubernatorial campaign. Michel died on March 13, 1962, at the age of 70.

GARY L. BROWNE

MILAM, ARTHUR YAGER (Florida, 1925) was born on October 26, 1889, in Leesburg, Florida. Educated in schools in Texas and Jacksonville, Florida, he earned a degree from Stetson University in De Land, Florida, in 1912. Milam then began practicing law in Jacksonville. In addition, he was district governor of the Kiwanis and a member of the Masons and the Episcopal Church. He was married.

A Democrat, Milam was a delegate to the 1920 Democratic National Convention and state chair of the Democratic National Finance Committee. He was elected to the Florida House of Representatives from Duval County in 1922 and 1924, and he was named as speaker for the 1925 session. After that he returned to his Jacksonville practice. Milam died on March 26, 1956, at the age of 66.

Robert J. Huckshorn, ed., *Government and Politics in Florida* (Gainesville: University of Florida Press, 1991); Allen Morris, *The Florida Handbook* (Tallahassee: Peninsular Publishing, 1947–).

GEORGE E. POZZETTA

MILLER, GEORGE OLIVER (Alabama, 1942, 1943) was born on April 4, 1891, in Pine Hill, Alabama. He attended local public schools and Massey Business College in Montgomery, Alabama. For twelve years he worked as a state court reporter. Miller studied law with his uncle in Linden, Alabama, before beginning a practice in Livingston, Alabama, in 1921. A Baptist, he married LaNelle Cox in 1912.

In 1926 Miller was elected to the Alabama House of Representatives as a Democrat from Sumter County. Serving five consecutive four-year terms, he was concurrently solicitor of Alabama's 17th Circuit Court. He was named to the speakership for the special session of November 1942 and the 1943 regular session. Miller was still speaker when he died of a cerebral hemorrhage in Selma, Alabama, on June 7, 1944, at age 53.

BENJAMIN B. WILLIAMS AND DONALD B. DODD

MILLER, JOHN ELDON (Arkansas, 1979) was born on March 2, 1929, in Melbourne, Arkansas, to Greene Hightower and Annie Margaret (Gray) Miller. Educated in local public schools, he earned a B.S. in chemistry from Arkansas State College (now University) in 1949. Miller became a traveling salesman, service station owner, and foreman for the Reynolds Metal Company. In 1957 he opened the John E. Miller Real Estate and Insurance Agency in Melbourne. He was also the owner of Izard County Abstract Company, vice-president of the M&M Construction Company, a surveyor, and a cattle rancher.

A Democrat, Miller was clerk of the Izard County Circuit Court in 1953–56 and president of the Arkansas County Clerks Association. He was elected to the Arkansas House of Representatives from Izard and Stone counties in 1958. Miller chaired the Revenue and Taxation Committee, Joint Budget Committee, and Joint Committee on Legislative Facilities. Chosen as speaker for the 1979 session, he chaired the Southern Legislative Conference (1982) and the Council of State Governments (1986).

Miller became a director of the American Red Cross in 1958 and vice-president of the Arkansas Board of Easter Seals in 1975. In addition, he belonged to the Masons, Lions, Arkansas Real Estate Association, Arkansas Insurance Association, Farm Bureau, and Baptist Church. He married Ruby Lenora Robertson in 1949, and the couple had three children. As of this writing Miller remains in the House and continues to operate his Melbourne realty business.

SUZANNE MABERRY

MILLIKEN, JOHN S. (Kentucky, 1928, 1930) was born in Louisville, Kentucky, on November 22, 1891, to Walter B. and Lillie (Givident) Milliken. Educated in local schools, he earned a degree from the Jefferson School of Law in Louisville. Milliken then practiced law in Franklin, Kentucky. He belonged to the Masons, and he married Olive Dragelis in 1919.

A Democrat, Milliken was town attorney of Franklin for six years. In 1925 he was elected to the Kentucky House of Representatives from Simpson County. He served three consecutive terms and was chosen as speaker for the 1928 and 1930 sessions. Milliken died on June 7, 1948, at the age of 56.

George T. Blakey, *Hard Times and the New Deal in Kentucky, 1929–1939* (Lexington: University Press of Kentucky, 1986); Malcolm E. Jewell and Everett W. Cunningham, *Kentucky Politics* (Lexington: University Press of Kentucky, 1968); Malcolm E. Jewell and Penny Miller, *The Kentucky Legislature: Two Decades of Change* (Lexington: University Press of Kentucky, 1988); Robert F. Sexton, ''Kentucky Politics and Society, 1919–1932'' (Ph.D. dissertation, University of Washington, 1970).

NANCY DISHER BAIRD

MILLS, JON L. (Florida, 1987) was born in Miami, Florida, on July 24, 1947, to Herb J. and Marguerite (Sweat) Mills. Earning a B.A. in economics from Stetson University in De Land, Florida, in 1969, he received a J.D. from the University of Florida in 1972. Mills served in the U.S. Army Reserve and worked in the Miami public defender's office. He then became a director of the University of Florida's Executive Impoundment Project and Center for Government Responsibility.

Beginning a law practice, Mills eventually became a partner in the firm of McGalliard, Mills, DeMontomollin, Monaco & Sieg in Gainesville, Florida. He was also an adjunct professor at Florida, writing several articles on political issues. Mills was a director of the Rotary as well as a member of the Jaycees and the American and Florida bar associations. A Methodist, he never married.

In 1978 Mills was elected to the Florida House of Representatives as a Democrat from Alachua County. Remaining there for five consecutive terms, he was named "Representative of the Year" by the Florida Association of Retarded Citizens in 1981 and "Outstanding Legislator" by the Florida Health Care Association the next year. He was chosen as speaker for the 1987 session. Mills then returned to Gainesville, where he continues to live at this writing.

GINA PETONITO

MILWEE, R. FRANK (Arkansas, 1911) was born on March 16, 1872, in Monroe County, Arkansas. After his father and his older brother died, he was forced to leave school. Milwee became the manager of a plantation when he was 15. He belonged to the Rotary and the Presbyterian Church.

A Democrat, Milwee served Monroe County as chief deputy sheriff and tax collector, sheriff (1900–04), and judge (1904–08). He successfully ran for the Arkansas House of Representatives from Monroe County in 1910. Concurrently he managed the successful reelection of Governor George W. Donaghey. Milwee was chosen as speaker for the 1911 term, his only one in the House. Returning to Monroe County, he was again sheriff in 1914–19.

Afterward Milwee operated the Milwee and Dunlap Furniture Company in Brinkley, Arkansas. Appointed state manager of the U.S. Home Owners' Loan Corporation in 1933, he remained in that position until 1946. He was also Arkansas revenue commissioner. Milwee died on January 29, 1955, at the age of 82.

Arkansas Democrat; Arkansas Gazette.

CARL H. MONEYHON

MINOR, FRED H. (Texas, 1931) was born in Denton County, Texas, on December 11, 1888. Educated in local schools, he earned a degree from North Texas State Normal College (now the University of North Texas) in Denton and worked as a teacher. Minor later received an LL.B. from the University of Texas and began practicing law in Denton. He was married.

A Democrat, Minor chaired the Denton County Democratic Executive Committee in 1918. He was elected to the Denton City Commission in 1922, becoming its chair two years later. In 1926 he successfully ran for the Texas House of Representatives from Denton County. Serving three consecutive terms, Minor often presided over the House in 1929 due to Speaker Wingate S. Barron's poor health. Consequently he was a natural choice for the speakership for the 1931 session.

In addition, Minor was a delegate to the 1932 and 1940 Democratic national conventions. He sat on the Texas Liquor Control Board (1943–48), Texas Civil Judicial Council, and Denton school board. President of the Chamber of Commerce, he belonged to the Masons, Knights of Pythias, Kiwanis, Texas and Denton County bar associations, and Christian Church (Disciples of Christ). Minor died on April 24, 1976, at the age of 87.

Frank Carter Adams, *Texas Democracy: A Centennial History of Politics and Personalities of the Democratic Party, 1836–1936*, 4 vols. (Austin: Democratic Historical Association, 1937), II: 58–61; Norman D. Brown, *Hood, Bonnet, and Little Brown Jug: Texas Politics, 1921–1928* (College Station: Texas A&M University Press, 1984); *Presiding Officers of the Texas Legislature, 1846–1982* (Austin: Texas Legislative Council, 1982), 168–169.

ALWYN BARR

MITCHELL, R. CLAYTON, Jr. (Maryland, 1987, 1991) was born in Chestertown, Maryland, on April 16, 1936. Attending local public schools, he served in the U.S. Army for one year. Mitchell earned a degree from Goldey-Beacom College in Wilmington, Delaware, in 1958. Afterward he became a businessman in Chestertown. He was married with three children, and he belonged to the Catholic Church.

A conservative Democrat, Mitchell was president of the Kent County Board of Commissioners from 1966 to 1970. In the latter year he won election to the Maryland House of Delegates from Kent County. Mitchell served six consecutive four–year terms, and he was named speaker for the 1987 and 1991 sessions. While in the speakership he emphasized restructuring the higher education system, economic development, and reforming criminal justice programs for juveniles. He survived a 1992 attempt to oust him. Resigning from the House in November 1993, Mitchell continues to live in Chestertown at this writing.

GINA PETONITO

MOATE, MARVIN E. (Georgia, 1955, 1957) was born in Sparta, Georgia, on September 22, 1910, to Robert H. and Eula (Smith) Moate. Earning a degree from the 10th District A&M School in Granite Hill, Georgia, (1927) and an LL.B. from the Atlanta Law School in Georgia (1932), he began practicing law in Sparta. Moate later owned a lumber company and a cotton gin. In addition, he belonged to the Masons, Elks, and Methodist Church. He married Margaret Carroll in 1942, and the couple had two children.

A Democrat, Moate won election to the Georgia Senate in 1938. He successfully ran for the Georgia House of Representatives from Hancock and Putnam counties in 1940 and 1942 before rejoining the Senate. In 1952 Moate was again elected to the House, where he served nine consecutive terms and was named speaker for the 1955 and 1957 sessions. Retiring from the House in 1970, he returned to his Sparta practice. Moate died on September 6, 1984, at the age of 73.

Georgia Department of History and Archives, *Georgia's Official Register* (Atlanta: Longino and Porter, 1923–1967/68).

JANE W. HERNDON

MOFFITT, H. LEE (Florida, 1983) was born on November 10, 1941, in Tampa, Florida, to Benjamen Bascum and Clara (Stewart) Moffitt. Educated in local public schools, he earned a B.S. in political science from the University of South Florida (1964) and a J.D. from Cumberland University in Lebanon, Tennessee (1967). Moffitt then began practicing law in Tampa. He married Karen Arlene Mathis in 1971, and the couple had one daughter.

A Democrat, Moffitt sat on the Tampa Study Commission in 1971–72. In 1974 he won election to the Florida House of Representatives from Hillsborough County. Moffitt served five consecutive terms and was nominated by the *St. Petersburg Times* as the most valuable House member in 1978 and 1982. He was chosen as speaker for the 1983 session.

Afterward Moffitt returned to his law practice. He was a director of the South Florida Alumni Association and a member of the American, Florida, and Hillsborough County bar associations, Florida Academy of Trial Lawyers, and Methodist Church. In addition he received the Tampa Chamber of Commerce's Community Leadership Award. Moffitt continues to live in Tampa at this writing.

GINA PETONITO

MOORE, EDGAR BLACKBURN (Virginia, 1950, 1952, 1954, 1956, 1958, 1960, 1962, 1964, 1966) was born in Washington, D.C., on April 26, 1897. He attended Davidson College in North Carolina and Cornell University in Ithaca, New York. Coming to Clarke County, Virginia, in 1921 to sell an apple orchard owned by his father, Moore instead expanded the business. In 1930 he cofounded the firm of Moore and Dorsey, Inc., which became one of the largest apple companies in Virginia.

A conservative Democrat, Moore was elected to the Virginia House of Delegates from Clarke and Frederick counties and the city of Winchester in a special election in 1933. He served seventeen consecutive terms, joining the faction led by U.S. Senator Harry F. Byrd, Sr., and opposing state tax increases. In addition, he supported Byrd's policy of "massive resistance" to the U.S. Supreme Court's decision to strike down racial segregation in *Brown v. Board of Education.* Moore was named speaker for the 1950, 1952, 1954, 1956, 1958, 1960, 1962, 1964, and 1966 sessions. While in the speakership he controlled committee assignments to ensure that members of the Byrd faction were given the most important responsibilities.

Afterward Moore returned to his apple business. In addition, he sat on the Virginia Water Control Board from 1946 to 1970. President of the National Apple Institute, Moore belonged to the Rotary and the Presbyterian Church. He married Dorothy Parker. Moore died on July 22, 1980, at the age of 83.

E. Griffith Dodson, ed., *Speakers and Clerks of the Virginia House of Delegates, 1776–1976,* rev. under the direction of Joseph H. Holleman, Jr. (Richmond, 1976), 120–143; *Richmond Times-Dispatch,* July 23–25, 1980; *Winchester Star,* July 23, 1980.

JAMES R. SWEENEY

MOORE, FRANK WASHINGTON (Tennessee, 1933) was born in South Pittsburg, Tennessee, on April 19, 1905, of Scotch-Irish ancestry. His father, Charles C. Moore, and his great-grandfather, Hugh L. W. Raulston, were state legislators. The younger Moore was educated in public and private schools in Chattanooga, Tennessee. Attending the University of the South in Sewanee, Tennessee, he earned a degree from Washington and Lee University in Lexington, Virginia, and an LL.B. from the University of Chattanooga (now the University of Tennessee at Chattanooga). He began practicing law in Chattanooga in 1929.

A Democrat, Moore was a charter member of the Hamilton County Young Democrats. In 1932 he successfully ran for the Tennessee House of Representatives from Hamilton County. He was chosen as speaker in 1933, his only term in the House.

Afterward Moore returned to his private practice. Active in the coal-mining business from 1940 to 1952, he was also exalted ruler of the Elks and a member of the Masons and the Presbyterian Church. He married Margaret Curtis in 1935, and the couple had one daughter. Moore died on May 10, 1982, at the age of 77.

Tennessee Blue Book (Nashville: Tennessee Secretary of State).

WILLIE H. PIGG

MOORE, LARRY ICHABOD, Jr. (North Carolina, 1955) was born in Greenville, North Carolina, on January 26, 1904, to Larry Ichabod and Ella (King) Moore. Educated in public schools in New Bern, North Carolina, he earned an A.B. (1922), a B.S. (1924), and an LL.B. (1926) from the University of North Carolina. Moore then began practicing law in Wilson, North Carolina, where he also worked as a dairyman. He married Grace Thompson in 1946, and the couple had five children.

A Democrat, Moore served Wilson County as solicitor of the General Court (1929–34) and as attorney (1943–55). In 1938 he was elected to the North

Carolina House of Representatives from Wilson County. Moore served eleven consecutive terms, becoming speaker for the 1955 regular session and for the special session of 1956. He also sat on the North Carolina Board of Health.

Leaving the House in 1960, Moore returned to his Wilson law practice. In addition, he was president of the Wilson County Young Democrats and the 2nd Judicial District Bar Association. He was master of the Masons and a member of the Elks, Grange, Moose, Farm Bureau, University of North Carolina Alumni Association, and Episcopal Church. Moore died on January 8, 1972, at the age of 67.

OTIENO OKELO

MORSE, ROBERT EMMETT (Texas, 1939) was born in Houston, Texas, on April 8, 1896. Educated in local schools, he sold real estate with his father. During World War I he served as a lieutenant in the U.S. Army. Morse was secretary of the Houston Real Estate Board and the Texas Association of Real Estate Boards. He was married.

In 1926 Morse won election to the Texas House of Representatives as a Democrat from Harris County. Remaining there for nine consecutive terms, he became a leader of the liberal faction. Morse gained a reputation as an expert on parliamentary procedure, helping to revise the rules of the House. He was named speaker for the 1939 session.

Earning a degree from Sommerville Law School in Dallas, Texas, Morse began a private practice in 1939. After leaving the House in 1944, Morse settled in Austin, Texas, where he was general counsel for the Texas Wholesale Liquor Dealers Association. In addition, he belonged to the Masons, Chamber of Commerce, American Legion, YMCA, and Baptist Church. Morse died on August 19, 1957, at the age of 61.

Austin *Statesman*, August 20, 1957; Norman D. Brown, *Hood, Bonnet, and Little Brown Jug: Texas Politics, 1921–1928* (College Station: Texas A&M University Press, 1984); Dallas *Morning News*, January 10, 1939; George Norris Green, *The Establishment in Texas Politics: The Primitive Years, 1938–1957* (Westport, CT: Greenwood Press, 1979); *Presiding Officers of the Texas Legislature, 1846–1982* (Austin: Texas Legislative Council, 1982), 174–175.

ALWYN BARR

MOSS, THOMAS WARREN, Jr. (Virginia, 1991, 1992, 1994) was born in Norfolk, Virginia, on October 3, 1928, to Thomas Warren and Laura (Burckard) Moss. Educated in local public schools, he received a B.S. from the Virginia Polytechnic Institute in Blacksburg in 1950. During the Korean conflict he served in the U.S. Army, rising to the rank of first lieutenant. Moss earned an LL.B. from the University of Richmond in Virginia in 1956 and began a private practice in Norfolk. He married Lorna Payne, and the couple had three children.

A Democrat, Moss was executive vice-president of the Virginia Young Democrats. In 1965 he was elected to the Virginia House of Delegates from the city of Norfolk. He opposed the state party's dominant conservative faction led by U.S. Senator Harry F. Byrd, Sr., but he eventually chaired the General Laws Committee and the Committee on Corporations, Insurance and Banking. While in office Moss worked for stricter regulation of the insurance industry, a consumers' bill of rights, and the unification of the ports in the Hampton Roads region. After narrowly defeating a feminist opponent in 1982, he agreed to support abortion rights and passage of the Equal Rights Amendment to the U.S. Constitution.

Moss attended the Democratic National Convention in 1980, the same year he became majority leader. He was chosen as speaker following the death of incumbent A. L. Philpott in November 1991, and he was renamed to the post for the 1992 and 1994 sessions. Outside of politics he belonged to the Masons, American Bar Association, Virginia Trial Lawyers Association, and Lutheran Church. As of this writing Moss remains in the speakership.

JAMES R. SWEENEY

MULL, ODUS McCOY (North Carolina, 1941) was born in Cleveland County, North Carolina, on September 18, 1880. Educated in public and private schools, he earned an A.B. *magna cum laude* (1902) and an LL.B. (1903) from Wake Forest College (now University) in North Carolina. While in college he was captain of the baseball team. Mull briefly worked as a teacher before beginning to practice law in Shelby, North Carolina. From 1930 to 1936 he was general manager and financial advisor of the Cleveland Cloth Mills. He was married.

A Democrat, Mull participated in a white supremacy campaign in the 1900 gubernatorial race. He was Shelby city attorney and attorney for the Cleveland County school board. Mull was elected to the North Carolina House of Representatives from Cleveland County in 1906, 1918, 1928, 1938, and 1940. While in office he coauthored a road construction bill and helped pass legislation establishing a state vocational education system. Chair of the Democratic executive committees of North Carolina (1928–32) and Cleveland County, he was executive counsel to Governor O. Max Gardner. He was named speaker for the 1941 session.

Resuming his Shelby law practice, Mull was an attorney for several banks and textile mills. He owned extensive farm land. In addition Mull was president of the Kiwanis and the Cleveland County Bar Association, chair of the Red Cross, a trustee of the Bowman Gray Memorial School of Medicine, and a member of the North Carolina Bar Association and the Baptist Church. Chair of the board of Wake Forest College, he was instrumental in moving the institution to Winston-Salem, North Carolina, in 1956. Mull died on November 27, 1962, at age 82.

William S. Powell, ed., *Dictionary of North Carolina Biography*, 6 vols. (Chapel Hill: University of North Carolina Press, 1979–1996).

CHARLES H. BOWMAN, JR.

MURPHY, THOMAS BAILEY (Georgia, 1974, 1975, 1977, 1979, 1981, 1983, 1985, 1987, 1989, 1991, 1993) was born in Bremen, Georgia, on March 10, 1924, to William Harvey and Leita (Jones) Murphy. Educated in local public schools, he received an A.B. from North Georgia College in Dahlonega in 1943. During World War II he served in the U.S. Navy. Murphy earned an LL.B. from the University of Georgia in 1949 and began a law practice in Bremen. He belonged to the Moose, American Legion, VFW, Fraternal Order of Police, and Baptist Church.

A Democrat, Murphy chaired the Bremen school board. He won election to the Georgia House of Representatives from Haralson and Paulding counties in 1960, becoming majority floor leader in 1967 and speaker *pro tem* in 1971. Murphy was chosen as speaker in 1974 following the death of incumbent George L. Smith, and he was renamed to the post for the 1975, 1977, 1979, 1981, 1983, 1985, 1987, 1989, 1991, and 1993 sessions. Although Murphy represented a rural district, he helped pass legislation beneficial to urban areas such as the development of Atlanta's rapid transit system and World Congress Center. In addition, he was instrumental in the successful 1982 gubernatorial campaign of Joe Frank Harris.

Active in the Council of State Governments (CSG), Murphy and Tennessee Speaker Ned R. McWherter originated the idea of a "Super Tuesday" primary during the 1975 CSG Southern legislative conference. Their goal was to persuade presidential candidates to pay more attention to Southern voters. In 1989 Murphy became chair of the CSG. He married Agnes Bennett, and the couple had four children before her death. At this writing Murphy remains in the speakership, having held the post longer than anyone in Georgia history.

Penkalski, Janice, "Georgia Legend Swings a Mean Gavel," *State Government News* 32 (February 1989), 5.

JAMES E. DORSEY

MURPHY, WALTER "Pete" (North Carolina, 1914, 1917) was born on October 27, 1872, in Salisbury, North Carolina. He earned an A.B. and an LL.B. from the University of North Carolina, where he founded the *Carolina Daily Tarheel* student newspaper. Murphy began to practice law in Salisbury in 1894. An Episcopalian, he was married.

Murphy won election to one term in the North Carolina House of Representatives as a Democrat from Rowan County in 1896. He was again elected to the House in 1902 and served sixteen consecutive terms, the longest tenure in state history at that time. From 1903 to 1908 Murphy was also Salisbury city attorney. Named speaker for the 1914 extra session and the regular session of 1917, he sought to increase appropriations for higher education, highways, and welfare programs.

In 1908 Murphy was a presidential elector and a delegate to the Democratic National Convention. He sat on the North Carolina Democratic Executive Committee in 1906–24, and he managed the 1924 presidential campaign of Senator Oscar W. Underwood of Alabama. Outside of politics he was president of the board of the University of North Carolina, a member of the Masons, Kiwanis, and American Bar Association, and a collector of Jacksonian memorabilia. Murphy died on January 12, 1946, at the age of 73.

John L. Cheney, Jr., *North Carolina Government, 1585–1974: A Narrative and Statistical History* (Raleigh: North Carolina Department of the Secretary of State, 1975); Hugh Talmadge Lefler and Albert Ray Newsome, *The History of a Southern State: North Carolina* (Chapel Hill: University of North Carolina Press, 1973); William S. Powell, *North Carolina through Four Centuries* (Chapel Hill: University of North Carolina Press, 1989).

CLAUDE HARGROVE

MURRAY, CHARLES EDWARD (Tennessee, 1987, 1989) was born in Decherd, Tennessee, on August 16, 1928, to Richard Oliver and Patty (Moffatt) Murray. Attending the University of the South in Sewanee, Tennessee, he earned a B.S. from Middle Tennessee State University in Murfreesboro in 1951. During the Korean conflict he served in the U.S. Navy. Murray received a J.D. from the YMCA Law School in Nashville, Tennessee, in 1965. He then began a private practice in Winchester, Tennessee.

A Democrat, Murray was assistant director of the Tennessee Aeronautical Commission in 1965–67. He was elected to the Tennessee House of Representatives from Franklin County in 1970 and remained there for ten consecutive terms. Murray was named speaker for the 1987 and 1989 sessions. In addition, he was vice-chair of the Southern Growth Policies Board.

President of the Chamber of Commerce, Murray was a member of the American Legion and the University of Tennessee Space Institute Support Council. He married Sandra Gail Fields in 1969. Murray continues to live in Winchester at this writing.

GINA PETONITO

MURRAY, PERRY EARL (Florida, 1949) was born in Vienna, Georgia, on December 16, 1899. He attended public schools in Vienna and Rochelle, Georgia. During World War I Murray served in the U.S. Navy as a radio operator on the U.S.S. *New Hampshire*. Earning a B.S. from the Georgia Normal and Business College in Douglas in 1919, he received an LL.B. (1921) and an A.B. (1922) from Mercer University in Macon, Georgia. Murray began a private practice in Macon in 1923. Three years later he moved to Frostproof, Florida, where he raised citrus crops. He was married, and he belonged to the Masons, Rotary, American Legion, and Methodist Church.

A Democrat, Murray became city attorney of Frostproof in 1926. In 1940 he was elected to the Florida House of Representatives from Polk County. Remaining there for eight consecutive terms, he emphasized issues concerning constitutional revision, government reorganization, appropriations, taxation, and the citrus industry. Murray was responsible for House reforms that outlawed proxy voting in committees, established permanent public recording of committee proceedings, and required the registration of lobbyists. He was named the legislator "rendering the most valuable service" in 1945 and 1947, and he received the Morris Cracker Politics Award.

Chair of the Judiciary Committee in 1943 and 1945 and the Finance and Taxation Committee in 1947, Murray was chosen as speaker for the 1949 session. During his speakership the House passed bills creating a state sales tax and increasing the cigarette tax. It also approved the formation of the Legislative Reference Bureau, but it failed to provide the revenues necessary to pay for a flood control project and improvements in public education. Murray was still serving in the House when he died in an automobile accident on December 12, 1955. He was 55.

Paul S. George, *A Guide to the History of Florida* (Westport, CT: Greenwood Press, 1989); *Miami Daily News; Miami Herald; Tallahassee Democrat; Tampa Tribune.*

PAUL S. GEORGE

MUTSCHER, GUS FRANKLIN (Texas, 1969, 1971) was born in Washington County, Texas, on November 19, 1932, to Gus and Gertie (Goeke) Mutscher. Educated in local public schools, he attended Blinn Junior College in Brenham, Texas, and earned a B.B.A. from the University of Texas in 1956. While at Blinn he played varsity baseball and participated on a state championship debate team. Mutscher served in the U.S. Army's Military Police for three years, rising to the rank of first lieutenant. He studied law at the University of Texas and South Texas College of Law in Houston, Texas. After working as a field representative for the Borden Company in Houston, he settled in Brenham.

In 1960 Mutscher was elected to the Texas House of Representatives as a Democrat from Washington, Austin, Burleson, Lee, and Waller counties. Remaining there for six consecutive terms, he chaired the Redistricting Committee and the Claims and Account Committee. Mutscher was chosen as speaker for the 1969 and 1971 sessions. While in the post he helped pass Texas's first minimum wage law and first solid waste disposal act. Other successful bills created several state medical schools, ratified the 26th Amendment to the U.S. Constitution lowering the voting age, and approved the selling of liquor by the drink.

Mutscher was indicted in 1971 due to his involvement in the Sharpstown financial scandal. He resigned from the speakership in March 1972 and was defeated for reelection to the House later that year. Convicted and sentenced to probation, Mutscher was appointed to the Washington County Court upon his release in 1976. In other affairs he was president of the Texas Association of Regional Councils and a member of the Texas Association of County Judges and Commissioners. A Lutheran, he married Donna Axum in 1969; the couple had one daughter. Mutscher owned a motor inn as well as real estate and cattle holdings.

Houston Chronicle, September 24, 1971.

LUTHER G. HAGARD, JR.

N

NAIFEH, JAMES O. (Tennessee, 1991, 1993) was born in Covington, Tennessee, on June 16, 1939. Earning a B.S. from the University of Tennessee in 1961, he served in the U.S. Army and rose to the rank of first lieutenant. Naifeh then helped operate his family's grocery store chain in Covington. He sat on the board of the St. Jude Children's Research Hospital. In addition, Naifeh was president of the Chamber of Commerce and a member of the Rotary, Tennessee Wholesale Grocers Association, and American Legion. An Episcopalian, he was married in 1962 and had three children.

Naifeh was elected to the Tennessee House of Representatives as a Democrat from Tipton and Fayette counties in 1974. Named majority floor leader in 1987, he was chosen as speaker for the 1991 and 1993 sessions. He also chaired the Rural West Tennessee Democratic Caucus. As of this writing Naifeh remains in the speakership.

Tennessee Blue Book (Nashville: Secretary of State).

JON L. WAKELYN

NANCE, JAMES CLARK (Oklahoma, 1929, 1953) was born on August 27, 1893, in Rogers, Arkansas. After studying law, he married a member of the Choctaw Indian Nation in 1913. The next year he moved to Weatherford, Oklahoma. Nance purchased the *Weatherford Democrat* and eventually co-owned eleven newspapers throughout the state. He moved to Stephens County, Oklahoma, and then to Cotton County, Oklahoma.

A Democrat, Nance successfully ran for the Oklahoma House of Representatives from Stephens County in 1920 and 1922. He was elected to the House from Cotton County in 1926, serving three consecutive terms and becoming floor leader. Nance was chosen as speaker in 1929 when incumbent Allen M. Street was forced to resign after just three hours in office. While in the post he helped impeach Governor Henry S. Johnston. In 1936 Nance settled in Purcell, Oklahoma. He won election to the House from McClain County in 1936, 1952, 1956, and 1958, and he was again named to the speakership for the 1953 session.

Nance won races for the Oklahoma Senate in 1932, 1940, 1944, and 1948. He was that body's floor leader in 1943 and president *pro tem* in 1947, joining William T. Anglin as the only persons to lead both chambers of the Oklahoma legislature. President of the Oklahoma Press Association in 1933, Nance was a member of the Masons, Odd Fellows, Rotary, and Presbyterian Church. In addition, he was inducted into the Oklahoma Hall of Fame in 1953. Nance died on September 3, 1984, a week following his ninety-first birthday.

Rex F. Harlow, comp., *Makers of Government in Oklahoma* (Oklahoma City: Harlow Publishing, 1930); Gaston Litton, *History of Oklahoma at the Golden Anniversary of Statehood*, 4 vols. (New York: Lewis Historical Publishing, 1957); Joseph B. Thoburn and Muriel H. Wright, *Oklahoma: A History of the State and Its People*, 4 vols. (New York: Lewis Historical Publishing, 1929); Jim Young, "Veteran Oklahoma Politician, Publisher James C. Nance Dies at 91," *The Daily Oklahoman*, September 4, 1984: 1–2.

DONOVAN L. REICHENBERGER

NEALE, IRVING C. (Arkansas, 1931) was born in Fort Smith, Arkansas, on October 10, 1894. Attending local public schools and Hendrix College in Conway, Arkansas, he received a B.A. from Drury College in Springfield, Missouri, in 1916. While in college he was a member of the varsity football team. Neale served in an ROTC unit in St. Louis, Missouri, during World War I. He earned an LL.B. from the University of Missouri in 1921 and afterward began a law practice in Fort Smith.

In 1924 Neale was elected to the Arkansas House of Representatives as a Democrat from Sebastian County. He served four consecutive terms and was chosen as speaker for the 1931 session. Outside of politics Neale belonged to the Knights of Pythias, Eagles, and Woodmen of the World. A Methodist, he was married. Neale still held the speakership when he died on October 28, 1932, at the age of 38.

Diane D. Blair, *Arkansas Politics and Government* (Lincoln: University of Nebraska Press, 1988), 160–184; Jerry E. Hinshaw, *Call the Roll* (Little Rock: Rose Publishing, 1986); *Historical Report of the Secretary of State, Arkansas* (Little Rock: Secretary of State, 1958–   ); Walter Nunn, *Readings in Arkansas Government* (Little Rock: Rose Publishing, 1973), 59–133.

CAL LEDBETTER, JR.

NEILL, WILLIAM CECIL (Georgia, 1921, 1923, 1925) was born in Columbus, Georgia, on March 26, 1880, of Scotch-Irish ancestry. Educated in local schools, he studied law and began a private practice in Columbus. Neill was a member of the Masons, Elks, Odd Fellows, Knights of Pythias, and Presbyterian Church. He was married.

A Democrat, Neill chaired the Muscogee County Democratic Executive Committee in 1908–12. In 1914 he was elected to the Georgia House of Representatives from Muscogee County. Neill served six consecutive terms and wrote several important bills. The best known of these was the Neill Primary Act of 1917, which provided for state legislative primaries and strengthened the county-unit electoral system through which power was concentrated in rural counties. He was named speaker for the 1921, 1923, and 1925 regular sessions and for two special sessions in 1926.

Announcing his candidacy for governor of Georgia in 1928, Neill was forced to withdraw following an automobile accident. Instead he won election to the Georgia Senate, becoming that body's president in 1929. While in office he authored an amendment to the Georgia Constitution moving legislative sessions from June to January. Neill was still Senate president when he died on March 16, 1932, from complications following an operation. He was 51. After Neill's death the *Atlanta Constitution* reported that "probably no other figure in the State boasted so many friends ranging from the governor down to . . . the newest janitor."

Atlanta Constitution, March 17, 1932; James F. Cook, *Governors of Georgia* (Huntsville, AL: Strode, 1979); *The Georgia Annual: A Compendium of Useful Information about Georgia* (Atlanta: A. B. Caldwell, 1911–   ); Lucian L. Knight, ed., *Encyclopedia of Georgia Biography* (Atlanta: A. H. Cawston, 1931); Bernice McCullar, *This Is Your Georgia* (Montgomery, AL: Viewpoint Publications, 1982).

CHARLES J. WEEKS

NESBITT, PAUL (Oklahoma, 1917) was born in 1872 in Nuckolls County, Nebraska, to James B. and Eveline Lee Nesbitt. He attended Cotner University in Lincoln, Nebraska, and earned an M.D. from Chicago Medical College in Illinois in 1895. Nesbitt practiced medicine in El Dorado Springs, Missouri, until 1898, when he moved to Watonga, Oklahoma Territory. From 1902 to 1906 he lived in St. Louis and Joplin, Missouri. Settling in South McAlester, Indian Territory (now Oklahoma) in 1906, he belonged to the Rotary. He married Carrie M. Lee in 1896, and the couple had two children.

A Democrat, Nesbitt avidly supported merging Indian Territory and Oklahoma Territory into the state of Oklahoma. He became his party's publicity director, helping to elect a strong Democratic majority to the 1906–07 Oklahoma Constitutional Convention. Nesbitt was appointed assistant state examiner and inspector in 1907 and clerk to Governor Charles N. Haskell two years later. While in the latter post he assisted in the 1910 relocation of the Oklahoma capital from Guthrie to Oklahoma City. In 1911 Nesbitt began editing the *New State Tribune* in McAlester, Oklahoma. He chaired the Pittsburg County Democratic Central Committee in 1912.

Elected to the Oklahoma House of Representatives from Pittsburg County in 1914 and 1916, Nesbitt was chair of the Penal Institution Committee and vice-chair of the Rules Committee. He was chosen as speaker for the 1917 session, working successfully with Governor Robert L. Williams. Afterward Nesbitt returned to his newspaper. Named to the Oklahoma Highway Commission in 1923, he lost the position later that year following Governor John C. Walton's impeachment. Nesbitt died in McAlester in July 1950.

GORDON MOORE

NEWMAN, CLARENCE BENTON "Buddie" (Mississippi, 1976, 1980, 1984) was born in Valley Park, Mississippi, on May 8, 1921. Educated in local public schools, he earned a degree from Copiah-Lincoln Junior College in Wesson, Mississippi. Newman served with the U.S. Army in the Pacific theater during World War II. He then began farming in Valley Park, where he was also active in the natural gas and manufacturing industries.

A Democrat, Newman successfully ran for the Mississippi Senate in 1947. In 1951 he was elected to the Mississippi House of Representatives. He remained there for nine consecutive four-year terms, representing Issaquena County and later Issaquena, Sharkey, and Warren counties. Newman chaired the Ways and Means Committee and became speaker *pro tem* in 1974 due to the illness of Speaker John R. Junkin. Named to the speakership for the 1976, 1980, and 1984 sessions, he advocated industrial development and fiscal conservatism.

Afterward Newman returned to his businesses. Active in the Council of State Governments, he sat on the Mississippi Economic Council and the Delta Council. In addition, Newman belonged to the Chamber of Commerce, Farm Bureau, Cattlemen's Association, American Legion, VFW, and Baptist Church. He was married. Newman continues to live in Valley Park at this writing.

Dale Krane and Stephen D. Shaffer, eds., *Mississippi Government & Politics: Modernizers versus Traditionalists* (Lincoln: University of Nebraska Press, 1992); Richard A. McLemore, *A History of Mississippi*, 2 vols. (Jackson: University and College Press of Mississippi, 1973); *Mississippi Official and Statistical Register* (Jackson: Secretary of State).

DAVID G. SANSING

NEWTON, CLARENCE PRICE (Arkansas, 1919) was born in Lonoke County, Arkansas, on July 31, 1879. He began working for the *England Courier* in 1903, later becoming its editor. Newton moved to Pulaski County, Arkansas, where he was superintendent of the state Confederate Soldiers' Home from 1913 to 1919. In addition, he was a member of the Masons and the Methodist Church.

A progressive Democrat, Newton entered politics in 1899 when he won election as Lonoke County justice of the peace. He successfully ran for the Arkansas House of Representatives from Lonoke County in 1908 and served three consecutive terms. While in office Newton introduced bills concerning state referenda, corruption, and the paroling of mental patients. Elected to the House from Pulaski County in 1918, he was named speaker for the 1919 session.

In 1920 Newton lost a bid for Arkansas secretary of state. However, he was then appointed a U.S. prohibition inspector and private secretary to Governor Thomas C. McRae. He sat on the Pulaski County Court in 1924–29, working to increase road construction and construct a new jail. Newton died in Little Rock, Arkansas, on December 4, 1958, at the age of 79.

Arkansas Democrat; Arkansas Gazette.

CARL H. MONEYHON

NORMAN, CHARLES DOZIER (Alabama, 1944) was born on September 18, 1886, in Union Springs, Alabama. His father, James Dean Norman, was mayor of Union Springs and a delegate to the 1901 Alabama Constitutional Convention, and his grandfather was a state senator. Educated in public schools, the younger Norman earned a B.S. from the University of Alabama in 1907. He then began publishing the *Union Springs Herald*. During World War I he served as a captain with the U.S. Army in Europe.

A conservative Democrat, Norman served Union Springs as an alderman and chair of the school board. In addition, he chaired the Bullock County Board of Public Welfare. He was elected to the Alabama House of Representatives from Bullock County in 1926 and remained there for six consecutive four-year terms. Norman was a firm believer in states' rights, but he was unsympathetic to the "Dixiecrat" movement to separate Southern Democrats from the national party. Supporting the successful 1942 gubernatorial campaign of Chauncey Sparks, he became floor leader and vice-chair of the Rules Committee in 1943.

In June 1944 Norman was chosen as speaker following the death of incumbent George O. Miller. However, he was not renamed to the post in 1947 due to his opposition to much of the reform program of Governor James E. Folsom. Defeated for reelection to the House in 1950, Norman returned to his newspaper. He belonged to the Presbyterian Church. Norman died on June 8, 1951, at the age of 64.

Alabama Official and Statistical Register (Montgomery: State of Alabama, Department of Archives and History, 1903–   ); Frank L. Grove, ed., *Library of Alabama Lives* (Hopkinsville, KY: Historical Records Association, 1961); Murray C. Havens, *City versus Farm: Urban-Rural Conflict in the Alabama Legislature* (University, AL: Bureau of Public Administration, University of Alabama, 1957); *A Manual for Alabama Legislators* (Montgomery: Legislative Reference Service, State of Alabama, 1942–   ); Henry S. Marks, *Alabama Past Leaders* (Huntsville: Strode Publishers, 1982); *Who's Who in Alabama* (Birmingham: Sayers Enterprises, 1965–   ).

                                                                        REID BADGER

NORTHCUTT, HORACE ALLEN (Arkansas, 1945) was born in Salem, Arkansas, on February 16, 1883, to Arch and Jennie (Brown) Northcutt. His father was sheriff of Fulton County. Educated in local public schools, he studied law and began a private practice around 1904. Northcutt belonged to the Masons and the Methodist Church. He was married.

A Democrat, Northcutt sat on the Salem school board and was prosecuting attorney for the 16th Judicial District of Arkansas in 1912–16. In 1924 and 1936 he successfully ran for the Arkansas Senate. Elected to the Arkansas House of Representatives from Fulton County in 1932, 1934, 1940, 1942, and 1944, Northcutt was named speaker for the 1945 session. While in the legislature he sponsored the Martineau Road Laws and the Revolving School Loan Fund. He later became president of the Bank of Salem. Northcutt died in Little Rock, Arkansas, on March 23, 1950, at age 67, and he was buried in Salem.

Arkansas Democrat, Arkansas Gazette; The Arkansas Handbook (Little Rock: Arkansas History Commission, 1936–   ).

RUSSELL PIERCE BAKER

O

O'DELL, JOHN ED (Tennessee, 1939, 1941) was born in Tennessee on March 10, 1906. Earning an A.B. from King College in Bristol, Tennessee (1924), and an LL.B. from the University of Virginia (1927), he began practicing law in Bristol. O'Dell was a member of the Elks and the Presbyterian Church. He married Frances Minton in 1926.

In 1936 O'Dell was elected to the Tennessee House of Representatives as a Democrat from Sullivan County. He served three consecutive terms and was chosen as speaker for the 1939 and 1941 sessions. Returning to Bristol, O'Dell later moved his practice to Nashville, Tennessee. Eventually he became an assistant attorney general of Tennessee. O'Dell died on December 21, 1956, at the age of 50.

LEE S. GREENE

OZLIN, THOMAS WILLIAM (Virginia, 1926, 1928) was born on July 12, 1884, in Lunenburg County, Virginia. Attending local public schools and LaCrosse Academy in Mecklenburg County, Virginia, he earned a B.A. and an LL.B. from Richmond College (now the University of Richmond) in Virginia in 1909. Ozlin briefly taught at Fork Union Military Academy in Virginia before beginning to practice law in Kenbridge, Virginia, in 1910. In 1917 he became secretary-treasurer of the Lunenburg County National Farm Loan Association.

A Democrat, Ozlin entered politics in 1912 when he was elected mayor of Kenbridge. He narrowly lost a race for the Virginia House of Delegates from Lunenburg County in 1915, but he won election in 1917 and served six consecutive terms. Ozlin was named speaker for the 1926 and 1928 sessions, coinciding with the tenure of Governor Harry F. Byrd, Sr. The two men had become close during the early 1920s, when they demanded reforms to the state Highway Department and successfully advocated the "pay-as-you-go" policy of funding road construction with revenues from the state gasoline tax and automobile license fees. While in the speakership Ozlin helped gather support for Byrd's government reorganization program.

Returning to his private practice, Ozlin was appointed to the Virginia Corporation Commission in 1933. He announced his intention to enter the 1941 race for governor of Virginia but then dropped out as a result of financial problems. Throughout his career he was known as a strong supporter of public education. Ozlin died on July 14, 1944, at the age of 60.

E. Griffith Dodson, ed., *Speakers and Clerks of the Virginia House of Delegates, 1776–1976*, rev. under the direction of Joseph H. Holleman, Jr. (Richmond, 1976), 120–143; *History of Virginia* (Chicago: American Historical Society, 1924): IV–VI; *Richmond Times-Dispatch*, July 15, 1944.

JAMES R. SWEENEY

P

PAULEY, HARRY R. (West Virginia, 1958, 1959) was born in Keystone, West Virginia, on February 19, 1907, to Emery P. and Etta (Redmond) Pauley. Graduating from public schools, he took business training courses. Pauley then became involved in contracting, real estate, and coal mining in Iaeger, West Virginia. He was also vice-president of the Bank of Iaeger.

A Democrat, Pauley was elected to the West Virginia House of Delegates from McDowell County in 1936, 1938, 1948, 1950, 1952, 1956, 1958, 1962, 1964, 1968, 1970, and 1972. He chaired the Roads and Transportation Committee, Education Committee, Finance Committee, and Joint Committee on Government and Finance. Pauley was chosen as speaker following the death of incumbent W. E. Flannery in March 1958, and he was renamed to the post for the 1959 session. Known as a skilled orator, he was, according to his colleagues, "endowed with a wit and humor of a modern-day Will Rogers."

In 1974 Pauley retired from the House and returned to his business interests in Iaeger. After farming in Christiansburg, Virginia, from 1977 to 1985, he moved to Beckley, West Virginia. Pauley was a member of the Masons, Odd Fellows, Rotary, and Methodist Church. He married Jessie M. Lambert in 1927, and the couple had one daughter. At this writing Pauley continues to live in Beckley.

LISLE G. BROWN

PEARSALL, THOMAS JENKINS (North Carolina, 1947) was born in Rocky Mount, North Carolina, on February 11, 1903, to Leon F. and Mary (Jenkins) Pearsall. Attending local public schools and the Georgia Military Academy in College Park, he won academic and athletic awards. In 1927 he received a law certificate from the University of North Carolina, where he managed the varsity baseball team. Pearsall then began a law practice in Rocky Mount. He married Elizabeth Braswell in 1930, and the couple had two sons.

A Democrat, Pearsall served Rocky Mount as a school board member and as solicitor of the Recorder's Court in 1928–33. He won a special election to the

North Carolina House of Representatives from Nash County in late 1940 and remained there for four consecutive terms. Pearsall was chair of the Committee on Agriculture and the Appropriations Committee before being named speaker for the 1947 session. The next year he comanaged the unsuccessful gubernatorial campaign of Charles M. Johnston. He chaired state committees addressing the U.S. Supreme Court's decision in favor of school desegregation in *Brown v. Board of Education* (1954) and reorganizing the University of North Carolina system (1962).

Returning to Rocky Mount, Pearsall owned farm land and the Pearsall Oil and Fuel Company. He was president of the Citizens Savings and Loan Association, general manager of the M. C. Braswell Company, and a director of the Planters National Bank and Trust Company. In addition, Pearsall was president of the North Carolina State University Agricultural Foundation. Chair of the board of North Carolina Wesleyan College, he was a trustee of North Carolina A&T State University and the Asheville School for Boys and a member of the Rotary and the Farm Bureau. Pearsall died on May 5, 1981, at the age of 78.

OTIENO OKELO

PELTER, JOHN J. (West Virginia, 1935) was born in Carlisle, West Virginia, on January 27, 1905, to English immigrants. After earning a B.A. from West Virginia University, he became a teacher in Logan County, West Virginia. In addition, Pelter studied law at the University of Kentucky. He never married.

Pelter successfully ran for the West Virginia House of Delegates as a Democrat from Logan County in 1932 and 1934. Named speaker for the 1935 session when he was only 29, he was the youngest person to hold the post in state history. In 1938 Pelter was elected to one term in the West Virginia Senate. He was mentioned as a candidate for higher office until becoming addicted to alcohol.

Returning to teaching in Logan County, Pelter's illness led to his eventual dismissal. He also lost a personnel management position at a coal mine. However, he was eventually able to overcome his alcoholism. Pelter died of a heart attack on March 28, 1974, at the age of 69.

Jim Comstock, ed., *The West Virginia Heritage Encyclopedia*, 25 vols. (Richwood, WV, 1976); Phil Conley, ed., *The West Virginia Encyclopedia* (Charleston: West Virginia Publishing, 1929).

PATRICK J. CHASE

PETTIGREW, RICHARD ALLEN (Florida, 1971) was born in Charleston, West Virginia, on June 10, 1930, to Grady Lewis and Otella (Overton) Pettigrew. The next year he moved with his family to Miami, Florida. Earning a B.A. from the University of Florida in 1953, he served with the U.S. Air Force's photointelligence division in Korea and Japan and rose to the rank of captain. Pettigrew received an LL.B. from Florida in 1957 and then practiced with the firm of Walton Lantaff. He founded his own law firm in Miami in 1967.

A Democrat, Pettigrew was president of the Florida Young Democrats. He won election to the Florida House of Representatives from Dade County in 1962 and remained there for five consecutive terms. Pettigrew chaired the Governmental Reorganization and Efficiency Committee and he sat on the commission that drafted the 1968 state constitution. Named speaker for the 1971 session, he backed progressive Governor Reubin O. Askew's reforms over opposition from state Senate leaders. As a result, legislation was passed that reduced the numbers of units in the executive branch from 150 to fewer than 25.

In 1972 Pettigrew was elected to the Florida Senate. Unsuccessfully running for the U.S. Senate from Florida in 1974, he returned to his law practice. Pettigrew was appointed an assistant to President Jimmy Carter in charge of reorganization in 1977. Outside of politics he was president of the junior branch of the Dade County Bar Association. A Congregationalist, Pettigrew married Ann Moorhead in 1954; the couple had two children.

JERRELL H. SHOFNER

PHARR, EDGAR WALTER (North Carolina, 1925) was born in Mecklenburg County, North Carolina, on March 4, 1889. Attending Charlotte University (now the University of North Carolina at Charlotte) and Erskine College in Due West, South Carolina, he studied law at the University of North Carolina. Pharr began a private practice in Mecklenburg County. He chaired the War Savings Committee during World War I and belonged to the Masons, Knights of Pythias, and American Bar Association. A Presbyterian, he was married.

In 1916 Pharr was elected to the North Carolina House of Representatives as a Democrat from Mecklenburg County. He served five consecutive terms and was chosen as speaker for the 1925 session. Returning to his law practice, he was appointed to the Federal Power Commission in 1935. Pharr died on December 15, 1936, at the age of 47.

John L. Cheney, Jr., *North Carolina Government, 1585–1974: A Narrative and Statistical History* (Raleigh: North Carolina Department of the Secretary of State, 1975); Hugh Talmadge Lefler and Albert Ray Newsome, *The History of a Southern State: North Carolina* (Chapel Hill: University of North Carolina Press, 1973); William S. Powell, *North Carolina through Four Centuries* (Chapel Hill: University of North Carolina Press, 1989).

CLAUDE HARGROVE

PHILLIPS, LEON CHASE "Red" (Oklahoma, 1935) was born in Worth County, Missouri, on December 9, 1890, of Scotch-Irish and German ancestry. Moving with his family to Arapaho, Oklahoma Territory, in 1892, he attended local public schools and became a teacher. Phillips studied for the ministry at Epworth (now Oklahoma City) University in Oklahoma and earned an LL.B. from the University of Oklahoma in 1916. He then began practicing law in

Okemah, Oklahoma. During World War I he served in the U.S. Army with the Artillery Officers' Training School.

A Democrat, Phillips was a special member of the Oklahoma Supreme Court in 1927–28. He successfully ran for the Oklahoma House of Representatives from Okfuskee County in 1932 and remained there for three consecutive terms. Phillips was chosen as speaker for the 1935 session. Elected governor of Oklahoma in 1938, his opposition to New Deal programs caused him to break from the national Democratic Party and support the 1942 Republican ticket.

After that Phillips returned to his Okemah law practice. In addition, he was a member of the Masons, Elks, Knights of Pythias, Kiwanis, American Legion, and Methodist Church. He was married. Phillips died on March 27, 1958, at the age of 67.

TIMOTHY A. ZWINK

PHILPOTT, ALBERT LEE (Virginia, 1980, 1982, 1984, 1986, 1988, 1990) was born in Henry County, Virginia, on July 29, 1919. Educated in local public schools, he received a B.A. from the University of Richmond in Virginia in 1941. During World War II he served in the U.S. Army Air Forces. Philpott earned a J.D. from Richmond in 1947 and began practicing law in Bassett, Virginia. He married Katherine Apperson, and the couple had two children.

A conservative Democrat, Philpott was commonwealth's attorney of Henry County from 1951 to 1957. In the latter year he successfully ran for the Virginia House of Delegates from Henry County and the city of Martinsville. Philpott remained there for seventeen consecutive terms, gaining respect for his debating skills, knowledge of the state's criminal code, and mastery of the legislative process. Close to the dominant Democratic faction led by U.S. Senator Harry F. Byrd, Sr., he chaired the Corporations, Insurance and Banking Committee and the Virginia Code Commission.

Philpott was named majority leader in 1978 and speaker for the 1980, 1982, 1984, 1986, 1988, and 1990 sessions. While in the speakership he was criticized for packing important committees with conservatives and for testifying at committee hearings. Feminists denounced his opposition to the Equal Rights Amendment to the U.S. Constitution, and blacks were irritated by remarks of his deemed racially insensitive. After surviving a challenge to his position in 1982, Philpott avoided additional controversies. He was deeply involved in passing 1989 legislation to improve an arterial road in southern Virginia through bond financing, marking a departure from the state's "pay-as-you-go" policy of highway construction.

In 1985 Philpott surprised observers by endorsing black state Senator L. Douglas Wilder's campaign for lieutenant governor of Virginia. He again supported Wilder in 1989, when the latter became the first African American to be elected governor of a U.S. state. Newspaper polls taken in 1987 and 1989 among government officials, lobbyists, and the media rated Philpott as the most effective Virginia legislator. Outside of politics he belonged to the Elks, Knights of Pythias, Moose, American Legion, American and Virginia bar associations, and Methodist Church. Philpott was still speaker when he died in Bassett on September 28, 1991, at age 72.

Norfolk Virginian-Pilot, September 29, 1991; *Richmond Times-Dispatch*, September 26, 29, 1991.

JAMES R. SWEENEY

POPE, THOMAS HARRINGTON (South Carolina, 1949) was born on July 28, 1913, in Kinards, South Carolina, to Thomas H. and Marie (Gary) Pope. He was raised in Newberry, South Carolina. Pope earned an A.B. from The Citadel in Charleston, South Carolina, in 1935, and an LL.B. from the University of South Carolina in 1938. After that he began practicing law in Newberry.

Pope successfully ran for the South Carolina House of Representatives as a Democrat from Newberry County in 1936, 1938, 1946, and 1948. During World War II he served in the U.S. Army, rising to the rank of lieutenant colonel. He lost the 1947 race for speaker, but he was named to the post in May 1949 following the resignation of incumbent C. Bruce Littlejohn.

In 1950 Pope was soundly defeated in the Democratic primary for governor of South Carolina by James F. Byrnes. He then returned to his law practice. President of The Citadel Alumni Association, he was also master of the Masons, commander of the American Legion, and a member of the Kiwanis, Chamber of Commerce, and Baptist Church. Pope continues to live in Newberry at this writing.

South Carolina Legislative Manual (Columbia: General Assembly of South Carolina, 1916–   ); *The State* (Columbia).

MARIAN ELIZABETH STROBEL

PRICE, WILLIAM RAYFORD (Texas, 1972) was born in Jacksonville, Texas, on February 9, 1937, to Quanah and Vaye (Baker) Price. Educated in public schools in Frankston, Texas, he attended Lon Morris College in Jacksonville and became student body president. Price worked as a printer before earning a bachelor's degree and an LL.B. (1967) from the University of Texas. Afterward he began a law practice in Palestine, Texas. He served in the Texas National Guard, rising to the rank of sergeant first class.

In 1960 Price was elected to the Texas House of Representatives as a Democrat from Anderson, Henderson, and Van Zandt counties. Remaining there for six consecutive terms, he chaired the Committee on Constitutional Amendments and the Committee on State Affairs. He was named speaker in March 1972 following the resignation of incumbent Gus F. Mutscher.

Price lost the 1972 Democratic primary for the House as a result of redistricting and opposition from the "Dirty Thirty," the group that had led the fight against Mutscher. He switched to the Republican Party in 1973. Moving to Dallas, Texas, he joined the law firm of Hutchison, Price, Boyle and Brooks.

In addition, he belonged to the Kiwanis, Chamber of Commerce, International Typographical Union, and Texas and Dallas bar associations. A Methodist, Price married Barbara Jean Ashley in 1961; the couple had two sons.

LUTHER G. HAGARD, JR.

PRIVETT, ARNOLD REX (Oklahoma, 1967, 1969, 1971) was born on May 28, 1924, in Maramec, Oklahoma, to Arnold Loyd and Muriel Privett. Educated in local public schools, he served as an engineer with the U.S. Army in the Pacific theater during World War II. He earned a B.A. in business administration from Oklahoma State University in 1949. Following that, Privett became a rancher in Maramec. A Methodist, he married Patricia Nichols; the couple had three children.

Privett successfully ran for the Oklahoma House of Representatives as a Democrat from Pawnee County in 1956. He remained there for eight consecutive terms and was chosen as speaker for the 1967, 1969, and 1971 sessions. While in the speakership Privett helped pass tax increases to fund the state government. In addition, he attended the 1968 Democratic National Convention and was active in the Council of State Governments and the National Conference of State Legislative Leaders. Elected to the Oklahoma Corporation Commission in 1972, he was that body's chair from 1975 to 1978.

In 1979 Privett entered the real estate business in Norman, Oklahoma. He became a vice-president of the First National Bank and Trust Company of Oklahoma City, Oklahoma, in 1980, specializing in matters relating to the Corporation Commission and banking legislation. After working as a lobbyist for the Oklahoma Bankers Association, he was named executive director of the Oklahoma Public Employees Retirement System in 1982. Privett was president of the Cattlemen's Association and a member of the Chamber of Commerce and the American Legion.

KENNY L. BROWN

Q

QUIN, HILLRIE MARSHALL (Mississippi, 1912) was born in Holmesville, Mississippi, on March 2, 1866. Educated in local public schools, he received a degree from the University of Mississippi in 1886. Quin was then a teacher and school principal in McComb and Fayette, Mississippi. From 1892 to 1902 he worked in the newspaper business, briefly becoming editor of the Centreville, Mississippi, *Jeffersonian*. He earned an LL.B. from Mississippi in 1904 and began practicing law in Jackson, Mississippi.

A Democrat, Quin was an alderman in Centreville. He was elected to the Mississippi House of Representatives from Wilkinson County in 1899 and from Hinds County in 1907 and 1911. While in office he belonged to a party faction led by James Vardaman. Quin lost a bid for speaker in 1908, but he was named to the post for the 1912 session. In 1915 he was defeated for governor of Mississippi by Theodore G. Bilbo.

After editing Vardaman's newspaper for a year, Quin moved his law practice to Meridian, Mississippi, in 1917. In other affairs he was a member of the Masons, Odd Fellows, Knights of Pythias, Rotary, and Methodist Church. He was married. Quin died on January 20, 1923, at the age of 56.

Albert Kirwan, *The Revolt of the Rednecks: Mississippi Politics, 1876–1925* (Lexington: University of Kentucky Press, 1951); Dale Krane and Stephen D. Shaffer, eds., *Mississippi Government & Politics: Modernizers versus Traditionalists* (Lincoln: University of Nebraska Press, 1992); Richard A. McLemore, *A History of Mississippi*, 2 vols. (Jackson: University and College Press of Mississippi, 1973); *Mississippi Official and Statistical Register* (Jackson: Secretary of State).

DAVID G. SANSING

R

RAMSAY, KERR CRAIGE (North Carolina, 1949) was born in Salisbury, North Carolina, on July 23, 1911, to John E. and Elizabeth Erwin (Craige) Ramsay. Educated in local public schools, he received an A.B. from the University of North Carolina in 1931. He studied law at North Carolina before earning an LL.B. from Yale University in 1934. Afterward Ramsay joined the law firm of Craige and Craige in Salisbury. A Presbyterian, he married Elenor Walton Newman in 1940; the couple had one daughter.

Ramsay was elected to the North Carolina House of Representatives as a Democrat from Rowan County in 1940. Remaining there for six consecutive terms, he was chosen as speaker for the 1949 session. He was named one of the most influential House members by his colleagues in 1951.

State chair of the American Cancer Society, Ramsay was president of the Chamber of Commerce and secretary of the Rowan County Bar Association. In addition, he was a trustee of Rowan Memorial Hospital as well as a member of the Rotary and the American, North Carolina, and Forsyth County bar associations. Ramsay was still serving in the House when he died of a heart attack on December 10, 1951. He was 40.

OTIENO OKELO

RAMSEY, JAMES EDWARD (North Carolina, 1973) was born in Woodsdale, North Carolina, on October 19, 1931, to John Talmadge and Otey (Wilkins) Ramsey. Educated in local schools, he received an A.B. from the University of North Carolina in 1953. He served in the U.S. Marine Corps for two years, rising to the rank of captain. Ramsey attended the University of Hawaii before earning an LL.B. from North Carolina in 1958. After that he began to practice law in Roxboro, North Carolina, with the firm of Ramsey, Jackson & Hubbard.

A Democrat, Ramsey was president of the Person County Young Democrats and sat on the Person County Recorder's Court from 1958 to 1962. In the latter year he was elected to the North Carolina House of Representatives from Person, Caswell, Granville, Vance, and Warren counties. He remained there for six consecutive terms, defining himself as "liberal on spending and taxing policy, but rather conservative on law and order." Ramsey was chosen as speaker for the 1973 session. While in the speakership he sought to establish annual sessions and to enlarge the legislative staff.

Returning to his law practice, Ramsey lost the 1982 Democratic primary for the U.S. House of Representatives from North Carolina's 2nd District. In addition, he was president of the Lions, Ruritan Club, and Person County Bar Association and a member of the Chamber of Commerce, American and North Carolina bar associations, and Methodist Church. Ramsey was named "Outstanding Young Man of Person County" in 1962. He married Eunice Saunders in 1953, and the couple had four children. At this writing Ramsey continues to live in Roxboro.

William S. Powell, ed., *Dictionary of North Carolina Biography*, 6 vols. (Chapel Hill: University of North Carolina Press, 1979–1996).

CHARLES H. BOWMAN, JR.

RAMSEY, LISTON BRYAN (North Carolina, 1981, 1983, 1985, 1987) was born on February 26, 1919, in Marshall, North Carolina, to John Morgan and Della Lee (Bryan) Ramsey. Educated in local public schools, he earned a business degree from Mars Hill College in North Carolina in 1938. Ramsey served as a sergeant in the U.S. Army Air Forces during World War II. Afterward he operated his family's retail building supply company in Marshall until 1961. Commander of the American Legion, Ramsey was a trustee of the Cherokee Historical Association and a member of the Masons, Elks, VFW, and Baptist Church. He married Florence McDevitt, and the couple had one daughter.

A Democrat, Ramsey was an alderman in Marshall (1949–61) and chair of the Madison County Democratic Executive Committee. He successfully ran for the North Carolina House of Representatives in 1960 and 1962. Ramsey was again elected to the House in 1966, representing Madison, Haywood, Jackson, and Swain counties until 1982 and Madison, Graham, Haywood, Jackson, and Swain counties thereafter. In addition, he attended the 1968 Democratic National Convention and sat on the executive committee of the Southern Legislative Conference.

Named speaker for the 1981, 1983, 1985, and 1987 sessions, Ramsey held the post for the longest tenure in state history. He received awards from the North Carolina Center for Public Policy Research, North Carolina Association of Educators, AFL-CIO, and Raleigh *News and Observer*. The Liston B. Ramsey Regional Activity Center at Western Carolina University was named for him in 1986. However, he drew increasing criticism within the House. In 1989 he was ousted from the speakership by a coalition of conservative Democrats and Republicans led by Josephus L. Mavretic. Ramsey remains in the House at this writing.

Christensen, Rob, "Growing Republican Ranks Help Topple Speaker in North Carolina," *State Legislatures* 15 (April 1989), 16–19; William S. Powell, ed., *Dictionary of*

North Carolina Biography, 6 vols. (Chapel Hill: University of North Carolina Press, 1979–1996).

CHARLES H. BOWMAN, JR.

RAYBURN, SAMUEL TALIAFERRO (Texas, 1911) was born in the Clinch River Valley of Tennessee on January 6, 1882, to William Marion and Martha (Waller) Rayburn. In 1887 he moved with his family to a cotton farm near Bonham, Texas, where they lived at a subsistence level. He made a personal goal of serving in the U.S. House after hearing a speech by Representative Joseph W. Bailey in 1894. Educated in local schools, Rayburn earned a B.S. from the Mayo Normal School (now Texas A&M University at Commerce) in 1903. For three years he worked as a teacher in Fannin County, Texas.

A Democrat, Rayburn entered politics when he successfully ran for the Texas House of Representatives from Fannin County in 1906. He remained there for three consecutive terms, and he was chosen as speaker for the 1911 session when he was only 29. Concurrently he received a law degree from the University of Texas.

Rayburn was narrowly elected to the U.S. House of Representatives from the 4th District of Texas in 1912, becoming that body's majority leader in 1937. Named to the speakership in 1940, he retained the position with the exception of the 1947 and 1953 terms when the Democrats lost control of the House. While in office Rayburn became one of the nation's most influential politicians. He was described as being sincerely modest, focusing upon his duties and avoiding publicity. A Baptist, he was divorced. Rayburn was still U.S. House speaker when he died in Bonham on November 16, 1961, at age 79.

THOMAS R. MYERS

REED, HOWARD (Arkansas, 1923) was born on September 29, 1883, in Salem, Kansas, to natives of New York. As a child he moved with his family to Heber Springs, Arkansas. Reed attended local public schools, Quitman College in Arkansas, and the University of Arkansas. After reading law with his father, he began a private practice around 1910. He served in the Arkansas National Guard in 1909–14, rising to the rank of captain.

A Democrat, Reed was Cleburne County tax assessor from 1907 to 1911. In 1918 he was elected to the Arkansas House of Representatives from Cleburne County. Reed remained there for three consecutive terms and was named speaker for the 1923 session. He was Arkansas comptroller and chief budget officer in 1927–32, but he unsuccessfully ran for governor of Arkansas in 1932 and 1934.

Returning to his Heber Springs law practice, Reed was also engaged in the bond and insurance business. During the 1930s he was an executive with the U.S. Works Project Administration. He was married. Reed died on November 16, 1942, at the age of 59.

Diane D. Blair, *Arkansas Politics and Government* (Lincoln: University of Nebraska Press, 1988), 160–184; Jerry E. Hinshaw, *Call the Roll* (Little Rock: Rose Publishing,

1986); *Historical Report of the Secretary of State, Arkansas* (Little Rock: Secretary of State, 1958–   ); Walter Nunn, *Readings in Arkansas Government* (Little Rock: Rose Publishing, 1973): 59–133.

                                                                         CAL LEDBETTER, JR.

REED, WILLIAM OTEY (Texas, 1947) was born in Dallas, Texas, on May 12, 1902, the youngest of ten children. Employed as a newspaper boy, he gained a reputation as an accomplished fighter able to control the more lucrative street corners. Reed quit school when he was 15, joining the Dallas Water Department. Later he worked as a clerk for the Texas and Pacific Railway Company. After attending Jefferson Law School in Dallas and earning a law license in 1933, he became an attorney for the railroad.

In 1932 Reed was elected to the Texas House of Representatives as a Democrat from Dallas County. Serving nine consecutive terms, he was unanimously named speaker for the 1947 session. Reed was known as an astute parliamentarian and a fiscal conservative, and he sponsored a state constitutional amendment to prevent the appropriation of funds for projects without first ensuring the availability of adequate tax revenues. He unsuccessfully ran for lieutenant governor of Texas in 1950.

Afterward Reed became counsel for the Texas railroad industry in Washington, D.C. In addition, he belonged to the Texas and Dallas bar associations. A Presbyterian, Reed was married. He often displayed showmanship in defying superstitions against the number thirteen, such as filing for reelection on Friday the 13th and wearing a horseshoe ring with a "13" on it. Reed died on October 28, 1969, at the age of 67.

                                                                         RICHARD B. RILEY

RIALES, ROY LEE, Sr. (Arkansas, 1947) was born in Nunley, Arkansas, on December 24, 1909, to William T. and Vi Biller (Ringgold) Riales. Educated in schools in Arkansas and Oklahoma, he attended the Georgia-Carolina School of Commerce in Brunswick, Georgia. Riales then settled in Mena, Arkansas. He joined the engineering division of the Arkansas Highway Department in 1925 and worked for the U.S. Forest Service and the U.S. Resettlement Administration during the 1930s.

Elected to the Arkansas House of Representatives as a Democrat from Polk County in 1938, Riales served five consecutive terms. Concurrently he was an aide to U.S. Representative Fadjo Cravens of Arkansas. Riales was named speaker for the 1947 session. After that he moved to Tulare, California, where he was postmaster in 1950–52. He lost a 1952 race for the U.S. House of Representatives from California.

Returning to Mena, Riales won election to the Arkansas Senate in 1954 and was that body's president *pro tem* in 1959. He withdrew from the 1964 race for lieutenant governor of Arkansas. That same year Riales was appointed postmaster of Mena, a post he held until 1969. A Methodist, he was married. Riales died on November 1, 1985, at the age of 75.

Arkansas Democrat; Arkansas Gazette; The Arkansas Handbook (Little Rock: Arkansas History Commission, 1936–   ).

RUSSELL PIERCE BAKER

RICHARDSON, BOBBY HAROLD (Kentucky, 1982, 1984) was born on November 25, 1944, in Glasgow, Kentucky, to Robert E. and Nina (Tucker) Richardson. Educated in local public schools, he earned an A.B. from Western Kentucky University in Bowling Green and a J.D. from the University of Kentucky. Richardson then began a law practice in Glasgow. He was also a director of the First Federal Savings and Loan Association.

A Democrat, Richardson was master commissioner of Barren County in 1968–72 and a delegate to the 1976 Democratic National Convention. In 1971 he was elected to the Kentucky House of Representatives from Barren and Metcalfe counties. He served ten consecutive terms. Named majority leader in 1976, Richardson worked with Speaker William G. Kenton to increase the House's independence from the governor. Richardson was named speaker for the 1982 and 1984 sessions. While in the post he kept a high profile, using the media to publicize House activities.

Forced to step down from the speakership in 1986, Richardson retired from the House in 1991. Outside of politics he was president of the Lions and a member of the Jaycees, Farm Bureau, American and Kentucky bar associations, and Baptist Church. He married Elaine Alexander in 1970. Richardson continues to live in Glasgow at this writing.

Malcolm E. Jewell, *Representation in State Legislatures* (Lexington: University Press of Kentucky, 1982); Malcolm E. Jewell and Penny Miller, *The Kentucky Legislature: Two Decades of Change* (Lexington: University Press of Kentucky, 1988); Malcolm E. Jewell and Samuel C. Patterson, *The Legislative Process in the United States*, 4th ed. (New York: Random House, 1986).

H. LEW WALLACE

RICHARDSON, OSCAR LEON (North Carolina, 1945) was born in Union County, North Carolina, on February 25, 1896. Educated in local public schools, he served in the U.S. Army Air Service during World War I. Richardson received an A.B. from Trinity College (now Duke University) in Durham, North Carolina, in 1921. While in college he was a member of the track and baseball teams. After taking graduate courses at the University of North Carolina, Richardson earned an LL.B. from Trinity in 1924. He then began a law practice in Monroe, North Carolina, where he also worked as a teacher.

A Democrat, Richardson was clerk of the Union County Superior Court for ten years and Monroe city attorney for fourteen years. In 1938 he was elected to the North Carolina House of Representatives from Union County. Richardson served four consecutive terms. Chair of the Judiciary Committee and vice-chair of the Appropriations Committee, he was chosen as speaker for the 1945 session. He successfully ran for the North Carolina Senate in 1946 and 1948.

Following that Richardson sat on the North Carolina Board of Education for five years. In addition, he belonged to the American Legion and the Methodist Church. He married Sara Cowan in 1930, and the couple had two children. Richardson died of a heart ailment on March 17, 1966, at the age of 70.

OTIENO OKELO

RIVERS, EURITH DICKINSON (Georgia, 1933, 1935) was born in Center Point, Arkansas, on December 1, 1895. Earning an A.A. from Young Harris College in Georgia in 1914, he became a teacher. Later he received an LL.B. through correspondence from LaSalle Extension University in Chicago, Illinois. Rivers practiced law in Cairo, Georgia, before moving to Lakeland, Georgia. He was married.

A Democrat, Rivers was a justice of the peace, city attorney of both Cairo and Lakeland, and attorney for Grady and Lanier counties. In 1924 he successfully ran for the Georgia House of Representatives from Lanier County. Rivers won races for the Georgia Senate in 1926 and 1928 and was that body's speaker *pro tem* for two terms. Losing the 1928 and 1930 Democratic primaries for governor of Georgia, he again won election to the House in 1932 and 1934. He was named speaker for the 1933 and 1935 sessions.

Elected governor in 1936 and 1938, Rivers instituted a "Little New Deal" program but was hurt by charges of a pardons racket and of corruption in the state highway department. He was defeated in the 1946 gubernatorial primary. Afterward Rivers purchased several radio stations in Georgia and Florida. In addition, he was president of the Woodmen of the World, master of the Masons, and a member of the Elks, Odd Fellows, Knights of Pythias, Ku Klux Klan, American and Georgia bar associations, and Baptist Church. Rivers was a millionaire when he died on June 11, 1967, at age 71.

Georgia Department of History and Archives, *Georgia's Official Register* (Atlanta: Longino and Porter, 1923–1967/68).

JANE W. HERNDON

ROGERS, W. E., Sr. (Kentucky, 1934) was born in Montgomery County, Tennessee, on December 20, 1880, to S. L. and Ellen Rogers. Later he moved with his family to Guthrie, Kentucky, where he became the owner of a hardware and grocery business. In addition, Rogers was president of a bank. He married Mary Mannion in 1904.

A Democrat, Rogers was city judge of Guthrie in 1904–12. He won election to the Kentucky House of Representatives from Todd County in 1913 and to the Kentucky Senate two years later. Again elected to the House in 1933, Rogers was chosen as speaker for the 1934 session. Afterward he returned to his Guthrie business interests. Rogers, a Methodist, died on April 25, 1951, at the age of 70.

George T. Blakey, *Hard Times and the New Deal in Kentucky, 1929–1939* (Lexington: University Press of Kentucky, 1986); Malcolm E. Jewell and Everett W. Cunningham, *Kentucky Politics* (Lexington: University Press of Kentucky, 1968); Malcolm E. Jewell and Penny Miller, *The Kentucky Legislature: Two Decades of Change* (Lexington: University Press of Kentucky, 1988); Robert F. Sexton, "Kentucky Politics and Society, 1919–1932" (Ph.D. dissertation, University of Washington, 1970).

NANCY DISHER BAIRD

ROWELL, E. C. (Florida, 1965) once called himself the "meanest man in the legislature." Born in Oxford, Florida, on October 1, 1914, to Cleveland and Edna (Collier) Rowell, he was the grandson of H. O. Collier, a state legislator and a county commissioner. After attending the University of Florida for one year, Rowell returned to his family's farm. During World War II he served with the U.S. Army Air Forces in England, rising to the rank of sergeant. He later owned a finance company in Wildwood, Florida.

In 1956 Rowell was narrowly elected to the Florida House of Representatives as a Democrat from Sumter County. He remained there for seven consecutive terms and was named speaker for the 1965 regular session and for three special sessions in 1965 and 1966. Although suffering from a thyroid condition that caused him to lose his voice and memory temporarily, he continued to exercise influence. Rowell pushed through Governor Haydon Burn's bond program for road construction and sharply cut the state's operating budget. During the special sessions he sought to limit the effects of reapportionment on the legislature's rural power base, but he failed when the U.S. Supreme Court rejected his plan.

Retiring from the House in 1970, Rowell became a lobbyist for the Florida Trucking Association and director of the Southeast Bank in Wildwood. In addition, he was director of the Florida Farm Bureau, commander of the American Legion, and a member of the Masons, Lions, Chamber of Commerce, and Baptist Church. He married Marjorie Aylotte in 1943, and the couple had two daughters. Rowell died on September 14, 1992, at the age of 77.

J. LARRY DURRENCE

RUSSELL, RICHARD BREVARD (Georgia, 1927, 1929) was born in Winder, Georgia, on November 3, 1897, to Richard Brevard and Ina (Dillard) Russell. His father was chief justice of the state Supreme Court from 1923 to 1938. Russell graduated from Gordon Military Academy in 1915, and he served in the U.S. Naval Reserve during World War I. Earning a B.L. from the University of Georgia in 1918, he began a law practice in Winder. In addition, Russell belonged to the Masons, Elks, Odd Fellows, Kiwanis, American Legion, American and Georgia bar associations, and Methodist Church. He never married.

A Democrat, Russell was elected to the Georgia House of Representatives from Barrow County in 1920 and remained there for five consecutive terms. He was named speaker *pro tem* in 1923 and 1925 and speaker for the 1927 and

1929 sessions. Russell successfully ran for governor of Georgia in 1930. While in the governorship he promoted a revision of the Georgia Constitution that significantly reorganized government.

In 1932 Russell won election to the U.S. Senate from Georgia. Serving seven consecutive terms, he chaired the Appropriations Committee and became president *pro tem* in 1969. He lost the 1948 Democratic nomination for President, and he sat on the President's Commission on the Assassination of President John F. Kennedy led by Earl Warren in 1963–64. Russell was still a member of the Senate when he died on January 22, 1971, at age 73.

Georgia Department of History and Archives, *Georgia's Official Register* (Atlanta: Longino and Porter, 1923–1967/68).

JANE W. HERNDON

S

SATTERWHITE, ROBERT LEE (Texas, 1925) was born in Nevada County, Arkansas, on January 28, 1871, and moved with his family to Texas in 1885. After attending local schools, he worked on a farm and as a printer in Freestone County, Texas. Satterwhite founded the Wortham, Texas, *Signal* in 1893, and he published the Wortham *Journal* in 1896–98. During the Spanish-American War he served in the U.S. Army with the 2nd Texas Infantry. He later operated the Tulia, Texas, *Enterprise* and the Panhandle, Texas, *Herald*.

A Democrat, Satterwhite won election to one term in the Texas House of Representatives from Freestone County in 1900. He was assistant House reading clerk in 1903. In 1918 and 1920 he successfully ran for the House from Carson, Dallam, Hansford, Hartley, Hutchinson, Moore, Oldham, Potter, and Sherman counties. Satterwhite then relocated to Amarillo, Texas, and he was again elected to the House in 1922, this time from Potter, Armstrong, Carson, Deaf Smith, Oldham, and Randall counties. Serving three consecutive terms, he was named speaker for the 1925 session because he lacked close ties to Governor Miriam Ferguson.

Around 1928 Satterwhite began ranching near Odessa, Texas. He won an additional House term from Ector, Andrews, Crane, Jeff Davis, Loving, Martin, Midland, Pecos, Presidio, Reeves, Upton, Ward, and Winkler counties in 1930. Losing races for lieutenant governor of Texas in 1944 and for the House two years later, Satterwhite settled in Houston, Texas, in 1947. In other affairs he was president of the Panhandle Press Association and a member of the Baptist Church. He was married. Satterwhite died on November 29, 1959, at the age of 78.

Norman D. Brown, *Hood, Bonnet, and Little Brown Jug: Texas Politics, 1921–1928* (College Station: Texas A&M University Press, 1984); Dallas *Morning News*, January 11–15, 1925, November 30, 1959; Lewis L. Gould, *Progressives and Prohibitionists: Texas Democrats in the Wilson Era* (Austin: University of Texas Press, 1973); George Norris Green, *The Establishment in Texas Politics: The Primitive Years, 1938–1957* (Westport, CT: Greenwood Press, 1979); Frank W. Johnson, *A History of Texas and*

Texans, 5 vols. (Chicago: American Historical Society, 1914), V: 2164; *Presiding Officers of the Texas Legislature, 1846–1982* (Austin: Texas Legislative Council, 1982), 162–163.

ALWYN BARR

SAWYER, LEWIS ERNEST (Arkansas, 1915) was born on June 24, 1867, in Shelby County, Alabama. Educated in public schools in Lee County, Mississippi, he earned a degree from the University of Mississippi and studied law. Sawyer began practicing law in Friar's Point, Mississippi, in 1895 and in Iuka, Mississippi, in 1900. During the Spanish-American War he served with the U.S. Army in the Philippines. He moved to Hot Springs, Arkansas, in 1908, becoming counsel for several businesses.

A Democrat, Sawyer was elected mayor of Friar's Point in 1896. In 1912 and 1914 he successfully ran for the Arkansas House of Representatives from Garland County. Sawyer was chosen as speaker for the 1915 session in a closely contested race. He apparently presided with a sense of humor, for at the end of his speakership he was presented with a hatchet for cutting an item in the general appropriation from $1,000 to $999.

Defeated for the U.S. House of Representatives from the 6th District of Arkansas by Sam Taylor in 1918, Sawyer won election to the post in 1922. In addition, he belonged to the Masons, Elks, Knights of Pythias, and Christian Church (Disciples of Christ). He was married. Sawyer was still a member of the U.S. House when he died in Hot Springs on May 5, 1923, at age 55.

Arkansas Democrat; Arkansas Gazette.

CARL H. MONEYHON

SCHULTZ, FREDERICK HENRY (Florida, 1969) was born on January 16, 1929, in Jacksonville, Florida, to Clifford G. and Mae (Wangler) Schultz. Attending the Bolles School and the Lawrenceville School in New Jersey, he earned an A.B. from Princeton University in 1952. Schultz served in the U.S. Army during the Korean conflict, rising to the rank of first lieutenant. He received a law degree from the University of Florida in 1956, and then he became an investment counselor in Jacksonville. A Catholic, he married Nancy Jane Reilly in 1951; the couple had four children.

In 1962 Schultz was elected to the Florida House of Representatives as a Democrat from Duval County. He remained there for four consecutive terms and was named speaker for the 1969 session. During his speakership the issue of state reapportionment was resolved by a U.S. court order. Schultz also worked to increase the professionalization of the House by attempting to implement recommendations for an expanded staff and increased salaries. These efforts were criticized by Governor Claude Kirk, the first Republican in that office since 1877.

Returning to his business interests, Schultz became an official of the Barnett Bank and was active in several life insurance and manufacturing firms. In addition, he was a member of the Jacksonville Expressway Authority, governor of the Chamber of Commerce, and trustee of Jacksonville University and Edward Waters College. He unsuccessfully ran for the U.S. Senate from Florida. Schultz continues to live in Jacksonville at this writing.

JERRELL H. SHOFNER

SCHWABE, GEORGE BLAINE (Oklahoma, 1921) was born in Missouri on July 26, 1886. After receiving an LL.B. from the University of Missouri in 1910, he began practicing law in Nowata, Oklahoma. Schwabe belonged to the Masons, Elks, Odd Fellows, and Christian Church (Disciples of Christ). He married Jeanette E. Simpson in 1914, and the couple had five children.

A Republican, Schwabe served Nowata as mayor (1913–15), city attorney (1916–19), and school board member (1916–22). In 1918 and 1920 he was elected to the Oklahoma House of Representatives from Nowata County. He was named speaker for the 1921 session, becoming the only Republican to hold the post during Oklahoma's statehood. While in the speakership Schwabe led an investigation into alleged wrongdoings in the executive and judiciary branches. Impeachment charges against Democratic Governor James B. A. Robertson failed by a single vote, but they were brought against the lieutenant governor and a Supreme Court justice.

Losing reelection to the House in 1922, Schwabe relocated his private practice to Tulsa, Oklahoma. He won election to the U.S. House of Representatives from the 1st District of Oklahoma in 1944. Schwabe still held that office when he died on April 7, 1952, at age 65.

GORDON MOORE

SCHWARTZ, RAMON, Jr. (South Carolina, 1980, 1981, 1983, 1985) was born on March 25, 1925, in Sumter, South Carolina, to Raymon and Madge (Grossman) Schwartz. Educated in local schools, he served with the U.S. Army in Europe during World War II. Schwartz earned an A.B. (1948) and an LL.B. (1949) from the University of South Carolina. He then began practicing law in Sumter with the firm of Schwartz & DuRant.

A Democrat, Schwartz served Sumter as city recorder (1953–57, 1960–64) and chair of the Housing Authority (1964–68). In 1968 he was elected to the South Carolina House of Representatives from Sumter County. Schwartz remained there for nine consecutive terms. Becoming speaker *pro tem* in 1976, he was chosen as speaker in September 1980 following the resignation of incumbent Rex L. Carter. He was renamed to the speakership for the 1981, 1983, and 1985 sessions.

Schwartz resigned from the House in October 1986, returning to his law practice. Chair of the Sumter County library board in 1961–68, he was president of the South Carolina Jaycees (1959–60), Rotary, and Chamber of Commerce. In addition, Schwartz belonged to the Elks, American Legion, VFW, and Episcopal Church. He married Rosa Weinberg in 1950, and the couple had four children. As of this writing Schwartz continues to live in Sumter.

South Carolina Legislative Manual (Columbia: General Assembly of South Carolina, 1916–   ); *The State* (Columbia).

MARIAN ELIZABETH STROBEL

SEAGLER, RICHARD E. (Texas, 1923) was born in Tennessee Colony, Texas, on December 3, 1883. Educated in local public schools, he earned a degree from North Texas State Normal College (now the University of North Texas) in Denton in 1908. He received a law degree from the University of Texas in 1912, and he began a private law practice in Palestine, Texas.

A Democrat, Seagler won election to the Texas House of Representatives from Anderson County in 1918. He served three consecutive terms, authoring several measures concerning judicial procedure. Seagler became chair of the Committee on Criminal Jurisprudence and vice-chair of the Rules Committee in 1921. Named speaker for the 1923 session, he helped pass bills to create Texas Technological College and to set state highway speed limits.

In 1924 Seagler was appointed an assistant attorney general of Texas. Becoming a counsel for the Humble Oil and Refining Company in 1925, he headed that firm's trial division from 1929 to 1948. He then briefly practiced law in Houston, Texas. Seagler died on January 6, 1956, at the age of 72.

Journal of the House of Representatives (Austin: Von Boeckmann-Jones Co., 1909–   ); *Members of the Texas Legislature, 1846–1980* (Austin: Texas Legislature, 1981); *Presiding Officers of the Texas Legislature, 1846–1982* (Austin: Texas Legislative Council, 1982).

RON LAW

SEE, CLYDE M., Jr. (West Virginia, 1979, 1981, 1983) was born on October 20, 1941, in Moorefield, West Virginia, to Clyde M. and Minnie (Crites) See. Educated in local public schools, he served in the U.S. Army from 1958 to 1962. See attended Concord College in Athens, West Virginia, and earned an A.B. (1967) and a J.D. (1970) from West Virginia University. He began practicing law in Moorefield, eventually becoming senior partner in the firm of See and Walters.

In 1974 See was elected to the West Virginia House of Delegates as a Democrat from Hardy, Hampshire, and Pendleton counties. He remained there for five consecutive terms. See was chair of the Commission on Special Investigations and vice-chair of the Judiciary Committee. Majority leader in 1977, he was chosen as speaker for the 1979, 1981, and 1983 sessions.

See lost the 1984 race for governor of West Virginia to Republican Arch A. Moore, Jr. He then returned to his private practice and worked as a legislative lobbyist. In addition, See belonged to the Moose, Farm Bureau, American Legion, and American and West Virginia bar associations. A Presbyterian, he married Judith Ann Robinson in 1968; the couple had four children. At this writing See continues to live in Moorefield.

LISLE G. BROWN

SENTERFITT, REUBEN (Texas, 1951, 1953) was born in San Saba County, Texas, on June 18, 1917. Graduating from local public schools as valedictorian, he received an LL.B. from the University of Texas. While in college he was editor of the *Texas Law Review*. Senterfitt then began practicing law in San Saba, Texas. He married Maurine Culton in 1940, and the couple adopted three children.

Elected to the Texas House of Representatives as a Democrat in 1940, Senterfitt remained there for seven consecutive terms. He represented San Saba, Lampasas, and McCulloch counties until 1952 and San Saba, Burnet, Gillespie, Lampasas, Llano, and McCulloch counties thereafter. Concurrently he served as a lieutenant (j.g.) with the U.S. Navy in the Pacific theater during World War II. Senterfitt sponsored legislation to establish the M.D. Anderson Hospital in Houston and to create the Texas Veterans Land Program. Named speaker for the 1951 and 1953 sessions, he helped reform the appropriations process and enact a bill authorizing construction of the Dallas–Fort Worth Turnpike.

In 1956 Senterfitt lost the Democratic nomination for governor of Texas. Returning to his private law practice, he was also attorney for San Saba (1955–60) and San Saba County (1962–64). He was president of the Rotary and the Jaycees as well as commander of the VFW. Senterfitt operates a cattle ranch near San Saba at this writing.

Eugene W. Jones, Joe E. Ericson, Lyle C. Brown, and Robert S. Trotter, Jr., *Practicing Texas Politics*, 8th ed. (Boston: Houghton Mifflin, 1992); *Presiding Officers of the Texas Legislature, 1846–1982* (Austin: Texas Legislative Council, 1982), 186–187.

L. GERALD FIELDER

SESSUMS, THOMAS TERRELL (Florida, 1973) was born on June 11, 1930, in Daytona Beach, Florida, to Thomas Little and Dorothy (Cornwall) Sessums. He received a B.A. (1952) and an LL.B. (1958) from the University of Florida. Sessums served in the U.S. Air Force in 1954–56, rising to the rank of captain. In 1961 he became a partner in the law firm of Albritton and Sessums in Tampa, Florida.

Elected to the Florida House of Representatives as a Democrat from Hillsborough and Citrus counties in 1962, Sessums remained there for six consecutive terms. He was speaker *pro tem* in 1969 and chair of the Education Committee for the 1971 session. While in the latter post he played a major role in authorizing a new College of Medicine and Nursing at the University of South Florida. Named speaker in 1973, Sessums helped enact an educational finance program that drew national praise. The legislature also instituted a statewide achievement exam for public school students and passed bills on financial disclosure and consumer protection.

Sessums then returned to practicing law and worked as a lobbyist. Appointed to the Florida Board of Regents, he was a trustee of Florida Southern College. In addition, Sessums belonged to the Kiwanis, Chamber of Commerce, American, Florida, and Hillsborough County bar associations, and Methodist Church. He married Neva Ann Steeves in 1958, and the couple had three children. At this writing Sessums continues to live in Tampa.

J. LARRY DURRENCE

SHAVER, JAMES LEVESQUE, Jr. (Arkansas, 1977) was born on November 23, 1927, in Wynne, Arkansas, to James Levesque and Louise (Davis) Shaver. After attending local public schools, he served in the U.S. Navy for one year. In 1951 Shaver received a J.D. from the University of Arkansas. He then joined his family's law firm of Shaver, Shaver and Smith.

Shaver was elected to the Arkansas House of Representatives as a Democrat from Cross County in 1954. He was chosen as speaker for the 1977 session. In addition, he chaired the Judiciary Committee, Committee to Study Improvement in Legislative Procedures, Interstate Cooperation Committee, and Joint Interim Committee on the Judiciary.

Outside of politics Shaver was president of the Rotary and the Arkansas Bar Association and treasurer of the Cross County Bar Association. He also belonged to the American Bar Association and the American College of Probate Counsel. A Presbyterian, he married Bonnie Wood in 1949; the couple had one daughter. As of this writing Shaver remains in the House and continues to practice law.

SUZANNE MABERRY

SHEHEEN, ROBERT J. (South Carolina, 1987, 1989, 1991, 1993) was born in Camden, South Carolina, on January 21, 1943, to Austin M. and Lucile (Toukos) Sheheen. Educated in local public schools, he earned a B.A. from Duke University in Durham, North Carolina, in 1965 and a J.D. from the University of South Carolina in 1968. Sheheen then began a law practice in Camden. A member of Kiwanis and the Catholic Church, he never married.

Sheheen entered politics when he was elected as a Democrat to the South Carolina House of Representatives from Kershaw County in 1976. He was named "Legislator of the Year" by the South Carolina Association of Counties (1980), Greenville *News* (1979, 1982), and South Carolina Chamber of Commerce (1986). Sheheen was chosen as speaker for the 1987, 1989, 1991, and 1993 sessions. As of this writing he remains in the House.

GINA PETONITO

SHIELDS, BENJAMIN FRANKLIN (Kentucky, 1940) was born in Nelson County, Kentucky, on January 2, 1881. After earning a B.S. from Transylvania College (now University) in Lexington, Kentucky, and an M.D. from the University of Louisville in Kentucky, he moved to Shelbyville, Kentucky. Shields practiced medicine for more than fifty years, sometimes making his rounds on foot, on horseback, or by boat. He was married, and he belonged to the Masons, Rotary, and Christian Church (Disciples of Christ).

A Democrat, Shields was elected to the Kentucky House of Representatives from Shelby and Spencer counties in 1919, 1931, 1935, 1939, and 1951. He was named speaker for the 1940 session. In 1953 he successfully ran for the Kentucky Senate, where he remained until retiring in 1958 due to failing eyesight. Shields died on March 10, 1969, at age 88, and he was buried in Shelbyville.

Louisville *Courier-Journal; Kentucky Directory for the Use of the Courts, State and County Officials and General Assembly of the State of Kentucky* (Frankfort, KY, 1914–); John E. Kleber, ed., *The Kentucky Encyclopedia* (Lexington: University Press of Kentucky, 1992); Penny M. Miller, *Kentucky Politics and Government* (Lincoln: University of Nebraska Press, 1994); Robert F. Sexton, ed., *The Public Papers of the Governors of Kentucky* (Lexington: University Press of Kentucky, 1975).

ROGER TATE

SHROPSHIRE, CLYDE MOORE (Tennessee, 1917) was born on January 22, 1866, in Rome, Georgia, to Wilson Monroe and Ann Eliza (Moore) Shropshire. He attended public schools, earned a B.A. from the University of Georgia, and studied law with his father. Becoming a U.S. diplomat in Paris, France, in 1889, he served as consul-general to France in 1893–97. Shropshire then practiced law in Rome until 1911, when he settled in Nashville, Tennessee. In addition, he purchased the Nashville Baseball Club in 1914 and was vice-president of the Southern Baseball League for several years. A Baptist, he married Josephine Egan in 1911.

Shropshire was elected to the Tennessee House of Representatives as a Democrat from Davidson County in 1914 and 1916. He was chosen as speaker for the 1917 session. After losing the 1918 Democratic nomination for governor of Tennessee, Shropshire returned to his private practice. In 1933 he moved to Washington, D.C., to work for the Federal Housing Authority. Shropshire still held that post when he died on January 6, 1949, at age 82.

Biographical file of Tennessee legislators, Tennessee State Library and Archives, Nashville; *Lawmakers and Public Men of Tennessee* (Nashville, 1915), 69; Nashville *Banner*, January 8, 1949; Nashville *Tennessean and American*, January 2, 1917.

FRED A. BAILEY

SILLERS, WALTER (Mississippi, 1944, 1948, 1952, 1956, 1960, 1964) was born in Rosedale, Mississippi, on April 13, 1888. His father and his father-in-law were state legislators. Attending local public schools and a college preparatory academy in Tennessee, Sillers earned an LL.B. from the University of Mississippi in 1909. Afterward he joined his father's law firm in Rosedale. He belonged to the Masons and the Rotary. A Methodist, he was married.

Sillers was elected to the Mississippi House of Representatives as a Democrat from Bolivar County in 1915, and he served thirteen consecutive four-year terms. Concurrently he was Rosedale city attorney and counsel for the Bolivar County Board of Supervisors. During his early years in the House, Sillers joined Thomas L. Bailey, Joseph W. George, and Lawrence T. Kennedy in a group known as the "Big Four," which controlled the fiscally conservative "low pressure" faction of the Democratic Party. He was named speaker for the 1944, 1948, 1952, 1956, 1960, and 1964 sessions, becoming recognized as the "most powerful figure in Mississippi."

After World War II Sillers refused to support the national Democratic platform. He helped lead the "Dixiecrat" movement in 1948, presiding over the faction's convention. When the U.S. Supreme Court backed school desegregation in its 1954 decision in *Brown v. Board of Education*, Sillers worked to prevent or postpone its implementation in Mississippi. In addition, he pushed for a right-to-work law. Sillers was still speaker when he died on September 24, 1966, at age 78.

Albert Kirwan, *The Revolt of the Rednecks: Mississippi Politics, 1876–1925* (Lexington: University of Kentucky Press, 1951); Dale Krane and Stephen D. Shaffer, eds., *Mississippi Government & Politics: Modernizers versus Traditionalists* (Lincoln: University of Nebraska Press, 1992); Richard A. McLemore, *A History of Mississippi*, 2 vols. (Jackson: University and College Press of Mississippi, 1973); *Mississippi Official and Statistical Register* (Jackson: Secretary of State).

DAVID G. SANSING

SIMPSON, RICHARD HENRY (Florida, 1943) was born in Chicago, Illinois, on January 9, 1905, and moved with his family to Monticello, Florida, when he was 6. Attending local public schools, the Georgia Military Academy in Atlanta, and Purdue University in West Lafayette, Indiana, he earned a B.S. in southern horticulture from the University of Florida in 1926. Simpson then joined his family's nursery business in Monticello. He and his brother developed one of the world's largest watermelon seed companies and also operated pecan orchards.

A Democrat, Simpson was mayor of Monticello for thirteen years. He was elected to the Florida House of Representatives from Jefferson County in 1938 and served six consecutive terms. While in office he emphasized agriculture, school appropriations, and rehabilitation of veterans, and he won acclaim for his support of the Minimum Foundation Program for Schools. Simpson was named speaker for the 1943 session. Working closely with Governor Spessard L. Holland, the legislature passed a cigarette tax and enacted laws concerning adoption, operation of child care institutions, and conservation. It also approved the transfer of state lands to Everglades National Park.

Receiving the Morris Cracker Politics Award as the outstanding House member in 1945 and 1947, Simpson left the House in 1950. Afterward he chaired the Florida Road Department and sat on the Florida Turnpike Authority. In addition, Simpson was president of the Southern Seedsmen Association and the Chamber of Commerce and a member of the Kiwanis, Jefferson County

Historical Society, and Presbyterian Church. He was married. Simpson died on November 2, 1968, at the age of 63.

Paul S. George, *A Guide to the History of Florida* (Westport, CT: Greenwood Press, 1989); *Miami Daily News; Miami Herald; Tallahassee Democrat; Tampa Tribune.*

PAUL S. GEORGE

SINGLETON, JULIUS W., Jr. (West Virginia, 1961, 1963) was born on March 4, 1921, in Charleston, West Virginia, to Julius W. and Mary (Cox) Singleton. He attended local public schools. Serving with the U.S. Army in the European theater during World War II, he rose to the rank of major. Singleton earned an LL.B. from West Virginia University in 1948. Afterward he began a law practice in Morgantown, West Virginia.

A Democrat, Singleton sat on the Monongalia County Democratic Committee. In addition, he was county assistant prosecutor (1949–51) and U.S. district attorney (1952). Singleton was elected to the West Virginia House of Delegates from Monongalia County in 1956 and remained there for four consecutive terms. He was named majority leader in 1958, chair of the Finance Committee in 1959, and speaker for the 1961 and 1963 sessions.

In 1964 Singleton lost reelection to the House. Becoming an administrative aide to Governor Hulett C. Smith, he was appointed to the West Virginia Court of Claims in 1967 but resigned due to ill health the next year. He married Marjorie Garlow in 1942, and the couple had three daughters. Singleton died on April 18, 1977, at the age of 56.

LISLE G. BROWN

SMITH, CHARLES F., Jr. (Arkansas, 1955) was born in Hot Springs, Arkansas, on July 6, 1912, to Charles F. and Mary (Helms) Smith. Educated in public schools in Crawfordsville, Arkansas, he earned an LL.B. from Southern University in Baton Rouge, Louisiana. From 1930 to 1935 he served as a petty officer in the U.S. Navy. Smith then began practicing law in West Memphis, Arkansas. In addition, he was secretary-treasurer of the Crittenden County Bar Association and a member of the Rotary and the Methodist Church. He was married.

A Democrat, Smith was a deputy clerk of the Crittenden County Circuit Court. He was elected to the Arkansas House of Representatives from Crittenden County in 1948. Remaining there for four consecutive terms, Smith was chosen as speaker for the 1955 session. The following year he successfully ran for the Arkansas Senate. Smith still held that position when he drowned on August 3, 1962, at age 50.

Arkansas Gazette, August 4, 1962.

JANE McBRIDE GATES

SMITH, GEORGE LEON, II (Georgia, 1959, 1961, 1967, 1969, 1971, 1973) was born in Stillmore, Georgia, on November 27, 1912, to DeSaussaure Dugas and Sarah (Wilder) Smith. After attending the University of Georgia and reading law, he began a private practice in Swainsboro, Georgia. Smith was state president of the Jaycees and a member of the Masons, Georgia Bar Association, and Methodist Church. He married Frances McWhorter Mobley in 1937, and the couple had one daughter.

A Democrat, Smith served Swainsboro as city court solicitor and city attorney. In 1944 he was elected to the Georgia House of Representatives from Emanuel County. Smith remained there for fifteen consecutive terms, becoming speaker *pro tem* in 1947. Governor S. Ernest Vandiver chose Smith as speaker for the 1959 and 1961 sessions. He was also state coleader for John F. Kennedy's 1960 presidential campaign. Known as a supporter of legislative independence, he was not reappointed by Governor Carl E. Sanders in 1963.

The House named Smith to the speakership again in 1967, thereby breaking a long-standing tradition of executive control of the post. Remaining in office for the 1969, 1971, and 1973 terms, he was widely credited with securing passage of Governor Jimmy Carter's governmental reorganization package. He also allowed daily taping of House proceedings by the press. Smith was still speaker when he died on December 9, 1973, at the age of 61.

JAMES E. DORSEY

SMITH, GEORGE THORNEWELL (Georgia, 1963, 1965) was born in Camilla, Georgia, on October 15, 1916. Attending Middle Georgia College in Cochran, he received an A.A. from Abraham Baldwin Agricultural College in Tifton, Georgia. During World War II he served as a lieutenant commander in the U.S. Navy. Smith earned an LL.B. from the University of Georgia in 1947, and he began a law practice in Cairo, Georgia. He married Eloise Taylor.

A Democrat, Smith was Grady County attorney as well as attorney and city court solicitor of Cairo. He won election to the Georgia House of Representatives from Grady County in 1958 and remained there for four consecutive terms. Smith was named speaker by Governor Carl E. Sanders for the 1963 and 1965 sessions. Presiding immediately after legislative reapportionment, he helped pass several progressive bills including one on educational reform.

Smith successfully ran for lieutenant governor of Georgia in 1966 and for the state Court of Appeals in 1976. Elected to the Georgia Supreme Court in 1981, he became the only person in state history to hold high office in all three branches of government. In 1991 Smith retired from the bench. He was district governor of the Kiwanis and a member of the Moose, Georgia Bar Association, American Legion, and Baptist Church. At this writing Smith practices law in Marietta, Georgia.

JAMES E. DORSEY

SMITH, MENDELL LAFAYETTE (South Carolina, 1911, 1913; also 1903, 1905) was a Democrat from Kershaw County. He served as speaker of the South

Carolina House of Representatives for the 1911 and 1913 sessions, having previously presided in 1903 and 1905.

Charles F. Ritter and Jon L. Wakelyn, *American Legislative Leaders, 1850–1910* (New York: Greenwood Press, 1989) 585.

KEVIN G. ATWATER

SMITH, RAY S., Jr. (Arkansas, 1971) was born in Hot Springs, Arkansas, on February 4, 1924. Earning an LL.B. from Washington and Lee University in Lexington, Virginia, in 1950, he began practicing law in Hot Springs. Smith was president of the Garland County Bar Association as well as a member of the American and Arkansas bar associations and the American Judicature Society. He married Patricia C. Floyd, and the couple had five children.

Smith was elected to the Arkansas House of Representatives as a Democrat from Garland County in 1954. He served fourteen consecutive terms. Speaking out against education bills backed by segregationist Governor Orval E. Faubus, Smith became identified with the ''Young Turk'' faction that opposed Faubus and his legislative allies in the ''Old Guard.'' In 1965 he was defeated for the speakership by John H. Cottrell, Jr.

The ''Old Guard'' suffered electoral setbacks in 1966 and 1970, and Smith was chosen as speaker for the 1971 session without opposition. While in the post he concentrated on improving the House's image by insisting on proper floor etiquette. He retired from the House in 1982, returning to his law practice. Smith continues to live in Hot Springs at this writing.

LEON C. MILLER

SMITH, WILLIS (North Carolina, 1931) was born in Norfolk, Virginia, on December 19, 1887. Attending public and private schools in Elizabeth City, North Carolina, he earned an A.B. (1910) and a law degree (1912) from Trinity College (now Duke University) in Durham, North Carolina. Smith began practicing law in Raleigh, North Carolina, becoming general counsel for several banking, insurance, railroad, and gas companies. During World War I he served in the U.S. Army. He was married.

A Democrat, Smith was appointed inheritance tax attorney of North Carolina in 1915. He won election to the North Carolina House of Representatives from Wake County in 1926 and remained there for three consecutive terms. Smith was chosen as speaker for the 1931 session. Afterward he sat on the board of the American Legislators Association and the commission to revise the rules for federal courts in North Carolina. Chair of the North Carolina Democratic Convention in 1940, he was a delegate to the 1944 Democratic National Convention.

Smith was an observer at the Nuremberg Trials (1946), a member of the U.S. Amnesty Board (1947), and chair of the U.S. delegation to the Interparliamentary Union in Bern, Switzerland (1952). In 1950 he was elected to the U.S. Senate from North Carolina. Chair of the board of Duke University, Smith was president of the Kiwanis and the American and North Carolina bar associations.

He also belonged to the Chamber of Commerce, Wake County Bar Association, American Judicature Society, American Legion, and Methodist Church. Smith was still serving in the Senate when he died on June 26, 1953, at age 65.

William S. Powell, ed., *Dictionary of North Carolina Biography*, 6 vols. (Chapel Hill: University of North Carolina Press, 1979–1996).

CHARLES H. BOWMAN, JR.

STANLEY, THOMAS BAHNSON (Virginia, 1942, 1944, 1946) was born in Henry County, Virginia, on July 16, 1890. After attending local schools and Eastman Business College in Poughkeepsie, New York, he held bookkeeping and banking jobs in Henry County for several years. In 1918 Stanley married Anne Pocahontas Bassett, whose father owned the Bassett Furniture Company. He joined that firm before founding the Stanley Furniture Company in 1924. The business grew rapidly, and the village of Stanleytown was constructed for its employees.

A conservative Democrat, Stanley sat on the Henry County school board. He won election to the Virginia House of Delegates from Henry County and the city of Martinsville in 1929. Stanley served nine consecutive terms and was named speaker for the 1942, 1944, and 1946 sessions. Elected to the U.S. House of Representatives from Virginia's 5th District in 1946, he remained there until successfully running for governor of Virginia in 1953.

Stanley's governorship was a troubled one. A group of state legislators known as the "Young Turks" forced party leaders to appropriate more money for public services in 1954. That same year the U.S. Supreme Court struck down school segregation with its decision in *Brown v. Board of Education*. Although Stanley initially appealed for "cool heads, calm study and sound judgments," the state's dominant Democratic faction led by U.S. Senator Harry F. Byrd, Sr., pressured him into following a policy of "massive resistance." As a result, the Virginia legislature adopted the "Stanley Plan," a package of laws requiring the closing of all schools under court order to integrate. The plan was later declared unconstitutional.

Leaving office in 1958, Stanley returned to his furniture company and also bred livestock. He was president of the Virginia Hereford Breeders Association and a member of the Masons, Chamber of Commerce, Virginia Manufacturers Association, and Methodist Church. From 1962 to 1964 he was chair of a state commission that studied tax reform measures. Stanley died on July 11, 1970, at the age of 79.

E. Griffith Dodson, ed., *Speakers and Clerks of the Virginia House of Delegates, 1776–1976*, rev. under the direction of Joseph H. Holleman, Jr. (Richmond, 1976), 120–143; Heinemann, Ronald L., "Thomas B. Stanley: Reluctant Resister," in Edward Younger and James Tice Moore, eds., *The Governors of Virginia, 1860–1978* (Charlottesville: University Press of Virginia, 1982), 333–347; *Richmond Times-Dispatch*, July 12, 1970.

JAMES R. SWEENEY

STANSEL, HORACE SYLVAN (Mississippi, 1936) was born in Columbus, Mississippi, on November 5, 1888. After attending local elementary schools, he began working. Stansel earned a degree in civil engineering from Mississippi Agricultural and Mechanical College (now Mississippi State University) in 1914. Afterward he moved to Ruleville, Mississippi. He was married, and he belonged to the Masons, Knights of Pythias, and Baptist Church.

In 1923 Stansel was elected to the Mississippi House of Representatives as a Democrat from Sunflower County. Serving four consecutive four-year terms, he was reelected with only token opposition. While in office Stansel sought to modernize the state road system, becoming known as the "Father of Mississippi's Highway Program." Concurrently he was state director of the U.S. Public Works Administration. He was named to the speakership for the 1936 session. Stansel was still speaker when he died on April 4, 1936, at age 47.

Albert Kirwan, *The Revolt of the Rednecks: Mississippi Politics, 1876–1925* (Lexington: University of Kentucky Press, 1951); Dale Krane and Stephen D. Shaffer, eds., *Mississippi Government & Politics: Modernizers versus Traditionalists* (Lincoln: University of Nebraska Press, 1992); Richard A. McLemore, *A History of Mississippi*, 2 vols. (Jackson: University and College Press of Mississippi, 1973); *Mississippi Official and Statistical Register* (Jackson: Secretary of State).

DAVID G. SANSING

STANTON, WILLIAM MORTIMER (Tennessee, 1913) was born on January 2, 1890, in Meridian, Mississippi, to Martin and Johanna (Shea) Stanton. Shortly thereafter he moved with his family to Memphis, Tennessee, where he attended public schools. Stanton earned an A.B. from Christian Brothers College (now University) in Memphis and a law degree from Vanderbilt University in Nashville, Tennessee. A Catholic, he never married.

In 1910 Stanton was elected to the Tennessee House of Representatives as a Democrat from Shelby County. Remaining there for three consecutive terms, he joined the "Fusionist" coalition of prohibitionist Democrats and East Tennessee Republicans. Stanton was named speaker in 1913 when he was only 23, becoming the youngest person to hold the post in state history. He did not seek renomination to the speakership for the 1915 session. Concurrently he was assistant city attorney of Memphis (1911–12) and a Juvenile Court judge (1916).

Retiring from the House in 1916, Stanton served as a captain with the U.S. Army during the Mexican border crisis and World War I. He sat on the Memphis Planning Commission for seven years and was clerk and master of the Chancery Court in 1933–47. From 1922 to 1937 Stanton belonged to the Shelby County Democratic Executive Committee. In addition, he was president of the Shelby County Bar Association, commander of the American Legion, and a member of the Chamber of Commerce, American Bar Association, and Knights of Columbus. Stanton died on July 15, 1957, at the age of 67.

Biographical file of Tennessee legislators, Tennessee State Library and Archives, Nashville; *Lawmakers and Public Men of Tennessee* (Nashville, 1915), 157; Robert M. McBride, *Preliminary Biographical Directory of Tennessee General Assembly* (Nashville, 1967–), XXXVII: 159; John Trotwood Moore, ed., *Tennessee: The Volunteer State, 1769–1923* (Chicago, 1923), IV: 462–63; Nashville *Banner*, January 6, 1913, January 4, 1915; Nashville *Tennessean and American*, January 7, 1913, January 5, 1915.

FRED A. BAILEY

STEVENSON, COKE ROBERT (Texas, 1933, 1935) was born in Mason County, Texas, on March 20, 1888, of Irish descent. He moved with his family to several communities in Texas and New Mexico before settling in Junction, Texas. During that time Stevenson attended elementary schools. After working for a telephone company and a freight company, he joined the First State Bank in Junction in 1906. Stevenson read law and began a private practice in 1913. In addition, he was a rancher, president of the First National Bank, and the operator of several other businesses in Junction.

A Democrat, Stevenson entered politics by serving Kimble County as attorney (1914–18) and judge (1918–20). He won election to the Texas House of Representatives from Kimble, Bandera, Crockett, Edwards, Kerr, Mason, Menard, Schleicher, and Sutton counties in 1928. Stevenson served five consecutive terms. Named speaker in 1933 and 1935, he became the first person in Texas history to hold the post for two terms.

Stevenson successfully ran for lieutenant governor of Texas in 1938, and he rose to governor in 1941 following the resignation of incumbent W. Lee O'Daniel. Elected to the governorship in 1942 and 1944, he followed conservative economic policies. In 1948 Stevenson lost a controversial Democratic primary for the U.S. Senate from Texas to Lyndon B. Johnson. Returning to his law and ranching careers in Junction, he was president of the Rotary and a member of the Masons, Chamber of Commerce, and Methodist Church. He was married. Stevenson died on June 28, 1975, at the age of 87.

George Norris Green, *The Establishment in Texas Politics: The Primitive Years, 1938–1957* (Westport, CT: Greenwood Press, 1979); *Presiding Officers of the Texas Legislature, 1846–1982* (Austin: Texas Legislative Council, 1982), 62–63, 170–171; Frederica Burt Wyatt and Hooper Shelton, comps., *Coke R. Stevenson: A Texas Legend* (Junction, TX: Shelton Press, 1976).

ALWYN BARR

STEWART, CARL JEROME, Jr. (North Carolina, 1977, 1979) was born in Gastonia, North Carolina, on October 2, 1936, to Carl Jerome and Hazel (Holland) Stewart. He attended local public schools and won awards for his debating skills. Stewart earned an A.B. (1958) and a J.D. (1961) from Duke University in Durham, North Carolina, where he was student body president. After serving as a lieutenant colonel in the U.S. National Guard, he began practicing law in Gastonia.

In 1966 Stewart was elected to the North Carolina House of Representatives as a Democrat from Gaston and Lincoln counties. Remaining there for seven consecutive terms, he successfully backed an open government meetings law in 1971. Stewart emerged as a leader of the moderate wing of his party, gaining recognition as an effective urban politician in a predominantly rural state. He was chosen as speaker in 1977 and broke precedent by being renamed for the 1979 session. While in the speakership Stewart emphasized budget and tax reform, governmental ethics, and environmental legislation. In addition, he helped pass the proposed Equal Rights Amendment to the U.S. Constitution, incurring the opposition of the religious right.

Narrowly losing the 1980 Democratic nomination for lieutenant governor of North Carolina to incumbent James C. Green, Stewart was again defeated for the post in 1984. He returned to his law practice, and he also entered the insurance and investment businesses. Stewart was president of the Optimists and the Duke Alumni Association and a member of the Masons, Elks, Jaycees, American and North Carolina bar associations, and Methodist Church. A Methodist, he was married. At this writing Stewart continues to live in Gastonia.

HENRY C. FERRELL, JR.

STOVALL, DAVID ANCIL (Oklahoma, 1927) was born in Bethel Springs, Tennessee, on January 25, 1882. Graduating from high school in Jackson, Tennessee, he earned a degree from Southwest Baptist University in Jackson and an LL.B. from the University of Tennessee in 1903. In 1905 Stovall began practicing law in Hugo, Indian Territory (now Oklahoma). He was married.

A Democrat, Stovall was city attorney of Hugo (1909 and 1917–18) and secretary of the Choctaw County Election Board (1909–12). During World War I he sat on the Oklahoma Election Commission. Stovall was elected to the Oklahoma House of Representatives from Choctaw County in 1918 and served six consecutive terms. He was chosen as speaker for the 1927 session. In addition, he was a delegate to the 1928 Democratic National Convention.

Leaving the House in 1930, Stovall returned to his Hugo law practice. He was appointed to the Oklahoma Securities Commission in 1951, but he resigned to become a U.S. commissioner in Muskogee, Oklahoma. Outside of politics he was Oklahoma president-general of the Sons of the American Revolution, president of the Lions and the Boy Scouts, and a member of the Masons and the Presbyterian Church. Stovall died on October 24, 1971, at the age of 89.

Rex F. Harlow, comp., *Makers of Government in Oklahoma* (Oklahoma City: Harlow Publishing, 1930); Gaston Litton, *History of Oklahoma at the Golden Anniversary of Statehood*, 4 vols. (New York: Lewis Historical Publishing, 1957); "Services Today in Hugo for Ex-Speaker of the House," *Tulsa World*, October 28, 1971; Joseph B. Thoburn and Muriel H. Wright, *Oklahoma: A History of the State and Its People*, 4 vols. (New York: Lewis Historical Publishing, 1929).

DONOVAN L. REICHENBERGER

STREET, ALLEN MORGAN (Oklahoma, 1929) was born in Mexia, Texas, on June 17, 1885. He moved with his family to Stonewall, Oklahoma Territory, in 1890 and to Oklahoma City, Oklahoma Territory, the next year. Educated in local public schools, he attended Vanderbilt University in Nashville, Tennessee. Street entered the funeral home business in Oklahoma City in 1907. In addition, he was a director of Mid-West Enterprises, Inc., and the Eichaltz Furniture Company in Muskogee, Oklahoma.

A Democrat, Street was elected to the Oklahoma House of Representatives from Oklahoma County in 1918, 1922, 1924, 1928, and 1930. He was unanimously named speaker for the 1929 session, but he was forced to resign just three hours later by a bipartisan coalition opposed to Governor Henry S. Johnston. After leaving the House, Street served Oklahoma City as a city councilman for four years and as mayor from 1946 to 1958. While in the latter post he was acknowledged for his fairness, overcoming his reputation in state politics of having a quick temper.

Outside of politics Street was active in the Boy Scouts, helping to organize the local council in 1910 and sitting on the National Scout Council. He was president of the Oklahoma Society for Crippled Children, vice-president of the Rotary, and a member of the Masons. A Presbyterian, he was married. Street died on May 10, 1969, at the age of 83.

"Former Mayor Street Dies," *The Daily Oklahoman*, May 11, 1969: 1; Rex F. Harlow, comp., *Makers of Government in Oklahoma* (Oklahoma City: Harlow Publishing, 1930); Gaston Litton, *History of Oklahoma at the Golden Anniversary of Statehood*, 4 vols. (New York: Lewis Historical Publishing, 1957); Joseph B. Thoburn and Muriel H. Wright, *Oklahoma: A History of the State and Its People*, 4 vols. (New York: Lewis Historical Publishing, 1929).

DONOVAN L. REICHENBERGER

SYBERT, CORNELIUS FERDINAND (Maryland, 1947) was born in Loretto, Pennsylvania, on September 16, 1900, to Alphonsus and Anne Marie Sybert. He moved with his family to Elkridge, Maryland, in 1904. Sybert attended Catholic schools in Elkridge and Baltimore, Maryland, and earned an A.B. from Loyola College in Baltimore in 1922. While working as a reporter for the *Baltimore News*, he received an LL.B. from University of Maryland in 1925. Afterward he began a law practice in Ellicott City, Maryland.

A Democrat, Sybert served Howard County as counsel to the Board of Commissioners (1931–34) and state's attorney (1934–46). In 1946 he won election to the Maryland House of Delegates from Howard County. Sybert was chosen as speaker in 1947, his only term in the House. He successfully ran for the Maryland Senate in 1950.

Elected attorney general of Maryland in 1954, Sybert's 1958 reelection was by the largest margin ever given to a state candidate at that time. From 1961 to 1965 he sat on the Maryland Court of Appeals. Outside of politics Sybert was president of the Howard County Bar Association and a member of the Rotary, Knights of Columbus, and American and Maryland bar associations. He married Elizabeth J. Johnson in 1927, and the couple had three children. Sybert died on March 29, 1982, at the age of 81.

MORGAN H. PRITCHETT

T

TAYLOR, CASPER R., Jr. (Maryland, 1994) was born on December 19, 1934, in Cumberland, Maryland. Educated in local Catholic schools, he earned a B.A. from the University of Notre Dame in Indiana in 1956. Afterward he served in the U.S. Air Force. Taylor became a businessman in Cumberland, eventually purchasing a restaurant. He married Mary Lenore, and he belonged to the Elks, Eagles, Chamber of Commerce, Knights of Columbus, and Maryland Wildlife Federation.

In 1974 Taylor won election to the Maryland House of Delegates as a Democrat from Allegany County. He was named chair of the Economic Matters Committee in 1987. Chosen as speaker in 1994 following the resignation of incumbent R. Clayton Mitchell, Taylor was the first person from western Maryland to hold the post since 1877. Taylor remains in the speakership at this writing.

JON L. WAKELYN

TAYLOR, CLAUDE AMBROSE (South Carolina, 1935) was born on August 24, 1902, in Gilbert, South Carolina, to Hutchinson S. and Margaret Cummings (Smith) Taylor. He received an LL.B. from the University of South Carolina in 1926. The following year Taylor began practicing law in Spartanburg, South Carolina. In addition, he was a member of the University of South Carolina Alumni Council and the Presbyterian Church.

Taylor won election to the South Carolina House of Representatives as a Democrat from Spartanburg County in 1930. Serving three consecutive terms, he was named speaker *pro tem* in 1933 and speaker for the 1935 session. He lost a 1936 bid for the U.S. House of Representatives from South Carolina. In 1940 and 1942 Taylor was again elected to the state House. Successfully running for the South Carolina Supreme Court in 1944, he was named its chief justice in 1961. Taylor still held that post when he died of a heart attack on January 21, 1966, at age 63.

South Carolina Legislative Manual (Columbia: General Assembly of South Carolina, 1916–); *The State* (Columbia).

MARIAN ELIZABETH STROBEL

TAYLOR, HOYT PATRICK, Jr. (North Carolina, 1965) was born in Wadesboro, North Carolina, on April 1, 1924, to Hoyt Patrick and Inez (Wooten) Taylor. His father was a state senator and lieutenant governor under W. Kerr Scott in 1949–52. Attending the McCallie School in Chattanooga, Tennessee, Taylor earned a B.S. (1945) and an LL.B. (1948) from the University of North Carolina. Afterward he began practicing law in Wadesboro with his father and A. Paul Kitchin, a former U.S. congressman. He served in the U.S. Marine Corps during World War II and the Korean conflict.

Taylor successfully ran for the North Carolina House of Representatives as a Democrat from Anson County in 1954. Remaining there for six consecutive terms, he lost a 1963 bid for speaker to H. Clifton Blue. He was named to the speakership for the 1965 regular session and the special session later that year. In 1968 Taylor was elected lieutenant governor of North Carolina on a ticket headed by Robert Scott, the son of W. Kerr Scott. This marked the only instance in state history when children of a governor and a lieutenant governor also held those posts. While in office Taylor helped mend a split within the state Democratic Party over the restructuring of higher education.

Defeated in the 1972 Democratic gubernatorial primary by Hargrove Bowles, Jr., Taylor returned to his law practice. In addition, he belonged to the American Legion, North Carolina Bar Association, and Methodist Church. He married Elizabeth Lockhart in 1951, and the couple had three children. Taylor continues to live in Wadesboro at this writing.

Hugh Talmage Lefler and Albert Ray Newsome, *The History of a Southern State: North Carolina* (Chapel Hill: University of North Carolina Press, 1973); *The News and Observer* (Raleigh, North Carolina); William S. Powell, *North Carolina through Four Centuries* (Chapel Hill: University of North Carolina Press, 1989).

FRED D. RAGAN

TAYLOR, JAMES ALFRED (West Virginia, 1931) was born on September 25, 1878, in Lawrence County, Ohio, to West Virginia natives James Clark and Malinda (Bryant) Taylor. Educated in local elementary schools, he began working for the Ironton, Ohio, *Irontonian* when he was 14. Taylor then moved to Fayette County, West Virginia, where he owned a newspaper. In addition, he belonged to the Masons, Odd Fellows, Moose, West Virginia Historical Society, and Presbyterian Church. He married Bina E. Taylor, a distant cousin, in 1905, and the couple had five children.

A Democrat, Taylor was elected to the West Virginia House of Delegates from Fayette County in 1916 and 1920. He was defeated in the 1918 race for the West Virginia Senate. Taylor successfully ran for the U.S. House of Representatives from West Virginia's 6th District in 1922 and 1924, but he narrowly lost reelection in 1926. Two years later he failed in a bid for governor of West Virginia. Returned to the state House in 1930, he was chosen as speaker for the 1931 session.

Taylor unsuccessfully sought the Democratic nominations for governor in 1932 and the U.S. Senate from West Virginia in 1934. He again won election to the state House in 1936, but he was defeated in a 1938 bid for the U.S. House from the 3rd District of West Virginia. Returning to his newspaper, Taylor was president of the Fayette County school board for two years. In 1956 he lost the Democratic nomination for the state Senate. Taylor died on June 9, 1956, at the age of 77.

ROBERT L. HUNT

TAYLOR, WALTER FRANK (North Carolina, 1951) was born on a farm near Faison, North Carolina, on April 4, 1889, to S. Luther and Ettie (Crow) Taylor. After earning an A.B. (1911) and an LL.B. (1914) from the University of North Carolina, he began to practice law in Goldsboro, North Carolina. Taylor served in the U.S. armed forces. He married Elizabeth Gibson in 1933, and the couple had one daughter.

A Democrat, Taylor successfully ran for the North Carolina Senate in 1920. From 1933 to 1939 he was a Goldsboro alderman. He won election to the North Carolina House of Representatives from Wayne County in 1938 and remained there for seven consecutive terms. Taylor was named speaker for the 1951 session. In addition, he served North Carolina as chair of the Motor Transportation Commission (1943–47) and as a member of the Recodification Commission, Board of Contracts and Awards, and Board of Law Examiners.

President of the North Carolina Bar Association in 1943–44, Taylor belonged to the American Legion, Wayne County Bar Association, American Judicature Society, and Methodist Church. He was a trustee of the University of North Carolina and the North Carolina College for Negroes (now North Carolina Central University). Taylor died on September 28, 1977, at the age of 88.

OTIENO OKELO

TERRELL, CHESTER H. (Texas, 1913) was born in Terrell, Texas, on December 23, 1882. His father was a state senator and an unsuccessful Republican candidate for governor of Texas in 1910. Moving with his family to San Antonio, Texas, in 1895, he attended San Antonio Academy. Terrell earned a bachelor's degree and a law degree (1904) from the University of Texas, where he played varsity baseball. He then began practicing law in San Antonio.

Terrell was elected to the Texas House of Representatives as a Democrat from Bexar County in 1908. Serving three consecutive terms, he gained a reputation for being "able, sincere, and devoted to his country." While in office Terrell unsuccessfully introduced bills to appoint matrons for female prisoners, enlarge the Southwestern Insane Asylum, and investigate state water resources.

He was named speaker for the 1913 session when he was only 30, and he helped pass one of the state's first major acts to control water pollution.

Returning to his San Antonio practice, Terrell was forced to withdraw from the 1916 race for governor of Texas as a result of illness. In 1917 he represented Speaker Franklin O. Fuller in successful impeachment proceedings against Governor James E. Ferguson. He supported Republican Warren G. Harding's 1920 bid for President. Terrell died on September 13, 1920, at the age of 37.

Austin American-Statesman, January 5, 10, 15, April 2, 1913, September 14, 1920; *Journal of the House of Representatives* (Austin: Von Boeckmann–Jones, 1909–   ); *Presiding Officers of the Texas Legislature, 1846–1982* (Austin: Texas Legislative Council, 1982).

                                                              TRACY ANDERS GREENLEE

TERRELL, CLAUDE B. (Kentucky, 1912, 1914) was born in Union County, Kentucky, on February 4, 1871, to George W. and Mary B. Terrell. Educated in public schools, he earned a law degree from the University of Louisville in Kentucky and began a private practice in Bedford, Kentucky. Terrell belonged to the Masons, Odd Fellows, Knights of Pythias, and Methodist Church. He never married.

A Democrat, Terrell was Trimble County attorney. He successfully ran for the Kentucky House of Representatives from Trimble County in 1911 and was reelected without opposition in 1913. Chosen as speaker in 1912 after a hotly contested caucus battle, Terrell was renamed to the post for the 1914 session. Afterward he returned to his law practice. Terrell died on July 18, 1922, at the age of 51.

Malcolm E. Jewell and Everett W. Cunningham, *Kentucky Politics* (Lexington: University Press of Kentucky, 1968); Malcolm E. Jewell and Penny Miller, *The Kentucky Legislature: Two Decades of Change* (Lexington: University Press of Kentucky, 1988); Robert F. Sexton, "Kentucky Politics and Society, 1919–1932" (Ph.D. dissertation, University of Washington, 1970).

                                                              CAROL CROWE-CARRACO

THOMAS, CHARLES GRAHAM (Texas, 1921) was born near Richardson, Texas, on December 10, 1879, and moved with his family to Lewisville, Texas, two years later. Educated in local public schools, he earned a degree from Baylor University in Waco, Texas. Thomas joined his father's dry goods business. He later began a retail lumber company and a real estate and insurance firm.

A Democrat, Thomas was elected to the Texas House of Representatives from Denton County in 1916. He served three consecutive terms. In 1919 he chaired the Committee on Appropriations, playing a crucial role in the passage of the State Depository Law. Thomas was chosen as speaker for the 1921 session. While in the post he was at the center of controversies involving Governor Patrick M. Neff, prohibitionists, and advocates of state regulation of corporations.

In other affairs Thomas was a director of the First National Bank of Lewisville. He was secretary of the Texas Relief Commission during the 1930s. Thomas died of a heart attack in Van Alstyne, Texas, on February 14, 1937, at age 57, and he was buried in Lewisville.

Austin Statesman, February 15, 1937; Norman D. Brown, *Hood, Bonnet, and Little Brown Jug: Texas Politics, 1921–1928* (College Station: Texas A&M University Press, 1984); *Fort Worth Star Telegram*, February 16, 1937; *Journal of the House of Representatives* (Austin: Von Boeckmann–Jones Co., 1909–); *Members of the Texas Legislature, 1846–1980* (Austin: Texas Legislature, 1981); *Presiding Officers of the Texas Legislature, 1846–1982* (Austin: Texas Legislative Council, 1982).

RON LAW

THOMAS, JAMES KAY (West Virginia, 1937, 1939) was born in Charleston, West Virginia, on February 23, 1902, to George E. and Jean Susan (Kay) Thomas. Educated in public schools, he received an LL.B. from Washington and Lee University in Lexington, Virginia, in 1926. Thomas began a law practice in Charleston. He was president of the board of Charleston General Hospital, a director of the Charleston National Bank, and a member of the Masons, Elks, Moose, Rotary, and American and West Virginia bar associations. A Methodist, he married Julia Lewis Roseberry in 1934; the couple had two children.

Thomas won election to the West Virginia House of Delegates as a Democrat from Kanawha County in 1932. He remained there for four consecutive terms. Chair of the Finance Committee in 1935, Thomas was chosen as speaker for the 1937 and 1939 sessions. While in the speakership he supported Governor Homer A. Holt's agenda, helping pass a general consumer sales tax and introducing legislation on education.

During World War II Thomas served with the U.S. Army Air Forces in the North African and European theaters, rising to the rank of lieutenant colonel. Elected attorney general of West Virginia in absentia in 1942, he named Ira Partlow to act in his place. Partlow successfully ran for the post in 1944, and the next year Thomas became his assistant. He lost the 1948 Democratic nomination for governor of West Virginia. Afterward he became a vice-president and general counsel for the Greyhound Corporation. Thomas was West Virginia motor vehicle commissioner in 1965–68, and he then returned to his Charleston practice.

WILLIAM T. DOHERTY

THOMAS, LEE EMMETT (Louisiana, 1912) was born in Marion, Louisiana, on September 23, 1866. Attending Concordia Institute in Shiloh, Louisiana, and Howard College (now Samford University) in Alabama, he earned an A.B. from Eastman Business College in Poughkeepsie, New York. Thomas received a master's degree from the University of Virginia in 1889. He then settled in Shreveport, Louisiana.

In 1907 and 1911 Thomas was elected to the Louisiana House of Representatives as a Democrat from Caddo Parish. He lost the speakership in 1908 to southern Louisianan Henry G. Dupre because it was customary to alternate the post between regions of the state. Thomas was chosen as speaker, an office he characterized as "purely honorary," for the 1912 session. Although he launched his career as a reformer and helped organize the Good Government League, he remained a conservative.

Later Thomas was mayor of Shreveport, Louisiana. While unsuccessfully running for the U.S. Senate from Louisiana against incumbent Joseph E. Ransdell in 1924, he became an opponent of political leader Huey P. Long. The latter continually used Thomas as an example of the kind of entrenched politician he was trying to drive from power. Such invective eventually provoked Thomas to sue Long for slander. Thomas died on February 16, 1935, at the age of 68.

Dave H. Brown, comp., *A History of Who's Who in Louisiana Politics in 1916* (New Orleans: Coste and Frichter, 1916); Patricia L. Meador, "Lee Emmett Thomas," *A Dictionary of Louisiana Biography* (New Orleans: Louisiana Historical Association, 1988), I: 788; *Membership in the Legislature of Louisiana, 1880–1980* (Baton Rouge, 1979).

                                                              RAYMOND O. NUSSBAUM

THOMASON, ROBERT EWING (Texas, 1919) was born in Shelbyville, Tennessee, on May 30, 1879, and moved with his family to Era, Texas, the next year. Educated in local public schools, he earned a B.A. from Southwestern University in Georgetown, Texas (1898), and an LL.B. from the University of Texas (1900). Thomason practiced law in Oklahoma and in Era before relocating to Gainesville, Texas. Contracting malarial fever in 1911, he settled in El Paso, Texas. He was married, and he belonged to the Masons.

A Democrat, Thomason was Cooke County district attorney in 1902–06. He won election to the Texas House of Representatives from El Paso County in 1916 and 1918 on a "clean government" ticket. Thomason was unanimously named speaker for the 1919 session. While in office he supported women's suffrage in state primaries and helped secure the state's ratification of the 19th Amendment to the U.S. Constitution, giving women the vote. In addition, he successfully backed legislation enacting the first workers' compensation law in Texas and creating the Texas Highway Commission.

Thomason lost the 1920 Democratic primary for governor of Texas to Patrick M. Neff. He was elected mayor of El Paso in 1926, overseeing construction of the municipal airport. In 1930 he won a race for the U.S. House of Representatives from Texas's 16th District. Serving eight consecutive terms, Thomason supported President Franklin D. Roosevelt's defense programs and chaired a special panel that toured European concentration camps in 1945. He was a federal judge for the Western District of Texas from 1947 to 1963. Thomason died on November 8, 1973, at the age of 94.

Austin Statesman, January 5, 10, 1919; *Presiding Officers of the Texas Legislature, 1846–1982* (Austin: Texas Legislative Council, 1982); *Texas Almanac and State Indus-*

trial Guide (Dallas: A. H. Belo, 1857–   ); "Thomason," *El Paso Times*, November 10, 1973.

EDWARD WELLER

THOMPSON, JAMES H. (Kentucky, 1922) was born in Montgomery County, Kentucky, on July 2, 1872, to G. C. and Rebekah Sparh (Scott) Thompson. Educated in public schools, he earned a degree from Transylvania University in Lexington, Kentucky. Thompson then began farming in Paris, Kentucky. He married Tillie Rennick Ferguson in 1894.

Thompson successfully ran for the Kentucky House of Representatives as a Democrat from Bourbon County in 1919 and 1921. He was minority leader for the 1920 session. When the Democrats gained control of the House in 1922, he was named speaker after veteran legislator Hugh C. Duffy withdrew his candidacy.

Afterward Thompson returned to his Paris farm. He was elected without opposition to the Kentucky Senate in 1933, chairing that body's Revenue and Taxation Committee. Outside of politics he belonged to the Masons, Elks, Knights of Pythias, and Christian Church (Disciples of Christ). Thompson died on February 9, 1950, at the age of 77.

Malcolm E. Jewell and Everett W. Cunningham, *Kentucky Politics* (Lexington: University Press of Kentucky, 1968); Malcolm E. Jewell and Penny Miller, *The Kentucky Legislature: Two Decades of Change* (Lexington: University Press of Kentucky, 1988); Robert F. Sexton, "Kentucky Politics and Society, 1919–1932" (Ph.D. dissertation, University of Washington, 1970).

CAROL CROWE-CARRACO

THOMPSON, JAMES HAROLD (Florida, 1985) was born on November 18, 1944, in Mobile, Alabama. Attending high school in Quincy, Florida, he received a B.A. (1966) and a J.D. (1969) from Florida State University. Thompson began a law practice in Quincy, eventually becoming a partner in the firm of Thompson and Arrington. He was married and had three children.

A Democrat, Thompson sat on the Gadsden County Small Claims Court in 1971–73. In 1974 he won election to the Florida House of Representatives from Gadsden County. He served six consecutive terms and was chosen as speaker for the 1985 session. Thompson then returned to Quincy, where he continues to live at this writing.

GINA PETONITO

THORN, HARVEY BELL, Sr. (Arkansas, 1935) was born in Harrisburg, Arkansas, on August 28, 1885, to Jesse A. and Margaret (Wilson) Thorn. Educated in local public schools, he earned a degree in education from the University of Arkansas. Thorn was a member of the Masons and the Methodist Church. He was married.

A Democrat, Thorn was Poinsett County school superintendent from 1910 to

1922. He gained a reputation as a strong advocate of rural education. Thorn successfully ran for the Arkansas House of Representatives from Poinsett County in 1930. He served three consecutive terms there. Named speaker for the 1935 session, he drafted a law that repealed prohibition in the state and regulated the retail liquor trade.

In 1936 Thorn was defeated for lieutenant governor of Arkansas. Moving to Little Rock, Arkansas, during World War II, he began a law practice. He lost a bid for Arkansas attorney general in 1956. Thorn died in Little Rock on October 3, 1962, at the age of 77.

Arkansas Democrat; Arkansas Gazette; The Arkansas Handbook (Little Rock: Arkansas History Commission, 1936–).

RUSSELL PIERCE BAKER

THURMOND, JOSEPH SAMUEL (West Virginia, 1917) was born in Fayette County, Virginia (later West Virginia), on May 9, 1855. Educated in local public schools, he earned a degree from Shelton College in St. Albans, West Virginia. Thurmond worked as a civil engineer, farmer, and coal operator before he began farming in Greenbrier County, West Virginia, in 1912. In addition, he belonged to the Baptist Church. He married Betty Rippetoe, and the couple had six children.

A Democrat, Thurmond was mayor of Thurmond, West Virginia. He was elected to the West Virginia House of Delegates from Greenbrier County in 1914 and served three consecutive terms. The Democrats took control of the House for the 1917 session, and Thurmond was chosen as speaker. When the Republicans regained a majority in 1919, he was forced to step down. Thurmond died in 1932.

ROBERT L. HUNT

TINSLEY, T. HERBERT (Kentucky, 1948) was born in Buffalo, Missouri, on December 29, 1889. He earned a B.A. from Transylvania University in Lexington, Kentucky, and a B.D. from Lexington Theological Seminary. After serving as a pastor of the Christian Church (Disciples of Christ) in Kentucky and Indiana, he moved to Warsaw, Kentucky. Tinsley joined the YMCA during World War I. He was married, and he belonged to the Masons and the American Legion.

A Democrat, Tinsley was elected to the Kentucky House of Representatives from Carroll County in 1941, 1947, 1949, 1955, 1957, and 1963. He was named speaker for the 1948 session under Governor Earle C. Clements. While in the post Tinsley helped pass legislation concerning education, conservation, and economic development. In 1951 he successfully ran for state auditor. Tinsley died in Warsaw on June 8, 1966, at the age of 76.

Louisville *Courier-Journal; Kentucky Directory for the Use of the Courts, State and County Officials, and General Assembly of the State of Kentucky* (Frankfort, KY, 1914–); John E. Kleber, ed., *The Kentucky Encyclopedia* (Lexington: University Press of Kentucky, 1992); Penny M. Miller, *Kentucky Politics and Government* (Lincoln: University of Nebraska Press, 1994); Robert F. Sexton, ed., *The Public Papers of the Governors of Kentucky* (Lexington: University Press of Kentucky, 1975).

ROGER TATE

TODD, ANDREW LEE (Tennessee, 1921) was born in Rutherford County, Tennessee, on July 27, 1872, to Aaron and Elizabeth (Prater) Todd. Educated in local public schools, he received a B.A. from Union University in Murfreesboro, Tennessee, and studied law at the University of the South in Sewanee, Tennessee. Todd earned a law degree from Cumberland University in Lebanon, Tennessee, and he began a private practice in Murfreesboro in 1903. He married Minneola Wilson in 1905.

A Democrat, Todd was chair of the Murfreesboro school board (1905), superintendent of the Rutherford County schools (1905–15), and a member of the Tennessee Board of Education (1903–15). In 1912 he won election to one term in the Tennessee House of Representatives from Rutherford County. Todd successfully ran for the Tennessee Senate in 1914 and 1918, becoming speaker of that body in 1919. Again elected to the House in 1920, he was named to the speakership for the 1921 session. He unsuccessfully sought the 1930 Democratic nomination for the U.S. Senate from Tennessee.

In other pursuits Todd was president of the Tennessee Public School Officers Association and a trustee of the Tennessee College for Women (now Middle Tennessee State University) and Union University. He presided over the State Baptist Association in 1926–27. President of the Murfreesboro Bank and Trust Company, he was also an insurance agent and the editor of the Murfreesboro *News-Journal*. Todd died in Murfreesboro on March 25, 1945, at the age of 72.

Biographical file of Tennessee legislators, Tennessee State Library and Archives, Nashville; *Lawmakers and Public Men of Tennessee* (Nashville, 1915), 39; Robert M. McBride, *Preliminary Biographical Directory of Tennessee General Assembly* (Nashville, 1967–   ), VI: 56–57; Murfreesboro *Daily News*, March 25, 1945; Nashville *Banner*, January 6, 1919; Nashville *Tennessean*, January 2, 4, 1921; Nashville *Tennessean and American*, January 6, 1919.

FRED A. BAILEY

TOMASELLO, PETER, Jr. (Florida, 1933) was born in January 1900 in Santa Rosa County, Florida. His father was an Italian immigrant. Educated in public schools, he served in the U.S. Army during World War I and rose to the rank of first sergeant. Tomasello became involved in the lumbering and manufacturing businesses, and he helped reorganize banks following the collapse of the state real estate boom in 1926. He then moved to Okeechobee County, Florida, where he became chair of the Citizens Bank.

Tomasello was elected to the Florida House of Representatives as a Democrat from Okeechobee County in 1928. Remaining there for three consecutive terms, he led the successful fight to create the Everglades Flood Control District and was named speaker for the 1933 session. During Tomasello's speakership Governor David Sholtz called for major cuts in the educational budget and an increased centralization of the school system, which was passed after a vicious debate. Sholtz also sought the formation of a commission that could control all public budgets in the state, but he was defeated by Tomasello and the Florida League of Municipalities.

After announcing his intention to run for governor of Florida in 1934, Tomasello withdrew from the race. In 1938 he was elected to one additional House term. He was married, and he belonged to the Presbyterian Church. Tomasello died on November 17, 1961, at the age of 61.

GARY R. MORMINO

TONEY, HARDIN KEMP (Arkansas, 1933) was born near Oxford, Mississippi, on March 2, 1876, and moved with his family to Pine Bluff, Arkansas, in 1890. Educated in local public schools, he earned a degree from the University of Mississippi. Around 1900 Toney began practicing law in Pine Bluff. He was district governor of the Rotary and president of the Jefferson County Bar Association. A Presbyterian, he was married.

Toney won election to the Arkansas House of Representatives as a Democrat from Jefferson County in 1898, when he was only 22, and he served three consecutive terms. He successfully ran for the Arkansas Senate in 1904 and 1908, becoming that body's president *pro tem* in 1911. After that Toney returned to his private practice. Again elected to the House in 1930, he remained there for another nine consecutive terms and was named speaker for the 1933 session. Toney died on March 9, 1955, at the age of 79.

Diane D. Blair, *Arkansas Politics and Government* (Lincoln: University of Nebraska Press, 1988), 160–184; Jerry E. Hinshaw, *Call the Roll* (Little Rock: Rose Publishing, 1986); *Historical Report of the Secretary of State, Arkansas* (Little Rock: Secretary of State, 1958–   ); Walter Nunn, *Readings in Arkansas Government* (Little Rock: Rose Publishing, 1973), 59–133.

CAL LEDBETTER, JR.

TRIPPE, JAMES McCONKY (Maryland, 1912, 1914) was born in Baltimore, Maryland, on March 4, 1874. His father, Andrew C. Trippe, was a general in the Confederate Army. After earning an A.B. from Johns Hopkins University in Baltimore (1896) and an LL.B. from the University of Maryland (1898), he began a law practice in Baltimore.

Trippe was elected to the Maryland House of Delegates as a progressive Democrat from the city of Baltimore in 1911 and 1913. He was chosen as speaker for the 1912 and 1914 sessions. In addition, Trippe was a presidential elector in 1913 and president of the Maryland Democratic Convention the following year. From 1915 to 1920 he sat on the Maryland Court of Appeals.

Outside of politics Trippe belonged to the Maryland and Baltimore bar associations and the Maryland Historical Society. He was a member of the boards of the Maryland Agricultural College and St. John's College. A Presbyterian, he was married. Trippe died on July 10, 1936, at the age of 62.

GARY L. BROWNE

TUCKER, ARLIE DANIEL (Georgia, 1931) was born in Ocilla, Georgia, on November 28, 1894. Graduating from local public schools, he read law and became counsel for two railroads. Following that he moved to Nashville, Georgia. Tucker was secretary of the Chamber of Commerce and a member of the Masons and the Baptist Church. He was married, and he served in the U.S. armed forces.

A Democrat, Tucker served Nashville as an alderman in 1923–24. In 1924 he was elected to the Georgia House of Representatives from Berrien County. Tucker remained there for four consecutive terms. He was chosen as speaker *pro tem* in 1927 and 1929 and as speaker for the 1931 session.

From 1937 to 1943 Tucker sat on the Georgia Industrial Board. After working as supervisor of claims for the Georgia Board of Workmen's Compensation, he was appointed to that body in 1945 and was its chair in 1949–53. He lost a 1970 race for the state Prisons and Parole Board. Tucker died on March 30, 1974, at the age of 79.

AMOS ST. GERMAIN

TUCKER, DONALD L. (Florida, 1975, 1977) was born on July 23, 1935, in Tallahassee, Florida. His father, Luther Tucker, was a state legislator and chair of the county commission. The younger Tucker attended Brigham Young University and the University of Utah, and he earned a law degree from the University of Florida in 1962. He served in the U.S. Army before starting a private practice in St. Marks, Florida.

In 1966 Tucker was elected to the Florida House of Representatives as a Democrat from Wakulla County. He served six consecutive terms and was named speaker for the 1975 and 1977 sessions. During his speakership Tucker helped pass two measures designed to improve the legislative process. The first restored the practice of having bills read three times to prevent mistakes, and the second required that amendments adding money to any general appropriations measure be coupled with provisions for subtracting a comparable amount from the bill.

Outside of politics Tucker was governor of Florida Boys State and chair of the Florida Youth Safety Council. He also belonged to the Jaycees, Chamber of Commerce, Florida and Tallahassee bar associations, and American Judicature Society. A member of the Church of Jesus Christ of Latter-day Saints, he was a missionary for two years. Tucker was named one of the "Outstanding Young Men in America" by the Jaycees in 1966.

JERRELL H. SHOFNER

TUNNELL, BYRON M. (Texas, 1963) was born on October 14, 1925, in Tyler, Texas. Educated in local schools, he served as a tail gunner with the U.S.

Naval Air Corps in Europe during World War II. Tunnell attended Tyler Junior College and earned a law degree from Baylor University in Waco, Texas, in 1952. Three years later he began a private practice in Tyler. He married Bette Lemons.

A Democrat, Tunnell was assistant district attorney for Smith County in 1952–55. In 1956 he won election to the Texas House of Representatives from Smith and Gregg counties. He remained there for four consecutive terms and was named speaker for the 1963 session. While in the speakership Tunnell helped pass the Texas Regulatory Loan Act. The House also approved bills that created the Texas Tourist Development Agency, merged existing agencies into the state Parks and Wildlife Department, and dealt with land the federal government would use for the Padre Island National Seashore.

Appointed to the Texas Railroad Commission in January 1965, Tunnell was eventually that body's chair. He resigned in 1973 to become vice-president for governmental affairs of Tenneco, Inc., an oil and gas firm in Houston, Texas. Tunnell was president of the Smith County Bar Association, vice-president of the Texas Jaycees, and a member of the Masons, Chamber of Commerce, American Legion, YMCA, and Methodist Church.

LUTHER G. HAGARD, JR.

TUNSTALL, ALFRED MOORE (Alabama, 1931; also 1903) was a Democrat from Hale County. He served as speaker of the Alabama House of Representatives for the 1931 session, having previously presided in 1903.

Charles F. Ritter and Jon L. Wakelyn, *American Legislative Leaders, 1850–1910* (New York: Greenwood Press, 1989), 638–639.

KEVIN G. ATWATER

TURLINGTON, RALPH DONALD (Florida, 1967) was born on October 5, 1920, in Gainesville, Florida. He received a degree from the University of Florida and an M.B.A. from Harvard University (1942). Turlington served as an officer in the U.S. Army during World War II. Afterward he became a professor of business administration at Florida.

A Democrat, Turlington won election to the Florida House of Representatives from Alachua County in 1950. He served twelve consecutive terms and was named speaker for the 1967 session. His speakership was highlighted by the completion of the 1968 state constitution, which required annual legislative sessions. Turlington supported Governor Reubin Askew's request for a "sunshine law" requiring all local government meetings to be open to the public. In addition, the House approved a corporate profits tax and created a state consumer protection agency and a division of aging.

Appointed education commissioner of Florida in April 1974, Turlington remained in the position until 1986. Outside of politics he belonged to the Elks, Exchange Club, American Legion, VFW, and Baptist Church. He married Ann

Gellerstedt, and the couple had two children. Turlington works as an educational consultant in Gainesville at this writing.

J. LARRY DURRENCE

TURMAN, JAMES A. (Texas, 1961) was born on November 29, 1927, in Gober, Texas. He received a bachelor's degree (1948) and a master's degree (1949) from East Texas State Teachers College (now Texas A&M University at Commerce). Turman then became a teacher and a farmer. During the Korean War he served in the U.S. Navy. Earning a doctorate in educational administration from the University of Texas in 1957, he was a professor and assistant to the president of Texas Woman's University in Denton for two years.

In 1954 Turman was elected to the Texas House of Representatives as a Democrat from Fannin County. He remained there for four consecutive terms. Turman was chosen as speaker for the 1961 session after defeating Wade Spilman of Hidalgo County. During his speakership Texas enacted a general sales tax despite opposition from Governor M. Price Daniel, Sr.

Losing the 1962 Democratic primary for lieutenant governor of Texas to Preston Smith, Turman worked as a consultant for the U.S. Department of Health, Education and Welfare (HEW) in Dallas, Texas. He held various positions within the HEW and its successor, the Department of Health and Human Services. Turman was named administrative assistant to U.S. Representative Jim Mattox of Texas in 1978. In addition, he belonged to the Rotary, Lions, and Farm Bureau. A Baptist, he married Ira Nell Wigley.

LUTHER G. HAGARD, JR.

TURNER, GROVER W. "Buddy," Jr. (Arkansas, 1973) was born in Thornton, Arkansas, on August 15, 1923. During World War II he served as an electrical engineer in the U.S. Army Air Forces, rising to the rank of staff sergeant. Turner earned a B.A. from Henderson State Teacher's College (now University) in Arkadelphia, Arkansas (1948), and a master's degree in school administration from the University of Arkansas (1952). After working as a principal in Pine Bluff, Arkansas, he founded the real estate and insurance firm of Turner and Company in 1962. He also chaired the boards of the Pine Bluff Abstract Company and the First Arkansas Title Insurance Company.

A Democrat, Turner was superintendent of schools in Tinsman, Arkansas. In 1960 he was elected to the Arkansas House of Representatives from Jefferson County. He remained there for sixteen consecutive terms, becoming chair of the Education Committee and vice-chair of the Insurance and Commerce Committee. Turner was named speaker in 1973, the first session with single-member districts and the first since Reconstruction to include black members. While in the speakership he helped pass the largest expansion of government services in state history, including the creation of public kindergartens and a junior college system, expansion of the University of Arkansas Medical Center, and improvements in the state prison system.

At the end of 1973 Turner tried to set a precedent for annual sessions by ruling a motion to recess to have passed without allowing a recount. However, a brief shoving match ensued and the attempt ultimately failed. Outside of politics he was president of the Jaycees and a member of the Kiwanis, National Association of Realtors, Arkansas Insurance Association, and Methodist Church. Turner was named Pine Bluff's "Outstanding Young Man" in 1958. He married Sue Dickerson, and the couple had three children. Leaving the House in 1992, Turner continues to live in Pine Bluff at this writing.

LEON C. MILLER

TYDINGS, MILLARD EVELYN (Maryland, 1920) was born in Havre de Grace, Maryland, on April 6, 1890. After earning a B.S. in mechanical engineering (1910) and an LL.B. (1913) from the University of Maryland, he began a law practice in Havre de Grace. He belonged to the Masons, Elks, Odd Fellows, Moose, Rotary, and American Legion.

In 1915 Tydings won election to the Maryland House of Delegates as a Democrat from Harford County. Resigning from the House in June 1916, he served in the U.S. Army during World War I and rose to the rank of lieutenant colonel. Tydings was again elected to the House in 1919 and was named speaker for the 1920 session. He successfully ran for the Maryland Senate in 1921.

Winning 1922 and 1924 races for the U.S. House of Representatives from Maryland's 2nd District, Tydings was elected to the U.S. Senate from Maryland in 1926 and remained there until losing reelection in 1950. He was renominated for the U.S. Senate in 1956 but withdrew due to ill health. In addition, Tydings was a regent of the University of Maryland and president of the university's Alumni Association. An Episcopalian, he was married in 1931. Tydings died on his farm near Havre de Grace on February 9, 1961, at age 70.

GARY L. BROWNE

V

VAUGHN, EARL W. (North Carolina, 1967, 1969) was born in Reidsville, North Carolina, on June 17, 1928, to John H. and Lelia F. Vaughn. Educated in local public schools, he served in the U.S. Army in 1945–47. Vaughn attended Pfeiffer Junior College (now College) in Misenheimer, North Carolina, and earned an A.B. (1950) and an LL.B. (1952) from the University of North Carolina. Afterward he began practicing law in Rockingham County, North Carolina. He married Eloise Freeland Maddry in 1952, and the couple had four children.

A Democrat, Vaughn was attorney for Draper, North Carolina, and solicitor of the Leaksville, North Carolina, Recorder's Court. Those municipalities merged into Eden, North Carolina, in 1967, and he became that city's attorney. Vaughn was also president of the Rockingham County Young Democrats and secretary-treasurer of the county Democratic Executive Committee. In 1960 he won election to the North Carolina House of Representatives from Rockingham County. Remaining there for five consecutive terms, Vaughn was majority leader. His perception of a concentration of political power at the national level led him to become active in the Commission on Interstate Cooperation, Council of State Governments, and National Conference of State Legislative Leaders.

Vaughn was chosen as speaker in late 1967 after the resignation of incumbent David M. Britt, and he was renamed to the post for the 1969 session. Near the end of 1969 he was appointed to the North Carolina Court of Appeals. Named to the North Carolina Supreme Court in 1984, Vaughn retired the next year. He was president of the Rotary and a member of the North Carolina Bar Association and the Methodist Church. Vaughn died in Raleigh, North Carolina, on April 1, 1986, at the age of 57.

Hugh Talmage Lefler and Albert Ray Newsome, *The History of a Southern State: North Carolina* (Chapel Hill: University of North Carolina Press, 1973); *The News and Observer* (Raleigh, North Carolina); William S. Powell, *North Carolina through Four Centuries* (Chapel Hill: University of North Carolina Press, 1989).

FRED D. RAGAN

W

WALDREP, THOMAS CARNES (Oklahoma, 1919) was born on February 16, 1889, in Birmingham, Alabama, to Thomas and Elizabeth (Murphy) Waldrep. He moved with his family to Ardmore, Indian Territory (now Oklahoma), in 1900, and to Shawnee, Oklahoma, in 1908. Waldrep earned a degree from Central State Normal School (now the University of Central Oklahoma) in Edmond, Oklahoma (1912), and an LL.B. from the University of Oklahoma (1915). Afterward he began practicing law in Shawnee with the firm of Waldrep and Haight. A Methodist, he was married.

In 1914 Waldrep successfully ran for the Oklahoma House of Representatives as a Democrat from Pottawatomie County. He served three consecutive terms and was named speaker for the 1919 session. Elected to the Oklahoma Senate in 1926, he remained there until being defeated for reelection in 1940. Waldrep pleaded guilty to charges of selling a state job in 1941, receiving a $1,000 fine and a six-month jail term.

GORDON MOORE

WALKER, RICHARD FLOURNOY (Louisiana, 1920) was born in Chickasaw County, Mississippi, on February 16, 1868. Educated in local schools, he received a B.S. from Mississippi State Normal College in 1891. For three years he was president of Norvilla College in Greensburg, Louisiana. Walker settled in Clinton, Louisiana, in 1896. He earned an LL.B. from Tulane University in New Orleans, Louisiana, in 1897, and began a law practice in Clinton.

A Democrat, Walker sat on the Clinton town council from 1898 to 1902. In 1903 he won election to one four-year term in the Louisiana House of Representatives from East Feliciana Parish. Walker was again elected to the House in 1919. He was named speaker for the 1920 session with the support of Governor John M. Parker.

In other affairs Walker was a delegate to the 1913 and 1921 Louisiana constitutional conventions and a member of the 6th Congressional Democratic Committee. He was married, and he belonged to the Masons, Elks, and Baptist Church. Walker died on July 17, 1949, at the age of 81.

Henry E. Chambers, *A History of Louisiana: Wilderness—Colony—Province—Territory—State—People* (Chicago: American Historical Society, 1925); Edwin Adams Davis, *The Story of Louisiana* (New Orleans: J. F. Hyer, 1960).

BEATRICE R. OWSLEY

WALKER, ROBERT HENRY "Harry" (Alabama, 1935) was born on March 18, 1875, in Limestone County, Alabama. After attending local public schools and the North Alabama Agricultural School in Athens, he became editor of the *Limestone Democrat* in Athens in 1893. Walker was secretary of the National Editorial Association and a member of the Knights of Pythias and the Baptist Church. He married Memory McClellan in 1901.

A Democrat, Walker was immigration commissioner of Alabama in 1910. In 1930 he was elected to one term in the Alabama Senate. Walker successfully ran for the Alabama House of Representatives from Limestone County in 1934, and he was named speaker for his only term in 1935. While in the speakership he opposed the adoption of a state sales tax and strongly advocated the creation of the Tennessee Valley Authority. He then returned to his newspaper. Moving to Columbia, Tennessee, Walker died there on September 22, 1952, at age 77.

BENJAMIN B. WILLIAMS AND DONALD B. DODD

WALKER, SETH McKINNEY (Tennessee, 1919) was born on March 6, 1892, in Chattanooga, Tennessee, to Seth McKinney and Mary J. (Stephenson) Walker. He received a law degree from Cumberland University in Lebanon, Tennessee. Walker began a private practice in Lebanon in 1914, and he belonged to the American Bar Association. A Presbyterian, he married Katherine Hooker in 1913.

In 1918 Walker was elected to the Tennessee House of Representatives as a Democrat from Wilson County. He was chosen as speaker without opposition for the 1919 term, his only one in the House. When Tennessee became the final state to approve the 19th Amendment to the U.S. Constitution granting women suffrage, Walker gained national attention by leading the legislative opposition. Afterward he moved his law practice to Nashville, Tennessee. Walker died on February 26, 1951, at the age of 58.

Biographical file of Tennessee legislators, Tennessee State Library and Archives, Nashville; Nashville *Tennessean*, February 27, 1951; Nashville *Tennessean and American*, January 6, 1919.

FRED A. BAILEY

WALTHER, GLENN F. (Arkansas, 1957) was born in Little Rock, Arkansas, August 15, 1908, to Carl Frederick and Laura Belle (Glenn) Walther. Attending local public schools and the University of Illinois, he earned an LL.B. from the

University of Arkansas. Walther then began practicing law in Little Rock. During World War II he served as a captain in the U.S. Army. He was married.

A Democrat, Walther became deputy prosecuting attorney of Pulaski County in 1940. He won election to the Arkansas House of Representatives from Pulaski County in 1946 and remained there for ten consecutive terms. Walther was chosen as speaker for the 1957 session. Leaving the House in 1966, he returned to his Little Rock practice. In addition, Walther was a member of the Elks, Lions, American Legion, VFW, Amvets, International Brotherhood of Magicians, Arkansas and Little Rock bar associations, and Lutheran Church.

The Arkansas Handbook (Little Rock: Arkansas History Commission, 1936–   ).

JANE McBRIDE GATES

WARD, DAVID LIVINGSTONE "Libby," Jr. (North Carolina, 1939) was born in New Bern, North Carolina, on June 23, 1903. Educated in local public schools, he earned an A.B. from the University of North Carolina in 1924 and a law degree from Wake Forest College (now University) in North Carolina in 1926. Ward then began a private practice in New Bern. He was married.

A Democrat, Ward was solicitor for the Craven County Recorder's Court (1928–30) and a member of the North Carolina Board of Conservation and Development (1933–37). In 1934 he was elected to the North Carolina House of Representatives from Craven County. Ward remained there for five consecutive terms and was named speaker for the 1939 session. He successfully ran for the North Carolina Senate in 1944. Secretary of the North Carolina Democratic Executive Committee, he was a delegate to the 1936 and 1940 Democratic national conventions.

After that Ward taught at the University of North Carolina. In addition, he was a director of the First Citizens Bank and Trust Company, Carolina Telephone and Telegraph Company, and Seaboard Transportation Company. Exalted ruler of the Elks, he belonged to the American, North Carolina, and Craven County bar associations and the Episcopal Church. Ward died on June 18, 1971, at the age of 67.

William S. Powell, ed., *Dictionary of North Carolina Biography*, 6 vols. (Chapel Hill: University of North Carolina Press, 1979–1996).

CHARLES H. BOWMAN, JR.

WATERFIELD, HARRY LEE (Kentucky, 1944, 1946) was born in Calloway County, Kentucky, on January 19, 1911, to Burnett and Lois (Burton) Waterfield. Educated in local public schools, he earned a B.S. in journalism from Murray State Teachers College (now University) in Kentucky in 1932. Waterfield then entered the newspaper business, eventually becoming owner of the *Hickman County Gazette* in Clinton, Kentucky. He married Laura Ferguson in 1933, and the couple had three children.

A Democrat, Waterfield won election to the Kentucky House of Representatives from Hickman and Fulton counties in 1937 and remained there for five consecutive terms. He was named speaker for the 1944 and 1946 regular sessions and the special session in 1944. Waterfield lost Democratic primaries for governor of Kentucky in 1947, 1959, and 1967, but he successfully ran for one additional House term in 1949. Elected lieutenant governor in 1955 and 1963, he became the first person in state history to serve two terms in that office.

In other affairs Waterfield was secretary of the Kentucky Democratic Party and a delegate to the 1968 Democratic National Convention. He began raising cattle and hogs in 1946. Around 1963 Waterfield opened an insurance agency in Frankfort, Kentucky. President of the Kentucky Press Association, he also belonged to the Masons, Elks, Rotary, Lions, Chamber of Commerce, Farm Bureau, and Christian Church (Disciples of Christ). Waterfield died in Frankfort on August 4, 1988, at the age of 77.

Louisville *Courier-Journal; Kentucky Directory for the Use of the Courts, State and County Officials and General Assembly of the State of Kentucky* (Frankfort, KY, 1914–); John E. Kleber, ed., *The Kentucky Encyclopedia* (Lexington: University Press of Kentucky, 1992); Penny M. Miller, *Kentucky Politics and Government* (Lincoln: University of Nebraska Press, 1994); Robert F. Sexton, ed., *The Public Papers of the Governors of Kentucky* (Lexington: University Press of Kentucky, 1975).

ROGER TATE

WEAVER, CARLTON (Oklahoma, 1931) was born in Mt. Vernon, Texas, on August 25, 1881. After attending local public schools, he moved to Ada, Indian Territory (now Oklahoma) and purchased an interest in the *Ada Weekly News*. In 1903 he and his brother founded the *Ada Daily News*. Weaver then attended the University of Kentucky and the University of Oklahoma, where he was class president. He became the owner of the *Latimer County News* (later *News-Democrat*) in Wilburton, Oklahoma, in 1914.

A Democrat, Weaver was a delegate to the 1906–07 Oklahoma Constitutional Convention. He won election to the Oklahoma House of Representatives from Latimer County in 1930 and was named speaker in 1931, his only term in the House. While in the speakership he worked closely with Governor William H. Murray.

After that Weaver returned to his newspaper. President of the Wilburton State Bank (1933–39), he was also vice-president of the Boy Scouts and a member of the Lions, Oklahoma Press Association, Izaak Walton League, Sons of the Confederacy, and Baptist Church. He donated or sold a total of 8,400 acres to Robbers Cave State Park, reserving his own grave site there. Weaver died on August 17, 1947, at the age of 65.

Charles Evans, "Carlton Weaver 1881–1947," *The Chronicles of Oklahoma* 25 (winter 1947/48), 410; Rex F. Harlow, comp., *Makers of Government in Oklahoma* (Oklahoma City: Harlow Publishing, 1930); Gaston Litton, *History of Oklahoma at the Golden Anniversary of Statehood*, 4 vols. (New York: Lewis Historical Publishing, 1957);

Joseph B. Thoburn and Muriel H. Wright, *Oklahoma: A History of the State and Its People*, 4 vols. (New York: Lewis Historical Publishing, 1929).

DONOVAN L. REICHENBERGER

WEINTRAUB, MORRIS (Kentucky, 1958) was born in Newport, Kentucky, on May 14, 1909, to Jewish immigrants. His father was from Warsaw, Poland, and his mother from Odessa, Ukraine. Weintraub attended local public schools and earned an LL.B. from Dayton Law School in Ohio. He then began practicing law in Newport.

A Democrat, Weintraub was Campbell County judge *pro tem*, U.S. conciliation commissioner, Newport city solicitor, and attorney for the Newport Housing Authority. He was secretary of the Kentucky Young Democrats from 1936 to 1939. In the latter year Weintraub successfully ran for the Kentucky Senate. Elected to the Kentucky House of Representatives from Campbell County in 1945, he served seven consecutive terms and was cited by state newspapers as the best all-around legislator. Weintraub was named speaker for the 1958 session with bipartisan support. He gained a reputation for innovation despite the fact that the speakership was sharply circumscribed by the power of the governor and a lack of resources.

After that Weintraub returned to his Newport practice. In addition, he was president of the Jaycees and a member of the Elks, Eagles, Moose, and American Trial Lawyers Association. He was married. Weintraub retired to Miami, Florida, where he continues to live at this writing.

Malcolm E. Jewell, *Representation in State Legislatures* (Lexington: University Press of Kentucky, 1982); Malcolm E. Jewell and Everett W. Cunningham, *Kentucky Politics* (Lexington: University Press of Kentucky, 1968); Malcolm E. Jewell and Penny Miller, *The Kentucky Legislature: Two Decades of Change* (Lexington: University Press of Kentucky, 1988); Malcolm E. Jewell and Samuel C. Patterson, *The Legislative Process in the United States*, 4th ed. (New York: Random House, 1986); John Ed Pearce, *Divide and Dissent: Kentucky Politics, 1930–1963* (Lexington: University Press of Kentucky, 1987); Seymour Sher, "Conditions for Legislative Control," *Journal of Politics* 25 (1963), 526–551.

H. LEW WALLACE

WELCH, WILLIAM DONOVAN, Sr. (Oklahoma, 1939) was born in Caston, Indian Territory (now Oklahoma), on October 22, 1898. Graduating from high school in Tonkawa, Oklahoma, he attended Oklahoma A&M College (now Oklahoma State University) and the University of Oklahoma. Welch served in the U.S. Army during World War I. He earned an LL.B. from Oklahoma in 1920 and joined the Antlers, Oklahoma, law firm of Welch and Welch. In 1921 he began a practice in Madill, Oklahoma. After living in Ada and Oklahoma City, Oklahoma, he returned to Madill by 1930.

Welch was elected to the Oklahoma House of Representatives as a Democrat from Marshall County in 1934. Remaining there for three consecutive terms, he was chosen as speaker for the 1939 session. In 1940 Welch was a delegate to the Democratic National Convention. He became the first director of the Selective Service in Oklahoma during World War II.

Afterward Welch was legislative counsel for the Association of American Railroads in Oklahoma. Known for his expertise in tax law, he influenced a state constitutional amendment on school finances and an institutional bond issue. In addition Welch aided the successful 1954 gubernatorial campaign of Raymond D. Gary. He belonged to the Rotary, Chamber of Commerce, American Legion, American, Oklahoma, and Marshall County bar associations, and Church of Christ. Welch died of a heart attack on October 13, 1955, at age 56.

TIMOTHY A. ZWINK

WETHERELL, THOMAS KENT (Florida, 1991) was born in Daytona Beach, Florida, on December 22, 1945. Educated in local public schools, he earned a B.S. (1967), M.S. (1968), and Ph.D. in educational administration (1974) from Florida State University. Wetherell was an administrator at Daytona Beach Community College and the University of Central Florida, and he taught at Bethune-Cookman College. Later he became president of Wetherell Enterprises, Inc., in Daytona Beach.

Wetherell was elected to the Florida House of Representatives as a Democrat from Volusia County in 1980 and served six consecutive terms. Majority floor leader in 1982–84, he chaired the Higher Education Committee and the Appropriations Committee. While in the House Wetherell became an ally of party leader Dempsey Barron. He was chosen as speaker for the 1991 session.

Afterward Wetherell returned to his business interests and was active in the construction of the Daytona Beach Convention Center. He belonged to the Masons, Farm Bureau, and NAACP. A Presbyterian, he married Virginia Bass; the couple had three children. Wetherell continues to live in Daytona Beach at this writing.

The Miami Herald Almanac of Florida Politics (Miami: Miami Herald Publishing, 1994–).

JON L. WAKELYN

WETZEL, CHARLES McCLUER (West Virginia, 1911) was born on August 17, 1850, in Knox County, Indiana, to Virginia natives Solomon and Eliza (Buriss) Wetzel. He practiced law in Indiana until 1885, when he was appointed to the U.S. Customs Service in Washington, D.C. Wetzel began operating a farm and an apple orchard in Keyes Ferry, West Virginia, in 1898. An Episcopalian, he married Margaret Anne Beck in 1886; the couple had two sons.

In 1901 Wetzel successfully ran for the West Virginia House of Delegates as a Democrat from Jefferson County in a special election. He was again elected in 1902, 1904, 1906, 1910, and 1912, and he was chosen as speaker for the 1911 session. Named chief deputy of the U.S. Bureau of Internal Revenue in Parkersburg, West Virginia, in 1913, Wetzel held the post until 1921. Afterward he returned to his businesses in Keyes Ferry. Wetzel died on June 6, 1929, at the age of 78.

ROBERT L. HUNT

WHITE, H. LABAN, Jr. (West Virginia, 1965, 1967) was born on May 1, 1916, in Spencer, West Virginia, to H. Laban and Nannie L. (Cox) White. Educated in local public schools, he earned an A.B. from Glenville State College in West Virginia (1937) and an LL.B. from West Virginia University (1942). White served in the U.S. Army during World War II, rising to the rank of captain. Later he became a lieutenant colonel in the Army Reserve. He began to practice law in Clarksburg, West Virginia, in 1946, eventually becoming a partner in the firm of Marstiller, Siegrist & White.

A Democrat, White was city attorney of Clarksburg in 1949–55 and Harrison County assistant prosecuting attorney in 1956–57. He was elected to the West Virginia House of Delegates from Harrison County in 1956 and remained for six consecutive terms. While in office White sponsored more than 2,500 successful pieces of legislation. Instrumental in the passage of the state's first minimum wage law, he was named speaker for the 1965 and 1967 sessions. Concurrently he was a director of the National Conference of Legislative Leaders.

After that White returned to his law practice. Commander of the West Virginia Amvets in 1950, he was president of the Lions and the Harrison County Bar Association. In addition, he belonged to the Elks, Moose, Chamber of Commerce, American Legion, YMCA, American and West Virginia bar associations, American Judicature Society, and Baptist Church. He married Gwendolyn Beall in 1943, and the couple had three daughters. White continues to live in Clarksburg at this writing.

LISLE G. BROWN

WHITE, JOHN S. (Maryland, 1943) was born around 1895 in Philadelphia, Pennsylvania, of Irish descent. After attending local public schools and the University of Pennsylvania, he joined the freight department of the Philadelphia and Reading Railroad. During World War I he served in the U.S. Navy. White worked for the U.S. Quartermaster General before earning an LL.B. from Georgetown University in Washington, D.C., in 1923. He settled in Colmar Manor, Maryland, and he began practicing law in Hyattsville, Maryland.

A Democrat, White entered politics when he was elected mayor of Colmar Manor in 1927. In 1935 he successfully ran for the Maryland House of Delegates from Prince George's County. White remained there for three consecutive four-year terms. Majority floor leader for the 1939 and 1943 sessions, he gained notoriety for leading a "sit down strike" to protest the state senate's failure to pass a bill. He was named speaker in July 1943 following the resignation of incumbent Thomas E. Conlon.

White was defeated for attorney general of Maryland in 1946. Returning to his private practice, he lost a 1952 bid for the U.S. House of Representatives from Maryland. In addition, White was a member of the Elks, Moose, Kiwanis, and Catholic Church. He married Mary O'Neill, and the couple had three children. While vacationing in the Bahamas, White died on May 15, 1960, at age 64.

"John S. White, Ex-Legislator," *Washington Post*, May 18, 1960.

MORGAN H. PRITCHETT

WILDER, GEORGE HAMILTON (Florida, 1918, 1919) was born on February 23, 1870, in a log cabin in Echebusassa (now Plant City), Florida. His father, Calfrey LaFayette Wilder, was a state legislator. Educated in local schools, the younger Wilder earned a B.A. from Stetson University in De Land, Florida, in 1893. The following year he moved to Washington, D.C., to work as an attache in the U.S. Senate. Wilder was secretary to U.S. Representative Stephen Sparkman of Florida for fourteen years. He was married.

In 1914 Wilder won election to the Florida House of Representatives as a Democrat from Hillsborough County. He served three consecutive terms, and he was named speaker for the special session of November 1918 and for the 1919 regular session. While in the speakership Wilder worked with maverick Democratic Governor Sidney J. Catts, known as the "Cracker Messiah," in ratifying the 18th Amendment to the U.S. Constitution in support of prohibition. The legislature also reformed the state school for boys and passed an automobile tax to fund road improvements. Appointed state motor vehicle commissioner in 1932, Wilder died on June 3, 1959, at age 89.

GARY R. MORMINO

WILKINSON, NORMAN MEANS (Arkansas, 1941) was born on October 26, 1910, in Greenwood, Arkansas, to William N. and Mary Myrtle (Means) Wilkinson. Educated in local public schools, he earned a B.A. from the University of Arkansas (1931) and an LL.B. from Cumberland University in Lebanon, Tennessee (1933). Wilkinson then began a law practice in Greenwood as well as publishing the *Greenwood Democrat* and the *Mansfield Messenger*. He joined the Farmers Bank of Greenwood in 1935.

In 1932 Wilkinson was elected to the Arkansas House of Representatives as a Democrat from Sebastian County. Remaining there for five consecutive terms, he was named speaker for the 1941 session. Wilkinson served in the U.S. Navy during World War II, rising to the rank of lieutenant commander and receiving several medals. He was appointed to the Arkansas Banking Board in 1948, Arkansas Board of Education in 1949, and Arkansas Industrial Development Commission in 1970.

Becoming president of his bank in 1955, Wilkinson also sat on the boards of the Arkansas Children's Colony in Conway, Sparks Regional Medical Center in Fort Smith, Arkansas, and Fort Smith Junior College. He was president of the Arkansas Bankers Association in 1970–71 and a member of the Masons. A

Presbyterian, Wilkinson was married. In addition, he wrote a history of his hometown entitled *Greenwood: 100 Years a County Seat, 1851–1951*. Wilkinson died on November 11, 1991, at the age of 81.

Arkansas Democrat; Arkansas Gazette; The Arkansas Handbook (Little Rock: Arkansas History Commission, 1936–   ).

RUSSELL PIERCE BAKER

WILKINSON, PERRY O. (Maryland, 1959) was born in Hebron, Maryland, on March 21, 1905. Educated in local public schools, he earned a B.A. (1928) and an M.A. (1936) from the University of Maryland. From 1929 to 1940 Wilkinson was a teacher, coach, and school administrator in Prince George's County, Maryland. He then established an insurance agency in Hyattsville, Maryland. A Methodist, he was married.

Wilkinson was elected to the Maryland House of Delegates as a Democrat from Prince George's County in 1942. He served five consecutive four-year terms, becoming speaker *pro tem* in 1948. With the support of Governor J. Millard Tawes, Wilkinson was named speaker for the 1959 session after defeating Majority Leader A. Gordon Boone in the party caucus.

In 1962 Wilkinson lost the Democratic primary for the U.S. House of Representatives from Maryland's 8th District to Carlton R. Sickles. Outside of politics he was president of the Kiwanis and the Chamber of Commerce and a member of the Masons, Elks, Moose, and Kiwanis. Suffering a brain hemorrhage in 1963, Wilkinson partially recovered after a long convalescence. He sold his insurance firm to his son in 1967. Wilkinson died on December 14, 1979, at the age of 74.

Baltimore *Evening Sun*; Baltimore *Sun*, January 4, 7, 1959, December 17, 1979; Robert J. Brugger, *Maryland: A Middle Temperament, 1634–1980* (Baltimore: Johns Hopkins University Press, 1988); George H. Callcott, *Maryland and America, 1940–1980* (Baltimore, Johns Hopkins University Press, 1985); *Maryland Manual: Annual Publication of State Officers* (Annapolis: Hall of Records Commission); Morris L. Radoff, *The Old Line State: A History of Maryland* (Hopkinsville, KY: Historical Records Association, 1956), II: 963–966.

WHITMAN H. RIDGWAY

WILLIS, WILLIAM PASCÁL (Oklahoma, 1973, 1975, 1977) was born on October 17, 1910, near Anadarko, Oklahoma, to Robert Garnett and Lulu (Wyatt) Willis. His mother was a Kiowa Indian. Attending public schools and the Haskell Indian Institute in Lawrence, Kansas, he earned a B.A. in English and history from East Central State Teachers College (now University) in Ada, Oklahoma, in 1935. Willis was a teacher in Spaulding and Mill Creek, Oklahoma, for two years. During World War II he served with the U.S. Army field artillery in the Pacific theater. He received an M.A. in history from the University of Tulsa in Oklahoma in 1948, and he operated a mercantile store in Tahlequah, Oklahoma.

A Democrat, Willis entered politics as mayor of Locust Grove, Oklahoma, from 1937 to 1944. In 1958 he was elected to the Oklahoma House of Representatives from Cherokee and Adair counties. Willis remained there for fourteen consecutive terms, gaining recognition as an expert on taxes and state finances. Named chair of the Appropriations Committee in 1964, he was chosen as speaker for the 1973, 1975, and 1977 sessions. While in the speakership Willis helped address problems with the Oklahoma prison system and opposed attacks on the state revenue base. He left the House in 1986.

Willis was a member of the Masons, Kiwanis, Chamber of Commerce, American Legion, and Baptist Church. In addition, he belonged to the Black Leggings, a Kiowa veterans organization. The American Indian Exposition in Anadarko named Willis its "Indian of the Year" in 1974. He married Zelma Bynum in 1936, and the couple had seven children. As of this writing Willis continues to live in Tahlequah.

KENNY L. BROWN

WIMBERLY, LORRIS M. (Louisiana, 1936, 1948, 1956) was born in Arcadia, Louisiana, in 1898. His father, J. Rush Wimberly, was a state legislator. The younger Wimberly worked as a page in the state House (1904) and Senate (1912). Attending public schools and the Gulf Coast Military Academy in Gulfport, Mississippi, he graduated from the Randolph-Macon Military Academy in Front Royal, Virginia. During World War I he served in the U.S. Army. Wimberly worked in the construction business in Arcadia in 1923–34 and later became an insurance agent. He was married.

A Democrat, Wimberly was a justice of the peace in Bienville Parish. He was elected to the Louisiana House of Representatives from Bienville Parish in 1927, 1935, 1947, 1951, and 1955. Wimberly chaired the Public Roads, State Debt, and Contingent Expense committees, and he helped support Governor Huey P. Long against impeachment proceedings in 1929. In addition, he was secretary of the Louisiana Tax Reform Commission and the Louisiana Civil Service Commission.

Chosen as speaker for the 1936 and 1948 terms, Wimberly enjoyed close working relationships with governors Earl K. Long, Richard Leche, and Oscar K. Allen. He was again named to the speakership in 1956, but he left the House in July of that year to become Louisiana public works director. Outside of politics he was a director of the First National Bank of Arcadia and a member of the Methodist Church. Wimberly died on May 3, 1962.

Edwin Adams Davis, *The Story of Louisiana* (New Orleans: J. F. Hyer, 1960).

BEATRICE R. OWSLEY

WOLFE, J. LUTHER (West Virginia, 1919) was born in Given, West Virginia, to G. B. and Laura Wolfe. Educated in local public schools, he earned a law degree from West Virginia University in 1900. The following year Wolfe began a private practice in Ripley, West Virginia. He also worked as a teacher. A Methodist, he married Ivy L. Guinn in 1902; the couple had one daughter.

Wolfe was elected to the West Virginia House of Delegates as a Republican from Jackson County in 1914 and 1918. He chaired the Committee on Railroads. When the GOP gained control of the House for the 1919 session, Wolfe was chosen as speaker. In 1926–27 he was assistant attorney general of West Virginia. Outside of politics he belonged to the Masons, Odd Fellows, and Knights of Pythias. Wolfe died on November 27, 1933.

Jim Comstock, ed., *The West Virginia Heritage Encyclopedia*, 25 vols. (Richwood, WV, 1976); Phil Conley, ed., *The West Virginia Encyclopedia* (Charleston: West Virginia Publishing, 1929).

PATRICK J. CHASE

WOOD, GEORGE PIERCE (Florida, 1939) was born in Attapulgus, Georgia, on August 26, 1895. He attended schools in Jackson County, Mississippi, Emory College (now University) in Atlanta, Georgia, and the University of Florida. While at the latter he earned letters in football and basketball. Wood served with the U.S. Army's 81st Headquarters Division in Europe during World War I, rising to the rank of first sergeant. Moving to Vilas, Florida, he operated a farm and was involved in the construction, naval stores, and lumber businesses. During the 1930s he became a purchasing agent for the St. Joe Paper Company.

A Democrat, Wood entered politics by sitting on the Liberty County board of Commissioners in 1926–29. He was elected to the Florida House of Representatives from Liberty County in 1928 and remained there for six consecutive terms. Wood gained prominence in 1931, when he helped shape state policy on gasoline taxation, road building, and parimutual wagering. In 1937 he chaired the Committee on Finance and Taxation and was chief lieutenant to Speaker William M. Christie.

Wood was chosen as speaker for the 1939 session. While in the post he attempted to lessen Florida's budget deficit of more than $2 million. However, the legislature failed to approve bills that would have levied a two percent general sales tax and legalized gambling casinos. The legislature did pass measures on controlling fires in the Everglades region and on extending county participation in gasoline tax revenues. Afterward Wood returned to his Vilas business interests. He belonged to the Methodist Church, and he was married and had three children. Wood died on July 8, 1945, at the age of 49.

PAUL S. GEORGE

WOODEN, HERBERT R. (Maryland, 1918) was born in Pennsylvania in 1877. He earned a degree from Princeton University and attended the Pennsylvania State College of Agriculture. Wooden then settled in Hampstead, Maryland, where he began farming. A Methodist, he never married.

In 1911 Wooden was elected to the Maryland House of Delegates as a Democrat from Carroll County. He served four consecutive terms and was chosen as speaker for the 1918 session. Returning to his farm, he was also part-owner of the Oak Grove Dairy in Baltimore, Maryland. Eventually he moved back to Pennsylvania. Wooden died on August 27, 1959.

GARY L. BROWNE

WOODS, GEORGE STANLEY (Tennessee, 1945) was born in Etowah, Tennessee, on June 25, 1913. Graduating from local schools, he began working in the retailing business in Etowah. Woods was a member of the Elks, Lions, and Baptist Church. He married Hannah Webb in 1931.

In 1940 Woods won election to the Tennessee House of Representatives as a Democrat from McMinn County. Serving three consecutive terms, he was chosen as speaker for the 1945 session. He was also purchasing agent for McMinn County (1944–46) and mayor of Etowah (1950–53). Woods then moved to Chattanooga, Tennessee.

Biographical Directory, Tennessee General Assembly, 1796–1969 (Nashville: State Library and Archives).

LEE S. GREENE

WOODS, JOHN WILLIAM (Texas, 1915) was born on September 4, 1875, in Denton County, Texas. When he moved with his family to Callahan County, Texas, in 1882, he helped drive a large herd of cattle. Later he became a cowboy. Woods graduated from high school in Mineral Wells, Texas. After working as a teacher, he received a law degree from the University of Texas. He practiced law in Baird, Texas, before settling in Rotan, Texas, in 1909.

A Democrat, Woods was prosecuting attorney of Callahan County for eight years and Rotan city attorney in 1909–13. In 1912 and 1914 he was elected to the Texas House of Representatives from Fisher, Mitchell, and Nolan counties. While in office he authored the Married Woman's Property Rights Act and sponsored a bill to create a girls' training school in Gainesville, and as a result he was appointed to the Southern Conference on Women and Child Labor in 1913. Woods was named speaker for the 1915 session, successfully backing legislation to make school attendance compulsory and to improve rural schools. His background led to his becoming known as the "Cowboy Speaker."

Losing two bids for attorney general of Texas, Woods returned to his private practice in Baird. Eventually he relocated to Abilene, Texas, and then to Dallas, Texas. He was married, and he belonged to the Methodist Church. Woods died in Dallas on April 18, 1933, at the age of 57.

Lewis L. Gould, *Progressives and Prohibitionists: Texas Democrats in the Wilson Era* (Austin: University of Texas Press, 1973), 151, 156; *Journal of the House of Representatives* (Austin: Von Boeckmann–Jones Co., 1909–); *Presiding Officers of the Texas Legislature, 1846–1982* (Austin: Texas Legislative Council, 1982), 153; "Woods, John William," *Fort Worth Star-Telegram*, April 19, 1933.

JANET SCHMELZER

WOOTEN, EMMETT ROBINSON (North Carolina, 1915) was born in Craven County, North Carolina, November 2, 1878. Educated in private schools in

Kinston, North Carolina, he earned an A.B. from Wake Forest College (now University) in North Carolina and studied law at the University of North Carolina. Wooten began a private practice in Kinston. He was married, and he belonged to the Masons, Odd Fellows, North Carolina Bar Association, and Episcopal Church.

A Democrat, Wooten was Lenoir County attorney (1903) and Kinston city attorney (1904–06). In 1908 he won election to the North Carolina House of Representatives from Lenoir County. He served four consecutive terms and was named to the speakership for the 1915 session. Wooten was still speaker when he died in an automobile accident on February 27, 1915, at age 36.

John L. Cheney, Jr., *North Carolina Government, 1585–1974: A Narrative and Statistical History* (Raleigh: North Carolina Department of the Secretary of State, 1975); Hugh Talmadge Lefler and Albert Ray Newsome, *The History of a Southern State: North Carolina* (Chapel Hill: University of North Carolina Press, 1973); William S. Powell, *North Carolina through Four Centuries* (Chapel Hill: University of North Carolina Press, 1989).

CLAUDE HARGROVE

WRIGHT, FIELDING LEWIS (Mississippi, 1936) was born in Rolling Fork, Mississippi, on May 16, 1895. Earning an LL.B. from the University of Alabama, he began practicing corporate law in Rolling Fork. Wright was a member of the Masons, Elks, American Legion, and Methodist Church. He was married.

A Democrat, Wright won election to the Mississippi Senate in 1927. He successfully ran for the Mississippi House of Representatives from Sharkey County in 1931 and 1935, becoming speaker *pro tem* in 1936. Wright was chosen as speaker in September 1936 following the death of incumbent Horace S. Stansel. Elected lieutenant governor of Mississippi in 1943, he was named governor after incumbent Thomas L. Bailey died in November 1946. He won a race for the governorship the next year.

In 1948 Wright helped organize many southern Democrats who opposed President Harry S. Truman's support for civil rights legislation into the States' Rights ("Dixiecrat") Party. He was named the party's vice presidential candidate under J. Strom Thurmond of South Carolina, and their ticket carried four states. Settling in Jackson, Mississippi, Wright lost a 1955 gubernatorial bid. Wright died in Jackson on May 8, 1956, at the age of 60.

Dale Krane and Stephen D. Shaffer, eds., *Mississippi Government & Politics: Modernizers versus Traditionalists* (Lincoln: University of Nebraska Press, 1992); Richard A. McLemore, *A History of Mississippi*, 2 vols. (Jackson: University and College Press of Mississippi, 1973); *Mississippi Official and Statistical Register* (Jackson: Secretary of State).

DAVID G. SANSING

BIBLIOGRAPHY

GENERAL

Administrative Officials Classified by Functions. Chicago: Council of State Governments, 1961–1965.

Almanac of American Politics. New York: E. P. Dutton, 1972– .

American College and Private School Directory. Chicago: Educational Aid Society, 1907–1916.

American Universities and Colleges. Washington, DC: American Council on Education, 1928– .

The Biographical Directory of the American Congress, 1774–1971. Washington, DC: U.S. Government Printing Office, 1971.

The Book of the States. Chicago: Council of State Governments, 1935– .

Citation World Atlas. Maplewood, NJ: Hammond, 1982.

College and Private School Directory of the United States. Chicago: Educational Aid Society, 1917/18–1936.

College and Private School Directory of the United States and Canada. Chicago: Educational Bureau, 1937– .

Congressional Quarterly's Guide to Congress. Washington, DC: Congressional Quarterly, 1971– .

Congressional Quarterly's Guide to U.S. Elections. 3rd ed. Washington, DC: Congressional Quarterly, 1994.

Election Results Directory. Denver: National Conference of State Legislatures, 1993– .

Encyclopedia of Associations. Detroit: Gale Research, 1961– .

Glashan, Roy R., *American Governors and Gubernatorial Elections, 1775–1978.* Westport, CT: Meckler Books, 1979.

The Handbook of State Legislative Leaders. Cambridge, MA: Ballinger Publishing, 1983/84–1992.

The Handbook of State Legislative Leaders. Centerville, MA: State Legislative Leaders Foundation, 1994– .

Inside the Legislature. Centerville, MA: State Legislative Leaders Foundation, 1993.

Mullaney, Marie Marmo, *American Governors and Gubernatorial Elections, 1979–1987.* Westport, CT: Meckler Books, 1988.

The National Directory of State Agencies. Washington, DC: Information Resources Press, 1974/75–1989.

Preuss, Arthur, *A Dictionary of Secret and Other Societies.* Detroit: Gale Research, 1966.

Rand McNally Commercial Atlas & Marketing Guide. Chicago: Rand McNally, 1983–   .

Ritter, Charles F., and Jon L. Wakelyn, eds., *American Legislative Leaders, 1850–1910.* New York: Greenwood Press, 1989.

Selected State Officials and the Legislatures. Lexington, KY: Council of State Governments, 1975.

State Administrative Officials Classified by Function. Lexington, KY: Council of State Governments, 1981/82–   .

State Administrative Officials Classified by Functions. Chicago: Council of State Governments, 1967–1979.

State Elective Officials and the Legislatures. Chicago: Council of State Governments, 1963–1973.

State Elective Officials and the Legislatures. Lexington, KY: Council of State Governments, 1977–   .

State Legislative Sourcebook. Topeka, KS: Government Research Service, 1986–   .

Who's Who in American Politics. New York: R. R. Bowker, 1967/68–   .

Who's Who in the East. Boston: Larkin, Roosevelt & Larkin, 1942/43–   .

Who's Who in the Midwest. Chicago: Marquis-Who's Who, 1949–   .

Who's Who in the South and Southwest. Chicago: Marquis-Who's Who, 1947–   .

Who's Who in the West. Chicago: Marquis-Who's Who, 1949–   .

The World Almanac and Book of Facts. New York: Press Publishing, 1923–   .

INTRODUCTION

Advisory Commission on Intergovernmental Relations, *The Question of State Government Capability.* Washington, DC: Advisory Commission on Intergovernmental Relations, 1985.

Beyle, Thad L., "Political Change in North Carolina: A Legislative Coup D'Etat," *Comparative State Politics Newsletter* 10 (April 1989): 3–15.

Brazil, Edward, and Andrew McNitt, "Speakers of the State Houses in an Era of Legislative Change." Paper presented at the April 1990 meeting of the Midwest Political Science Association, Chicago.

Browning, Robert X., "Indiana Elects Democratic Governor and Equally Divided House," *Comparative State Politics Newsletter* 10 (April 1989): 1–2.

Campbell, Ballard, "The State Legislature in American History: A Review Essay," *Historical Methods Newsletter* 9 (September 1976): 185–194.

Chaffey, Douglas Camp, and Malcolm E. Jewell, "Selection and Tenure of State Legislative Party Leaders: A Comparative Analysis," *The Journal of Politics* 34 (November 1972): 1278–1286.

Christensen, Rob, "Growing Republican Ranks Help Topple Speaker in North Carolina," *State Legislatures* 15 (April 1989): 16–19.

Eulau, Heinz, William Buchanan, LeRoy Ferguson, and John C. Wahlke, "Career Perspectives of American State Legislators," in Dwaine Marvick, ed., *Political Decision-Makers.* New York: Free Press of Glencoe, 1961: 218–263.

Hansen, Karen, "To the Democrats Go the Spoils," *State Legislatures* 16 (November/December 1990): 15–20.

Jacklin, Michele, "Conservative Democrats Are Victorious in Connecticut House," *State Legislatures* 15 (April 1989): 13–15.

Jewell, Malcolm E., "Editor's Introduction: The State of U.S. State Legislative Research," *Legislative Studies Quarterly* 6 (February 1981): 1–25.

Leonard, Lee, "Pro among Pros," *State Legislatures* 15 (November/December 1989): 13–15.

Maddox, Russell W., and Robert F. Fuquay, *State and Local Government*. 4th ed. New York: D. Van Nostrand, 1981.

Matthews, Donald R., "Legislative Recruitment and Legislative Careers," in Gerhard Loewenberg, Samuel C. Patterson, and Malcolm E. Jewell, eds., *Handbook of Legislative Research*. Cambridge, MA: Harvard University Press, 1985: 17–55.

McNeely, Dave, "Last of the Good Old Boys," *State Legislatures* 15 (November/December 1989): 27–29.

McNitt, Andrew, and Edward Brazil, "Speakers of the State Houses: 1960–1989," *Comparative State Politics* 14 (February 1993): 31–42.

Morandi, Larry, "She's Got Clout," *State Legislatures* 15 (November/December 1989): 16–17.

Morgan, Lucy, "In Florida a Coalition Saves Speaker-Designee," *State Legislatures* 15 (April 1989): 22–23.

"Oklahoma Ousts Speaker," *State Legislatures* 15 (July 1989): 9.

Paddock, Richard C., "A Speaker of Prominence," *State Legislatures* 15 (November/December 1989): 22–24.

Paterson, Andrea, "Is the Citizen Legislator Becoming Extinct?" *State Legislatures* 12 (July 1986): 22–25.

Polsby, Nelson W., "The Institutionalization of the U.S. House of Representatives," *The American Political Science Review* 62 (March 1968): 144–168.

Price, H. Douglas, "Congress and the Evolution of Legislative 'Professionalism,' " in Norman J. Ornstein, ed., *Congress in Change: Evolution and Reform*. New York: Praeger, 1975: 2–23.

Price, H. Douglas, "The Congressional Career: Then and Now," in Nelson W. Polsby, ed., *Congressional Behavior*. New York: Random House, 1971.

Ray, David, "Membership Stability in Three State Legislatures: 1893–1969," *The American Political Science Review* 68 (March 1974): 106–112.

Ray, David, "Voluntary Retirement and Electoral Defeat in Eight State Legislatures," *The Journal of Politics* 38 (May 1976): 426–433.

Rosenthal, Alan, "Turnover in State Legislatures," *American Journal of Political Science* 18 (August 1974): 609–616.

Shin, Kwang S., and John S. Jackson, III, "Membership Turnover in U.S. State Legislatures: 1931–1976," *Legislative Studies Quarterly* 4 (February 1979): 95–104.

Simon, Lucinda, "When Leaders Leave," *State Legislatures* 13 (February 1987): 16–18.

Stonecash, Jeffrey M., "Observations from New York: The Limits of 50-State Studies and the Case for Case Studies," *Comparative State Politics* 12 (August 1991): 1–9.

"Survey on Selection of State Legislative Leaders," *Comparative State Politics Newsletter* 1 (May 1980): 7–21.

Thompson, Joel A., "The 1989 North Carolina General Assembly: Beirut on a Bad Day," *Comparative State Politics* 10 (December 1989): 13–17.

Traub, Patrick J., "Speakers du Jour in Indiana," *State Legislatures* 15 (July 1989): 17–22.

Urdang, Laurence, ed., *The Timetables of American History*. New York: Simon and Schuster, 1981.

U.S. Bureau of the Census, *Historical Statistics of the United States, Colonial Times to 1957*. Washington, DC: U.S. Government Printing Office, 1960.

U.S. Bureau of the Census, *Statistical Abstract of the United States*. 111th ed. Washington, DC: U.S. Government Printing Office, 1991.

Weeks, George, and Don Weeks, "Taking Turns," *State Legislatures* 19 (July 1993): 19–25.

ALABAMA

Alabama Official and Statistical Register. Montgomery: State of Alabama, Department of Archives and History, 1903– .

Grove, Frank L., comp., *Library of Alabama Lives*. Hopkinsville, KY: Historical Records Association, 1961.

Havens, Murray Clark, *City versus Farm? Urban-Rural Conflict in the Alabama Legislature*. University, AL: Bureau of Public Administration, University of Alabama, 1957.

A Manual for Alabama Legislators. Montgomery: Legislative Reference Service, State of Alabama, 1942– .

Marks, Henry S., and Marsha Kass Marks, *Alabama Past Leaders*. Huntsville, AL: Strode Publishers, 1982.

Stewart, John Craig, *The Governors of Alabama*. Gretna, LA: Pelican Publishing, 1975.

Thomas, James D., and William H. Stewart, *Alabama Government & Politics*. Lincoln: University of Nebraska Press, 1988.

Who's Who in Alabama. Birmingham: Sayers Enterprises, 1965– .

ARKANSAS

Anderson, Peg, *Government in Arkansas*. Little Rock: League of Women Voters of Arkansas, 1989.

Arkansas Almanac: The Encyclopedia of Arkansas. Little Rock: Arkansas Almanac, 1954/55–1972.

The Arkansas Handbook. Little Rock: Arkansas History Commission, 1936– .

Blair, Diane D., *Arkansas Politics & Government: Do the People Rule?* Lincoln: University of Nebraska Press, 1988.

Herndon, Dallas Tabor, *Annals of Arkansas, 1947*. 4 vols. Hopkinsville, KY: Historical Records Association, 1947.

Hinshaw, Jerry E., *Call the Roll: The First One Hundred Fifty Years of the Arkansas Legislature*. Little Rock: Department of Arkansas Heritage, 1986.

Historical Report of the Secretary of State, Arkansas. Little Rock: Secretary of State, 1958– .

Nunn, Walter, ed., *Readings in Arkansas Government*. Little Rock: Rose Publishing, 1973.

Wells, Donald T., "The Arkansas Legislature," in Alex B. Lacy, Jr., ed., *Power in American State Legislatures: Case Studies of the Arkansas, Louisiana, Mississippi, and Oklahoma Legislatures*. New Orleans: Tulane University, 1967: 1–41.

FLORIDA

The Florida Handbook. Tallahassee: Peninsular Publishing, 1947/48–   .

Gatlin, Douglas S., "The Development of a Responsible Party System in the Florida Legislature," in James A. Robinson, ed., *State Legislative Innovation: Case Studies of Washington, Ohio, Florida, Illinois, Wisconsin, and California*. New York: Praeger, 1973: 1–45.

George, Paul S., ed., *A Guide to the History of Florida*. New York: Greenwood Press, 1989.

Guidebook to Florida Legislators. Baltimore: Legislative Guidebooks, 1993/94–   .

Havard, William C., and Loren P. Beth, *The Politics of Mis-Representation: Rural-Urban Conflict in the Florida Legislature*. Baton Rouge: Louisiana State University Press, 1962.

Huckshorn, Robert J., ed., *Government and Politics in Florida*. Gainesville: University of Florida Press, 1991.

The Miami Herald Almanac of Florida Politics. Miami: Miami Herald Publishing, 1994–   .

Morgan, Lucy, "In Florida a Coalition Saves Speaker-Designee," *State Legislatures* 15 (April 1989): 22–23.

Smith, C. Lynwood, Jr., *Strengthening the Florida Legislature*. New Brunswick, NJ: Rutgers University Press, 1970.

GEORGIA

Cook, James F., *Governors of Georgia*. Huntsville, AL: Strode Publishers, 1979.

The Georgia Annual: A Compendium of Useful Information about Georgia. Atlanta: A. B. Caldwell, 1911–   .

Georgia's Official Register. Atlanta: Georgia Department of Archives and History, 1923–1967/68.

Knight, Lucian Lamar, ed., *Encyclopedia of Georgia Biography*. Atlanta: A. H. Cawston, 1931.

McCullar, Bernice, *This Is Your Georgia*. Montgomery, AL: Viewpoint Publications, 1982.

Penkalski, Janice, "Georgia Legend Swings a Mean Gavel," *State Government News* 32 (February 1989): 5.

KENTUCKY

Blakey, George T., *Hard Times and New Deal in Kentucky, 1929–1939*. Lexington: University Press of Kentucky, 1986.

Cox, Gary S., "The Kentucky Legislative Interim Committee System, 1968–1974." Ph.D. dissertation, University of Kentucky, 1975.

Harrison, Lowell H., ed., *Kentucky's Governors, 1792–1985*. Lexington: University Press of Kentucky, 1985.

Jewell, Malcolm E., and Everett W. Cunningham, *Kentucky Politics*. Lexington: University of Kentucky Press, 1968.

Jewell, Malcolm E., and Penny M. Miller, *The Kentucky Legislature: Two Decades of Change*. Lexington: University Press of Kentucky, 1988.

Kentucky Directory for the Use of Courts, State and County Officials, and General Assembly of the State of Kentucky. Frankfort, 1914– .

Kleber, John E., ed., *The Kentucky Encyclopedia*. Lexington: University Press of Kentucky, 1992.

Loftus, Tom, and Al Cross, "Lies, Bribes and Videotapes," *State Legislatures* 19 (July 1993): 42–47.

Miller, Penny M., *Kentucky Politics & Government: Do We Stand United?* Lincoln: University of Nebraska Press, 1994.

Pearce, John Ed, *Divide and Dissent: Kentucky Politics, 1930–1963*. Lexington: University Press of Kentucky, 1987.

Scher, Seymour, "Conditions for Legislative Control," *The Journal of Politics* 25 (August 1963): 526–551.

Sexton, Robert F., "Kentucky Politics and Society, 1919–1932." Ph.D. dissertation, University of Washington, 1970.

LOUISIANA

Bolner, James, ed., *Louisiana Politics: Festival in a Labyrinth*. Baton Rouge: Louisiana State University Press, 1982.

Brown, Dave H., comp., *A History of Who's Who in Louisiana Politics in 1916*. New Orleans: Coste and Frichter, 1916.

Chambers, Henry E., *A History of Louisiana: Wilderness—Colony—Province—Territory—State—People*. Chicago: American Historical Society, 1925.

Davis, Edwin Adams, *The Story of Louisiana*. New Orleans: J. F. Hyer, 1960.

A Dictionary of Louisiana Biography. New Orleans: Louisiana Historical Association, 1988.

Lacy, Alex B., Jr., "The Louisiana Legislature," in Alex B. Lacy, Jr., ed., *Power in American State Legislatures: Case Studies of the Arkansas, Louisiana, Mississippi, and Oklahoma Legislatures*. New Orleans: Tulane University, 1967: 42–80.

Louisiana Legislature, 1992–1996: Grass Roots Guide. Lafayette, LA: Louisiana Governmental Studies, 1992.

Membership in the Legislature of Louisiana, 1880–1980. Baton Rouge: Louisiana Legislative Council, 1979.

MARYLAND

Brugger, Robert J., *Maryland: A Middle Temperament, 1634–1980*. Baltimore: Johns Hopkins University Press, 1988.

Callcott, George H., *Maryland & America, 1940–1980*. Baltimore: Johns Hopkins University Press, 1985.

Douglas, Robert, "Ben Cardin and the Family Dilemma," *Baltimore Magazine* 74 (February 1981): 56–61.

Maryland Manual. Annapolis: Hall of Records Commission.

Radoff, Morris L., *The Old Line State: A History of Maryland*. Hopkinsville, KY: Historical Records Association, 1956.

Rosenthal, Alan, *Strengthening the Maryland Legislature*. New Brunswick, NJ: Rutgers University Press, 1968.

MISSISSIPPI

Coleman, Mary DeLorse, *Legislators, Law, and Public Policy: Political Change in Mississippi and the South*. Westport, CT: Greenwood Press, 1993.

Fortenberry, C. N., "The Mississippi Legislature," in Alex B. Lacy, Jr., ed., *Power in American State Legislatures: Case Studies of the Arkansas, Louisiana, Mississippi, and Oklahoma Legislatures*. New Orleans: Tulane University, 1967: 81–130.

Kirwan, Albert Dennis, *The Revolt of the Rednecks: Mississippi Politics, 1876–1925*. Lexington: University of Kentucky Press, 1951.

Krane, Dale, and Stephen D. Shaffer, eds., *Mississippi Government & Politics: Modernizers versus Traditionalists*. Lincoln: University of Nebraska Press, 1992.

McLemore, Richard Aubrey, ed., *A History of Mississippi*. 2 vols. Jackson: University and College Press of Mississippi, 1973.

Mississippi Official and Statistical Register. Jackson: Secretary of State.

Ogle, David B., *Strengthening the Mississippi Legislature*. New Brunswick, NJ: Rutgers University Press, 1971.

NORTH CAROLINA

Beyle, Thad L., "Political Change in North Carolina: A Legislative Coup D'Etat," *Comparative State Politics Newsletter* 10 (April 1989): 3–15.

Cheney, John L., Jr., *North Carolina Government, 1585–1974: A Narrative and Statistical History*. Raleigh: North Carolina Department of the Secretary of State, 1975.

Christensen, Rob, "Growing Republican Ranks Help Topple Speaker in North Carolina," *State Legislatures* 15 (April 1989): 16–19.

Fleer, Jack D., *North Carolina Government & Politics*. Lincoln: University of Nebraska Press, 1994.

Lefler, Hugh Talmage, and Albert Ray Newsome, *The History of a Southern State: North Carolina*. Chapel Hill: University of North Carolina Press, 1973.

Luebke, Paul, *Tar Heel Politics: Myths and Realities*. Chapel Hill: University of North Carolina Press, 1990.

North Carolina Manual. Raleigh: North Carolina Historical Commission, 1917– .

Powell, William S., *North Carolina through Four Centuries*. Chapel Hill: University of North Carolina Press, 1989.

Powell, William S., ed., *Dictionary of North Carolina Biography*. 6 vols. Chapel Hill: University of North Carolina Press, 1979–1996.

Thompson, Joel A., "The 1989 North Carolina General Assembly: Beirut on a Bad Day," *Comparative State Politics* 10 (December 1989): 13–17.

OKLAHOMA

Directory of Oklahoma: State Almanac. Oklahoma City: Oklahoma Department of Libraries.
Harlow, Rex F., comp., *Makers of Government in Oklahoma.* Oklahoma City: Harlow Publishing, 1930.
Jones, Stephen, *Oklahoma Politics: In State and Nation.* Enid, OK: Haymaker Press, 1974– .
Kirkpatrick, Samuel A., *The Legislative Process in Oklahoma: Policy Making, People, & Politics.* Norman: University of Oklahoma Press, 1978.
Litton, Gaston, *History of Oklahoma at the Golden Anniversary of Statehood.* 4 vols. New York: Lewis Historical Publishing, 1957.
Morgan, David R., Robert E. England, and George G. Humphreys, *Oklahoma Politics & Policies: Governing the Sooner State.* Lincoln: University of Nebraska Press, 1991.
"Oklahoma Ousts Speaker," *State Legislatures* 15 (July 1989): 9.
Thoburn, Joseph B., and Muriel H. Wright, *Oklahoma: A History of the State and Its People.* 4 vols. New York: Lewis Historical Publishing, 1929.
Wood, John W., "The Oklahoma Legislature," in Alex B. Lacy, Jr., ed., *Power in American State Legislatures: Case Studies of the Arkansas, Louisiana, Mississippi, and Oklahoma Legislatures.* New Orleans: Tulane University, 1967: 131–171.

SOUTH CAROLINA

Bailey, N. Louise, Mary L. Morgan, and Carolyn R. Taylor, eds., *Biographical Directory of the South Carolina Senate, 1776–1985.* 3 vols. Columbia: University of South Carolina Press, 1986.
Biographical Directory of the South Carolina House of Representatives. Columbia: University of South Carolina Press, 1974– .
Carter, Luther F., and David S. Mann, eds., *Government in the Palmetto State.* Columbia: Bureau of Governmental Research and Service, 1983.
Cauthen, John K., *Speaker Blatt: His Challenges Were Greater.* Columbia: University of South Carolina Press, 1978.
Littlejohn, Bruce, *Littlejohn's Half Century at the Bench and Bar.* Columbia: South Carolina Bar Foundation, 1987.
South Carolina Legislative Manual. Columbia: General Assembly of South Carolina, 1916– .

TENNESSEE

Biographical file of Tennessee legislators, Tennessee State Library and Archives, Nashville.

Biographical Directory: Tennessee General Assembly, 1796–1969. Nashville: Tennessee State Library and Archives.

Blake, Morgan, and Stuart Towe, *Lawmakers and Public Men of Tennessee*. Nashville: Eagle Printing, 1915.

Greene, Lee Seifert, David H. Grubbs, and Victor C. Hobday. *Government in Tennessee*. 4th ed. Knoxville: University of Tennessee Press, 1982.

Hamer, Philip M., ed., *Tennessee: A History, 1673–1932*. 4 vols. New York: American Historical Society, 1933.

Moore, John Trotwood, ed., *Tennessee: The Volunteer State, 1769–1923*. 5 vols. Chicago: S. J. Clarke Publishing, 1923.

Tennessee Blue Book. Nashville: Secretary of State.

TEXAS

Adams, Frank Carter, *Texas Democracy: A Centennial History of Politics and Personalities of the Democratic Party, 1836–1936*. 4 vols. Austin: Democratic Historical Association, 1937.

Bailey, Emory E., ed., *Who's Who in Texas: A Biographical Directory*. Dallas: Who's Who Publishing, 1931.

Branda, Eldon Stephen, ed., *The Handbook of Texas: A Supplement*. Austin: Texas State Historical Association, 1976.

Brown, Norman D., *Hood, Bonnet, and Little Brown Jug: Texas Politics, 1921–1928*. College Station: Texas A&M University Press, 1984.

Calvert, Robert W., *Here Comes the Judge: From State Home to State House*. Waco, TX: Texian Press, 1977.

Gould, Lewis L., *Progressives and Prohibitionists: Texas Democrats in the Wilson Era*. Austin: University of Texas Press, 1973.

Green, George Norris, *The Establishment in Texas Politics: The Primitive Years, 1938–1957*. Westport, CT: Greenwood Press, 1979.

Johnson, Frank W., *A History of Texas and Texans*. 5 vols. Chicago: American Historical Society, 1914.

Jones, Eugene W., Joe E. Ericson, Lyle C. Brown, and Robert S. Trotter, Jr., *Practicing Texas Politics*. 8th ed. Boston: Houghton Mifflin, 1992.

Journal of the House of Representatives. Austin: Von Boeckmann-Jones, 1909– .

McNeely, Dave, "Last of the Good Old Boys," *State Legislatures* 15 (November/December 1989): 27–29.

Members of the Texas Legislature, 1846–1980. Austin: Texas Legislature, 1981.

Presiding Officers of the Texas Legislature, 1846–1982. Austin: Texas Legislative Council, 1982.

Texas Almanac and State Industrial Guide. Dallas: A. H. Belo, 1857– .

Wyatt, Frederica Burt, and Hooper Shelton, comps., *Coke R. Stevenson: A Texas Legend*. Junction, TX: Shelton Press, 1976.

VIRGINIA

Cooper, Weldon, and Thomas R. Morris, *Virginia Government and Politics: Readings and Comments*. Charlottesville: University Press of Virginia, 1976.

Dodson, E. Griffith, ed., *Speakers and Clerks of the Virginia House of Delegates, 1776–1976*. Rev. under the direction of Joseph H. Holleman, Jr. Richmond, 1976.

Heinemann, Ronald L., "Thomas B. Stanley: Reluctant Resister," in Edward Younger and James Tice Moore, eds., *The Governors of Virginia, 1860–1978*. Charlottesville: University Press of Virginia, 1982: 333–347.

History of Virginia. 6 vols. Chicago: American Historical Society, 1924.

WEST VIRGINIA

Brisbin, Richard A., Jr., Robert Jay Dilger, Allan S. Hammock, and Christopher Z. Mooney, *West Virginia Politics & Government*. Lincoln: University of Nebraska Press, 1996.

Comstock, Jim, ed., *The West Virginia Heritage Encyclopedia*. 25 vols. Richwood, WV, 1976.

Conley, Phil, ed., *The West Virginia Encyclopedia*. Charleston: West Virginia Publishing, 1929.

Appendix 1:
Political Party and Home County

1ST SPKR	NAME	POL PARTY	HOME COUNTY

ALABAMA

1911	ALMON EDWARD BERTON	DEM	COLBERT
1919	MERRITT HENRY PAUL	DEM	MACON
1920	LYNNE SEABOURN ARTHUR	DEM	MORGAN
1923	MERRILL HUGH DAVIS	DEM	CALHOUN
1927	LONG JOHN LEE	DEM	BUTLER
1935	WALKER ROBERT HENRY	DEM	LIMESTONE
1942	MILLER GEORGE OLIVER	DEM	SUMTER
1944	NORMAN CHARLES DOZIER	DEM	BULLOCK
1947	BECK WILLIAM MORRIS	DEM	DE KALB
1951	BROWN ROBERTS HENRY	DEM	LEE
1955	FITE ERNEST RANKIN	DEM	MARION
1959	ADAMS CHARLES CRAYTON III	DEM	TALLAPOOSA
1961	ASHWORTH VIRGIS MARION	DEM	BIBB
1963	BREWER ALBERT PRESTON	DEM	MORGAN
1971	LYONS GEORGE SAGE	DEM	MOBILE
1975	MCCORQUODALE JOSEPH CHARLES JR	DEM	CLARKE
1983	DRAKE THOMAS E	DEM	CULLMAN
1987	CLARK JAMES STERLING	DEM	BARBOUR

ARKANSAS

1911	MILWEE R FRANK	DEM	MONROE
1913	HARDAGE JOSIAH	DEM	CLARK
1915	SAWYER LEWIS ERNEST	DEM	GARLAND
1917	CAZORT WILLIAM LEE SR	DEM	JOHNSON
1919	NEWTON CLARENCE PRICE	DEM	PULASKI
1921	JOINER JOSEPH WILLIAM	DEM	COLUMBIA
1923	REED HOWARD	DEM	CLEBURNE
1925	HILL THOMAS AUSTIN	DEM	JEFFERSON
1927	CAUDLE REECE ARTHUR	DEM	POPE
1929	ABINGTON WILLIAM H	DEM	WHITE
1931	NEALE IRVING C	DEM	SEBASTIAN
1933	TONEY HARDIN KEMP	DEM	JEFFERSON
1935	THORN HARVEY BELL SR	DEM	POINSETT
1937	BRANSFORD JOHN MCKINNIS	DEM	LONOKE
1941	WILKINSON NORMAN MEANS	DEM	SEBASTIAN
1943	GRIFFITH ROBERT WILLIAM	DEM	PULASKI

STATE

1ST   NAME   POL   HOME COUNTY
SPKR   PARTY

ARKANSAS (*CONT.*)

1945   NORTHCUTT HORACE ALLEN   DEM   FULTON
1947   RIALES ROY LEE SR   DEM   POLK
1949   HENDRIX CARL EDWARD   DEM   SEVIER
1951   CAMPBELL JAMES R JR   DEM   GARLAND
1953   HOLLENSWORTH CARROLL C   DEM   BRADLEY
1955   SMITH CHARLES F JR   DEM   CRITTENDEN
1957   WALTHER GLENN F   DEM   PULASKI
1959   FLEEMAN EUGENE CECIL   DEM   MISSISSIPPI
1961   BETHELL JOHN PINCKNEY SR   DEM   PRAIRIE
1963   CRANK MARION HARLAN   DEM   LITTLE RIVER
1965   COTTRELL JOHN HALL JR   DEM   PULASKI
1967   COCKRILL STERLING ROBERTSON JR   DEM   PULASKI
1969   MCCLERKIN HAYES CANDOR   DEM   MILLER
1971   SMITH RAY S JR   DEM   GARLAND
1973   TURNER GROVER W JR   DEM   JEFFERSON
1975   ALEXANDER CECIL LEWIS   DEM   CLEBURNE
1977   SHAVER JAMES LEVESQUE JR   DEM   CROSS
1979   MILLER JOHN ELDON   DEM   IZARD
1981   MCCUISTON LLOYD CARLISLE JR   DEM   CRITTENDEN
1983   CAPPS JOHN PAUL   DEM   WHITE
1985   LANDERS H LACY   DEM   SALINE
1987   CUNNINGHAM ERNEST G   DEM   HELENA
1989   HENDRIX B G   DEM   SEBASTIAN

FLORIDA

1911   JENNINGS THOMAS ALBERT   DEM   ESCAMBIA
1915   HARDEE CARY AUGUSTUS   DEM   SUWANNEE
1918   WILDER GEORGE HAMILTON   DEM   HILLSBOROUGH
1921   JENNINGS FRANK E   DEM   DUVAL
1923   EDGE L DAY   DEM   LAKE
1925   MILAM ARTHUR YAGER   DEM   DUVAL
1927   DAVIS FRED HENRY   DEM   LEON
1929   GETZEN SAMUEL WYCHE   DEM   SUMTER
1931   LEWIS E CLAY JR   DEM   GULF
1933   TOMASELLO PETER JR   DEM   OKEECHOBEE
1935   BISHOP WILLIAM BURTON   DEM   JEFFERSON
1937   CHRISTIE WILLIAM MCLEAN   DEM   DUVAL
1939   WOOD GEORGE PIERCE   DEM   LIBERTY
1941   MCCARTY DANIEL THOMAS   DEM   SAINT LUCIE
1943   SIMPSON RICHARD HENRY   DEM   JEFFERSON
1945   CRARY EVANS SR   DEM   MARTIN
1947   BEASLEY THOMAS DEKALB   DEM   WALTON
1949   MURRAY PERRY EARL   DEM   POLK
1951   ELLIOTT ELMER B   DEM   PALM BEACH
1953   BRYANT CECIL FARRIS   DEM   MARION
1955   DAVID THOMAS E   DEM   BROWARD
1957   CONNER DOYLE E   DEM   BRADFORD
1961   CHAPPELL WILLIAM VENROE JR   DEM   MARION
1962   HORNE MALLORY ELI   DEM   LEON
1965   ROWELL E C   DEM   SUMTER

STATE

1ST SPKR	NAME	POL PARTY	HOME COUNTY

FLORIDA (*CONT.*)

1967	TURLINGTON RALPH DONALD	DEM	ALACHUA
1969	SCHULTZ FREDERICK HENRY	DEM	DUVAL
1971	PETTIGREW RICHARD ALLEN	DEM	DADE
1973	SESSUMS THOMAS TERRELL	DEM	HILLSBOROUGH
1975	TUCKER DONALD L	DEM	WAKULLA
1979	BROWN JAMES HYATT	DEM	VOLUSIA
1981	HABEN RALPH H JR	DEM	MANATEE
1983	MOFFITT H LEE	DEM	HILLSBOROUGH
1985	THOMPSON JAMES HAROLD	DEM	GADSDEN
1987	MILLS JON L	DEM	ALACHUA
1989	GUSTAFSON TOM	DEM	BROWARD

GEORGIA

1913	BURWELL WILLIAM HIX	DEM	HANCOCK
1921	NEILL WILLIAM CECIL	DEM	MUSCOGEE
1927	RUSSELL RICHARD BREVARD	DEM	BARROW
1931	TUCKER ARLIE DANIEL	DEM	BERRIEN
1933	RIVERS EURITH DICKINSON	DEM	LANIER
1937	HARRIS ROY VINCENT	DEM	RICHMOND
1941	EVANS RANDALL JR	DEM	MCDUFFIE
1947	HAND FREDRICK BARROW	DEM	MITCHELL
1955	MOATE MARVIN E	DEM	HANCOCK
1959	SMITH GEORGE LEON II	DEM	EMANUEL
1963	SMITH GEORGE THORNEWELL	DEM	GRADY
1974	MURPHY THOMAS BAILEY	DEM	HARALSON

KENTUCKY

1912	TERRELL CLAUDE B	DEM	TRIMBLE
1916	DUFFY HUGH CORNELIUS	DEM	HARRISON
1918	CROWE ROBERT T	DEM	OLDHAM
1920	BOSWORTH JOE F	REP	BELL
1922	THOMPSON JAMES H	DEM	BOURBON
1924	ADAMS SAMUEL W	DEM	KENTON
1926	DRURY GEORGE LUCIAN	DEM	UNION
1928	MILLIKEN JOHN S	DEM	SIMPSON
1932	BROWN JOHN YOUNG	DEM	FAYETTE
1933	LEBUS FRANK	DEM	HARRISON
1934	ROGERS W E SR	DEM	TODD
1935	BROWN WALLACE	DEM	NELSON
1936	KIRTLEY JOHN D	DEM	MCLEAN
1940	SHIELDS BENJAMIN FRANKLIN	DEM	SHELBY
1942	DICKSON STANLEY S	DEM	BOURBON
1944	WATERFIELD HARRY LEE	DEM	HICKMAN
1948	TINSLEY T HERBERT	DEM	CARROLL
1950	DORAN ADRON	DEM	CALLOWAY
1952	BURNLEY CHARLES W	DEM	MCCRACKEN
1956	FITZPATRICK THOMAS P	DEM	KENTON
1958	WEINTRAUB MORRIS	DEM	CAMPBELL

STATE

1ST SPKR	NAME	POL PARTY	HOME COUNTY

KENTUCKY (*CONT.*)

1960	LOWMAN HARRY KING	DEM	BOYD
1964	MCCALLUM SHELBY	DEM	MARSHALL
1968	CARROLL JULIAN MORTON	DEM	MCCRACKEN
1972	BLUME NORBERT	DEM	JEFFERSON
1976	KENTON WILLIAM G	DEM	FAYETTE
1982	RICHARDSON BOBBY HAROLD	DEM	BARREN
1986	BLANDFORD DONALD JOSEPH	DEM	DAVIESS

LOUISIANA

1912	THOMAS LEE EMMETT	DEM	CADDO
1916	BOUANCHAUD HEWITT LEONIDAS	DEM	POINTE COUPEE
1920	WALKER RICHARD FLOURNOY	DEM	EAST FELICIANA
1924	DOUGLAS JAMES STUART	DEM	CADDO
1926	HUGHES WILLIAM CLARK	DEM	BOSSIER
1928	FOURNET JOHN BAPTISTE	DEM	JEFFERSON DAVIS
1932	ELLENDER ALLEN JOSEPH	DEM	TERREBONNE
1936	WIMBERLY LORRIS M	DEM	BIENVILLE
1940	BAUER RALPH NORMAN	DEM	SAINT MARY
1952	AYCOCK CLARENCE C	DEM	SAINT MARY
1957	ANGELLE ROBERT	DEM	SAINT MARTIN
1960	JEWELL J THOMAS	DEM	POINTE COUPEE
1964	DELONY VAIL MONTGOMERY	DEM	EAST CARROLL
1968	GARRETT JOHN SIDNEY	DEM	CLAIBORNE
1972	HENRY EDGERTON L	DEM	JACKSON
1980	HAINKEL JOHN JOSEPH JR	DEM	ORLEANS
1984	ALARIO JOHN A JR	DEM	JEFFERSON
1988	DIMOS JIMMY N	DEM	OUACHITA

MARYLAND

1912	TRIPPE JAMES MCCONKY	DEM	BALTIMORE (IC)
1916	LAIRD PHILIP DANDRIDGE	DEM	MONTGOMERY
1917	MCINTOSH DAVID GREGG JR	DEM	BALTIMORE
1918	WOODEN HERBERT R	DEM	CARROLL
1920	TYDINGS MILLARD EVELYN	DEM	HARFORD
1922	LEE JOHN L G	DEM	HARFORD
1924	CURTIS FRANCIS P	DEM	BALTIMORE (IC)
1927	LEE EDWARD BROOKE	DEM	MONTGOMERY
1931	MICHEL FRANCIS A	DEM	BALTIMORE (IC)
1933	HARRINGTON T BARTON	DEM	BALTIMORE (IC)
1935	GORFINE EMANUEL	DEM	BALTIMORE (IC)
1939	CONLON THOMAS EDWARD	DEM	BALTIMORE (IC)
1943	WHITE JOHN S	DEM	PRINCE GEORGE'S
1947	SYBERT CORNELIUS FERDINAND	DEM	HOWARD
1951	LUBER JOHN CHRISTOPHER	DEM	BALTIMORE (IC)
1959	WILKINSON PERRY O	DEM	PRINCE GEORGE'S
1963	BOONE A GORDON	DEM	BALTIMORE
1964	MANDEL MARVIN	DEM	BALTIMORE (IC)
1969	LOWE THOMAS HUNTER	DEM	TALBOT

STATE

1ST SPKR	NAME	POL PARTY	HOME COUNTY

MARYLAND (CONT.)

1973	BRISCOE JOHN HANSON	DEM	SAINT MARY'S
1979	CARDIN BENJAMIN LOUIS	DEM	BALTIMORE (IC)
1987	MITCHELL R CLAYTON JR	DEM	KENT

MISSISSIPPI

1912	QUIN HILLRIE MARSHALL	DEM	HINDS
1916	CONNER MARTIN SENNETT	DEM	COVINGTON
1924	BAILEY THOMAS LOWRY	DEM	LAUDERDALE
1936	STANSEL HORACE SYLVAN	DEM	SUNFLOWER
1936	WRIGHT FIELDING LEWIS	DEM	SHARKEY
1940	LUMPKIN SAMUEL E	DEM	LEE
1944	SILLERS WALTER	DEM	BOLIVAR
1966	JUNKIN JOHN RICHARD	DEM	ADAMS
1976	NEWMAN CLARENCE BENTON	DEM	ISSAQUENA
1988	FORD TIMOTHY ALAN	DEM	LEE

NORTH CAROLINA

1911	DOWD WILLIAM CAREY	DEM	MECKLENBURG
1913	CONNOR GEORGE WHITFIELD	DEM	WILSON
1914	MURPHY WALTER	DEM	ROWAN
1915	WOOTEN EMMETT ROBINSON	DEM	LENOIR
1919	BRUMMITT DENNIS GARFIELD	DEM	GRANVILLE
1921	GRIER HARRY PERCY	DEM	IREDELL
1923	DAWSON JOHN GILMER	DEM	LENOIR
1925	PHARR EDGAR WALTER	DEM	MECKLENBURG
1927	FOUNTAIN RICHARD TILLMAN	DEM	EDGECOMBE
1929	GRAHAM ALEXANDER HAWKINS	DEM	ORANGE
1931	SMITH WILLIS	DEM	WAKE
1933	HARRIS REGINALD LEE	DEM	PERSON
1935	JOHNSON ROBERT GRADY	DEM	PENDER
1936	CHERRY ROBERT GREGG	DEM	GASTON
1939	WARD DAVID LIVINGSTONE JR	DEM	CRAVEN
1941	MULL ODUS MCCOY	DEM	CLEVELAND
1943	KERR JOHN HOSEA JR	DEM	WARREN
1945	RICHARDSON OSCAR LEON	DEM	UNION
1947	PEARSALL THOMAS JENKINS	DEM	NASH
1949	RAMSAY KERR CRAIGE	DEM	ROWAN
1951	TAYLOR WALTER FRANK	DEM	WAYNE
1953	BOST EUGENE THOMPSON JR	DEM	CABARRUS
1955	MOORE LARRY ICHABOD JR	DEM	WILSON
1957	DOUGHTON JAMES KEMP	DEM	ALLEGHANY
1959	HEWLETT ADDISON JR	DEM	NEW HANOVER
1961	HUNT JOSEPH MARVIN	DEM	GUILFORD
1963	BLUE HERBERT CLIFTON	DEM	MOORE
1965	TAYLOR HOYT PATRICK JR	DEM	ANSON
1967	BRITT DAVID MAXWELL	DEM	ROBESON
1967	VAUGHN EARL W	DEM	ROCKINGHAM
1969	GODWIN PHILIP PITTMAN	DEM	GATES

STATE

1ST SPKR	NAME	POL PARTY	HOME COUNTY

NORTH CAROLINA (*CONT.*)

1973	RAMSEY JAMES EDWARD	DEM	PERSON
1975	GREEN JAMES COLLINS	DEM	BLADEN
1977	STEWART CARL JEROME JR	DEM	GASTON
1981	RAMSEY LISTON BRYAN	DEM	MADISON
1989	MAVRETIC JOSEPHUS L	DEM	EDGECOMBE

OKLAHOMA

1910	ANTHONY WILLIAM BRUCE	DEM	STEPHENS
1911	DURANT WILLIAM ALEXANDER	DEM	BRYAN
1913	MAXEY JAMES HARVEY	DEM	MUSKOGEE
1915	MCCRORY ALONZO	DEM	JEFFERSON
1917	NESBITT PAUL	DEM	PITTSBURG
1919	WALDREP THOMAS CARNES	DEM	POTTAWATOMIE
1921	SCHWABE GEORGE BLAINE	REP	NOWATA
1923	GIBBONS MURRAY F	DEM	MCCLAIN
1923	MCBEE WILLIAM DALTON	DEM	STEPHENS
1925	HARPER JESSE B	DEM	LE FLORE
1927	STOVALL DAVID ANCIL	DEM	CHOCTAW
1929	STREET ALLEN MORGAN	DEM	OKLAHOMA
1929	NANCE JAMES CLARK	DEM	COTTON
1931	WEAVER CARLTON	DEM	LATIMER
1933	ANGLIN WILLIAM THOMAS	DEM	HUGHES
1935	PHILLIPS LEON CHASE	DEM	OKFUSKEE
1937	DANIEL J T	DEM	JEFFERSON
1939	WELCH WILLIAM DONOVAN SR	DEM	MARSHALL
1941	BLUMHAGEN E	DEM	BLAINE
1943	FREEMAN HAROLD	DEM	GARVIN
1944	LANSDEN JOSEPH MERLE	DEM	BEAVER
1945	HILL JOHNSON DAVIS	DEM	TULSA
1945	HINDS H IREDELLE	DEM	CHEROKEE
1947	BOARD CHARLES RAYMOND	DEM	CIMARRON
1949	BILLINGSLEY WALTER ASBURY	DEM	SEMINOLE
1951	BULLARD JAMES MARVIN	DEM	STEPHENS
1955	HARKEY BYRON E	DEM	OKLAHOMA
1959	LIVINGSTON CLINT GRAHAM	DEM	LOVE
1961	MCCARTY J D	DEM	OKLAHOMA
1967	PRIVETT ARNOLD REX	DEM	PAWNEE
1973	WILLIS WILLIAM PASCAL	DEM	CHEROKEE
1979	DRAPER DANIEL DAVID JR	DEM	PAYNE
1984	BARKER JIM L	DEM	MUSKOGEE
1989	LEWIS STEPHEN C	DEM	POTTAWATOMIE

SOUTH CAROLINA

1915	HOYT JAMES ALFRED	DEM	GREENVILLE
1918	COTHRAN THOMAS PERRIN	DEM	GREENVILLE
1921	ATKINSON JAMES BUFORD	DEM	SPARTANBURG
1923	MCMILLAN THOMAS SANDERS	DEM	CHARLESTON
1925	BROWN EDGAR ALLAN	DEM	BARNWELL

STATE

1ST SPKR	NAME	POL PARTY	HOME COUNTY

SOUTH CAROLINA (*CONT.*)

1927	HAMBLIN JOHN KNAPP	DEM	UNION
1933	GIBSON JAMES BREEDEN	DEM	MARLBORO
1935	TAYLOR CLAUDE AMBROSE	DEM	SPARTANBURG
1937	BLATT SOLOMON	DEM	BARNWELL
1947	LITTLEJOHN CAMERON BRUCE	DEM	SPARTANBURG
1949	POPE THOMAS HARRINGTON	DEM	NEWBERRY
1973	CARTER REX LYLE	DEM	GREENVILLE
1980	SCHWARTZ RAMON JR	DEM	SUMTER
1987	SHEHEEN ROBERT J	DEM	KERSHAW

TENNESSEE

1911	LEACH ALBERT MARTIN	DEM	MONTGOMERY
1913	STANTON WILLIAM MORTIMER	DEM	SHELBY
1915	COOPER WILLIAM PRENTICE	DEM	BEDFORD
1917	SHROPSHIRE CLYDE MOORE	DEM	DAVIDSON
1919	WALKER SETH MCKINNEY	DEM	WILSON
1921	TODD ANDREW LEE	DEM	RUTHERFORD
1923	HALL FRANK SAMPSON	DEM	DICKSON
1925	BARRY WILLIAM FRANCIS JR	DEM	MADISON
1927	MAIDEN SELDEN LONGLEY	DEM	WEAKLEY
1929	LOVE CHARLES HOWARD	DEM	ROBERTSON
1931	HAYNES WALTER MILLER	DEM	FRANKLIN
1933	MOORE FRANK WASHINGTON	DEM	HAMILTON
1939	O'DELL JOHN ED	DEM	SULLIVAN
1943	BROOME JAMES JESSE	DEM	MONTGOMERY
1945	WOODS GEORGE STANLEY	DEM	MCMINN
1947	LEWALLEN W BUFORD	DEM	ANDERSON
1949	FOUTCH MCALLEN	DEM	DE KALB
1953	BOMAR JAMES LA FAYETTE JR	DEM	BEDFORD
1963	BARRY WILLIAM LOGAN	DEM	HENDERSON
1967	CUMMINGS JAMES HARVEY II	DEM	CANNON
1969	JENKINS WILLIAM LEWIS	REP	HAWKINS
1971	MCKINNEY JAMES ROBIN	DEM	DAVIDSON
1973	MCWHERTER NED RAY	DEM	WEAKLEY
1987	MURRAY CHARLES EDWARD	DEM	FRANKLIN

TEXAS

1911	RAYBURN SAMUEL TALIAFERRO	DEM	FANNIN
1913	TERRELL CHESTER H	DEM	BEXAR
1915	WOODS JOHN WILLIAM	DEM	FISHER
1917	FULLER FRANKLIN OLIVER	DEM	SAN JACINTO
1919	THOMASON ROBERT EWING	DEM	EL PASO
1921	THOMAS CHARLES GRAHAM	DEM	DENTON
1923	SEAGLER RICHARD E	DEM	ANDERSON
1925	SATTERWHITE ROBERT LEE	DEM	POTTER
1927	BOBBITT ROBERT LEE	DEM	WEBB
1929	BARRON WINGATE STUART	DEM	BRAZOS
1931	MINOR FRED H	DEM	DENTON

STATE

1ST SPKR	NAME	POL PARTY	HOME COUNTY

TEXAS (*CONT.*)

1933	STEVENSON COKE ROBERT	DEM	KIMBLE
1937	CALVERT ROBERT WILBURN	DEM	HILL
1939	MORSE ROBERT EMMETT	DEM	HARRIS
1941	LEONARD HOMER L	DEM	HIDALGO
1943	DANIEL MARION PRICE SR	DEM	LIBERTY
1945	GILMER CLAUD H	DEM	EDWARDS
1947	REED WILLIAM OTEY	DEM	DALLAS
1949	MANFORD THOMAS DURWOOD JR	DEM	GONZALES
1951	SENTERFITT REUBEN	DEM	SAN SABA
1955	LINDSEY JIM THURSTON	DEM	BOWIE
1957	CARR WAGGONER	DEM	LUBBOCK
1961	TURMAN JAMES A	DEM	FANNIN
1963	TUNNELL BYRON M	DEM	SMITH
1965	BARNES BEN FRANK	DEM	COMANCHE
1969	MUTSCHER GUS FRANKLIN	DEM	WASHINGTON
1972	PRICE WILLIAM RAYFORD	DEM	ANDERSON
1973	DANIEL MARION PRICE JR	DEM	LIBERTY
1975	CLAYTON BILLY WAYNE	DEM	LAMB
1983	LEWIS GIBSON D	DEM	TARRANT

VIRGINIA

1914	COX EDWIN PIPER	DEM	RICHMOND (IC)
1916	HOUSTON HARRY RUTHERFORD	DEM	HAMPTON (IC)
1920	BREWER RICHARD LEWIS JR	DEM	SUFFOLK (IC)
1926	OZLIN THOMAS WILLIAM	DEM	LUNENBURG
1930	BROWN J SINCLAIR	DEM	ROANOKE
1936	DOVELL GROVER ASHTON	DEM	WILLIAMSBURG (IC)
1942	STANLEY THOMAS BAHNSON	DEM	HENRY
1947	MASSENBURG GEORGE ALVIN	DEM	HAMPTON (IC)
1950	MOORE EDGAR BLACKBURN	DEM	CLARKE
1968	COOKE JOHN WARREN	DEM	MATHEWS
1980	PHILPOTT ALBERT LEE	DEM	HENRY

WEST VIRGINIA

1911	WETZEL CHARLES MCCLUER	DEM	JEFFERSON
1913	GEORGE WILLIAM TAYLOR	REP	BARBOUR
1915	JOHNSON VERNON EMIL	REP	MORGAN
1917	THURMOND JOSEPH SAMUEL	DEM	GREENBRIER
1919	WOLFE J LUTHER	REP	JACKSON
1921	KEATLEY EDWIN MINER	REP	KANAWHA
1923	BYRNE WILLIAM ESTON RANDOLPH	DEM	KANAWHA
1929	CUMMINS JOHN WILLIAM	REP	OHIO
1931	TAYLOR JAMES ALFRED	DEM	FAYETTE
1933	HINER RALPH MCCLUNG	DEM	PENDLETON
1935	PELTER JOHN J	DEM	LOGAN
1937	THOMAS JAMES KAY	DEM	KANAWHA
1941	ARNOLD MALCOLM R	DEM	BOONE
1943	AMOS JOHN ELLISON	DEM	KANAWHA

STATE

1ST SPKR	NAME	POL PARTY	HOME COUNTY

WEST VIRGINIA (*CONT.*)

1949	FLANNERY W E	DEM	LOGAN
1958	PAULEY HARRY R	DEM	MCDOWELL
1961	SINGLETON JULIUS W JR	DEM	MONONGALIA
1965	WHITE H LABAN JR	DEM	HARRISON
1969	BOIARSKY IVOR F	DEM	KANAWHA
1971	MCMANUS LEWIS NICHOLS	DEM	RALEIGH
1977	KOPP DONALD LEE	DEM	HARRISON
1979	SEE CLYDE M JR	DEM	HARDY
1985	ALBRIGHT JOSEPH PAUL	DEM	WOOD
1987	CHAMBERS ROBERT C	DEM	CABELL

KEY:

1ST SPKR = YEAR FIRST SERVED AS SPEAKER

POL PARTY = POLITICAL PARTY AFFILIATION DURING SPEAKERSHIP
DEM = DEMOCRAT
REP = REPUBLICAN

HOME COUNTY = HOME COUNTY / PARISH DURING SPEAKERSHIP
(IC) = (INDEPENDENT CITY)

Appendix 2: Years in Speakership and House

STATE 1ST SPKR	NAME	1ST HSE	YRS BEF	YRS SPK	LAST SPKR	YRS HSE	LAST HSE
ALABAMA							
1911	ALMON EDWARD BERTON	1910	0	4	1914	4	1914
1919	MERRITT HENRY PAUL	1910	8	1	1919	9	1919
1920	LYNNE SEABOURN ARTHUR	1918	1	3	1922	4	1922
1923	MERRILL HUGH DAVIS	1899	2	8	1942	14	1942
1927	LONG JOHN LEE	1906	16	2	1929	18	1929
1935	WALKER ROBERT HENRY	1934	0	4	1938	4	1938
1942	MILLER GEORGE OLIVER	1926	16	2	1944	18	1944
1944	NORMAN CHARLES DOZIER	1926	18	2	1946	24	1950
1947	BECK WILLIAM MORRIS	1938	1	4	1950	5	1950
1951	BROWN ROBERTS HENRY	1938	9	4	1954	17	1958
1955	FITE ERNEST RANKIN	1950	4	8	1970	20	1974
1959	ADAMS CHARLES CRAYTON III	1950	8	2	1960	10	1960
1961	ASHWORTH VIRGIS MARION	1954	6	2	1962	8	1962
1963	BREWER ALBERT PRESTON	1954	8	4	1966	12	1966
1971	LYONS GEORGE SAGE	1969	2	4	1974	6	1974
1975	MCCORQUODALE JOSEPH CHARLES	1958	16	8	1982	24	1982
1983	DRAKE THOMAS E	1962	16	4	1986	28	N/A
1987	CLARK JAMES STERLING	1984	2	8	N/A	10	N/A
ARKANSAS							
1911	MILWEE R FRANK	1910	0	2	1912	2	1912
1913	HARDAGE JOSIAH	1910	2	2	1914	6	1918
1915	SAWYER LEWIS ERNEST	1912	2	2	1916	4	1916
1917	CAZORT WILLIAM LEE SR	1914	2	2	1918	4	1918
1919	NEWTON CLARENCE PRICE	1908	6	2	1920	8	1920
1921	JOINER JOSEPH WILLIAM	1914	4	2	1922	6	1922
1923	REED HOWARD	1918	4	2	1924	6	1924
1925	HILL THOMAS AUSTIN	1918	6	2	1926	8	1926
1927	CAUDLE REECE ARTHUR	1922	4	2	1928	6	1928
1929	ABINGTON WILLIAM H	1926	2	2	1930	10	1946
1931	NEALE IRVING C	1924	6	2	1932	8	1932
1933	TONEY HARDIN KEMP	1898	8	2	1934	24	1948
1935	THORN HARVEY BELL SR	1930	4	2	1936	6	1936
1937	BRANSFORD JOHN MCKINNIS	1930	6	4	1940	10	1940
1941	WILKINSON NORMAN MEANS	1932	8	1	1942	9	1942
1943	GRIFFITH ROBERT WILLIAM	1938	4	2	1944	6	1944

STATE

1ST SPKR	NAME	1ST HSE	YRS BEF	YRS SPK	LAST SPKR	YRS HSE	LAST HSE

ARKANSAS (CONT.)

1ST SPKR	NAME	1ST HSE	YRS BEF	YRS SPK	LAST SPKR	YRS HSE	LAST HSE
1945	NORTHCUTT HORACE ALLEN	1932	8	2	1946	10	1946
1947	RIALES ROY LEE SR	1938	8	2	1948	10	1948
1949	HENDRIX CARL EDWARD	1944	4	2	1950	6	1950
1951	CAMPBELL JAMES R JR	1928	18	2	1952	22	1954
1953	HOLLENSWORTH CARROLL C	1934	18	2	1954	25	1959
1955	SMITH CHARLES F JR	1948	6	2	1956	8	1956
1957	WALTHER GLENN F	1946	10	2	1958	20	1966
1959	FLEEMAN EUGENE CECIL	1944	14	2	1960	17	1962
1961	BETHELL JOHN PINCKNEY SR	1948	12	2	1962	24	1972
1963	CRANK MARION HARLAN	1950	12	2	1964	18	1968
1965	COTTRELL JOHN HALL JR	1954	10	2	1966	12	1966
1967	COCKRILL STERLING ROBERTSON	1956	10	2	1968	14	1970
1969	MCCLERKIN HAYES CANDOR	1960	8	2	1970	10	1970
1971	SMITH RAY S JR	1954	16	2	1972	28	1982
1973	TURNER GROVER W JR	1960	12	2	1974	32	1992
1975	ALEXANDER CECIL LEWIS	1962	12	2	1976	16	1978
1977	SHAVER JAMES LEVESQUE JR	1954	22	2	1978	40	N/A
1979	MILLER JOHN ELDON	1958	20	2	1980	36	N/A
1981	MCCUISTON LLOYD CARLISLE JR	1960	20	2	1982	34	N/A
1983	CAPPS JOHN PAUL	1962	20	2	1984	32	N/A
1985	LANDERS H LACY	1962	22	2	1986	32	N/A
1987	CUNNINGHAM ERNEST G	1968	18	2	1988	26	N/A
1989	HENDRIX B G	1962	26	2	1990	32	N/A

FLORIDA

1ST SPKR	NAME	1ST HSE	YRS BEF	YRS SPK	LAST SPKR	YRS HSE	LAST HSE
1911	JENNINGS THOMAS ALBERT	1910	0	2	1912	2	1912
1915	HARDEE CARY AUGUSTUS	1914	0	4	1918	.	.
1918	WILDER GEORGE HAMILTON	1914	3	3	1920	6	1920
1921	JENNINGS FRANK E	1920	0	2	1922	2	1922
1923	EDGE L DAY	1914	8	2	1924	10	1924
1925	MILAM ARTHUR YAGER	1922	2	2	1926	4	1926
1927	DAVIS FRED HENRY	1920	6	1	1927	7	1927
1929	GETZEN SAMUEL WYCHE	1922	6	2	1930	10	1936
1931	LEWIS E CLAY JR	1926	4	2	1932	12	1944
1933	TOMASELLO PETER JR	1928	4	2	1934	8	1940
1935	BISHOP WILLIAM BURTON	1920	8	2	1936	10	1936
1937	CHRISTIE WILLIAM MCLEAN	1932	4	2	1938	7	1939
1939	WOOD GEORGE PIERCE	1928	10	2	1940	12	1940
1941	MCCARTY DANIEL THOMAS	1936	4	1	1941	5	1941
1943	SIMPSON RICHARD HENRY	1938	4	2	1944	12	1950
1945	CRARY EVANS SR	1936	8	2	1946	10	1946
1947	BEASLEY THOMAS DEKALB	1938	6	4	1960	20	1962
1949	MURRAY PERRY EARL	1940	8	2	1950	15	1955
1951	ELLIOTT ELMER B	1944	6	2	1952	8	1952
1953	BRYANT CECIL FARRIS	1942	6	2	1954	10	1956
1955	DAVID THOMAS E	1948	6	2	1956	8	1956
1957	CONNER DOYLE E	1950	6	2	1958	10	1960
1961	CHAPPELL WILLIAM VENROE JR	1954	6	1	1961	12	1968
1962	HORNE MALLORY ELI	1954	7	3	1964	10	1964
1965	ROWELL E C	1956	8	2	1966	14	1970

STATE

1ST SPKR	NAME	1ST HSE	YRS BEF	YRS SPK	LAST SPKR	YRS HSE	LAST HSE
FLORIDA (*CONT.*)							
1967	TURLINGTON RALPH DONALD	1950	16	2	1968	24	1974
1969	SCHULTZ FREDERICK HENRY	1962	6	2	1970	8	1970
1971	PETTIGREW RICHARD ALLEN	1962	8	2	1972	10	1972
1973	SESSUMS THOMAS TERRELL	1962	10	2	1974	12	1974
1975	TUCKER DONALD L	1966	8	4	1978	12	1978
1979	BROWN JAMES HYATT	1972	6	2	1980	8	1980
1981	HABEN RALPH H JR	1972	8	2	1982	10	1982
1983	MOFFITT H LEE	1974	8	2	1984	10	1984
1985	THOMPSON JAMES HAROLD	1974	10	2	1986	12	1986
1987	MILLS JON L	1978	8	2	1988	10	1988
1989	GUSTAFSON TOM	1976	12	2	1990	14	1990
GEORGIA							
1913	BURWELL WILLIAM HIX	1894	8	4	1916	14	1918
1921	NEILL WILLIAM CECIL	1914	6	6	1926	12	1926
1927	RUSSELL RICHARD BREVARD	1920	6	4	1930	10	1930
1931	TUCKER ARLIE DANIEL	1924	6	2	1932	8	1932
1933	RIVERS EURITH DICKINSON	1924	2	4	1936	6	1936
1937	HARRIS ROY VINCENT	1920	12	8	1946	22	1946
1941	EVANS RANDALL JR	1930	8	2	1942	10	1942
1947	HAND FREDRICK BARROW	1932	12	8	1954	20	1954
1955	MOATE MARVIN E	1940	6	4	1958	22	1970
1959	SMITH GEORGE LEON II	1944	14	11	1973	29	1973
1963	SMITH GEORGE THORNEWELL	1958	4	4	1966	8	1966
1974	MURPHY THOMAS BAILEY	1960	13	21	N/A	34	N/A
KENTUCKY							
1912	TERRELL CLAUDE B	1911	0	4	1915	4	1915
1916	DUFFY HUGH CORNELIUS	1909	4	2	1917	12	1925
1918	CROWE ROBERT T	1915	2	2	1919	4	1919
1920	BOSWORTH JOE F	1905	2	2	1921	10	1933
1922	THOMPSON JAMES H	1919	2	2	1923	4	1923
1924	ADAMS SAMUEL W	1901	6	2	1925	8	1925
1926	DRURY GEORGE LUCIAN	1911	6	2	1927	8	1927
1928	MILLIKEN JOHN S	1925	2	4	1931	6	1931
1932	BROWN JOHN YOUNG	1929	2	1	1932	11	1967
1933	LEBUS FRANK	1933	0	1	1933	1	1933
1934	ROGERS W E SR	1913	2	1	1934	3	1934
1935	BROWN WALLACE	1911	3	1	1935	6	1937
1936	KIRTLEY JOHN D	1933	2	3	1938	5	1938
1940	SHIELDS BENJAMIN FRANKLIN	1919	6	2	1941	10	1953
1942	DICKSON STANLEY S	1933	6	2	1943	8	1943
1944	WATERFIELD HARRY LEE	1937	6	4	1947	12	1951
1948	TINSLEY T HERBERT	1941	2	2	1949	12	1965
1950	DORAN ADRON	1943	6	2	1951	8	1951
1952	BURNLEY CHARLES W	1943	8	4	1955	14	1957
1956	FITZPATRICK THOMAS P	1933	11	2	1957	18	1962
1958	WEINTRAUB MORRIS	1945	12	2	1959	14	1959

STATE

1ST SPKR	NAME	1ST HSE	YRS BEF	YRS SPK	LAST SPKR	YRS HSE	LAST HSE
KENTUCKY (*CONT.*)							
1960	LOWMAN HARRY KING	1941	16	4	1963	20	1963
1964	MCCALLUM SHELBY	1951	10	4	1967	16	1969
1968	CARROLL JULIAN MORTON	1961	6	4	1971	10	1971
1972	BLUME NORBERT	1963	8	4	1975	14	1977
1976	KENTON WILLIAM G	1969	6	6	1981	12	1981
1982	RICHARDSON BOBBY HAROLD	1971	10	4	1985	19	1990
1986	BLANDFORD DONALD JOSEPH	1967	18	7	1992	26	1993
LOUISIANA							
1912	THOMAS LEE EMMETT	1907	4	4	1915	8	1915
1916	BOUANCHAUD HEWITT LEONIDAS	1907	8	4	1919	12	1919
1920	WALKER RICHARD FLOURNOY	1903	4	4	1923	8	1923
1924	DOUGLAS JAMES STUART	1915	8	1	1924	9	1924
1926	HUGHES WILLIAM CLARK	1903	22	2	1927	27	1930
1928	FOURNET JOHN BAPTISTE	1927	0	4	1931	4	1931
1932	ELLENDER ALLEN JOSEPH	1923	8	4	1935	12	1935
1936	WIMBERLY LORRIS M	1927	8	9	1957	21	1957
1940	BAUER RALPH NORMAN	1927	8	8	1947	16	1947
1952	AYCOCK CLARENCE C	1951	0	4	1955	8	1959
1957	ANGELLE ROBERT	1935	21	3	1959	28	1963
1960	JEWELL J THOMAS	1935	24	4	1963	32	1967
1964	DELONY VAIL MONTGOMERY	1939	24	4	1967	28	1967
1968	GARRETT JOHN SIDNEY	1947	20	4	1971	24	1971
1972	HENRY EDGERTON L	1967	4	8	1979	12	1979
1980	HAINKEL JOHN JOSEPH JR	1967	12	4	1983	20	1987
1984	ALARIO JOHN A JR	1971	12	7	N/A	23	N/A
1988	DIMOS JIMMY N	1975	12	4	1991	19	N/A
MARYLAND							
1912	TRIPPE JAMES MCCONKY	1911	0	4	1915	4	1915
1916	LAIRD PHILIP DANDRIDGE	1885	20	1	1917	21	1917
1917	MCINTOSH DAVID GREGG JR	1913	3	1	1917	6	1919
1918	WOODEN HERBERT R	1911	6	2	1919	8	1919
1920	TYDINGS MILLARD EVELYN	1915	1	2	1921	3	1921
1922	LEE JOHN L G	1917	4	2	1923	6	1923
1924	CURTIS FRANCIS P	1899	10	3	1926	13	1926
1927	LEE EDWARD BROOKE	1926	0	4	1930	4	1930
1931	MICHEL FRANCIS A	1923	7	2	1932	9	1932
1933	HARRINGTON T BARTON	1930	2	2	1934	4	1934
1935	GORFINE EMANUEL	1930	4	4	1938	8	1938
1939	CONLON THOMAS EDWARD	1934	4	5	1943	9	1943
1943	WHITE JOHN S	1934	9	3	1946	12	1946
1947	SYBERT CORNELIUS FERDINAND	1946	0	4	1950	4	1950
1951	LUBER JOHN CHRISTOPHER	1938	12	8	1958	20	1958
1959	WILKINSON PERRY O	1942	16	4	1962	20	1962
1963	BOONE A GORDON	1946	16	1	1963	17	1964
1964	MANDEL MARVIN	1952	11	5	1968	16	1968
1969	LOWE THOMAS HUNTER	1958	10	5	1973	15	1973

STATE

1ST SPKR	NAME	1ST HSE	YRS BEF	YRS SPK	LAST SPKR	YRS HSE	LAST HSE
	MARYLAND (*CONT.*)						
1973	BRISCOE JOHN HANSON	1962	11	5	1978	16	1978
1979	CARDIN BENJAMIN LOUIS	1966	12	8	1986	20	1986
1987	MITCHELL R CLAYTON JR	1970	16	7	1993	23	1993
	MISSISSIPPI						
1912	QUIN HILLRIE MARSHALL	1899	8	4	1915	12	1915
1916	CONNER MARTIN SENNETT	1915	0	8	1923	8	1923
1924	BAILEY THOMAS LOWRY	1915	8	12	1935	24	1939
1936	STANSEL HORACE SYLVAN	1923	12	1	1936	13	1936
1936	WRIGHT FIELDING LEWIS	1931	5	3	1939	8	1939
1940	LUMPKIN SAMUEL E	1931	8	3	1942	11	1942
1944	SILLERS WALTER	1915	28	23	1966	51	1966
1966	JUNKIN JOHN RICHARD	1943	23	9	1975	32	1975
1976	NEWMAN CLARENCE BENTON	1951	24	12	1987	36	1987
1988	FORD TIMOTHY ALAN	1983	4	7	N/A	11	N/A
	NORTH CAROLINA						
1911	DOWD WILLIAM CAREY	1906	4	2	1912	8	1914
1913	CONNOR GEORGE WHITFIELD	1900	4	1	1913	5	1913
1914	MURPHY WALTER	1896	13	3	1918	34	1934
1915	WOOTEN EMMETT ROBINSON	1908	6	1	1915	7	1915
1919	BRUMMITT DENNIS GARFIELD	1914	4	2	1920	6	1920
1921	GRIER HARRY PERCY	1912	8	2	1922	10	1922
1923	DAWSON JOHN GILMER	1918	4	2	1924	6	1924
1925	PHARR EDGAR WALTER	1916	8	2	1926	10	1926
1927	FOUNTAIN RICHARD TILLMAN	1918	8	2	1928	10	1928
1929	GRAHAM ALEXANDER HAWKINS	1920	8	2	1930	10	1930
1931	SMITH WILLIS	1926	4	2	1932	6	1932
1933	HARRIS REGINALD LEE	1926	6	2	1934	14	1950
1935	JOHNSON ROBERT GRADY	1930	4	2	1936	6	1936
1936	CHERRY ROBERT GREGG	1930	6	2	1938	10	1940
1939	WARD DAVID LIVINGSTONE JR	1934	4	2	1940	10	1944
1941	MULL ODUS MCCOY	1906	8	2	1942	10	1942
1943	KERR JOHN HOSEA JR	1928	6	2	1944	22	1964
1945	RICHARDSON OSCAR LEON	1938	6	2	1946	8	1946
1947	PEARSALL THOMAS JENKINS	1940	6	2	1948	8	1948
1949	RAMSAY KERR CRAIGE	1940	8	2	1950	11	1951
1951	TAYLOR WALTER FRANK	1938	12	2	1952	14	1952
1953	BOST EUGENE THOMPSON JR	1936	16	2	1954	20	1958
1955	MOORE LARRY ICHABOD JR	1938	16	2	1956	22	1960
1957	DOUGHTON JAMES KEMP	1948	8	2	1958	10	1958
1959	HEWLETT ADDISON JR	1950	8	2	1960	10	1960
1961	HUNT JOSEPH MARVIN	1952	8	2	1962	10	1962
1963	BLUE HERBERT CLIFTON	1946	16	2	1964	18	1964
1965	TAYLOR HOYT PATRICK JR	1954	10	2	1966	12	1966
1967	BRITT DAVID MAXWELL	1958	8	1	1967	9	1967
1967	VAUGHN EARL W	1960	7	2	1969	9	1969
1969	GODWIN PHILIP PITTMAN	1960	9	3	1972	12	1972

STATE

1ST SPKR	NAME	1ST HSE	YRS BEF	YRS SPK	LAST SPKR	YRS HSE	LAST HSE

NORTH CAROLINA (*CONT.*)

1ST SPKR	NAME	1ST HSE	YRS BEF	YRS SPK	LAST SPKR	YRS HSE	LAST HSE
1973	RAMSEY JAMES EDWARD	1962	10	2	1974	12	1974
1975	GREEN JAMES COLLINS	1960	12	2	1976	14	1976
1977	STEWART CARL JEROME JR	1966	10	4	1980	14	1980
1981	RAMSEY LISTON BRYAN	1960	18	8	1988	32	N/A
1989	MAVRETIC JOSEPHUS L	1980	8	2	1990	14	N/A

OKLAHOMA

1ST SPKR	NAME	1ST HSE	YRS BEF	YRS SPK	LAST SPKR	YRS HSE	LAST HSE
1910	ANTHONY WILLIAM BRUCE	1907	4	0	1910	6	1912
1911	DURANT WILLIAM ALEXANDER	1907	4	2	1912	10	1916
1913	MAXEY JAMES HARVEY	.	.	2	1914	.	1916
1915	MCCRORY ALONZO	1912	2	2	1916	4	1916
1917	NESBITT PAUL	1914	2	2	1918	4	1918
1919	WALDREP THOMAS CARNES	1914	4	2	1920	6	1920
1921	SCHWABE GEORGE BLAINE	1918	2	2	1922	4	1922
1923	GIBBONS MURRAY F	1920	2	1	1923	3	1923
1923	MCBEE WILLIAM DALTON	1922	1	1	1924	2	1924
1925	HARPER JESSE B	1916	8	2	1926	10	1926
1927	STOVALL DAVID ANCIL	1918	8	2	1928	12	1930
1929	STREET ALLEN MORGAN	1918	6	0	1929	10	1932
1929	NANCE JAMES CLARK	1920	5	4	1954	17	1960
1931	WEAVER CARLTON	1930	0	2	1932	2	1932
1933	ANGLIN WILLIAM THOMAS	1918	2	2	1934	4	1934
1935	PHILLIPS LEON CHASE	1932	2	2	1936	6	1938
1937	DANIEL J T	1926	8	2	1938	12	1942
1939	WELCH WILLIAM DONOVAN SR	1934	4	2	1940	6	1940
1941	BLUMHAGEN E	1936	4	2	1942	6	1942
1943	FREEMAN HAROLD	1934	8	1	1943	9	1943
1944	LANSDEN JOSEPH MERLE	1940	3	1	1944	8	1964
1945	HILL JOHNSON DAVIS	1942	2	0	1945	2	1945
1945	HINDS H IREDELLE	1930	6	2	1946	8	1946
1947	BOARD CHARLES RAYMOND	1940	6	2	1948	8	1948
1949	BILLINGSLEY WALTER ASBURY	1940	8	2	1950	10	1950
1951	BULLARD JAMES MARVIN	1938	10	2	1952	22	1962
1955	HARKEY BYRON E	1950	4	4	1958	8	1958
1959	LIVINGSTON CLINT GRAHAM	1950	6	2	1960	8	1960
1961	MCCARTY J D	1940	20	6	1966	26	1966
1967	PRIVETT ARNOLD REX	1956	10	6	1972	16	1972
1973	WILLIS WILLIAM PASCAL	1958	14	6	1978	28	1986
1979	DRAPER DANIEL DAVID JR	1970	8	5	1983	14	1984
1984	BARKER JIM L	1976	7	6	1989	14	1990
1989	LEWIS STEPHEN C	1981	9	1	1990	10	1990

SOUTH CAROLINA

1ST SPKR	NAME	1ST HSE	YRS BEF	YRS SPK	LAST SPKR	YRS HSE	LAST HSE
1915	HOYT JAMES ALFRED	1914	0	3	1917	3	1917
1918	COTHRAN THOMAS PERRIN	1904	9	3	1921	12	1921
1921	ATKINSON JAMES BUFORD	1916	4	2	1922	8	1924
1923	MCMILLAN THOMAS SANDERS	1916	6	2	1924	8	1924
1925	BROWN EDGAR ALLAN	1920	4	2	1926	6	1926

1ST SPKR	NAME	1ST HSE	YRS BEF	YRS SPK	LAST SPKR	YRS HSE	LAST HSE
SOUTH CAROLINA (*CONT.*)							
1927	HAMBLIN JOHN KNAPP	1916	10	6	1932	16	1932
1933	GIBSON JAMES BREEDEN	1930	2	2	1934	4	1934
1935	TAYLOR CLAUDE AMBROSE	1930	4	2	1936	10	1944
1937	BLATT SOLOMON	1932	4	33	1973	54	1986
1947	LITTLEJOHN CAMERON BRUCE	1936	7	3	1949	10	1949
1949	POPE THOMAS HARRINGTON	1936	7	1	1950	8	1950
1973	CARTER REX LYLE	1952	21	7	1980	28	1980
1980	SCHWARTZ RAMON JR	1968	12	6	1986	18	1986
1987	SHEHEEN ROBERT J	1976	10	8	N/A	18	N/A
TENNESSEE							
1911	LEACH ALBERT MARTIN	1908	2	2	1912	4	1912
1913	STANTON WILLIAM MORTIMER	1910	2	2	1914	6	1916
1915	COOPER WILLIAM PRENTICE	1914	0	2	1916	2	1916
1917	SHROPSHIRE CLYDE MOORE	1914	2	2	1918	4	1918
1919	WALKER SETH MCKINNEY	1918	0	2	1920	2	1920
1921	TODD ANDREW LEE	1912	2	2	1922	4	1922
1923	HALL FRANK SAMPSON	1918	2	2	1924	8	1944
1925	BARRY WILLIAM FRANCIS JR	1922	2	2	1926	4	1926
1927	MAIDEN SELDEN LONGLEY	1914	4	2	1928	6	1928
1929	LOVE CHARLES HOWARD	1904	4	2	1930	6	1930
1931	HAYNES WALTER MILLER	1922	8	6	1938	18	1962
1933	MOORE FRANK WASHINGTON	1932	0	2	1934	2	1934
1939	O'DELL JOHN ED	1936	2	4	1942	6	1942
1943	BROOME JAMES JESSE	1942	0	2	1944	6	1950
1945	WOODS GEORGE STANLEY	1940	4	2	1946	6	1946
1947	LEWALLEN W BUFORD	1946	0	2	1948	2	1948
1949	FOUTCH MCALLEN	1942	6	4	1952	14	1958
1953	BOMAR JAMES LA FAYETTE JR	1942	4	10	1962	14	1962
1963	BARRY WILLIAM LOGAN	1954	8	4	1966	12	1966
1967	CUMMINGS JAMES HARVEY II	1930	16	2	1968	22	1972
1969	JENKINS WILLIAM LEWIS	1962	6	2	1970	8	1970
1971	MCKINNEY JAMES ROBIN	1968	2	2	1972	16	1984
1973	MCWHERTER NED RAY	1968	4	14	1986	18	1986
1987	MURRAY CHARLES EDWARD	1970	16	4	1990	20	1990
TEXAS							
1911	RAYBURN SAMUEL TALIAFERRO	1906	4	2	1912	6	1912
1913	TERRELL CHESTER H	1908	4	2	1914	6	1914
1915	WOODS JOHN WILLIAM	1912	2	2	1916	4	1916
1917	FULLER FRANKLIN OLIVER	1906	8	2	1918	10	1918
1919	THOMASON ROBERT EWING	1916	2	2	1920	4	1920
1921	THOMAS CHARLES GRAHAM	1916	4	2	1922	6	1922
1923	SEAGLER RICHARD E	1918	4	2	1924	6	1924
1925	SATTERWHITE ROBERT LEE	1900	8	2	1926	14	1932
1927	BOBBITT ROBERT LEE	1922	4	2	1928	6	1928
1929	BARRON WINGATE STUART	1924	4	2	1930	6	1930
1931	MINOR FRED H	1926	4	2	1932	6	1932

STATE

1ST SPKR	NAME	1ST HSE	YRS BEF	YRS SPK	LAST SPKR	YRS HSE	LAST HSE

TEXAS (*CONT.*)

1ST SPKR	NAME	1ST HSE	YRS BEF	YRS SPK	LAST SPKR	YRS HSE	LAST HSE
1933	STEVENSON COKE ROBERT	1928	4	4	1936	10	1938
1937	CALVERT ROBERT WILBURN	1932	4	2	1938	6	1938
1939	MORSE ROBERT EMMETT	1926	12	2	1940	18	1944
1941	LEONARD HOMER L	1930	10	2	1942	15	1945
1943	DANIEL MARION PRICE SR	1938	4	2	1944	6	1944
1945	GILMER CLAUD H	1938	6	2	1946	10	1948
1947	REED WILLIAM OTEY	1932	14	2	1948	18	1950
1949	MANFORD THOMAS DURWOOD JR	1940	8	2	1950	10	1950
1951	SENTERFITT REUBEN	1940	10	4	1954	14	1954
1955	LINDSEY JIM THURSTON	1948	6	2	1956	8	1956
1957	CARR WAGGONER	1950	6	4	1960	10	1960
1961	TURMAN JAMES A	1954	6	2	1962	8	1962
1963	TUNNELL BYRON M	1956	6	2	1964	8	1964
1965	BARNES BEN FRANK	1960	4	4	1968	8	1968
1969	MUTSCHER GUS FRANKLIN	1960	8	3	1972	12	1972
1972	PRICE WILLIAM RAYFORD	1960	11	1	1972	12	1972
1973	DANIEL MARION PRICE JR	1968	4	2	1974	6	1974
1975	CLAYTON BILLY WAYNE	1962	12	8	1982	20	1982
1983	LEWIS GIBSON D	1970	12	10	1992	22	1992

VIRGINIA

1ST SPKR	NAME	1ST HSE	YRS BEF	YRS SPK	LAST SPKR	YRS HSE	LAST HSE
1914	COX EDWIN PIPER	1903	10	2	1915	12	1915
1916	HOUSTON HARRY RUTHERFORD	1905	8	4	1919	14	1925
1920	BREWER RICHARD LEWIS JR	1911	8	6	1925	22	1933
1926	OZLIN THOMAS WILLIAM	1917	8	4	1929	12	1929
1930	BROWN J SINCLAIR	1915	14	6	1935	20	1935
1936	DOVELL GROVER ASHTON	1923	12	6	1941	18	1941
1942	STANLEY THOMAS BAHNSON	1929	12	5	1946	17	1946
1947	MASSENBURG GEORGE ALVIN	1925	21	3	1949	24	1949
1950	MOORE EDGAR BLACKBURN	1933	17	18	1967	35	1967
1968	COOKE JOHN WARREN	1941	26	12	1979	38	1979
1980	PHILPOTT ALBERT LEE	1957	22	12	1991	34	1991

WEST VIRGINIA

1ST SPKR	NAME	1ST HSE	YRS BEF	YRS SPK	LAST SPKR	YRS HSE	LAST HSE
1911	WETZEL CHARLES MCCLUER	1901	7	2	1912	10	1913
1913	GEORGE WILLIAM TAYLOR	1912	0	2	1914	2	1914
1915	JOHNSON VERNON EMIL	1910	4	4	1928	.	1928
1917	THURMOND JOSEPH SAMUEL	1914	2	2	1918	6	1920
1919	WOLFE J LUTHER	1914	2	2	1920	4	1920
1921	KEATLEY EDWIN MINER	1920	0	4	1926	8	1930
1923	BYRNE WILLIAM ESTON R	1922	0	2	1924	2	1924
1929	CUMMINS JOHN WILLIAM	1926	2	2	1930	8	1940
1931	TAYLOR JAMES ALFRED	1916	4	2	1932	8	1938
1933	HINER RALPH MCCLUNG	1928	4	2	1934	8	1936
1935	PELTER JOHN J	1932	2	2	1936	4	1936
1937	THOMAS JAMES KAY	1932	4	4	1940	10	1942
1941	ARNOLD MALCOLM R	1940	0	2	1942	4	1944
1943	AMOS JOHN ELLISON	1934	6	6	1948	12	1948

STATE

1ST SPKR	NAME	1ST HSE	YRS BEF	YRS SPK	LAST SPKR	YRS HSE	LAST HSE

WEST VIRGINIA (*CONT.*)

1ST SPKR	NAME	1ST HSE	YRS BEF	YRS SPK	LAST SPKR	YRS HSE	LAST HSE
1949	FLANNERY W E	1944	4	10	1958	14	1958
1958	PAULEY HARRY R	1936	12	2	1960	24	1974
1961	SINGLETON JULIUS W JR	1956	4	4	1964	8	1964
1965	WHITE H LABAN JR	1956	8	4	1968	12	1968
1969	BOIARSKY IVOR F	1958	10	3	1971	13	1971
1971	MCMANUS LEWIS NICHOLS	1964	7	5	1976	12	1976
1977	KOPP DONALD LEE	1964	12	2	1978	16	1982
1979	SEE CLYDE M JR	1974	4	6	1984	10	1984
1985	ALBRIGHT JOSEPH PAUL	1970	12	2	1986	14	1986
1987	CHAMBERS ROBERT C	1978	8	8	N/A	16	N/A

KEY:

   1ST SPKR = YEAR FIRST SERVED AS SPEAKER

   1ST HSE = YEAR FIRST ELECTED / APPOINTED TO HOUSE
      . = MISSING DATA

   YRS BEF = NUMBER OF YEARS SERVED IN HOUSE BEFORE SPEAKERSHIP
   YRS SPK = NUMBER OF YEARS SERVED AS SPEAKER AS OF 1994
   YRS HSE = NUMBER OF YEARS SERVED IN HOUSE AS OF 1994
      . = MISSING DATA

   LAST SPKR = YEAR LAST SERVED AS SPEAKER
   LAST HSE = YEAR LAST SERVED IN HOUSE
      . = MISSING DATA
      N/A = NOT APPLICABLE, STILL SERVING

Appendix 3: Legislative Pathways

1ST SPKR	NAME	LEAD	CHOS BY	LEAVE SPEAKER	LEAVE HOUSE
ALABAMA					
1911	ALMON EDWARD BERTON	NO	GOV	OTH ELEC	OTH ELEC
1919	MERRITT HENRY PAUL	NO	GOV	APPT ST	APPT ST
1920	LYNNE SEABOURN ARTHUR	YES	GOV	RET HSE	RET HSE
1923	MERRILL HUGH DAVIS	NO	GOV	RET HSE	RET HSE
1927	LONG JOHN LEE	NO	GOV	DEATH	DEATH
1935	WALKER ROBERT HENRY	NO	GOV	RET HSE	RET HSE
1942	MILLER GEORGE OLIVER	NO	GOV	DEATH	DEATH
1944	NORMAN CHARLES DOZIER	YES	GOV	LOST SPK	LOST HSE
1947	BECK WILLIAM MORRIS	NO	GOV	OTH ELEC	OTH ELEC
1951	BROWN ROBERTS HENRY	NO	GOV	LOST SPK	RET HSE
1955	FITE ERNEST RANKIN	NO	GOV	LOST SPK	ILLNESS
1959	ADAMS CHARLES CRAYTON III	NO	GOV	APPT ST	APPT ST
1961	ASHWORTH VIRGIS MARION	YES	GOV	RET HSE	RET HSE
1963	BREWER ALBERT PRESTON	NO	GOV	OTH ELEC	OTH ELEC
1971	LYONS GEORGE SAGE	NO	GOV	RET HSE	RET HSE
1975	MCCORQUODALE JOSEPH CHARLES	YES	MAJ	OTH ELEC	OTH ELEC
1983	DRAKE THOMAS E	NO	MAJ	RET SPK	N/A
1987	CLARK JAMES STERLING	YES	MAJ	N/A	N/A
ARKANSAS					
1911	MILWEE R FRANK	NO	MAJ	RET HSE	RET HSE
1913	HARDAGE JOSIAH	NO	MAJ	RET HSE	RET HSE
1915	SAWYER LEWIS ERNEST	NO	MAJ	RET HSE	RET HSE
1917	CAZORT WILLIAM LEE SR	NO	MAJ	OTH ELEC	OTH ELEC
1919	NEWTON CLARENCE PRICE	NO	MAJ	OTH ELEC	OTH ELEC
1921	JOINER JOSEPH WILLIAM	NO	MAJ	RET HSE	RET HSE
1923	REED HOWARD	NO	MAJ	.	.
1925	HILL THOMAS AUSTIN	NO	MAJ		
1927	CAUDLE REECE ARTHUR	NO	MAJ	APPT ST	APPT ST
1929	ABINGTON WILLIAM H	NO	MAJ	OTH ELEC	.
1931	NEALE IRVING C	NO	MAJ	DEATH	DEATH
1933	TONEY HARDIN KEMP	NO	MAJ	RET SPK	.
1935	THORN HARVEY BELL SR	NO	MAJ	OTH ELEC	OTH ELEC
1937	BRANSFORD JOHN MCKINNIS	YES	MAJ	OTH ELEC	OTH ELEC
1941	WILKINSON NORMAN MEANS	NO	MAJ	RET HSE	RET HSE
1943	GRIFFITH ROBERT WILLIAM	NO	MAJ	RET HSE	RET HSE

STATE

1ST SPKR	NAME	LEAD	CHOS BY	LEAVE SPEAKER	LEAVE HOUSE

ARKANSAS (*CONT.*)

1945	NORTHCUTT HORACE ALLEN	NO	MAJ	RET HSE	RET HSE
1947	RIALES ROY LEE SR	NO	MAJ	RET HSE	RET HSE
1949	HENDRIX CARL EDWARD	NO	MAJ	.	.
1951	CAMPBELL JAMES R JR	NO	MAJ	RET SPK	.
1953	HOLLENSWORTH CARROLL C	YES	MAJ	RET SPK	DEATH
1955	SMITH CHARLES F JR	NO	MAJ	OTH ELEC	OTH ELEC
1957	WALTHER GLENN F	NO	MAJ	RET SPK	.
1959	FLEEMAN EUGENE CECIL	NO	MAJ	RET SPK	DEATH
1961	BETHELL JOHN PINCKNEY SR	YES	MAJ	RET SPK	RET HSE
1963	CRANK MARION HARLAN	YES	MAJ	RET SPK	OTH ELEC
1965	COTTRELL JOHN HALL JR	YES	MAJ	LOST HSE	LOST HSE
1967	COCKRILL STERLING ROBERTSON	YES	MAJ	RET SPK	OTH ELEC
1969	MCCLERKIN HAYES CANDOR	YES	MAJ	OTH ELEC	OTH ELEC
1971	SMITH RAY S JR	YES	MAJ	RET SPK	RET HSE
1973	TURNER GROVER W JR	YES	MAJ	RET SPK	.
1975	ALEXANDER CECIL LEWIS	NO	MAJ	RET SPK	OTH ELEC
1977	SHAVER JAMES LEVESQUE JR	YES	MAJ	RET SPK	N/A
1979	MILLER JOHN ELDON	YES	MAJ	RET SPK	N/A
1981	MCCUISTON LLOYD CARLISLE JR	NO	MAJ	RET SPK	N/A
1983	CAPPS JOHN PAUL	YES	MAJ	RET SPK	N/A
1985	LANDERS H LACY	YES	MAJ	RET SPK	N/A
1987	CUNNINGHAM ERNEST G	NO	MAJ	RET SPK	N/A
1989	HENDRIX B G	YES	MAJ	RET SPK	N/A

FLORIDA

1911	JENNINGS THOMAS ALBERT	NO	MAJ	.	.
1915	HARDEE CARY AUGUSTUS	NO	MAJ	.	.
1918	WILDER GEORGE HAMILTON	NO	MAJ	RET HSE	RET HSE
1921	JENNINGS FRANK E	NO	MAJ	.	.
1923	EDGE L DAY	YES	MAJ	OTH ELEC	OTH ELEC
1925	MILAM ARTHUR YAGER	NO	MAJ	.	.
1927	DAVIS FRED HENRY	NO	MAJ	OTH ELEC	OTH ELEC
1929	GETZEN SAMUEL WYCHE	YES	MAJ	OTH ELEC	RET HSE
1931	LEWIS E CLAY JR	NO	MAJ	APPT ST	APPT ST
1933	TOMASELLO PETER JR	NO	MAJ	RET HSE	RET HSE
1935	BISHOP WILLIAM BURTON	NO	MAJ	RET HSE	RET HSE
1937	CHRISTIE WILLIAM MCLEAN	NO	MAJ	RET SPK	DEATH
1939	WOOD GEORGE PIERCE	YES	MAJ	RET HSE	RET HSE
1941	MCCARTY DANIEL THOMAS	NO	MAJ	RET HSE	RET HSE
1943	SIMPSON RICHARD HENRY	NO	MAJ	RET SPK	RET HSE
1945	CRARY EVANS SR	NO	MAJ	OTH ELEC	OTH ELEC
1947	BEASLEY THOMAS DEKALB	NO	MAJ	RET HSE	RET HSE
1949	MURRAY PERRY EARL	YES	MAJ	RET SPK	DEATH
1951	ELLIOTT ELMER B	NO	MAJ	RET HSE	RET HSE
1953	BRYANT CECIL FARRIS	NO	MAJ	RET SPK	OTH ELEC
1955	DAVID THOMAS E	NO	MAJ	.	.
1957	CONNER DOYLE E	NO	MAJ	RET SPK	OTH ELEC
1961	CHAPPELL WILLIAM VENROE JR	NO	MAJ	.	OTH ELEC
1962	HORNE MALLORY ELI	NO	MAJ	.	.
1965	ROWELL E C	NO	MAJ	RET SPK	RET HSE

STATE

1ST SPKR	NAME	LEAD	CHOS BY	LEAVE SPEAKER	LEAVE HOUSE

FLORIDA (CONT.)

1ST SPKR	NAME	LEAD	CHOS BY	LEAVE SPEAKER	LEAVE HOUSE
1967	TURLINGTON RALPH DONALD	NO	MAJ	RET SPK	APPT ST
1969	SCHULTZ FREDERICK HENRY	NO	MAJ	.	.
1971	PETTIGREW RICHARD ALLEN	YES	MAJ	OTH ELEC	OTH ELEC
1973	SESSUMS THOMAS TERRELL	YES	MAJ	RET HSE	RET HSE
1975	TUCKER DONALD L	NO	MAJ	.	.
1979	BROWN JAMES HYATT	YES	MAJ	RET HSE	RET HSE
1981	HABEN RALPH H JR	NO	MAJ	RET HSE	RET HSE
1983	MOFFITT H LEE	YES	MAJ	.	.
1985	THOMPSON JAMES HAROLD	NO	MAJ	.	.
1987	MILLS JON L	YES	MAJ	.	.
1989	GUSTAFSON TOM	NO	COAL	.	.

GEORGIA

1ST SPKR	NAME	LEAD	CHOS BY	LEAVE SPEAKER	LEAVE HOUSE
1913	BURWELL WILLIAM HIX	NO	GOV	LOST SPK	RET HSE
1921	NEILL WILLIAM CECIL	NO	GOV	.	.
1927	RUSSELL RICHARD BREVARD	YES	GOV	OTH ELEC	OTH ELEC
1931	TUCKER ARLIE DANIEL	YES	GOV	.	.
1933	RIVERS EURITH DICKINSON	NO	GOV	OTH ELEC	OTH ELEC
1937	HARRIS ROY VINCENT	NO	GOV	LOST HSE	LOST HSE
1941	EVANS RANDALL JR	NO	GOV	.	.
1947	HAND FREDRICK BARROW	YES	GOV	OTH ELEC	OTH ELEC
1955	MOATE MARVIN E	NO	GOV	LOST SPK	RET HSE
1959	SMITH GEORGE LEON II	YES	GOV	DEATH	DEATH
1963	SMITH GEORGE THORNEWELL	NO	GOV	OTH ELEC	OTH ELEC
1974	MURPHY THOMAS BAILEY	YES	MAJ	N/A	N/A

KENTUCKY

1ST SPKR	NAME	LEAD	CHOS BY	LEAVE SPEAKER	LEAVE HOUSE
1912	TERRELL CLAUDE B	NO	MAJ	RET HSE	RET HSE
1916	DUFFY HUGH CORNELIUS	NO	MAJ	RET HSE	RET HSE
1918	CROWE ROBERT T	YES	MAJ	RET HSE	RET HSE
1920	BOSWORTH JOE F	NO	MAJ	LOST SPK	RET HSE
1922	THOMPSON JAMES H	YES	MAJ	RET HSE	RET HSE
1924	ADAMS SAMUEL W	NO	MAJ	OTH ELEC	OTH ELEC
1926	DRURY GEORGE LUCIAN	NO	MAJ	RET HSE	RET HSE
1928	MILLIKEN JOHN S	NO	MAJ	RET HSE	RET HSE
1932	BROWN JOHN YOUNG	NO	MAJ	OTH ELEC	.
1933	LEBUS FRANK	NO	MAJ	.	.
1934	ROGERS W E SR	NO	MAJ	.	.
1935	BROWN WALLACE	NO	MAJ	RET SPK	OTH ELEC
1936	KIRTLEY JOHN D	NO	MAJ	APPT ST	APPT ST
1940	SHIELDS BENJAMIN FRANKLIN	NO	MAJ	RET HSE	.
1942	DICKSON STANLEY S	NO	MAJ	.	.
1944	WATERFIELD HARRY LEE	NO	MAJ	OTH ELEC	OTH ELEC
1948	TINSLEY T HERBERT	NO	MAJ	RET SPK	.
1950	DORAN ADRON	NO	MAJ	.	.
1952	BURNLEY CHARLES W	NO	MAJ	RET SPK	APPT ST
1956	FITZPATRICK THOMAS P	NO	MAJ	RET SPK	DEATH
1958	WEINTRAUB MORRIS	NO	MAJ	RET HSE	RET HSE

STATE

1ST SPKR	NAME	LEAD	CHOS BY	LEAVE SPEAKER	LEAVE HOUSE

KENTUCKY (*CONT.*)

1ST SPKR	NAME	LEAD	CHOS BY	LEAVE SPEAKER	LEAVE HOUSE
1960	LOWMAN HARRY KING	YES	MAJ	LOST HSE	LOST HSE
1964	MCCALLUM SHELBY	NO	MAJ	LOST SPK	RET HSE
1968	CARROLL JULIAN MORTON	NO	MAJ	OTH ELEC	OTH ELEC
1972	BLUME NORBERT	NO	MAJ	RET SPK	LOST HSE
1976	KENTON WILLIAM G	NO	MAJ	DEATH	DEATH
1982	RICHARDSON BOBBY HAROLD	YES	MAJ	LOST SPK	RET HSE
1986	BLANDFORD DONALD JOSEPH	NO	MAJ	RESN SPK	RESN HSE

LOUISIANA

1ST SPKR	NAME	LEAD	CHOS BY	LEAVE SPEAKER	LEAVE HOUSE
1912	THOMAS LEE EMMETT	NO	GOV	.	.
1916	BOUANCHAUD HEWITT LEONIDAS	NO	GOV	OTH ELEC	OTH ELEC
1920	WALKER RICHARD FLOURNOY	NO	GOV	RET HSE	RET HSE
1924	DOUGLAS JAMES STUART	NO	GOV	DEATH	DEATH
1926	HUGHES WILLIAM CLARK	NO	GOV	LOST SPK	DEATH
1928	FOURNET JOHN BAPTISTE	NO	GOV	OTH ELEC	OTH ELEC
1932	ELLENDER ALLEN JOSEPH	YES	GOV	.	.
1936	WIMBERLY LORRIS M	YES	GOV	APPT ST	APPT ST
1940	BAUER RALPH NORMAN	NO	GOV	RET HSE	RET HSE
1952	AYCOCK CLARENCE C	NO	GOV	LOST SPK	OTH ELEC
1957	ANGELLE ROBERT	NO	GOV	LOST SPK	.
1960	JEWELL J THOMAS	NO	GOV	LOST SPK	RET HSE
1964	DELONY VAIL MONTGOMERY	NO	GOV	DEATH	DEATH
1968	GARRETT JOHN SIDNEY	NO	GOV	RET HSE	RET HSE
1972	HENRY EDGERTON L	NO	GOV	OTH ELEC	OTH ELEC
1980	HAINKEL JOHN JOSEPH JR	NO	GOV	LOST SPK	OTH ELEC
1984	ALARIO JOHN A JR	YES	GOV	N/A	N/A
1988	DIMOS JIMMY N	NO	GOV	RET SPK	N/A

MARYLAND

1ST SPKR	NAME	LEAD	CHOS BY	LEAVE SPEAKER	LEAVE HOUSE
1912	TRIPPE JAMES MCCONKY	NO	MAJ	APPT ST	APPT ST
1916	LAIRD PHILIP DANDRIDGE	NO	MAJ	ILLNESS	ILLNESS
1917	MCINTOSH DAVID GREGG JR	NO	MAJ	RET SPK	RET HSE
1918	WOODEN HERBERT R	NO	MAJ	RET HSE	RET HSE
1920	TYDINGS MILLARD EVELYN	NO	MAJ	OTH ELEC	OTH ELEC
1922	LEE JOHN L G	NO	MAJ	.	.
1924	CURTIS FRANCIS P	NO	MAJ	APPT ST	APPT ST
1927	LEE EDWARD BROOKE	NO	MAJ	RET HSE	RET HSE
1931	MICHEL FRANCIS A	NO	MAJ	RET HSE	RET HSE
1933	HARRINGTON T BARTON	NO	MAJ	APPT FED	APPT FED
1935	GORFINE EMANUEL	NO	MAJ	OTH ELEC	OTH ELEC
1939	CONLON THOMAS EDWARD	NO	MAJ	OTH ELEC	OTH ELEC
1943	WHITE JOHN S	YES	MAJ	.	.
1947	SYBERT CORNELIUS FERDINAND	NO	MAJ	OTH ELEC	OTH ELEC
1951	LUBER JOHN CHRISTOPHER	YES	MAJ	LOST HSE	LOST HSE
1959	WILKINSON PERRY O	YES	MAJ	OTH ELEC	OTH ELEC
1963	BOONE A GORDON	YES	MAJ	RESN SPK	RESN HSE
1964	MANDEL MARVIN	YES	MAJ	APPT ST	APPT ST
1969	LOWE THOMAS HUNTER	YES	MAJ	APPT ST	APPT ST

STATE

1ST SPKR	NAME	LEAD	CHOS BY	LEAVE SPEAKER	LEAVE HOUSE

MARYLAND (CONT.)

1ST SPKR	NAME	LEAD	CHOS BY	LEAVE SPEAKER	LEAVE HOUSE
1973	BRISCOE JOHN HANSON	YES	MAJ	RET HSE	RET HSE
1979	CARDIN BENJAMIN LOUIS	YES	MAJ	OTH ELEC	OTH ELEC
1987	MITCHELL R CLAYTON JR	NO	MAJ	RET HSE	RET HSE

MISSISSIPPI

1ST SPKR	NAME	LEAD	CHOS BY	LEAVE SPEAKER	LEAVE HOUSE
1912	QUIN HILLRIE MARSHALL	NO	MAJ	OTH ELEC	OTH ELEC
1916	CONNER MARTIN SENNETT	NO	MAJ	OTH ELEC	OTH ELEC
1924	BAILEY THOMAS LOWRY	NO	MAJ	LOST SPK	OTH ELEC
1936	STANSEL HORACE SYLVAN	NO	MAJ	DEATH	DEATH
1936	WRIGHT FIELDING LEWIS	YES	MAJ	RET HSE	RET HSE
1940	LUMPKIN SAMUEL E	NO	MAJ	RET HSE	RET HSE
1944	SILLERS WALTER	NO	MAJ	DEATH	DEATH
1966	JUNKIN JOHN RICHARD	YES	MAJ	DEATH	DEATH
1976	NEWMAN CLARENCE BENTON	YES	MAJ	.	.
1988	FORD TIMOTHY ALAN	NO	MAJ	N/A	N/A

NORTH CAROLINA

1ST SPKR	NAME	LEAD	CHOS BY	LEAVE SPEAKER	LEAVE HOUSE
1911	DOWD WILLIAM CAREY	NO	MAJ	RET SPK	RET HSE
1913	CONNOR GEORGE WHITFIELD	NO	MAJ	APPT ST	APPT ST
1914	MURPHY WALTER	NO	MAJ	LOST SPK	RET HSE
1915	WOOTEN EMMETT ROBINSON	NO	MAJ	DEATH	DEATH
1919	BRUMMITT DENNIS GARFIELD	NO	MAJ	RET HSE	RET HSE
1921	GRIER HARRY PERCY	NO	MAJ	OTH ELEC	OTH ELEC
1923	DAWSON JOHN GILMER	NO	MAJ	LOST HSE	LOST HSE
1925	PHARR EDGAR WALTER	NO	MAJ	APPT ST	APPT ST
1927	FOUNTAIN RICHARD TILLMAN	NO	MAJ	OTH ELEC	OTH ELEC
1929	GRAHAM ALEXANDER HAWKINS	NO	MAJ	RET HSE	RET HSE
1931	SMITH WILLIS	NO	MAJ	RET HSE	RET HSE
1933	HARRIS REGINALD LEE	NO	MAJ	RET SPK	RET HSE
1935	JOHNSON ROBERT GRADY	NO	MAJ	.	.
1936	CHERRY ROBERT GREGG	NO	MAJ	RET SPK	RET HSE
1939	WARD DAVID LIVINGSTONE JR	NO	MAJ	RET SPK	OTH ELEC
1941	MULL ODUS MCCOY	NO	MAJ	RET HSE	RET HSE
1943	KERR JOHN HOSEA JR	NO	MAJ	RET SPK	RET HSE
1945	RICHARDSON OSCAR LEON	YES	MAJ	OTH ELEC	OTH ELEC
1947	PEARSALL THOMAS JENKINS	YES	MAJ	.	.
1949	RAMSAY KERR CRAIGE	NO	MAJ	RET SPK	DEATH
1951	TAYLOR WALTER FRANK	NO	MAJ	.	.
1953	BOST EUGENE THOMPSON JR	YES	MAJ	RET HSE	LOST HSE
1955	MOORE LARRY ICHABOD JR	NO	MAJ	RET SPK	RET HSE
1957	DOUGHTON JAMES KEMP	YES	MAJ	RET HSE	RET HSE
1959	HEWLETT ADDISON JR	YES	MAJ	OTH ELEC	OTH ELEC
1961	HUNT JOSEPH MARVIN	NO	MAJ	OTH ELEC	OTH ELEC
1963	BLUE HERBERT CLIFTON	NO	MAJ	OTH ELEC	OTH ELEC
1965	TAYLOR HOYT PATRICK JR	NO	MAJ	RET HSE	RET HSE
1967	BRITT DAVID MAXWELL	YES	MAJ	APPT ST	APPT ST
1967	VAUGHN EARL W	YES	MAJ	APPT ST	APPT ST
1969	GODWIN PHILIP PITTMAN	YES	MAJ	OTH ELEC	OTH ELEC

STATE

1ST SPKR	NAME	LEAD	CHOS BY	LEAVE SPEAKER	LEAVE HOUSE

NORTH CAROLINA (*CONT.*)

1ST SPKR	NAME	LEAD	CHOS BY	LEAVE SPEAKER	LEAVE HOUSE
1973	RAMSEY JAMES EDWARD	YES	MAJ	RET HSE	RET HSE
1975	GREEN JAMES COLLINS	YES	MAJ	OTH ELEC	OTH ELEC
1977	STEWART CARL JEROME JR	YES	MAJ	OTH ELEC	OTH ELEC
1981	RAMSEY LISTON BRYAN	YES	MAJ	LOST SPK	N/A
1989	MAVRETIC JOSEPHUS L	NO	COAL	LOST SPK	N/A

OKLAHOMA

1ST SPKR	NAME	LEAD	CHOS BY	LEAVE SPEAKER	LEAVE HOUSE
1910	ANTHONY WILLIAM BRUCE	YES	GOV	LOST SPK	.
1911	DURANT WILLIAM ALEXANDER	NO	GOV	LOST SPK	APPT ST
1913	MAXEY JAMES HARVEY	NO	GOV	LOST SPK	.
1915	MCCRORY ALONZO	NO	GOV	APPT ST	APPT ST
1917	NESBITT PAUL	YES	GOV	RET HSE	RET HSE
1919	WALDREP THOMAS CARNES	NO	GOV	RET HSE	RET HSE
1921	SCHWABE GEORGE BLAINE	NO	MAJ	LOST HSE	LOST HSE
1923	GIBBONS MURRAY F	NO	GOV	RESN HSE	RESN HSE
1923	MCBEE WILLIAM DALTON	NO	COAL	RET HSE	RET HSE
1925	HARPER JESSE B	NO	GOV	OTH ELEC	OTH ELEC
1927	STOVALL DAVID ANCIL	NO	GOV	LOST SPK	RET HSE
1929	STREET ALLEN MORGAN	NO	GOV	RESN SPK	LOST HSE
1929	NANCE JAMES CLARK	YES	COAL	LOST SPK	RET HSE
1931	WEAVER CARLTON	NO	GOV	RET HSE	RET HSE
1933	ANGLIN WILLIAM THOMAS	NO	GOV	OTH ELEC	OTH ELEC
1935	PHILLIPS LEON CHASE	NO	GOV	LOST SPK	OTH ELEC
1937	DANIEL J T	YES	GOV	.	.
1939	WELCH WILLIAM DONOVAN SR	NO	GOV	.	.
1941	BLUMHAGEN E	NO	GOV	.	.
1943	FREEMAN HAROLD	NO	GOV	RET HSE	RET HSE
1944	LANSDEN JOSEPH MERLE	NO	GOV	LOST SPK	RET HSE
1945	HILL JOHNSON DAVIS	NO	GOV	RET HSE	RET HSE
1945	HINDS H IREDELLE	NO	GOV	RET HSE	RET HSE
1947	BOARD CHARLES RAYMOND	NO	GOV	RET HSE	RET HSE
1949	BILLINGSLEY WALTER ASBURY	YES	GOV	RET HSE	RET HSE
1951	BULLARD JAMES MARVIN	NO	GOV	LOST SPK	OTH ELEC
1955	HARKEY BYRON E	NO	GOV	OTH ELEC	OTH ELEC
1959	LIVINGSTON CLINT GRAHAM	NO	GOV	APPT ST	APPT ST
1961	MCCARTY J D	NO	GOV	LOST HSE	LOST HSE
1967	PRIVETT ARNOLD REX	NO	MAJ	OTH ELEC	OTH ELEC
1973	WILLIS WILLIAM PASCAL	YES	MAJ	RET SPK	.
1979	DRAPER DANIEL DAVID JR	NO	MAJ	RESN HSE	RET HSE
1984	BARKER JIM L	NO	MAJ	LOST SPK	.
1989	LEWIS STEPHEN C	YES	COAL	.	.

SOUTH CAROLINA

1ST SPKR	NAME	LEAD	CHOS BY	LEAVE SPEAKER	LEAVE HOUSE
1915	HOYT JAMES ALFRED	NO	MAJ	RET HSE	RET HSE
1918	COTHRAN THOMAS PERRIN	NO	MAJ	APPT ST	APPT ST
1921	ATKINSON JAMES BUFORD	YES	MAJ	RET SPK	RET HSE
1923	MCMILLAN THOMAS SANDERS	YES	MAJ	OTH ELEC	OTH ELEC
1925	BROWN EDGAR ALLAN	NO	MAJ	OTH ELEC	OTH ELEC

STATE

1ST SPKR	NAME	LEAD	CHOS BY	LEAVE SPEAKER	LEAVE HOUSE

SOUTH CAROLINA (*CONT.*)

1ST SPKR	NAME	LEAD	CHOS BY	LEAVE SPEAKER	LEAVE HOUSE
1927	HAMBLIN JOHN KNAPP	NO	MAJ	.	.
1933	GIBSON JAMES BREEDEN	NO	MAJ	RET HSE	RET HSE
1935	TAYLOR CLAUDE AMBROSE	YES	MAJ	OTH ELEC	OTH ELEC
1937	BLATT SOLOMON	YES	MAJ	RET SPK	DEATH
1947	LITTLEJOHN CAMERON BRUCE	NO	MAJ	RET SPK	OTH ELEC
1949	POPE THOMAS HARRINGTON	NO	MAJ	OTH ELEC	OTH ELEC
1973	CARTER REX LYLE	YES	MAJ	RET HSE	RET HSE
1980	SCHWARTZ RAMON JR	YES	MAJ	RET HSE	RET HSE
1987	SHEHEEN ROBERT J	YES	MAJ	N/A	N/A

TENNESSEE

1ST SPKR	NAME	LEAD	CHOS BY	LEAVE SPEAKER	LEAVE HOUSE
1911	LEACH ALBERT MARTIN	NO	COAL	RET HSE	RET HSE
1913	STANTON WILLIAM MORTIMER	NO	COAL	RET SPK	RET HSE
1915	COOPER WILLIAM PRENTICE	NO	MAJ	RET HSE	RET HSE
1917	SHROPSHIRE CLYDE MOORE	NO	MAJ	OTH ELEC	OTH ELEC
1919	WALKER SETH MCKINNEY	NO	MAJ	RET HSE	RET HSE
1921	TODD ANDREW LEE	NO	MAJ	RET HSE	RET HSE
1923	HALL FRANK SAMPSON	NO	MAJ	OTH ELEC	RET HSE
1925	BARRY WILLIAM FRANCIS JR	NO	MAJ	APPT ST	APPT ST
1927	MAIDEN SELDEN LONGLEY	NO	MAJ	RET HSE	RET HSE
1929	LOVE CHARLES HOWARD	NO	MAJ	APPT ST	APPT ST
1931	HAYNES WALTER MILLER	NO	MAJ	RET HSE	RET HSE
1933	MOORE FRANK WASHINGTON	NO	MAJ	RET HSE	RET HSE
1939	O'DELL JOHN ED	NO	MAJ	.	.
1943	BROOME JAMES JESSE	NO	MAJ	RET SPK	.
1945	WOODS GEORGE STANLEY	NO	MAJ	.	.
1947	LEWALLEN W BUFORD	NO	MAJ	RET HSE	RET HSE
1949	FOUTCH MCALLEN	NO	MAJ	LOST SPK	RET HSE
1953	BOMAR JAMES LA FAYETTE JR	NO	MAJ	OTH ELEC	OTH ELEC
1963	BARRY WILLIAM LOGAN	YES	MAJ	RET HSE	RET HSE
1967	CUMMINGS JAMES HARVEY II	NO	MAJ	LOST SPK	RET HSE
1969	JENKINS WILLIAM LEWIS	NO	MAJ	APPT ST	APPT ST
1971	MCKINNEY JAMES ROBIN	YES	MAJ	LOST SPK	LOST HSE
1973	MCWHERTER NED RAY	YES	MAJ	OTH ELEC	OTH ELEC
1987	MURRAY CHARLES EDWARD	NO	MAJ	.	.

TEXAS

1ST SPKR	NAME	LEAD	CHOS BY	LEAVE SPEAKER	LEAVE HOUSE
1911	RAYBURN SAMUEL TALIAFERRO	NO	MAJ	OTH ELEC	OTH ELEC
1913	TERRELL CHESTER H	NO	MAJ	RET HSE	RET HSE
1915	WOODS JOHN WILLIAM	NO	MAJ	OTH ELEC	OTH ELEC
1917	FULLER FRANKLIN OLIVER	NO	MAJ	RET HSE	RET HSE
1919	THOMASON ROBERT EWING	NO	MAJ	OTH ELEC	OTH ELEC
1921	THOMAS CHARLES GRAHAM	YES	MAJ	.	.
1923	SEAGLER RICHARD E	YES	MAJ	APPT ST	APPT ST
1925	SATTERWHITE ROBERT LEE	NO	MAJ	RET SPK	RET HSE
1927	BOBBITT ROBERT LEE	NO	MAJ	APPT ST	APPT ST
1929	BARRON WINGATE STUART	NO	MAJ	RET HSE	RET HSE
1931	MINOR FRED H	NO	MAJ	RET HSE	RET HSE

STATE

1ST SPKR	NAME	LEAD	CHOS BY	LEAVE SPEAKER	LEAVE HOUSE

TEXAS (CONT.)

1ST SPKR	NAME	LEAD	CHOS BY	LEAVE SPEAKER	LEAVE HOUSE
1933	STEVENSON COKE ROBERT	NO	MAJ	RET SPK	OTH ELEC
1937	CALVERT ROBERT WILBURN	NO	MAJ	OTH ELEC	OTH ELEC
1939	MORSE ROBERT EMMETT	NO	MAJ	RET SPK	RET HSE
1941	LEONARD HOMER L	NO	MAJ	RET SPK	RET HSE
1943	DANIEL MARION PRICE SR	NO	MAJ	RET HSE	RET HSE
1945	GILMER CLAUD H	NO	MAJ	RET SPK	RET HSE
1947	REED WILLIAM OTEY	NO	MAJ	LOST SPK	OTH ELEC
1949	MANFORD THOMAS DURWOOD JR	NO	MAJ	RET HSE	RET HSE
1951	SENTERFITT REUBEN	NO	MAJ	RET HSE	RET HSE
1955	LINDSEY JIM THURSTON	NO	MAJ	RET HSE	RET HSE
1957	CARR WAGGONER	NO	MAJ	OTH ELEC	OTH ELEC
1961	TURMAN JAMES A	NO	MAJ	OTH ELEC	OTH ELEC
1963	TUNNELL BYRON M	NO	MAJ	APPT ST	APPT ST
1965	BARNES BEN FRANK	YES	MAJ	OTH ELEC	OTH ELEC
1969	MUTSCHER GUS FRANKLIN	YES	MAJ	RESN SPK	LOST HSE
1972	PRICE WILLIAM RAYFORD	YES	MAJ	LOST HSE	LOST HSE
1973	DANIEL MARION PRICE JR	NO	MAJ	RET HSE	RET HSE
1975	CLAYTON BILLY WAYNE	NO	MAJ	RET HSE	RET HSE
1983	LEWIS GIBSON D	YES	MAJ	.	.

VIRGINIA

1ST SPKR	NAME	LEAD	CHOS BY	LEAVE SPEAKER	LEAVE HOUSE
1914	COX EDWIN PIPER	YES	MAJ	RET HSE	RET HSE
1916	HOUSTON HARRY RUTHERFORD	NO	MAJ	RET HSE	RET HSE
1920	BREWER RICHARD LEWIS JR	YES	MAJ	RET SPK	RET HSE
1926	OZLIN THOMAS WILLIAM	NO	MAJ	RET HSE	RET HSE
1930	BROWN J SINCLAIR	YES	MAJ	RET HSE	RET HSE
1936	DOVELL GROVER ASHTON	YES	MAJ	RET HSE	RET HSE
1942	STANLEY THOMAS BAHNSON	NO	MAJ	OTH ELEC	OTH ELEC
1947	MASSENBURG GEORGE ALVIN	NO	MAJ	LOST HSE	LOST HSE
1950	MOORE EDGAR BLACKBURN	NO	MAJ	RET HSE	RET HSE
1968	COOKE JOHN WARREN	YES	MAJ	RET HSE	RET HSE
1980	PHILPOTT ALBERT LEE	YES	MAJ	DEATH	DEATH

WEST VIRGINIA

1ST SPKR	NAME	LEAD	CHOS BY	LEAVE SPEAKER	LEAVE HOUSE
1911	WETZEL CHARLES MCCLUER	NO	MAJ	LOST SPK	APPT FED
1913	GEORGE WILLIAM TAYLOR	NO	MAJ	.	.
1915	JOHNSON VERNON EMIL	NO	MAJ	APPT FED	APPT FED
1917	THURMOND JOSEPH SAMUEL	NO	MAJ	LOST SPK	.
1919	WOLFE J LUTHER	NO	MAJ	.	.
1921	KEATLEY EDWIN MINER	NO	MAJ	LOST SPK	LOST HSE
1923	BYRNE WILLIAM ESTON R	NO	MAJ	RET HSE	RET HSE
1929	CUMMINS JOHN WILLIAM	NO	MAJ	LOST SPK	.
1931	TAYLOR JAMES ALFRED	NO	MAJ	OTH ELEC	OTH ELEC
1933	HINER RALPH MCCLUNG	NO	MAJ	RET SPK	.
1935	PELTER JOHN J	NO	MAJ	.	.
1937	THOMAS JAMES KAY	YES	MAJ	RET SPK	RET HSE
1941	ARNOLD MALCOLM R	NO	MAJ	RET SPK	RESN HSE
1943	AMOS JOHN ELLISON	NO	MAJ	OTH ELEC	OTH ELEC

<u>STATE</u>

1ST SPKR	NAME	LEAD	CHOS BY	LEAVE SPEAKER	LEAVE HOUSE

<u>WEST VIRGINIA</u> (*CONT.*)

1949	FLANNERY W E	NO	MAJ	DEATH	DEATH
1958	PAULEY HARRY R	YES	MAJ	RET SPK	RET HSE
1961	SINGLETON JULIUS W JR	YES	MAJ	RET HSE	RET HSE
1965	WHITE H LABAN JR	NO	MAJ	RET HSE	RET HSE
1969	BOIARSKY IVOR F	YES	MAJ	DEATH	DEATH
1971	MCMANUS LEWIS NICHOLS	YES	MAJ	APPT ST	APPT ST
1977	KOPP DONALD LEE	YES	MAJ	LOST HSE	APPT ST
1979	SEE CLYDE M JR	YES	MAJ	OTH ELEC	OTH ELEC
1985	ALBRIGHT JOSEPH PAUL	YES	MAJ	.	.
1987	CHAMBERS ROBERT C	YES	MAJ	N/A	N/A

KEY:

1ST SPKR = YEAR FIRST SERVED AS SPEAKER

LEAD = MEMBER OF HOUSE LEADERSHIP BEFORE SPEAKERSHIP

CHOS BY = AUTHORITY RESPONSIBLE FOR CHOOSING SPEAKER
   MAJ = MAJORITY PARTY
   COAL = MULTIPARTY COALITION / COMPROMISE
   GOV = GOVERNOR

LEAVE SPEAKER = REASON FOR LEAVING SPEAKERSHIP
LEAVE HOUSE = REASON FOR LEAVING HOUSE
   . = MISSING DATA
   N/A = NOT APPLICABLE, STILL SERVING
   OTH ELEC = SOUGHT OTHER ELECTIVE OFFICE
   APPT ST = APPOINTED TO STATE OFFICE
   APPT FED = APPOINTED TO FEDERAL OFFICE
   RET HSE = VOLUNTARILY RETIRED FROM HOUSE
   LOST HSE = LOST ELECTION TO HOUSE
   RESN HSE = FORCED TO RESIGN FROM HOUSE
   RET SPK = VOLUNTARILY RETIRED / BARRED BY TRADITION FROM
        SPEAKERSHIP
   LOST SPK = LOST MAJORITY SUPPORT FOR SPEAKERSHIP
   RESN SPK = FORCED TO RESIGN FROM SPEAKERSHIP

Appendix 4:
Gender, Racial
Background, Birth, and
Death

1ST SPKR	NAME	GEN	RACE	BIRTHPLACE	YEAR BORN	YEAR DIED

ALABAMA

1911	ALMON EDWARD BERTON	M	W	ALABAMA	1860	1933
1919	MERRITT HENRY PAUL	M	W	ALABAMA	1873	1923
1920	LYNNE SEABOURN ARTHUR	M	W	ALABAMA	1877	1960
1923	MERRILL HUGH DAVIS	M	W	GEORGIA	1877	1954
1927	LONG JOHN LEE	M	W	ALABAMA	1867	1929
1935	WALKER ROBERT HENRY	M	W	ALABAMA	1875	1952
1942	MILLER GEORGE OLIVER	M	W	ALABAMA	1891	1944
1944	NORMAN CHARLES DOZIER	M	W	ALABAMA	1886	1951
1947	BECK WILLIAM MORRIS	M	W	ALABAMA	1903	1990
1951	BROWN ROBERTS HENRY	M	W	ALABAMA	1907	1971
1955	FITE ERNEST RANKIN	M	W	ALABAMA	1916	1980
1959	ADAMS CHARLES CRAYTON III	M	W	ALABAMA	1912	1982
1961	ASHWORTH VIRGIS MARION	M	W	ILLINOIS	1911	1975
1963	BREWER ALBERT PRESTON	M	W	TENNESSEE	1928	N/A
1971	LYONS GEORGE SAGE	M	W	ALABAMA	1936	N/A
1975	MCCORQUODALE JOSEPH CHARLES	M	W	ALABAMA	1920	N/A
1983	DRAKE THOMAS E	M	W	ALABAMA	1930	N/A
1987	CLARK JAMES STERLING	M	W	ALABAMA	1921	N/A

ARKANSAS

1911	MILWEE R FRANK	M	W	ARKANSAS	1872	1955
1913	HARDAGE JOSIAH	M	W	ARKANSAS	1868	1928
1915	SAWYER LEWIS ERNEST	M	W	ALABAMA	1867	1923
1917	CAZORT WILLIAM LEE SR	M	W	ARKANSAS	1887	1969
1919	NEWTON CLARENCE PRICE	M	W	ARKANSAS	1879	1958
1921	JOINER JOSEPH WILLIAM	M	W	ARKANSAS	1888	1932
1923	REED HOWARD	M	W	KANSAS	1883	1942
1925	HILL THOMAS AUSTIN	M	W	ARKANSAS	1889	1937
1927	CAUDLE REECE ARTHUR	M	W	ARKANSAS	1888	1955
1929	ABINGTON WILLIAM H	M	W	ARKANSAS	1871	1951
1931	NEALE IRVING C	M	W	ARKANSAS	1894	1932
1933	TONEY HARDIN KEMP	M	W	MISSISSIPP	1876	1955
1935	THORN HARVEY BELL SR	M	W	ARKANSAS	1885	1962
1937	BRANSFORD JOHN MCKINNIS	M	W	ARKANSAS	1901	1967
1941	WILKINSON NORMAN MEANS	M	W	ARKANSAS	1910	1991
1943	GRIFFITH ROBERT WILLIAM	M	W	ARKANSAS	1906	1960

STATE

1ST SPKR	NAME	GEN	RACE	BIRTHPLACE	YEAR BORN	YEAR DIED

ARKANSAS (*CONT.*)

1ST SPKR	NAME	GEN	RACE	BIRTHPLACE	YEAR BORN	YEAR DIED
1945	NORTHCUTT HORACE ALLEN	M	W	ARKANSAS	1883	1950
1947	RIALES ROY LEE SR	M	W	ARKANSAS	1909	1985
1949	HENDRIX CARL EDWARD	M	W	ARKANSAS	1906	.
1951	CAMPBELL JAMES R JR	M	W	ALABAMA	1893	1981
1953	HOLLENSWORTH CARROLL C	M	W	ARKANSAS	.	1959
1955	SMITH CHARLES F JR	M	W	ARKANSAS	1912	1962
1957	WALTHER GLENN F	M	W	ARKANSAS	1908	.
1959	FLEEMAN EUGENE CECIL	M	W	ARKANSAS	1907	1962
1961	BETHELL JOHN PINCKNEY SR	M	W	TENNESSEE	1907	1981
1963	CRANK MARION HARLAN	M	W	ARKANSAS	1915	N/A
1965	COTTRELL JOHN HALL JR	M	W	ARKANSAS	1917	N/A
1967	COCKRILL STERLING ROBERTSON	M	W	ARKANSAS	1925	N/A
1969	MCCLERKIN HAYES CANDOR	M	W	ARKANSAS	1931	N/A
1971	SMITH RAY S JR	M	W	ARKANSAS	1924	N/A
1973	TURNER GROVER W JR	M	W	ARKANSAS	1923	N/A
1975	ALEXANDER CECIL LEWIS	M	W	ARKANSAS	1935	N/A
1977	SHAVER JAMES LEVESQUE JR	M	W	ARKANSAS	1927	N/A
1979	MILLER JOHN ELDON	M	W	ARKANSAS	1929	N/A
1981	MCCUISTON LLOYD CARLISLE JR	M	W	TENNESSEE	1918	N/A
1983	CAPPS JOHN PAUL	M	W	ARKANSAS	1934	N/A
1985	LANDERS H LACY	M	W	ARKANSAS	1927	N/A
1987	CUNNINGHAM ERNEST G	M	W	ARKANSAS	1936	N/A
1989	HENDRIX B G	M	W	ARKANSAS	1922	N/A

FLORIDA

1ST SPKR	NAME	GEN	RACE	BIRTHPLACE	YEAR BORN	YEAR DIED
1911	JENNINGS THOMAS ALBERT	M	W	FLORIDA	1865	1917
1915	HARDEE CARY AUGUSTUS	M	W	FLORIDA	1876	1957
1918	WILDER GEORGE HAMILTON	M	W	FLORIDA	1870	1959
1921	JENNINGS FRANK E	M	W	KANSAS	1877	1966
1923	EDGE L DAY	M	W	GEORGIA	1891	1971
1925	MILAM ARTHUR YAGER	M	W	FLORIDA	1889	1956
1927	DAVIS FRED HENRY	M	W	S CAROLINA	1894	1937
1929	GETZEN SAMUEL WYCHE	M	W	FLORIDA	1898	1960
1931	LEWIS E CLAY JR	M	W	FLORIDA	1901	1961
1933	TOMASELLO PETER JR	M	W	FLORIDA	1900	1961
1935	BISHOP WILLIAM BURTON	M	W	FLORIDA	1890	1954
1937	CHRISTIE WILLIAM MCLEAN	M	W	FLORIDA	1892	1939
1939	WOOD GEORGE PIERCE	M	W	GEORGIA	1895	1945
1941	MCCARTY DANIEL THOMAS	M	W	FLORIDA	1912	1953
1943	SIMPSON RICHARD HENRY	M	W	ILLINOIS	1905	1968
1945	CRARY EVANS SR	M	W	FLORIDA	1905	1968
1947	BEASLEY THOMAS DEKALB	M	W	ALABAMA	1904	1988
1949	MURRAY PERRY EARL	M	W	GEORGIA	1899	1955
1951	ELLIOTT ELMER B	M	W	TEXAS	1903	1960
1953	BRYANT CECIL FARRIS	M	W	FLORIDA	1914	N/A
1955	DAVID THOMAS E	M	W	GEORGIA	1920	.
1957	CONNER DOYLE E	M	W	FLORIDA	1928	N/A
1961	CHAPPELL WILLIAM VENROE JR	M	W	FLORIDA	1922	1989
1962	HORNE MALLORY ELI	M	W	FLORIDA	1925	N/A
1965	ROWELL E C	M	W	FLORIDA	1914	1992

STATE

1ST SPKR	NAME	GEN	RACE	BIRTHPLACE	YEAR BORN	YEAR DIED

FLORIDA (*CONT.*)

1ST SPKR	NAME	GEN	RACE	BIRTHPLACE	YEAR BORN	YEAR DIED
1967	TURLINGTON RALPH DONALD	M	W	FLORIDA	1920	N/A
1969	SCHULTZ FREDERICK HENRY	M	W	FLORIDA	1929	N/A
1971	PETTIGREW RICHARD ALLEN	M	W	W VIRGINIA	1930	N/A
1973	SESSUMS THOMAS TERRELL	M	W	FLORIDA	1930	N/A
1975	TUCKER DONALD L	M	W	FLORIDA	1935	.
1979	BROWN JAMES HYATT	M	W	FLORIDA	1937	N/A
1981	HABEN RALPH H JR	M	W	GEORGIA	1941	N/A
1983	MOFFITT H LEE	M	W	FLORIDA	1941	N/A
1985	THOMPSON JAMES HAROLD	M	W	ALABAMA	1944	N/A
1987	MILLS JON L	M	W	FLORIDA	1947	N/A
1989	GUSTAFSON TOM	M	W	NEW JERSEY	1949	N/A

GEORGIA

1ST SPKR	NAME	GEN	RACE	BIRTHPLACE	YEAR BORN	YEAR DIED
1913	BURWELL WILLIAM HIX	M	W	MARYLAND	1869	1953
1921	NEILL WILLIAM CECIL	M	W	GEORGIA	1880	1932
1927	RUSSELL RICHARD BREVARD	M	W	GEORGIA	1897	1971
1931	TUCKER ARLIE DANIEL	M	W	GEORGIA	1894	1974
1933	RIVERS EURITH DICKINSON	M	W	ARKANSAS	1895	1967
1937	HARRIS ROY VINCENT	M	W	GEORGIA	1895	1985
1941	EVANS RANDALL JR	M	W	GEORGIA	1906	.
1947	HAND FREDRICK BARROW	M	W	GEORGIA	1904	1978
1955	MOATE MARVIN E	M	W	GEORGIA	1910	1984
1959	SMITH GEORGE LEON II	M	W	GEORGIA	1912	1973
1963	SMITH GEORGE THORNEWELL	M	W	GEORGIA	1916	N/A
1974	MURPHY THOMAS BAILEY	M	W	GEORGIA	1924	N/A

KENTUCKY

1ST SPKR	NAME	GEN	RACE	BIRTHPLACE	YEAR BORN	YEAR DIED
1912	TERRELL CLAUDE B	M	W	KENTUCKY	1871	1922
1916	DUFFY HUGH CORNELIUS	M	W	TENNESSEE	1854	1941
1918	CROWE ROBERT T	M	W	CANADA	1875	1937
1920	BOSWORTH JOE F	M	W	KENTUCKY	1867	1939
1922	THOMPSON JAMES H	M	W	KENTUCKY	1872	1950
1924	ADAMS SAMUEL W	M	W	KENTUCKY	1873	1954
1926	DRURY GEORGE LUCIAN	M	W	KENTUCKY	1875	1940
1928	MILLIKEN JOHN S	M	W	KENTUCKY	1891	1948
1932	BROWN JOHN YOUNG	M	W	KENTUCKY	1900	1985
1933	LEBUS FRANK	M	W	KENTUCKY	1882	1962
1934	ROGERS W E SR	M	W	TENNESSEE	1880	1951
1935	BROWN WALLACE	M	W	KENTUCKY	1874	1964
1936	KIRTLEY JOHN D	M	W	KENTUCKY	1900	1978
1940	SHIELDS BENJAMIN FRANKLIN	M	W	KENTUCKY	1881	1969
1942	DICKSON STANLEY S	M	W	KENTUCKY	1897	1973
1944	WATERFIELD HARRY LEE	M	W	KENTUCKY	1911	1988
1948	TINSLEY T HERBERT	M	W	MISSOURI	1889	1966
1950	DORAN ADRON	M	W	TENNESSEE	1909	N/A
1952	BURNLEY CHARLES W	M	W	KENTUCKY	1904	1962
1956	FITZPATRICK THOMAS P	M	W	KENTUCKY	1894	1962
1958	WEINTRAUB MORRIS	M	W	KENTUCKY	1909	N/A

STATE

1ST SPKR	NAME	GEN	RACE	BIRTHPLACE	YEAR BORN	YEAR DIED

KENTUCKY (*CONT.*)

1ST SPKR	NAME	GEN	RACE	BIRTHPLACE	YEAR BORN	YEAR DIED
1960	LOWMAN HARRY KING	M	W	KENTUCKY	1913	1977
1964	MCCALLUM SHELBY	M	W	KENTUCKY	1918	1987
1968	CARROLL JULIAN MORTON	M	W	KENTUCKY	1931	N/A
1972	BLUME NORBERT	M	W	KENTUCKY	1922	N/A
1976	KENTON WILLIAM G	M	W	KENTUCKY	1941	1981
1982	RICHARDSON BOBBY HAROLD	M	W	KENTUCKY	1944	N/A
1986	BLANDFORD DONALD JOSEPH	M	W	.	1938	N/A

LOUISIANA

1ST SPKR	NAME	GEN	RACE	BIRTHPLACE	YEAR BORN	YEAR DIED
1912	THOMAS LEE EMMETT	M	W	LOUISIANA	1866	1935
1916	BOUANCHAUD HEWITT LEONIDAS	M	W	LOUISIANA	1877	1950
1920	WALKER RICHARD FLOURNOY	M	W	MISSISSIPP	1868	1949
1924	DOUGLAS JAMES STUART	M	W	LOUISIANA	1876	1924
1926	HUGHES WILLIAM CLARK	M	W	LOUISIANA	1868	1930
1928	FOURNET JOHN BAPTISTE	M	W	LOUISIANA	1895	1984
1932	ELLENDER ALLEN JOSEPH	M	W	LOUISIANA	1890	1972
1936	WIMBERLY LORRIS M	M	W	LOUISIANA	1898	1962
1940	BAUER RALPH NORMAN	M	W	LOUISIANA	1899	1963
1952	AYCOCK CLARENCE C	M	W	LOUISIANA	.	1987
1957	ANGELLE ROBERT	M	W	LOUISIANA	1896	1979
1960	JEWELL J THOMAS	M	W	LOUISIANA	1909	1993
1964	DELONY VAIL MONTGOMERY	M	W	LOUISIANA	1901	1967
1968	GARRETT JOHN SIDNEY	M	W	LOUISIANA	1922	N/A
1972	HENRY EDGERTON L	M	W	LOUISIANA	1936	N/A
1980	HAINKEL JOHN JOSEPH JR	M	W	LOUISIANA	1938	N/A
1984	ALARIO JOHN A JR	M	W	LOUISIANA	1943	N/A
1988	DIMOS JIMMY N	M	W	.	1938	N/A

MARYLAND

1ST SPKR	NAME	GEN	RACE	BIRTHPLACE	YEAR BORN	YEAR DIED
1912	TRIPPE JAMES MCCONKY	M	W	MARYLAND	1874	1936
1916	LAIRD PHILIP DANDRIDGE	M	W	MARYLAND	1847	1920
1917	MCINTOSH DAVID GREGG JR	M	W	MARYLAND	1877	1940
1918	WOODEN HERBERT R	M	W	PENNSYLVAN	1877	1959
1920	TYDINGS MILLARD EVELYN	M	W	MARYLAND	1890	1961
1922	LEE JOHN L G	M	W	MARYLAND	.	1952
1924	CURTIS FRANCIS P	M	W	MARYLAND	1866	1933
1927	LEE EDWARD BROOKE	M	W	DIST COLUM	1892	1984
1931	MICHEL FRANCIS A	M	W	MARYLAND	1892	1962
1933	HARRINGTON T BARTON	M	W	MARYLAND	1897	1974
1935	GORFINE EMANUEL	M	W	MARYLAND	1895	1984
1939	CONLON THOMAS EDWARD	M	W	OHIO	1883	1943
1943	WHITE JOHN S	M	W	PENNSYLVAN	.	1960
1947	SYBERT CORNELIUS FERDINAND	M	W	PENNSYLVAN	1900	1982
1951	LUBER JOHN CHRISTOPHER	M	W	MARYLAND	1903	1962
1959	WILKINSON PERRY O	M	W	MARYLAND	1905	1979
1963	BOONE A GORDON	M	W	MARYLAND	1910	1988
1964	MANDEL MARVIN	M	W	MARYLAND	1920	N/A
1969	LOWE THOMAS HUNTER	M	W	MARYLAND	1928	1984

STATE

1ST SPKR	NAME	GEN	RACE	BIRTHPLACE	YEAR BORN	YEAR DIED

MARYLAND (*CONT.*)

1ST SPKR	NAME	GEN	RACE	BIRTHPLACE	YEAR BORN	YEAR DIED
1973	BRISCOE JOHN HANSON	M	W	MARYLAND	1934	N/A
1979	CARDIN BENJAMIN LOUIS	M	W	MARYLAND	1943	N/A
1987	MITCHELL R CLAYTON JR	M	W	MARYLAND	1936	N/A

MISSISSIPPI

1ST SPKR	NAME	GEN	RACE	BIRTHPLACE	YEAR BORN	YEAR DIED
1912	QUIN HILLRIE MARSHALL	M	W	MISSISSIPP	1866	1923
1916	CONNER MARTIN SENNETT	M	W	MISSISSIPP	1891	1950
1924	BAILEY THOMAS LOWRY	M	W	MISSISSIPP	1888	1946
1936	STANSEL HORACE SYLVAN	M	W	MISSISSIPP	1888	1936
1936	WRIGHT FIELDING LEWIS	M	W	MISSISSIPP	1895	1956
1940	LUMPKIN SAMUEL E	M	W	MISSISSIPP	1908	1964
1944	SILLERS WALTER	M	W	MISSISSIPP	1888	1966
1966	JUNKIN JOHN RICHARD	M	W	MISSISSIPP	1896	1975
1976	NEWMAN CLARENCE BENTON	M	W	MISSISSIPP	1921	N/A
1988	FORD TIMOTHY ALAN	M	W	FLORIDA	1951	N/A

NORTH CAROLINA

1ST SPKR	NAME	GEN	RACE	BIRTHPLACE	YEAR BORN	YEAR DIED
1911	DOWD WILLIAM CAREY	M	W	N CAROLINA	1865	1927
1913	CONNOR GEORGE WHITFIELD	M	W	N CAROLINA	1872	1938
1914	MURPHY WALTER	M	W	N CAROLINA	1872	1946
1915	WOOTEN EMMETT ROBINSON	M	W	N CAROLINA	1878	1915
1919	BRUMMITT DENNIS GARFIELD	M	W	N CAROLINA	1881	1935
1921	GRIER HARRY PERCY	M	W	S CAROLINA	1871	1932
1923	DAWSON JOHN GILMER	M	W	N CAROLINA	1882	1966
1925	PHARR EDGAR WALTER	M	W	N CAROLINA	1889	1936
1927	FOUNTAIN RICHARD TILLMAN	M	W	N CAROLINA	1885	1945
1929	GRAHAM ALEXANDER HAWKINS	M	W	N CAROLINA	1890	1977
1931	SMITH WILLIS	M	W	VIRGINIA	1887	1953
1933	HARRIS REGINALD LEE	M	W	N CAROLINA	1890	1959
1935	JOHNSON ROBERT GRADY	M	W	N CAROLINA	1895	1951
1936	CHERRY ROBERT GREGG	M	W	S CAROLINA	1891	1957
1939	WARD DAVID LIVINGSTONE JR	M	W	N CAROLINA	1903	1971
1941	MULL ODUS MCCOY	M	W	N CAROLINA	1880	1962
1943	KERR JOHN HOSEA JR	M	W	N CAROLINA	1900	1968
1945	RICHARDSON OSCAR LEON	M	W	N CAROLINA	1896	1966
1947	PEARSALL THOMAS JENKINS	M	W	N CAROLINA	1903	1981
1949	RAMSAY KERR CRAIGE	M	W	N CAROLINA	1911	1951
1951	TAYLOR WALTER FRANK	M	W	N CAROLINA	1889	1977
1953	BOST EUGENE THOMPSON JR	M	W	N CAROLINA	1907	1977
1955	MOORE LARRY ICHABOD JR	M	W	N CAROLINA	1904	1972
1957	DOUGHTON JAMES KEMP	M	W	N CAROLINA	1884	1972
1959	HEWLETT ADDISON JR	M	W	N CAROLINA	1912	N/A
1961	HUNT JOSEPH MARVIN	M	W	N CAROLINA	1906	1978
1963	BLUE HERBERT CLIFTON	M	W	N CAROLINA	1910	1990
1965	TAYLOR HOYT PATRICK JR	M	W	N CAROLINA	1924	N/A
1967	BRITT DAVID MAXWELL	M	W	N CAROLINA	1917	N/A
1967	VAUGHN EARL W	M	W	N CAROLINA	1928	1986
1969	GODWIN PHILIP PITTMAN	M	W	N CAROLINA	1925	N/A

STATE

1ST SPKR	NAME	GEN	RACE	BIRTHPLACE	YEAR BORN	YEAR DIED

NORTH CAROLINA (*CONT.*)

1ST SPKR	NAME	GEN	RACE	BIRTHPLACE	YEAR BORN	YEAR DIED
1973	RAMSEY JAMES EDWARD	M	W	N CAROLINA	1931	N/A
1975	GREEN JAMES COLLINS	M	W	VIRGINIA	1921	N/A
1977	STEWART CARL JEROME JR	M	W	N CAROLINA	1936	N/A
1981	RAMSEY LISTON BRYAN	M	W	N CAROLINA	1919	N/A
1989	MAVRETIC JOSEPHUS L	M	W	N CAROLINA	1934	N/A

OKLAHOMA

1ST SPKR	NAME	GEN	RACE	BIRTHPLACE	YEAR BORN	YEAR DIED
1910	ANTHONY WILLIAM BRUCE	M	W	TENNESSEE	1871	1933
1911	DURANT WILLIAM ALEXANDER	M	IN	OKLAHOMA	1866	1948
1913	MAXEY JAMES HARVEY	M	W	.	.	.
1915	MCCRORY ALONZO	M	W	TEXAS	1878	.
1917	NESBITT PAUL	M	W	NEBRASKA	1872	1950
1919	WALDREP THOMAS CARNES	M	W	ALABAMA	1889	.
1921	SCHWABE GEORGE BLAINE	M	W	MISSOURI	1886	1952
1923	GIBBONS MURRAY F	M	W	OKLAHOMA	1891	.
1923	MCBEE WILLIAM DALTON	M	W	TEXAS	1876	1965
1925	HARPER JESSE B	M	W	ARKANSAS	.	.
1927	STOVALL DAVID ANCIL	M	W	TENNESSEE	1882	1971
1929	STREET ALLEN MORGAN	M	W	TEXAS	1885	1969
1929	NANCE JAMES CLARK	M	W	ARKANSAS	1893	1984
1931	WEAVER CARLTON	M	W	TEXAS	1881	1947
1933	ANGLIN WILLIAM THOMAS	M	W	VIRGINIA	1883	1953
1935	PHILLIPS LEON CHASE	M	W	MISSOURI	1890	1958
1937	DANIEL J T	M	W	TEXAS	1893	1965
1939	WELCH WILLIAM DONOVAN SR	M	W	OKLAHOMA	1898	1955
1941	BLUMHAGEN E	M	W	N DAKOTA	1907	N/A
1943	FREEMAN HAROLD	M	W	OKLAHOMA	1902	N/A
1944	LANSDEN JOSEPH MERLE	M	W	OKLAHOMA	1907	1989
1945	HILL JOHNSON DAVIS	M	W	MISSOURI	1887	1977
1945	HINDS H IREDELLE	M	W	ARKANSAS	1895	1972
1947	BOARD CHARLES RAYMOND	M	W	MISSOURI	1901	.
1949	BILLINGSLEY WALTER ASBURY	M	W	ARKANSAS	1890	1985
1951	BULLARD JAMES MARVIN	M	W	OKLAHOMA	1901	1978
1955	HARKEY BYRON E	M	W	TEXAS	1911	N/A
1959	LIVINGSTON CLINT GRAHAM	M	W	OKLAHOMA	1918	N/A
1961	MCCARTY J D	M	W	OKLAHOMA	1916	1981
1967	PRIVETT ARNOLD REX	M	W	OKLAHOMA	1924	N/A
1973	WILLIS WILLIAM PASCAL	M	IN	OKLAHOMA	1910	N/A
1979	DRAPER DANIEL DAVID JR	M	W	OKLAHOMA	1940	N/A
1984	BARKER JIM L	M	W	OKLAHOMA	1935	N/A
1989	LEWIS STEPHEN C	M	W	OKLAHOMA	1943	N/A

SOUTH CAROLINA

1ST SPKR	NAME	GEN	RACE	BIRTHPLACE	YEAR BORN	YEAR DIED
1915	HOYT JAMES ALFRED	M	W	VIRGINIA	1837	.
1918	COTHRAN THOMAS PERRIN	M	W	S CAROLINA	1857	1934
1921	ATKINSON JAMES BUFORD	M	W	S CAROLINA	1872	1942
1923	MCMILLAN THOMAS SANDERS	M	W	S CAROLINA	1888	1939
1925	BROWN EDGAR ALLAN	M	W	S CAROLINA	1888	1975

STATE

1ST SPKR	NAME	GEN	RACE	BIRTHPLACE	YEAR BORN	YEAR DIED

SOUTH CAROLINA (*CONT.*)

1927	HAMBLIN JOHN KNAPP	M	W	N CAROLINA	1881	1933
1933	GIBSON JAMES BREEDEN	M	W	S CAROLINA	1879	1934
1935	TAYLOR CLAUDE AMBROSE	M	W	S CAROLINA	1902	1966
1937	BLATT SOLOMON	M	W	S CAROLINA	1896	1986
1947	LITTLEJOHN CAMERON BRUCE	M	W	S CAROLINA	1913	N/A
1949	POPE THOMAS HARRINGTON	M	W	S CAROLINA	1913	N/A
1973	CARTER REX LYLE	M	W	S CAROLINA	1925	N/A
1980	SCHWARTZ RAMON JR	M	W	S CAROLINA	1925	N/A
1987	SHEHEEN ROBERT J	M	W	S CAROLINA	1943	N/A

TENNESSEE

1911	LEACH ALBERT MARTIN	M	W	TENNESSEE	1859	1926
1913	STANTON WILLIAM MORTIMER	M	W	MISSISSIPP	1890	1957
1915	COOPER WILLIAM PRENTICE	M	W	KENTUCKY	.	1961
1917	SHROPSHIRE CLYDE MOORE	M	W	GEORGIA	1866	1949
1919	WALKER SETH MCKINNEY	M	W	TENNESSEE	1892	1951
1921	TODD ANDREW LEE	M	W	TENNESSEE	1872	1945
1923	HALL FRANK SAMPSON	M	W	TENNESSEE	1890	1958
1925	BARRY WILLIAM FRANCIS JR	M	W	TENNESSEE	1900	1967
1927	MAIDEN SELDEN LONGLEY	M	W	TENNESSEE	1883	1949
1929	LOVE CHARLES HOWARD	M	W	KENTUCKY	1874	1950
1931	HAYNES WALTER MILLER	M	W	TENNESSEE	1897	1967
1933	MOORE FRANK WASHINGTON	M	W	TENNESSEE	1905	1982
1939	O'DELL JOHN ED	M	W	TENNESSEE	1906	1956
1943	BROOME JAMES JESSE	M	W	TENNESSEE	1884	1952
1945	WOODS GEORGE STANLEY	M	W	TENNESSEE	1913	N/A
1947	LEWALLEN W BUFORD	M	W	TENNESSEE	1920	N/A
1949	FOUTCH MCALLEN	M	W	TENNESSEE	1909	.
1953	BOMAR JAMES LA FAYETTE JR	M	W	TENNESSEE	1914	N/A
1963	BARRY WILLIAM LOGAN	M	W	TENNESSEE	1926	N/A
1967	CUMMINGS JAMES HARVEY II	M	W	TENNESSEE	1890	1979
1969	JENKINS WILLIAM LEWIS	M	W	MICHIGAN	1936	N/A
1971	MCKINNEY JAMES ROBIN	M	W	TENNESSEE	1931	N/A
1973	MCWHERTER NED RAY	M	W	TENNESSEE	1930	N/A
1987	MURRAY CHARLES EDWARD	M	W	TENNESSEE	1928	N/A

TEXAS

1911	RAYBURN SAMUEL TALIAFERRO	M	W	TENNESSEE	1882	1961
1913	TERRELL CHESTER H	M	W	TEXAS	1882	1920
1915	WOODS JOHN WILLIAM	M	W	TEXAS	1875	1933
1917	FULLER FRANKLIN OLIVER	M	W	TEXAS	1873	1934
1919	THOMASON ROBERT EWING	M	W	TENNESSEE	1879	1973
1921	THOMAS CHARLES GRAHAM	M	W	TEXAS	1879	1937
1923	SEAGLER RICHARD E	M	W	TEXAS	1883	1956
1925	SATTERWHITE ROBERT LEE	M	W	ARKANSAS	1871	1959
1927	BOBBITT ROBERT LEE	M	W	TEXAS	1888	1972
1929	BARRON WINGATE STUART	M	W	TEXAS	1889	1984
1931	MINOR FRED H	M	W	TEXAS	1888	1976

STATE

1ST SPKR	NAME	GEN	RACE	BIRTHPLACE	YEAR BORN	YEAR DIED

TEXAS (*CONT.*)

1ST SPKR	NAME	GEN	RACE	BIRTHPLACE	YEAR BORN	YEAR DIED
1933	STEVENSON COKE ROBERT	M	W	TEXAS	1888	1975
1937	CALVERT ROBERT WILBURN	M	W	TENNESSEE	1905	N/A
1939	MORSE ROBERT EMMETT	M	W	TEXAS	1896	1957
1941	LEONARD HOMER L	M	W	MISSOURI	1899	1979
1943	DANIEL MARION PRICE SR	M	W	TEXAS	1910	1988
1945	GILMER CLAUD H	M	W	TEXAS	1901	1983
1947	REED WILLIAM OTEY	M	W	TEXAS	1902	1969
1949	MANFORD THOMAS DURWOOD JR	M	W	TEXAS	1917	1988
1951	SENTERFITT REUBEN	M	W	TEXAS	1917	N/A
1955	LINDSEY JIM THURSTON	M	W	TEXAS	1927	N/A
1957	CARR WAGGONER	M	W	TEXAS	1918	N/A
1961	TURMAN JAMES A	M	W	TEXAS	1927	N/A
1963	TUNNELL BYRON M	M	W	TEXAS	1925	N/A
1965	BARNES BEN FRANK	M	W	TEXAS	1938	N/A
1969	MUTSCHER GUS FRANKLIN	M	W	TEXAS	1932	N/A
1972	PRICE WILLIAM RAYFORD	M	W	TEXAS	1937	N/A
1973	DANIEL MARION PRICE JR	M	W	TEXAS	1941	1981
1975	CLAYTON BILLY WAYNE	M	W	TEXAS	1928	N/A
1983	LEWIS GIBSON D	M	W	TEXAS	1936	N/A

VIRGINIA

1ST SPKR	NAME	GEN	RACE	BIRTHPLACE	YEAR BORN	YEAR DIED
1914	COX EDWIN PIPER	M	W	VIRGINIA	1870	1938
1916	HOUSTON HARRY RUTHERFORD	M	W	VIRGINIA	1878	1960
1920	BREWER RICHARD LEWIS JR	M	W	VIRGINIA	1864	1947
1926	OZLIN THOMAS WILLIAM	M	W	VIRGINIA	1884	1944
1930	BROWN J SINCLAIR	M	W	VIRGINIA	1880	1965
1936	DOVELL GROVER ASHTON	M	W	VIRGINIA	1885	1949
1942	STANLEY THOMAS BAHNSON	M	W	VIRGINIA	1890	1970
1947	MASSENBURG GEORGE ALVIN	M	W	VIRGINIA	1894	1968
1950	MOORE EDGAR BLACKBURN	M	W	DIST COLUM	1897	1980
1968	COOKE JOHN WARREN	M	W	VIRGINIA	1915	N/A
1980	PHILPOTT ALBERT LEE	M	W	VIRGINIA	1919	1991

WEST VIRGINIA

1ST SPKR	NAME	GEN	RACE	BIRTHPLACE	YEAR BORN	YEAR DIED
1911	WETZEL CHARLES MCCLUER	M	W	INDIANA	1850	1929
1913	GEORGE WILLIAM TAYLOR	M	W	W VIRGINIA	1870	1957
1915	JOHNSON VERNON EMIL	M	W	W VIRGINIA	1880	1944
1917	THURMOND JOSEPH SAMUEL	M	W	W VIRGINIA	1855	1932
1919	WOLFE J LUTHER	M	W	W VIRGINIA	1875	1933
1921	KEATLEY EDWIN MINER	M	W	NEW YORK	1868	1933
1923	BYRNE WILLIAM ESTON R	M	W	VIRGINIA	1862	1937
1929	CUMMINS JOHN WILLIAM	M	W	W VIRGINIA	1881	1965
1931	TAYLOR JAMES ALFRED	M	W	OHIO	1878	1956
1933	HINER RALPH MCCLUNG	M	W	W VIRGINIA	1896	.
1935	PELTER JOHN J	M	W	W VIRGINIA	1905	1974
1937	THOMAS JAMES KAY	M	W	W VIRGINIA	1902	.
1941	ARNOLD MALCOLM R	M	W	W VIRGINIA	1909	1979
1943	AMOS JOHN ELLISON	M	W	W VIRGINIA	1905	.

STATE

1ST SPKR	NAME	GEN	RACE	BIRTHPLACE	YEAR BORN	YEAR DIED

WEST VIRGINIA (CONT.)

1ST SPKR	NAME	GEN	RACE	BIRTHPLACE	YEAR BORN	YEAR DIED
1949	FLANNERY W E	M	W	KENTUCKY	1904	1958
1958	PAULEY HARRY R	M	W	W VIRGINIA	1907	N/A
1961	SINGLETON JULIUS W JR	M	W	W VIRGINIA	1921	1977
1965	WHITE H LABAN JR	M	W	W VIRGINIA	1916	N/A
1969	BOIARSKY IVOR F	M	W	W VIRGINIA	1920	1971
1971	MCMANUS LEWIS NICHOLS	M	W	W VIRGINIA	1929	N/A
1977	KOPP DONALD LEE	M	W	W VIRGINIA	1935	N/A
1979	SEE CLYDE M JR	M	W	W VIRGINIA	1941	N/A
1985	ALBRIGHT JOSEPH PAUL	M	W	W VIRGINIA	1938	N/A
1987	CHAMBERS ROBERT C	M	W	W VIRGINIA	1952	N/A

KEY:

1ST SPKR = YEAR FIRST SERVED AS SPEAKER

GEN = GENDER OF SPEAKER
  M = MALE

RACE = RACIAL BACKGROUND OF SPEAKER
  W = WHITE
  IN = NATIVE AMERICAN

BIRTHPLACE = STATE / COUNTRY OF SPEAKER'S BIRTH
  (SOME RESPONSES TRUNCATED)
  . = MISSING DATA

YEAR BORN
YEAR DIED
  . = MISSING DATA
  N/A = NOT APPLICABLE, STILL ALIVE

Appendix 5:
Education

1ST SPKR	NAME	HIGHEST LEVEL	COLLEGE GRANTING HIGHEST DEGREE

ALABAMA

1ST SPKR	NAME	HIGHEST LEVEL	COLLEGE GRANTING HIGHEST DEGREE
1911	ALMON EDWARD BERTON	PROFESS	ALABAMA
1919	MERRITT HENRY PAUL	PROFESS	VIRGINIA
1920	LYNNE SEABOURN ARTHUR	PROFESS	ALABAMA
1923	MERRILL HUGH DAVIS	PROFESS	ALABAMA
1927	LONG JOHN LEE	ATTD H S	NONE
1935	WALKER ROBERT HENRY	ATTD H S	NONE
1942	MILLER GEORGE OLIVER	ATTD COLL	MASSEY BUSINESS
1944	NORMAN CHARLES DOZIER	GRAD COLL	ALABAMA
1947	BECK WILLIAM MORRIS	PROFESS	BIRMINGHAM-SOUTH
1951	BROWN ROBERTS HENRY	PROFESS	GEORGIA
1955	FITE ERNEST RANKIN	PROFESS	ALABAMA
1959	ADAMS CHARLES CRAYTON III	GRAD COLL	AUBURN
1961	ASHWORTH VIRGIS MARION	GRAD COLL	BIRMINGHAM LAW
1963	BREWER ALBERT PRESTON	PROFESS	ALABAMA
1971	LYONS GEORGE SAGE	PROFESS	ALABAMA
1975	MCCORQUODALE JOSEPH CHARLES	ATTD COLL	ALABAMA
1983	DRAKE THOMAS E	PROFESS	ALABAMA
1987	CLARK JAMES STERLING	ATTD COLL	.

ARKANSAS

1ST SPKR	NAME	HIGHEST LEVEL	COLLEGE GRANTING HIGHEST DEGREE
1911	MILWEE R FRANK	ELEMENT	NONE
1913	HARDAGE JOSIAH	PROFESS	CUMBERLAND
1915	SAWYER LEWIS ERNEST	GRAD COLL	MISSISSIPPI
1917	CAZORT WILLIAM LEE SR	PROFESS	WASHINGTON & LEE
1919	NEWTON CLARENCE PRICE	.	.
1921	JOINER JOSEPH WILLIAM	PROFESS	ARKANSAS
1923	REED HOWARD	ATTD COLL	ARKANSAS
1925	HILL THOMAS AUSTIN	GRAD H S	NONE
1927	CAUDLE REECE ARTHUR	GRAD COLL	ARKANSAS
1929	ABINGTON WILLIAM H	PROFESS	ARKANSAS MEDICAL
1931	NEALE IRVING C	PROFESS	MISSOURI
1933	TONEY HARDIN KEMP	GRAD COLL	MISSISSIPPI
1935	THORN HARVEY BELL SR	GRAD COLL	ARKANSAS
1937	BRANSFORD JOHN MCKINNIS	GRAD COLL	ARKANSAS
1941	WILKINSON NORMAN MEANS	PROFESS	CUMBERLAND
1943	GRIFFITH ROBERT WILLIAM	PROFESS	ARKANSAS LAW

STATE

1ST SPKR	NAME	HIGHEST LEVEL	COLLEGE GRANTING HIGHEST DEGREE

ARKANSAS (CONT.)

1945	NORTHCUTT HORACE ALLEN	GRAD H S	NONE
1947	RIALES ROY LEE SR	ATTD COLL	GA-CAR COMMERCE
1949	HENDRIX CARL EDWARD	GRAD COLL	ARKANSAS
1951	CAMPBELL JAMES R JR	PROFESS	CUMBERLAND
1953	HOLLENSWORTH CARROLL C	PROFESS	CHICAGO LAW
1955	SMITH CHARLES F JR	PROFESS	SOUTHERN
1957	WALTHER GLENN F	PROFESS	ARKANSAS
1959	FLEEMAN EUGENE CECIL	GRAD H S	NONE
1961	BETHELL JOHN PINCKNEY SR	ATTD COLL	ARKANSAS
1963	CRANK MARION HARLAN	PROFESS	ARKANSAS
1965	COTTRELL JOHN HALL JR	PROFESS	ARKANSAS
1967	COCKRILL STERLING ROBERTSON	GRAD COLL	ARKANSAS
1969	MCCLERKIN HAYES CANDOR	PROFESS	ARKANSAS
1971	SMITH RAY S JR	PROFESS	WASHINGTON & LEE
1973	TURNER GROVER W JR	PROFESS	ARKANSAS
1975	ALEXANDER CECIL LEWIS	GRAD COLL	HENDRIX
1977	SHAVER JAMES LEVESQUE JR	PROFESS	ARKANSAS
1979	MILLER JOHN ELDON	GRAD COLL	ARKANSAS ST
1981	MCCUISTON LLOYD CARLISLE JR	GRAD COLL	ARKANSAS
1983	CAPPS JOHN PAUL	ATTD COLL	ARKANSAS ST
1985	LANDERS H LACY	ATTD COLL	LITTLE ROCK JR COL
1987	CUNNINGHAM ERNEST G	GRAD COLL	ARKANSAS
1989	HENDRIX B G	ATTD COLL	CENTRAL

FLORIDA

1911	JENNINGS THOMAS ALBERT	ATTD COLL	EMORY
1915	HARDEE CARY AUGUSTUS	GRAD H S	NONE
1918	WILDER GEORGE HAMILTON	GRAD COLL	STETSON
1921	JENNINGS FRANK E	PROFESS	MISSOURI
1923	EDGE L DAY	PROFESS	FLORIDA
1925	MILAM ARTHUR YAGER	GRAD COLL	STETSON
1927	DAVIS FRED HENRY	GRAD H S	NONE
1929	GETZEN SAMUEL WYCHE	PROFESS	FLORIDA
1931	LEWIS E CLAY JR	PROFESS	FLORIDA
1933	TOMASELLO PETER JR	ATTD H S	NONE
1935	BISHOP WILLIAM BURTON	GRAD COLL	FLORIDA NORMAL
1937	CHRISTIE WILLIAM MCLEAN	PROFESS	FLORIDA
1939	WOOD GEORGE PIERCE	ATTD COLL	FLORIDA
1941	MCCARTY DANIEL THOMAS	GRAD COLL	FLORIDA
1943	SIMPSON RICHARD HENRY	GRAD COLL	FLORIDA
1945	CRARY EVANS SR	PROFESS	FLORIDA
1947	BEASLEY THOMAS DEKALB	PROFESS	CUMBERLAND
1949	MURRAY PERRY EARL	GRAD COLL	MERCER
1951	ELLIOTT ELMER B	.	.
1953	BRYANT CECIL FARRIS	PROFESS	HARVARD
1955	DAVID THOMAS E	PROFESS	MIAMI (FL)
1957	CONNER DOYLE E	GRAD COLL	FLORIDA
1961	CHAPPELL WILLIAM VENROE JR	PROFESS	FLORIDA
1962	HORNE MALLORY ELI	PROFESS	FLORIDA
1965	ROWELL E C	ATTD COLL	FLORIDA

STATE

1ST SPKR	NAME	HIGHEST LEVEL	COLLEGE GRANTING HIGHEST DEGREE

FLORIDA (*CONT.*)

1ST SPKR	NAME	HIGHEST LEVEL	COLLEGE GRANTING HIGHEST DEGREE
1967	TURLINGTON RALPH DONALD	PROFESS	HARVARD
1969	SCHULTZ FREDERICK HENRY	PROFESS	FLORIDA
1971	PETTIGREW RICHARD ALLEN	PROFESS	FLORIDA
1973	SESSUMS THOMAS TERRELL	PROFESS	FLORIDA
1975	TUCKER DONALD L	PROFESS	FLORIDA
1979	BROWN JAMES HYATT	GRAD COLL	FLORIDA
1981	HABEN RALPH H JR	PROFESS	CUMBERLAND
1983	MOFFITT H LEE	PROFESS	CUMBERLAND
1985	THOMPSON JAMES HAROLD	PROFESS	FLORIDA ST
1987	MILLS JON L	PROFESS	FLORIDA
1989	GUSTAFSON TOM	PROFESS	FLORIDA

GEORGIA

1ST SPKR	NAME	HIGHEST LEVEL	COLLEGE GRANTING HIGHEST DEGREE
1913	BURWELL WILLIAM HIX	GRAD H S	NONE
1921	NEILL WILLIAM CECIL	GRAD H S	NONE
1927	RUSSELL RICHARD BREVARD	PROFESS	GEORGIA
1931	TUCKER ARLIE DANIEL	GRAD H S	NONE
1933	RIVERS EURITH DICKINSON	PROFESS	LASALLE EXTENSION
1937	HARRIS ROY VINCENT	PROFESS	GEORGIA
1941	EVANS RANDALL JR	PROFESS	MAYNARD'S LAW
1947	HAND FREDRICK BARROW	GRAD COLL	GEORGIA
1955	MOATE MARVIN E	PROFESS	ATLANTA LAW
1959	SMITH GEORGE LEON II	ATTD COLL	GEORGIA
1963	SMITH GEORGE THORNEWELL	PROFESS	GEORGIA
1974	MURPHY THOMAS BAILEY	PROFESS	GEORGIA

KENTUCKY

1ST SPKR	NAME	HIGHEST LEVEL	COLLEGE GRANTING HIGHEST DEGREE
1912	TERRELL CLAUDE B	PROFESS	LOUISVILLE
1916	DUFFY HUGH CORNELIUS	PROFESS	VIRGINIA
1918	CROWE ROBERT T	GRAD COLL	S.U.N.Y.
1920	BOSWORTH JOE F	PROFESS	VIRGINIA
1922	THOMPSON JAMES H	GRAD COLL	TRANSYLVANIA
1924	ADAMS SAMUEL W	PROFESS	CHICAGO-KENT LAW
1926	DRURY GEORGE LUCIAN	PROFESS	LOUISVILLE
1928	MILLIKEN JOHN S	PROFESS	JEFFERSON LAW
1932	BROWN JOHN YOUNG	PROFESS	KENTUCKY
1933	LEBUS FRANK	ELEMENT	NONE
1934	ROGERS W E SR	.	.
1935	BROWN WALLACE	GRAD COLL	CENTRE
1936	KIRTLEY JOHN D	GRAD H S	NONE
1940	SHIELDS BENJAMIN FRANKLIN	PROFESS	LOUISVILLE
1942	DICKSON STANLEY S	ATTD COLL	PRINCETON
1944	WATERFIELD HARRY LEE	GRAD COLL	MURRAY ST
1948	TINSLEY T HERBERT	GRAD COLL	LEXINGTON SEMINARY
1950	DORAN ADRON	PROFESS	KENTUCKY
1952	BURNLEY CHARLES W	GRAD H S	NONE
1956	FITZPATRICK THOMAS P	GRAD H S	NONE
1958	WEINTRAUB MORRIS	PROFESS	DAYTON LAW

STATE

1ST SPKR	NAME	HIGHEST LEVEL	COLLEGE GRANTING HIGHEST DEGREE

KENTUCKY (CONT.)

1960	LOWMAN HARRY KING	PROFESS	KENTUCKY
1964	MCCALLUM SHELBY	GRAD H S	NONE
1968	CARROLL JULIAN MORTON	PROFESS	KENTUCKY
1972	BLUME NORBERT	ATTD COLL	LOUISVILLE
1976	KENTON WILLIAM G	PROFESS	KENTUCKY
1982	RICHARDSON BOBBY HAROLD	PROFESS	KENTUCKY
1986	BLANDFORD DONALD JOSEPH	GRAD H S	NONE

LOUISIANA

1912	THOMAS LEE EMMETT	PROFESS	VIRGINIA
1916	BOUANCHAUD HEWITT LEONIDAS	PROFESS	TULANE
1920	WALKER RICHARD FLOURNOY	PROFESS	TULANE
1924	DOUGLAS JAMES STUART	ATTD H S	NONE
1926	HUGHES WILLIAM CLARK	ATTD COLL	TULANE
1928	FOURNET JOHN BAPTISTE	PROFESS	LOUISIANA ST
1932	ELLENDER ALLEN JOSEPH	PROFESS	TULANE
1936	WIMBERLY LORRIS M	GRAD COLL	RANDOLPH-MACON
1940	BAUER RALPH NORMAN	PROFESS	LOUISIANA ST
1952	AYCOCK CLARENCE C	PROFESS	LOYOLA (LA)
1957	ANGELLE ROBERT	GRAD COLL	SW LOUISIANA
1960	JEWELL J THOMAS	GRAD COLL	LOUISIANA ST
1964	DELONY VAIL MONTGOMERY	GRAD COLL	.
1968	GARRETT JOHN SIDNEY	GRAD COLL	LOUISIANA TECH
1972	HENRY EDGERTON L	PROFESS	LOUISIANA ST
1980	HAINKEL JOHN JOSEPH JR	PROFESS	TULANE
1984	ALARIO JOHN A JR	GRAD COLL	SE LOUISIANA
1988	DIMOS JIMMY N	PROFESS	TULANE

MARYLAND

1912	TRIPPE JAMES MCCONKY	PROFESS	MARYLAND
1916	LAIRD PHILIP DANDRIDGE	GRAD H S	NONE
1917	MCINTOSH DAVID GREGG JR	PROFESS	MARYLAND
1918	WOODEN HERBERT R	GRAD COLL	PRINCETON
1920	TYDINGS MILLARD EVELYN	PROFESS	MARYLAND
1922	LEE JOHN L G	.	.
1924	CURTIS FRANCIS P	GRAD H S	NONE
1927	LEE EDWARD BROOKE	PROFESS	GEORGE WASHINGTON
1931	MICHEL FRANCIS A	PROFESS	MARYLAND
1933	HARRINGTON T BARTON	PROFESS	MARYLAND
1935	GORFINE EMANUEL	PROFESS	MARYLAND
1939	CONLON THOMAS EDWARD	PROFESS	BALTIMORE
1943	WHITE JOHN S	PROFESS	GEORGETOWN
1947	SYBERT CORNELIUS FERDINAND	PROFESS	MARYLAND
1951	LUBER JOHN CHRISTOPHER	ATTD H S	NONE
1959	WILKINSON PERRY O	PROFESS	MARYLAND
1963	BOONE A GORDON	PROFESS	MARYLAND
1964	MANDEL MARVIN	PROFESS	MARYLAND
1969	LOWE THOMAS HUNTER	PROFESS	MARYLAND

STATE

1ST SPKR	NAME	HIGHEST LEVEL	COLLEGE GRANTING HIGHEST DEGREE

MARYLAND (*CONT.*)

1973	BRISCOE JOHN HANSON	PROFESS	MARYLAND
1979	CARDIN BENJAMIN LOUIS	PROFESS	MARYLAND
1987	MITCHELL R CLAYTON JR	ATTD COLL	GOLDEY-BEACOM

MISSISSIPPI

1912	QUIN HILLRIE MARSHALL	PROFESS	MISSISSIPPI
1916	CONNER MARTIN SENNETT	PROFESS	YALE
1924	BAILEY THOMAS LOWRY	PROFESS	MILLSAPS
1936	STANSEL HORACE SYLVAN	GRAD COLL	MISSISSIPPI ST
1936	WRIGHT FIELDING LEWIS	PROFESS	ALABAMA
1940	LUMPKIN SAMUEL E	PROFESS	CUMBERLAND
1944	SILLERS WALTER	PROFESS	MISSISSIPPI
1966	JUNKIN JOHN RICHARD	GRAD H S	NONE
1976	NEWMAN CLARENCE BENTON	ATTD COLL	COPIAH-LINCOLN JR
1988	FORD TIMOTHY ALAN	PROFESS	MISSISSIPPI

NORTH CAROLINA

1911	DOWD WILLIAM CAREY	GRAD COLL	WAKE FOREST
1913	CONNOR GEORGE WHITFIELD	PROFESS	NORTH CAROLINA
1914	MURPHY WALTER	PROFESS	NORTH CAROLINA
1915	WOOTEN EMMETT ROBINSON	PROFESS	NORTH CAROLINA
1919	BRUMMITT DENNIS GARFIELD	PROFESS	WAKE FOREST
1921	GRIER HARRY PERCY	GRAD H S	NONE
1923	DAWSON JOHN GILMER	PROFESS	NORTH CAROLINA
1925	PHARR EDGAR WALTER	PROFESS	NORTH CAROLINA
1927	FOUNTAIN RICHARD TILLMAN	PROFESS	NORTH CAROLINA
1929	GRAHAM ALEXANDER HAWKINS	PROFESS	HARVARD
1931	SMITH WILLIS	PROFESS	DUKE
1933	HARRIS REGINALD LEE	ATTD COLL	VIRGINIA MILITARY
1935	JOHNSON ROBERT GRADY	ATTD COLL	WAKE FOREST
1936	CHERRY ROBERT GREGG	PROFESS	DUKE
1939	WARD DAVID LIVINGSTONE JR	PROFESS	WAKE FOREST
1941	MULL ODUS MCCOY	PROFESS	WAKE FOREST
1943	KERR JOHN HOSEA JR	PROFESS	WAKE FOREST
1945	RICHARDSON OSCAR LEON	PROFESS	DUKE
1947	PEARSALL THOMAS JENKINS	PROFESS	NORTH CAROLINA
1949	RAMSAY KERR CRAIGE	PROFESS	YALE
1951	TAYLOR WALTER FRANK	PROFESS	NORTH CAROLINA
1953	BOST EUGENE THOMPSON JR	PROFESS	DUKE
1955	MOORE LARRY ICHABOD JR	PROFESS	NORTH CAROLINA
1957	DOUGHTON JAMES KEMP	ATTD COLL	NORTH CAROLINA
1959	HEWLETT ADDISON JR	PROFESS	WAKE FOREST
1961	HUNT JOSEPH MARVIN	ATTD COLL	DUKE
1963	BLUE HERBERT CLIFTON	GRAD H S	NONE
1965	TAYLOR HOYT PATRICK JR	PROFESS	NORTH CAROLINA
1967	BRITT DAVID MAXWELL	PROFESS	WAKE FOREST
1967	VAUGHN EARL W	PROFESS	NORTH CAROLINA
1969	GODWIN PHILIP PITTMAN	PROFESS	WAKE FOREST

STATE

1ST SPKR	NAME	HIGHEST LEVEL	COLLEGE GRANTING HIGHEST DEGREE

NORTH CAROLINA (*CONT.*)

1973	RAMSEY JAMES EDWARD	PROFESS	NORTH CAROLINA
1975	GREEN JAMES COLLINS	ATTD COLL	WASHINGTON & LEE
1977	STEWART CARL JEROME JR	PROFESS	DUKE
1981	RAMSEY LISTON BRYAN	GRAD COLL	MARS HILL
1989	MAVRETIC JOSEPHUS L	PROFESS	GEORGE WASHINGTON

OKLAHOMA

1910	ANTHONY WILLIAM BRUCE	GRAD COLL	TERRILL
1911	DURANT WILLIAM ALEXANDER	PROFESS	ARKANSAS COLL
1913	MAXEY JAMES HARVEY	.	.
1915	MCCRORY ALONZO	ATTD COLL	BAYLOR
1917	NESBITT PAUL	PROFESS	CHICAGO MEDICAL
1919	WALDREP THOMAS CARNES	PROFESS	OKLAHOMA
1921	SCHWABE GEORGE BLAINE	GRAD COLL	MISSOURI
1923	GIBBONS MURRAY F	GRAD COLL	OKLAHOMA
1923	MCBEE WILLIAM DALTON	GRAD H S	NONE
1925	HARPER JESSE B	GRAD COLL	COLUMBIA
1927	STOVALL DAVID ANCIL	PROFESS	TENNESSEE
1929	STREET ALLEN MORGAN	ATTD COLL	VANDERBILT
1929	NANCE JAMES CLARK	GRAD H S	NONE
1931	WEAVER CARLTON	ATTD COLL	OKLAHOMA
1933	ANGLIN WILLIAM THOMAS	PROFESS	VIRGINIA
1935	PHILLIPS LEON CHASE	PROFESS	OKLAHOMA
1937	DANIEL J T	PROFESS	OKLAHOMA
1939	WELCH WILLIAM DONOVAN SR	PROFESS	OKLAHOMA
1941	BLUMHAGEN E	PROFESS	CUMBERLAND
1943	FREEMAN HAROLD	PROFESS	CUMBERLAND
1944	LANSDEN JOSEPH MERLE	PROFESS	OKLAHOMA
1945	HILL JOHNSON DAVIS	PROFESS	MISSOURI
1945	HINDS H IREDELLE	ATTD COLL	NE OKLAHOMA
1947	BOARD CHARLES RAYMOND	PROFESS	CUMBERLAND
1949	BILLINGSLEY WALTER ASBURY	ATTD COLL	E CEN OKLAHOMA
1951	BULLARD JAMES MARVIN	GRAD COLL	CHICKASHA BUSINESS
1955	HARKEY BYRON E	PROFESS	OKLAHOMA CITY
1959	LIVINGSTON CLINT GRAHAM	PROFESS	OKLAHOMA
1961	MCCARTY J D	GRAD COLL	OKLAHOMA
1967	PRIVETT ARNOLD REX	GRAD COLL	OKLAHOMA ST
1973	WILLIS WILLIAM PASCAL	PROFESS	TULSA
1979	DRAPER DANIEL DAVID JR	PROFESS	GEORGE WASHINGTON
1984	BARKER JIM L	GRAD COLL	NE OKLAHOMA
1989	LEWIS STEPHEN C	PROFESS	OKLAHOMA

SOUTH CAROLINA

1915	HOYT JAMES ALFRED	.	.
1918	COTHRAN THOMAS PERRIN	ATTD COLL	VIRGINIA
1921	ATKINSON JAMES BUFORD	PROFESS	SOUTH CAROLINA
1923	MCMILLAN THOMAS SANDERS	PROFESS	SOUTH CAROLINA
1925	BROWN EDGAR ALLAN	ATTD COLL	OSBORNE'S BUSINESS

STATE

1ST SPKR	NAME	HIGHEST LEVEL	COLLEGE GRANTING HIGHEST DEGREE

SOUTH CAROLINA (*CONT.*)

1927	HAMBLIN JOHN KNAPP	PROFESS	NORTH CAROLINA
1933	GIBSON JAMES BREEDEN	PROFESS	NORTH CAROLINA
1935	TAYLOR CLAUDE AMBROSE	PROFESS	SOUTH CAROLINA
1937	BLATT SOLOMON	PROFESS	SOUTH CAROLINA
1947	LITTLEJOHN CAMERON BRUCE	PROFESS	SOUTH CAROLINA
1949	POPE THOMAS HARRINGTON	PROFESS	SOUTH CAROLINA
1973	CARTER REX LYLE	PROFESS	SOUTH CAROLINA
1980	SCHWARTZ RAMON JR	PROFESS	SOUTH CAROLINA
1987	SHEHEEN ROBERT J	PROFESS	SOUTH CAROLINA

TENNESSEE

1911	LEACH ALBERT MARTIN	.	.
1913	STANTON WILLIAM MORTIMER	PROFESS	VANDERBILT
1915	COOPER WILLIAM PRENTICE	PROFESS	VANDERBILT
1917	SHROPSHIRE CLYDE MOORE	GRAD COLL	GEORGIA
1919	WALKER SETH MCKINNEY	PROFESS	CUMBERLAND
1921	TODD ANDREW LEE	PROFESS	CUMBERLAND
1923	HALL FRANK SAMPSON	PROFESS	CUMBERLAND
1925	BARRY WILLIAM FRANCIS JR	PROFESS	CUMBERLAND
1927	MAIDEN SELDEN LONGLEY	PROFESS	MEMPHIS
1929	LOVE CHARLES HOWARD	.	.
1931	HAYNES WALTER MILLER	PROFESS	CUMBERLAND
1933	MOORE FRANK WASHINGTON	PROFESS	CHATTANOOGA
1939	O'DELL JOHN ED	PROFESS	VIRGINIA
1943	BROOME JAMES JESSE	ELEMENT	NONE
1945	WOODS GEORGE STANLEY	GRAD H S	NONE
1947	LEWALLEN W BUFORD	PROFESS	TENNESSEE
1949	FOUTCH MCALLEN	PROFESS	ANDREW JACKSON
1953	BOMAR JAMES LA FAYETTE JR	PROFESS	CUMBERLAND
1963	BARRY WILLIAM LOGAN	PROFESS	VANDERBILT
1967	CUMMINGS JAMES HARVEY II	PROFESS	CUMBERLAND
1969	JENKINS WILLIAM LEWIS	PROFESS	TENNESSEE
1971	MCKINNEY JAMES ROBIN	PROFESS	NASHVILLE YMCA
1973	MCWHERTER NED RAY	GRAD H S	NONE
1987	MURRAY CHARLES EDWARD	PROFESS	NASHVILLE YMCA

TEXAS

1911	RAYBURN SAMUEL TALIAFERRO	PROFESS	TEXAS
1913	TERRELL CHESTER H	PROFESS	TEXAS
1915	WOODS JOHN WILLIAM	PROFESS	TEXAS
1917	FULLER FRANKLIN OLIVER	PROFESS	SOUTHERN NORMAL
1919	THOMASON ROBERT EWING	PROFESS	TEXAS
1921	THOMAS CHARLES GRAHAM	GRAD COLL	BAYLOR
1923	SEAGLER RICHARD E	PROFESS	TEXAS
1925	SATTERWHITE ROBERT LEE	ATTD H S	NONE
1927	BOBBITT ROBERT LEE	PROFESS	TEXAS
1929	BARRON WINGATE STUART	PROFESS	TEXAS
1931	MINOR FRED H	PROFESS	TEXAS

STATE

1ST SPKR	NAME	HIGHEST LEVEL	COLLEGE GRANTING HIGHEST DEGREE

TEXAS (CONT.)

1933	STEVENSON COKE ROBERT	ELEMENT	NONE
1937	CALVERT ROBERT WILBURN	PROFESS	TEXAS
1939	MORSE ROBERT EMMETT	PROFESS	SOMMERVILLE LAW
1941	LEONARD HOMER L	GRAD COLL	MISSOURI
1943	DANIEL MARION PRICE SR	PROFESS	BAYLOR
1945	GILMER CLAUD H	ATTD COLL	MERIDIAN JR COLL
1947	REED WILLIAM OTEY	PROFESS	JEFFERSON LAW
1949	MANFORD THOMAS DURWOOD JR	PROFESS	TEXAS
1951	SENTERFITT REUBEN	PROFESS	TEXAS
1955	LINDSEY JIM THURSTON	PROFESS	BAYLOR
1957	CARR WAGGONER	PROFESS	TEXAS
1961	TURMAN JAMES A	PROFESS	TEXAS
1963	TUNNELL BYRON M	PROFESS	BAYLOR
1965	BARNES BEN FRANK	GRAD COLL	TEXAS
1969	MUTSCHER GUS FRANKLIN	PROFESS	TEXAS
1972	PRICE WILLIAM RAYFORD	PROFESS	TEXAS
1973	DANIEL MARION PRICE JR	PROFESS	BAYLOR
1975	CLAYTON BILLY WAYNE	GRAD COLL	TEXAS A&M
1983	LEWIS GIBSON D	GRAD COLL	TEXAS CHRISTIAN

VIRGINIA

1914	COX EDWIN PIPER	PROFESS	VIRGINIA
1916	HOUSTON HARRY RUTHERFORD	GRAD COLL	HAMPDEN-SYDNEY
1920	BREWER RICHARD LEWIS JR	GRAD H S	NONE
1926	OZLIN THOMAS WILLIAM	GRAD COLL	RICHMOND
1930	BROWN J SINCLAIR	ATTD COLL	VIRGINIA
1936	DOVELL GROVER ASHTON	PROFESS	VIRGINIA
1942	STANLEY THOMAS BAHNSON	ATTD COLL	EASTMAN BUSINESS
1947	MASSENBURG GEORGE ALVIN	ATTD H S	NONE
1950	MOORE EDGAR BLACKBURN	ATTD COLL	CORNELL (NY)
1968	COOKE JOHN WARREN	ATTD COLL	VIRGINIA MILITARY
1980	PHILPOTT ALBERT LEE	PROFESS	RICHMOND

WEST VIRGINIA

1911	WETZEL CHARLES MCCLUER	GRAD H S	NONE
1913	GEORGE WILLIAM TAYLOR	PROFESS	STOCKTON NORMAL
1915	JOHNSON VERNON EMIL	ATTD COLL	EASTMAN BUSINESS
1917	THURMOND JOSEPH SAMUEL	GRAD COLL	SHELTON
1919	WOLFE J LUTHER	PROFESS	WEST VIRGINIA
1921	KEATLEY EDWIN MINER	GRAD COLL	WYOMING SEMINARY
1923	BYRNE WILLIAM ESTON R	GRAD H S	NONE
1929	CUMMINS JOHN WILLIAM	PROFESS	GEORGETOWN
1931	TAYLOR JAMES ALFRED	ELEMENT	NONE
1933	HINER RALPH MCCLUNG	PROFESS	WEST VIRGINIA
1935	PELTER JOHN J	PROFESS	KENTUCKY
1937	THOMAS JAMES KAY	PROFESS	WASHINGTON & LEE
1941	ARNOLD MALCOLM R	PROFESS	COLUMBIA
1943	AMOS JOHN ELLISON	PROFESS	WEST VIRGINIA

STATE

1ST SPKR	NAME	HIGHEST LEVEL	COLLEGE GRANTING HIGHEST DEGREE

WEST VIRGINIA (*CONT.*)

1ST SPKR	NAME	HIGHEST LEVEL	COLLEGE GRANTING HIGHEST DEGREE
1949	FLANNERY W E	PROFESS	KENTUCKY
1958	PAULEY HARRY R	GRAD H S	NONE
1961	SINGLETON JULIUS W JR	PROFESS	WEST VIRGINIA
1965	WHITE H LABAN JR	PROFESS	WEST VIRGINIA
1969	BOIARSKY IVOR F	PROFESS	VIRGINIA
1971	MCMANUS LEWIS NICHOLS	PROFESS	CHARLESTON
1977	KOPP DONALD LEE	GRAD H S	NONE
1979	SEE CLYDE M JR	PROFESS	WEST VIRGINIA
1985	ALBRIGHT JOSEPH PAUL	PROFESS	NOTRE DAME
1987	CHAMBERS ROBERT C	PROFESS	WEST VIRGINIA

KEY:

1ST SPKR = YEAR FIRST SERVED AS SPEAKER

HIGHEST LEVEL = HIGHEST LEVEL OF EDUCATION DURING LIFETIME
. = MISSING DATA
ELEMENT = ELEMENTARY SCHOOL
ATTD H S = ATTENDED HIGH SCHOOL
GRAD H S = GRADUATED FROM HIGH SCHOOL
ATTD COLL = ATTENDED COLLEGE
GRAD COLL = GRADUATED FROM COLLEGE
PROFESS = PROFESSIONAL EDUCATION

COLLEGE GRANTING HIGHEST DEGREE
(SOME RESPONSES TRUNCATED)
. = MISSING DATA / NAME UNKNOWN

Appendix 6:
Religious, Military, and
Marital Background

1ST SPKR	NAME	RELIGION	MILITARY RANK	MARITAL STATUS
ALABAMA				
1911	ALMON EDWARD BERTON	METHODIST	NONE	MARRIED
1919	MERRITT HENRY PAUL	METHODIST	NONE	MARRIED
1920	LYNNE SEABOURN ARTHUR	BAPTIST	NONE	MARRIED
1923	MERRILL HUGH DAVIS	BAPTIST	NONE	MARRIED
1927	LONG JOHN LEE	EPISCOPAL	OFFICER	MARRIED
1935	WALKER ROBERT HENRY	BAPTIST	NONE	MARRIED
1942	MILLER GEORGE OLIVER	BAPTIST	NONE	MARRIED
1944	NORMAN CHARLES DOZIER	PRESBYTER	OFFICER	MARRIED
1947	BECK WILLIAM MORRIS	BAPTIST	ENLISTED	MARRIED
1951	BROWN ROBERTS HENRY	PRESBYTER	ENLISTED	MARRIED
1955	FITE ERNEST RANKIN	METHODIST	OFFICER	MARRIED
1959	ADAMS CHARLES CRAYTON III	METHODIST	OFFICER	MARRIED
1961	ASHWORTH VIRGIS MARION	BAPTIST	.	MARRIED
1963	BREWER ALBERT PRESTON	BAPTIST	ENLISTED	MARRIED
1971	LYONS GEORGE SAGE	EPISCOPAL	OFFICER	MARRIED
1975	MCCORQUODALE JOSEPH CHARLES	METHODIST	OFFICER	MARRIED
1983	DRAKE THOMAS E	BAPTIST	ENLISTED	MARRIED
1987	CLARK JAMES STERLING	METHODIST	ENLISTED	MARRIED
ARKANSAS				
1911	MILWEE R FRANK	PRESBYTER	.	.
1913	HARDAGE JOSIAH	BAPTIST	.	.
1915	SAWYER LEWIS ERNEST	DISCIPLES	ENLISTED	MARRIED
1917	CAZORT WILLIAM LEE SR	METHODIST	.	MARRIED
1919	NEWTON CLARENCE PRICE	METHODIST	.	.
1921	JOINER JOSEPH WILLIAM	BAPTIST	ENLISTED	.
1923	REED HOWARD	.	OFFICER	MARRIED
1925	HILL THOMAS AUSTIN	METHODIST	.	MARRIED
1927	CAUDLE REECE ARTHUR	DISCIPLES	.	MARRIED
1929	ABINGTON WILLIAM H	DISCIPLES	OFFICER	MARRIED
1931	NEALE IRVING C	METHODIST	OFFICER	NEV MARR
1933	TONEY HARDIN KEMP	PRESBYTER	.	MARRIED
1935	THORN HARVEY BELL SR	METHODIST	NONE	MARRIED
1937	BRANSFORD JOHN MCKINNIS	DISCIPLES	NONE	MARRIED
1941	WILKINSON NORMAN MEANS	PRESBYTER	OFFICER	MARRIED
1943	GRIFFITH ROBERT WILLIAM	EPISCOPAL	NONE	MARRIED

<u>STATE</u>

1ST SPKR	NAME	RELIGION	MILITARY RANK	MARITAL STATUS

<u>ARKANSAS</u> (*CONT.*)

1ST SPKR	NAME	RELIGION	MILITARY RANK	MARITAL STATUS
1945	NORTHCUTT HORACE ALLEN	METHODIST	NONE	MARRIED
1947	RIALES ROY LEE SR	METHODIST	.	MARRIED
1949	HENDRIX CARL EDWARD	BAPTIST	NONE	MARRIED
1951	CAMPBELL JAMES R JR	METHODIST	OFFICER	MARRIED
1953	HOLLENSWORTH CARROLL C	PRESBYTER	.	MARRIED
1955	SMITH CHARLES F JR	METHODIST	ENLISTED	MARRIED
1957	WALTHER GLENN F	LUTHERAN	OFFICER	MARRIED
1959	FLEEMAN EUGENE CECIL	METHODIST	.	MARRIED
1961	BETHELL JOHN PINCKNEY SR	PRESBYTER	NONE	MARRIED
1963	CRANK MARION HARLAN	EPISCOPAL	NONE	MARRIED
1965	COTTRELL JOHN HALL JR	DISCIPLES	OFFICER	MARRIED
1967	COCKRILL STERLING ROBERTSON	EPISCOPAL	OFFICER	MARRIED
1969	MCCLERKIN HAYES CANDOR	PRESBYTER	OFFICER	MARRIED
1971	SMITH RAY S JR	.	.	MARRIED
1973	TURNER GROVER W JR	METHODIST	ENLISTED	MARRIED
1975	ALEXANDER CECIL LEWIS	METHODIST	ENLISTED	MARRIED
1977	SHAVER JAMES LEVESQUE JR	PRESBYTER	ENLISTED	MARRIED
1979	MILLER JOHN ELDON	BAPTIST	ENLISTED	MARRIED
1981	MCCUISTON LLOYD CARLISLE JR	BAPTIST	OFFICER	MARRIED
1983	CAPPS JOHN PAUL	DISCIPLES	ENLISTED	MARRIED
1985	LANDERS H LACY	BAPTIST	ENLISTED	MARRIED
1987	CUNNINGHAM ERNEST G	EPISCOPAL	ENLISTED	MARRIED
1989	HENDRIX B G	METHODIST	ENLISTED	MARRIED

<u>FLORIDA</u>

1ST SPKR	NAME	RELIGION	MILITARY RANK	MARITAL STATUS
1911	JENNINGS THOMAS ALBERT	METHODIST	.	MARRIED
1915	HARDEE CARY AUGUSTUS	BAPTIST	NONE	MARRIED
1918	WILDER GEORGE HAMILTON	UNKN PROT	NONE	MARRIED
1921	JENNINGS FRANK E	DISCIPLES	ENLISTED	MARRIED
1923	EDGE L DAY	.	NONE	.
1925	MILAM ARTHUR YAGER	EPISCOPAL	.	MARRIED
1927	DAVIS FRED HENRY	.	ENLISTED	.
1929	GETZEN SAMUEL WYCHE	METHODIST	OFFICER	MARRIED
1931	LEWIS E CLAY JR	.	NONE	MARRIED
1933	TOMASELLO PETER JR	PRESBYTER	ENLISTED	MARRIED
1935	BISHOP WILLIAM BURTON	METHODIST	.	MARRIED
1937	CHRISTIE WILLIAM MCLEAN	EPISCOPAL	OFFICER	MARRIED
1939	WOOD GEORGE PIERCE	METHODIST	ENLISTED	MARRIED
1941	MCCARTY DANIEL THOMAS	EPISCOPAL	NONE	MARRIED
1943	SIMPSON RICHARD HENRY	PRESBYTER	.	MARRIED
1945	CRARY EVANS SR	METHODIST	NONE	MARRIED
1947	BEASLEY THOMAS DEKALB	METHODIST	.	MARRIED
1949	MURRAY PERRY EARL	METHODIST	ENLISTED	MARRIED
1951	ELLIOTT ELMER B	METHODIST	.	MARRIED
1953	BRYANT CECIL FARRIS	METHODIST	OFFICER	MARRIED
1955	DAVID THOMAS E	.	OFFICER	.
1957	CONNER DOYLE E	BAPTIST	NONE	MARRIED
1961	CHAPPELL WILLIAM VENROE JR	METHODIST	OFFICER	MARRIED
1962	HORNE MALLORY ELI	.	ENLISTED	.
1965	ROWELL E C	BAPTIST	ENLISTED	MARRIED

STATE

1ST SPKR	NAME	RELIGION	MILITARY RANK	MARITAL STATUS

FLORIDA (*CONT.*)

1ST SPKR	NAME	RELIGION	MILITARY RANK	MARITAL STATUS
1967	TURLINGTON RALPH DONALD	BAPTIST	OFFICER	MARRIED
1969	SCHULTZ FREDERICK HENRY	CATHOLIC	OFFICER	MARRIED
1971	PETTIGREW RICHARD ALLEN	CONGREGAT	OFFICER	MARRIED
1973	SESSUMS THOMAS TERRELL	METHODIST	OFFICER	MARRIED
1975	TUCKER DONALD L	MORMON	ENLISTED	.
1979	BROWN JAMES HYATT	BAPTIST	NONE	MARRIED
1981	HABEN RALPH H JR	.	ENLISTED	.
1983	MOFFITT H LEE	METHODIST	NONE	MARRIED
1985	THOMPSON JAMES HAROLD	PRESBYTER	NONE	MARRIED
1987	MILLS JON L	METHODIST	OFFICER	NEV MARR
1989	GUSTAFSON TOM	.	NONE	MARRIED

GEORGIA

1ST SPKR	NAME	RELIGION	MILITARY RANK	MARITAL STATUS
1913	BURWELL WILLIAM HIX	PRESBYTER	NONE	MARRIED
1921	NEILL WILLIAM CECIL	PRESBYTER	NONE	MARRIED
1927	RUSSELL RICHARD BREVARD	METHODIST	ENLISTED	NEV MARR
1931	TUCKER ARLIE DANIEL	BAPTIST	ENLISTED	MARRIED
1933	RIVERS EURITH DICKINSON	BAPTIST	NONE	MARRIED
1937	HARRIS ROY VINCENT	METHODIST	OFFICER	MARRIED
1941	EVANS RANDALL JR	BAPTIST	.	MARRIED
1947	HAND FREDRICK BARROW	METHODIST	NONE	MARRIED
1955	MOATE MARVIN E	METHODIST	NONE	MARRIED
1959	SMITH GEORGE LEON II	METHODIST	NONE	MARRIED
1963	SMITH GEORGE THORNEWELL	BAPTIST	OFFICER	MARRIED
1974	MURPHY THOMAS BAILEY	BAPTIST	ENLISTED	MARRIED

KENTUCKY

1ST SPKR	NAME	RELIGION	MILITARY RANK	MARITAL STATUS
1912	TERRELL CLAUDE B	METHODIST	.	NEV MARR
1916	DUFFY HUGH CORNELIUS	.	.	MARRIED
1918	CROWE ROBERT T	METHODIST	.	MARRIED
1920	BOSWORTH JOE F	BAPTIST	.	REMARR
1922	THOMPSON JAMES H	DISCIPLES	.	MARRIED
1924	ADAMS SAMUEL W	BAPTIST	.	MARRIED
1926	DRURY GEORGE LUCIAN	CATHOLIC	.	MARRIED
1928	MILLIKEN JOHN S	UNKN PROT	.	MARRIED
1932	BROWN JOHN YOUNG	METHODIST	ENLISTED	MARRIED
1933	LEBUS FRANK	.	.	MARRIED
1934	ROGERS W E SR	METHODIST	.	MARRIED
1935	BROWN WALLACE	METHODIST	.	MARRIED
1936	KIRTLEY JOHN D	METHODIST	NONE	MARRIED
1940	SHIELDS BENJAMIN FRANKLIN	DISCIPLES	NONE	MARRIED
1942	DICKSON STANLEY S	DISCIPLES	ENLISTED	MARRIED
1944	WATERFIELD HARRY LEE	DISCIPLES	NONE	MARRIED
1948	TINSLEY T HERBERT	DISCIPLES	ENLISTED	MARRIED
1950	DORAN ADRON	DISCIPLES	NONE	MARRIED
1952	BURNLEY CHARLES W	DISCIPLES	NONE	MARRIED
1956	FITZPATRICK THOMAS P	CATHOLIC	ENLISTED	MARRIED
1958	WEINTRAUB MORRIS	JEWISH	NONE	MARRIED

STATE

1ST SPKR	NAME	RELIGION	MILITARY RANK	MARITAL STATUS

KENTUCKY (*CONT.*)

1ST SPKR	NAME	RELIGION	MILITARY RANK	MARITAL STATUS
1960	LOWMAN HARRY KING	DISCIPLES	ENLISTED	MARRIED
1964	MCCALLUM SHELBY	METHODIST	ENLISTED	MARRIED
1968	CARROLL JULIAN MORTON	PRESBYTER	OFFICER	MARRIED
1972	BLUME NORBERT	CATHOLIC	ENLISTED	MARRIED
1976	KENTON WILLIAM G	BAPTIST	NONE	MARRIED
1982	RICHARDSON BOBBY HAROLD	BAPTIST	NONE	MARRIED
1986	BLANDFORD DONALD JOSEPH	CATHOLIC	ENLISTED	MARRIED

LOUISIANA

1ST SPKR	NAME	RELIGION	MILITARY RANK	MARITAL STATUS
1912	THOMAS LEE EMMETT	UNKN PROT	.	.
1916	BOUANCHAUD HEWITT LEONIDAS	CATHOLIC	.	.
1920	WALKER RICHARD FLOURNOY	BAPTIST	NONE	MARRIED
1924	DOUGLAS JAMES STUART	PRESBYTER	NONE	MARRIED
1926	HUGHES WILLIAM CLARK	.	.	.
1928	FOURNET JOHN BAPTISTE	.	ENLISTED	.
1932	ELLENDER ALLEN JOSEPH	CATHOLIC	ENLISTED	MARRIED
1936	WIMBERLY LORRIS M	METHODIST	.	MARRIED
1940	BAUER RALPH NORMAN	UNKN PROT	ENLISTED	MARRIED
1952	AYCOCK CLARENCE C	CATHOLIC	OFFICER	MARRIED
1957	ANGELLE ROBERT	.	.	MARRIED
1960	JEWELL J THOMAS	CATHOLIC	NONE	MARRIED
1964	DELONY VAIL MONTGOMERY	EPISCOPAL	NONE	MARRIED
1968	GARRETT JOHN SIDNEY	METHODIST	ENLISTED	.
1972	HENRY EDGERTON L	BAPTIST	NONE	MARRIED
1980	HAINKEL JOHN JOSEPH JR	CATHOLIC	NONE	MARRIED
1984	ALARIO JOHN A JR	CATHOLIC	NONE	MARRIED
1988	DIMOS JIMMY N	EPISCOPAL	ENLISTED	MARRIED

MARYLAND

1ST SPKR	NAME	RELIGION	MILITARY RANK	MARITAL STATUS
1912	TRIPPE JAMES MCCONKY	PRESBYTER	NONE	MARRIED
1916	LAIRD PHILIP DANDRIDGE	.	NONE	MARRIED
1917	MCINTOSH DAVID GREGG JR	EPISCOPAL	NONE	MARRIED
1918	WOODEN HERBERT R	METHODIST	.	NEV MARR
1920	TYDINGS MILLARD EVELYN	EPISCOPAL	OFFICER	NEV MARR
1922	LEE JOHN L G	LUTHERAN	.	MARRIED
1924	CURTIS FRANCIS P	CATHOLIC	NONE	MARRIED
1927	LEE EDWARD BROOKE	EPISCOPAL	OFFICER	MARRIED
1931	MICHEL FRANCIS A	CATHOLIC	NONE	MARRIED
1933	HARRINGTON T BARTON	CATHOLIC	NONE	.
1935	GORFINE EMANUEL	JEWISH	ENLISTED	MARRIED
1939	CONLON THOMAS EDWARD	CATHOLIC	NONE	MARRIED
1943	WHITE JOHN S	CATHOLIC	OFFICER	MARRIED
1947	SYBERT CORNELIUS FERDINAND	CATHOLIC	NONE	MARRIED
1951	LUBER JOHN CHRISTOPHER	CATHOLIC	NONE	MARRIED
1959	WILKINSON PERRY O	METHODIST	NONE	MARRIED
1963	BOONE A GORDON	EPISCOPAL	OFFICER	DIVORCED
1964	MANDEL MARVIN	JEWISH	ENLISTED	MARRIED
1969	LOWE THOMAS HUNTER	EPISCOPAL	ENLISTED	MARRIED

STATE

1ST SPKR	NAME	RELIGION	MILITARY RANK	MARITAL STATUS

MARYLAND (CONT.)

1973	BRISCOE JOHN HANSON	CATHOLIC	NONE	MARRIED
1979	CARDIN BENJAMIN LOUIS	JEWISH	NONE	MARRIED
1987	MITCHELL R CLAYTON JR	CATHOLIC	ENLISTED	MARRIED

MISSISSIPPI

1912	QUIN HILLRIE MARSHALL	METHODIST	NONE	MARRIED
1916	CONNER MARTIN SENNETT	METHODIST	NONE	MARRIED
1924	BAILEY THOMAS LOWRY	METHODIST	NONE	MARRIED
1936	STANSEL HORACE SYLVAN	BAPTIST	NONE	MARRIED
1936	WRIGHT FIELDING LEWIS	METHODIST	ENLISTED	MARRIED
1940	LUMPKIN SAMUEL E	METHODIST	NONE	MARRIED
1944	SILLERS WALTER	METHODIST	.	MARRIED
1966	JUNKIN JOHN RICHARD	CATHOLIC	ENLISTED	MARRIED
1976	NEWMAN CLARENCE BENTON	BAPTIST	ENLISTED	MARRIED
1988	FORD TIMOTHY ALAN	PRESBYTER	NONE	MARRIED

NORTH CAROLINA

1911	DOWD WILLIAM CAREY	BAPTIST	NONE	MARRIED
1913	CONNOR GEORGE WHITFIELD	EPISCOPAL	NONE	MARRIED
1914	MURPHY WALTER	EPISCOPAL	ENLISTED	MARRIED
1915	WOOTEN EMMETT ROBINSON	EPISCOPAL	.	MARRIED
1919	BRUMMITT DENNIS GARFIELD	UNKN PROT	.	MARRIED
1921	GRIER HARRY PERCY	CONGREGAT	NONE	MARRIED
1923	DAWSON JOHN GILMER	EPISCOPAL	.	MARRIED
1925	PHARR EDGAR WALTER	PRESBYTER	.	MARRIED
1927	FOUNTAIN RICHARD TILLMAN	PRESBYTER	NONE	MARRIED
1929	GRAHAM ALEXANDER HAWKINS	EPISCOPAL	OFFICER	MARRIED
1931	SMITH WILLIS	METHODIST	ENLISTED	MARRIED
1933	HARRIS REGINALD LEE	METHODIST	NONE	MARRIED
1935	JOHNSON ROBERT GRADY	UNKN PROT	ENLISTED	NEV MARR
1936	CHERRY ROBERT GREGG	METHODIST	OFFICER	MARRIED
1939	WARD DAVID LIVINGSTONE JR	EPISCOPAL	NONE	MARRIED
1941	MULL ODUS MCCOY	BAPTIST	NONE	MARRIED
1943	KERR JOHN HOSEA JR	BAPTIST	ENLISTED	MARRIED
1945	RICHARDSON OSCAR LEON	METHODIST	ENLISTED	MARRIED
1947	PEARSALL THOMAS JENKINS	UNKN PROT	OFFICER	MARRIED
1949	RAMSAY KERR CRAIGE	PRESBYTER	.	MARRIED
1951	TAYLOR WALTER FRANK	METHODIST	OFFICER	MARRIED
1953	BOST EUGENE THOMPSON JR	METHODIST	.	MARRIED
1955	MOORE LARRY ICHABOD JR	EPISCOPAL	NONE	MARRIED
1957	DOUGHTON JAMES KEMP	METHODIST	NONE	REMARR
1959	HEWLETT ADDISON JR	BAPTIST	OFFICER	MARRIED
1961	HUNT JOSEPH MARVIN	METHODIST	NONE	MARRIED
1963	BLUE HERBERT CLIFTON	PRESBYTER	NONE	MARRIED
1965	TAYLOR HOYT PATRICK JR	METHODIST	OFFICER	MARRIED
1967	BRITT DAVID MAXWELL	BAPTIST	ENLISTED	MARRIED
1967	VAUGHN EARL W	METHODIST	ENLISTED	MARRIED
1969	GODWIN PHILIP PITTMAN	BAPTIST	ENLISTED	MARRIED

STATE

1ST SPKR	NAME	RELIGION	MILITARY RANK	MARITAL STATUS

NORTH CAROLINA (*CONT.*)

1973	RAMSEY JAMES EDWARD	METHODIST	OFFICER	MARRIED
1975	GREEN JAMES COLLINS	PRESBYTER	ENLISTED	MARRIED
1977	STEWART CARL JEROME JR	METHODIST	OFFICER	MARRIED
1981	RAMSEY LISTON BRYAN	BAPTIST	ENLISTED	MARRIED
1989	MAVRETIC JOSEPHUS L	METHODIST	OFFICER	MARRIED

OKLAHOMA

1910	ANTHONY WILLIAM BRUCE	METHODIST	.	MARRIED
1911	DURANT WILLIAM ALEXANDER	PRESBYTER	.	MARRIED
1913	MAXEY JAMES HARVEY	.	.	.
1915	MCCRORY ALONZO	BAPTIST	NONE	MARRIED
1917	NESBITT PAUL	.	NONE	MARRIED
1919	WALDREP THOMAS CARNES	METHODIST	.	MARRIED
1921	SCHWABE GEORGE BLAINE	DISCIPLES	NONE	MARRIED
1923	GIBBONS MURRAY F	.	NONE	MARRIED
1923	MCBEE WILLIAM DALTON	METHODIST	NONE	MARRIED
1925	HARPER JESSE B	BAPTIST	NONE	MARRIED
1927	STOVALL DAVID ANCIL	PRESBYTER	NONE	MARRIED
1929	STREET ALLEN MORGAN	PRESBYTER	NONE	MARRIED
1929	NANCE JAMES CLARK	PRESBYTER	NONE	MARRIED
1931	WEAVER CARLTON	BAPTIST	ENLISTED	MARRIED
1933	ANGLIN WILLIAM THOMAS	DISCIPLES	.	MARRIED
1935	PHILLIPS LEON CHASE	METHODIST	ENLISTED	MARRIED
1937	DANIEL J T	BAPTIST	.	MARRIED
1939	WELCH WILLIAM DONOVAN SR	DISCIPLES	ENLISTED	MARRIED
1941	BLUMHAGEN E	NONE	NONE	MARRIED
1943	FREEMAN HAROLD	PRESBYTER	ENLISTED	MARRIED
1944	LANSDEN JOSEPH MERLE	CATHOLIC	OFFICER	MARRIED
1945	HILL JOHNSON DAVIS	EPISCOPAL	NONE	MARRIED
1945	HINDS H IREDELLE	METHODIST	ENLISTED	MARRIED
1947	BOARD CHARLES RAYMOND	BAPTIST	NONE	MARRIED
1949	BILLINGSLEY WALTER ASBURY	DISCIPLES	OFFICER	MARRIED
1951	BULLARD JAMES MARVIN	BAPTIST	NONE	MARRIED
1955	HARKEY BYRON E	EPISCOPAL	ENLISTED	MARRIED
1959	LIVINGSTON CLINT GRAHAM	METHODIST	ENLISTED	MARRIED
1961	MCCARTY J D	METHODIST	ENLISTED	MARRIED
1967	PRIVETT ARNOLD REX	METHODIST	ENLISTED	MARRIED
1973	WILLIS WILLIAM PASCAL	BAPTIST	ENLISTED	MARRIED
1979	DRAPER DANIEL DAVID JR	DISCIPLES	NONE	MARRIED
1984	BARKER JIM L	METHODIST	OFFICER	MARRIED
1989	LEWIS STEPHEN C	.	ENLISTED	MARRIED

SOUTH CAROLINA

1915	HOYT JAMES ALFRED	BAPTIST	OFFICER	.
1918	COTHRAN THOMAS PERRIN	PRESBYTER	.	WIDOWED
1921	ATKINSON JAMES BUFORD	.	.	.
1923	MCMILLAN THOMAS SANDERS	BAPTIST	.	MARRIED
1925	BROWN EDGAR ALLAN	METHODIST	ENLISTED	MARRIED

STATE

1ST SPKR	NAME	RELIGION	MILITARY RANK	MARITAL STATUS

SOUTH CAROLINA (*CONT.*)

1ST SPKR	NAME	RELIGION	MILITARY RANK	MARITAL STATUS
1927	HAMBLIN JOHN KNAPP	BAPTIST	.	REMARR
1933	GIBSON JAMES BREEDEN	METHODIST	.	MARRIED
1935	TAYLOR CLAUDE AMBROSE	PRESBYTER	NONE	MARRIED
1937	BLATT SOLOMON	JEWISH	ENLISTED	MARRIED
1947	LITTLEJOHN CAMERON BRUCE	BAPTIST	OFFICER	MARRIED
1949	POPE THOMAS HARRINGTON	BAPTIST	OFFICER	MARRIED
1973	CARTER REX LYLE	UNKN PROT	ENLISTED	MARRIED
1980	SCHWARTZ RAMON JR	EPISCOPAL	ENLISTED	MARRIED
1987	SHEHEEN ROBERT J	CATHOLIC	NONE	NEV MARR

TENNESSEE

1ST SPKR	NAME	RELIGION	MILITARY RANK	MARITAL STATUS
1911	LEACH ALBERT MARTIN	METHODIST	NONE	MARRIED
1913	STANTON WILLIAM MORTIMER	CATHOLIC	NONE	NEV MARR
1915	COOPER WILLIAM PRENTICE	METHODIST	NONE	MARRIED
1917	SHROPSHIRE CLYDE MOORE	BAPTIST	NONE	MARRIED
1919	WALKER SETH MCKINNEY	PRESBYTER	NONE	MARRIED
1921	TODD ANDREW LEE	BAPTIST	NONE	MARRIED
1923	HALL FRANK SAMPSON	PRESBYTER	ENLISTED	MARRIED
1925	BARRY WILLIAM FRANCIS JR	BAPTIST	ENLISTED	NEV MARR
1927	MAIDEN SELDEN LONGLEY	METHODIST	.	MARRIED
1929	LOVE CHARLES HOWARD	METHODIST	NONE	MARRIED
1931	HAYNES WALTER MILLER	EPISCOPAL	NONE	MARRIED
1933	MOORE FRANK WASHINGTON	PRESBYTER	NONE	MARRIED
1939	O'DELL JOHN ED	PRESBYTER	.	MARRIED
1943	BROOME JAMES JESSE	PRESBYTER	NONE	MARRIED
1945	WOODS GEORGE STANLEY	BAPTIST	.	MARRIED
1947	LEWALLEN W BUFORD	BAPTIST	ENLISTED	MARRIED
1949	FOUTCH MCALLEN	BAPTIST	.	MARRIED
1953	BOMAR JAMES LA FAYETTE JR	PRESBYTER	OFFICER	MARRIED
1963	BARRY WILLIAM LOGAN	BAPTIST	OFFICER	NEV MARR
1967	CUMMINGS JAMES HARVEY II	.	NONE	MARRIED
1969	JENKINS WILLIAM LEWIS	BAPTIST	OFFICER	MARRIED
1971	MCKINNEY JAMES ROBIN	BAPTIST	ENLISTED	MARRIED
1973	MCWHERTER NED RAY	METHODIST	OFFICER	DIVORCED
1987	MURRAY CHARLES EDWARD	UNKN PROT	ENLISTED	MARRIED

TEXAS

1ST SPKR	NAME	RELIGION	MILITARY RANK	MARITAL STATUS
1911	RAYBURN SAMUEL TALIAFERRO	BAPTIST	NONE	NEV MARR
1913	TERRELL CHESTER H	.	NONE	.
1915	WOODS JOHN WILLIAM	METHODIST	NONE	MARRIED
1917	FULLER FRANKLIN OLIVER	UNKN PROT	OFFICER	MARRIED
1919	THOMASON ROBERT EWING	PRESBYTER	NONE	MARRIED
1921	THOMAS CHARLES GRAHAM	.	.	.
1923	SEAGLER RICHARD E	.	.	.
1925	SATTERWHITE ROBERT LEE	BAPTIST	ENLISTED	MARRIED
1927	BOBBITT ROBERT LEE	PRESBYTER	OFFICER	MARRIED
1929	BARRON WINGATE STUART	BAPTIST	NONE	NEV MARR
1931	MINOR FRED H	DISCIPLES	NONE	MARRIED

STATE

1ST SPKR	NAME	RELIGION	MILITARY RANK	MARITAL STATUS

TEXAS (*CONT.*)

1ST SPKR	NAME	RELIGION	MILITARY RANK	MARITAL STATUS
1933	STEVENSON COKE ROBERT	METHODIST	NONE	MARRIED
1937	CALVERT ROBERT WILBURN	BAPTIST	NONE	MARRIED
1939	MORSE ROBERT EMMETT	BAPTIST	OFFICER	MARRIED
1941	LEONARD HOMER L	BAPTIST	ENLISTED	MARRIED
1943	DANIEL MARION PRICE SR	BAPTIST	OFFICER	MARRIED
1945	GILMER CLAUD H	BAPTIST	NONE	MARRIED
1947	REED WILLIAM OTEY	PRESBYTER	NONE	MARRIED
1949	MANFORD THOMAS DURWOOD JR	METHODIST	NONE	MARRIED
1951	SENTERFITT REUBEN	UNKN PROT	OFFICER	MARRIED
1955	LINDSEY JIM THURSTON	BAPTIST	ENLISTED	MARRIED
1957	CARR WAGGONER	METHODIST	OFFICER	MARRIED
1961	TURMAN JAMES A	BAPTIST	ENLISTED	MARRIED
1963	TUNNELL BYRON M	METHODIST	ENLISTED	MARRIED
1965	BARNES BEN FRANK	METHODIST	NONE	MARRIED
1969	MUTSCHER GUS FRANKLIN	LUTHERAN	OFFICER	NEV MARR
1972	PRICE WILLIAM RAYFORD	METHODIST	ENLISTED	MARRIED
1973	DANIEL MARION PRICE JR	METHODIST	NONE	MARRIED
1975	CLAYTON BILLY WAYNE	BAPTIST	NONE	MARRIED
1983	LEWIS GIBSON D	DISCIPLES	ENLISTED	MARRIED

VIRGINIA

1ST SPKR	NAME	RELIGION	MILITARY RANK	MARITAL STATUS
1914	COX EDWIN PIPER	EPISCOPAL	NONE	MARRIED
1916	HOUSTON HARRY RUTHERFORD	PRESBYTER	NONE	MARRIED
1920	BREWER RICHARD LEWIS JR	METHODIST	NONE	.
1926	OZLIN THOMAS WILLIAM	BAPTIST	NONE	WIDOWED
1930	BROWN J SINCLAIR	PRESBYTER	NONE	MARRIED
1936	DOVELL GROVER ASHTON	EPISCOPAL	ENLISTED	MARRIED
1942	STANLEY THOMAS BAHNSON	METHODIST	NONE	MARRIED
1947	MASSENBURG GEORGE ALVIN	METHODIST	OFFICER	MARRIED
1950	MOORE EDGAR BLACKBURN	PRESBYTER	NONE	MARRIED
1968	COOKE JOHN WARREN	EPISCOPAL	NONE	MARRIED
1980	PHILPOTT ALBERT LEE	METHODIST	OFFICER	MARRIED

WEST VIRGINIA

1ST SPKR	NAME	RELIGION	MILITARY RANK	MARITAL STATUS
1911	WETZEL CHARLES MCCLUER	EPISCOPAL	NONE	MARRIED
1913	GEORGE WILLIAM TAYLOR	METHODIST	NONE	MARRIED
1915	JOHNSON VERNON EMIL	.	.	MARRIED
1917	THURMOND JOSEPH SAMUEL	BAPTIST	NONE	WIDOWED
1919	WOLFE J LUTHER	METHODIST	NONE	MARRIED
1921	KEATLEY EDWIN MINER	EPISCOPAL	NONE	REMARR
1923	BYRNE WILLIAM ESTON R	PRESBYTER	NONE	MARRIED
1929	CUMMINS JOHN WILLIAM	CATHOLIC	OFFICER	MARRIED
1931	TAYLOR JAMES ALFRED	PRESBYTER	ENLISTED	MARRIED
1933	HINER RALPH MCCLUNG	.	OFFICER	MARRIED
1935	PELTER JOHN J	EPISCOPAL	NONE	NEV MARR
1937	THOMAS JAMES KAY	METHODIST	OFFICER	MARRIED
1941	ARNOLD MALCOLM R	PRESBYTER	OFFICER	MARRIED
1943	AMOS JOHN ELLISON	METHODIST	NONE	MARRIED

STATE

1ST SPKR	NAME	RELIGION	MILITARY RANK	MARITAL STATUS

WEST VIRGINIA (CONT.)

1ST SPKR	NAME	RELIGION	MILITARY RANK	MARITAL STATUS
1949	FLANNERY W E	METHODIST	.	MARRIED
1958	PAULEY HARRY R	METHODIST	NONE	MARRIED
1961	SINGLETON JULIUS W JR	PRESBYTER	OFFICER	MARRIED
1965	WHITE H LABAN JR	BAPTIST	OFFICER	MARRIED
1969	BOIARSKY IVOR F	JEWISH	OFFICER	MARRIED
1971	MCMANUS LEWIS NICHOLS	PRESBYTER	NONE	NEV MARR
1977	KOPP DONALD LEE	METHODIST	NONE	MARRIED
1979	SEE CLYDE M JR	PRESBYTER	ENLISTED	MARRIED
1985	ALBRIGHT JOSEPH PAUL	CATHOLIC	NONE	MARRIED
1987	CHAMBERS ROBERT C	METHODIST	NONE	MARRIED

KEY:

  1ST SPKR = YEAR FIRST SERVED AS SPEAKER

  RELIGION = RELIGIOUS AFFILIATION DURING SPEAKERSHIP
    (SOME RESPONSES TRUNCATED)
    . = MISSING DATA
    CONGREGAT = CONGREGATIONALIST / UNITED CHURCH OF CHRIST
    DISCIPLES = DISCIPLES OF CHRIST / CHURCH OF CHRIST
    UNITARIAN = UNITARIAN / UNIVERSALIST
    CHRST SCI = CHRISTIAN SCIENTIST
    PROTEST = UNIDENTIFIED PROTESTANT AFFILIATION

  MILITARY RANK = HIGHEST MILITARY RANK BEFORE SPEAKERSHIP
    . = MISSING DATA

  MARITAL STATUS = MARITAL STATUS DURING SPEAKERSHIP
    . = MISSING DATA
    NEV MARR = NEVER MARRIED
    REMARR = REMARRIED

Appendix 7: Occupations

1ST SPKR	NAME	BEFORE SPEAKER	CONTINUE AFTER	BEGUN AFTER
ALABAMA				
1911	ALMON EDWARD BERTON	LAWYER	NONE	NONE
1919	MERRITT HENRY PAUL	LAWYER	NONE	NONE
1920	LYNNE SEABOURN ARTHUR	LAWYER	LAWYER	NONE
1923	MERRILL HUGH DAVIS	LAWYER	LAWYER	NONE
1927	LONG JOHN LEE	WHOLESAL	NONE	NONE
1935	WALKER ROBERT HENRY	NEWSPAP	NEWSPAP	NONE
1942	MILLER GEORGE OLIVER	LAWYER	LAWYER	NONE
1944	NORMAN CHARLES DOZIER	NEWSPAP	NEWSPAP	NONE
1947	BECK WILLIAM MORRIS	LAWYER	LAWYER	NONE
1951	BROWN ROBERTS HENRY	LAWYER	LAWYER	NONE
1955	FITE ERNEST RANKIN	LAWYER	LAWYER	BANKING
1959	ADAMS CHARLES CRAYTON III	REAL EST	NONE	NONE
1961	ASHWORTH VIRGIS MARION	LAWYER	LAWYER	NONE
1963	BREWER ALBERT PRESTON	LAWYER	LAWYER	PROFESSO
1971	LYONS GEORGE SAGE	LAWYER	LAWYER	NONE
1975	MCCORQUODALE JOSEPH CHARLES	RETAIL	RETAIL	NONE
1983	DRAKE THOMAS E	LAWYER	LAWYER	NONE
1987	CLARK JAMES STERLING	REAL EST	REAL EST	NONE
ARKANSAS				
1911	MILWEE R FRANK	AGRICULT	NONE	RETAIL
1913	HARDAGE JOSIAH	LAWYER	NONE	NONE
1915	SAWYER LEWIS ERNEST	LAWYER	LAWYER	NONE
1917	CAZORT WILLIAM LEE SR	LAWYER	NONE	NONE
1919	NEWTON CLARENCE PRICE	NEWSPAP	NONE	GOV AIDE
1921	JOINER JOSEPH WILLIAM	LAWYER	LAWYER	NONE
1923	REED HOWARD	LAWYER	LAWYER	NONE
1925	HILL THOMAS AUSTIN	PUB REL	PUB REL	NONE
1927	CAUDLE REECE ARTHUR	LAWYER	LAWYER	NONE
1929	ABINGTON WILLIAM H	DOCTOR	DOCTOR	NONE
1931	NEALE IRVING C	LAWYER	NONE	NONE
1933	TONEY HARDIN KEMP	LAWYER	LAWYER	NONE
1935	THORN HARVEY BELL SR	TEACHER	NONE	LAWYER
1937	BRANSFORD JOHN MCKINNIS	BANKING	BANKING	NONE
1941	WILKINSON NORMAN MEANS	LAWYER	BANKING	NONE
1943	GRIFFITH ROBERT WILLIAM	LAWYER	LAWYER	NONE

STATE

1ST SPKR	NAME	BEFORE SPEAKER	CONTINUE AFTER	BEGUN AFTER
	ARKANSAS (CONT.)			
1945	NORTHCUTT HORACE ALLEN	LAWYER	NONE	BANKING
1947	RIALES ROY LEE SR	ENGINEER	NONE	NONE
1949	HENDRIX CARL EDWARD	BANKING	.	.
1951	CAMPBELL JAMES R JR	LAWYER	NONE	NONE
1953	HOLLENSWORTH CARROLL C	LAWYER	NONE	NONE
1955	SMITH CHARLES F JR	LAWYER	NONE	NONE
1957	WALTHER GLENN F	LAWYER	LAWYER	NONE
1959	FLEEMAN EUGENE CECIL	BANKING	NONE	NONE
1961	BETHELL JOHN PINCKNEY SR	TEACHER	NONE	AGRICULT
1963	CRANK MARION HARLAN	REAL EST	REAL EST	NONE
1965	COTTRELL JOHN HALL JR	BANKING	BANKING	NONE
1967	COCKRILL STERLING ROBERTSON	INSURANC	NONE	NONE
1969	MCCLERKIN HAYES CANDOR	LAWYER	LAWYER	NONE
1971	SMITH RAY S JR	LAWYER	LAWYER	NONE
1973	TURNER GROVER W JR	REAL EST	REAL EST	NONE
1975	ALEXANDER CECIL LEWIS	REAL EST	REAL EST	LOBBYIST
1977	SHAVER JAMES LEVESQUE JR	LAWYER	LAWYER	NONE
1979	MILLER JOHN ELDON	REAL EST	REAL EST	NONE
1981	MCCUISTON LLOYD CARLISLE JR	AGRICULT	AGRICULT	NONE
1983	CAPPS JOHN PAUL	RADIO/TV	RADIO/TV	NONE
1985	LANDERS H LACY	MINING	NONE	NONE
1987	CUNNINGHAM ERNEST G	MINING	MINING	NONE
1989	HENDRIX B G	REAL EST	REAL EST	NONE
	FLORIDA			
1911	JENNINGS THOMAS ALBERT	RETAIL	RETAIL	NONE
1915	HARDEE CARY AUGUSTUS	LAWYER	NONE	BANKING
1918	WILDER GEORGE HAMILTON	GOV AIDE	NONE	NONE
1921	JENNINGS FRANK E	LAWYER	LAWYER	NONE
1923	EDGE L DAY	RETAIL	RETAIL	AGRICULT
1925	MILAM ARTHUR YAGER	LAWYER	LAWYER	NONE
1927	DAVIS FRED HENRY	LAWYER	NONE	NONE
1929	GETZEN SAMUEL WYCHE	LAWYER	NONE	NONE
1931	LEWIS E CLAY JR	LAWYER	NONE	NONE
1933	TOMASELLO PETER JR	BANKING	NONE	LOBBYIST
1935	BISHOP WILLIAM BURTON	AGRICULT	AGRICULT	NONE
1937	CHRISTIE WILLIAM MCLEAN	LAWYER	NONE	NONE
1939	WOOD GEORGE PIERCE	MILLING	MILLING	NONE
1941	MCCARTY DANIEL THOMAS	AGRICULT	AGRICULT	NONE
1943	SIMPSON RICHARD HENRY	RETAIL	AGRICULT	NONE
1945	CRARY EVANS SR	LAWYER	LAWYER	NONE
1947	BEASLEY THOMAS DEKALB	LAWYER	LAWYER	NONE
1949	MURRAY PERRY EARL	LAWYER	AGRICULT	NONE
1951	ELLIOTT ELMER B	AGRICULT	AGRICULT	NONE
1953	BRYANT CECIL FARRIS	LAWYER	LAWYER	NONE
1955	DAVID THOMAS E	LAWYER	LAWYER	NONE
1957	CONNER DOYLE E	AGRICULT	AGRICULT	NONE
1961	CHAPPELL WILLIAM VENROE JR	LAWYER	LAWYER	CRAFT
1962	HORNE MALLORY ELI	LAWYER	LAWYER	LOBBYIST
1965	ROWELL E C	BANKING	BANKING	LOBBYIST

STATE

1ST SPKR	NAME	BEFORE SPEAKER	CONTINUE AFTER	BEGUN AFTER

FLORIDA (CONT.)

1ST SPKR	NAME	BEFORE SPEAKER	CONTINUE AFTER	BEGUN AFTER
1967	TURLINGTON RALPH DONALD	PROFESSO	NONE	NONE
1969	SCHULTZ FREDERICK HENRY	BANKING	BANKING	NONE
1971	PETTIGREW RICHARD ALLEN	LAWYER	LAWYER	NONE
1973	SESSUMS THOMAS TERRELL	LAWYER	LAWYER	NONE
1975	TUCKER DONALD L	LAWYER	.	.
1979	BROWN JAMES HYATT	INSURANC	INSURANC	NONE
1981	HABEN RALPH H JR	LAWYER	NONE	NONE
1983	MOFFITT H LEE	LAWYER	LAWYER	NONE
1985	THOMPSON JAMES HAROLD	LAWYER	LAWYER	NONE
1987	MILLS JON L	LAWYER	LAWYER	NONE
1989	GUSTAFSON TOM	LAWYER	LAWYER	NONE

GEORGIA

1ST SPKR	NAME	BEFORE SPEAKER	CONTINUE AFTER	BEGUN AFTER
1913	BURWELL WILLIAM HIX	LAWYER	LAWYER	NONE
1921	NEILL WILLIAM CECIL	LAWYER	NONE	NONE
1927	RUSSELL RICHARD BREVARD	LAWYER	NONE	NONE
1931	TUCKER ARLIE DANIEL	LAWYER	NONE	NONE
1933	RIVERS EURITH DICKINSON	LAWYER	NONE	RADIO/TV
1937	HARRIS ROY VINCENT	LAWYER	LAWYER	NONE
1941	EVANS RANDALL JR	LAWYER	NONE	NONE
1947	HAND FREDRICK BARROW	AGRICULT	AGRICULT	NONE
1955	MOATE MARVIN E	LAWYER	LAWYER	NONE
1959	SMITH GEORGE LEON II	LAWYER	LAWYER	NONE
1963	SMITH GEORGE THORNEWELL	LAWYER	LAWYER	NONE
1974	MURPHY THOMAS BAILEY	LAWYER	LAWYER	NONE

KENTUCKY

1ST SPKR	NAME	BEFORE SPEAKER	CONTINUE AFTER	BEGUN AFTER
1912	TERRELL CLAUDE B	LAWYER	LAWYER	NONE
1916	DUFFY HUGH CORNELIUS	LAWYER	LAWYER	NONE
1918	CROWE ROBERT T	LAWYER	LAWYER	NONE
1920	BOSWORTH JOE F	LAWYER	NONE	NONE
1922	THOMPSON JAMES H	AGRICULT	AGRICULT	NONE
1924	ADAMS SAMUEL W	LAWYER	LAWYER	NONE
1926	DRURY GEORGE LUCIAN	LAWYER	LAWYER	NONE
1928	MILLIKEN JOHN S	LAWYER	.	.
1932	BROWN JOHN YOUNG	LAWYER	LAWYER	NONE
1933	LEBUS FRANK	AGRICULT	.	.
1934	ROGERS W E SR	RETAIL	RETAIL	NONE
1935	BROWN WALLACE	LAWYER	NONE	NONE
1936	KIRTLEY JOHN D	AGRICULT	NONE	NONE
1940	SHIELDS BENJAMIN FRANKLIN	DOCTOR	DOCTOR	NONE
1942	DICKSON STANLEY S	AGRICULT	.	.
1944	WATERFIELD HARRY LEE	NEWSPAP	NEWSPAP	BANKING
1948	TINSLEY T HERBERT	CLERGY	NONE	NONE
1950	DORAN ADRON	CLERGY	CLERGY	COLL ADM
1952	BURNLEY CHARLES W	CRAFT	NONE	NONE
1956	FITZPATRICK THOMAS P	INSURANC	NONE	NONE
1958	WEINTRAUB MORRIS	LAWYER	LAWYER	NONE

STATE

1ST SPKR	NAME	BEFORE SPEAKER	CONTINUE AFTER	BEGUN AFTER

KENTUCKY (*CONT.*)

1ST SPKR	NAME	BEFORE SPEAKER	CONTINUE AFTER	BEGUN AFTER
1960	LOWMAN HARRY KING	REAL EST	REAL EST	NONE
1964	MCCALLUM SHELBY	RADIO/TV	RADIO/TV	NONE
1968	CARROLL JULIAN MORTON	LAWYER	LAWYER	NONE
1972	BLUME NORBERT	UNION	UNION	LOBBYIST
1976	KENTON WILLIAM G	LAWYER	LAWYER	NONE
1982	RICHARDSON BOBBY HAROLD	LAWYER	LAWYER	NONE
1986	BLANDFORD DONALD JOSEPH	AGRICULT	AGRICULT	NONE

LOUISIANA

1ST SPKR	NAME	BEFORE SPEAKER	CONTINUE AFTER	BEGUN AFTER
1912	THOMAS LEE EMMETT	.	NONE	NONE
1916	BOUANCHAUD HEWITT LEONIDAS	LAWYER	LAWYER	AGRICULT
1920	WALKER RICHARD FLOURNOY	LAWYER	LAWYER	NONE
1924	DOUGLAS JAMES STUART	RETAIL	NONE	NONE
1926	HUGHES WILLIAM CLARK	RETAIL	NONE	NONE
1928	FOURNET JOHN BAPTISTE	LAWYER	NONE	NONE
1932	ELLENDER ALLEN JOSEPH	LAWYER	NONE	NONE
1936	WIMBERLY LORRIS M	CONSTRUC	NONE	INSURANC
1940	BAUER RALPH NORMAN	LAWYER	LAWYER	NONE
1952	AYCOCK CLARENCE C	LAWYER	NONE	NONE
1957	ANGELLE ROBERT	MINING	NONE	BANKING
1960	JEWELL J THOMAS	LAWYER	LAWYER	NONE
1964	DELONY VAIL MONTGOMERY	AGRICULT	NONE	NONE
1968	GARRETT JOHN SIDNEY	BANKING	BANKING	NONE
1972	HENRY EDGERTON L	LAWYER	LAWYER	NONE
1980	HAINKEL JOHN JOSEPH JR	LAWYER	LAWYER	NONE
1984	ALARIO JOHN A JR	ACCOUNT	ACCOUNT	NONE
1988	DIMOS JIMMY N	LAWYER	LAWYER	NONE

MARYLAND

1ST SPKR	NAME	BEFORE SPEAKER	CONTINUE AFTER	BEGUN AFTER
1912	TRIPPE JAMES MCCONKY	LAWYER	NONE	NONE
1916	LAIRD PHILIP DANDRIDGE	LAWYER	LAWYER	NONE
1917	MCINTOSH DAVID GREGG JR	LAWYER	NONE	NONE
1918	WOODEN HERBERT R	AGRICULT	AGRICULT	NONE
1920	TYDINGS MILLARD EVELYN	LAWYER	NONE	AGRICULT
1922	LEE JOHN L G	.	NONE	NONE
1924	CURTIS FRANCIS P	LAWYER	NONE	NONE
1927	LEE EDWARD BROOKE	REAL EST	REAL EST	AGRICULT
1931	MICHEL FRANCIS A	LAWYER	LAWYER	NONE
1933	HARRINGTON T BARTON	LAWYER	LAWYER	NONE
1935	GORFINE EMANUEL	LAWYER	NONE	NONE
1939	CONLON THOMAS EDWARD	TRANSPOR	NONE	NONE
1943	WHITE JOHN S	LAWYER	LAWYER	NONE
1947	SYBERT CORNELIUS FERDINAND	LAWYER	LAWYER	NONE
1951	LUBER JOHN CHRISTOPHER	ACCOUNT	ACCOUNT	LOBBYIST
1959	WILKINSON PERRY O	INSURANC	INSURANC	NONE
1963	BOONE A GORDON	LAWYER	NONE	NONE
1964	MANDEL MARVIN	LAWYER	NONE	RADIO/TV
1969	LOWE THOMAS HUNTER	LAWYER	LAWYER	NONE

STATE

1ST SPKR	NAME	BEFORE SPEAKER	CONTINUE AFTER	BEGUN AFTER

MARYLAND (*CONT.*)

1ST SPKR	NAME	BEFORE SPEAKER	CONTINUE AFTER	BEGUN AFTER
1973	BRISCOE JOHN HANSON	LAWYER	LAWYER	LOBBYIST
1979	CARDIN BENJAMIN LOUIS	LAWYER	LAWYER	NONE
1987	MITCHELL R CLAYTON JR	.	NONE	NONE

MISSISSIPPI

1ST SPKR	NAME	BEFORE SPEAKER	CONTINUE AFTER	BEGUN AFTER
1912	QUIN HILLRIE MARSHALL	LAWYER	LAWYER	NONE
1916	CONNER MARTIN SENNETT	LAWYER	LAWYER	RECREAT
1924	BAILEY THOMAS LOWRY	LAWYER	NONE	NONE
1936	STANSEL HORACE SYLVAN	ENGINEER	NONE	NONE
1936	WRIGHT FIELDING LEWIS	LAWYER	LAWYER	NONE
1940	LUMPKIN SAMUEL E	LAWYER	LAWYER	NONE
1944	SILLERS WALTER	LAWYER	NONE	NONE
1966	JUNKIN JOHN RICHARD	CONSTRUC	CONSTRUC	NONE
1976	NEWMAN CLARENCE BENTON	AGRICULT	AGRICULT	NONE
1988	FORD TIMOTHY ALAN	LAWYER	LAWYER	NONE

NORTH CAROLINA

1ST SPKR	NAME	BEFORE SPEAKER	CONTINUE AFTER	BEGUN AFTER
1911	DOWD WILLIAM CAREY	NEWSPAP	NEWSPAP	NONE
1913	CONNOR GEORGE WHITFIELD	LAWYER	NONE	NONE
1914	MURPHY WALTER	LAWYER	LAWYER	NONE
1915	WOOTEN EMMETT ROBINSON	LAWYER	NONE	NONE
1919	BRUMMITT DENNIS GARFIELD	LAWYER	LAWYER	NONE
1921	GRIER HARRY PERCY	LAWYER	NONE	NONE
1923	DAWSON JOHN GILMER	LAWYER	LAWYER	RADIO/TV
1925	PHARR EDGAR WALTER	LAWYER	LAWYER	NONE
1927	FOUNTAIN RICHARD TILLMAN	LAWYER	LAWYER	NONE
1929	GRAHAM ALEXANDER HAWKINS	LAWYER	LAWYER	NONE
1931	SMITH WILLIS	LAWYER	LAWYER	NONE
1933	HARRIS REGINALD LEE	MILLING	MILLING	NONE
1935	JOHNSON ROBERT GRADY	LAWYER	LAWYER	NONE
1936	CHERRY ROBERT GREGG	LAWYER	LAWYER	NONE
1939	WARD DAVID LIVINGSTONE JR	LAWYER	LAWYER	PROFESSO
1941	MULL ODUS MCCOY	LAWYER	LAWYER	AGRICULT
1943	KERR JOHN HOSEA JR	LAWYER	LAWYER	NONE
1945	RICHARDSON OSCAR LEON	LAWYER	NONE	NONE
1947	PEARSALL THOMAS JENKINS	LAWYER	NONE	BANKING
1949	RAMSAY KERR CRAIGE	LAWYER	NONE	NONE
1951	TAYLOR WALTER FRANK	LAWYER	LAWYER	NONE
1953	BOST EUGENE THOMPSON JR	LAWYER	LAWYER	MILLING
1955	MOORE LARRY ICHABOD JR	LAWYER	LAWYER	NONE
1957	DOUGHTON JAMES KEMP	BANKING	BANKING	NONE
1959	HEWLETT ADDISON JR	LAWYER	LAWYER	NONE
1961	HUNT JOSEPH MARVIN	INSURANC	INSURANC	NONE
1963	BLUE HERBERT CLIFTON	NEWSPAP	NEWSPAP	NONE
1965	TAYLOR HOYT PATRICK JR	LAWYER	LAWYER	NONE
1967	BRITT DAVID MAXWELL	LAWYER	LAWYER	NONE
1967	VAUGHN EARL W	LAWYER	NONE	NONE
1969	GODWIN PHILIP PITTMAN	LAWYER	LAWYER	NONE

STATE

1ST SPKR	NAME	BEFORE SPEAKER	CONTINUE AFTER	BEGUN AFTER

NORTH CAROLINA (CONT.)

1ST SPKR	NAME	BEFORE SPEAKER	CONTINUE AFTER	BEGUN AFTER
1973	RAMSEY JAMES EDWARD	LAWYER	LAWYER	NONE
1975	GREEN JAMES COLLINS	AGRICULT	AGRICULT	REAL EST
1977	STEWART CARL JEROME JR	LAWYER	LAWYER	BANKING
1981	RAMSEY LISTON BRYAN	RETAIL	NONE	NONE
1989	MAVRETIC JOSEPHUS L	AGRICULT	AGRICULT	NONE

OKLAHOMA

1ST SPKR	NAME	BEFORE SPEAKER	CONTINUE AFTER	BEGUN AFTER
1910	ANTHONY WILLIAM BRUCE	NEWSPAP	NONE	UTILITY
1911	DURANT WILLIAM ALEXANDER	LAWYER	NONE	LABORER
1913	MAXEY JAMES HARVEY	.	.	.
1915	MCCRORY ALONZO	BANKING	BANKING	NONE
1917	NESBITT PAUL	NEWSPAP	NEWSPAP	NONE
1919	WALDREP THOMAS CARNES	LAWYER	LAWYER	NONE
1921	SCHWABE GEORGE BLAINE	LAWYER	LAWYER	NONE
1923	GIBBONS MURRAY F	LAWYER	LAWYER	NONE
1923	MCBEE WILLIAM DALTON	LAWYER	LAWYER	REAL EST
1925	HARPER JESSE B	LAWYER	NONE	NONE
1927	STOVALL DAVID ANCIL	LAWYER	LAWYER	NONE
1929	STREET ALLEN MORGAN	MORTUARY	MORTUARY	NONE
1929	NANCE JAMES CLARK	NEWSPAP	NEWSPAP	NONE
1931	WEAVER CARLTON	NEWSPAP	NEWSPAP	BANKING
1933	ANGLIN WILLIAM THOMAS	LAWYER	LAWYER	NONE
1935	PHILLIPS LEON CHASE	LAWYER	LAWYER	NONE
1937	DANIEL J T	TEACHER	NONE	NEWSPAP
1939	WELCH WILLIAM DONOVAN SR	LAWYER	LAWYER	NONE
1941	BLUMHAGEN E	LAWYER	LAWYER	NONE
1943	FREEMAN HAROLD	NONE	NONE	LAWYER
1944	LANSDEN JOSEPH MERLE	LAWYER	LAWYER	NONE
1945	HILL JOHNSON DAVIS	LAWYER	INSURANC	NONE
1945	HINDS H IREDELLE	RETAIL	RETAIL	GOV AIDE
1947	BOARD CHARLES RAYMOND	LAWYER	LAWYER	NONE
1949	BILLINGSLEY WALTER ASBURY	LAWYER	LAWYER	NONE
1951	BULLARD JAMES MARVIN	AGRICULT	AGRICULT	NONE
1955	HARKEY BYRON E	LAWYER	LAWYER	NONE
1959	LIVINGSTON CLINT GRAHAM	LAWYER	LAWYER	CLERGY
1961	MCCARTY J D	INSURANC	INSURANC	LOBBYIST
1967	PRIVETT ARNOLD REX	AGRICULT	NONE	LOBBYIST
1973	WILLIS WILLIAM PASCAL	RETAIL	NONE	NONE
1979	DRAPER DANIEL DAVID JR	LAWYER	NONE	NONE
1984	BARKER JIM L	WHOLESAL	WHOLESAL	NONE
1989	LEWIS STEPHEN C	LAWYER	LAWYER	NONE

SOUTH CAROLINA

1ST SPKR	NAME	BEFORE SPEAKER	CONTINUE AFTER	BEGUN AFTER
1915	HOYT JAMES ALFRED	NEWSPAP	NONE	NONE
1918	COTHRAN THOMAS PERRIN	LAWYER	NONE	NONE
1921	ATKINSON JAMES BUFORD	LAWYER	LAWYER	NONE
1923	MCMILLAN THOMAS SANDERS	LAWYER	NONE	NONE
1925	BROWN EDGAR ALLAN	LAWYER	LAWYER	NONE

STATE

1ST SPKR	NAME	BEFORE SPEAKER	CONTINUE AFTER	BEGUN AFTER

SOUTH CAROLINA (*CONT.*)

1ST SPKR	NAME	BEFORE SPEAKER	CONTINUE AFTER	BEGUN AFTER
1927	HAMBLIN JOHN KNAPP	LAWYER	NONE	NONE
1933	GIBSON JAMES BREEDEN	LAWYER	LAWYER	NONE
1935	TAYLOR CLAUDE AMBROSE	LAWYER	LAWYER	NONE
1937	BLATT SOLOMON	LAWYER	LAWYER	NONE
1947	LITTLEJOHN CAMERON BRUCE	LAWYER	NONE	NONE
1949	POPE THOMAS HARRINGTON	LAWYER	LAWYER	NONE
1973	CARTER REX LYLE	LAWYER	LAWYER	LOBBYIST
1980	SCHWARTZ RAMON JR	LAWYER	LAWYER	NONE
1987	SHEHEEN ROBERT J	LAWYER	LAWYER	NONE

TENNESSEE

1ST SPKR	NAME	BEFORE SPEAKER	CONTINUE AFTER	BEGUN AFTER
1911	LEACH ALBERT MARTIN	MANUFACT	MANUFACT	NONE
1913	STANTON WILLIAM MORTIMER	NONE	NONE	LAWYER
1915	COOPER WILLIAM PRENTICE	LAWYER	BANKING	NONE
1917	SHROPSHIRE CLYDE MOORE	LAWYER	LAWYER	NONE
1919	WALKER SETH MCKINNEY	LAWYER	LAWYER	NONE
1921	TODD ANDREW LEE	LAWYER	NONE	INSURANC
1923	HALL FRANK SAMPSON	LAWYER	LAWYER	NONE
1925	BARRY WILLIAM FRANCIS JR	LAWYER	LAWYER	NONE
1927	MAIDEN SELDEN LONGLEY	LAWYER	LAWYER	BANKING
1929	LOVE CHARLES HOWARD	NEWSPAP	NONE	NONE
1931	HAYNES WALTER MILLER	LAWYER	LAWYER	NONE
1933	MOORE FRANK WASHINGTON	LAWYER	LAWYER	MINING
1939	O'DELL JOHN ED	LAWYER	LAWYER	NONE
1943	BROOME JAMES JESSE	AGRICULT	AGRICULT	NONE
1945	WOODS GEORGE STANLEY	RETAIL	RETAIL	NONE
1947	LEWALLEN W BUFORD	NONE	NONE	LAWYER
1949	FOUTCH MCALLEN	LAWYER	LAWYER	NONE
1953	BOMAR JAMES LA FAYETTE JR	LAWYER	LAWYER	NONE
1963	BARRY WILLIAM LOGAN	LAWYER	LAWYER	GOV AIDE
1967	CUMMINGS JAMES HARVEY II	LAWYER	LAWYER	NONE
1969	JENKINS WILLIAM LEWIS	LAWYER	LAWYER	AGRICULT
1971	MCKINNEY JAMES ROBIN	LAWYER	NONE	NONE
1973	MCWHERTER NED RAY	WHOLESAL	WHOLESAL	NONE
1987	MURRAY CHARLES EDWARD	LAWYER	LAWYER	NONE

TEXAS

1ST SPKR	NAME	BEFORE SPEAKER	CONTINUE AFTER	BEGUN AFTER
1911	RAYBURN SAMUEL TALIAFERRO	TEACHER	NONE	NONE
1913	TERRELL CHESTER H	LAWYER	LAWYER	NONE
1915	WOODS JOHN WILLIAM	LAWYER	LAWYER	NONE
1917	FULLER FRANKLIN OLIVER	LAWYER	LAWYER	NONE
1919	THOMASON ROBERT EWING	LAWYER	LAWYER	NONE
1921	THOMAS CHARLES GRAHAM	RETAIL	NONE	NONE
1923	SEAGLER RICHARD E	LAWYER	LAWYER	NONE
1925	SATTERWHITE ROBERT LEE	NEWSPAP	AGRICULT	NONE
1927	BOBBITT ROBERT LEE	LAWYER	LAWYER	NONE
1929	BARRON WINGATE STUART	LAWYER	LAWYER	NONE
1931	MINOR FRED H	LAWYER	LAWYER	NONE

STATE

1ST SPKR	NAME	BEFORE SPEAKER	CONTINUE AFTER	BEGUN AFTER

TEXAS (CONT.)

1ST SPKR	NAME	BEFORE SPEAKER	CONTINUE AFTER	BEGUN AFTER
1933	STEVENSON COKE ROBERT	LAWYER	LAWYER	NONE
1937	CALVERT ROBERT WILBURN	LAWYER	LAWYER	NONE
1939	MORSE ROBERT EMMETT	REAL EST	NONE	LAWYER
1941	LEONARD HOMER L	SERV IND	SERV IND	LOBBYIST
1943	DANIEL MARION PRICE SR	LAWYER	LAWYER	NONE
1945	GILMER CLAUD H	LAWYER	LAWYER	AGRICULT
1947	REED WILLIAM OTEY	LAWYER	LAWYER	LOBBYIST
1949	MANFORD THOMAS DURWOOD JR	LAWYER	NONE	RETAIL
1951	SENTERFITT REUBEN	LAWYER	LAWYER	AGRICULT
1955	LINDSEY JIM THURSTON	NONE	NONE	LOBBYIST
1957	CARR WAGGONER	NONE	NONE	LAWYER
1961	TURMAN JAMES A	COLL ADM	NONE	GOV AIDE
1963	TUNNELL BYRON M	LAWYER	NONE	MINING
1965	BARNES BEN FRANK	NONE	NONE	REAL EST
1969	MUTSCHER GUS FRANKLIN	PUB REL	NONE	AGRICULT
1972	PRICE WILLIAM RAYFORD	LAWYER	LAWYER	NONE
1973	DANIEL MARION PRICE JR	LAWYER	LAWYER	NONE
1975	CLAYTON BILLY WAYNE	AGRICULT	AGRICULT	NONE
1983	LEWIS GIBSON D	SERV IND	SERV IND	NONE

VIRGINIA

1ST SPKR	NAME	BEFORE SPEAKER	CONTINUE AFTER	BEGUN AFTER
1914	COX EDWIN PIPER	LAWYER	LAWYER	NONE
1916	HOUSTON HARRY RUTHERFORD	NEWSPAP	NEWSPAP	NONE
1920	BREWER RICHARD LEWIS JR	RETAIL	RETAIL	BANKING
1926	OZLIN THOMAS WILLIAM	LAWYER	LAWYER	NONE
1930	BROWN J SINCLAIR	BANKING	BANKING	INSURANC
1936	DOVELL GROVER ASHTON	LAWYER	LAWYER	NONE
1942	STANLEY THOMAS BAHNSON	MANUFACT	MANUFACT	AGRICULT
1947	MASSENBURG GEORGE ALVIN	CRAFT	CRAFT	NONE
1950	MOORE EDGAR BLACKBURN	AGRICULT	AGRICULT	NONE
1968	COOKE JOHN WARREN	NEWSPAP	NEWSPAP	NONE
1980	PHILPOTT ALBERT LEE	LAWYER	LAWYER	NONE

WEST VIRGINIA

1ST SPKR	NAME	BEFORE SPEAKER	CONTINUE AFTER	BEGUN AFTER
1911	WETZEL CHARLES MCCLUER	LAWYER	AGRICULT	NONE
1913	GEORGE WILLIAM TAYLOR	LAWYER	LAWYER	NONE
1915	JOHNSON VERNON EMIL	INSURANC	NONE	NONE
1917	THURMOND JOSEPH SAMUEL	AGRICULT	AGRICULT	NONE
1919	WOLFE J LUTHER	LAWYER	NONE	NONE
1921	KEATLEY EDWIN MINER	LAWYER	LAWYER	NONE
1923	BYRNE WILLIAM ESTON R	LAWYER	LAWYER	NONE
1929	CUMMINS JOHN WILLIAM	LAWYER	LAWYER	NONE
1931	TAYLOR JAMES ALFRED	NEWSPAP	NEWSPAP	NONE
1933	HINER RALPH MCCLUNG	LAWYER	.	.
1935	PELTER JOHN J	TEACHER	TEACHER	MINING
1937	THOMAS JAMES KAY	LAWYER	LAWYER	NONE
1941	ARNOLD MALCOLM R	SCH ADM	SCH ADM	LABORER
1943	AMOS JOHN ELLISON	LAWYER	LAWYER	TRANSPOR

STATE

1ST SPKR	NAME	BEFORE SPEAKER	CONTINUE AFTER	BEGUN AFTER

WEST VIRGINIA (*CONT.*)

1ST SPKR	NAME	BEFORE SPEAKER	CONTINUE AFTER	BEGUN AFTER
1949	FLANNERY W E	SCH ADM	NONE	NONE
1958	PAULEY HARRY R	REAL EST	REAL EST	AGRICULT
1961	SINGLETON JULIUS W JR	LAWYER	LAWYER	GOV AIDE
1965	WHITE H LABAN JR	LAWYER	LAWYER	NONE
1969	BOIARSKY IVOR F	LAWYER	LAWYER	NONE
1971	MCMANUS LEWIS NICHOLS	REAL EST	NONE	LOBBYIST
1977	KOPP DONALD LEE	LABORER	NONE	RETAIL
1979	SEE CLYDE M JR	LAWYER	LAWYER	LOBBYIST
1985	ALBRIGHT JOSEPH PAUL	LAWYER	LAWYER	NONE
1987	CHAMBERS ROBERT C	LAWYER	LAWYER	NONE

KEY:

1ST SPKR = YEAR FIRST SERVED AS SPEAKER

BEFORE SPEAKER = PRIMARY OCCUPATION BEFORE SPEAKERSHIP
CONTINUE AFTER = PRIMARY OCCUPATION CONTINUED AFTER
    SPEAKERSHIP
BEGUN AFTER = PRIMARY OCCUPATION BEGUN AFTER SPEAKERSHIP
    (SOME RESPONSES TRUNCATED)
    . = MISSING DATA

Appendix 8:
Voluntary Organizations

1ST SPKR	NAME	FRAT ORG	PROF ORG	BUS ORG	CIV ORG	OTH ORG	TOT VOL
ALABAMA							
1911	ALMON EDWARD BERTON	YES	NO	YES	NO	YES	8
1919	MERRITT HENRY PAUL	YES	NO	NO	NO	YES	5
1920	LYNNE SEABOURN ARTHUR	YES	NO	NO	NO	NO	2
1923	MERRILL HUGH DAVIS	YES	NO	NO	YES	YES	6
1927	LONG JOHN LEE	NO	NO	NO	NO	YES	1
1935	WALKER ROBERT HENRY	YES	NO	YES	NO	NO	2
1942	MILLER GEORGE OLIVER	NO	NO	NO	NO	NO	0
1944	NORMAN CHARLES DOZIER	YES	NO	NO	NO	NO	1
1947	BECK WILLIAM MORRIS	YES	YES	NO	YES	YES	10
1951	BROWN ROBERTS HENRY	YES	NO	NO	YES	YES	4
1955	FITE ERNEST RANKIN	YES	NO	NO	YES	NO	2
1959	ADAMS CHARLES CRAYTON III	YES	NO	YES	YES	YES	6
1961	ASHWORTH VIRGIS MARION	NO	NO	YES	YES	YES	4
1963	BREWER ALBERT PRESTON	YES	YES	NO	YES	YES	8
1971	LYONS GEORGE SAGE	YES	YES	YES	YES	YES	16
1975	MCCORQUODALE JOSEPH CHARLES	YES	NO	YES	YES	YES	7
1983	DRAKE THOMAS E	YES	YES	NO	NO	YES	9
1987	CLARK JAMES STERLING	NO	NO	YES	YES	YES	4
ARKANSAS							
1911	MILWEE R FRANK	NO	NO	NO	YES	NO	1
1913	HARDAGE JOSIAH	NO	NO	NO	NO	NO	0
1915	SAWYER LEWIS ERNEST	YES	NO	NO	NO	NO	3
1917	CAZORT WILLIAM LEE SR	YES	NO	YES	NO	NO	3
1919	NEWTON CLARENCE PRICE	YES	NO	NO	NO	NO	1
1921	JOINER JOSEPH WILLIAM	YES	NO	NO	NO	NO	4
1923	REED HOWARD	NO	NO	NO	NO	NO	0
1925	HILL THOMAS AUSTIN	YES	NO	YES	NO	NO	4
1927	CAUDLE REECE ARTHUR	YES	NO	YES	NO	YES	3
1929	ABINGTON WILLIAM H	YES	NO	NO	NO	NO	4
1931	NEALE IRVING C	YES	NO	NO	NO	NO	4
1933	TONEY HARDIN KEMP	YES	YES	NO	YES	NO	3
1935	THORN HARVEY BELL SR	YES	NO	NO	NO	NO	1
1937	BRANSFORD JOHN MCKINNIS	YES	NO	YES	NO	NO	3
1941	WILKINSON NORMAN MEANS	YES	NO	YES	NO	YES	5
1943	GRIFFITH ROBERT WILLIAM	YES	YES	NO	NO	NO	2

STATE

1ST SPKR	NAME	FRAT ORG	PROF ORG	BUS ORG	CIV ORG	OTH ORG	TOT VOL
ARKANSAS *(CONT.)*							
1945	NORTHCUTT HORACE ALLEN	YES	NO	NO	NO	NO	1
1947	RIALES ROY LEE SR	NO	NO	NO	NO	NO	0
1949	HENDRIX CARL EDWARD	YES	NO	NO	NO	YES	3
1951	CAMPBELL JAMES R JR	YES	YES	NO	NO	YES	4
1953	HOLLENSWORTH CARROLL C	YES	YES	NO	YES	YES	7
1955	SMITH CHARLES F JR	NO	YES	NO	YES	NO	2
1957	WALTHER GLENN F	YES	YES	NO	YES	YES	8
1959	FLEEMAN EUGENE CECIL	NO	NO	NO	YES	NO	2
1961	BETHELL JOHN PINCKNEY SR	YES	NO	NO	YES	YES	4
1963	CRANK MARION HARLAN	NO	NO	YES	YES	NO	3
1965	COTTRELL JOHN HALL JR	NO	NO	NO	NO	NO	0
1967	COCKRILL STERLING ROBERTSON	NO	NO	YES	YES	YES	6
1969	MCCLERKIN HAYES CANDOR	YES	YES	NO	YES	YES	10
1971	SMITH RAY S JR	YES	YES	NO	NO	YES	7
1973	TURNER GROVER W JR	NO	NO	YES	YES	NO	4
1975	ALEXANDER CECIL LEWIS	NO	NO	YES	NO	NO	3
1977	SHAVER JAMES LEVESQUE JR	YES	YES	YES	YES	YES	9
1979	MILLER JOHN ELDON	YES	YES	YES	YES	YES	8
1981	MCCUISTON LLOYD CARLISLE JR	YES	YES	YES	YES	YES	9
1983	CAPPS JOHN PAUL	NO	NO	YES	YES	YES	9
1985	LANDERS H LACY	NO	NO	NO	NO	NO	0
1987	CUNNINGHAM ERNEST G	NO	NO	NO	NO	NO	0
1989	HENDRIX B G	YES	NO	YES	NO	YES	6
FLORIDA							
1911	JENNINGS THOMAS ALBERT	YES	NO	NO	NO	NO	3
1915	HARDEE CARY AUGUSTUS	YES	NO	NO	NO	NO	3
1918	WILDER GEORGE HAMILTON	NO	NO	NO	NO	YES	1
1921	JENNINGS FRANK E	YES	NO	YES	NO	YES	4
1923	EDGE L DAY	NO	NO	NO	NO	NO	0
1925	MILAM ARTHUR YAGER	YES	NO	NO	YES	YES	7
1927	DAVIS FRED HENRY	YES	NO	NO	NO	YES	4
1929	GETZEN SAMUEL WYCHE	YES	NO	NO	NO	NO	4
1931	LEWIS E CLAY JR	YES	YES	NO	YES	YES	7
1933	TOMASELLO PETER JR	NO	NO	NO	NO	NO	0
1935	BISHOP WILLIAM BURTON	YES	NO	YES	NO	NO	3
1937	CHRISTIE WILLIAM MCLEAN	YES	NO	NO	NO	YES	2
1939	WOOD GEORGE PIERCE	NO	NO	NO	NO	NO	0
1941	MCCARTY DANIEL THOMAS	YES	NO	YES	YES	YES	9
1943	SIMPSON RICHARD HENRY	NO	NO	YES	YES	YES	4
1945	CRARY EVANS SR	YES	YES	YES	YES	YES	6
1947	BEASLEY THOMAS DEKALB	NO	NO	NO	YES	NO	1
1949	MURRAY PERRY EARL	YES	NO	NO	YES	YES	3
1951	ELLIOTT ELMER B	YES	NO	NO	NO	NO	2
1953	BRYANT CECIL FARRIS	YES	YES	YES	YES	YES	19
1955	DAVID THOMAS E	NO	NO	NO	NO	YES	1
1957	CONNER DOYLE E	YES	NO	YES	YES	YES	8
1961	CHAPPELL WILLIAM VENROE JR	YES	YES	NO	NO	YES	6
1962	HORNE MALLORY ELI	NO	YES	NO	YES	YES	3
1965	ROWELL E C	YES	NO	YES	YES	YES	8

STATE

1ST SPKR	NAME	FRAT ORG	PROF ORG	BUS ORG	CIV ORG	OTH ORG	TOT VOL

FLORIDA (*CONT.*)

1967	TURLINGTON RALPH DONALD	YES	NO	NO	YES	YES	4
1969	SCHULTZ FREDERICK HENRY	YES	NO	YES	NO	YES	5
1971	PETTIGREW RICHARD ALLEN	YES	YES	NO	NO	YES	4
1973	SESSUMS THOMAS TERRELL	YES	YES	YES	YES	YES	15
1975	TUCKER DONALD L	NO	YES	YES	YES	YES	7
1979	BROWN JAMES HYATT	YES	NO	YES	YES	YES	10
1981	HABEN RALPH H JR	NO	NO	NO	NO	NO	0
1983	MOFFITT H LEE	YES	YES	NO	YES	YES	11
1985	THOMPSON JAMES HAROLD	NO	NO	NO	NO	NO	0
1987	MILLS JON L	YES	YES	NO	YES	YES	9
1989	GUSTAFSON TOM	NO	YES	YES	YES	YES	9

GEORGIA

1913	BURWELL WILLIAM HIX	YES	NO	NO	NO	NO	2
1921	NEILL WILLIAM CECIL	YES	NO	NO	NO	YES	7
1927	RUSSELL RICHARD BREVARD	YES	YES	NO	YES	YES	10
1931	TUCKER ARLIE DANIEL	YES	NO	YES	NO	NO	2
1933	RIVERS EURITH DICKINSON	YES	YES	NO	NO	YES	10
1937	HARRIS ROY VINCENT	YES	NO	NO	YES	YES	5
1941	EVANS RANDALL JR	NO	NO	NO	NO	NO	0
1947	HAND FREDRICK BARROW	YES	NO	NO	YES	NO	2
1955	MOATE MARVIN E	YES	NO	NO	NO	YES	3
1959	SMITH GEORGE LEON II	YES	YES	NO	YES	YES	8
1963	SMITH GEORGE THORNEWELL	YES	YES	NO	YES	YES	5
1974	MURPHY THOMAS BAILEY	YES	NO	NO	NO	YES	7

KENTUCKY

1912	TERRELL CLAUDE B	YES	NO	NO	NO	NO	4
1916	DUFFY HUGH CORNELIUS	NO	YES	NO	NO	NO	1
1918	CROWE ROBERT T	YES	NO	NO	NO	YES	3
1920	BOSWORTH JOE F	YES	NO	YES	NO	NO	2
1922	THOMPSON JAMES H	YES	NO	NO	NO	NO	3
1924	ADAMS SAMUEL W	YES	NO	NO	NO	YES	5
1926	DRURY GEORGE LUCIAN	NO	NO	NO	YES	YES	2
1928	MILLIKEN JOHN S	YES	NO	NO	NO	NO	1
1932	BROWN JOHN YOUNG	YES	YES	NO	YES	YES	10
1933	LEBUS FRANK	NO	NO	NO	NO	NO	0
1934	ROGERS W E SR	NO	NO	NO	NO	NO	0
1935	BROWN WALLACE	YES	NO	NO	NO	YES	2
1936	KIRTLEY JOHN D	YES	NO	NO	NO	NO	2
1940	SHIELDS BENJAMIN FRANKLIN	YES	NO	NO	YES	NO	2
1942	DICKSON STANLEY S	NO	NO	NO	NO	YES	1
1944	WATERFIELD HARRY LEE	YES	NO	YES	YES	YES	10
1948	TINSLEY T HERBERT	YES	NO	NO	NO	YES	3
1950	DORAN ADRON	YES	NO	NO	YES	NO	2
1952	BURNLEY CHARLES W	NO	NO	NO	NO	YES	1
1956	FITZPATRICK THOMAS P	YES	NO	NO	NO	YES	3
1958	WEINTRAUB MORRIS	YES	YES	NO	YES	YES	10

STATE

1ST SPKR	NAME	FRAT ORG	PROF ORG	BUS ORG	CIV ORG	OTH ORG	TOT VOL

KENTUCKY (CONT.)

1ST SPKR	NAME	FRAT ORG	PROF ORG	BUS ORG	CIV ORG	OTH ORG	TOT VOL
1960	LOWMAN HARRY KING	NO	NO	NO	NO	YES	2
1964	MCCALLUM SHELBY	YES	NO	NO	YES	NO	2
1968	CARROLL JULIAN MORTON	YES	YES	YES	YES	YES	11
1972	BLUME NORBERT	NO	NO	NO	NO	YES	6
1976	KENTON WILLIAM G	NO	YES	NO	YES	YES	6
1982	RICHARDSON BOBBY HAROLD	NO	YES	YES	YES	NO	5
1986	BLANDFORD DONALD JOSEPH	NO	NO	YES	YES	YES	5

LOUISIANA

1ST SPKR	NAME	FRAT ORG	PROF ORG	BUS ORG	CIV ORG	OTH ORG	TOT VOL
1912	THOMAS LEE EMMETT	NO	NO	NO	NO	NO	0
1916	BOUANCHAUD HEWITT LEONIDAS	NO	NO	NO	NO	NO	0
1920	WALKER RICHARD FLOURNOY	YES	NO	NO	NO	YES	4
1924	DOUGLAS JAMES STUART	NO	NO	NO	NO	YES	1
1926	HUGHES WILLIAM CLARK	NO	NO	NO	NO	NO	0
1928	FOURNET JOHN BAPTISTE	YES	YES	NO	NO	YES	4
1932	ELLENDER ALLEN JOSEPH	NO	NO	NO	NO	YES	1
1936	WIMBERLY LORRIS M	NO	NO	NO	NO	YES	1
1940	BAUER RALPH NORMAN	YES	YES	NO	YES	NO	5
1952	AYCOCK CLARENCE C	NO	YES	NO	NO	NO	1
1957	ANGELLE ROBERT	NO	NO	NO	NO	NO	0
1960	JEWELL J THOMAS	YES	YES	YES	YES	YES	17
1964	DELONY VAIL MONTGOMERY	NO	NO	NO	NO	NO	0
1968	GARRETT JOHN SIDNEY	YES	NO	YES	YES	YES	6
1972	HENRY EDGERTON L	YES	YES	NO	YES	YES	8
1980	HAINKEL JOHN JOSEPH JR	YES	YES	YES	YES	YES	11
1984	ALARIO JOHN A JR	NO	YES	NO	YES	YES	4
1988	DIMOS JIMMY N	NO	NO	NO	YES	YES	3

MARYLAND

1ST SPKR	NAME	FRAT ORG	PROF ORG	BUS ORG	CIV ORG	OTH ORG	TOT VOL
1912	TRIPPE JAMES MCCONKY	NO	YES	NO	NO	YES	9
1916	LAIRD PHILIP DANDRIDGE	NO	NO	NO	NO	NO	0
1917	MCINTOSH DAVID GREGG JR	YES	YES	NO	NO	YES	6
1918	WOODEN HERBERT R	NO	NO	NO	NO	NO	0
1920	TYDINGS MILLARD EVELYN	YES	NO	NO	YES	YES	8
1922	LEE JOHN L G	NO	NO	NO	NO	NO	0
1924	CURTIS FRANCIS P	NO	NO	NO	YES	YES	5
1927	LEE EDWARD BROOKE	NO	NO	YES	NO	YES	3
1931	MICHEL FRANCIS A	YES	YES	NO	YES	YES	10
1933	HARRINGTON T BARTON	NO	YES	NO	NO	YES	12
1935	GORFINE EMANUEL	YES	YES	YES	NO	YES	16
1939	CONLON THOMAS EDWARD	NO	NO	YES	YES	YES	4
1943	WHITE JOHN S	NO	NO	NO	YES	NO	1
1947	SYBERT CORNELIUS FERDINAND	NO	YES	NO	YES	YES	8
1951	LUBER JOHN CHRISTOPHER	YES	YES	NO	NO	YES	9
1959	WILKINSON PERRY O	YES	NO	YES	YES	YES	10
1963	BOONE A GORDON	NO	NO	NO	NO	NO	0
1964	MANDEL MARVIN	NO	YES	NO	NO	YES	6
1969	LOWE THOMAS HUNTER	YES	YES	YES	YES	YES	13

STATE

1ST SPKR	NAME	FRAT ORG	PROF ORG	BUS ORG	CIV ORG	OTH ORG	TOT VOL
MARYLAND *(CONT.)*							
1973	BRISCOE JOHN HANSON	YES	YES	NO	YES	YES	6
1979	CARDIN BENJAMIN LOUIS	YES	YES	NO	NO	YES	12
1987	MITCHELL R CLAYTON JR	NO	NO	NO	NO	YES	1
MISSISSIPPI							
1912	QUIN HILLRIE MARSHALL	YES	NO	NO	YES	YES	5
1916	CONNER MARTIN SENNETT	YES	NO	NO	NO	NO	1
1924	BAILEY THOMAS LOWRY	NO	NO	NO	YES	NO	2
1936	STANSEL HORACE SYLVAN	YES	NO	NO	NO	NO	3
1936	WRIGHT FIELDING LEWIS	YES	NO	NO	NO	YES	3
1940	LUMPKIN SAMUEL E	YES	NO	NO	YES	YES	7
1944	SILLERS WALTER	YES	NO	YES	YES	NO	3
1966	JUNKIN JOHN RICHARD	NO	NO	NO	NO	YES	1
1976	NEWMAN CLARENCE BENTON	NO	NO	YES	NO	YES	14
1988	FORD TIMOTHY ALAN	NO	NO	NO	NO	NO	0
NORTH CAROLINA							
1911	DOWD WILLIAM CAREY	YES	NO	YES	YES	YES	7
1913	CONNOR GEORGE WHITFIELD	YES	NO	NO	NO	YES	3
1914	MURPHY WALTER	YES	YES	NO	YES	YES	9
1915	WOOTEN EMMETT ROBINSON	YES	YES	NO	NO	YES	6
1919	BRUMMITT DENNIS GARFIELD	YES	YES	NO	NO	YES	8
1921	GRIER HARRY PERCY	NO	NO	NO	NO	YES	2
1923	DAWSON JOHN GILMER	YES	YES	NO	NO	YES	6
1925	PHARR EDGAR WALTER	YES	YES	NO	NO	YES	4
1927	FOUNTAIN RICHARD TILLMAN	YES	YES	NO	YES	YES	9
1929	GRAHAM ALEXANDER HAWKINS	YES	YES	NO	NO	YES	11
1931	SMITH WILLIS	YES	YES	YES	YES	YES	22
1933	HARRIS REGINALD LEE	YES	NO	YES	YES	YES	12
1935	JOHNSON ROBERT GRADY	YES	YES	NO	NO	YES	5
1936	CHERRY ROBERT GREGG	YES	YES	NO	YES	YES	14
1939	WARD DAVID LIVINGSTONE JR	YES	YES	NO	NO	YES	10
1941	MULL ODUS MCCOY	NO	YES	NO	YES	YES	11
1943	KERR JOHN HOSEA JR	NO	YES	NO	NO	YES	4
1945	RICHARDSON OSCAR LEON	NO	NO	NO	NO	YES	1
1947	PEARSALL THOMAS JENKINS	YES	NO	YES	YES	YES	13
1949	RAMSAY KERR CRAIGE	YES	YES	YES	YES	YES	11
1951	TAYLOR WALTER FRANK	NO	YES	NO	NO	YES	6
1953	BOST EUGENE THOMPSON JR	NO	YES	NO	NO	YES	4
1955	MOORE LARRY ICHABOD JR	YES	YES	YES	NO	YES	11
1957	DOUGHTON JAMES KEMP	NO	NO	NO	NO	NO	0
1959	HEWLETT ADDISON JR	YES	YES	NO	YES	YES	6
1961	HUNT JOSEPH MARVIN	NO	NO	YES	YES	YES	7
1963	BLUE HERBERT CLIFTON	YES	NO	YES	YES	YES	6
1965	TAYLOR HOYT PATRICK JR	YES	YES	NO	YES	YES	8
1967	BRITT DAVID MAXWELL	YES	YES	NO	YES	YES	11
1967	VAUGHN EARL W	YES	YES	NO	YES	YES	8
1969	GODWIN PHILIP PITTMAN	YES	YES	NO	NO	YES	6

STATE

1ST SPKR	NAME	FRAT ORG	PROF ORG	BUS ORG	CIV ORG	OTH ORG	TOT VOL
NORTH CAROLINA (*CONT.*)							
1973	RAMSEY JAMES EDWARD	YES	YES	YES	YES	YES	14
1975	GREEN JAMES COLLINS	YES	NO	YES	YES	YES	15
1977	STEWART CARL JEROME JR	YES	YES	NO	YES	YES	18
1981	RAMSEY LISTON BRYAN	YES	NO	NO	NO	YES	7
1989	MAVRETIC JOSEPHUS L	YES	NO	NO	YES	YES	8
OKLAHOMA							
1910	ANTHONY WILLIAM BRUCE	YES	NO	NO	NO	NO	3
1911	DURANT WILLIAM ALEXANDER	YES	NO	NO	NO	NO	3
1913	MAXEY JAMES HARVEY	NO	NO	NO	NO	NO	0
1915	MCCRORY ALONZO	YES	NO	NO	YES	YES	4
1917	NESBITT PAUL	NO	NO	NO	YES	YES	2
1919	WALDREP THOMAS CARNES	YES	NO	NO	NO	NO	2
1921	SCHWABE GEORGE BLAINE	YES	NO	NO	YES	NO	4
1923	GIBBONS MURRAY F	NO	NO	NO	NO	NO	0
1923	MCBEE WILLIAM DALTON	YES	NO	NO	YES	YES	5
1925	HARPER JESSE B	YES	NO	NO	YES	NO	2
1927	STOVALL DAVID ANCIL	YES	YES	YES	YES	YES	11
1929	STREET ALLEN MORGAN	YES	NO	NO	YES	YES	6
1929	NANCE JAMES CLARK	YES	NO	YES	YES	NO	5
1931	WEAVER CARLTON	NO	NO	YES	YES	YES	8
1933	ANGLIN WILLIAM THOMAS	YES	NO	YES	YES	YES	6
1935	PHILLIPS LEON CHASE	YES	NO	NO	YES	YES	5
1937	DANIEL J T	NO	YES	NO	NO	NO	1
1939	WELCH WILLIAM DONOVAN SR	YES	YES	YES	YES	YES	8
1941	BLUMHAGEN E	NO	YES	NO	YES	NO	3
1943	FREEMAN HAROLD	YES	NO	YES	YES	YES	6
1944	LANSDEN JOSEPH MERLE	YES	YES	NO	NO	NO	3
1945	HILL JOHNSON DAVIS	YES	NO	YES	NO	YES	5
1945	HINDS H IREDELLE	YES	NO	NO	NO	YES	4
1947	BOARD CHARLES RAYMOND	YES	YES	YES	YES	NO	5
1949	BILLINGSLEY WALTER ASBURY	YES	YES	NO	YES	YES	6
1951	BULLARD JAMES MARVIN	YES	NO	YES	YES	YES	8
1955	HARKEY BYRON E	YES	NO	YES	YES	YES	5
1959	LIVINGSTON CLINT GRAHAM	YES	NO	NO	YES	NO	3
1961	MCCARTY J D	NO	NO	YES	YES	YES	5
1967	PRIVETT ARNOLD REX	YES	NO	YES	NO	YES	6
1973	WILLIS WILLIAM PASCAL	YES	NO	YES	YES	YES	6
1979	DRAPER DANIEL DAVID JR	YES	YES	YES	YES	YES	8
1984	BARKER JIM L	NO	NO	YES	NO	YES	2
1989	LEWIS STEPHEN C	NO	NO	NO	YES	NO	1
SOUTH CAROLINA							
1915	HOYT JAMES ALFRED	NO	NO	NO	NO	YES	4
1918	COTHRAN THOMAS PERRIN	YES	NO	NO	YES	NO	4
1921	ATKINSON JAMES BUFORD	NO	NO	NO	NO	NO	0
1923	MCMILLAN THOMAS SANDERS	YES	NO	NO	YES	YES	3
1925	BROWN EDGAR ALLAN	YES	NO	NO	NO	YES	9

STATE

1ST SPKR	NAME	FRAT ORG	PROF ORG	BUS ORG	CIV ORG	OTH ORG	TOT VOL

SOUTH CAROLINA (*CONT.*)

1ST SPKR	NAME	FRAT ORG	PROF ORG	BUS ORG	CIV ORG	OTH ORG	TOT VOL
1927	HAMBLIN JOHN KNAPP	NO	NO	NO	NO	YES	1
1933	GIBSON JAMES BREEDEN	YES	NO	NO	NO	NO	4
1935	TAYLOR CLAUDE AMBROSE	NO	NO	NO	NO	YES	1
1937	BLATT SOLOMON	YES	NO	NO	NO	YES	4
1947	LITTLEJOHN CAMERON BRUCE	YES	YES	NO	YES	YES	10
1949	POPE THOMAS HARRINGTON	YES	YES	YES	YES	YES	10
1973	CARTER REX LYLE	YES	NO	NO	NO	YES	6
1980	SCHWARTZ RAMON JR	NO	NO	YES	YES	YES	9
1987	SHEHEEN ROBERT J	NO	NO	NO	YES	YES	2

TENNESSEE

1ST SPKR	NAME	FRAT ORG	PROF ORG	BUS ORG	CIV ORG	OTH ORG	TOT VOL
1911	LEACH ALBERT MARTIN	NO	NO	NO	NO	NO	0
1913	STANTON WILLIAM MORTIMER	YES	YES	YES	NO	YES	8
1915	COOPER WILLIAM PRENTICE	YES	NO	NO	YES	YES	3
1917	SHROPSHIRE CLYDE MOORE	NO	NO	YES	NO	NO	1
1919	WALKER SETH MCKINNEY	YES	YES	NO	NO	NO	2
1921	TODD ANDREW LEE	NO	NO	NO	NO	YES	4
1923	HALL FRANK SAMPSON	YES	YES	NO	NO	YES	4
1925	BARRY WILLIAM FRANCIS JR	YES	YES	YES	NO	YES	11
1927	MAIDEN SELDEN LONGLEY	YES	NO	NO	NO	NO	1
1929	LOVE CHARLES HOWARD	YES	NO	YES	NO	YES	6
1931	HAYNES WALTER MILLER	YES	YES	NO	NO	NO	6
1933	MOORE FRANK WASHINGTON	YES	YES	NO	NO	YES	7
1939	O'DELL JOHN ED	YES	NO	NO	NO	NO	1
1943	BROOME JAMES JESSE	YES	NO	NO	NO	NO	3
1945	WOODS GEORGE STANLEY	YES	NO	NO	YES	NO	2
1947	LEWALLEN W BUFORD	YES	NO	NO	NO	YES	3
1949	FOUTCH MCALLEN	YES	NO	NO	YES	YES	4
1953	BOMAR JAMES LA FAYETTE JR	YES	YES	YES	YES	YES	13
1963	BARRY WILLIAM LOGAN	YES	YES	YES	YES	YES	10
1967	CUMMINGS JAMES HARVEY II	YES	NO	YES	YES	NO	5
1969	JENKINS WILLIAM LEWIS	YES	YES	YES	YES	NO	7
1971	MCKINNEY JAMES ROBIN	YES	NO	NO	YES	YES	6
1973	MCWHERTER NED RAY	YES	NO	YES	YES	YES	9
1987	MURRAY CHARLES EDWARD	NO	NO	YES	NO	YES	4

TEXAS

1ST SPKR	NAME	FRAT ORG	PROF ORG	BUS ORG	CIV ORG	OTH ORG	TOT VOL
1911	RAYBURN SAMUEL TALIAFERRO	NO	NO	NO	NO	NO	0
1913	TERRELL CHESTER H	YES	NO	NO	NO	NO	1
1915	WOODS JOHN WILLIAM	NO	NO	NO	NO	NO	0
1917	FULLER FRANKLIN OLIVER	NO	NO	NO	NO	YES	1
1919	THOMASON ROBERT EWING	YES	NO	NO	NO	NO	3
1921	THOMAS CHARLES GRAHAM	NO	NO	NO	NO	NO	0
1923	SEAGLER RICHARD E	NO	NO	NO	NO	NO	0
1925	SATTERWHITE ROBERT LEE	NO	NO	YES	NO	NO	1
1927	BOBBITT ROBERT LEE	YES	YES	YES	YES	YES	10
1929	BARRON WINGATE STUART	YES	YES	NO	NO	NO	2
1931	MINOR FRED H	YES	YES	YES	YES	YES	8

STATE

1ST SPKR	NAME	FRAT ORG	PROF ORG	BUS ORG	CIV ORG	OTH ORG	TOT VOL

TEXAS *(CONT.)*

1ST SPKR	NAME	FRAT ORG	PROF ORG	BUS ORG	CIV ORG	OTH ORG	TOT VOL
1933	STEVENSON COKE ROBERT	YES	NO	YES	YES	NO	3
1937	CALVERT ROBERT WILBURN	NO	NO	YES	YES	YES	5
1939	MORSE ROBERT EMMETT	YES	NO	YES	NO	YES	8
1941	LEONARD HOMER L	YES	NO	NO	YES	YES	4
1943	DANIEL MARION PRICE SR	YES	YES	NO	NO	YES	6
1945	GILMER CLAUD H	YES	NO	YES	NO	NO	2
1947	REED WILLIAM OTEY	NO	YES	NO	NO	NO	2
1949	MANFORD THOMAS DURWOOD JR	YES	YES	NO	NO	NO	3
1951	SENTERFITT REUBEN	YES	NO	NO	YES	YES	5
1955	LINDSEY JIM THURSTON	YES	NO	YES	YES	YES	4
1957	CARR WAGGONER	YES	YES	YES	YES	YES	9
1961	TURMAN JAMES A	NO	NO	YES	YES	NO	3
1963	TUNNELL BYRON M	YES	YES	YES	YES	YES	6
1965	BARNES BEN FRANK	YES	NO	YES	YES	NO	4
1969	MUTSCHER GUS FRANKLIN	NO	NO	NO	NO	YES	7
1972	PRICE WILLIAM RAYFORD	YES	YES	YES	YES	YES	6
1973	DANIEL MARION PRICE JR	YES	YES	NO	YES	YES	7
1975	CLAYTON BILLY WAYNE	YES	NO	NO	YES	YES	5
1983	LEWIS GIBSON D	NO	NO	YES	YES	YES	11

VIRGINIA

1ST SPKR	NAME	FRAT ORG	PROF ORG	BUS ORG	CIV ORG	OTH ORG	TOT VOL
1914	COX EDWIN PIPER	YES	NO	NO	NO	YES	4
1916	HOUSTON HARRY RUTHERFORD	YES	NO	YES	YES	YES	7
1920	BREWER RICHARD LEWIS JR	YES	NO	YES	NO	YES	5
1926	OZLIN THOMAS WILLIAM	YES	NO	NO	NO	NO	2
1930	BROWN J SINCLAIR	YES	NO	YES	YES	YES	6
1936	DOVELL GROVER ASHTON	YES	YES	NO	YES	YES	5
1942	STANLEY THOMAS BAHNSON	YES	NO	YES	NO	YES	6
1947	MASSENBURG GEORGE ALVIN	YES	NO	YES	YES	YES	13
1950	MOORE EDGAR BLACKBURN	NO	NO	YES	YES	NO	2
1968	COOKE JOHN WARREN	NO	NO	NO	YES	YES	2
1980	PHILPOTT ALBERT LEE	YES	YES	NO	YES	YES	8

WEST VIRGINIA

1ST SPKR	NAME	FRAT ORG	PROF ORG	BUS ORG	CIV ORG	OTH ORG	TOT VOL
1911	WETZEL CHARLES MCCLUER	NO	NO	NO	NO	NO	0
1913	GEORGE WILLIAM TAYLOR	YES	NO	NO	NO	NO	1
1915	JOHNSON VERNON EMIL	YES	NO	YES	NO	YES	3
1917	THURMOND JOSEPH SAMUEL	NO	NO	NO	NO	YES	1
1919	WOLFE J LUTHER	YES	NO	NO	NO	NO	3
1921	KEATLEY EDWIN MINER	YES	NO	YES	YES	NO	3
1923	BYRNE WILLIAM ESTON R	NO	NO	NO	NO	NO	0
1929	CUMMINS JOHN WILLIAM	YES	NO	NO	YES	YES	5
1931	TAYLOR JAMES ALFRED	YES	NO	NO	NO	YES	6
1933	HINER RALPH MCCLUNG	YES	NO	NO	NO	YES	4
1935	PELTER JOHN J	NO	NO	NO	NO	NO	0
1937	THOMAS JAMES KAY	YES	YES	YES	YES	YES	11
1941	ARNOLD MALCOLM R	YES	NO	NO	NO	YES	3
1943	AMOS JOHN ELLISON	YES	NO	YES	NO	YES	6

STATE

1ST SPKR	NAME	FRAT ORG	PROF ORG	BUS ORG	CIV ORG	OTH ORG	TOT VOL
	WEST VIRGINIA *(CONT.)*						
1949	FLANNERY W E	NO	NO	NO	NO	NO	0
1958	PAULEY HARRY R	YES	NO	NO	YES	YES	4
1961	SINGLETON JULIUS W JR	YES	NO	NO	NO	YES	6
1965	WHITE H LABAN JR	YES	YES	YES	YES	YES	22
1969	BOIARSKY IVOR F	NO	NO	NO	NO	NO	0
1971	MCMANUS LEWIS NICHOLS	YES	NO	YES	NO	YES	5
1977	KOPP DONALD LEE	YES	NO	NO	NO	YES	4
1979	SEE CLYDE M JR	YES	YES	YES	NO	YES	6
1985	ALBRIGHT JOSEPH PAUL	YES	YES	YES	NO	YES	7
1987	CHAMBERS ROBERT C	NO	YES	NO	NO	YES	7

KEY:

1ST SPKR = YEAR FIRST SERVED AS SPEAKER

FRAT ORG = MEMBERSHIP IN FRATERNAL ORGANIZATION
PROF ORG = MEMBERSHIP IN VOLUNTARY PROFESSIONAL ORGANIZATION
BUS ORG = MEMBERSHIP IN VOLUNTARY BUSINESS ORGANIZATION
CIV ORG = MEMBERSHIP IN VOLUNTARY CIVIC ORGANIZATION
OTH ORG = MEMBERSHIP IN OTHER VOLUNTARY ORGANIZATION

TOT VOL = TOTAL NUMBER OF VOLUNTARY MEMBERSHIPS DURING LIFETIME

Appendix 9:
Public Offices before
Speakership

STATE

1ST SPKR	NAME	HIGHEST LOCAL	HIGHEST STATE	HIGH FEDER	TOT PUB
ALABAMA					
1911	ALMON EDWARD BERTON	NONE	JUDGE	NONE	2
1919	MERRITT HENRY PAUL	NONE	SENATE	NONE	1
1920	LYNNE SEABOURN ARTHUR	BUREAU	SENATE	NONE	2
1923	MERRILL HUGH DAVIS	BUREAU	JUDGE	NONE	2
1927	LONG JOHN LEE	EXECUT	NONE	NONE	4
1935	WALKER ROBERT HENRY	NONE	SENATE	NONE	2
1942	MILLER GEORGE OLIVER	NONE	BUREAU	NONE	2
1944	NORMAN CHARLES DOZIER	CO REPR	NONE	NONE	3
1947	BECK WILLIAM MORRIS	CO JUD	NONE	NONE	1
1951	BROWN ROBERTS HENRY	BUREAU	NONE	NONE	1
1955	FITE ERNEST RANKIN	NONE	SENATE	NONE	1
1959	ADAMS CHARLES CRAYTON III	NONE	NONE	NONE	0
1961	ASHWORTH VIRGIS MARION	CO BUR	NONE	NONE	2
1963	BREWER ALBERT PRESTON	BUREAU	NONE	NONE	1
1971	LYONS GEORGE SAGE	NONE	BUREAU	NONE	1
1975	MCCORQUODALE JOSEPH CHARLES	REPRES	NONE	NONE	1
1983	DRAKE THOMAS E	NONE	NONE	NONE	0
1987	CLARK JAMES STERLING	MAYOR	SENATE	NONE	3
ARKANSAS					
1911	MILWEE R FRANK	CO JUD	NONE	NONE	3
1913	HARDAGE JOSIAH	CO JUD	NONE	NONE	1
1915	SAWYER LEWIS ERNEST	MAYOR	NONE	NONE	1
1917	CAZORT WILLIAM LEE SR	NONE	NONE	NONE	0
1919	NEWTON CLARENCE PRICE	JUDGE	NONE	NONE	1
1921	JOINER JOSEPH WILLIAM	NONE	NONE	NONE	0
1923	REED HOWARD	CO BUR	NONE	NONE	1
1925	HILL THOMAS AUSTIN	NONE	NONE	NONE	0
1927	CAUDLE REECE ARTHUR	CO BUR	NONE	NONE	1
1929	ABINGTON WILLIAM H	MAYOR	NONE	NONE	3
1931	NEALE IRVING C	NONE	NONE	NONE	0
1933	TONEY HARDIN KEMP	NONE	SENATE	NONE	1
1935	THORN HARVEY BELL SR	CO BUR	NONE	NONE	1
1937	BRANSFORD JOHN MCKINNIS	NONE	NONE	NONE	0
1941	WILKINSON NORMAN MEANS	NONE	NONE	NONE	0
1943	GRIFFITH ROBERT WILLIAM	NONE	NONE	NONE	0

STATE

1ST SPKR	NAME	HIGHEST LOCAL	HIGHEST STATE	HIGH FEDER	TOT PUB

ARKANSAS (*CONT.*)

1945	NORTHCUTT HORACE ALLEN	REPRES	SENATE	NONE	3
1947	RIALES ROY LEE SR	NONE	NONE	NONE	0
1949	HENDRIX CARL EDWARD	NONE	NONE	NONE	0
1951	CAMPBELL JAMES R JR	CO BUR	NONE	NONE	3
1953	HOLLENSWORTH CARROLL C	NONE	NONE	NONE	0
1955	SMITH CHARLES F JR	CO BUR	BUREAU	NONE	2
1957	WALTHER GLENN F	CO BUR	NONE	NONE	1
1959	FLEEMAN EUGENE CECIL	NONE	NONE	NONE	0
1961	BETHELL JOHN PINCKNEY SR	MAYOR	NONE	NONE	1
1963	CRANK MARION HARLAN	NONE	BUREAU	BUREAU	2
1965	COTTRELL JOHN HALL JR	REPRES	NONE	NONE	1
1967	COCKRILL STERLING ROBERTSON	NONE	NONE	NONE	0
1969	MCCLERKIN HAYES CANDOR	NONE	NONE	NONE	0
1971	SMITH RAY S JR	NONE	NONE	NONE	0
1973	TURNER GROVER W JR	CO BUR	NONE	NONE	1
1975	ALEXANDER CECIL LEWIS	NONE	NONE	NONE	0
1977	SHAVER JAMES LEVESQUE JR	CO BUR	NONE	NONE	1
1979	MILLER JOHN ELDON	CO BUR	NONE	NONE	1
1981	MCCUISTON LLOYD CARLISLE JR	JUDGE	NONE	NONE	2
1983	CAPPS JOHN PAUL	NONE	NONE	NONE	0
1985	LANDERS H LACY	NONE	NONE	NONE	0
1987	CUNNINGHAM ERNEST G	NONE	NONE	NONE	0
1989	HENDRIX B G	JUDGE	NONE	BUREAU	5

FLORIDA

1911	JENNINGS THOMAS ALBERT	BUREAU	NONE	NONE	1
1915	HARDEE CARY AUGUSTUS	NONE	BUREAU	NONE	1
1918	WILDER GEORGE HAMILTON	NONE	NONE	NONE	0
1921	JENNINGS FRANK E	BUREAU	BUREAU	NONE	2
1923	EDGE L DAY	NONE	NONE	NONE	0
1925	MILAM ARTHUR YAGER	NONE	NONE	NONE	0
1927	DAVIS FRED HENRY	CO BUR	NONE	NONE	2
1929	GETZEN SAMUEL WYCHE	NONE	NONE	NONE	0
1931	LEWIS E CLAY JR	CO JUD	NONE	NONE	1
1933	TOMASELLO PETER JR	NONE	NONE	NONE	0
1935	BISHOP WILLIAM BURTON	NONE	NONE	NONE	0
1937	CHRISTIE WILLIAM MCLEAN	NONE	NONE	BUREAU	1
1939	WOOD GEORGE PIERCE	CO REPR	NONE	NONE	1
1941	MCCARTY DANIEL THOMAS	NONE	NONE	NONE	0
1943	SIMPSON RICHARD HENRY	MAYOR	NONE	NONE	1
1945	CRARY EVANS SR	JUDGE	NONE	NONE	3
1947	BEASLEY THOMAS DEKALB	CO BUR	NONE	NONE	1
1949	MURRAY PERRY EARL	CO REPR	NONE	NONE	2
1951	ELLIOTT ELMER B	NONE	NONE	NONE	0
1953	BRYANT CECIL FARRIS	NONE	JUDGE	NONE	1
1955	DAVID THOMAS E	NONE	NONE	NONE	0
1957	CONNER DOYLE E	NONE	NONE	NONE	0
1961	CHAPPELL WILLIAM VENROE JR	CO BUR	NONE	NONE	1
1962	HORNE MALLORY ELI	NONE	NONE	NONE	0
1965	ROWELL E C	NONE	NONE	NONE	0

STATE

1ST SPKR	NAME	HIGHEST LOCAL	HIGHEST STATE	HIGH FEDER	TOT PUB

FLORIDA (*CONT.*)

1ST SPKR	NAME	HIGHEST LOCAL	HIGHEST STATE	HIGH FEDER	TOT PUB
1967	TURLINGTON RALPH DONALD	NONE	NONE	NONE	0
1969	SCHULTZ FREDERICK HENRY	BUREAU	NONE	NONE	1
1971	PETTIGREW RICHARD ALLEN	NONE	BUREAU	NONE	1
1973	SESSUMS THOMAS TERRELL	NONE	NONE	BUREAU	1
1975	TUCKER DONALD L	NONE	NONE	NONE	0
1979	BROWN JAMES HYATT	NONE	NONE	NONE	0
1981	HABEN RALPH H JR	JUDGE	BUREAU	NONE	3
1983	MOFFITT H LEE	CO BUR	NONE	NONE	2
1985	THOMPSON JAMES HAROLD	CO JUD	NONE	NONE	1
1987	MILLS JON L	BUREAU	NONE	NONE	1
1989	GUSTAFSON TOM	NONE	NONE	NONE	0

GEORGIA

1ST SPKR	NAME	HIGHEST LOCAL	HIGHEST STATE	HIGH FEDER	TOT PUB
1913	BURWELL WILLIAM HIX	MAYOR	SENATE	NONE	2
1921	NEILL WILLIAM CECIL	NONE	NONE	NONE	0
1927	RUSSELL RICHARD BREVARD	CO BUR	NONE	NONE	2
1931	TUCKER ARLIE DANIEL	REPRES	NONE	NONE	1
1933	RIVERS EURITH DICKINSON	JUDGE	SENATE	NONE	4
1937	HARRIS ROY VINCENT	NONE	SENATE	NONE	1
1941	EVANS RANDALL JR	MAYOR	SENATE	NONE	4
1947	HAND FREDRICK BARROW	NONE	SENATE	NONE	1
1955	MOATE MARVIN E	NONE	SENATE	NONE	1
1959	SMITH GEORGE LEON II	BUREAU	NONE	NONE	2
1963	SMITH GEORGE THORNEWELL	CO BUR	NONE	NONE	3
1974	MURPHY THOMAS BAILEY	REPRES	NONE	NONE	1

KENTUCKY

1ST SPKR	NAME	HIGHEST LOCAL	HIGHEST STATE	HIGH FEDER	TOT PUB
1912	TERRELL CLAUDE B	CO BUR	NONE	NONE	1
1916	DUFFY HUGH CORNELIUS	NONE	NONE	NONE	0
1918	CROWE ROBERT T	CO BUR	NONE	NONE	1
1920	BOSWORTH JOE F	REPRES	NONE	NONE	3
1922	THOMPSON JAMES H	NONE	NONE	NONE	0
1924	ADAMS SAMUEL W	NONE	NONE	NONE	0
1926	DRURY GEORGE LUCIAN	NONE	NONE	NONE	0
1928	MILLIKEN JOHN S	BUREAU	NONE	NONE	1
1932	BROWN JOHN YOUNG	NONE	NONE	NONE	0
1933	LEBUS FRANK	JUDGE	NONE	NONE	1
1934	ROGERS W E SR	JUDGE	NONE	NONE	1
1935	BROWN WALLACE	CO JUD	SENATE	NONE	3
1936	KIRTLEY JOHN D	NONE	NONE	NONE	0
1940	SHIELDS BENJAMIN FRANKLIN	NONE	NONE	NONE	0
1942	DICKSON STANLEY S	NONE	NONE	NONE	0
1944	WATERFIELD HARRY LEE	NONE	NONE	NONE	0
1948	TINSLEY T HERBERT	NONE	NONE	NONE	0
1950	DORAN ADRON	NONE	NONE	NONE	0
1952	BURNLEY CHARLES W	NONE	NONE	BUREAU	1
1956	FITZPATRICK THOMAS P	MAYOR	NONE	NONE	2
1958	WEINTRAUB MORRIS	CO JUD	SENATE	BUREAU	5

STATE

1ST SPKR	NAME	HIGHEST LOCAL	HIGHEST STATE	HIGH FEDER	TOT PUB
KENTUCKY (*CONT.*)					
1960	LOWMAN HARRY KING	NONE	NONE	NONE	0
1964	MCCALLUM SHELBY	NONE	NONE	NONE	0
1968	CARROLL JULIAN MORTON	NONE	NONE	NONE	0
1972	BLUME NORBERT	NONE	NONE	NONE	0
1976	KENTON WILLIAM G	NONE	NONE	NONE	0
1982	RICHARDSON BOBBY HAROLD	NONE	NONE	CO REPR	1
1986	BLANDFORD DONALD JOSEPH	NONE	NONE	BUREAU	1
LOUISIANA					
1912	THOMAS LEE EMMETT	NONE	NONE	NONE	0
1916	BOUANCHAUD HEWITT LEONIDAS	NONE	NONE	NONE	0
1920	WALKER RICHARD FLOURNOY	REPRES	NONE	NONE	1
1924	DOUGLAS JAMES STUART	NONE	NONE	NONE	0
1926	HUGHES WILLIAM CLARK	NONE	NONE	NONE	0
1928	FOURNET JOHN BAPTISTE	NONE	NONE	NONE	0
1932	ELLENDER ALLEN JOSEPH	CO BUR	NONE	NONE	2
1936	WIMBERLY LORRIS M	JUDGE	NONE	NONE	1
1940	BAUER RALPH NORMAN	NONE	NONE	NONE	0
1952	AYCOCK CLARENCE C	NONE	NONE	NONE	0
1957	ANGELLE ROBERT	MAYOR	NONE	NONE	1
1960	JEWELL J THOMAS	NONE	BUREAU	NONE	2
1964	DELONY VAIL MONTGOMERY	MAYOR	NONE	NONE	1
1968	GARRETT JOHN SIDNEY	NONE	NONE	NONE	0
1972	HENRY EDGERTON L	NONE	NONE	NONE	0
1980	HAINKEL JOHN JOSEPH JR	NONE	NONE	NONE	0
1984	ALARIO JOHN A JR	NONE	BUREAU	NONE	1
1988	DIMOS JIMMY N	NONE	NONE	NONE	0
MARYLAND					
1912	TRIPPE JAMES MCCONKY	NONE	NONE	NONE	0
1916	LAIRD PHILIP DANDRIDGE	NONE	BUREAU	NONE	2
1917	MCINTOSH DAVID GREGG JR	NONE	NONE	NONE	0
1918	WOODEN HERBERT R	NONE	NONE	NONE	0
1920	TYDINGS MILLARD EVELYN	NONE	NONE	NONE	0
1922	LEE JOHN L G	NONE	NONE	NONE	0
1924	CURTIS FRANCIS P	REPRES	NONE	NONE	2
1927	LEE EDWARD BROOKE	NONE	EXECUT	NONE	3
1931	MICHEL FRANCIS A	NONE	NONE	NONE	0
1933	HARRINGTON T BARTON	NONE	NONE	NONE	0
1935	GORFINE EMANUEL	NONE	NONE	NONE	0
1939	CONLON THOMAS EDWARD	NONE	NONE	NONE	0
1943	WHITE JOHN S	MAYOR	NONE	NONE	1
1947	SYBERT CORNELIUS FERDINAND	CO BUR	NONE	NONE	1
1951	LUBER JOHN CHRISTOPHER	NONE	NONE	NONE	0
1959	WILKINSON PERRY O	NONE	NONE	NONE	0
1963	BOONE A GORDON	CO BUR	NONE	NONE	1
1964	MANDEL MARVIN	JUDGE	BUREAU	NONE	2
1969	LOWE THOMAS HUNTER	BUREAU	NONE	NONE	1

<u>STATE</u>

1ST SPKR	NAME	HIGHEST LOCAL	HIGHEST STATE	HIGH FEDER	TOT PUB

<u>MARYLAND</u> (*CONT.*)

1ST SPKR	NAME	HIGHEST LOCAL	HIGHEST STATE	HIGH FEDER	TOT PUB
1973	BRISCOE JOHN HANSON	NONE	NONE	NONE	0
1979	CARDIN BENJAMIN LOUIS	NONE	NONE	NONE	0
1987	MITCHELL R CLAYTON JR	CO REPR	NONE	NONE	1

<u>MISSISSIPPI</u>

1ST SPKR	NAME	HIGHEST LOCAL	HIGHEST STATE	HIGH FEDER	TOT PUB
1912	QUIN HILLRIE MARSHALL	REPRES	NONE	NONE	1
1916	CONNER MARTIN SENNETT	NONE	NONE	NONE	0
1924	BAILEY THOMAS LOWRY	NONE	NONE	NONE	0
1936	STANSEL HORACE SYLVAN	NONE	NONE	BUREAU	1
1936	WRIGHT FIELDING LEWIS	NONE	SENATE	NONE	1
1940	LUMPKIN SAMUEL E	NONE	NONE	NONE	0
1944	SILLERS WALTER	CO BUR	NONE	NONE	2
1966	JUNKIN JOHN RICHARD	CO REPR	NONE	NONE	1
1976	NEWMAN CLARENCE BENTON	NONE	SENATE	NONE	1
1988	FORD TIMOTHY ALAN	NONE	NONE	NONE	0

<u>NORTH CAROLINA</u>

1ST SPKR	NAME	HIGHEST LOCAL	HIGHEST STATE	HIGH FEDER	TOT PUB
1911	DOWD WILLIAM CAREY	NONE	SENATE	NONE	1
1913	CONNOR GEORGE WHITFIELD	REPRES	NONE	NONE	2
1914	MURPHY WALTER	BUREAU	NONE	NONE	1
1915	WOOTEN EMMETT ROBINSON	CO BUR	NONE	NONE	2
1919	BRUMMITT DENNIS GARFIELD	MAYOR	NONE	NONE	2
1921	GRIER HARRY PERCY	MAYOR	NONE	NONE	2
1923	DAWSON JOHN GILMER	BUREAU	NONE	NONE	1
1925	PHARR EDGAR WALTER	NONE	NONE	NONE	0
1927	FOUNTAIN RICHARD TILLMAN	REPRES	NONE	NONE	2
1929	GRAHAM ALEXANDER HAWKINS	CO BUR	NONE	NONE	1
1931	SMITH WILLIS	NONE	BUREAU	NONE	1
1933	HARRIS REGINALD LEE	NONE	BUREAU	NONE	2
1935	JOHNSON ROBERT GRADY	CO REPR	NONE	NONE	3
1936	CHERRY ROBERT GREGG	MAYOR	NONE	NONE	1
1939	WARD DAVID LIVINGSTONE JR	CO BUR	BUREAU	NONE	3
1941	MULL ODUS MCCOY	BUREAU	NONE	NONE	1
1943	KERR JOHN HOSEA JR	NONE	NONE	NONE	0
1945	RICHARDSON OSCAR LEON	CO BUR	BUREAU	NONE	3
1947	PEARSALL THOMAS JENKINS	REPRES	NONE	NONE	2
1949	RAMSAY KERR CRAIGE	NONE	BUREAU	NONE	1
1951	TAYLOR WALTER FRANK	NONE	SENATE	NONE	7
1953	BOST EUGENE THOMPSON JR	NONE	NONE	NONE	0
1955	MOORE LARRY ICHABOD JR	CO BUR	NONE	NONE	1
1957	DOUGHTON JAMES KEMP	NONE	BUREAU	BUREAU	3
1959	HEWLETT ADDISON JR	NONE	NONE	NONE	0
1961	HUNT JOSEPH MARVIN	REPRES	NONE	NONE	2
1963	BLUE HERBERT CLIFTON	REPRES	NONE	NONE	1
1965	TAYLOR HOYT PATRICK JR	NONE	NONE	NONE	0
1967	BRITT DAVID MAXWELL	BUREAU	BUREAU	NONE	4
1967	VAUGHN EARL W	BUREAU	NONE	NONE	2
1969	GODWIN PHILIP PITTMAN	NONE	NONE	NONE	0

STATE

1ST SPKR	NAME	HIGHEST LOCAL	HIGHEST STATE	HIGH FEDER	TOT PUB

NORTH CAROLINA (*CONT.*)

1973	RAMSEY JAMES EDWARD	JUDGE	NONE	NONE	1
1975	GREEN JAMES COLLINS	CO REPR	SENATE	NONE	2
1977	STEWART CARL JEROME JR	NONE	NONE	NONE	0
1981	RAMSEY LISTON BRYAN	REPRES	BUREAU	NONE	3
1989	MAVRETIC JOSEPHUS L	REPRES	BUREAU	NONE	2

OKLAHOMA

1910	ANTHONY WILLIAM BRUCE	MAYOR	NONE	NONE	1
1911	DURANT WILLIAM ALEXANDER	REPRES	BUREAU	NONE	4
1913	MAXEY JAMES HARVEY	NONE	NONE	NONE	0
1915	MCCRORY ALONZO	NONE	NONE	NONE	0
1917	NESBITT PAUL	NONE	BUREAU	NONE	2
1919	WALDREP THOMAS CARNES	NONE	NONE	NONE	0
1921	SCHWABE GEORGE BLAINE	MAYOR	NONE	NONE	3
1923	GIBBONS MURRAY F	NONE	NONE	NONE	0
1923	MCBEE WILLIAM DALTON	CO JUD	SENATE	NONE	6
1925	HARPER JESSE B	NONE	NONE	NONE	0
1927	STOVALL DAVID ANCIL	CO BUR	BUREAU	NONE	4
1929	STREET ALLEN MORGAN	NONE	NONE	NONE	0
1929	NANCE JAMES CLARK	NONE	NONE	NONE	0
1931	WEAVER CARLTON	REPRES	NONE	NONE	1
1933	ANGLIN WILLIAM THOMAS	NONE	SEN PRES	NONE	1
1935	PHILLIPS LEON CHASE	NONE	JUDGE	NONE	1
1937	DANIEL J T	BUREAU	NONE	NONE	1
1939	WELCH WILLIAM DONOVAN SR	NONE	NONE	NONE	0
1941	BLUMHAGEN E	NONE	NONE	NONE	0
1943	FREEMAN HAROLD	CO BUR	NONE	NONE	1
1944	LANSDEN JOSEPH MERLE	CO BUR	NONE	NONE	1
1945	HILL JOHNSON DAVIS	NONE	NONE	NONE	0
1945	HINDS H IREDELLE	CO BUR	NONE	NONE	1
1947	BOARD CHARLES RAYMOND	CO JUD	NONE	NONE	3
1949	BILLINGSLEY WALTER ASBURY	CO BUR	JUDGE	NONE	6
1951	BULLARD JAMES MARVIN	CO EXEC	NONE	NONE	2
1955	HARKEY BYRON E	NONE	JUDGE	NONE	2
1959	LIVINGSTON CLINT GRAHAM	CO BUR	NONE	NONE	1
1961	MCCARTY J D	NONE	NONE	NONE	0
1967	PRIVETT ARNOLD REX	NONE	NONE	NONE	0
1973	WILLIS WILLIAM PASCAL	MAYOR	NONE	NONE	1
1979	DRAPER DANIEL DAVID JR	BUREAU	NONE	NONE	1
1984	BARKER JIM L	NONE	NONE	NONE	0
1989	LEWIS STEPHEN C	CO BUR	NONE	NONE	2

SOUTH CAROLINA

1915	HOYT JAMES ALFRED	NONE	BUREAU	NONE	1
1918	COTHRAN THOMAS PERRIN	NONE	NONE	NONE	0
1921	ATKINSON JAMES BUFORD	NONE	NONE	BUREAU	1
1923	MCMILLAN THOMAS SANDERS	NONE	NONE	NONE	0
1925	BROWN EDGAR ALLAN	NONE	BUREAU	NONE	1

STATE

1ST SPKR	NAME	HIGHEST LOCAL	HIGHEST STATE	HIGH FEDER	TOT PUB
SOUTH CAROLINA (*CONT.*)					
1927	HAMBLIN JOHN KNAPP	CO BUR	NONE	BUREAU	3
1933	GIBSON JAMES BREEDEN	NONE	NONE	NONE	0
1935	TAYLOR CLAUDE AMBROSE	NONE	NONE	NONE	0
1937	BLATT SOLOMON	NONE	NONE	NONE	0
1947	LITTLEJOHN CAMERON BRUCE	NONE	NONE	NONE	0
1949	POPE THOMAS HARRINGTON	NONE	NONE	NONE	0
1973	CARTER REX LYLE	NONE	NONE	NONE	0
1980	SCHWARTZ RAMON JR	BUREAU	NONE	NONE	2
1987	SHEHEEN ROBERT J	NONE	NONE	NONE	0
TENNESSEE					
1911	LEACH ALBERT MARTIN	NONE	NONE	NONE	0
1913	STANTON WILLIAM MORTIMER	BUREAU	NONE	NONE	1
1915	COOPER WILLIAM PRENTICE	NONE	NONE	NONE	0
1917	SHROPSHIRE CLYDE MOORE	NONE	NONE	BUREAU	1
1919	WALKER SETH MCKINNEY	NONE	NONE	NONE	0
1921	TODD ANDREW LEE	REPRES	SEN PRES	NONE	4
1923	HALL FRANK SAMPSON	NONE	SENATE	NONE	1
1925	BARRY WILLIAM FRANCIS JR	NONE	NONE	NONE	0
1927	MAIDEN SELDEN LONGLEY	NONE	SENATE	NONE	1
1929	LOVE CHARLES HOWARD	CO BUR	NONE	BUREAU	3
1931	HAYNES WALTER MILLER	NONE	BUREAU	NONE	1
1933	MOORE FRANK WASHINGTON	NONE	NONE	NONE	0
1939	O'DELL JOHN ED	NONE	NONE	NONE	0
1943	BROOME JAMES JESSE	CO REPR	SENATE	NONE	3
1945	WOODS GEORGE STANLEY	CO BUR	NONE	NONE	1
1947	LEWALLEN W BUFORD	NONE	NONE	NONE	0
1949	FOUTCH MCALLEN	BUREAU	NONE	NONE	3
1953	BOMAR JAMES LA FAYETTE JR	NONE	SENATE	NONE	1
1963	BARRY WILLIAM LOGAN	REPRES	NONE	NONE	1
1967	CUMMINGS JAMES HARVEY II	CO BUR	EXECUT	NONE	3
1969	JENKINS WILLIAM LEWIS	NONE	NONE	NONE	0
1971	MCKINNEY JAMES ROBIN	NONE	NONE	NONE	0
1973	MCWHERTER NED RAY	NONE	NONE	NONE	0
1987	MURRAY CHARLES EDWARD	NONE	BUREAU	BUREAU	2
TEXAS					
1911	RAYBURN SAMUEL TALIAFERRO	NONE	NONE	NONE	0
1913	TERRELL CHESTER H	NONE	NONE	NONE	0
1915	WOODS JOHN WILLIAM	CO BUR	NONE	NONE	2
1917	FULLER FRANKLIN OLIVER	CO BUR	NONE	NONE	1
1919	THOMASON ROBERT EWING	CO BUR	NONE	NONE	1
1921	THOMAS CHARLES GRAHAM	NONE	NONE	NONE	0
1923	SEAGLER RICHARD E	NONE	NONE	NONE	0
1925	SATTERWHITE ROBERT LEE	NONE	NONE	NONE	0
1927	BOBBITT ROBERT LEE	NONE	NONE	NONE	0
1929	BARRON WINGATE STUART	CO BUR	NONE	NONE	1
1931	MINOR FRED H	REPRES	NONE	NONE	1

STATE

1ST SPKR	NAME	HIGHEST LOCAL	HIGHEST STATE	HIGH FEDER	TOT PUB
TEXAS (*CONT.*)					
1933	STEVENSON COKE ROBERT	CO JUD	NONE	NONE	2
1937	CALVERT ROBERT WILBURN	NONE	NONE	NONE	0
1939	MORSE ROBERT EMMETT	NONE	NONE	NONE	0
1941	LEONARD HOMER L	NONE	NONE	NONE	0
1943	DANIEL MARION PRICE SR	NONE	NONE	NONE	0
1945	GILMER CLAUD H	CO JUD	NONE	NONE	1
1947	REED WILLIAM OTEY	NONE	NONE	NONE	0
1949	MANFORD THOMAS DURWOOD JR	NONE	NONE	NONE	0
1951	SENTERFITT REUBEN	NONE	NONE	NONE	0
1955	LINDSEY JIM THURSTON	NONE	NONE	NONE	0
1957	CARR WAGGONER	CO BUR	BUREAU	NONE	2
1961	TURMAN JAMES A	NONE	NONE	NONE	0
1963	TUNNELL BYRON M	CO BUR	NONE	NONE	1
1965	BARNES BEN FRANK	NONE	NONE	NONE	0
1969	MUTSCHER GUS FRANKLIN	NONE	NONE	NONE	0
1972	PRICE WILLIAM RAYFORD	NONE	NONE	NONE	0
1973	DANIEL MARION PRICE JR	JUDGE	NONE	NONE	1
1975	CLAYTON BILLY WAYNE	NONE	NONE	NONE	0
1983	LEWIS GIBSON D	REPRES	NONE	NONE	2
VIRGINIA					
1914	COX EDWIN PIPER	NONE	NONE	NONE	0
1916	HOUSTON HARRY RUTHERFORD	NONE	NONE	NONE	0
1920	BREWER RICHARD LEWIS JR	MAYOR	BUREAU	NONE	2
1926	OZLIN THOMAS WILLIAM	MAYOR	NONE	NONE	1
1930	BROWN J SINCLAIR	CO EXEC	NONE	NONE	2
1936	DOVELL GROVER ASHTON	BUREAU	BUREAU	NONE	2
1942	STANLEY THOMAS BAHNSON	CO REPR	NONE	NONE	1
1947	MASSENBURG GEORGE ALVIN	NONE	NONE	NONE	0
1950	MOORE EDGAR BLACKBURN	NONE	BUREAU	NONE	1
1968	COOKE JOHN WARREN	BUREAU	NONE	NONE	1
1980	PHILPOTT ALBERT LEE	NONE	BUREAU	NONE	1
WEST VIRGINIA					
1911	WETZEL CHARLES MCCLUER	NONE	NONE	BUREAU	1
1913	GEORGE WILLIAM TAYLOR	NONE	NONE	NONE	0
1915	JOHNSON VERNON EMIL	REPRES	BUREAU	NONE	3
1917	THURMOND JOSEPH SAMUEL	MAYOR	NONE	NONE	1
1919	WOLFE J LUTHER	NONE	NONE	NONE	0
1921	KEATLEY EDWIN MINER	NONE	BUREAU	BUREAU	2
1923	BYRNE WILLIAM ESTON R	CO BUR	BUREAU	NONE	3
1929	CUMMINS JOHN WILLIAM	NONE	NONE	NONE	0
1931	TAYLOR JAMES ALFRED	NONE	NONE	HOUSE	1
1933	HINER RALPH MCCLUNG	NONE	NONE	NONE	0
1935	PELTER JOHN J	NONE	NONE	NONE	0
1937	THOMAS JAMES KAY	NONE	NONE	NONE	0
1941	ARNOLD MALCOLM R	CO BUR	NONE	NONE	1
1943	AMOS JOHN ELLISON	NONE	NONE	NONE	0

STATE

1ST SPKR	NAME	HIGHEST LOCAL	HIGHEST STATE	HIGH FEDER	TOT PUB

WEST VIRGINIA (*CONT.*)

1ST SPKR	NAME	HIGHEST LOCAL	HIGHEST STATE	HIGH FEDER	TOT PUB
1949	FLANNERY W E	NONE	NONE	NONE	0
1958	PAULEY HARRY R	NONE	NONE	NONE	0
1961	SINGLETON JULIUS W JR	CO BUR	NONE	BUREAU	2
1965	WHITE H LABAN JR	CO BUR	NONE	NONE	2
1969	BOIARSKY IVOR F	NONE	BUREAU	NONE	1
1971	MCMANUS LEWIS NICHOLS	NONE	NONE	NONE	0
1977	KOPP DONALD LEE	NONE	NONE	NONE	0
1979	SEE CLYDE M JR	NONE	NONE	NONE	0
1985	ALBRIGHT JOSEPH PAUL	CO BUR	SENATE	NONE	4
1987	CHAMBERS ROBERT C	NONE	BUREAU	NONE	1

KEY:

   1ST SPKR = YEAR FIRST SERVED AS SPEAKER

   HIGHEST LOCAL = HIGHEST LOCAL OFFICE BEFORE SPEAKERSHIP
      CO EXEC = COUNTY EXECUTIVE
      CO REPR = COUNTY REPRESENTATIVE
      MAYOR = MAYOR / TOWN SUPERVISOR
      EXECUT = LOCAL LOWER EXECUTIVE POSITION
      REPRES = LOCAL REPRESENTATIVE
      CO JUD = COUNTY JUDGE
      JUDGE = LOCAL JUDGE
      CO BUR = COUNTY BUREAUCRATIC POSITION
      BUREAU = LOCAL BUREAUCRATIC POSITION

   HIGHEST STATE = HIGHEST STATE OFFICE BEFORE SPEAKERSHIP
      EXECUT = LOWER EXECUTIVE POSITION
      SEN PRES = SENATE PRESIDENT
      SENATE = SENATE / OTHER STATE'S HOUSE
      BUREAU = BUREAUCRATIC POSITION

   HIGH FEDER = HIGHEST FEDERAL OFFICE BEFORE SPEAKERSHIP
      BUREAU = BUREAUCRATIC POSITION

   TOT PUB = TOTAL NUMBER OF PUBLIC OFFICES BEFORE SPEAKERSHIP

Appendix 10:
Public Offices after
Speakership

1ST SPKR	NAME	HIGHEST STATE	2ND HIGH STATE	HIGHEST FEDERAL

ALABAMA

1ST SPKR	NAME	HIGHEST STATE	2ND HIGH STATE	HIGHEST FEDERAL
1911	ALMON EDWARD BERTON	NONE	NONE	HOUSE
1919	MERRITT HENRY PAUL	JUDGE	NONE	NONE
1920	LYNNE SEABOURN ARTHUR	JUDGE	NONE	NONE
1923	MERRILL HUGH DAVIS	LT GOV	NONE	NONE
1927	LONG JOHN LEE	NONE	NONE	NONE
1935	WALKER ROBERT HENRY	NONE	NONE	NONE
1942	MILLER GEORGE OLIVER	NONE	NONE	NONE
1944	NORMAN CHARLES DOZIER	NONE	NONE	NONE
1947	BECK WILLIAM MORRIS	BUREAU	NONE	NONE
1951	BROWN ROBERTS HENRY	NONE	NONE	NONE
1955	FITE ERNEST RANKIN	NONE	NONE	NONE
1959	ADAMS CHARLES CRAYTON III	JUDGE	NONE	BUREAU
1961	ASHWORTH VIRGIS MARION	JUDGE	LOCAL	NONE
1963	BREWER ALBERT PRESTON	GOVERNOR	LT GOV	NONE
1971	LYONS GEORGE SAGE	BUREAU	BUREAU	NONE
1975	MCCORQUODALE JOSEPH CHARLES	BUREAU	BUREAU	NONE
1983	DRAKE THOMAS E	BUREAU	NONE	NONE
1987	CLARK JAMES STERLING	NONE	NONE	NONE

ARKANSAS

1ST SPKR	NAME	HIGHEST STATE	2ND HIGH STATE	HIGHEST FEDERAL
1911	MILWEE R FRANK	BUREAU	LOCAL	BUREAU
1913	HARDAGE JOSIAH	JUDGE	BUREAU	NONE
1915	SAWYER LEWIS ERNEST	NONE	NONE	HOUSE
1917	CAZORT WILLIAM LEE SR	LT GOV	NONE	BUREAU
1919	NEWTON CLARENCE PRICE	LOCAL	NONE	BUREAU
1921	JOINER JOSEPH WILLIAM	LOCAL	LOCAL	NONE
1923	REED HOWARD	BUREAU	NONE	BUREAU
1925	HILL THOMAS AUSTIN	NONE	NONE	NONE
1927	CAUDLE REECE ARTHUR	BUREAU	BUREAU	NONE
1929	ABINGTON WILLIAM H	SENATE	NONE	NONE
1931	NEALE IRVING C	NONE	NONE	NONE
1933	TONEY HARDIN KEMP	NONE	NONE	NONE
1935	THORN HARVEY BELL SR	NONE	NONE	NONE
1937	BRANSFORD JOHN MCKINNIS	BUREAU	NONE	NONE
1941	WILKINSON NORMAN MEANS	BUREAU	BUREAU	NONE
1943	GRIFFITH ROBERT WILLIAM	NONE	NONE	NONE

STATE

1ST SPKR	NAME	HIGHEST STATE	2ND HIGH STATE	HIGHEST FEDERAL

ARKANSAS (CONT.)

1945	NORTHCUTT HORACE ALLEN	NONE	NONE	NONE
1947	RIALES ROY LEE SR	SEN PRES	NONE	BUREAU
1949	HENDRIX CARL EDWARD	.	.	.
1951	CAMPBELL JAMES R JR	NONE	NONE	NONE
1953	HOLLENSWORTH CARROLL C	NONE	NONE	NONE
1955	SMITH CHARLES F JR	SENATE	NONE	NONE
1957	WALTHER GLENN F	NONE	NONE	NONE
1959	FLEEMAN EUGENE CECIL	NONE	NONE	NONE
1961	BETHELL JOHN PINCKNEY SR	NONE	NONE	NONE
1963	CRANK MARION HARLAN	BUREAU	LOCAL	NONE
1965	COTTRELL JOHN HALL JR	NONE	NONE	NONE
1967	COCKRILL STERLING ROBERTSON	BUREAU	NONE	BUREAU
1969	MCCLERKIN HAYES CANDOR	BUREAU	NONE	NONE
1971	SMITH RAY S JR	NONE	NONE	NONE
1973	TURNER GROVER W JR	NONE	NONE	NONE
1975	ALEXANDER CECIL LEWIS	NONE	NONE	NONE
1977	SHAVER JAMES LEVESQUE JR	NONE	NONE	NONE
1979	MILLER JOHN ELDON	NONE	NONE	NONE
1981	MCCUISTON LLOYD CARLISLE JR	NONE	NONE	NONE
1983	CAPPS JOHN PAUL	NONE	NONE	NONE
1985	LANDERS H LACY	NONE	NONE	NONE
1987	CUNNINGHAM ERNEST G	NONE	NONE	NONE
1989	HENDRIX B G	NONE	NONE	NONE

FLORIDA

1911	JENNINGS THOMAS ALBERT	NONE	NONE	NONE
1915	HARDEE CARY AUGUSTUS	GOVERNOR	NONE	NONE
1918	WILDER GEORGE HAMILTON	BUREAU	NONE	NONE
1921	JENNINGS FRANK E	NONE	NONE	NONE
1923	EDGE L DAY	SENATE	LOCAL	NONE
1925	MILAM ARTHUR YAGER	NONE	NONE	NONE
1927	DAVIS FRED HENRY	CHF JUST	EXECUT	NONE
1929	GETZEN SAMUEL WYCHE	SENATE	LOCAL	NONE
1931	LEWIS E CLAY JR	JUDGE	BUREAU	BUREAU
1933	TOMASELLO PETER JR	NONE	NONE	NONE
1935	BISHOP WILLIAM BURTON	NONE	NONE	NONE
1937	CHRISTIE WILLIAM MCLEAN	NONE	NONE	NONE
1939	WOOD GEORGE PIERCE	NONE	NONE	NONE
1941	MCCARTY DANIEL THOMAS	GOVERNOR	NONE	NONE
1943	SIMPSON RICHARD HENRY	BUREAU	BUREAU	NONE
1945	CRARY EVANS SR	SENATE	NONE	NONE
1947	BEASLEY THOMAS DEKALB	NONE	NONE	NONE
1949	MURRAY PERRY EARL	NONE	NONE	NONE
1951	ELLIOTT ELMER B	NONE	NONE	NONE
1953	BRYANT CECIL FARRIS	GOVERNOR	NONE	BUREAU
1955	DAVID THOMAS E	BUREAU	LOCAL	NONE
1957	CONNER DOYLE E	EXECUT	NONE	NONE
1961	CHAPPELL WILLIAM VENROE JR	NONE	NONE	HOUSE
1962	HORNE MALLORY ELI	SEN PRES	NONE	NONE
1965	ROWELL E C	NONE	NONE	NONE

STATE

1ST SPKR	NAME	HIGHEST STATE	2ND HIGH STATE	HIGHEST FEDERAL
FLORIDA (*CONT.*)				
1967	TURLINGTON RALPH DONALD	EXECUT	NONE	NONE
1969	SCHULTZ FREDERICK HENRY	NONE	NONE	NONE
1971	PETTIGREW RICHARD ALLEN	SENATE	NONE	BUREAU
1973	SESSUMS THOMAS TERRELL	BUREAU	NONE	NONE
1975	TUCKER DONALD L	.	.	.
1979	BROWN JAMES HYATT	NONE	NONE	NONE
1981	HABEN RALPH H JR	NONE	NONE	NONE
1983	MOFFITT H LEE	NONE	NONE	NONE
1985	THOMPSON JAMES HAROLD	NONE	NONE	NONE
1987	MILLS JON L	NONE	NONE	BUREAU
1989	GUSTAFSON TOM	NONE	NONE	NONE
GEORGIA				
1913	BURWELL WILLIAM HIX	NONE	NONE	NONE
1921	NEILL WILLIAM CECIL	SEN PRES	NONE	NONE
1927	RUSSELL RICHARD BREVARD	GOVERNOR	NONE	SENATE
1931	TUCKER ARLIE DANIEL	BUREAU	BUREAU	NONE
1933	RIVERS EURITH DICKINSON	GOVERNOR	NONE	NONE
1937	HARRIS ROY VINCENT	LOCAL	NONE	NONE
1941	EVANS RANDALL JR	JUDGE	NONE	NONE
1947	HAND FREDRICK BARROW	NONE	NONE	NONE
1955	MOATE MARVIN E	NONE	NONE	NONE
1959	SMITH GEORGE LEON II	NONE	NONE	NONE
1963	SMITH GEORGE THORNEWELL	LT GOV	JUDGE	NONE
1974	MURPHY THOMAS BAILEY	NONE	NONE	NONE
KENTUCKY				
1912	TERRELL CLAUDE B	NONE	NONE	NONE
1916	DUFFY HUGH CORNELIUS	NONE	NONE	NONE
1918	CROWE ROBERT T	BUREAU	LOCAL	NONE
1920	BOSWORTH JOE F	NONE	NONE	NONE
1922	THOMPSON JAMES H	SENATE	NONE	NONE
1924	ADAMS SAMUEL W	SENATE	NONE	NONE
1926	DRURY GEORGE LUCIAN	NONE	NONE	NONE
1928	MILLIKEN JOHN S	.	.	.
1932	BROWN JOHN YOUNG	BUREAU	NONE	HOUSE
1933	LEBUS FRANK	.	.	.
1934	ROGERS W E SR	NONE	NONE	NONE
1935	BROWN WALLACE	LOCAL	NONE	NONE
1936	KIRTLEY JOHN D	BUREAU	NONE	NONE
1940	SHIELDS BENJAMIN FRANKLIN	SENATE	NONE	NONE
1942	DICKSON STANLEY S	.	.	.
1944	WATERFIELD HARRY LEE	LT GOV	BUREAU	NONE
1948	TINSLEY T HERBERT	EXECUT	NONE	NONE
1950	DORAN ADRON	NONE	NONE	NONE
1952	BURNLEY CHARLES W	BUREAU	NONE	NONE
1956	FITZPATRICK THOMAS P	NONE	NONE	NONE
1958	WEINTRAUB MORRIS	NONE	NONE	NONE

STATE

1ST SPKR	NAME	HIGHEST STATE	2ND HIGH STATE	HIGHEST FEDERAL

KENTUCKY (CONT.)

1ST SPKR	NAME	HIGHEST STATE	2ND HIGH STATE	HIGHEST FEDERAL
1960	LOWMAN HARRY KING	NONE	NONE	NONE
1964	MCCALLUM SHELBY	NONE	NONE	NONE
1968	CARROLL JULIAN MORTON	GOVERNOR	LT GOV	NONE
1972	BLUME NORBERT	NONE	NONE	NONE
1976	KENTON WILLIAM G	BUREAU	NONE	NONE
1982	RICHARDSON BOBBY HAROLD	NONE	NONE	NONE
1986	BLANDFORD DONALD JOSEPH	NONE	NONE	NONE

LOUISIANA

1ST SPKR	NAME	HIGHEST STATE	2ND HIGH STATE	HIGHEST FEDERAL
1912	THOMAS LEE EMMETT	LOCAL	NONE	NONE
1916	BOUANCHAUD HEWITT LEONIDAS	LT GOV	BUREAU	NONE
1920	WALKER RICHARD FLOURNOY	NONE	NONE	NONE
1924	DOUGLAS JAMES STUART	NONE	NONE	NONE
1926	HUGHES WILLIAM CLARK	NONE	NONE	NONE
1928	FOURNET JOHN BAPTISTE	CHF JUST	LT GOV	NONE
1932	ELLENDER ALLEN JOSEPH	NONE	NONE	SENATE
1936	WIMBERLY LORRIS M	BUREAU	BUREAU	NONE
1940	BAUER RALPH NORMAN	LOCAL	NONE	NONE
1952	AYCOCK CLARENCE C	LT GOV	NONE	NONE
1957	ANGELLE ROBERT	NONE	NONE	NONE
1960	JEWELL J THOMAS	NONE	NONE	NONE
1964	DELONY VAIL MONTGOMERY	NONE	NONE	NONE
1968	GARRETT JOHN SIDNEY	NONE	NONE	NONE
1972	HENRY EDGERTON L	BUREAU	NONE	NONE
1980	HAINKEL JOHN JOSEPH JR	SENATE	NONE	NONE
1984	ALARIO JOHN A JR	NONE	NONE	NONE
1988	DIMOS JIMMY N	NONE	NONE	NONE

MARYLAND

1ST SPKR	NAME	HIGHEST STATE	2ND HIGH STATE	HIGHEST FEDERAL
1912	TRIPPE JAMES MCCONKY	JUDGE	NONE	NONE
1916	LAIRD PHILIP DANDRIDGE	NONE	NONE	NONE
1917	MCINTOSH DAVID GREGG JR	SEN PRES	NONE	NONE
1918	WOODEN HERBERT R	NONE	NONE	NONE
1920	TYDINGS MILLARD EVELYN	NONE	NONE	SENATE
1922	LEE JOHN L G	NONE	NONE	NONE
1924	CURTIS FRANCIS P	LOCAL	NONE	NONE
1927	LEE EDWARD BROOKE	NONE	BUREAU	NONE
1931	MICHEL FRANCIS A	LOCAL	NONE	BUREAU
1933	HARRINGTON T BARTON	NONE	NONE	BUREAU
1935	GORFINE EMANUEL	SENATE	BUREAU	NONE
1939	CONLON THOMAS EDWARD	LOCAL	NONE	NONE
1943	WHITE JOHN S	NONE	NONE	NONE
1947	SYBERT CORNELIUS FERDINAND	EXECUT	JUDGE	NONE
1951	LUBER JOHN CHRISTOPHER	NONE	NONE	NONE
1959	WILKINSON PERRY O	NONE	NONE	NONE
1963	BOONE A GORDON	NONE	NONE	NONE
1964	MANDEL MARVIN	GOVERNOR	NONE	NONE
1969	LOWE THOMAS HUNTER	JUDGE	NONE	NONE

STATE

1ST SPKR	NAME	HIGHEST STATE	2ND HIGH STATE	HIGHEST FEDERAL

MARYLAND (*CONT.*)

1ST SPKR	NAME	HIGHEST STATE	2ND HIGH STATE	HIGHEST FEDERAL
1973	BRISCOE JOHN HANSON	JUDGE	NONE	NONE
1979	CARDIN BENJAMIN LOUIS	BUREAU	NONE	HOUSE
1987	MITCHELL R CLAYTON JR	NONE	NONE	NONE

MISSISSIPPI

1ST SPKR	NAME	HIGHEST STATE	2ND HIGH STATE	HIGHEST FEDERAL
1912	QUIN HILLRIE MARSHALL	NONE	NONE	NONE
1916	CONNER MARTIN SENNETT	GOVERNOR	NONE	NONE
1924	BAILEY THOMAS LOWRY	GOVERNOR	NONE	NONE
1936	STANSEL HORACE SYLVAN	NONE	NONE	NONE
1936	WRIGHT FIELDING LEWIS	GOVERNOR	LT GOV	NONE
1940	LUMPKIN SAMUEL E	LT GOV	LOCAL	NONE
1944	SILLERS WALTER	NONE	NONE	NONE
1966	JUNKIN JOHN RICHARD	NONE	NONE	NONE
1976	NEWMAN CLARENCE BENTON	NONE	NONE	NONE
1988	FORD TIMOTHY ALAN	NONE	NONE	NONE

NORTH CAROLINA

1ST SPKR	NAME	HIGHEST STATE	2ND HIGH STATE	HIGHEST FEDERAL
1911	DOWD WILLIAM CAREY	NONE	NONE	NONE
1913	CONNOR GEORGE WHITFIELD	JUDGE	JUDGE	NONE
1914	MURPHY WALTER	NONE	NONE	NONE
1915	WOOTEN EMMETT ROBINSON	NONE	NONE	NONE
1919	BRUMMITT DENNIS GARFIELD	EXECUT	NONE	NONE
1921	GRIER HARRY PERCY	SENATE	NONE	NONE
1923	DAWSON JOHN GILMER	SENATE	NONE	NONE
1925	PHARR EDGAR WALTER	NONE	NONE	BUREAU
1927	FOUNTAIN RICHARD TILLMAN	LT GOV	BUREAU	BUREAU
1929	GRAHAM ALEXANDER HAWKINS	LT GOV	BUREAU	NONE
1931	SMITH WILLIS	NONE	NONE	SENATE
1933	HARRIS REGINALD LEE	LT GOV	BUREAU	NONE
1935	JOHNSON ROBERT GRADY	BUREAU	BUREAU	NONE
1936	CHERRY ROBERT GREGG	GOVERNOR	SENATE	NONE
1939	WARD DAVID LIVINGSTONE JR	SENATE	BUREAU	BUREAU
1941	MULL ODUS MCCOY	NONE	NONE	NONE
1943	KERR JOHN HOSEA JR	SENATE	NONE	NONE
1945	RICHARDSON OSCAR LEON	BUREAU	NONE	NONE
1947	PEARSALL THOMAS JENKINS	BUREAU	NONE	NONE
1949	RAMSAY KERR CRAIGE	NONE	NONE	NONE
1951	TAYLOR WALTER FRANK	NONE	NONE	NONE
1953	BOST EUGENE THOMPSON JR	NONE	NONE	NONE
1955	MOORE LARRY ICHABOD JR	NONE	NONE	NONE
1957	DOUGHTON JAMES KEMP	NONE	NONE	NONE
1959	HEWLETT ADDISON JR	NONE	NONE	NONE
1961	HUNT JOSEPH MARVIN	NONE	NONE	NONE
1963	BLUE HERBERT CLIFTON	NONE	NONE	NONE
1965	TAYLOR HOYT PATRICK JR	LT GOV	NONE	NONE
1967	BRITT DAVID MAXWELL	JUDGE	NONE	NONE
1967	VAUGHN EARL W	JUDGE	LOCAL	NONE
1969	GODWIN PHILIP PITTMAN	SENATE	NONE	NONE

STATE

1ST SPKR	NAME	HIGHEST STATE	2ND HIGH STATE	HIGHEST FEDERAL

NORTH CAROLINA (CONT.)

1ST SPKR	NAME	HIGHEST STATE	2ND HIGH STATE	HIGHEST FEDERAL
1973	RAMSEY JAMES EDWARD	NONE	NONE	NONE
1975	GREEN JAMES COLLINS	LT GOV	BUREAU	NONE
1977	STEWART CARL JEROME JR	NONE	NONE	BUREAU
1981	RAMSEY LISTON BRYAN	NONE	NONE	NONE
1989	MAVRETIC JOSEPHUS L	NONE	NONE	NONE

OKLAHOMA

1ST SPKR	NAME	HIGHEST STATE	2ND HIGH STATE	HIGHEST FEDERAL
1910	ANTHONY WILLIAM BRUCE	BUREAU	LOCAL	NONE
1911	DURANT WILLIAM ALEXANDER	NONE	NONE	NONE
1913	MAXEY JAMES HARVEY	.	.	.
1915	MCCRORY ALONZO	BUREAU	NONE	NONE
1917	NESBITT PAUL	BUREAU	NONE	NONE
1919	WALDREP THOMAS CARNES	SENATE	NONE	NONE
1921	SCHWABE GEORGE BLAINE	NONE	NONE	HOUSE
1923	GIBBONS MURRAY F	NONE	NONE	NONE
1923	MCBEE WILLIAM DALTON	NONE	NONE	NONE
1925	HARPER JESSE B	SENATE	BUREAU	NONE
1927	STOVALL DAVID ANCIL	BUREAU	NONE	BUREAU
1929	STREET ALLEN MORGAN	LOCAL	LOCAL	NONE
1929	NANCE JAMES CLARK	SEN PRES	NONE	NONE
1931	WEAVER CARLTON	NONE	NONE	NONE
1933	ANGLIN WILLIAM THOMAS	SEN PRES	BUREAU	NONE
1935	PHILLIPS LEON CHASE	GOVERNOR	NONE	NONE
1937	DANIEL J T	LOCAL	NONE	NONE
1939	WELCH WILLIAM DONOVAN SR	NONE	NONE	NONE
1941	BLUMHAGEN E	LOCAL	NONE	NONE
1943	FREEMAN HAROLD	NONE	NONE	NONE
1944	LANSDEN JOSEPH MERLE	JUDGE	NONE	NONE
1945	HILL JOHNSON DAVIS	NONE	NONE	NONE
1945	HINDS H IREDELLE	BUREAU	LOCAL	BUREAU
1947	BOARD CHARLES RAYMOND	JUDGE	JUDGE	NONE
1949	BILLINGSLEY WALTER ASBURY	JUDGE	NONE	NONE
1951	BULLARD JAMES MARVIN	EXECUT	BUREAU	NONE
1955	HARKEY BYRON E	NONE	NONE	NONE
1959	LIVINGSTON CLINT GRAHAM	JUDGE	NONE	NONE
1961	MCCARTY J D	NONE	NONE	NONE
1967	PRIVETT ARNOLD REX	EXECUT	BUREAU	NONE
1973	WILLIS WILLIAM PASCAL	NONE	NONE	NONE
1979	DRAPER DANIEL DAVID JR	NONE	NONE	NONE
1984	BARKER JIM L	NONE	NONE	NONE
1989	LEWIS STEPHEN C	NONE	NONE	NONE

SOUTH CAROLINA

1ST SPKR	NAME	HIGHEST STATE	2ND HIGH STATE	HIGHEST FEDERAL
1915	HOYT JAMES ALFRED	NONE	NONE	NONE
1918	COTHRAN THOMAS PERRIN	JUDGE	NONE	NONE
1921	ATKINSON JAMES BUFORD	NONE	NONE	NONE
1923	MCMILLAN THOMAS SANDERS	NONE	NONE	HOUSE
1925	BROWN EDGAR ALLAN	SEN PRES	NONE	NONE

STATE

1ST SPKR	NAME	HIGHEST STATE	2ND HIGH STATE	HIGHEST FEDERAL

SOUTH CAROLINA (CONT.)

1ST SPKR	NAME	HIGHEST STATE	2ND HIGH STATE	HIGHEST FEDERAL
1927	HAMBLIN JOHN KNAPP	NONE	NONE	NONE
1933	GIBSON JAMES BREEDEN	NONE	NONE	NONE
1935	TAYLOR CLAUDE AMBROSE	CHF JUST	NONE	NONE
1937	BLATT SOLOMON	NONE	NONE	NONE
1947	LITTLEJOHN CAMERON BRUCE	CHF JUST	JUDGE	NONE
1949	POPE THOMAS HARRINGTON	NONE	NONE	NONE
1973	CARTER REX LYLE	NONE	NONE	NONE
1980	SCHWARTZ RAMON JR	NONE	NONE	NONE
1987	SHEHEEN ROBERT J	NONE	NONE	NONE

TENNESSEE

1ST SPKR	NAME	HIGHEST STATE	2ND HIGH STATE	HIGHEST FEDERAL
1911	LEACH ALBERT MARTIN	LOCAL	NONE	NONE
1913	STANTON WILLIAM MORTIMER	LOCAL	LOCAL	NONE
1915	COOPER WILLIAM PRENTICE	NONE	NONE	NONE
1917	SHROPSHIRE CLYDE MOORE	NONE	NONE	BUREAU
1919	WALKER SETH MCKINNEY	NONE	NONE	NONE
1921	TODD ANDREW LEE	NONE	NONE	NONE
1923	HALL FRANK SAMPSON	SENATE	EXECUT	NONE
1925	BARRY WILLIAM FRANCIS JR	EXECUT	BUREAU	NONE
1927	MAIDEN SELDEN LONGLEY	NONE	NONE	NONE
1929	LOVE CHARLES HOWARD	BUREAU	BUREAU	BUREAU
1931	HAYNES WALTER MILLER	LT GOV	SEN PRES	NONE
1933	MOORE FRANK WASHINGTON	NONE	NONE	NONE
1939	O'DELL JOHN ED	BUREAU	NONE	NONE
1943	BROOME JAMES JESSE	NONE	NONE	NONE
1945	WOODS GEORGE STANLEY	LOCAL	NONE	NONE
1947	LEWALLEN W BUFORD	LOCAL	NONE	NONE
1949	FOUTCH MCALLEN	SENATE	NONE	NONE
1953	BOMAR JAMES LA FAYETTE JR	LT GOV	NONE	NONE
1963	BARRY WILLIAM LOGAN	BUREAU	NONE	NONE
1967	CUMMINGS JAMES HARVEY II	NONE	NONE	NONE
1969	JENKINS WILLIAM LEWIS	EXECUT	NONE	BUREAU
1971	MCKINNEY JAMES ROBIN	NONE	NONE	NONE
1973	MCWHERTER NED RAY	GOVERNOR	NONE	NONE
1987	MURRAY CHARLES EDWARD	NONE	NONE	NONE

TEXAS

1ST SPKR	NAME	HIGHEST STATE	2ND HIGH STATE	HIGHEST FEDERAL
1911	RAYBURN SAMUEL TALIAFERRO	NONE	NONE	HSE SPKR
1913	TERRELL CHESTER H	NONE	NONE	NONE
1915	WOODS JOHN WILLIAM	NONE	NONE	NONE
1917	FULLER FRANKLIN OLIVER	NONE	NONE	NONE
1919	THOMASON ROBERT EWING	LOCAL	NONE	HOUSE
1921	THOMAS CHARLES GRAHAM	BUREAU	NONE	NONE
1923	SEAGLER RICHARD E	BUREAU	NONE	NONE
1925	SATTERWHITE ROBERT LEE	NONE	NONE	NONE
1927	BOBBITT ROBERT LEE	JUDGE	EXECUT	NONE
1929	BARRON WINGATE STUART	JUDGE	NONE	NONE
1931	MINOR FRED H	BUREAU	BUREAU	NONE

STATE

1ST SPKR	NAME	HIGHEST STATE	2ND HIGH STATE	HIGHEST FEDERAL
TEXAS (*CONT.*)				
1933	STEVENSON COKE ROBERT	GOVERNOR	LT GOV	NONE
1937	CALVERT ROBERT WILBURN	CHF JUST	BUREAU	NONE
1939	MORSE ROBERT EMMETT	NONE	NONE	NONE
1941	LEONARD HOMER L	NONE	NONE	NONE
1943	DANIEL MARION PRICE SR	GOVERNOR	EXECUT	SENATE
1945	GILMER CLAUD H	BUREAU	NONE	NONE
1947	REED WILLIAM OTEY	NONE	NONE	NONE
1949	MANFORD THOMAS DURWOOD JR	BUREAU	BUREAU	NONE
1951	SENTERFITT REUBEN	LOCAL	LOCAL	NONE
1955	LINDSEY JIM THURSTON	NONE	NONE	NONE
1957	CARR WAGGONER	EXECUT	NONE	NONE
1961	TURMAN JAMES A	NONE	NONE	BUREAU
1963	TUNNELL BYRON M	BUREAU	NONE	NONE
1965	BARNES BEN FRANK	LT GOV	NONE	BUREAU
1969	MUTSCHER GUS FRANKLIN	JUDGE	BUREAU	NONE
1972	PRICE WILLIAM RAYFORD	NONE	NONE	NONE
1973	DANIEL MARION PRICE JR	NONE	NONE	NONE
1975	CLAYTON BILLY WAYNE	NONE	NONE	NONE
1983	LEWIS GIBSON D	NONE	NONE	NONE
VIRGINIA				
1914	COX EDWIN PIPER	JUDGE	NONE	NONE
1916	HOUSTON HARRY RUTHERFORD	BUREAU	NONE	BUREAU
1920	BREWER RICHARD LEWIS JR	NONE	NONE	NONE
1926	OZLIN THOMAS WILLIAM	BUREAU	NONE	NONE
1930	BROWN J SINCLAIR	BUREAU	NONE	NONE
1936	DOVELL GROVER ASHTON	NONE	NONE	NONE
1942	STANLEY THOMAS BAHNSON	GOVERNOR	BUREAU	HOUSE
1947	MASSENBURG GEORGE ALVIN	BUREAU	BUREAU	NONE
1950	MOORE EDGAR BLACKBURN	NONE	NONE	NONE
1968	COOKE JOHN WARREN	BUREAU	NONE	NONE
1980	PHILPOTT ALBERT LEE	NONE	NONE	NONE
WEST VIRGINIA				
1911	WETZEL CHARLES MCCLUER	NONE	NONE	BUREAU
1913	GEORGE WILLIAM TAYLOR	NONE	NONE	NONE
1915	JOHNSON VERNON EMIL	BUREAU	NONE	BUREAU
1917	THURMOND JOSEPH SAMUEL	NONE	NONE	NONE
1919	WOLFE J LUTHER	BUREAU	NONE	NONE
1921	KEATLEY EDWIN MINER	NONE	NONE	NONE
1923	BYRNE WILLIAM ESTON R	BUREAU	NONE	NONE
1929	CUMMINS JOHN WILLIAM	NONE	NONE	NONE
1931	TAYLOR JAMES ALFRED	NONE	NONE	NONE
1933	HINER RALPH MCCLUNG	.	.	.
1935	PELTER JOHN J	SENATE	NONE	NONE
1937	THOMAS JAMES KAY	BUREAU	BUREAU	NONE
1941	ARNOLD MALCOLM R	NONE	NONE	NONE
1943	AMOS JOHN ELLISON	SENATE	NONE	NONE

STATE

1ST SPKR	NAME	HIGHEST STATE	2ND HIGH STATE	HIGHEST FEDERAL

WEST VIRGINIA (*CONT.*)

1ST SPKR	NAME	HIGHEST STATE	2ND HIGH STATE	HIGHEST FEDERAL
1949	FLANNERY W E	NONE	NONE	NONE
1958	PAULEY HARRY R	NONE	NONE	NONE
1961	SINGLETON JULIUS W JR	JUDGE	NONE	NONE
1965	WHITE H LABAN JR	BUREAU	BUREAU	NONE
1969	BOIARSKY IVOR F	NONE	NONE	NONE
1971	MCMANUS LEWIS NICHOLS	BUREAU	NONE	NONE
1977	KOPP DONALD LEE	BUREAU	NONE	NONE
1979	SEE CLYDE M JR	NONE	NONE	NONE
1985	ALBRIGHT JOSEPH PAUL	NONE	NONE	NONE
1987	CHAMBERS ROBERT C	NONE	NONE	NONE

KEY:

   1ST SPKR = YEAR FIRST SERVED AS SPEAKER

   HIGHEST STATE = HIGHEST STATE OFFICE AFTER SPEAKERSHIP
   2ND HIGH STATE = SECOND HIGHEST STATE OFFICE AFTER SPEAKERSHIP
      . = MISSING DATA
      LT GOV = LIEUTENANT GOVERNOR
      EXECUT = LOWER EXECUTIVE POSITION
      SEN PRES = SENATE PRESIDENT
      SENATE = SENATE / OTHER STATE'S HOUSE
      CHF JUST = SUPREME COURT CHIEF JUSTICE
      BUREAU = BUREAUCRATIC POSITION

   HIGHEST FEDERAL = HIGHEST FEDERAL OFFICE AFTER SPEAKERSHIP
      . = MISSING DATA
      BUREAU = BUREAUCRATIC POSITION

INDEX

ABOUT THE CONTRIBUTORS

KEVIN G. ATWATER: E. S. Bird Library, Syracuse University, Syracuse, NY.

REID BADGER: Department of American Studies, University of Alabama, Tuscaloosa, AL.

FRED A. BAILEY: Abilene Christian University, Abilene, TX.

NANCY DISHER BAIRD: Department of Library Special Collections, Western Kentucky University, Bowling Green, KY.

RUSSELL PIERCE BAKER: Arkansas History Commission, Little Rock, AR.

ALWYN BARR: Department of History, Texas Tech University, Lubbock, TX.

CHARLES H. BOWMAN, JR.: Fayetteville State University, Fayetteville, NC.

KENNY L. BROWN: University of Central Oklahoma, Edmond, OK.

LISLE G. BROWN: Department of Special Collections, Morrow Library, Marshall University, Huntington, WV.

LYLE C. BROWN: Department of Political Science, Baylor University, Waco, TX.

GARY L. BROWNE: History Department, University of Maryland Baltimore County, Baltimore, MD.

PATRICK J. CHASE: Shepherd College, Shepherdstown, WV.

NANCY VANCE ASHMORE COOPER: Institute for Southern Studies, University of South Carolina, Columbia, SC.

CAROL CROWE-CARRACO: Department of History, Western Kentucky University, Bowling Green, KY.

DONALD B. DODD: History Department, Auburn University at Montgomery, Montgomery, AL.

WILLIAM T. DOHERTY: History Department, West Virginia University, Morgantown, West Virginia (retired).

JAMES E. DORSEY: Chestatee Regional Library System, Gainesville, GA.

J. LARRY DURRENCE: Department of Revenue, State of Florida, Tallahassee, FL.

WALTER B. EDGAR: Institute for Southern Studies, University of South Carolina, Columbia, SC.

JAMES H. EDMONSON: Emmanuel College, Franklin Springs, GA.

HENRY C. FERRELL, JR.: Department of History, East Carolina University, Greenville, NC.

L. GERALD FIELDER: Department of Political Science, Baylor University, Waco, TX.

JANE McBRIDE GATES: Department of Political Science, Arkansas State University, State University, AR.

PAUL S. GEORGE: Social Science Department, Miami-Dade Community College, Miami, FL.

LEE S. GREENE (deceased): University of Tennessee, Knoxville, TN.

TRACY ANDERS GREENLEE: Texas Christian University, Fort Worth, TX.

LUTHER G. HAGARD, JR.: Department of Political Science, University of Texas at Arlington, Arlington, TX.

CLAUDE HARGROVE: Fayetteville State University, Fayetteville, NC.

JANE W. HERNDON: DeKalb College, Clarkston, GA.

ROBERT L. HUNT: West Virginia Wesleyan College, Buckhannon, WV (retired).

RON LAW: Texas Christian University, Fort Worth, TX.

CAL LEDBETTER, JR.: Political Science Department, University of Arkansas at Little Rock, Little Rock, AR.

SUZANNE MABERRY: History Department, University of Arkansas, Fayetteville, AR.

LEON C. MILLER: Department of Special Collections, Mullins Library, University of Arkansas, Fayetteville, AR.

CARL H. MONEYHON: Department of History, University of Arkansas at Little Rock, Little Rock, AR.

GORDON MOORE: Department of Human Services, State of Oklahoma, Oklahoma City, OK.

GARY R. MORMINO: History Department, University of South Florida, Tampa, FL.

THOMAS R. MYERS: Department of Political Science, Baylor University, Waco, TX.

RAYMOND O. NUSSBAUM: New Orleans Notarial Archives, New Orleans, LA.

OTIENO OKELO: School of Socio-Cultural and Development Studies, Moi University, Eldoret, Kenya.

BEATRICE R. OWSLEY: Archives and Manuscripts/Special Collections Department, Earl K. Long Library, University of New Orleans, New Orleans, LA.

GINA PETONITO: Department of Sociology, Alma College, Alma, MI.

WILLIE H. PIGG: Social Science Department, California University of Pennsylvania, California, PA.

GEORGE E. POZZETTA: Department of History, University of Florida, Gainesville, FL.

MORGAN H. PRITCHETT (deceased): Enoch Pratt Free Library, Baltimore, MD.

FRED D. RAGAN: Department of History, East Carolina University, Greenville, NC.

DONOVAN L. REICHENBERGER: Northwestern Oklahoma State University, Alva, OK (retired).

WHITMAN H. RIDGWAY: Department of History, University of Maryland, College Park, MD.

RICHARD B. RILEY: Department of Political Science, Baylor University, Waco, TX.

AMOS ST. GERMAIN: Department of Humanities, Social Science and Management, Wentworth Institute of Technology, Boston, MA.

DAVID G. SANSING: Department of History, University of Mississippi, University, MS (retired).

JANET SCHMELZER: Department of Social Sciences, Tarleton State University, Stephenville, TX.

JERRELL H. SHOFNER: Department of History, University of Central Florida, Orlando, FL.

WILLIAM H. STEWART: Department of Political Science, University of Alabama, Tuscaloosa, AL.

MARIAN ELIZABETH STROBEL: Department of History, Furman University, Greenville, SC.

JAMES R. SWEENEY: Department of History, Old Dominion University, Norfolk, VA.

ROGER TATE: Somerset Community College, Somerset, KY.

JON L. WAKELYN: Department of History, Kent State University, Kent, OH.

H. LEW WALLACE: Department of History, Northern Kentucky University, Highland Heights, KY.

CHARLES J. WEEKS: Department of History, Southern Technical Institute, Marietta, GA.

EDWARD WELLER: San Jacinto College South, Houston, TX.

BENJAMIN B. WILLIAMS: Department of English, Auburn University at Montgomery, Montgomery, AL (retired).

TIMOTHY A. ZWINK: Northwestern Oklahoma State University, Alva, OK.

ISBN 0-313-30213-8

EAN

9 780313 302138

90000>

HARDCOVER BAR CODE